Europe Today

Europe Today

A Twenty-first Century Introduction

Fourth Edition

EDITED BY RONALD TIERSKY
AND ERIK JONES
WITH SASKIA VAN GENUGTEN

ROWMAN & LITTLEFIELD PUBLISHERS, INC.
Lanham • Boulder • New York • Toronto • Plymouth, UK

Published by Rowman & Littlefield Publishers, Inc.
A wholly owned subsidiary of The Rowman & Littlefield Publishing Group, Inc.
4501 Forbes Boulevard, Suite 200, Lanham, Maryland 20706
http://www.rowmanlittlefield.com

Estover Road, Plymouth PL6 7PY, United Kingdom

British Library Cataloguing in Publication Information Available

Library of Congress Cataloging-in-Publication Data

Europe today : a twenty-first century introduction / edited by Ronald Tiersky and Erik Jones, with Saskia van Genugten.—4th ed.
    p.   cm.
    Includes bibliographical references and index.
    ISBN 978-0-7425-6773-3 (pbk. : alk. paper)
    ISBN 978-0-7425-6774-0 (electronic)
    1. European Union countries—Politics and government—21st century.   2. Europe—Politics and government—21st century.   3. Europe—Forecasting.   I. Tiersky, Ronald, 1944–   II. Jones, Erik.   III. Genugten, Saskia van.
JN30.E82478   2011
320.94—dc22   2011004173

∞ ™ The paper used in this publication meets the minimum requirements of American National Standard for Information Sciences—Permanence of Paper for Printed Library Materials, ANSI/NISO Z39.48-1992.

Printed in the United States of America

Contents

Preface   vii

Timeline of Events Leading to the Current State of the European Union   xi

Acronyms   xv

Illustrations and Supplementary Material   xvii

Introduction: The European Outlook   1
Ronald Tiersky, Saskia van Genugten, and Erik Jones

PART ONE: COUNTRY STUDIES

1   France: The Sarkozy Presidency in Historical Perspective   25
Gabriel Goodliffe

2   Great Britain: From New Labour to New Politics?   67
Jonathan Hopkin

3   Germany: Two Decades of Passage from Bonn to Berlin   99
Helga A. Welsh

4   Italy: Politics in the Age of Berlusconi   133
Gianfranco Baldini

5   Scandinavia: Still the Middle Way?   161
Eric S. Einhorn and John Logue

6   Russia: European or Not?   207
Bruce Parrott

7   Poland 20 Years Later: The Long Arm of Transition   243
Ben Stanley

PART TWO: THEMATIC CHAPTERS

8   European Integration: Progress and Uncertainty   277
John Van Oudenaren

9   Economic Governance and Varieties of Capitalism   303
Benedicta Marzinotto

10   Europe and the Global Economic Crisis   327
Erik Jones

11   European Law and Politics   351
     R. Daniel Kelemen

12   Migration in Europe   371
     Jonathon W. Moses

13   Still at the Crossroads: Europe, the United States, and NATO   399
     Simon Duke and Roberta Haar

Notes   433

Glossary   465

Index   473

About the Contributors   487

Preface

A Note to Students

Introductory textbooks are notoriously difficult for professors to write. Success demands from authors not only a mastery of subject matter but an ability to explain things to beginning students without talking down to them. The job isn't easy.

For your part, you, the student, must be willing to read seriously and to engage the book in good faith. You must be willing to try to imagine what many or most of you have not yet seen, that is, Europe and its vividly different countries and societies. You must begin with nothing more than a willingness to get interested—an intellectual curiosity about the world outside the United States. We can assure you that cosmopolitan knowledge will repay you in ways that you will understand only later. You will discover the empowerment of traveling with your mind. You will, we hope, go to Europe and feel after a day or two that you are not completely a stranger in London, Paris, Berlin, Rome, Stockholm, or Warsaw, or even Brussels, home of the often-confusing European Union (EU).

Understanding international politics first requires familiarity with particular countries so as to possess a sort of foundational stone of knowledge upon which to build a progressively larger view of the world. One must be a specialist before becoming a generalist. You will find several country chapters in this book, but you will find the separate countries again in every European-gauge chapter. Be aware that your job is to hold the two ends of a rope—to know separate countries and to understand the European Union as a whole.

As students just arriving on the scene, you have the advantage of naïveté, meaning a relative lack of prejudices and stereotypes. How fortunate you are, we think, not to begin with the heavy baggage of the past! Yet how much you don't know of what you need to know—that is, the past!

A Note to Teachers

In our note to students, we've put teachers on the spot. We've asked students for imagination in addition to information; we're asking the same of teachers.

We hope that at the end of your courses you will feel that this book has done its part by giving you what you need to do an important job.

Some teachers have raised the issue of whether the country chapters or the European-integration chapters should come first. There is no obvious or completely satisfactory answer. At those moments when integration stalls, as in the context of the economic and financial crisis, putting the country chapters first seems best. That is what we have chosen for this edition. Teachers, obviously, can use the book from either direction according to their own inclinations.

Nor should teachers feel obliged to teach entirely "with the book" in order to get the most out of it. Each chapter in some way is an argument rather than a description. Teaching partly against rather than with the author of a chapter can be a powerful pedagogical strategy.

Above all, this fourth edition of *Europe Today* strives to be teacher- as well as student-friendly. We welcome comments about how the book can be improved.

In closing, we should give credit where credit is due. This book would not have been possible without the support of Amherst College, the SAIS Bologna Center, and Nuffield College in Oxford (where Erik Jones was on sabbatical during the completion of the manuscript). A particular thanks goes to Peter Mannisi for compiling the country-specific statistical data that leads off the country chapters.

Finally, it's a pleasure once again to thank Susan McEachern, our editor at Rowman & Littlefield, who has been so important in the success of the Europe Today series. She makes a great deal happen and she saves us from many mistakes.

Ronald Tiersky, Erik Jones, and Saskia van Genugten
January 2011

The European Union

Member States

Candidate Countries

⊛ Capitals (selected)

Country Abbreviations:

Belg. = Belgium
Cr. = Croatia
L. = Liechtenstein
Lux. = Luxembourg
Mac. = Macedonia
Mon. = Monoco

Mont. = Montenegro
Neth. = Netherlands
Sl. = Slovenia
Slov. = Slovak Republic
S.M. = San Marino
Switz. = Switzerland

City Abbreviations:

Br. = Bratislava
L. = Ljubljana
P.= Podgorica
S. = Skojpe

Sa. = Sarajevo
T. = Tirana
Z. = Zagreb

*As of June 2010, Iceland is also a candidate for EU membership.

European Union
Statistical Information

Population (million)	499.8 (January 2009)
Area in Square Miles	1,669,808
GDP (trillion, PPP)	$14.43 (2009 est.)
GDP per capita (PPP)	$31,900 (2009 est.)

Performance of Key Political Parties in Parliamentary Elections of June 4–7, 2009

Group of the European People's Party (Christian-Democrats, EPP)	36%
Group of the Progressive Alliance of Socialists and Democrats in the European Parliament (S&D)	25%
Group of the Alliance of Liberals and Democrats for Europe (ALDE)	11.4%
Group of the Greens/European Free Alliance (GREENS/EFA)	7.5%
European Conservatives and Reformists Group (ECR)	7.3%
Confederal Group of the European United Left–Nordic Green Left (GUE/NGL)	4.8%
Europe of Freedom and Democracy Group (EFD)	4.3%
Non-Attached (NA)	3.7%

Main Office Holders: President of the European Parliament: Jerzy Buzek (Poland)—EPP—in office since 2009; President of the European Commission: José Manuel Durão Barroso (Portugal)—EPP—in office since 2004, reelected in 2009; Permanent President to the European Council: Herman Van Rompuy (Belgium)—EPP—in office since 2009; High Representative for CFSP: Lady Catherine Ashton (Britain)—S&D—in office since 2009.

Timeline of Events Leading to the Current State of the European Union

May 1945	End of World War II in Europe.
June 1945	United Nations is founded.
June 1947	Marshall Plan (European Recovery Program) is launched.
April 1948	Organization for European Economic Cooperation (OEEC) is established.
May 1949	Council of Europe is founded.
April 1951	Treaty of Paris is signed, which establishes the European Coal and Steel Community (ECSC).
March 1957	Treaties of Rome are signed, which establish the European Atomic Energy Community (Euratom) and the European Economic Community (EEC). Members of the EEC are France, the Netherlands, Belgium, Luxembourg, Germany, and Italy.
February 1958	Benelux Economic Union is founded.
July 1958	Common Agricultural Policy (CAP) is proposed.
December 1960	OEEC is reorganized into the Organization for Economic Cooperation and Development (OECD).
August 1961	Denmark, Ireland, and the UK apply for EEC membership. (President de Gaulle of France vetoes British application twice, in January 1963 and November 1967.)
April 1962	Norway applies for EEC membership.
April 1965	Merger Treaty signed, which consolidates the institutions created by the Treaty of Paris and the Treaties of Rome.
July 1968	EEC customs union is finalized, and the CAP is enacted.
January 1972	EEC negotiations are concluded with UK, Denmark, Ireland, and Norway.
September 1972	National referendum in Norway goes against its membership in the EEC.
January 1973	UK, Denmark, and Ireland join the EEC.
January 1974	European Social Fund is created.
January 1975	European Regional Development Fund is created.

June 1975	Greece applies for EC membership.
March 1977	Portugal applies for EEC membership.
July 1977	Spain applies for EEC membership.
March 1979	European Monetary System (EMS) is established.
June 1979	First direct elections of the European Parliament (EP) are held.
January 1981	Greece joins the EEC.
January 1986	Spain and Portugal join the EEC.
February 1986	Single European Act is signed in Luxembourg, removing most of the remaining physical, fiscal, and technical barriers to the formation of a European common market. The EEC is now referred to simply as EC.
June 1987	Turkey applies for EC membership.
July 1989	Austria applies for EC membership.
December 1989	Turkey's membership application is rejected.
July 1990	Malta and Cyprus apply for EC membership.
October 1990	German reunification brings the former East Germany into the EC.
July 1991	Sweden applies for EC membership.
February 1992	Treaty on European Union (Maastricht Treaty) is signed, which expands the process of European integration and creates a timetable for the European Monetary Union (EMU). The European Community (EC) is now referred to as the European Union (EU).
March 1992	Finland applies for EU membership.
June 1992	Danish voters reject the Maastricht Treaty.
May 1993	Danish voters approve the Maastricht Treaty after certain compromises are inserted into treaty.
January 1995	Austria, Sweden, and Finland join the EU after respective national referendums favor membership. A national referendum in Norway rejects EU membership.
October 1997	Treaty of Amsterdam is signed, which aims, among other things, to equalize tax structures among members of the EU in preparation for upcoming monetary union.
January 1999	EMU goes into effect. The eleven EU member states participating are Austria, Belgium, Finland, France, Germany, Ireland, Italy, Luxembourg, the Netherlands, Portugal, and Spain.
May 1999	Treaty of Amsterdam enters into force.
September 1999	EP approves the new European Commission (EC) led by Romano Prodi.
December 1999	European Council meeting in Helsinki decides to open accession negotiations with Bulgaria, Latvia, Lithuania,

	Malta, Romania, and the Slovak Republic and to recognize Turkey as a candidate country.
June 2000	A new partnership agreement (2000–2020) between the EU and the African-Caribbean-Pacific (ACP) countries is signed in Cotonou, Benin.
December 2000	European Council agrees on Treaty of Nice (to be ratified by all member states). EU leaders formally proclaim the charter of Fundamental Rights of the European Union.
January 2001	Greece joins the eurozone.
February 2001	Regulation adopted establishing the Rapid Reaction Force.
Jan.–Feb. 2002	The euro becomes legal tender and permanently replaces national currencies in EMU countries.
December 2002	Copenhagen European Council declares that Cyprus, Czech Republic, Estonia, Hungary, Latvia, Lithuania, Malta, Poland, Slovak Republic, and Slovenia will become EU members by May 1, 2004.
February 2003	Treaty of Nice enters into force.
April 2003	Treaty of Accession (2003) is signed in Athens.
May 2004	Cyprus, Czech Republic, Estonia, Hungary, Latvia, Lithuania, Malta, Poland, Slovak Republic, and Slovenia become EU member states.
October 2004	President-designate of the European Commission, José Manuel Barroso, is forced to withdraw his proposal for the EC membership by the European Parliament. EU leaders sign the treaty establishing a constitution for Europe.
November 2004	EP approves the new commission proposed by Barroso.
February 2005	Spain holds the first referendum on the European Constitution; the Spanish people accept it.
April 2005	EP gives its approval to the accession of Bulgaria and Romania to the EU by 2007.
May 2005	The French electorate rejects the European Constitution in a national referendum.
June 2005	The Dutch electorate rejects the European Constitution in a national referendum; a "reflection period" on treaty reform initiates.
October 2005	European accession negotiations open with Croatia and Turkey.
January 2007	Bulgaria and Romania become EU member states; Slovenia joins the eurozone.
June 2007	German EU presidency ends "reflection period" and relaunches negotiations for a new treaty.
December 2007	The Lisbon Treaty, a slightly slimmed-down alternative to the European Constitution, is signed by the EU heads of

	state or government. Only Ireland is obliged to ratify by referendum.
January 2008	Cyprus and Malta join the eurozone.
June 2008	First Irish referendum on the Lisbon Treaty is held; the treaty is rejected.
June 2008	Negotiations for a new EU-Russia agreement are launched at the EU-Russia summit.
July 2008	At the Paris summit, French president Nicolas Sarkozy launches the Union for the Mediterranean, aimed at revitalizing the Euro-Mediterranean Partnership.
August 2008	Russia and Georgia fight a war over the provinces of South Ossetia and Abkhazia.
January 2009	Slovakia joins the eurozone.
June 2009	European Parliamentary elections; the European People's Party (EPP) becomes the largest party.
September 2009	Parliament confirms second term for European Commission president José Manuel Barroso.
October 2009	Second Irish referendum on the Lisbon Treaty is held; the treaty is ratified.
November 2009	Appointments take place for the two newly created EU top jobs in the Lisbon Treaty. Herman Van Rompuy is elected EU Council president and Catherine Ashton is elected high representative for foreign affairs and security policy.
December 2009	The Lisbon Treaty enters into force, thereby amending the Maastricht Treaty (TEU).
December 2009	Greek sovereign debt crisis escalates, leading to a crisis in the eurozone.
May 2010	Member states and the European Central Bank agree on the setup of a European Financial Stability Facility (EFSF) to help weaker eurozone members remain financially stable.
December 2010	EU approves the 2011 budget, after disagreements between the member states and the EP. Despite national austerity measures, the EU budget will increase 2.9 percent.
January 2011	Estonia joins the eurozone.

Acronyms

CAP	Common Agricultural Policy
CEEC	Central and Eastern European Countries
CFSP	Common Foreign and Security Policy
CMEA	Council for Mutual Economic Assistance
COREU	CORespondance EUropéenne
CSCE	Conference on Security and Cooperation in Europe
CSDP	Common Security and Defense Policy
EAPC	Euro-Atlantic Partnership Council
EBRD	European Bank for Reconstruction and Development
EC	European Community/European Council
ECB	European Central Bank
ECHR	European Convention/Court on Human Rights
ECJ	European Court of Justice
ECSC	European Coal and Steel Community
EDA	European Defense Agency
EEA	European Economic Area
EEAS	European External Action Service
EEC	European Economic Community
EFTA	European Free Trade Association
EMS	European Monetary System
EMU	Economic and Monetary Union
ENP	European Neighborhood Policy
EP	European Parliament
EPC	European Political Cooperation
EPU	European Political Union
ERM	Exchange Rate Mechanism
ERRF	European Rapid Reaction Force
ESDI	European Security and Defense Identity
ESS	European Security Strategy
GATT	General Agreement on Tariffs and Trade
IGC	Inter-Governmental Conference
IMF	International Monetary Fund
JHA	Justice and Home Affairs
MNC	multinational corporation
NACC	North Atlantic Cooperation Council

NATO	North Atlantic Treaty Organization
OECD	Organization for Economic Cooperation and Development
OEEC	Organization for European Economic Cooperation
OSCE	Organization for Security and Cooperation in Europe
PFP	Partnership for Peace
QMV	Qualified Majority Voting
SEA	Single European Act
SGP	Stability and Growth Pact
TCN	Third-Country Nationals
TEU	Treaty on European Union
WEU	Western European Union
WTO	World Trade Organization

List of Illustrations and Supplementary Material

Boxes

1.1	The Institutions of the French Fifth Republic	28
1.2	Fifth Republic Presidents and the Three Cohabitation Periods	30
1.3	Douelle: A Mirror of France?	42
1.4	The Marseille Exception	47
1.5	De Gaulle on Gaullism	57
2.1	From "Old" to "New" Labour: The End of Socialism?	75
2.2	An Awkward Partner: Margaret Thatcher on Europe	90
2.3	Blair on Iraq	95
3.1	The Nervousness about Facing the Positive Aspects of German History	106
3.2	Berlin: City on the Move	114
3.3	Speech by Federal Chancellor Angela Merkel before the United States Congress	127
4.1	The Crisis of the First Republic (Chronology)	148
4.2	Silvio Berlusconi: A Very Peculiar Politician	152
5.1	Why Do the Scandinavian Welfare States Survive?	170
5.2	Cartoons and Immigrants: No Laughing Matter	190
6.1	From a Speech by Deputy Head of the Presidential Administration Vladislav Surkov to Workers of the United Russia Political Party	212
6.2	Excerpts from Mikhail Gorbachev, *Perestroika*	236
6.3	From the Declaration on Human Rights and Dignity of the Tenth World Council of Russian People	238
7.1	Major Personalities	247
7.2	Chronology of Major Elections and Changes in Government	250
9.1	European Council Conclusions, Brussels, June 17, 2010	325
10.1	Treaty Provisions Pertaining to the "No-Bailout Clause"	340
10.2	Franco-German Declaration: Statement for the France-Germany-Russia Summit, Deauville, Monday, October 18, 2010	348
11.1	The European Court of Justice	356
11.2	Direct Effect and Supremacy	357

11.3 The Preliminary Ruling Procedure   358
13.1 Extracts from the North Atlantic Treaty, Adopted in
      Washington, D.C., April 4, 1949   424

Figures

4.1   Parties and Electoral Alliances (1994–2010)   156
10.1 Greek-German Interest Rate Differential   330
10.2 Long-term Interest Rates and Current Account Balances in
      Greece   332
10.3 Interest Rate Convergence and Macroeconomic Imbalances   334
10.4 Irish Long-term Sovereign Yield Differentials with Germany   349
12.1 Net Migration, EU-27   374
12.2 Net Migration in 2007, by Country   374
12.3 Share of Foreign Population by State, 2009   376
12.4 Muslim Population   391
12.5 Unemployment Spreads in Europe, by Country, 2008   392
13.1 European Security Organizations   414

Maps

The European Union   ix
France   25
Great Britain   67
Germany   99
Italy   133
Scandinavia   161
Russia   207
Poland   243

Tables

0.0   European Union Statistical Information   x
2.1   Prime Ministers and Governing Parties in the United Kingdom,
      1945–2010   72
3.1   2009 Parliamentary Election   110
3.2   Federal Elections, Coalition Governments, and Chancellors,
      1949–2009   112
4.1   Italy's First Republic National Elections   140

4.2   Coalition Governance and Governments in Italy, 1948–2010   142
5.1   Party Parliamentary Strength in October 2010   183
5.2   Public Social Security Transfers as a Percentage of GDP,
      1960–2008   187
5.3   European Community/European Union Referenda   202
7.1   Genealogy and Ideology of Major Political Parties / Electoral
      Coalitions   260
8.1   Rounds of EU Enlargement   284
9.1   Institutional Features of LMEs and CMEs   313
12.1 International Migration Stocks by World Region, 2010   377
12.2 Evolving EU Control over Immigration Issues   385
13.1 Timeline of NATO, the European Union, and the West
      European Union   402

Introduction

The European Outlook

Ronald Tiersky, Saskia van Genugten, and Erik Jones

Europe in the second decade of the twenty-first century finds itself once again at a turning point. Some of its dilemmas are familiar ones, in particular the recurrent choice to make between "more Europe" and "less Europe" as a response to difficulties. That is, between ever deeper institutional integration of the continent's nation-states and peoples or, to the contrary, a great hesitation about further commitment to the European Union (EU). Other choices are new, or, more often, new forms of old issues. The greatest of these is the existential choice: Will the Europeans reestablish a historic dynamism, or are they in some broad sense an exhausted civilization?

The Old Continent is buffeted between three major forces: geopolitical peace and security on one side, economic and financial turmoil on the other, and encompassing globalization trends that raise unprecedented doubts about Europe's ability to compete successfully for international political influence and economic prosperity. Given continued American global centrality and rising Chinese influence everywhere on the planet, the European outlook is clouded with forecasts of historical decline. It is up to the Europeans to demonstrate that they can rise to the challenge.

The continent in 2011 is no longer threatened from without in military terms, other than by the now ever-present danger of catastrophic terrorist attacks. Simultaneously, however, the European Union has been badly shaken by the international financial crisis that began at the end of 2007. Several European national financial systems have required costly bailouts by EU partners. The euro, the common currency—the crowning achievement of European integration thus far—has been destabilized, and the political solidarity that lies behind the European monetary union has been tested. As a consequence, the entire edifice built up over decades of European integration is currently being put to its severest test.

In many ways, European integration is a victim of its own success. The original union structures were founded at the end of the Second World War on the promise that Europe would one day be united whole and free. Over the intervening decades, it has achieved that goal. Now, the question is where to go from there. The debate centers on whether progress toward an ever more united Europe is more desirable than the current, delicate equilibrium between supra-national institutions and still vibrant nation-states. The euro reflects this ambiguity. The economic advantages and simple convenience of having a single currency are obvious, but the need for bailouts has led to questions about whether the financial cost and the restrictions on national autonomy were not too great.

In the past, political or economic crisis in one or another country has always been surmounted. Stagnation in the larger EU has sooner or later led to a resurgence of political will and more thoroughgoing European integration. The sudden collapse of the Soviet Union in 1989–1991 was accommodated by a huge and ultimately successful eastern enlargement of EU membership. In other words, the way out of crisis, stagnation, and uncertainty has always been "more Europe" rather than "less Europe." The interplay and conflicts of national interests at the European level have in general been resolved, however reluctantly, through displays of mutual solidarity and sacrifice rather than uncompromising national egotism. Each for their own reasons, European countries have in effect acted on the principle that their own national interest is best served by coming to the aid of partner member states because, strong and weak alike, the benefits of European integration in a globalized world outweigh the costs.

Will this pattern of the past govern the current period and the years ahead into the twenty-first century? A number of prominent American writers such as Robert Kagan and Christopher Caldwell have been quick to point to evidence of Europe's decline.[1] Kagan notes that the European Union is not like the United States, that it is unable to hold its own against either the United States or the rise of China, and that it is even too weak and divided to stand up to its near neighbors, meaning not just Russia but in a certain sense a newly empowered Turkey as well. Caldwell points out that Europe's populations are aging, its welfare states seem unsustainable, and it has problematic relations with recent immigrants. Such criticisms carry an obvious grain of truth but can also be pushed too far.

Europe's critics seem overly pessimistic, and yet its supporters—like T. R. Reid, Jeremy Rifkin, and Steven Hill—seem to exaggerate in the opposite direction.[2] They suggest that Europe has fostered a new paradigm for global governance, that it has created a new model for innovation and competitiveness, and that it has lifted the pursuit of social justice to new and inspiring heights.

The debate between the two groups makes for an unintelligible conversation; it is almost as though they are writing about different places. The question they raise is nonetheless important. Does Europe still matter in geopolitical and geostrategic terms? This is not an idle concern of outside observers. Today, many Europeans are haunted by the prospect of their own long-term decline, not just as a world power but also as a model for successful international relations. Some, like Mark Leonard, try gamely to insist that Europe will lead the world into the future; others, like Anand Menon, are more measured in their analysis; and still others, like Simon Hix, are openly worried that Europe faces an existential crisis.[3] Unlike their counterparts in the United States, moreover, these voices are engaged in a sustained and broad-ranging debate that offers few prospects for clear resolution. Indeed, this conversation has become all absorbing. It is as though, faced with the prospect of their own obsolescence, Europeans have become ever more introspective, and as a result they have also become unable to shape a coherent response to the challenges coming from the world around them.[4]

The more Europeans argue with one another over the process of integration, the more easily non-Europeans find it to write Europe off. Indeed, other global powers have started to take Europe's decline as an assumption, some even as a given. In 2008, the Democratic presidential candidate Barack Obama made an unprecedented trip to Europe—the culmination was the future president's speech to a couple hundred thousand Berliners (most of whom were anti–George W. Bush or even anti-American) on the famous Unter den Linden boulevard—to burnish his foreign policy credentials. Yet, only a few years later, Washington seems disillusioned by what continued strategic partnership with Europe has to offer.[5]

President Obama continues to insist both in his administration's National Security Strategy and in his public writing and speeches that Europe remains the cornerstone for America's engagement with the outside world.[6] Nevertheless, it is clear that Obama administration officials are disappointed that Europeans do not contribute more to help stabilize Afghanistan or to beef up the NATO alliance. Europe's earlier promise to rival the United States economically is also discounted. No longer is there, for example, a great debate as to whether the euro will soon challenge the dollar as a global reserve currency. Instead the debate is about how long and with what membership the European currency will continue.

Some of this Euro-pessimism stems from Europe's inability to live up to self-generated high expectations and from the almost continuous criticism it receives in the media. Yet some of the disappointment is fueled by the obvious trends in the data. In economic terms, the EU countries' share in world real GDP has declined from around 35 percent in the 1970s to around 27 percent in 2009. By 2030, it is expected to fall to around 20 percent. Europe has grown (and will continue to do so), but China, India, and other parts of the world have grown faster. Also, while Europe still dominates world trade, its relative terms of trade are deteriorating. The gap between imports and exports is shrinking, mainly to the benefit of China, which has made substantial inroads in the European marketplace. Relative population sizes have shifted as well. According to demographic projections, Europeans will constitute only 7 percent of the world population in 2050. At the beginning of the twentieth century, it was still 20 percent. And, as the UN predicts, while in 1900 Europeans outnumbered Africans at a 3-to-1 ratio, by 2050 this is likely to be the other way around.[7]

Such trends should not be overemphasized. Despite its relative decline, Europe remains in many ways enviable. For example, Europe is the wealthiest world region, and several of its individual countries rival the United States in terms of income per capita and surpass it in quality of life, considering social, cultural, and environmental factors that wealth alone cannot measure. The creation and development of what is now the European Union is one of modern history's greatest political achievements. After all, the continent that initiated two world wars in the last century is now comparatively peaceful. Several other world regions look to Europe as an example of how to reconcile once historic enemies, how to promote democratic political systems where there were once dictatorships, and how to create legitimate institutions of supranational governance on a foundation of traditional national sovereignty and national interest.[8] Europeans take these things for granted, but it is worth remembering that there are many parts of the world that do not know peace and for which the unity that Europeans share is only a distant aspiration.

Even more impressive, the scope of Europe's achievement continues to widen in the face of incredible obstacles. Hence, the EU's enlargement from the original six countries in 1958 to twenty-seven by 2007 included epoch-making accomplishments. At the very start, France and (then West) Germany were reconciled, with Germany becoming emphatically European. In the 1970s, postfascist and military authoritarian governance were channeled into democracy in Spain, Portugal, and Greece. With the exception of Romania and the Balkans, the Cold War in Europe ended without violence. The Central and East European countries (CEECs) quickly found their way forward after decades of Soviet control, in great part thanks to the very reform process through which they became members of the European Union. When that process ended, the entry of the CEECs into the European Union in 2004 and 2007 created a truly continent-wide political framework.[9]

Altogether, seemingly contradictory judgments are justifiable about Europe today. It is both growing and weakening at the same time. Moreover, this situation will only become more complicated—and thus more difficult to interpret—given the wide range of challenges the countries of Europe face in the coming decades. Many of these are addressed in the chapters that follow, either generally or on a country-by-country basis. This introduction sketches several large themes: the economic crisis; European Union institutional reforms; European foreign policies, including dealing with Russia, Turkey, and international terrorism; and the future of the welfare state.

The Economic Crisis

The financial and economic crisis that set in at the end of 2007 did not leave Europe untouched. Although Great Britain, Iceland, and Ireland were hard hit from the outset, many of the core continental and Scandinavian countries seemed less directly affected than the United States. This was especially true for those with the least integrated banking systems—such as Italy—but it was true for countries like France and Poland as well.[10] Nevertheless, the feeling of relative strength turned out to be illusory. Banks and bank insurance conglomerates in several countries, including Germany, the Netherlands, and Belgium, revealed a surprisingly large exposure to U.S. mortgage markets and staggered under the weight of bad investments. Ultimately, some had to be bailed out. Whatever the hope that Europe was somehow decoupled from the United States, it was clear in the aftermath of the September 2008 Lehman Brothers default in New York that the two sides of the Atlantic remained deeply intertwined.[11]

The European Union also had problems that were uniquely its own. This became clear in late 2009 when financial markets began to question the solidarity among those countries that use the euro as their currency—the "euro zone."[12] The euro was introduced as a common currency in the financial markets in 1999 and in physical form three years later, and while it experienced some difficult moments at the outset, most observers viewed its first decade as a record of success. Initial estimates of the euro's performance during the financial crisis were positive as well. But problems started to emerge in October 2009 when a newly appointed Greek prime minister announced that his government would need to borrow considerably more from financial markets than his predecessor had admitted. The announcement itself was hardly surprising. Bond traders had known for a long time that Greek debt statistics were inaccurate, and these revisions had become something of an annual affair. The political reaction to the announcement was nevertheless unexpected. European leaders first refused to talk about the Greek crisis and then became openly divided over what should be done. In the resulting confusion, bond traders began to question whether Greece would be able to raise sufficient money in the markets to cover its existing debts and whether other European countries, Germany in particular, would step in to ensure that Greece did not default. European solidarity was tested.

Unfortunately, the European response was too little and too late. From one European Council summit to the next, it was clear that Europe's financial leaders were both unwilling and unable to agree on how to handle the Greek situation. In response, the banks and investment houses that trade in sovereign debt started to panic, and eventually the market for Greek bonds went into a rout. That panic proved difficult to stop, even though the member states in the end managed to come up with a €115 billion package for Greece, including substantial participation from the International Monetary Fund (IMF). Instead, the panic only widened, and the sovereign debt crisis that ensued rapidly spread far beyond the borders of Greece to encompass other countries with sizeable debts, both public and private. Soon opinion makers were putting Spain, Portugal, Ireland, and Italy together with stricken Greece in a new category, making for the latest European acronym: the "PIIGS." Within a week of their announcement of the Greek bailout, Europe's leaders already had to come up with a €750 billion commitment to a broader European stabilization fund. This seems like an enormous amount of money. Yet once Ireland tapped into the resources committed, voices immediately expressed concern that it would not be enough.[13]

There were more fundamental concerns as well. While throwing money at an issue—especially this one—can ease the symptoms of a crisis, only a deeper structural change can prevent it from being repeated. New rules seemed to be needed, and so the European Council instructed its new president, Herman Van Rompuy, to lead a task force to come up with suggestions for improving the coordination of macroeconomic governance. Van Rompuy's task force faced a considerable challenge, both to find agreement on a package of reforms and to ensure that the changes could be made to work within the existing framework of legislation. This last hurdle proved to be almost insurmountable because, for Europe, adding new rules—limits to budget deficits, limits to sovereign debt, a mechanism for when things go wrong—to such a fundamentally important issue often means treaty revisions, and in this particular case, it would mean reopening the Lisbon Treaty, which could be Europe's Pandora's box. The German chancellor, Angela Merkel, has been an advocate of another round of such treaty revisions to provide a facility for countries to manage an orderly default, but many others seem reluctant. Where this current reluctance for institutional reform comes from will be the topic of the next section of this introduction, but before we move there, it is good to take note of two other important developments that have been exposed by the crisis.

First of all, Germany positioned itself as a bulwark of monetary conservatism and expressed great reluctance to bail out countries that had borrowed beyond their means. This hard-line position was not the only possibility for Germany. In fact, the initial view expressed by then German finance minister Peer Steinbrück in February 2009 was that Germany would of course show solidarity, and no country using the euro would be allowed to default. Subsequent elections resulted in Steinbrück's Social Democratic Party having to leave the coalition. As head of a new center-right government, Chancellor Merkel adopted a more critical and less generous view. Given the changeover from center-left to center-right, this alternation in policy was understandable. What was striking about the shift was the assertiveness with which the new center-right coalition made itself heard. Chancellor Merkel's brusque manner in dismissing concerns about Greek solvency in the face of increasingly unsettled bond markets was quite unfamiliar to a postwar Germany that normally moves along with calmness and shrewdness. The fact that this put her at odds with French president Nicolas Sarkozy compounded the unfamiliarity of the situation. Not only was Germany being more assertive, but it was also creating tension within the Franco-German relationship, which is the traditional motor for European integration.

The second development that took place during the sovereign debt crisis reveals the extent to which Europeans were willing to challenge their own fundamental assumptions about how integration should work. In a remarkable turnaround, for the first time in its history, the European Central Bank (ECB) went beyond its assigned role of controlling inflation and bought national government bonds in secondary markets. The goal of the ECB's Governing Council was not to finance governments but to dampen volatility in the bond markets. Aware as they were of the possible chain of consequences, the ECB governors—conservative stewards of the currency—clearly realized that the sovereign debt crisis was not just about money but about market stability as well. Once again, though, differences in opinion became unexpectedly prominent. In contrast to the traditional discipline of "speaking with one voice" within the central banking community, the president of the German Bundesbank (central bank), Axel Weber, criticized the ECB for having abandoned its traditional role. Since Weber sits on the Governing Council of the ECB, this criticism could only mean that he refused to accept collective responsibility for the decision that body had made. The ECB president, Jean Claude Trichet, quickly defended the organization, denying that it was engaged in politics or inflationary public financing, and insisted that without market stability there would be no future for the euro. What Trichet obviously could not say was that not all of his colleagues on the Governing Council were in agreement. This led markets to speculate as to how deeply the members of the Governing Council might be divided and what the policy implications of that division might be. Market observers (including bond traders) also speculated as to whether Weber would be picked to follow Trichet as president of the ECB.[14]

With the situation still uncertain at the beginning of 2011, the question that remains to be answered is whether a European currency can remain viable without a European government to administer it. From the start of the project, many analysts have questioned whether the uncertainties of a common currency would not intensify the already substantive differences in political interests and policies among EU governments. The most extreme version of this argument came from the American economist Martin Feldstein who predicted that the euro would lead to war.[15] The point has been reiterated (albeit in much less extreme forms) across the political spectrum in Europe as well—most prominently by the Belgian economist Paul De Grauwe, but also by members of the central banking and legal communities.[16]

Again, during the first decade of its existence, from 1999 to 2009, developments seemed to prove the stability of the euro, the strength of it, and even its potential as a rival global reserve currency. But the recent crisis reveals that a currency is only as stable as the political will to support it. In turn, that forces us to reconsider precisely what it is that underpins European political will. The sovereign debt crisis shows that Europeans can either choose to hang together or they will hang separately. That lesson can be generalized beyond financial markets as well, to institutional reforms of the EU, to its common foreign and security policies, and to many other areas, as you will realize throughout this book.

Institutional Reform

The history of European integration has never been an unbroken chain of success. If anything, it is a tale of crisis and recovery. Moreover, this pattern is hardly unique. We could say much the same thing about the North Atlantic Treaty Organization (NATO) as well.[17] Still, admitting that Europe has often experienced moments of crisis in the past should not lead us to assume that it will always find some way to recover. Especially in the last couple of years, setbacks have been numerous, and the episodes of progress have been fewer and farther between. This is particularly evident in the uncomfortable interaction between the process of enlargement to include new member states in the European Union (or "widening") and the process of endowing the institutions of Europe with new competences while at the same time working to streamline their functioning in order to make them more accountable and more effective ("deepening"). Deepening and widening do not have to come into conflict, but the tension between them is not always productive.

Consider the events of the middle 2000s. During the run-up to the historic eastern enlargement in May 2004, EU leaders fashioned a draft constitutional treaty for Europe, including all kinds of nation-building paraphernalia aimed at streamlining Europe's institutional framework in order to finally stop "punching below its weight." This treaty was the culmination of a long process of adapting the institutions of the European Union to the challenge of enlargement. That process started with the 1996 intergovernmental conference, which was a meeting of the heads of state and government of the member nations organized with the express objective of reforming the treaties of the European Union. It continued through the 2000 Nice Treaty and the 2002–2003 constitutional convention. Along the way, the European Union added on significant responsibilities for labor market policy and welfare state reform, foreign and security policy, and justice and home affairs. The result was a dramatic change in expectations both about what Europe might do and about what it could not. A number of books and articles were published to predict the emergence of a European global power, a European superstate, or a European empire.[18] Yet for all the attention these celebrations of Europe received, they were matched by a growing unease that the European constitutional treaty was more than many Europeans wanted or would support.

This notion of popular support is important because institutional reforms require changes to the treaties that make up (or constitute) the process of European integration. In turn, these treaty changes usually have to be approved by the national parliaments and sometimes also by popular referenda. Such referenda have the potential to create embarrassing surprises, as when the Danish voted narrowly to reject the Maastricht Treaty in June 2002 or when the Irish voted to reject the Nice Treaty nine years later. The French government had referendum problems of its own in a hard-fought campaign in the summer of 1992 over the Maastricht Treaty. That French referendum only narrowly passed.

Despite this record of unexpected disappointment, however, most European politicians assumed that they could count on a solid majority of pro-European supporters, particularly in the core member states. For many, the widespread skepticism of the British toward European integration was simply the exception that proved the rule. Hence, the shock and disillusionment was great when this turned out not to be the case. In May and June of 2005, the long-worked-on and much-hailed EU constitutional treaty failed ratification by large majorities in popular referenda held in France and the Netherlands.[19]

Struggling to find a balance between pleasing their domestic audiences and moving the European project forward, political leaders engaged in a "year of reflection." That year ended in 2007 when they decided to do it all over again, but without any of the constitutional pretensions. There would be no flag, no anthem, and no foreign minister (at least in name). The new provisions would not be called a "constitutional" treaty but a "reform" treaty, thereby avoiding the need for a referendum in many member states. Also, it would be written for lawyers and not for the average citizen. But beyond these changes in form, much of the substance (meaning most of the reforms) remained the same. Unsurprisingly, then, getting this treaty through was a close-run thing. The Irish electorate—the only ones required by their national constitution to call a popular referendum—initially rejected this new series of amendments. It took sixteen months and a second referendum before the Irish could be brought around. By that time, however, the economic crisis was in full swing.

The Lisbon Treaty entered into force on December 1, 2009. As with all the other major revisions since Maastricht, its primary justification had been to accommodate the last enlargement of the European Union and to prepare for the next. The reasoning was straightforward. In the past decade, the European Union had grown from fifteen to twenty-seven members, and countries such as Serbia, Croatia, and Turkey were knocking on its door. To accommodate this growth, the decision-making mechanisms of the EU had to be reformed in order to work smoothly with a larger group of countries and votes. This held true for virtually all of the institutions, from the Council of the European Union to the European Commission and the European Parliament. Hence, for example, the Lisbon Treaty offered countries fewer opportunities to veto decisions in the Council, both by changing the majority thresholds and by creating more opportunities for the Council to take decisions by majority vote. At the same time, the Lisbon Treaty helped to close the "democratic deficit" of Europe both by giving more power to the European Parliament and by engaging national parliaments more closely in the legislative processes under way at the EU level.

Europe's Influence in the World

Another goal of the institutional reforms introduced in the Lisbon Treaty was to make it easier to coordinate and project European interests abroad.[20] Over the past two decades, the European Union has developed a Common Foreign and Security Policy and a European Security and Defense Policy (now called the Common Security and Defense Policy). And for most of that time, these two policy areas have been much less ambitious in practice than on paper. The Common Foreign and Security Policy only operated when the member states agreed on a policy that they could pursue in common, and the European Security and Defense Policy only worked when some member state accepted to send its military forces under the flag of Europe. The result was that the policies were always more fragmented than the names would seem to suggest—because countries had very little in common in their relations with the outside world and because few EU member states have either the desire or the resources to deploy their security or peacekeeping forces on behalf of Europe.

This situation is less alarming than it sounds, particularly when viewed in its proper historical context. When the Europeans decided to build common economic institutions back in the 1950s, ideas were floated for having a similar project in political affairs and defense. Both proposals for a European Defense Community and a Europe Political Community failed. Whatever the putative advantages of acting together, political leaders were unwilling to give up sovereignty in the realms of foreign policy or defense. Depending on how you look at it, further economic integration was either a least common denominator or a greatest common factor.

That reluctance to cede power in foreign and security policy remained firm up through the 1960s. By the early 1970s, however, European states started to consult each other and align their external political reactions whenever possible. This was done on a strictly ad hoc basis outside the formal institutions for European integration. It did not result in radical changes in the foreign policy of even the smallest member state, and yet it did offer some advantages over the alternative of facing the world alone—even for the largest European countries like Germany and France. That importance only grew as the 1970s gave way to the 1980s. The changes taking place within the Soviet Union, coupled with the rise of economic competition in Japan and other parts of Asia, underscored the importance of speaking with a common voice. Such factors did not make having a common foreign policy any easier; they just made it seem more attractive.

By the beginning of the 1990s, the French and the Germans sought to capitalize on these advantages by elaborating a Common Foreign and Security Policy within the institutional framework for European integration as one of the three principal competences of the European Union. Again, the success of the Maastricht Treaty was modest in this regard, and yet the incentive to build on that success remained apparent. In the follow-up Treaty of Amsterdam, the office of a high representative of the Common Foreign and Security Policy was created. The first person selected to occupy this position was former Spanish foreign minister Javier Solana, who brought to the job both foreign *and* security policy experience, since his previous position had been secretary general of NATO. Solana was also named secretary general of the West European Union, which was the organization developed in the 1950s when the first attempt at foreign and security policy integration failed.

This West European Union affiliation was important because the Amsterdam Treaty anticipated that the European Union would make further efforts in the domain of security and defense. Most of these would focus on crisis management, but they could also extend to peacekeeping and humanitarian intervention—the so-called Petersberg tasks (named after the 1992 West European Union summit where they were elaborated). The nucleus for this greater defense and security cooperation is the Anglo-French relationship, because these are the two countries that have both the military resources for foreign deployment and the political will to use them. What is unclear is whether the close cooperation of these two great powers will prove to be sufficient. In 1998, the French and British governments met in France at St. Malo to declare their ambition to push European integration in security and defense. In 2010, they met again to sign a joint defense treaty, but they made no mention of Europe.

Certainly the capacity for Europe to play a positive security role is greater than often estimated. While Americans tend to downplay the potential of the Common Security and Defense Policy (CSDP, previously the ESDP), it is worth noting that in a rather short time, quite a lot has been achieved. This includes progress toward a deployable force of 60,000 troops drawn from across the member states and also from countries outside the European Union (like Turkey); progress toward the creation of European "Battlegroups" for joint deployment; a European command headquarters; and a series of other support facilities related to command, control, communication, and intelligence that are important for having a credible defense apparatus. While not yet capable or willing to engage in high-profile military missions like those undertaken by the United States in Iraq and Afghanistan, the European Union has nevertheless deployed numerous peacekeeping and postconflict stabilization missions in places like Kosovo, Macedonia, Georgia, East Timor, and the Democratic Republic of the Congo. It has also deployed police missions in Gaza and Afghanistan and a naval mission to combat piracy near the Somali coast.[21]

The European Union has also worked hard to simplify its administrative structures. Most of the complexity developed naturally as a result of the piecemeal and incremental process of European integration. Consider, for example, the complicated division of labor between the Council of Ministers and the European Commission. Going into the 2000s, the Council of Ministers controlled the Common Foreign and Security Policy and even had the high representative of that policy as the ranking civil servant in its secretariat. Meanwhile, the Commission retained competence for a range of policies that cut deep into the "foreign policy" domain—like European Union enlargement, relations with neighboring countries (the "neighborhood" policy), international trade, and development assistance. The explanation for this division is simple: as we have seen, foreign and security policy were added relatively late in the process of European integration and remain primarily an intergovernmental project—hence the predominance of the Council; economic policy, including all manner of economic relations with the outside world, came much sooner in the process and tended to center on the Commission. The fact that the division of labor is easy to understand, however, does not make it easy to manage. From an outsider's perspective, the different institutional lines of authority made it difficult to identify who actually represents "Europe."

Thus, another goal of the Lisbon Treaty was to untangle this division of labor and so construct a more streamlined and efficient organization. Two positions were added at the top of the pyramid, a high representative of the Common Foreign and Security Policy and a permanent (rather than rotating) president of the Council of the European Union. The high representative has feet both in the Council and in the Commission and can draw upon the resources of a 1,100-person strong European External Action Service, which is the European Union's official diplomatic corps. The effectiveness of this new foreign policy establishment remains to be seen. All that can be suggested at this point is that the selection of the first high representative, Lady Catherine Ashton, was more heavily influenced by the necessity of meeting the requirements of a complex negotiation between the member states than by the aspiration of providing the most capable person for the job. Lady Ashton may yet prove to be an extraordinary political talent, but those skills are not what brought her to the position in the first place.

The new permanent Council president, Herman Van Rompuy, came in as part of the same complex negotiation. Unlike Lady Ashton, however, he did not need to establish a new large bureaucracy in order to launch himself into his work. Instead it was events—and not bureau shaping—that constituted his greatest challenge. The first six months of Van Rompuy's tenure were consumed by the Greek sovereign debt crisis. He began by playing an honest broker between France and Germany, and many believe he excelled at the job. Very soon, however, it began to seem that he was being pushed to the background as the two most powerful countries using the euro opted to negotiate with one another directly.[22] Efforts to institutionalize his role at the center of the crisis failed to turn the tide. As mentioned above, the European Council named Van Rompuy to head a high-level task force to make proposals for improving European macroeconomic governance. Once again, Van Rompuy worked hard to act as honest broker, cobbling together positions from any number of important euro-zone member states. In the end, however, France and Germany chose to reassert their prerogative as the most powerful euro-zone members. On the very day that Van Rompuy was to announce the final fruits of his negotiations, October 18, 2010, Merkel and Sarkozy declared that they had reached a separate agreement. This Franco-German declaration triggered the Irish sovereign debt crisis.[23]

It is too early to tell whether the Lisbon Treaty provisions will truly furnish the union with a more agile mind and more efficient decision-making processes, or whether it will fail in practice to live up to its potential on paper. Meanwhile, the importance of having a more streamlined and effective organization has only increased. The case for this increasing importance can be made in general terms with reference to generic challenges like the rise of China or the problem of failed states, but it is even more obvious in the context of relations with the EU's two largest neighbors: Russia and Turkey.[24] Both of these countries are hugely important, both to individual member states and to the European Union as a whole. Nonetheless, both are subject to important differences of interest and opinion across the member states as well.

RUSSIA

The end of the Cold War was supposed to bring calm to the eastern borders of Europe. The implacable ideological threat of Soviet communism was no more. The volatile threat of nationalism in Russia and elsewhere was problematic but could be managed and ultimately tamed. The Central and Eastern European countries would quickly catch up with Western Europe in terms of output and income. They may even challenge the West to achieve higher levels of productivity and dynamism along the way. NATO was to redefine its goals and operations, and cooperation with Russia was considered possible and desirable. Contrasting visits to NATO headquarters in Brussels in 1989 and 1996 give a sense of the transformation. In 1989, there were passport controls outside NATO as well as checkpoints within it—all ostensibly to keep the Soviets out. Less than a decade later, these facilities were no longer used, and the Russians had their own offices inside the security fence.

But the victory of Vladimir Putin in the 2000 presidential elections and his reelection four years later made the West suspicious once again. During

Ukraine's 2004 general election, the European Union and Russia found themselves on different sides of what was to be called the Orange Revolution. When in 2007 Russia declared a moratorium of observance on the Conventional Forces in Europe (CFE) treaty, openly challenged NATO enlargement, and evoked old-style Cold War rhetoric, the European Union reconsidered its stances on its eastern neighbor. There was a short illusion that Putin's successor as Russian president, Dmitry Medvedev, would be more "Western oriented" and "cooperative," despite the fact that he appointed Putin as his prime minister. It soon became obvious, however, that the two—Putin and Medvedev— were a carefully matched pair.[25]

The main sources of distrust between Russia and the European states are two. For core Europe, the main threat is not so much one of military aggression as it is a concern about the security of energy supplies. Russia uses its natural gas supplies and its pipelines for geostrategic influence; it did so in Lithuania as well as in Ukraine. Russia itself insists that cutting supplies had to do with economic contracts, not manipulative politics, but its neighbors are not convinced, to say the least. And the political game affects Western Europe as well. The last crisis left parts of Europe running on reserves—and that in the middle of winter.

Also, as Europe's periphery has experienced, Russia has proven itself willing to put its military into the equation. Europe did not expect the war in Georgia that erupted suddenly in August 2008 and had no particularly strong answer to it. For many of the former Soviet countries, like Ukraine or the Baltic states, this military threat makes for a second source of distrust. The fact is that none of these countries believes that either the European Union or NATO could intervene decisively in the highly unlikely event that Russia would invade. The question then becomes one of "when" European support for those countries on Russia's borders could tip the balance in their favor, and "when" Russia will retain the upper hand.[26]

The picture gets ever more complicated if one considers the country-specific differences in Europe. While the Central and Eastern European countries are not in any sense close to trusting their former Russian occupier, personal ties between the Russian leadership and prominent Western European politicians like Silvio Berlusconi, Gerhard Schröder, and Jacques Chirac have always been strong and friendly. And even within Western Europe and within single countries, divisions exist. For example, the former Russian president Vladimir Putin was always cordial with European Commission president and then Italian prime minister Romano Prodi, but with Berlusconi he can do real (and not just diplomatic or political) business. To this mixture, we also have to add the structural concerns. While some countries, such as the Baltic states, Bulgaria, or (increasingly) Poland, are almost completely dependent on Russian energy, others, Spain for example, have no stake in the debate. And, as has been shown, all these divisions are not just shades of grey. The recent diplomatic rows between

Russia and Britain over a range of issues from energy and trade to expatriates, espionage, and assassination show that between these two actors an undeniable mutual antagonism remains.

TURKEY

Turkey's long and troubled partnership with the process of European integration has made for a paradoxical situation.[27] For more than four decades, Turkey has aspired to EU membership. It filed its first application in the early 1960s, it has been an associated member since 1963, and it filed again for full membership in 1987. Throughout most of the 1990s, its application lay dormant, only to resurface toward the end of the decade when the European Union agreed to treat Turkey as a candidate "like any other." Negotiations for membership finally took off in 2005, but even then the exercise has been anything but smooth. Indeed, the process of negotiating Turkey's accession to the European Union may even prove to be damaging to certain aspects of EU-Turkey relations. That a majority of EU citizens have expressed themselves against Turkish membership clearly does not help. The prospect that countries like Austria and France will hold referenda on whether Turkey should be allowed to join is even more problematic.

The question of Turkish membership in the European Union has become a symbolic issue of heroic dimensions. Narratives of national history make many Europeans remember the Turks knocking on Europe's doors before; now one would just say, "Google 'siege of Vienna.'" As a result, the two entities, "Islamic Turkey" and "Christian Europe," have often been presented as mutually exclusive and unable to coexist. At heart, a large number of Europeans see Turkey's desire to be European as a fundamental threat. Turkey, many say, is simply not European, whether in geographic, demographic, or economic terms, or in psychological, cultural, or political terms. Turkey's population is perceived as being too large, too poor, and, for many, too Muslim. Breaking this black-and-white view is one of the main obstacles to Turkish membership within the European Union. It is a challenge for Turkey as well. As so often is the case, the talk is international relations, but the real issues are domestic.[28]

Over the forty years that Turkey has been trying to join the European Union (and the European Community before that), conditions within Turkey and within the European Union have changed considerably. In part this transformation is due to the progress that has been made in terms of economic integration. First through its associate membership and later once it entered into a customs union with the European Union, Turkey has industrialized its way from being a poor undeveloped economy to a much more vibrant middle-income country. Along the way, Turkey has witnessed huge migrations from its countryside into its cities. A rapidly growing Anatolian middle class has emerged to challenge the old Kemalist elites of Ankara and Istanbul. Hence it has become more economically successful, but it has also become more socially conservative and more openly religious. Whoever travels Turkey is immediately aware of the country's two faces. One is outspokenly secular; the other is modestly, but devoutly, Islamic. The secular face is the one advocated by Mustafa Kemal "Atatürk" (or father of the Turks), the founder of the modern Turkish state. The second face is the one long oppressed by the same Kemalists but recently brought back into the picture, not least by the current Turkish prime minister, Recep Tayyip Erdogan, and the president, Abdullah Gül.[29]

For decades, EU membership was associated with Atatürk's dream of becoming permanently a "Western" country. But currently, attitudes toward Europe are not easy to anticipate. For all that it is pro-Western, the secular group tends to be skeptical about Turkey's readiness to join the European Union, and they are uncomfortable with the influence that the European Union exercises over domestic Turkish politics. Meanwhile, the more Islamic—or, in its own terms, "conservative"—group is more accepting of both the goal of European Union membership and the influence of the European Union in Turkish affairs, especially where it advocates more pluralism and more religious freedoms.

Just as with Russia, EU member states have difficulties agreeing about the Turkish candidacy, not least because of prevailing negative public opinions. The official policy is that Turkey is a candidate country like any other. Nevertheless, Nicolas Sarkozy has stated that Turkey will not become a member while he is president of France, and German chancellor Angela Merkel has suggested that the most she could support would be a second-class "privileged partnership." British prime minister David Cameron, on the other hand, has declared himself very much in favor of a quick accession.

At the same time, Turkey has been reassessing its own opinions about the European Union. Strong economic growth, renewed self-confidence, and the opportunities that are presented to it in a more multipolar world have created alternative options. Turkey has regional aspirations as well as European ones, and it is acutely aware of its strategic—though therefore also vulnerable—location. In 2009, Foreign Minister Ahmet Davutoğlu introduced the policy of having a foreign policy that turns the whole "360 degrees" around the country. Turkey will take a new look at its relations with the European Union, and it will also reconsider its relations with the United States, Iran, Egypt, Syria, and Russia. Even the historically close ties between Turkey and Israel have come under scrutiny, and several recent clashes over Israeli treatment of Palestinians in Gaza signal that Turkey is willing to assert its interests forcefully if necessary.[30]

While many can be found, we want to give one illustration of the shift in power relations that is taking place between the European Union and Turkey. Consider diplomacy toward Iran. For years, the West has sought the right mixture of international pressure to persuade Iran to abandon what the international community perceives as a plan to build nuclear weapons capability. The balance over time has shifted between negotiations (preferred by Europeans) and sanctions (preferred by the United States), but without finding a compromise position or achieving much success. The European negotiation team—Germany, France, and the United Kingdom—is often derided as the "Three Dwarfs." But then in the spring of 2010, Turkey, together with Brazil, appeared as a new diplomatic force in trying to head off Iran's nuclear program. From the standpoint of the United States, this activism on the part of two middle-income countries was almost as unwelcome as it was unexpected.

Our point here is not to pass judgment on the policy itself. Rather, it is only to suggest that this Turkey-Brazil initiative is significant.[31] It suggests that the new rising economic and diplomatic powers, not Europe, might try to impose themselves as an alternative to American leadership—not on every issue, perhaps, but at least in some cases where they think they can make a difference. Hence the Turkey-Brazil initiative has an importance that extends well beyond either its content or its substantive impact on the Iranian nuclear program. The fact that Brazil and Turkey were willing to work outside the traditional Western tutelage ought to encourage EU governments to consider soberly the future of Europe in the international order.

TERRORISM AND INTERNAL SECURITY

A more general case for the increasing importance of both a Common Foreign and Security Policy and a Common Security and Defense Policy can be made in the context of international terrorism. More than that, however, terrorism is also important for the domestic security challenge it represents. A decade has passed since the al-Qaeda attack on the Twin Towers and the Pentagon. The U.S.-led "war on terror" that followed has ultimately changed the way we travel, the way we think about personal privacy, the way we perceive "strangers," the way we speak, and the like. Meanwhile, the wars in Iraq and Afghanistan, and the efforts to combat terrorism in Somalia and Yemen—not to mention the millions of dollars and euros worth of investments in increased security or the horrific toll in civilian and military casualties—seem not to have made the situation any better. Rather, terrorism has become more "creative" and better organized, and it now taps into an expanding pool of angry and disillusioned youth.

Europe had its own encounters with Islamic terrorism in Istanbul (2003), Madrid (2004), and London (2005), plus numerous attempts that were less destructive or were successfully intercepted. Moreover, the threat has not abated, and the newspapers regularly contain stories about threats of attacks or arrested suspects—many of whom are either second- or third-generation immigrants or recent converts to Islam. Despite the close proximity of the threat, however,

European reactions have been less ardent and extreme than in the United States. Instead of a "war on terror," Europe has preferred to conduct to a "fight against terrorism." It also is less eager to couple terrorism to Islam alone, not least because Europeans still face many domestic terrorist threats inspired by other beliefs and ideologies. There has been, and still is, nationalist-based terrorism such as that of the Irish Republican Army (IRA) and the Basque *Euskadi Ta Askatasuna* (ETA) in Spain. And there has been ideology-based terrorism from the Left as well as from the Right, such as in the 1970s by the *Rote Armee Fraktion* (RAF) in Germany, the *Brigate Rosse* (BR) and several right-wing groupuscules in Italy, and *Action Directe* (AD) and the Algerian GIA in France.[32]

With every wave of terrorism, European governments have stepped up their cooperation and coordination of policing and counterterrorism policies. However, a slight shift in objectives seems to be taking place. Most tellingly, while the UK has been the European state most convincingly involved in the war on terror, recently, even there, a "new realism" seems to be taking root. In November 2010, the head of the (British) armed forces stated that the threat from militant groups such as al-Qaeda can only be contained by the West but can never be defeated.

Especially with regard to containment of the new "globalized" forms of terrorism, coordination is key.[33] However, the sharing of intelligence is a precarious exercise, especially in an ever larger union or with partners that are judged more corrupt than oneself. The UK, not least because of its intelligence relationship with the rest of the Anglo-Saxon world—indeed with the United States in particular—is most reluctant to share classified information. The succession of "WikiLeaks" scandals that unfolded in 2010 will most likely make that reluctance even greater.

Nonetheless, terrorism remains a threat, and the fear that it generates has permeated into society. This has been reflected in a new wave of "populist politics" that is making headway in Europe. Politicians running on anti-immigration and anti-Islamic political programs seem to cash in rather easily on now permanent and pervasive worries about new terrorist attacks. But while these politicians are often referred to as "from the extreme Right," this holds true only with regard to their nationalist and xenophobic ideas. They are "Right" in terms of social and cultural conservatism, but "Left" in terms of their support for the benefits on offer via the welfare state. This combination is unexpected. During the early to mid-1990s, for example, most students of right-wing extremism identified those groups with other traditional right-wing issues like free-market liberalism.[34] This consensus started to break down shortly before September 11, 2001; now it is in tatters.[35] Indeed, given the many challenges to the European welfare state, it is even possible to find anti-Islamic xenophobia anchored firmly on the traditional "Left" of the European political spectrum. This brings us to our last introductory point.

Limits to the "European Social Model"?

As we read everywhere these days, Europe faces difficulties maintaining the current provisions of its generous welfare systems. An important element in the story is demography. The populations of many West European countries are among the oldest in the world, and their birthrates are well below replacement level. The countries of Central and Eastern Europe fare little better than those in the west. Their birthrates collapsed after the fall of communism in 1989, and for some, like Russia, this only accelerated the rate at which the population was already declining.

The European experience contrasts sharply with the United States, which remains a young and vibrant population thanks largely to its constant renewal through immigration. While several postwar European countries actively sought large numbers of immigrants to fill out a depleted labor force, most countries are currently reconsidering the impact of immigration across a range of dimensions. "Germany does away with itself," warns one German firebrand considering the implications of these demographic trends.[36] Many worry that he was speaking for Europe as a whole.

The relative declines in Europe's wealth, trade, and demographic importance will have repercussions for the vaunted "European social model" because they will restrict Europeans' disposable income even as they raise the cost of providing social welfare. This was the conclusion that former Dutch prime minister Wim Kok announced at the end of his review of welfare state reform measures in Europe in 2004, a trend that is only increasing. Moreover, the situation in Europe is in many ways more complex than the reform of health care or social security in the United States—which is hard enough to accomplish.

After the two devastating world wars, Keynesian economic policies were adopted to curb inequality, poverty, and economic conflict in general. They succeeded better than could have been expected. Decades of economic well-being meant that the systems could grow into all-encompassing social safety nets. Currently, as the late Tony Judt in his skillfully argued article "What Is Living and What Is Dead in Social Democracy?" stated, "Social democracy, in one form or another is the prose of contemporary European politics." And indeed, as he writes, "There are very few European politicians, and certainly fewer still in positions of influence, who would dissent from core social democratic assumptions about the duties of the state, however much they might be different as to their scope."[37]

In several countries, notably in Great Britain after Margaret Thatcher, the social democratic mentality was challenged by a new emphasis on social and cultural individualism, and on private property as the key to an individual's sense of being a citizen and a stakeholder in society.[38] The old ideological cleavage between, on the one hand, an economic liberalism based on market efficiency and individual success and, on the other hand, a socialism based on solidarity and mutual responsibility was resurrected.

In many ways, the debate on immigration is evolving much like the debate on welfare state reform. In postwar Europe, equality had not only an economic meaning, but also a cultural meaning. The legacy of the Holocaust and the persecution of other minorities loomed large in European policies regarding immigration. In the 1950s and 1960s, cheap labor was imported, predominantly from Turkey and North Africa. Initially, cultural differences did not become politically explosive issues. Until the 1990s, there was a kind of taboo on divisive cultural arguments in public opinion, as well as disregard toward the potential for intercultural antagonism. But, while intellectually noble, it made European governments insensitive to the gut feelings of a large part of their native electorate, which became increasingly resentful about the dramatically growing immigrant presence.

In the last decade, cultural arguments against minority communities have come to the fore in public debate, with politically successful, often racist, appeals to native populations that feel their way of life being threatened.[39] Some politicians have argued that these majority/minority cultural antagonisms are mainly socioeconomic in nature. Economic growth, increased job opportunities, and a generally more optimistic view of the future can therefore act as a solvent for what may appear to be irreconcilable differences. By contrast, if social antagonisms are assessed as being essentially cultural, political life can become enmeshed in the dangerous perception of a permanent and irreconcilable clash of cultures, not to say clash of civilizations.

Conclusion

Our conclusion returns to the matter of Europe's existential choice. The challenges confronting European development are daunting, but they can be met with greater or lesser success. No one should expect that the twenty-first century will be Europe's or that the European Union will become a superpower, as some overoptimistic observers suggested when the European Union was drafting an ultimately unratified constitutional treaty. A true United States of Europe is unlikely as far as anyone can reasonably forecast what is to come. Nevertheless, a European renewal with growth and optimism is not to be excluded as a more practical matter. However, given the current deficits of political, economic, and cultural dynamism across the continent, the most important motivating force will probably not be internal. Rather, that force is likely to stem from the necessity of responding to external challenges, to the various forces of global competition for prosperity and influence that press on the European future from the outside.

Suggested Readings

Anderson, Jeffrey, G. John Ikenberry, and Thomas Risse (eds.), *The End of the West: Crisis and Change in the Atlantic Order*, Ithaca, NY: Cornell University Press, 2008.

Dettke, Dieter, *Germany Says NO: The Iraq War and the Future of German Foreign and Security Policy*, Baltimore: Johns Hopkins University Press, 2009.

Judt, Tony, *Postwar: A History of Europe since 1945*, New York: Penguin, 2005.

Menon, Anand, *Europe: The State of the Union*, London: Atlantic Books, 2008.

Taras, Ray, *Europe, Old and New: Transnationalism, Belonging, Xenophobia*, Lanham, MD: Rowman & Littlefield, 2008.

Thies, Wallace J., *Why NATO Endures*, Cambridge: Cambridge University Press, 2009.

Tiersky, Ronald, and John Van Oudenaren (eds.), *European Foreign Policies: Does Europe Still Matter?* Lanham, MD: Rowman & Littlefield, 2010.

Yavuz, M. Hakan, *Secularism and Muslim Democracy in Turkey*, Cambridge: Cambridge University Press, 2009.

PART ONE

COUNTRY STUDIES

CHAPTER 1

France: The Sarkozy Presidency in Historical Perspective

Gabriel Goodliffe

France

Population (million):	64.5
Area in Square Miles:	212,934
Population Density per Square Mile:	303
GDP (in billion dollars, 2009):	$2,172.3
GDP per capita (PPP, 2005):	$29,597
Joined EC/EU:	January 1, 1958

Performance of Key Political Parties in Parliamentary Elections of June 2007

Greens	3.4%
French Communist Party (PCF)	4.3%
National Front (FN)	4.3%
Socialist Party (PS)	24.7%
Democratic Movement (MoDem)	7.6%
Union for a Presidential Majority (now Union for a Popular Movement) (UMP)	39.5%
New Centre (NC)	2.4%

Main Office Holders: President: Nicolas Sarkozy—UMP (2007); Prime Minister: François Fillon—UMP (2007).

The election of Nicolas Sarkozy to the French presidency in April 2007 was a cause of great excitement both in France and abroad. As a function of his background, dynamism, and avowed reformism, Sarkozy was cast by supporters at home and abroad as the man France needed in order to overcome the challenges she faces at the dawn of the twenty-first century. During the election campaign, Sarkozy encouraged this perception by presenting himself as the candidate of "rupture" (breaking with the past) in domestic and foreign affairs. Through his leadership style and policy choices, he pledged to modernize the French economy and political systems in order to bring France into the new century. Accordingly, domestic and foreign pundits were quick to brand Sarkozy a transformative figure and his election a transformative moment in the country's sociopolitical development.

At the political level, Sarkozy's victory was held to signal the end of a generation of professional politicians of both the Left and the Right who, in the image of his two predecessors in the Élysée Palace, traced the beginning of their political careers to, as in the case of Jacques Chirac (president from 1995 to 2007), the inception of the Fifth Republic (1958–), or, as in the case of François Mitterrand (president from 1981 to 1995), to the Fourth Republic (1946–1958). At the same time, Sarkozy's election was also seen to herald a return to an orderly bipolar system of party competition, thereby laying to rest the polarization and fragmentation that had marred French politics during the 1980s and 1990s, culminating in the accession of the far-right National Front (FN) candidate, Jean-Marie Le Pen, to the second-round runoff in the 2002 presidential election. For many pundits, Sarkozy's victory, which had depended on siphoning off the votes of many erstwhile Le Pen voters, sounded the death knell for the FN, now supposedly condemned to electoral irrelevance. In turn, on the economic front, the margin of Sarkozy's victory (he won by 53 percent of the vote) was interpreted as giving him a strong mandate to liberalize the French economy and thereby resolve the problems of mass unemployment and social unrest, notably involving the country's immigrant population.

Finally, in the realm of foreign policy, Sarkozy's election was seen to signal a new age of French comity and responsibility on the international stage. The assertive Gaullism of his predecessor, most pointedly expressed in the threat to veto a UN resolution authorizing the invasion of Iraq in March 2003, was expected to give way to a moderate Atlanticist course under the new president, with France resuming her rightful place within the American-led Western alliance. Correlatively, following the country's de facto withdrawal from European affairs in the wake of the May 2005 referendum in which French voters rejected the EU draft constitution, Sarkozy pledged to bring France back into the European fold and to resume its constructive role within the European Union.

The purpose of the present chapter is to assess how well Sarkozy has lived up to these expectations during the first three years of his presidential term. In

> ## Box 1.1   The Institutions of the French Fifth Republic
>
> The constitution introduced by General Charles de Gaulle in 1958 established a hybrid presidential-parliamentary system of government for the new Fifth Republic, which is still operative today. This system installed a division of labor between a nationally elected president in charge of foreign and security policy and a prime minister, appointed by the president and assumed to issue from the same party, who would be in charge of governing on domestic issues. In actual fact, there has been considerable blurring of the line between these two functions, as the prime minister usually decides on domestic matters with the president's approval when he or she is not doing his actual bidding. By the same token, the prime minister serves as a kind of fuse for the president by deflecting the unpopularity of domestic policies from the latter who, when the situation grows dire, can always name a new prime minister.
>
> However, since the president and prime minister, as leader of the majority party or coalition, are both electorally accountable, it is also possible for them to come from rival political camps, leading to instances of divided government, known under the French term of *cohabitation*. Such an outcome was long facilitated by the discrepancy between presidential and parliamentary elections, the former taking place every seven years, the latter, unless the president dissolved the National Assembly, occurring at five-year intervals. In part to limit the likelihood of *cohabitation*, since 2002 the presidential term has been shortened to five years and parliamentary elections scheduled to coincide with presidential elections, both of which involve two rounds of voting in which the top two recipients of votes in the first round, whether at the national level or within a parliamentary constituency, square off in a winner-take-all runoff in the second round.

so doing, it will seek to flesh out the continuities and departures represented by his policy agenda and leadership style within the longer run of French socio-political development.

Contemporary France: A Museum Country or a Modern Country?

By any measure, France is a wealthy country. Counting a population of 64 million, it is the sixth largest economy in the world with a GDP of $2.2 trillion in 2009. The country possesses a well-educated workforce and an advanced industrial base, and it is a global leader in a number of sectors, including nuclear energy, aerospace, and luxury goods. Its national infrastructure, symbolized by a cheap and efficient high-speed rail system, is second to none, and the country is a global leader in high-speed Internet usage. Likewise, France accounts for the third highest level of foreign direct investment in the world after the United States and the UK, testifying to the global competitiveness of French multinational firms. At the same time, the country is blessed with the largest territory in Europe and great geographical diversity. France's natural beauty and rich cultural and historical heritage—not to mention its world-renowned cuisine—make it the most visited tourist destination in the world. In short, France's identity is split between its vocation as an advanced high-tech country on the one hand and as a bucolic *pays musée* (museum country) on the other, with the French themselves often lurching from one identification to the other in their representation of it.

The latter designation, though it highlights the richness of France's historical and cultural patrimony, also carries a derogatory connotation. The term *pays musée* is often used by critics to refer to the country's economic and social immobility, underscoring the fact that, on account of its refusal to change, the country is being progressively left behind by more forward-thinking and adaptive competitors. This image of a France that is stuck in the past particularly resonates with those who argue that she has failed to sufficiently liberalize her economy in order to meet the challenges of globalization. According to these critics, due to her continuing adherence to statist economic policies and her development of an unsustainable welfare state, France is condemned to a course of anemic economic growth and unacceptably high unemployment, thereby creating dangerous divisions between the dwindling constituency of workers who continue to benefit under the present system and the growing mass of workers who do not.

In turn, the social exclusion fueled by the dysfunction of the French economy is seen to threaten France's one-law-for-all model of social integration and citizenship, the failure of which was spectacularly underscored by the month-long rioting that inflamed largely immigrant *banlieues* (suburbs) throughout the country in November 2005. For the more alarmist of these commentators, the failings of the French economic model could in turn facilitate the diffusion of Islamic fundamentalism among the country's Muslim immigrants, who, largely excluded from the country's economic life, are bound to become receptive to its entreaties.[1] More broadly, this perception of France's economic, social, and cultural decline is also to be seen in the cottage industry of books that has sprung up in recent years warning of the country's impending economic, demographic, and cultural demise. A cursory list of titles highlighting this despondent national mood includes *La France qui tombe* (The France That Is Falling, 2003); *Le malheur français* (The French Misfortune, 2005); *Le crépuscule des elites* (The Twilight of the Elites, 2008); and most recently, *Mélancolie française* (French Melancholy, 2010).

It is on this general backdrop of pessimism and anxiety that Nicolas Sarkozy was elected France's president in April 2007, marking the accession of a new generation of political and corporate leaders who would finally, after years of timid and ineffectual half measures, resolutely embrace reform and bring the country into the twenty-first century. In the following, we will seek to evaluate the first three years of the Sarkozy presidency and how well it has lived up to this promise of rupture by examining its achievements in three principal areas. First, the effectiveness of Sarkozy's economic reforms will be assessed, particularly in comparison with the policies of his predecessors. Second, after outlining the broader challenges posed by globalization to France's cultural identity and her social and political cohesion, his government's initiatives, particularly in the areas of social and immigration policy, as well as his performance as a leader, will be examined, once again with an eye to identifying the continuities and departures from what went before. Finally, a similar démarche will be followed in the area of foreign policy, the hope being that the reader will gain a greater sense of the ambitions and achievements of the Sarkozy presidency and of its significance within the broader course of French economic, social, and political development.

Economic Rupture? Between Statism and Liberalization

The area in which Sarkozy's agenda of rupture has been most eagerly awaited is in the economic arena. This is not surprising, since the problems attending the country's economic performance are serious and have proven notoriously difficult to resolve. Since 1970, the average unemployment rate has hovered at around 8 percent and has frequently topped 10 percent from the mid-1980s on (compared to a median unemployment rate of 4 to 5 percent in the United States for that period). Certain groups have been particularly hard hit, with joblessness among the young plateauing at around 20 percent since the mid-1980s and reaching 28 percent for immigrant youth. To make matters worse, a sub-

---

Box 1.2   Fifth Republic Presidents and the Three Cohabitation Periods

1958–1969	Charles de Gaulle (Conservative)
1969–1974	Georges Pompidou (Conservative)
1974–1981	Valéry Giscard d'Estaing (Conservative)
1981–1995	François Mitterrand (Socialist)
1986–1988	Prime Minister Jacques Chirac (Conservative)
1993–1995	Prime Minister Édouard Balladur (Conservative)
1995–2007	Jacques Chirac (Conservative)
1997–2002	Prime Minister Lionel Jospin (Socialist)
2007–	Nicolas Sarkozy (Conservative)

stantial proportion of existing jobs are government subsidized, meaning that they would not exist at all without the state's largesse.

As many analysts have pointed out, this persistently high unemployment rate is attributable to the unresponsiveness of the French labor market to changing economic circumstances due to the rigidity of labor laws—many extending back half a century—which focus on protecting existing jobs rather than spurring economic and hence job growth. At the same time, the cost burdens placed on French firms in order to pay for government-mandated fringe benefits make it more expensive for firms to hire new workers, while an excessive minimum wage exceeds the productivity of workers, thereby reducing the number of full-time minimum-wage jobs. In turn, long-paying and generous unemployment benefits lessen the incentive for the unemployed to seek new jobs. Finally, the labor market's rigidity is exacerbated by the traditional French resistance to moving to a new city or region for work or switching professions in midcareer, as well as the growing incompatibility between the technical skills demanded by companies in the modern economy and those developed by students in the general university system. As a result, a surprising number of good jobs remain unfilled in the private sector for lack of qualified candidates.

In short, the Fordist institutions that were introduced during the *Trente Glorieuses* (the thirty boom years following World War II) when France was a relatively self-enclosed economy shielded from international competition, were ill adapted to an increasingly integrated global economy subject to intensifying trade competition and international capital flows.[2] These include labor laws protecting employees from dismissal, wage growth to stimulate consumption, generous welfare and social security regimes, and statist-corporatist arrangements to oversee these institutions. As French firms became less and less competitive and were forced to lay off growing numbers of workers, French society grew increasingly divided between "insiders"—the shrinking core of workers whose jobs remain protected and who continue to enjoy the benefits of the Fordist welfare state—and "outsiders"—the growing number of unemployed or underemployed workers, particularly among the young and unskilled, who are excluded from the system and are exposed to worsening professional and socioeconomic uncertainty as a result.

These developments have fed a narrative, particularly within French conservative circles (not to mention among many American academics), that France needs to modernize its economic and social system by discarding or radically reforming the regulatory institutions inherited from the Fordist era in order to give its economy the requisite flexibility to cope with globalization. First and foremost, this narrative calls for getting the state out of the economy by limiting its control over investment and production decisions (i.e., planning), diminishing state ownership and the size of the public sector, and reducing state constraints on product and labor markets (i.e., protections and subsidies in the case of the former, and regulations in the case of the latter). Secondly, it prescribes reducing the welfare contributions falling on firms and, correspondingly, cutting the benefits guaranteed to French citizens under the social model that emerged in France and other European countries after World War II. Finally, this narrative calls for curtailing the influence of the corporative and class actors and their political allies—namely trade unions and left-wing parties—who are the principal benefactors of these interventions and would obstruct such a liberalizing agenda. According to this view, France's current economic and social problems can be attributed to the reluctance of political elites to undertake these reforms or, when they choose to do so, the negation of the impact of such reforms through the provision of welfare outlays to affected sectors and groups. Hence the enthusiasm elicited by Sarkozy's promises of economic rupture among business interests and economic liberals in both France and abroad.

A closer study of French economic policy over the past three decades calls into question this critique of France's supposed economic immobility. As Jonah Levy has shown, since the mid-1980s, a two-step process of reform has unfolded in the country which has increased economic flexibility while trying to attenuate the social pain and political fallout elicited by this process.[3] In the first stage, this has involved redeploying the remit of the state from economic planning and regulation to expanding the welfare state. In turn, in the second stage, social obligations are to be progressively reduced until they become fiscally and economically sustainable.

FROM *DÉPLANIFICATION* TO THE SOCIAL ANESTHESIA STATE

The roots of this process can be traced back to the 1970s, during which, as a result of the two oil shocks and the growth of international trade and financial flows, France experienced mass unemployment for the first time in the postwar period combined with spiraling inflation. The Socialist-Communist coalition that came to power following François Mitterrand's election in 1981 attempted to overcome the cycle of economic stagnation by stimulating consumption through a dual strategy of reflation and statist economic management. However, the failure of this strategy to achieve growth forced the government to embrace *déplanification* (abandonment of economic planning) combined with social management, a course that was in turn adopted by the Right when it reassumed power in 1986–1988 and 1993–1995, and then alternately pursued by the Right and the Left throughout Jacques Chirac's presidency.

During the first two years of Mitterrand's presidency, the Socialist-Communist government pursued a sweeping reflationary program that amounted to a 12 percent increase in government spending in real terms. This program was accompanied by the most comprehensive nationalization campaign since the liberation and by the resumption of industrial policies, including setting production targets for a large contingent of industries as well as a national champions policy that called for small and medium enterprises (SMEs) to be fused into larger, often state-controlled firms. This return to *dirigisme* was accompanied by a series of unemployment-reduction measures that would become a staple of French economic and social management in subsequent years, including reducing the work week from forty to thirty-nine hours, extending paid vacations from four to five weeks, making older workers eligible for early retirement, and subsidizing firms to hire younger workers. In addition, a slew of policies were promulgated to placate the political base of the Socialist-Communist coalition, principally industrial workers and civil servants, including reforms giving workers a greater say in running their firms and reinforcing their collective bargaining rights, as well as redistributive policies that benefited the poor as well as the fast-growing population of retirees. Last but not least, the government raised taxes on capital owners and businesses in order to pay for these benefits, notably instituting the highest capital gains tax in the industrialized world, which triggered massive capital flight from France to more investor-friendly markets.

The failure of reflation and nationalization to return the economy to a path of growth, however, forced the Socialist government to reappraise its policies and reverse course. In a radical turnabout, it embarked on a more comprehensive liberalization program than had hitherto ever been attempted. The proximate causes for this shift were the spiraling inflation and gaping budget and trade deficits that had been generated by the increase in government spending, combined with the contraction of demand for French goods due to the global economic slowdown. These conditions in turn wrought unsustainable pressure on the franc, triggering a run that threatened its inclusion in the European Monetary System.

By the end of 1982, the government was forced to implement a harsh austerity program in order to rein in inflation and relieve pressure on the franc. Under the stewardship of Finance Minister Jacques Delors, a series of strict price and wage controls, compulsory savings measures, and most significantly, painful spending cuts were enacted to stabilize the deficit at 3 percent of GDP. These measures were intensified under Delors' successor, Pierre Bérégovoy, who in turn did away with wage indexation and reduced price controls. As a corollary to this austerity package, Bérégovoy also introduced the *franc fort* (strong franc) policy, which sought to maintain the franc at a higher exchange parity with the deutschmark, thereby forcing French firms to lower their costs so as to remain internationally competitive. This policy of competitive disinflation implied severely tightening the money supply and markedly raising interest rates in order to buttress the franc and reduce inflation by curbing investment.

This combination of budgetary austerity and monetary rigor allowed France to achieve one of the lowest inflation rates in Western Europe while initiating a period of steady balance-of-trade surpluses. However, by choking investment borrowing and depressing consumer demand, the new policy caused, in the words of one observer, "damage to the economy . . . so severe and persistent" that growth was effectively strangled and unemployment shot up to 10 percent.[4] At the same time, these restrictive macroeconomic policies were accompanied by microeconomic reforms that aimed to enhance the flexibility of the economy by disengaging the state from its workings. This disengagement, overseen by the new finance minister and subsequent prime minister Laurent Fabius (1984–1986), meant eliminating state outlays to nationalized industries, exposing public enterprises to market competition, and lifting state restrictions on closures or layoffs within them. In the private sector, meanwhile, the state abandoned efforts to steer industry toward planning targets, while restrictions on firing workers and raising capital were lifted in exchange for firms no longer receiving government assistance. In turn, price controls were fully eliminated in 1986, a measure that forced public and private firms to become more competitive in order to remain economically viable.

Thirdly, *déplanification* was accompanied by comprehensive legislative deregulation. At one level, a series of measures were enacted to diversify financial markets and facilitate the provision of credit to French businesses. The most important was the reintroduction of private competition in the banking sector and lifting of controls on the free movement of capital, making it easier for firms to leave the country if they found conditions not to their liking. At a second level, deregulation also extended to the labor market, with wage deindexation and the lifting of administrative constraints on managers reinforcing the capacity of employers to impose their terms on workers and effect layoffs when they needed to. Similarly, the expansion of workshop bargaining paradoxically strengthened the hand of employers in dealing with their employees, the weak implantation of unions in the workplace and the context of high unemployment enabling them to secure derogations from national- and branch-level collective agreements within their firms.

The *déplanification* and deregulation campaign launched by the Fabius government was expanded by the second Chirac ministry of 1986–1988 and finalized by governments of both the Left and the Right in the early 1990s. These governments reversed the nationalizations undertaken between 1982 and 1984 and returned most public firms to private ownership. In addition, beginning with the ministry of Michel Rocard (1988–1991), a raft of measures was introduced to promote the growth of SMEs as the agents of the country's economic revival, including state subsidies and performance-conditioned loans to help them modernize their production and upgrade their product lines.

The implementation of these microeconomic reforms did much to rationalize the structure and liberalize the operation of the French economy. The elimination of subsidies to public and private enterprises resulted in a large number of bankruptcies, financial deregulation spurred greater firm reliance on finan-

cial markets, and labor market deregulation enhanced wage flexibility and reduced production costs, increasing firm profits. As an indication of the lack of
control over the French economy relative to the selective *dirigisme* (state economic management) of the 1970s and the Socialist *étatisme* (statism) of the early
1980s, these reforms marked a profound shift away from the direct management
of public and private enterprises by the state toward its essential disengagement
from the economy.

However, this retreat from *dirigisme* did not spell the end of state intervention in all its forms, but instead marked its displacement to the realm of social
policy. It is no small paradox that despite the abandonment of planning and
the decline of state intervention in the economy, overall government spending
continued to increase despite the end of the neo-Keynesian experiment in the
early 1980s and the ensuing process of *déplanification*, rising from 42.6 percent
of GDP in 1983 to 46 percent in 1999. This upsurge in government expenditure
was almost wholly attributable to the growth of the welfare state in order to
attenuate the social dislocations caused by the retreat from *dirigisme* and economic liberalization. First, the growth in welfare spending underwrote labor
market programs designed to dampen the rise in unemployment triggered by
economic restructuring and the deflationary policies that accompanied it—
mostly early-retirement programs intended to allow firms to pare down their
workforces without provoking a new increase in unemployment. By the early
1990s, given their failure to reduce unemployment, successive Socialist and center-Right governments supplemented these early-retirement programs with
various work subsidization measures and business-friendly tax incentives to encourage low-wage hires, particularly among young workers. In turn, in the second half of the decade, these were followed by two further initiatives introduced by the government of Lionel Jospin, including subsidizing nonprofit and
public sector organizations to encourage youth hires and, most famously, the
Aubry Law—named after Jospin's labor minister, Martine Aubry—which reduced the work week from thirty-nine to thirty-five hours. Overall, the number
of workers affected by these labor-reduction measures increased from 1.2 million in 1984 to 3 million in 1999. Adding this figure to the approximately 2
million unemployed, this meant that by the close of the century, France had
one of the lowest labor force participation rates—particularly among the
youngest and oldest workers—and the shortest average duration of employment in the industrialized world.

The second major area of expenditure increases designed to offset the effect
of *déplanification* concerned welfare programs proper. In the 1990s, France
evolved the largest welfare state outside of Scandinavia, with welfare spending
increasing from 21.3 percent of GDP in 1980 to 29.5 percent in 1998 as new
specialized benefit programs were launched to assist those worst affected by
deindustrialization and economic restructuring. A "social anesthesia state"
emerged under the stewardship of both the Left and the Right as the purview

of state intervention shifted from the *étatiste* stance it had assumed at the start of Mitterrand's first term to the welfarist function it evolved from the mideighties on.

As the 1990s drew to a close, however, retrenchment of the welfare state became an increasingly urgent priority. Domestically, the ballooning social security obligations imposed on French firms in order to fund this welfare expansion hurt their cost competitiveness and impeded their ability to hire more workers. Externally, the growth in welfare spending threatened France's position within the Stability and Growth Pact, the country eventually being placed on notice by the European Commission of its transgression of the 3 percent yearly limit on budgetary expenditures in 2003. Thus, political elites finally accepted the need to shrink the French welfare state, notably through reductions in benefits, pension reform, and cuts to the public sector.

Beginning with the Jospin government and especially under the succeeding governments of Jean-Pierre Raffarin (2002–2005) and Dominique de Villepin (2005–2007), there have been concerted attempts to reduce both government expenditures and tax obligations on firms, specifically by cutting welfare benefits for certain categories of the population, such as the long-term unemployed, and attempting to peel back social security taxes for employers. These were accompanied by a series of cost-cutting reforms of the health system that achieved savings by increasing personal deductibles and reducing the number of services that could be reimbursed by the state. In turn, the Jospin government drew up plans to reduce corporate and income taxes, including for the highest income brackets, in order to encourage savings and investment. These measures were intensified by the Raffarin and Villepin ministries, which in addition to reducing inheritance taxes and the rate on the highest earners, further cut corporate tax rates while continuing to shift the burden of social security taxes away from firms and toward employees. Finally, the cost burden attaching to the payment of welfare benefits was further diminished through the decentralization of income supports to the poor in 2004 and the replacement of the *Revenu Mensuel d'Insertion* (Monthly Integration Benefit), which had been introduced in 1988 to preserve the long-term unemployed from pauperization, by a less generous *Revenu de Solidarité Active* (Professional Solidarity Benefit) designed to serve as a complement to poorly paid short-term or part-time work. These retrenchment measures continued to be accompanied by various proposals to encourage employment, notably among affected groups such as the young, through activist policies exempting firms from having to pay social security taxes on certain types of jobs.[5]

At the same time, successive governments sought to limit government expenditures by reducing the size of the public sector as well as through reforms to the country's pension system. A symbolic threshold was crossed as the totemic public enterprises Electricité de France (EDF) and Gaz de France (GDF) were respectively opened to private capital in 2004 and 2006. Likewise, the post office was restructured to comply with EU directives on the liberalization of services, while its banking division was sloughed off to create a legally separate entity, La Banque Postale. Finally, on pension reform, after the effort of Alain Juppé's government (1995–1997) to overhaul the existing system came to naught in the strike wave of November–December 1995, beginning in 2003 the Raffarin ministry adopted a more discreet approach by extending the retirement age at which private sector workers would be eligible to receive a full pension.

SARKOZY'S ECONOMIC RUPTURE

This course of economic liberalization combined with budgetary retrenchment that has been pursued by the Jospin, Raffarin, and Villepin governments provided the template for the economic policies that would be enacted by the new president beginning in 2007. In this sense, rather than breaking from the policies of preceding governments, Nicolas Sarkozy and his prime minister François Fillon have sought to intensify them in the aim of completing the process of economic liberalization that began in the mid-1980s.

In keeping with the two-track approach outlined above, at the heart of the new government's economic reforms is the law "in favor of work, employment, and purchasing power"—or Fillon Law for short—which continues the structural reforms implemented by previous governments while reducing the size of the French welfare state. In terms of structural reform, the Fillon Law pursues two principal objectives. First and foremost, it instituted a number of measures to enhance the flexibility of the French labor market. These include increasing the opportunities available to workers within a firm to derogate from national- or branch-level collective agreements, exempting temporary or part-time workers from such agreements, eliminating the administrative constraints on firms to enact layoffs, relaxing the thirty-five-hour work week by making it easier to work overtime, and reducing the social security tax on firms by offsetting it with an increase in the value-added tax. In turn, the Fillon Law calls for privatizing not only formerly nationalized firms, as seen in the government's authorization of the takeover of GDF by Groupe Suez, but for extending such privatizations to public services as well. Accordingly, the capital of the post office has been opened to private investors since March 2010.

In terms of reducing state spending, the Fillon Law pursues three paths of retrenchment. At one level, it seeks to further reduce the state's welfare obligations by increasing individual health care liabilities as well as diminishing unemployment benefits for those who refuse to take a job. Secondly, it attempts to streamline the public sector, notably through the suppression of 30,000 civil servant posts. Finally, and perhaps most controversially, the government has sought to lighten its budgetary burden by standardizing civil service pensions with private sector ones, making full pensions for both categories of workers contingent on paying into the social security system for forty-one years. Finally, the government has accompanied these retrenchment measures with policies to stimulate saving and encourage people to work more. Most notably, it exempts employers and employees from social security taxes on overtime work, while further reducing corporate and income tax rates—particularly on the highest brackets—and cutting the wealth tax in an effort to create a supply-side confidence shock.[6]

The onset of the global economic crisis as a result of the collapse of the U.S. housing market in 2008 and 2009 signaled a temporary halt to this retrenchment agenda and a resumption of state spending to restore consumption and investment. In December 2008, a €26 million stimulus plan was approved to support the construction and automobile sectors, subsidize new SME hires, invest in public infrastructure, and provide income assistance to poor households. Following a 1.5 percent fall in GDP in 2009, further reflationary measures were enacted that specifically targeted ailing car builders and poor families.

However, despite this policy reversal and Sarkozy's denunciations of speculative capitalism, it is not clear that he has abandoned the course of deregulation and retrenchment with which he started his term. For one thing, the emphasis of state support has squarely been, as in the United States, on propping up firms and the financial sector rather than providing assistance to jobseekers and consumers. Moreover, despite the crisis, the government has persevered in many of its original reforms. Thus it is continuing to reduce the number of civil servant posts, maintain tax breaks for the highest earners, and reform unemployment benefits through the elimination of hiring subsidies and the reduction of income supports for the long-term unemployed. In short, Sarkozy has adopted ad hoc firefighting measures in order to dampen the worst impacts of the crisis while continuing to implement structural reforms and budgetary retrenchment. Rather than representing a break with the past, his economic and social reforms have continued or intensified the liberalizing course set out by his predecessors.

By the same token, contrary to critiques that portray these reforms as inconsequential, it could be argued that France has in fact substantially liberalized its economy since the mid-1980s. Though this liberalization process has occurred in a piecemeal fashion and has not unfolded as quickly as some critics called for, such was perhaps the best outcome that could be expected in a country as prone to social conflict and upheaval as France. Likewise, though this process has been accompanied by unacceptably high unemployment and worsening social inequality, it is far from certain that more rapid or radical liberalization would have produced a superior outcome. In this connection, Britain and the United States, despite achieving lower unemployment, continue to display dramatically higher levels of income and wealth inequality than France, which suggests that merely providing jobs to people is not in itself a guarantee against poverty and its attendant social blights.

By the same token, it is important not to minimize the social costs attached to this process of liberal reform. Even if the latter was necessary to make the French economy more competitive, the price exacted in terms of unemployment, inequality, and collapsing living standards for those who have been negatively impacted should not be underestimated. In turn, these costs have fueled a general fear and rejection of globalization, the sociopolitical manifestations of which will be examined in the next section.

French Politics and Society in the Face of Globalization

Since the early 1980s and the beginning of economic reform halfway through François Mitterrand's first term, income inequality has increased markedly in the country, and the living standards of certain groups—notably industrial workers but also a growing proportion of service-sector employees—have eroded substantially. Correspondingly, the corporative and partisan organizations that have traditionally defended these groups, notably the trade unions and the Communist Party (PCF), have been severely weakened or have collapsed over this period. For better or worse, this has been blamed—chiefly by people on the Left but not only—on a U.S.- and EU-led process of liberal economic globalization whose goal is to maximize returns to corporate leaders and the holders of capital at the expense of wage earners and stakeholders. According to these critics, advanced social democracies like France are being forced to dismantle their welfare states so as to satiate the greed of increasingly mobile financial and corporate actors who have been empowered by this process. In turn, the socioeconomic fears linked to the decline of formerly dominant producer groups dovetail with broader anxieties that, as a result of globalization's homogenizing effects, France is losing her cultural distinctiveness and identity. For growing numbers of people, the disorienting impact of globalization is putting into question what it means to be French by eroding the structural and symbolic foundations of their identity.

SAFEGUARDING *LA FRANCE PROFONDE*

The first of these foundations is the notion of *La France profonde* and the ensuing conception of rural rootedness held by French people to subtend their collective identity. Despite having experienced rapid urbanization following World War II, the French remain strongly attached to their country's rural past. The latter is predicated on the concept of *terroir*, which refers to the distinctive rural microregions or *pays*, often no larger than a town or village and its environs, which endow France with the richness and diversity of its countryside, its craft and culinary cultures, and its folk traditions and historical memory.

Politically, this attachment to the *terroir* can be traced to the Jacobin republican belief, born in the Revolution and disseminated during the Third Republic (1875–1940), in the universal accession of the people to small-scale property in the form of a farm or small artisanal business as the key to preserving the republican order. This accounts for the sectoral dominance of the agricultural and artisanal sectors during the third and fourth republics and explains why France still boasts more artisans and small shopkeepers as a proportion of its population than any other advanced industrial country, with the possible exception of Italy. Symbolically, these microregions have a special resonance for native-born French people because they represent the historical and cultural repository from which their families issued and to which—either in old age or, if they are lucky, on the weekend—they hope to return. This long-standing attachment of the French to *la France profonde* is to be seen in the perennial appeal enjoyed by children's books and films that turn on this theme, whether in *Bécassine*—the cartoon stories of a Breton peasant girl first published in 1905—or René Clément's *Jeux interdits* (Forbidden Games) (1952) of yesteryear, or the adventures of Astérix the Gaul (1959 to 2001) and Dany Boon's *Bienvenue chez les Ch'tis* (Welcome to the Sticks, 2008) on a more contemporary note. Likewise, whereas from the 1960s through the 1980s rural France experienced a large-scale exodus, since the 1990s, a reverse trend, known as *rurbanisation*, has developed whereby people who work in towns and cities are moving back to the countryside, speaking to the continuing pull of the country's rural identity.

In turn, the strength of these local identifications has translated into strong regional identities, which, despite the historic centralism of the French state, have sometimes given rise to demands for cultural, and in some cases political, autonomy or independence. The most obvious contemporary example is in Corsica, where an irredentist organization, the Corsican National Liberation Front (FLNC), and the various splinter groups that have issued from it have engaged in acts of vandalism, extortion, and attacks on the symbols and representatives of the French state—the most spectacular being the assassination of the island's prefect, Claude Érignac, in 1998. However, this is far from the only case, with autonomist or independence movements also active, though not to the same extremes, in Alsace, Brittany, Languedoc-Roussillon, and the French Basque country.[7]

Partly in an effort to recognize the specificity of these different regions and to preempt future demands for autonomy or independence, since the 1980s the French state has sought to decentralize its competencies, particularly in matters of infrastructure and technological investment and fiscal and welfare policy, and has officially recognized regional cultures and languages and promoted their teaching, particularly in primary school. However, the inherent tension posed by these initiatives between granting greater autonomy to the regions and maintaining the central authority of the state was underscored when the Constitutional Council—the highest authority on legislative matters—struck down a law granting special autonomous status to Corsica in January 2002. Accordingly, tensions between the state and local or regional collectivities are likely to persist, especially as the particularistic identities bound up in the latter are inflamed with the advances of globalization.

Indeed, local and regional identities are seen to be increasingly under attack by the supposed agents of globalization, whether this be the European Commission, which is seeking to open up the system of *appellations controlées*—the system of designations attesting to the origins and quality of a particular good—to include products that are made elsewhere, or the World Trade Organization (WTO), which is looking to eliminate production subsidies and tariff protections for French farmers, or the advent of new technologies threatening time-honored methods of production. Consequently, rural areas are undergoing the most profound structural and demographic transformation they have experienced since the rural exodus that accompanied the *Trente Glorieuses*.

Not surprisingly, these transformations have provoked a strong backlash in France against globalization. As pointed out in the previous edition of this book, this backlash provides in the figure of José Bové the most recognizable face of the antiglobalization movement. An activist and author who once served a prison sentence for ransacking a McDonald's restaurant and now a European parliamentary representative for the Europe Écologie Party, Bové has been a long-standing presence at antiglobalization protests against the WTO and Bretton Woods institutions, as well as at the alter-globalization meetings organized each year to coincide with the World Economic Forum, which assembles global political and business leaders in Davos, Switzerland. Bové is something of a folk hero in France, where he acts as the self-appointed defender of the products of the *terroir*—recall his smuggling and distribution of Roquefort cheese at the Seattle WTO Ministerial of 1999—against the homogenization and debasement of food products by the global agro and food industries, as summed up in his campaign against *la malbouffe* (bad food). In this capacity, he has led the opposition to the importation of hormone-treated beef and the use of genetically modified organisms in Europe, citing how the outsized profits made possible by these technologies outweigh the health and environmental hazards they pose for the multinational corporations and international organizations that promote their use.

In turn, even though farmers represent a dwindling proportion of the country's demographic and productive base—today, less than 4 percent of the population earns a living from the land, as opposed to 20 percent in 1970—French people continue to defend their economic interests, notably in the form of the EU's Common Agricultural Policy (CAP), even if this means having to

Box 1.3   Douelle: A Mirror of France?

A recent profile by *Le Monde* on the village of Douelle in the Lot exemplifies these changes. The object of Jean Fourastié's famous study which coined the term the *Trente Glorieuses*, Douelle continues to present the postcard picture of a village of the Quercy region of southwestern France. Yet, whereas in the past its inhabitants had been overwhelmingly tied to the land, today they present the professional and social profiles of city dwellers. Testifying to the phenomenon of *rurbanisation* (see above), these are principally white-collar workers employed in the service sector. Conversely, the number of farms has almost entirely disappeared. Only seven struggling winemakers are left today, compared to the thirty-nine farms that were attached to the village in 1970 and the ninety-two in 1945. Likewise, testifying to the effects of economic globalization, whereas in 1950 Douelle grew strawberries that were exported to England, by 2009 it was possible to buy a bottle of South African wine at the local supermarket for less than a bottle of the local product. Finally, testifying to the demographic decline of *la France profonde*, although Douelle counts 750 inhabitants today versus 670 in 1970, the village's population has substantially aged: although the total number of deaths was roughly the same in 2009 as in 1970, the number of births had fallen by half.

(*Source*: Marie-Pierre Subtil, "La France en son miroir," *Le Monde*, November 19, 2009. See also Jean Fourastié, *Les trente glorieuses ou la révolution invisible de 1946 à 1975*, Paris: Livre de poche, 1980.)

pay higher food prices and impoverishing small farmers in developing countries. At one level, this appeal is reflected in the disproportionate power that continues to be wielded by the rural sector within the country's political institutions and among its political leaders. This is most evident in the Senate, whose members are elected by officials from the country's 36,000 communes, the overwhelming majority of which are rural.

Secondly, popular sympathy for the plight of French farmers derives from the conception of *ruralité* or rootedness in the countryside, which casts them as fulfilling not only an economic function, but also as custodians of the French countryside, charged with safeguarding its natural beauty and cultural specificity. This romanticized view of farmers is largely mythical, of course, since large agro-industrial interests today dominate the country's agricultural production. However, in part because it continues to articulate with the rurally based representation that French people have of themselves, these large agricultural interests have been extremely successful in getting successive governments to defend the CAP despite growing opposition from France's European and international trading partners.

The history of the CAP highlights the extent to which the French state has been willing to play the protectionist card and interfere in the internal management of firms if this is deemed to be in the national interest. For example, appealing to the imperative of economic patriotism, in the summer of 2005 the Villepin government facilitated the merger of publicly traded Suez SA with state-controlled GDF in order to prevent the potential takeover of the latter by the Italian firm Enel. Four years later, President Sarkozy replicated this strategic protectionism by creating a $25 billion investment fund in order to shield French companies from foreign takeover. This policy has been accompanied by increased state investment in research and development as well as to extend France's high-speed rail and highway networks in order to better connect domestic and European markets. In short, the present government has largely followed the path laid out by its predecessors by pursuing an ad hoc mix of liberal reforms and state intervention so as to prepare the nation for the challenges of globalization while simultaneously trying to protect it—or certain groups within it—from globalization's most dislocating impacts.

Immigration and Identity in the Age of Globalization

If the economic and cultural transformations occasioned by globalization provide the general context fueling fears over the loss of France's cultural identity and specificity, no single issue has more vividly crystallized these fears than that of immigration. This is understandable since the debate over immigration brings into play a second great pillar of French identity and self-definition: the republican model of citizenship constructed around the twin principles of *laïcité* (secular-ness) and equality under the law. Inherited from the Revolution and shaped by the Catholic-republican culture wars that dominated the early decades of the Third Republic, this model strives in theory to assimilate foreigners and their French-born children into the national community, no matter their country of origin or ethnic or religious background, in the name of the republican ideal of civic equality. Viewing the nation as an elective community into which citizens freely enter, rather than a predetermined organic one based on blood or kinship ties, such a conception of citizenship implies an open definition of the nation which is accepting of immigrants so long as they are prepared to accept the universal republican rights and duties devolving to the citizen. This means in practice that individual immigrants are neither to be granted special privileges nor to suffer discriminatory treatment on account of their appurtenance to a particular religious, ethnic, or national group.

However, the growth of a large immigrant population of non-European descent in France has sorely tested the limits of this republican model of citizenship and is increasingly seen in some quarters as posing a threat to the civic identity of the nation. These shortcomings are highlighted by the negative indicators reflecting the exclusion of these immigrants from the country's economic and social life. These are especially dire for immigrants from North and Sub-Saharan Africa, who suffer from unusually high rates of unemployment, poverty, and educational failure. Members of these groups are often concentrated in government-subsidized housing projects (*cités*) situated on the fringes of French cities and towns, which are bereft of public services, civil society organizations, and economic opportunities. Such conditions contribute to periodic explosions of unrest in these areas—the most spectacular instance of which was the monthlong wave of rioting that swept the country in November 2005—which serve to further criminalize immigrants in the eyes of their cocitizens.

These developments have raised growing doubts about the viability of the republican model in some quarters. On the one hand, there are those who argue that the latter has failed to live up to its ideal of equality for all, condemning certain categories of immigrants to de facto underclass status within French society. For these critics, official appeals to this model have become a pretext for inaction that dispenses politicians and the broader society from correcting the profound structural inequities and social injustices that are faced by many immigrants in France. The answer, they aver, is to replace the universalist model of republican integration with a multicultural one in which communal differences are officially recognized and in which the state takes action to remedy the discriminations to which certain immigrant groups are subjected in the aim of facilitating their integration into society. Not surprisingly, these critics hold up the United States and the UK as successful examples of this multicultural model of integration and argue that France would be well served to recast her integration policies along similar lines.

Conversely, there are those who argue that the predominantly Islamic character of France's immigrant population places an unmanageable strain on the capacity of the republican model to integrate what they consider to be an irreducibly alien and inassimilable religious minority.[8] According to these critics, the hegemonic political as well as spiritual ambitions of Islam, as well as the inability of its practitioners to distinguish between the public and private spheres, render this model inoperable when it comes to integrating a large Islamic population into a secular society defined by the republican principle of *laïcité*. The debates over wearing a headscarf in the public schools or a burka in the street crystallized for them the cultural intractability of Islam and the incapacity of the republican model to integrate its denizens, instead marking the emergence of a de facto communitarianism in the midst of secular French society.

The debate over wearing a headscarf in the public schools first emerged to prominence in the late 1980s. Those who opposed it claimed that the headscarf was an overt religious symbol that, when worn in an official public space such as a public school, constituted an affront to the republican principle of *laïcité*. Meanwhile, those who supported the right to wear it claimed that it was not incompatible with the latter, but instead that banning it was an attack on an individual's right to practice her religion. The government reaction was initially confused, with the Constitutional Council defending in 1989 the right of Muslim girls to wear the headscarf in schools "unless it threatened [their] orderly functioning," followed by a decree in 1994 which sought to differentiate between discreet versus ostentatious symbols, without distinguishing into which category the headscarf fell. The expulsion and ensuing cases involving around one hundred Muslim girls for wearing a headscarf in public schools under this decree, as well as continuing demonstrations and counterdemonstrations on both sides, forced the government to take an unequivocal stand, resulting in a law in March 2004 banning the wearing of overt religious symbols, including headscarves, yarmulkes, and large crosses, in state schools.

This debate over the wearing of religious symbols in public places was reignited in the summer of 2010, when the Fillon government passed a law banning the wearing of a burka—a robelike garment covering the eyes and hands of women as used in Afghanistan—or a niqab—the burka's equivalent in the Arab world—in any public space, whether official or not. Notwithstanding the enforcement difficulties it poses and the fact that it would only concern about 1,900 out of 1.5 to 2 million Muslim women in France, the law's advocates see it as necessary to defend the principle of *laïcité* against the encroachments of fundamentalist Islam on a secular society.[9] And even though the overwhelming majority of Muslims in France are against their use, the mere presence of the burka and niqab in France, no matter how infinitesimal, attests for these critics to the fundamental incompatibility of Islam with the secular values of the republic and the insuperable difficulty of integrating Muslims into French society.

Yet, in actual fact, the French situation is not as dire as all that. In the first place, the republican model has functioned much better than its critics give it credit for given the size of the immigrant communities concerned and the short period of time the society has had to integrate them. Indeed, a few basic indicators show that despite everything, integration of these immigrants is progressing. The overwhelming majority of them almost exclusively speak French in their daily lives. Mixed marriages among these immigrants and their children, in particular those from the Maghreb, are rising fast, while birthrates among women from these groups approximate the national norm. Likewise, the attitudes of immigrants in general and Muslims in particular suggest that they have internalized the values of universalism and tolerance associated with republican citizenship. At the same time, Muslim immigrants are adopting strategies similar to those employed by previous immigrant groups in order to maximize their political leverage vis-à-vis the state and its agents as a means to speed their assimilation. In this capacity, civil society groups have been active at both the local and national levels in organizing immigrants and trying to articulate their needs and demands to politicians and officials.[10] The fact that these immigrants are resorting to time-proven strategies that facilitated the integration of previous groups into French society should be seen as encouraging testimony to the viability of the republican model.

As Jonathan Laurence and Justin Vaïsse have pointed out, the liberal critique that imputes the failure of the republican model to take into account the structural and social obstacles faced by French immigrants is belied by the actual flexibility it has displayed in attempting to integrate the latter.[11] Indeed, despite the republican injunction against implementing specific policies targeting immigrant groups, the country has actually been experimenting with various forms of affirmative action for two decades now, mostly under the cover of addressing the plight of the country's most deprived areas and populations. These have included the establishment of education priority zones (ZEPs) and tax-exempt zones to boost educational attainment and economic activity in poor urban—that is, immigrant—areas, the allocation of funds to rehabilitate public housing projects that have large immigrant populations, and the creation of subsidized jobs programs targeting unemployed youth, many from the *banlieues*. At the same time, private actors such as firms and *grandes écoles* like Sciences Po in Paris have reached out to minorities in order to diversify their workforces and student bodies. The most explicit moves in this direction were the creation of the High Authority for the Struggle against Discrimination and for Equality (HALDE) in 2004 and the promulgation of the Charter on the Equality of Chances in 2005 in order to improve the access of at-risk youth to higher education. In short, the French republican model has shown itself to be much more adaptive to the situation of immigrants than multiculturalist critics would admit, even though more remains to be done in order to advance their integration into French society.

The real problem in this regard appears to reside less in the republican model itself than in the general recalcitrance of the French to make it a reality. The social context for the November 2005 riots as well as smaller subsequent episodes of urban unrest is particularly illustrative in this regard. Unemployment among youth of immigrant descent living in the *cités* is often as high as 40 percent, testifying not only to the country's subpar economic performance but also to the deep-seated racism confronted by immigrants and their children in the labor market.[12] In turn, reflecting negative popular stereotypes associated with these populations, many of them dating back to colonial times, this socially widespread racism is magnified by official racism on the part of civil servants and the police who are much too often implicated in racial profiling and violence against immigrants. Lest we forget, the detonator of the November 2005 riots was the death of two teenagers of Tunisian and Malian descent who were electrocuted while trying to hide from the police in an electric power substation. Likewise, the most recent wave of unrest that swept the eastern city of Grenoble in July 2010 followed the police shooting of a suspect of Algerian descent who was being sought following a bank robbery.

In turn, these various forms of prejudice combine with the ghettoization of immigrant populations in the concrete confines of the *cités*, which, isolated from downtown areas and bereft of recreational and associative outlets, have morphed into architecturally conditioned "zones of highly concentrated social pathology."[13] Given this environment, what is surprising is not that the *banlieues* have periodically erupted in rioting, but that such explosions have not been more frequent. Finally, these conditions are exacerbated by the neglect of the state. As an example, in the two years leading up to the 2005 riots, the Raffarin government had reduced government aid and cut neighborhood policing initiatives in at-risk urban areas as cost-saving budgetary measures, thus contributing to the sense of isolation and alienation within them.

Seen from this standpoint, the problems of rioting, or more prosaically, of *délinquance* (petty crime), translate the frustration of immigrants with the failure of the republican model to live up to its promise of integration, rather than their rejection of it. This is suggested by the conspicuous absence of religious overtones to the 2005 riots, confounding critics who contend that, due to the political vocation of their religion, Muslim immigrants are inassimilable within secular Western societies. Indeed, French Islamist leaders were caught short by the violence. They were able neither to channel the alienation that had sparked the rioting nor, once the violence had spread, to quell or moderate it.

Confirming the insignificance of religion as a factor explaining the failure of Muslim immigrants to integrate into French society is the consistent loyalty displayed by Muslim leaders to the French state, particularly in the context of conflicts opposing the Islamic world and the West. Despite the often painful claims placed on their Muslim identity during the Gulf Wars of 1990–1991 and 2003, the wave of Islamic terrorism that swept France during the Algerian Civil War in 1995–1996, and the Second Intifada that began in September 2002, the vast majority of French Muslims harbored no intention of endangering their

Box 1.4   The Marseille Exception

The experience of the Mediterranean port city of Marseille, France's third largest city and the only significant urban center in which large-scale rioting failed to break out in November 2005, demonstrates the preponderance of social versus religious factors in explaining the unrest. Due to the relative vigor of the associative sector there, the integration of immigrants into the city's urban landscape, and the relative absence of racism among the police and broader population, the social fabric in Marseille's *cités* was able to resist the wave of violence that caused such damage elsewhere.

(*Source*: Luc Bronner, "Quartiers sensibles: l'exception marseillaise," *Le Monde*, hors série, July–August 2010, pp. 36–39.)

right to peaceful residence in their adopted country. On the contrary, this self-restraint highlighted the same desire that paradoxically underlay the violent demonstrations of immigrant youth: that Muslims in France want to be absorbed on equal terms within the broader society.

In this sense, when considered on its own merits, the challenge of integrating non-European immigrants into French society does not appear to be insuperable, especially in the long term. What is required is a civil rights revolution that, by addressing the structural and social inequalities that impede integration, will make the one-law-for-all republican model work in fact and not just in theory. After all, programs that guarantee the political and social equality of minorities who have been the historic victims of discrimination have been more or less successful elsewhere, and there is no reason to think that they could not be in France. Yet the impediments to such a program remain numerous, with politicians on both the Left and the Right attempting to thread the needle between improving the life chances of immigrants in French society on the one hand, while trying to address broader societal fears tying immigration to sociostructural problems such as unemployment, crime, and declining social services on the other.

SARKOZY'S IMMIGRATION POLICY: BETWEEN QUOTAS AND THE KÄRCHER

Nicolas Sarkozy's election has been particularly instructive in this regard, not least because it perpetuates the schizophrenic character of previous attempts to address the problem. On the one hand, the new president has actively promoted integrative policies that recognize the need for affirmative action in order to improve the lot of immigrant youth. Accordingly, he named two ministers with immigrant backgrounds to his cabinet (Rama Yade and Rachida Dati) while pushing for more diversity in the civil service and television sectors. Similarly, his government has also attempted to broaden the affirmative action mechanisms called for in the Charter of Equality, notably by further facilitating the access of members of poor minorities to better schooling and higher education.

Yet, by the same token, Sarkozy has also displayed a troubling willingness to exploit the immigration issue and pander to the xenophobia of the electorate for political gain. Since his election rested in large part on the siphoning off of a substantial number of votes from the National Front, his various hard-line pronouncements on immigration could be interpreted as part of a strategy to win over these voters and keep them electorally on his side. Already as interior minister, his reference to the November 2005 rioters as scum and subsequent call for the *cités* to be cleaned out with a hose (*au Kärcher*) raised eyebrows in many quarters. In turn, a number of initiatives undertaken by the present government have created doubts about the seriousness of Sarkozy's commitment to the goal of integration, since they single out immigrants for discriminatory treatment. The establishment of a Ministry of Immigration and National Identity, for example, was condemned by some as a throwback to the Vichy regime's Commissariat General of Jewish Affairs, while the hardening of sentences for repeat offenders was attacked as discriminatory since a disproportionate number of the latter issue from immigrant backgrounds. Likewise, the government's attempt to institute DNA testing as a precondition for reuniting immigrant families was seen as explicitly pandering to the Far Right, while the encouragement of immigration from certain regions (Europe and India) and not others (North and Sub-Saharan Africa) was viewed as implicitly racist by immigrant groups. Finally, the banning of the burka and niqab in all public spaces starting in early 2011, despite the fact that it will concern only several hundred people, is understandably viewed by French Muslims as a way of singling them out for discrimination by implicitly underscoring the incompatibility of Islam with French republican values.

At the same time, the government has gone further in drawing a link between immigration and crime by proposing a law that would strip immigrants or their children of their French nationality should they threaten a police officer's life, thus putting paid to the republican principle that the state not distinguish between its citizens on the basis of origin. This was followed in September 2010 with the mooting of a proposal to impose a probationary period of ten years for new citizens, during which their nationality could be rescinded if they committed certain crimes.[14] Finally, the forced deportation of *sans papiers* (undocumented immigrants) has been relentlessly stepped up under Sarkozy, leading to abuses that have provoked strong condemnation both at home and abroad. The expulsion of nearly 1,000 Roma in July and August 2010, bringing the total to 8,000 for 2010 alone, elicited an international outcry and could lead the European Commission to start proceedings against France for violating the EU's free-movement-of-citizens clause.

The ambiguities of Sarkozy's approach to immigration are best exemplified by the debate on national identity launched by his government in 2008. At one level, such a debate could be salutary if it facilitates an open discussion of the status of immigrants within French society and yields a positive agenda for facilitating their integration within it. However, it could also have a negative effect by explicitly tying the issues of national identity and immigration. On the one hand, it may radicalize those who, particularly on the Far Right, are opposed to regularizing the status of Muslim immigrants within French society. On the other, it could provoke a communitarian backlash among French Muslims and bring them to reject the republican model of integration in favor of asserting their own religious and ethnic particularities. In this sense, Sarkozy's recent hardening of immigration policy and opening of this debate on national identity may impede the flexibility of this model in assimilating Muslim immigrants while allowing them to assert their cultural and religious specificity under the formal framework of equality. Instead, his insistence on keeping immigration at the front and center of public debate could erode the capacity of the republican model to effectively integrate immigrants and their children into French society.

French Politics in the Age of Globalization

The challenges posed by immigration and globalization, and the difficulties of the French state in dealing with them, highlight the incapacity of the French political system and establishment to address the principal issues of concern to French voters. The political system has been wracked by a mounting crisis of representation and legitimacy as it proves incapable of aggregating people's demands and translating them into effective policies. This has fueled a negative dynamic of political alternation by which unhappy voters—60 percent of which declared "having little confidence in the political parties" in 2007—vote incumbent politicians and governing parties out of power with each electoral cycle.[15] The result is an increasingly fragmented party system on the one hand and governmental blockage or one-party rule on the other.

At one level, this fragmentation is to be seen in the erosion during the 1980s and 1990s of the bipolar pattern of party competition that had developed in the 1970s with an alliance of the Socialist Party (PS) and PCF on the Left opposing the Union for the French Democracy (UDF) and Rally for the Republic (RPR) on the Right. The most obvious beneficiary of this trend has been the National Front, but this splintering occurred on the Left as well, with the emergence of smaller parties to the left of the PS that occupied the space opened up by the collapse of the PCF. These include the Greens, the Revolutionary Communist League (LCR), the New Anti-Capitalist Party (NPA), and Workers' Struggle (LO). This process of fragmentation reached its apogee in the first round of the 2002 presidential election. With the electoral field dispersed among a record sixteen candidates, enough votes were siphoned off from Socialist Party candidate Lionel Jospin to result in his elimination and the accession of the National Front's Jean-Marie Le Pen to the second-round runoff.

At a second level, the hybrid presidential-parliamentary system instituted by General de Gaulle at the inception of the Fifth Republic has proved increasingly dysfunctional in the age of globalization (see box 1.1). On the one hand, this system reinforces the power of the executive at the expense of the legislature, where, except on the most controversial pieces of legislation, the opposition fulfills basically a ceremonial function. When the prime minister comes from the same party as the president, the National Assembly's role is essentially to rubber-stamp the initiatives of the president, with little real debate or amendment. At the same time, as voters grew increasingly dissatisfied with the policy records of sitting governments, instances of *cohabitation* grew increasingly frequent beginning in the 1980s. Characterized by intense policy rivalry between the president and prime minister, these periods of *cohabitation* often resulted in political stalemate and paralysis, contributing to the delegitimization of the country's political institutions among the electorate.

In turn, these institutional failings have become coupled in the public mind with the staleness and mediocrity of the nation's political establishment. As we saw earlier, until Sarkozy's election, France's political leaders, notably Jacques Chirac and François Mitterrand, had begun their careers half a century earlier if not more. These men had been the virtual faces of French politics for over three decades, and those who served under them represented an equally long-standing clique of professional politicians and party notables. The sense of permanence attaching to the political class is reinforced by their exclusive backgrounds, reflecting the fact that the country's political and economic elites almost all issue from highly selective schools (*grandes écoles*) such as the École Polytechnique and the ÉNA (National School of Administration). In their preparation for the task of steering the state bureaucracy and the country's leading firms, these future leaders develop tight-knit social and professional networks that facilitate their movement between the highest positions in the public and private sectors. To French voters, this exclusive and incestuous elite appears at best out of touch, and at worst corrupt.

This impression is reinforced by the numerous political and financial scandals that have embroiled leading French politicians over the years. In recent years, for example, the country has seen a former minister of the interior, Charles Pasqua, jailed for his role in facilitating illegal arms sales to Angola in 1995; the alleged involvement of former prime minister Dominique de Villepin in forging bank account statements implicating then minister of the economy, finances, and industry in the Raffarin government, Nicolas Sarkozy, in the receipt of kickbacks in the 1991 sale of frigates to Taiwan; and, most recently, the charging of former president Jacques Chirac—a first in the history of the Fifth Republic—with corruption during his tenure as mayor of Paris during the 1980s and 1990s. Similarly, the current government of Nicolas Sarkozy itself has not been free from scandal (see below). Given this unsavory track record, French voters might be forgiven for thinking that, not content to govern the country in order to advance their political careers and secure plum private sector jobs once their public tenure is over, French politicians would go to the lengths of breaking the law, such is the sense of entitlement and impunity they develop while in office.

Given this generalized distrust of the political establishment, it is not surprising that significant protest parties have emerged on both the Far Right and the Far Left since the 1980s, the most significant by far being the National Front (FN). Assembling former Vichy sympathizers, neofascists, Catholic fundamentalists, and dissidents from the mainstream Right, the FN first broke through on the national political scene in the mid-1980s and then went from strength to strength, its charismatic leader Jean-Marie Le Pen reaching the second round of the 2002 presidential election and winning 18 percent of the vote. The manifestation of an exclusivist nationalist and authoritarian plebiscitarian tradition whose roots can be traced back to the late 19th century, the FN has made the fight against immigration and linking it to France's current social and economic ills the cornerstone of its political message.

For many observers, the 2007 presidential election marked a critical setback for the National Front, its poor score—10.4 percent, its worst result since its electoral breakthrough in the mid-1980s—combined with its lack of a clear successor to the 82-year-old Le Pen, perhaps signaling the start of its definitive decline. However, the party's strong performance in the March 2010 regional elections, in which it garnered an average of 17 percent in the twelve three-way races in which its candidates were involved in the second round, have confounded these predictions. Indeed, given the morose social and economic climate and Sarkozy's mounting unpopularity, an even stronger electoral resurgence of the FN may be in the cards should it manage to peaceably resolve the question of who will succeed Le Pen as the party's leader. And even if its prospects for taking power remain remote, its already substantial capacity to shape the French political debate could well grow in the years ahead.

Sarkozy—A New Man for a New Time?

If Nicolas Sarkozy is today one of the most unpopular presidents in the history of the Fifth Republic—as of October 2010, only 31 percent of the French had a positive view of him—it is worth remembering that this was not always so. As we saw, his election was perceived in many quarters as marking a new beginning in French politics. Sarkozy had not attended a *grande école* and could thus legitimately pose as an outsider and reformer.[16] Likewise, his language of rupture elicited hope, particularly among conservative voters but also among some on the Left, that the French state and economy would finally be reformed. Lastly, as we have seen, Sarkozy's muscular discourse on immigration and his willingness to go further than previous presidents in linking it to crime was successful in attracting many voters from the Far Right.

At the same time, Sarkozy's election was also interpreted as a momentous shift in French politics because it appeared to herald the return to a stable system of party competition and democratic alternation. For many observers, the election's most salutary outcome was that it yielded the worst result for the FN since 1981 when Le Pen failed to garner the requisite number of signatures to present himself as a candidate, leading to predictions of the party's impending demise. Meanwhile, parties of the Far Left also fared much worse in 2007 compared to 2002, presaging an end to the fragmented party system that had plagued French politics over the previous two decades.[17] Finally, the healthy majority achieved by the Union for a Popular Movement (UMP) in the June 2007 parliamentary elections ensured that Sarkozy would have the support necessary to implement his ambitious reform agenda.

Not surprisingly, Sarkozy's accomplishments have not lived up to these expectations. He has shown himself to be more similar in many ways to his predecessors than to represent a new breed of politician. His administration is viewed as high-handed and domineering, an impression reinforced by Sarkozy's hyperactive style and micromanagement of issues that would normally fall to the prime minister. And though he himself is not an *énarque* (a graduate of ÉNA), his frequentation of people who are, notably his cozy relations with magnates of French industry and media, have fueled suspicions that he is no less immune to the trafficking of influence than his predecessors. Perhaps most troubling in this respect has been his attempt to use these connections to silence media that are critical of him. In the latest instance of this pattern, in September 2010 the center-left newspaper *Le Monde* launched a lawsuit against the Élysée Palace alleging that it had commissioned the French secret service to identify the paper's sources in linking the government and specifically the president himself to illegal campaign contributions in the context of the Bettencourt affair (see below).

Similarly, Sarkozy himself has not been immune to scandal. In the fall of 2009, he was widely accused of nepotism in promoting his son Jean, who was only twenty-three at the time, for the job of running the organization charged with overseeing the business quarter of La Défense just outside Paris, despite his total lack of managerial experience. More recently and perhaps more damaging has been the scandal linking Eric Woerth, one of Sarkozy's closest aides and the cabinet minister charged with pushing through the current pension reforms, to the Bettencourt affair, the dynastic court case surrounding Liliane Bettencourt, France's richest woman and heiress to the l'Oréal cosmetics empire, in an illegal party financing scandal. That he should choose to maintain Woerth as the government's point man on pension reform despite his being tainted by this scandal speaks for the president's critics to his political tone deafness and arrogant leadership style. Finally, the whiff of scandal swirling around Sarkozy is compounded by his hyperpublicized persona as the bling-bling president surrounded by celebrities and feted by the country's rich and famous. In this context, it is hardly surprising that his luxury vacations, yacht trips, Rolex watches, and public divorce and remarriage to a former model turned rock singer would alienate French voters struggling to make ends meet, let alone violate the traditional gravitas they have come to expect in their presidents. When coupled with his proximity to moneyed interests, these ostentatious displays confirm for many Frenchmen that the president is not in fact in their camp when it comes to defending their economic interests and preserving their social well-being.

Most significantly, however, like his predecessors, Sarkozy is confronted by a recalcitrant electorate that, though it understands the need to liberalize the economy and reform the welfare state in the age of globalization, wants the state to continue to protect it from the latter. More than anything, it is this historically ingrained dependence on the French state that makes substantial reforms so difficult to achieve. As Tiersky and de Boisgrollier noted in the previous edition of this book, France evolved as the nation-state par excellence, meaning that the processes of social and economic development were steered by a political elite that was centralized in Paris, first under the auspices of an absolute ruler and then, following the Revolution, under the guidance of a series of constitutional regimes. Accordingly, the country developed a top-down, state-centered relationship to the society, a pattern that was intensified as economic planning was adopted by the Vichy regime and the succeeding Fourth Republic. As we saw earlier, *dirigisme* and state oversight of collective bargaining remained the dominant paradigm until the 1980s, when the government retreated from its role in managing the economy and instead focused on managing the social fallout from this process.

As a result of this long history of statism, it is not surprising that the French people have grown to expect the state to take the lead in resolving economic problems and social conflicts, thus making it difficult to reduce its role in the society and economy without incurring public protest. At one level, the problem is structural; the state sector still accounts for a quarter of full-time jobs in the country. Attempts to cut this sector, let alone to eliminate or reduce the privileges attaching to it, are likely to incur the wrath of the trade unions—the public sector representing the one area where these remain strong—who are well placed to paralyze the country's public and transport services and bring the economy to a halt. As we saw, the most spectacular instance of such protests occurred in the fall and winter of 1995, following the Juppé government's attempt to push through comprehensive pension reform. Monthlong strikes resulted in the proposal being withdrawn and the government's ultimate collapse, forcing Jacques Chirac to call fresh parliamentary elections, which brought a Socialist majority to power. Fifteen years later, similarly widespread demonstrations have met the Fillon government's plans to cut the public sector by one-third and to align civil servants' pensions with those of private sector workers, bringing between 1.2 and 3.5 million protestors into the streets of French cities in October 2010.

At the same time, dependence on the state is reinforced by laws that affirm its capacity to moderate the effects of liberal capitalism and protect French workers from the ravages of globalization. Hence the legal obligation of French firms to consult with the government before downsizing their workforces in order to minimize layoffs and facilitate access for those laid off to new jobs or training programs. This Social Plan provision reinforces the idea that the state can counter the forces of global competition and force firms to act as responsible stakeholders in French society. Similarly, French political leaders often give the impression of being able to mitigate market forces in cases of corporate downsizing when this is increasingly not the case. For example, in February 2009, the government lent the Renault and Peugeot-Citroën automobile groups €8 billion in order to help them through the economic crisis. In exchange, the latter were forced to maintain employment in France and agree not to proceed to any layoffs or offshoring of their operations even though this would make them more competitive in the long run. Affirming this tutelary role of the state, Sarkozy proclaimed, "I welcome the commitment on the part of Renault [and Peugeot-Citroën] not to close any of their sites of production for the duration of these loans . . . because this will ensure that the current crisis does not destroy part of our industrial base."[18] In actual fact, despite such interventions, the state has proved increasingly powerless to prevent the dismantling of former French national champions (Alsthom), the offshoring of their productive operations (Alsthom, Airbus), or the foreign takeover of French firms (Pechiney, Arcelor) in the face of greater international competition.

In short, when confronted by the gap between politicians' assertions of the state's protective capacity and global economic realities, it is no wonder that more and more French people are frustrated by the state's inability to shield them from the forces of globalization, let alone turn them to their advantage. And in the face of this contradiction, Sarkozy has been forced to adopt the same ad hoc, one-step-forward, two-steps-back approach as that employed by his predecessors, a strategy that also risks alienating those who initially supported his reform agenda. In this sense, Sarkozy has replicated the same timidity and inertia in the pursuit of reform that he so vigorously lambasted during his election campaign, thereby testifying to the truism that, in a country like France, only a piecemeal course of reform is possible.

FRENCH FOREIGN POLICY UNDER SARKOZY: BEYOND GAULLISM?

As in other areas, the agenda of rupture touted by Sarkozy during his election campaign and at the outset of his presidency also extended to the realm of foreign policy. First, in calling for an ethical foreign policy, Sarkozy advocated abandoning the traditional Gaullist policy based on self-interest, especially in regard to North and Sub-Saharan Africa where France has overlooked the unsavory behavior of dictators who were seen as acting in conformity with her interests. Second, Sarkozy also appeared to downgrade this Gaullist tradition through well-publicized pronouncements that he was an Atlanticist bent on returning France to a full partnership role in the Western alliance. More broadly, in recognition of the emergence of a more globalized world, Sarkozy has asserted the need for France to fasten onto new vectors of influence in which horizontal multilateral relationships and issues would come to supplant hierarchical bilateral ones. In a symbolic gambit reflecting these shifts, he broke with the presidential convention of naming politicians from his own party to head French diplomacy by appointing the former Socialist Bernard Kouchner as his minister of foreign affairs as well as two other Socialists to serve as his first secretaries for state cooperation and European affairs.

In order to assess the true extent of this shift, it is necessary to say something about France's postwar foreign policy persona, specifically the legacy of Gaullism. At the center of General de Gaulle's conception of French foreign policy was the imperative of making France count as a world power by striving to maintain her "independence, sovereignty, and *grandeur.*" This implied an assertive discourse that was marked by a willingness to break with U.S. or European allies as a means of reaffirming France's global role. Likewise, the Gaullist assertion of French independence was also manifest in spectacular acts of diplomacy, such as the veto of the UK's EEC accession bids in 1963 and 1967, France's pullout from NATO-integrated military command in 1966, and de Gaulle's Phnom Penh speech denouncing the American war in Vietnam later the same year. At the same time, de Gaulle's foreign policy aimed to establish France as an indispensable intermediary between the Eastern and Western blocs on the one hand, and the developed and developing worlds on the other. By playing such a role, he believed, France would be able to recapture the global prestige she had enjoyed prior to the defeat of 1940 and thus punch above her weight as a middling power.

With different styles, we find a similar assertion of the imperatives of French independence and *grandeur* among de Gaulle's successors. Georges Pompidou, though he finally acceded to the UK's admission to the EEC, also indulged in sometimes virulent criticism of the United States (as in the case of the latter's arming of Israel during the Yom Kippur War of 1973). Valéry Giscard d'Estaing irritated Washington by characterizing the Soviet invasion of Afghanistan in 1979 as an act of self-defense and refusing to boycott the Moscow Olympics in 1980. François Mitterrand, while accommodating U.S. strategic aims by accepting the installation of Pershing and cruise missiles in Europe; supporting Chad in its war against Libya, a Soviet ally; and participating in the U.S.-led coalition to expel Iraqi troops from Kuwait, was also determined to act on his own on certain issues. Thus he resisted U.S. and UK pressures to rescind energy contracts with the USSR and called, alongside German chancellor Helmut Kohl, for the pursuit of an independent European Common Foreign and Security Policy. Finally, Jacques Chirac's two terms as president were characterized by a mix of foreign policy activism combined with independent policies vis-à-vis the United States. His hardening of the French line against Serbia in 1995 and his decision to resume French nuclear testing in the South Pacific were examples of the former, while his threat to veto a UN Security Council resolution authorizing a U.S.-led invasion of Iraq in 2003 was the most dramatic instance of the latter.

Alongside this traditional commitment to independence, French foreign

Box 1.5   De Gaulle on Gaullism

"All my life I have thought of France in a [special] way. This is inspired by sentiment as much as by reason. The emotional side of me tends to imagine France, like the princess in the fairy stories or the Madonna in the frescoes, as dedicated to an exalted and exceptional destiny. Instinctively I have the feeling that Providence has created her either for complete successes or for exemplary misfortunes. If, in spite of this, mediocrity shows in her acts and deeds, it strikes me as an absurd anomaly, to be imputed to the faults of Frenchmen, not to the genius of the [country]. But the [rational] side of my mind also assures me that France is not really herself unless in the front rank; that only vast enterprises are capable of counterbalancing the ferments of dispersal which are inherent in her people; that our country, as it is, surrounded by the others, as they are, must aim high and hold itself straight, on pain of mortal danger. In short, to my mind, France cannot be France without [grandeur]."

Charles de Gaulle, *War Memoirs*, quoted in Ronald Tiersky and Nicolas de Boisgrollier, "France: Hopes and Fears of a New Generation," in Ronald Tiersky and Erik Jones (eds.), *Europe Today*, 3rd ed., Lanham, MD: Rowman & Littlefield, 2005, p. 45.

policy has been focused since the war on three geographically defined areas or circles of activity: the Atlantic or Western alliance, Europe, and the francophone space (*francophonie*) incorporating France's former colonies, particularly in North and Sub-Saharan Africa and the Arab world. French foreign policy in these three areas has been remarkably consistent.

In the Atlantic area, relations between France and the U.S.-led Western alliance have been simultaneously characterized by mutual wariness and support. Relations hit a new low in the run-up to the Iraq war in 2003, marking the first time that France had openly and actively opposed the United States in an international crisis. However, even in the wake of this episode, the two countries continued to work together behind the scenes and cooperated on issues of vital interest to both, such as the fight against global terrorist networks. This mixed relationship is best summed up in former foreign minister Hubert Védrine's quip that the two countries remain "friends, allies, [but] non-aligned."

At the European level, French policy has been consistent since the Élysée Treaty of 1963, which attempted to cement the economic rapprochement with West Germany under the auspices of French foreign policy leadership. This policy reflected the belief that European economic and political integration could only be advanced on the basis of cooperation between France and Germany—the famous Franco-German engine. However, this conviction was tempered by the recognition that only through cooperation with London could Europe assume an independent military capability under Franco-British leadership.

Outwardly at least, it is perhaps at the level of *francophonie* that things have changed the most. Although France still ascribes great importance to what goes on in Algiers, Rabat, or Tunis, it no longer enjoys the influence to shape policy in these places that it once did. Likewise, though France continues to maintain a military presence in Sub-Saharan Africa, this presence is much less significant than before. Finally, although French leaders continue to dream of influencing developments in the Middle East, particularly in resolving the Israeli-Palestinian conflict, they harbor no illusion about their lack of leverage to do so.

What the foregoing suggests is that the central dilemma facing contemporary French diplomacy has less to do with defining her foreign policy aims than with how to go about fulfilling them. Despite boasting the second largest diplomatic corps in the world after the United States, broader structural and cultural changes in the global system have diminished France's influence. Signs of this loss of stature can be seen at a number of levels: the ascendancy of English as the undisputed lingua franca of diplomacy as well as business; the hegemony, even following the financial and economic crises of 2008–2009, of liberal economic ideas; and continued American economic and political dominance, combined with the emergence of new world powers such as China and India. More than ever before, these developments are forcing French policymakers to confront the reality of the country's relative decline in a globalized world.

The challenge of decline is not new, of course. Mitterrand was the first to try to negotiate the transition from a bipolar to a plural global system complicated by the tension between America's unipolar pretensions and the emergence of a multipolar order in which France would be reduced to the rank of a middling power. Likewise, Chirac made it a priority to prepare French diplomacy for the challenges posed by the horizontal supranational forces shaping the contemporary international system, and hence to move beyond the bilateral focus of interstate relations inherited from the Cold War. Still, the question of France's place in the world is especially urgent today because it poses the challenge of how France is to negotiate her post–Cold War decline while minimizing her loss of influence and prestige.

SARKOZY'S FOREIGN POLICY: A BREAK WITH GAULLISM OR GAULLISM REAFFIRMED?

Where does Nicolas Sarkozy's foreign policy fit in terms of this attempt to compensate for France's loss of influence in an increasingly plural and globalized world? How is it to be assessed in respect to the Gaullist heritage that informed the foreign policies of his predecessors? An examination of the principal circles of French diplomacy identified above makes it possible to identify the areas of continuity and discontinuity that characterize Sarkozy's approach to international affairs.

The Atlantic circle, and specifically France's relationship with the United

States, is in many ways the area in which Sarkozy's foreign policy displays the most continuities with the past. This is perhaps surprising given that, throughout his presidential campaign and upon arriving in office, Sarkozy had gone out of his way to define himself as an Atlanticist. In fact, as Justin Vaïsse has argued, there is a good case to be made that Sarkozy remains a Gaullist in terms of both the underlying beliefs and the actual initiatives that characterize his foreign policy.[19]

In the first place, Sarkozy's convictions in this area dovetail with many of those evinced by the general and his followers. Like de Gaulle before him, Sarkozy posits a multipolar world in which France, through the EU, rightfully exercises its diplomatic, security, and economic influence. This translates the Gaullist belief that it is not enough to simply defend the national interest, but that French foreign policy should also aim to secure the country's independence, influence, and *grandeur*. Accordingly, Sarkozy has expanded French weapons sales not only to advance French economic interests, but also to promote the country's technological independence, notably from NATO. Likewise, he is the first French president since de Gaulle to have established a military base outside of France's traditional zone of influence, in the United Arab Emirates.

Likewise, despite his rhetoric, Sarkozy has not substantially moved French foreign policy in a more Atlanticist direction, suggesting another continuity with his Gaullist predecessors. For example, there has been no great inflection in the French position on Israel-Palestine, despite the claim of greater even-handedness in attempting to mediate between the two sides. Likewise, on Iran, there has been only a slight hardening of France's position compared to the Chirac years, though the volume of investment by French companies has decreased. And on Afghanistan, after a slight increase in French troop commitments to the NATO coalition following Sarkozy's election, there are growing indications that French troops will be drawn down in the face of mounting military difficulties and the growing unpopularity of the Afghanistan war at home. Even Sarkozy's much-publicized decision to return France to NATO-integrated command in 2009 was prefigured by Chirac's failed attempt to do so in the mid-1990s.

In fact, on issues where the French position has shifted, it has often been in the wrong direction from the U.S. perspective. In the Middle East, Sarkozy's opposition to Turkish accession to the EU, as well as his willingness to negotiate with the Assad regime in Syria and Hezbollah in Lebanon, has caused displeasure in Washington. In international economic affairs, his propping up of French firms, his call for the establishment of EU trade preferences, and his condemnation of the weak dollar have run afoul of the United States' free-trade agenda, while he has attacked, in a manner reminiscent of de Gaulle, the dollar's status as the international reserve currency. Finally, on a host of issues ranging from global warming to cultivating relations with Venezuela's Hugo Chavez or

Iran's Mahmoud Ahmadinejad, Sarkozy's diplomacy has embraced a contrary course to the United States.

In short, the Atlanticist hype aside, these foreign policy choices suggest that, much like his predecessors, Sarkozy views the world in terms of an emerging multipolar dispensation that the United States and the West more generally will find increasingly difficult to control. In such a world, he believes that France has a crucial role to play in reaching out to and bridging divides with other states and regions. However, whereas during the Cold War France played this intermediary role between the Eastern and Western blocs, today this involves facilitating dialogue across regional and cultural fault lines in order to diminish the risk of a clash of civilizations, particularly between the Muslim and Western worlds—hence Sarkozy's proposal to establish a Union of the Mediterranean during the French presidency of the EU in 2008, as well as his "AREVA" diplomacy promoting the development of civilian nuclear energy in Arab countries such as Algeria, Morocco, Libya, and the UAE. Finally, in keeping with his vision of a more plural and multipolar post-post-Cold War world, Sarkozy has called for adapting international institutions to reflect this new reality. In this vein, he has advocated enlarging the G-8 into a G-13, incorporating China, India, Brazil, Mexico, and South Africa, as well as increasing the permanent members of the UN Security Council to include Germany, Japan, Brazil, and India, as well as a major African country.

Sarkozy's Gaullist persona has also influenced the second circle of French foreign policy, the country's relationship to Europe. This is reflected in the policy objectives set out during France's presidency of the EU from June to December 2008. First, the latter was informed by the imperative to put the EU back on the post–Iraq war international map, as seen in Sarkozy's intermediation in the Russo-Georgian conflict as well as in his attempt to fashion a leading role for the EU in tackling the global financial crisis. Second, Sarkozy strove to assert himself as the dominant leader in the EU, even at the risk of alienating France's EU partners, notably Germany. Linked to this assertion of strong leadership, Sarkozy sought to renew the manner in which the EU functions by demonstrating that political will can override institutional questions. Accordingly, following the Irish rejection of the Lisbon Treaty in June 2008, the French presidency strongly pushed for its adoption by the parliaments of member states so as to enact the institutional reforms initially called for in the defeated EU Constitution. Fourth and finally, the French presidency also reaffirmed the primacy of intergovernmentalism over a community-based approach, principally by reasserting the authority of the European Council over the Commission in a number of areas. This was in keeping with the Gaullist conception of a Europe of states, in which national governments retain considerable freedom of action over policy, as opposed to a federalist conception according to which the autonomy of the states is limited by pooling decision-making authority in centralized European instances of leadership.

In terms of its achievements, the French presidency of the European Union has been generally viewed as a success. First and foremost, it brought France squarely back to the center of the EU after its years in the European wilderness following the May 2005 "no" vote on the Constitution. In turn, the French presidency managed to enact two measures that had been at the top of French priorities for the EU. First, it was able to push through a European Pact on Immigration and Asylum, which harmonized political asylum laws and forbade large-scale amnesties for illegal immigrants within the EU. Second, it also gained assent for a Climate Energy Package in which member states agreed to reduce their greenhouse gas emissions and increase energy efficiency by 20 percent by 2020. These achievements are all the more noteworthy in that they were accomplished despite a number of unforeseen complications which could have derailed the French presidency, including the Irish rejection of the Lisbon Treaty in June 2008, the Russo-Georgian war two months later, and the outbreak of the global financial crisis in the fall of 2008.[20]

Despite these immediate successes, however, over the longer term an assessment of the French EU presidency appears less rosy. At one level, the Gaullist emphasis on weakening the European Commission is a potential source of concern because of the EU's need for an independent organ capable of representing and pursuing its collective interests rather than those of individual states. Perhaps more worrying from the perspective of French diplomacy has been the breakdown in Franco-German relations, which the presidency helped to precipitate. Sarkozy's assertion of strong French leadership chafed with Chancellor Angela Merkel and other German leaders who were used to more consultation and deference in addressing the EU's problems.

Two examples in particular illustrate this deterioration in relations. At one level, Sarkozy's unilateral announcement of the establishment of a Union of the Mediterranean provoked misgivings in Germany, which saw in this initiative an attempt to shift the EU's center of influence from Eastern to southern Europe. Secondly, this Franco-German dysfunction has been reflected in the lack of coordination and failure to agree on policies to address the 2008 financial meltdown and the ensuing economic crisis. Whereas Paris was fearful that the crisis would bring deflation and unemployment unless a course of reflationary spending was adopted, Germany feared that such a course would trigger inflation—a divergence that came to a head over the Greek sovereign debt crisis in the spring of 2010. Finally, French complaints about Germany's underconsumption and reliance on its exports to boost its savings at the expense of its EU partners is not likely to be allayed by the vigorous resumption of German economic growth during the third quarter of 2010, compared to France's anemic recovery over the same period.

In short, though France's new assertiveness in the EU has borne fruit, it has also had negative consequences that may end up detracting from the effectiveness of its foreign policy in this circle vital to its national interest. As in the Gaullist era, France's relations with its European partners continue to be complicated. In a newly expanded EU, however, she will not be able to get her way as easily as in de Gaulle's time. Instead, she is likely to more frequently find herself isolated on a growing number of issues.

On the face of it, it is in the circle of *francophonie* that Sarkozy's agenda of rupture in the realm of foreign policy is most evident. This was most vividly symbolized by his affirmation of an ethical foreign policy in which France's former colonial dependencies, particularly in Africa, were no longer to be treated as an exclusively French stomping ground and where the advancement of human rights was to hold sway, thereby presumably stripping friendly dictators of their former privileges and support. In turn, France has pledged to use her leverage to resolve regional conflicts in areas where she once had influence, notably by adopting a more balanced approach in helping to resolve the Israeli-Palestinian conflict and by using her weight with certain regional players, such as Lebanon and Syria, in order to advance that goal.

Again, however, the intrusion of political realities has brought into question how serious or capable France is about putting these new orientations into practice. In Chad, for example, the Sarkozy government stood by while the government of its former protégé, Idriss Deby, disappeared a number of democratic dissidents and political opponents in response to rebel attacks on the capital of Djamena in February 2008. This reminded people that when it came to Africa, the old political, military, and financial networks of the past continue to operate and shape French policy, Sarkozy's talk of *rupture* with these old colonial habits notwithstanding. Similarly, France's pretension to play the role of honest broker in the Middle East continues to be hampered by the perception that she is too pro-Arab, as well as by the EU's relative lack of clout in the region.

Indeed, if change is today the operative theme in this circle, it may well be for reasons that the French foreign policy establishment would rather not admit. Since the Cold War, France's weight in its traditional spheres of influence—the Maghreb, Western Africa, and the Machrek (Syria and Lebanon)—has considerably diminished. On the one hand, this reflects the emergence of new leaders who do not enjoy the traditional clientelistic ties to France that their predecessors did. On the other hand, this is the result of the encroachment of global powers such as the United States and China into these areas, notably Africa, thereby reducing France's historic influence there.

In short, the limitations of French power that became obvious after the Cold War are making it increasingly difficult for the country to live up to its self-perception as a global power, even in areas where it formerly held uncontested sway. In turn, this loss of power underscores the fact that the foreign policy challenge facing Sarkozy remains fundamentally the same as that confronting his predecessors: that France needs to redefine her foreign policy in the context of an increasingly multipolar and integrated international system, without relinquishing the balancing capacity that had allowed her to punch above her weight for most of the postwar period.

Conclusion

As the foregoing shows, Nicolas Sarkozy's agenda of rupture, whether in the realm of foreign or domestic policy, has run up against deep-seated structural and cultural impediments that have moderated or even deflected the much-heralded changes he announced at the start of his presidential term. On domestic policy, anxieties over globalization, the survival of the welfare state, and the spread of savage liberal capitalism have forced Sarkozy to embrace the path of slow and piecemeal reform initiated under his predecessors. As was most recently illustrated by the mass protests elicited by his (rather modest) plan to reform the nation's pension system, the atavistic opposition of the French to change could not but temper his initial ambitions of sweeping economic liberalization and social retrenchment. Similarly, on the foreign policy front, despite his rhetorical disavowal of France's Gaullist heritage, the reality of the erosion of French influence since the end of the Cold War could only translate into an effectively neo-Gaullist policy of trying to count in the world, whether in France's traditional spheres of influence such as Europe, Africa, and the Middle East, or in areas where her influence had historically been more circumscribed, such as within the Western alliance. In short, these structural and cultural impediments to change have meant that Sarkozy's reform program has been much more modest in scope than he initially announced and many of his supporters expected. Instead of representing a momentous break from the past, it has more often than not perpetuated and intensified courses of reform that had previously been set down.

Finally, Sarkozy's temperament and style as a leader have oftentimes been an obstacle to executing his reform agenda. At one level, his micromanagement of reforms has cost him dearly in popularity and effectiveness. His refusal to delegate prevents him from blaming the prime minister, thus exposing him to the brunt of public dissatisfaction when things go wrong. In turn, it has bred a highhandedness and arrogance in exercising power that is off-putting to his domestic and foreign interlocutors and creates a clannish atmosphere in the Élysée Palace that makes it difficult for his advisers to contradict him. As we saw above, this arrogance and insularity have led to blunders and scandals that have damaged Sarkozy's standing with the public.

Second, the president's hyperactivity, combined with his omnipresence in the media, has bred confusion about his motives and fatigue with his persona. Contradictory statements, such as urging the French to reconcile themselves to globalization while declaring that "laissez-faire capitalism is finished," or his advocacy of greater economic competition while at the same time calling for expanded EU trade protections, make it difficult for the French to distinguish between what is conviction and what rhetoric in their president's words, fueling a general sense of drift in the country as 2010 draws to a close.

Combined with the negative impact of the recession, this sense of listlessness and confusion about his motives has considerably weakened Sarkozy's political position. The March 2010 regional elections yielded the worst-ever results for the party in power, the UMP losing 22 out of 25 regions and retaining control only of Alsace in metropolitan France. Ominously for Sarkozy, 11.5 million voters who had backed him in 2007 failed to support the UMP in the regional elections. In turn, looking forward to the presidential election of 2012, in September 2010, 55 percent of the French said that they wished for the return of the Left to power. Polls indicate that both Dominique Strauss-Kahn, the most likely Socialist candidate, and Martine Aubry, the PS's current leader, would defeat Sarkozy in the second round of a presidential election if it were held today. Sensing this weakness, rival candidates are emerging on the Right, notably former prime minister Dominique de Villepin who has launched his own party in order to recoup Gaullist voters disillusioned with Sarkozy.

In short, less than two years from the next presidential election, Sarkozy finds himself politically embattled, and there is a serious question as to whether he will be reelected. Although there is still time to turn things around before 2012, the window of opportunity for him to make good on his reform agenda, let alone pull France out of recession, is closing fast. In this sense, it is not just Sarkozy's reform agenda but his very political survival that hangs in the balance over the coming year.

One thing is certain, however. Whoever does end up as France's next president will have to confront the same challenges and blockages that have been faced by Sarkozy during his first term. The question is whether, on a backdrop of persistent economic crisis and worsening social and political polarization, the future president will continue on the path of reform traced by Sarkozy and his predecessors, or instead revert to the protective policies of the past, even if these are increasingly unviable in the age of globalization. Whatever happens, France is likely to persist in her uneven course of development and thus retain her specificity as a society and economy.

Suggested Readings

Andrews, William, and Stanley Hoffman (eds.), *The Impact of the Fifth Republic on France*, Albany: State University of New York Press, 1981.

Ardaugh, John, *France in the New Century: Portrait of a Changing Society*, London: Viking Press, 1999.

Boltanski, Luc, *The Making of a Class: Cadres in French Society*, trans. A. Goldhammer, New York: Cambridge University Press, 1987.

Boy, Daniel, and Nonna Mayer (eds.), *The French Voter Decides*, trans. C. Schoch, Ann Arbor: University of Michigan Press, 1993.

Culpepper, Pepper, and Peter Hall, *Changing France: The Politics That Markets Make*, New York: Palgrave Macmillan, 2006.

DeClair, Edward, *Politics on the Fringe: The People, Policies, and Organization of the French National Front*, Durham, NC: Duke University Press, 1999.

Gordon, Philip, and Jeremy Shapiro, *Allies at War: America, Europe, and the Crisis over Iraq*, New York: McGraw-Hill, 2004.

Hall, Peter, *Governing the Economy: The Politics of State Intervention in Britain and France*, Cambridge, UK: Polity Press, 1986.

Hayward, Jack, and Vincent Wright (eds.), *Governing from the Center: Core Executive Coordination in France*, New York: Oxford University Press, 2002.

Hélias, Pierre-Jakez, *The Horse of Pride: Life in a Breton Village*, trans. J. Guicharnaud, New Haven, CT: Yale University Press, 1980.

Hoffmann, Stanley, "Paradoxes of the French Political Community," in S. Hoffmann (ed.), *In Search of France*, Cambridge, MA: Harvard University Press, 1963, pp. 1–117.

Kriegel, Annie, *The French Communists: Profile of a People*, trans. E. Halperin, Chicago: University of Chicago Press, 1972.

Kuisel, Richard, *Capitalism and the State in Modern France*, New York: Cambridge University Press, 1981.

Laurence, Jonathan, and Justin Vaïsse, *Integrating Islam: Political and Religious Challenges in Contemporary France*, Washington, DC: Brookings Institution Press, 2006.

Noiriel, Gérard, *The French Melting Pot: Immigration, Citizenship, and National Identity*, trans. G. de Laforcade, Minneapolis: University of Minnesota Press, 1996.

Nord, Philip, *France's New Deal: From the Thirties to the Postwar Era*, Princeton, NJ: Princeton University Press, 2010.

Rémond, René, *The Right Wing in France: From 1815 to de Gaulle*, trans. J. Laux, 2nd ed., Philadelphia: University of Pennsylvania Press, 1969.

Tiersky, Ronald, *France in the New Europe*, Belmont, CA: Wadsworth, 1994.

Weil, Patrick, *How to Be French*, trans. C. Porter, Durham, NC: Duke University Press, 2008.

Wright, Gordon, *Rural Revolution in France: The Peasantry in the Twentieth Century*, Stanford: Stanford University Press, 1964.

CHAPTER 2

Great Britain: From New Labour to New Politics?

Jonathan Hopkin

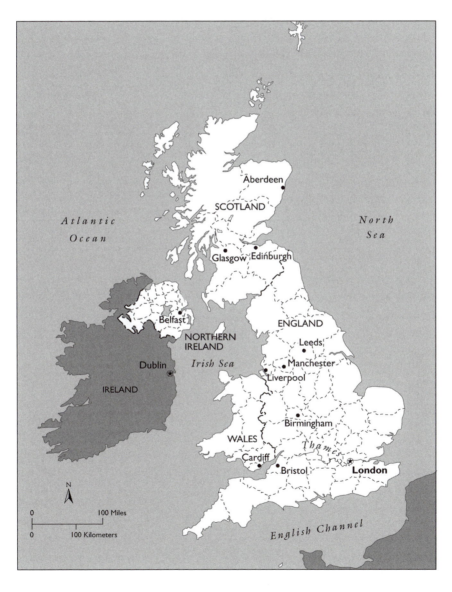

United Kingdom

Population (million):	61.8
Area in Square Miles:	94,548
Population Density per Square Mile:	654
GDP (in billion dollars, 2009):	$2,251.9
GDP per capita (PPP, 2005):	$32,001
Joined EC/EU:	January 1, 1973

Performance of Key Political Parties in Parliamentary Elections of May 2010

Conservative and Unionist Party	36.1% (306 seats)
Democratic Unionist Party (DUP)	0.6% (8 seats)
Labour Party	29.0% (258 seats)
Liberal Democrats	23.0% (57 seats)
Party of Wales (Plaid Cymru)	0.6% (3 seats)
Scottish National Party (SNP)	1.7% (6 seats)
Sinn Fein	0.6% (5 seats)
UK Independence Party (UKIP)	3.1% (0 seats)
Ulster Unionist Party (UUP)	0.3% (0 seats)

Main Office Holders: Prime Minister: David Cameron—Conservative (2010); Head of State: Queen Elizabeth II.

On May 6, 2010, Britain went to the polls to take part in one of the most uncertain elections for decades. The ruling Labour Party, having won a third general election in a row five years earlier, was desperately battling to avoid a crushing defeat under its new leader, Gordon Brown, the former chancellor of the Exchequer (Treasury minister) under Tony Blair. The Conservative Party, under its young, fresh-faced leader David Cameron, hoped to exploit the unpopularity of the Labour government to win the keys to Number 10 Downing Street. But opinion polls suggested that, unusually for the United Kingdom, there was a strong chance that no party would win an overall majority in the House of Commons, the main chamber of the British Parliament. The centrist Liberal Democrats, led by another ambitious young politician, Nick Clegg, hoped that such a "hung parliament" would turn his party into kingmaker, allowing the Liberals to enter government for the first time in eighty years. In most British elections, the winner is declared just a few hours after the polling stations close, but such was the tightness of this election that the outcome was still not clear at daybreak on May 7.

What followed was an entirely new situation in contemporary UK politics. The Labour prime minister Gordon Brown had suffered a humiliating defeat, his party shedding almost a million votes and ninety-one parliamentary seats, registering one of Labour's worst electoral performances in its history. Yet instead of driving to Buckingham Palace the following day to offer his resignation, as is the convention for a defeated prime minister, Brown stayed put in Downing Street. As the Chancellor of the Exchequer (based at Number 11) and then prime minister (Number 10), Brown had been resident in Downing Street for thirteen years, and hostile newspapers accused him of "squatting" in the prime ministerial quarters. However, Brown's delayed resignation was consistent with constitutional practice: the sitting prime minister does not resign until his or her successor can command majority support in parliament, and David Cameron's Conservatives had 306 seats, 20 short of an overall majority. The impasse was only resolved when, after five days of negotiations, Cameron reached an agreement with Liberal Democrat leader Clegg to form a coalition government, the first multiparty administration in Britain since the Second World War.

The 2010 election marked the end of a thirteen-year period in which British politics had been dominated by Tony Blair's Labour Party. On May 1, 1997, almost two decades of continuous Conservative governments came to an end with a landslide election victory for Labour. This was a remarkable achievement for the party's youthful leader Blair, who remolded the party to his image, even to the point of informally renaming it "New Labour" and promising that the rebranded party offered a "New Britain." Blair's Labour Party went on to win two further elections: another landslide in 2001, and a third, narrower, victory in 2005, making him the most successful Labour leader ever. But by 2005, Blair was increasingly embattled, haunted by his decision to join

George W. Bush in his unpopular invasion of Iraq, and constantly pressured to leave office by his ambitious deputy Gordon Brown. He resigned in the summer of 2007, but Brown very quickly came under pressure as the lurking financial crisis and other political difficulties exposed his weaknesses as a political leader.

Labour's defeat is therefore the end of an era, and a chance to take stock of the achievements and failures of the "New Labour" project. With a parliamentary majority even bigger than those enjoyed by Margaret Thatcher in her heyday of the 1980s, and an initially benign economic climate, the Labour government had an unprecedented opportunity to make its mark on British society and politics. So, has New Labour made a "New Britain"? With Labour's exit from office, it has now become possible to provide an answer to this question. This chapter will seek to draw a balance sheet on the Blair administration's achievements and failures by analyzing the transformations brought about by this historically unprecedented period of left-of-center political dominance. In doing so, it will also assess another historic transformation: the birth, or more accurately rebirth, of multiparty politics in Britain. For only the second time since the war, the British electorate defeated the governing party without providing the party of opposition with a ruling majority. Alongside the constitutional reforms carried out by the Blair governments, the formation of a coalition government in 2010 suggests a dramatic shift in the nature of British politics.

This chapter will trace the origins of this dramatic shift and tentatively assess its implications. It will look at three broad areas: the British economy and the impact of the financial crisis of 2007–2010, the important changes made to the British Constitution since 1997 and the implications of multiparty politics for the UK political system, and Britain's foreign policy under the leadership of Blair, Brown, and Cameron. The discussion will focus on recent developments over the past decade or so, but in doing so will also provide a general overview of the main trends and developments in contemporary British politics.

The British Economy: From Boom to Bust

WINNING CREDIBILITY: NEW LABOUR'S ECONOMIC STRATEGY

In many respects, 1997 was a good time for Labour to win an election. From a short-term perspective, the British economy was in good shape by historical standards. After the pound's devaluation and dramatic exit from the European Exchange Rate Mechanism in September 1992, the British economy very quickly began to emerge from the deep recession that had begun in 1990. By

1997, unemployment had been falling continuously for five years, but without sparking inflation. Britain appeared to be on the road to recovering from its postwar history of macroeconomic instability. Labour had hoped to win power in 1992, when an election was held in the middle of a recession and the Conservatives appeared weak and divided. However, in retrospect, Labour was fortunate to have lost the 1992 election: the Conservatives were left to sort out the crisis, and when Labour finally won, they inherited a healthy economy.

Tony Blair's priority as Labour leader was to win credibility as a competent manager of the economy. Labour needed to earn the support of middle-income voters in order to win election. Blair perceived that for many voters, Labour were not regarded as responsible custodians of the British economy. Moreover, it had become clear that a growing share of Labour's traditional working-class supporters felt that the Conservatives, with their stress on property ownership and low personal taxation, offered greater opportunities for improving their living standards. In order to win an election, Labour needed to convince such people that the party was on their side. Labour's manifesto for the 1997 election sought to do precisely that. Labour would be fiscally responsible, promising to follow clear fiscal rules to keep government borrowing low. There would be no increase in income tax rates, and the party would effectively freeze public spending for the first two years in office. At the same time, Labour promised to increase investment in key areas of the public sector, particularly in the health service and education systems. This greater spending would be paid for by a one-off "windfall" tax on the excessive profits of utility companies privatized by the Conservatives, and through a program aimed at slashing long-term unemployment and its related social costs.

As well as winning over wavering Conservative voters, Labour also had to make new friends in the business community. In a world of globalized capital flows, the financial services industry based in London had become indisputably the key strategic sector of the British economy, and the Conservatives had traditionally been the party closest to the City's interests. Labour's leaders felt that any lack of confidence in the new Labour government among City institutions could lead to capital flight and currency instability, which would derail their plans. In order to win over City elites, Blair and his economics spokesman, Gordon Brown, had embarked on a so-called prawn cocktail offensive, meeting key City figures over lunch to reassure them that Labour's economic plans would safeguard City interests. Once in office, Blair and Brown had a clear plan to consolidate this new relationship between the UK's financial elite and the party that had traditionally represented organized labor.

First, Labour had to address its reputation for fiscal irresponsibility. By signing up to the previous Conservative administration's budgetary plans for the first two years of the new Parliament, Labour was committing itself to a tough approach to public spending; after all, the Conservatives were expecting to lose and felt free to make unrealistically restrictive plans about how much

Table 2.1   Prime Ministers and Governing Parties in the United Kingdom, 1945–2010

Dates	Prime Minister	Governing Party
1945–1951	Clement Attlee	Labour
1951–1955	Winston Churchill	Conservative
1955–1957	Anthony Eden	Conservative
1957–1963	Harold MacMillan	Conservative
1963–1964	Alec Douglas-Home	Conservative
1964–1970	Harold Wilson	Labour
1970–1974	Edward Heath	Conservative
1974–1976	Harold Wilson	Labour
1976–1979	James Callaghan	Labour
1979–1990	Margaret Thatcher	Conservative
1990–1997	John Major	Conservative
1997–2007	Tony Blair	Labour
2007–2010	Gordon Brown	Labour
2010–	David Cameron	Conservative-Liberal Democrat

the government would need to spend. By sticking to these heroically frugal plans, Labour aimed to show the financial and business elite that it could be trusted to keep government borrowing low. It reinforced this approach with a so-called golden rule—a commitment that government would not borrow to fund current spending over the business cycle—and a further commitment to keep total government debt below 40 percent of gross domestic product. These policies were followed so strictly that the Labour government managed to run a budget surplus for every year of the 1997–2001 Parliament.[1]

A second fundamental reform was not trailed before the election. In his first act after being named Chancellor of the Exchequer, Gordon Brown announced that the new government would no longer set interest rates, which would become the responsibility of the UK's central bank, the Bank of England. By putting monetary policy at arm's length, Labour hoped to enhance its credibility as a responsible manager of the UK macroeconomy. This policy also quickly appeared vindicated, as interest rates and inflation both dropped to historically low levels within Labour's first term of office. Remarkably for recent British economic history, unemployment also continued to fall without sparking price increases. The immediate success of these policy decisions was a boost to Labour's fortunes. First, they vindicated one of Labour's most prominent messages in their political campaigns—that they would put an end to the "boom and bust" of the Thatcher period and lay the foundations for more stable economic growth. Second, the success in reducing both inflation and unemployment at the same time allowed Brown to follow a cautious economic policy without having to demand too many sacrifices of Labour's traditional supporters.

By granting independence to the Bank of England and committing itself to tough fiscal rules, Labour was signing up to the reigning economic orthodoxy of the 1990s. Significantly, Blair and Brown were also enthusiastic about a further plank of this orthodoxy: financial market deregulation. Unlike in monetary policy, New Labour did not embark on major reforms in the regulation of financial services, largely because a series of deregulatory measures had already been adopted by the Thatcher governments in the 1980s, removing a range of restrictions on financial activity and promoting a modernization and rapid expansion of the financial sector. The so-called Big Bang of 1986—which removed some key regulations and established electronic trading in the London stock exchange—brought a surge in capital flows to the City of London and a boom in lending to British consumers. Also in 1986, the Thatcher government passed the Building Societies Act, deregulating the usually small mutual financial institutions that financed most housing purchases in the UK. The majority of building societies converted to banks owned by shareholders as a direct result of this legislation and adopted more expansionary lending practices. This led to a rapid increase in property prices, followed by an equally rapid collapse of the property market in the early 1990s.

These changes to the financial sector, along with most other reforms promoted by the Thatcher governments, were strongly opposed by the Labour Party at the time, but by the mid-1990s, Labour had begun to adopt a much less confrontational strategy under Tony Blair. Blair's centrist orientation had two clear consequences for Labour's attitude to finance. First, Labour became very anxious to court middle-class voters who, notwithstanding the collapse of property prices, were supportive of many aspects of the Thatcherite economic programme. Second, Labour was desperate to win over the City of London by reassuring powerful figures in the banking world that Labour would not only protect and nurture the financial sector but promote its expansion as a motor of economic growth. One of Blair's key allies, the current business secretary Peter Mandelson, famously stated that "we are intensely relaxed about people getting filthy rich, as long as they pay their taxes." Such thinking was informed by the "third way" advocated by Blairite sociologist Anthony Giddens, who argued that progressive politics needed to move "beyond left and right."[2] In practice, this meant that once in power, Labour would maintain the deregulatory approach to the financial sector pioneered by the Conservatives. The housing market reached its bottom in 1995–1996 and had entered another rapidly expansionary phase once Labour was elected in 1997. This time, the rise in the housing market was bolstered by trends in the world economy, in particular the spectacular housing boom in the United States and the associated innovations in the financial sector. Securitization of residential housing mortgages—in which banks lent money for housing purchases but then sold on the debt to investors—was also adopted by British banks, and the City of London became a major center for hedge funds dealing in a range of sophisticated and risky financial products.

GROWING THE STATE: PUBLIC SPENDING AND REDISTRIBUTION

Of course Labour's success in managing the macroeconomy was hardly enough to satisfy the party's core left-wing supporters, who demanded action to reduce poverty and achieve a more equitable distribution of wealth. So, in addition to adopting an orthodox approach to monetary and fiscal matters, the government also proposed other, more traditionally social democratic policies. The high levels of poverty among British pensioners were addressed by introducing a "minimum income guarantee" for the elderly, providing increased state pensions for those without private pension entitlements. The "New Deal" program, financed by a windfall tax on privatized utility companies, provided assistance to the long-term unemployed to encourage them back into the labor market. This formed part of a series of measures called "Welfare to Work," aimed at increasing employment as a way of reducing poverty without increasing the burden on the welfare state. The Labour chancellor Gordon Brown had identified low wages for unskilled workers as a "poverty trap"—many of the unemployed could not easily earn enough to move out of welfare. The government attacked this problem by establishing a minimum wage and by providing tax credits for low earners with family responsibilities, topping up low wages to encourage work over welfare. Although some observers remain skeptical about the specific impact of the New Deal on employment, the Labour government was able to point to a continued decline in joblessness through its first term in office as proof of its success.[3]

Falling unemployment and healthy tax revenues allowed Labour, after a cautious start, to increase public spending in a number of areas, most notably health care and education. Despite the Thatcher and Major governments' commitment to a healthy private market in health and education services, the vast majority of British citizens remained reliant on state provision in these two areas. Moreover, opinion polls had long shown that voters demanded higher spending on these services, and that many of them even claimed to be willing to pay higher taxes to achieve this. As regards spending, there is little question that Labour has met this demand for greater resources. Education spending, for example, rose from £38 billion in 1997 to £73 billion in 2006, a spectacular increase in times of low inflation. Health spending, in turn, grew even faster, from £33 billion in 1997 to £96 billion in 2006.[4] Visible evidence of this greater largesse can be found in the new school and hospital buildings that sprang up

Box 2.1   From "Old" to "New" Labour: The End of Socialism?

Clause IV of the Labour Party constitution approved in 1918:

> To secure for the workers by hand or by brain the full fruits of their industry and the most equitable distribution thereof that may be possible upon the basis of the common ownership of the means of production, distribution and exchange, and the best obtainable system of popular administration and control of each industry or service.

Excerpt from Tony Blair's first speech to the Labour Party conference as leader, October 4, 1994:

> Market forces cannot educate us or equip us for this world of rapid technological and economic change. We must do it together. . . .
> That is our insight: A belief in society. Working together. Solidarity.
> Cooperation. Partnership. These are our words. This is my socialism. And we should stop apologizing for using the word.
> It is not the socialism of Marx or state control. It is rooted in a straight forward view of society. In the understanding that the individual does best in a strong and decent community of people with principles and standards and common aims and values.
> We are the Party of the individual because we are the Party of community. Our task is to apply those values to the modern world.
> It will change the traditional dividing lines between right and left. And it calls for a new politics.

(*Source:* http://www.australianpolitics.com/uk/labour/941004blair-new-labour-speech.shtml)

The "New" Clause IV approved by the Labour Party conference in 1995:

> The Labour Party is a democratic socialist party. It believes that by the strength of our common endeavor we achieve more than we achieve alone, so as to create for each of us the means to realize our true potential and for all of us a community in which power, wealth and opportunity are in the hands of the many, not the few. Where the rights we enjoy reflect the duties we owe. And where we live together, freely, in a spirit of solidarity, tolerance and respect.

around the country in the years after 2000. Evidence of increased performance in the delivery of services has been more controversial, however. Official government targets for cutting medical waiting times and achieving better school exam results have been met, but public skepticism over the effective improvement in services abounds. For some Labour opponents, the prioritization of public health and education over private consumption has simply increased the pay of public sector workers without any clear productivity gains.

The growth of government spending was the "big story" of Labour's second term as far as domestic politics were concerned. Much political debate therefore revolved around the question of how to pay for this higher spending. This question could be elided for some time thanks to the buoyant budgetary position built up during Labour's first term of office. However, as soon as the economic cycle began to turn downward, budget surpluses quickly turned to deficits in 2003 and by 2005 had breached the euro area's 3 percent limit. The problem of how to pay for higher spending was met in a combination of ways. First, Labour was obliged to allow some slippage in the observance of its own fiscal rules, which required budgets to balance over the economic cycle. In 2005, Brown's Treasury recalculated the dates of the economic cycle in order to make the rules easier to meet, allowing higher borrowing to continue. Second, Labour responded by raising taxes. Although Brown stuck to Labour's promise not to increase income tax rates, he did increase revenues through fiscal drag, and he also increased the British payroll tax—National Insurance—for high-end wage earners. Third, the government's budgetary position was helped by the consistent economic growth enjoyed from the mid-1990s, which reduced the costs of unemployment and brought increased tax receipts from property sales and consumption. In short, Labour seemed to have pulled off a difficult balancing act by significantly increasing public spending without a dramatic increase in personal taxation.

THE TRAIN HITS THE BUFFERS: GORDON BROWN AND THE FINANCIAL CRISIS

In June 2007, Tony Blair finally left Number 10 Downing Street, handing over to Gordon Brown, who had been pressuring him to resign for several years. Although reluctant to leave, Blair could point to several achievements in the fields of economic and social policy in his decade as prime minister. Most obviously, Labour had presided over one of the longest periods of uninterrupted economic growth in British history, with high levels of employment, historically low inflation, and an average growth rate of 2.5 percent between 1997 and 2007, well above trend. However, just two months later, the first unmistakable signs of economic collapse could be detected. A small regional bank, Northern Rock, requested liquidity support from the Bank of England, a clear sign of financial difficulty. The immediate response was panic: the bank's shares collapsed, and depositors rushed to withdraw their savings, leading to scenes reminiscent of *Mary Poppins* as desperate account holders queued in the streets outside Northern Rock branches. This was the first run on a bank in the UK since the 19th century, a huge embarrassment for a country whose economy had revolved around the financial sector in recent decades. By the second quarter of 2008, Britain had entered what was proving to be its longest recession since the 1930s.

The run on Northern Rock and its subsequent rescue by the government was a defining moment in the recent economic and political history of the UK. Although the financial crisis was obviously not solely a British problem—the Northern Rock bank run began on September 15, 2007, but on the same date a year later Lehman Brothers' bankruptcy provoked a world financial meltdown—it has had particularly powerful consequences, both economic and political, in the UK. It also made the defeat of the Labour government in the 2010 general election almost inevitable. The financial crisis plunged Britain into recession, destroying Gordon Brown's oft-repeated claim that New Labour had put an "end to boom and bust." But the crisis also exposed two key weaknesses at the heart of New Labour's economic strategy: its closeness to the City of London, and its enthusiasm for public spending.

New Labour's prawn cocktail offensive in the mid-1990s had succeeded in convincing the City that a Labour government would be competent custodians of the economy and friendly to the interests of the financial sector. However, this success came at a price, as Labour embraced a deregulatory approach to finance, allowing the financial sector to expand lending to households and companies at unprecedented rates, generating a credit-fueled consumer boom. UK consumers borrowed to buy houses, cars, holidays, and even everyday purchases. The influx of credit into the housing market led to a rapid rise in house prices, to which consumers responded by increasing their borrowing, including extracting equity from their homes to finance other spending. This borrowing fueled economic growth, which enhanced consumer confidence and encouraged further increases in indebtedness. In 2006, UK household debt exceeded £1 trillion, comfortably higher than annual GDP. Meanwhile, the City of London enjoyed spectacular growth in its revenues, with the financial sector growing to the extent that total financial assets in the UK amounted to 440 percent of GDP in 2006 (from 100 percent in 1980).

The growth of finance contributed to Britain's comparatively strong economic performance between the mid-1990s and the mid-2000s and generated unexpectedly high tax revenues, allowing Labour to expand public spending rapidly. Ironically, the financial boom had the curious outcome of allowing Blair and Brown, alone among center-left politicians in recent European history, to significantly expand the role of the state in the economy. Public spending increased substantially, from £315.9 billion in 1996–1997, the last year of Conservative government, to £550 billion in 2006–2007, a real-terms increase of 37 percent. Although tax rates and borrowing paid for part of this growth, a significant part of the expansion was made possible by the buoyant tax revenues from the booming financial sector, in particular the overheated housing market. When the financial sector entered a catastrophic crisis in autumn 2008, a huge shortfall in the government's budget opened up with frightening speed, with the UK Treasury reporting a double-digit budget deficit for both 2009 and 2010.

The financial meltdown of the late 2000s undermined all of the policy successes claimed by Gordon Brown and New Labour over their decade in power. The "light-touch" regulation of finance had allowed an asset price bubble to develop that destabilized the whole economy, and Blair and Brown had apparently not noticed that banks had built balance sheets that left them dangerously exposed to any turbulence in the financial markets. Moreover, the Labour governments had built up public spending to levels that quickly became unsustainable when the credit-fueled growth of consumption ceased, leaving the UK with one of the biggest fiscal deficits in the world. Gordon Brown's direct responsibility for the economy over a thirteen-year period, first as chancellor of the Exchequer, then as prime minister, left him politically accountable for the disaster. In the 2010 election, the British voters deserted Labour in sufficient numbers to relieve the party of its parliamentary majority, bringing Brown's short premiership to an end. However, if Labour undeniably lost the election, it was not clear if anyone had actually won it. The Conservatives, although clearly the winning party in terms of votes and seats, were short of an overall majority in parliament and could not form a new government without outside support. Britain was faced with an unusual situation, for only the second time since the Second World War. The way in which this situation was resolved has important implications for the way Britain is governed, as the next section will explain.

The British Constitution: A Modern Democracy?

Although epitaphs for the New Labour administration have mostly focused on its economic and social successes and failures, and the consequences of Tony Blair's foreign policy choices, the period since 1997 has also seen major constitutional innovation. The Third Way thinking that formed the basis of Tony Blair's governing strategy was not solely concerned with governing the economy and managing the social consequences of economic change. The Third Way also contemplated addressing the workings of democracy itself in order to make the political system more open, transparent, and effective. Labour had developed a coherent and powerful critique of the failings of British democracy, which it saw as excessively centralized and elitist, governed by an unaccountable metropolitan elite. The 1997 Labour manifesto therefore proposed a number of reforms in a bid to modernize and open up the UK political system, and these reforms have been described by some as the most radical in decades. However, perhaps the most important change was ushered in by the election result of 2010, which gave Britain a coalition government and brought an end to half a century of alternation between the two main political parties. This section provides an overview of the nature of the British constitution and assesses the implications of recent developments in the working of the UK political system.

THE BACKGROUND: THE UNITED KINGDOM'S "WESTMINSTER MODEL"

The United Kingdom is often described as the oldest democracy in the world. With the Magna Charta of 1215, the English king became subject to legal constraints long before most other monarchs, and the House of Commons—the lower house of the British Parliament—is the oldest legislative institution in the world, sitting continuously in the Palace of Westminster in central London since 1547. Unlike in many other countries, in Britain there has been no specific founding moment at which a democratic system became established. Instead, British democracy was the result of a centuries-long process whereby political power gradually passed from the monarch to the parliament, and the British Parliament itself won democratic legitimacy by progressively expanding voting rights until—with votes for women—universal suffrage was finally attained in 1928. This conventional interpretation of a smooth transition from absolute monarchy to full democracy of course glosses over the political violence and social conflict that has marked several periods of British history, such as the religious tensions sparked by the Protestant Reformation in the sixteenth century, the civil war of 1642–1649, and the working-class mobilization of the nineteenth and early twentieth centuries, not to mention the frequently changing borders of the British state. However, it does accurately reflect the remarkable institutional continuity the UK has enjoyed since at least the late seventeenth century, with a stable parliamentary monarchy that has managed to avoid the violent revolutions and foreign invasions suffered by many of its European neighbors.

This remarkable history has left the UK with a rather anomalous constitutional system. First of all, Britain does not even have a written constitution: there is no single text codifying and recording the rules regulating the political system. Instead, the British constitution, such as it exists, consists of a mixture of legislation and conventions, many of which are only written down in academic texts. As a result, "much of the substance of the contemporary constitution remains shrouded in uncertainty,"[5] something which in normal times matters little, but becomes more important at times of political flux, such as the 2010 election. Second, a number of features of Britain's "constitution" appear out of date and inappropriate for a modern, twenty-first-century democracy. For example, although the monarchy appears for the most part to play a purely symbolic role in British politics, a number of powers exercised by the British government, including the decision to engage British troops in combat, formally belong to the monarch through the so-called Royal Prerogative. This reflects the British political elite's reluctance to address the thorny issue of the constitution, rather than any particular enthusiasm for extending the powers of the Queen. The anachronistic and sometimes dysfunctional nature of the British system of government can be best understood in terms of the British elites' preference for working around the constitution rather than openly and systematically updating it.[6]

This peculiar approach to defining the way government works has some advantages. The British constitution is inherently very flexible. When laws regulating the broader political system become obsolete, they can easily be changed. One of the defining principles of the British political system is "parliamentary sovereignty," which means that no Parliament can bind future Parliaments, and that legislation is not subject to judicial review. This gives the Parliament of the day unlimited freedom to legislate on any matter with a simple majority vote, making reform of the political system much more straightforward than in other democracies, where constitutional reforms usually require enhanced majorities, and often popular referenda too. Parliamentary sovereignty explains in part why British governments have often preferred to leave the constitution alone: as long as a government enjoys a parliamentary majority, there are relatively few limits to its freedom of action.

This very flexibility is also a problem. Because there are few constitutional restraints on a parliamentary majority, a strong-willed government with sufficient parliamentary support can force through unpopular measures relatively easily. Moreover, through the Royal Prerogative, many powers once belonging to the monarchy are now exercised by the head of the government, the prime minister, in the monarch's name. These powers, such as government appointments, are not subject to any consultation with parliament and imply a greater concentration of power around the head of the executive than is usual in parliamentary democracies. Parliamentary sovereignty, of course, also means that the executive is ultimately dependent on the majority support of the House of Commons in order to continue governing. British prime ministers, unlike U.S. presidents, can be forced to step down at short notice by a majority vote of censure, known as a "vote of no confidence." But provided the prime minister retains the support of a parliamentary majority, there are few limits on his or her power, since Parliament can pass any law and there is no higher judicial power to review legislation.

In practice, therefore, the British parliamentary system has tended to create strong governments subject to few checks and balances. British political parties tend to be fairly cohesive, and individual members of Parliament (MPs) are usually heavily dependent on their party's support in their efforts to win reelection. As a result, governing majorities in Parliament are mostly disciplined in their support for the executive in general and the prime minister (who is also party leader) in particular. Moreover, members of the House of Commons are elected in small, single-member constituencies, which leads to a heavy overrepresentation of the winning party. Governments often enjoy very large majorities in the Commons that make their parliamentary positions almost unassailable. The upper house of Parliament, the House of Lords, is traditionally an unelected body of nobility and party appointees, and it therefore lacks the political legitimacy to challenge the power of the government. The House of

Lords can return legislation to the Commons for redrafting, but ultimately it must acquiesce in passing the legislation without amendment if the Commons stands firm. Until 1999, the House of Lords had a built-in Conservative majority due to the predominance of hereditary peers (nobles) and tended only to use its delaying powers against Labour governments. The Blair government abolished the voting rights of hereditary peers in 1999, leaving only ninety-two in place, with the remainder of the Lords consisting of retired party politicians and prominent members of civil society, all appointed by government. However, the Lords still lack the democratic legitimacy to challenge the government, leaving the UK without any effective separation of lawmaking powers.

The Thatcher government of the 1980s, for many of its opponents, epitomized the abuse of executive power made possible by the UK's constitutional vagueness and the distortions of its electoral system. With a little over 40 percent of the vote but a comfortable majority in the House of Commons, the Conservative administration forced a number of controversial and divisive measures through Parliament in the face of great popular unrest. Thatcher's own robust style was criticized as authoritarian, as she refused to consult with interest groups and trade unions, and even rode roughshod over Conservative opponents within her own government. In response, demands for constitutional reform grew, with the Electoral Reform Society arguing for the House of Commons to be elected by proportional representation, while a group named Charter 88 campaigned for a wholesale updating of Britain's constitutional arrangements, including the democratization of the House of Lords and greater transparency in government.

Ironically, Margaret Thatcher's own demise was a timely reminder that parliamentary sovereignty was not a blank check for the prime minister. Faced with an economic crisis and growing unpopularity over the reform of local taxes and her European policy, opposition mounted to Thatcher's leadership within the Conservative Party itself. At the end of 1990, a rival challenged Thatcher to a leadership election; although she won the election, the number of votes against her signaled that a substantial portion of her parliamentary party wanted a new leader. Persuaded by her own ministers that she was in an unsustainable position, she resigned, only three years after winning her third general election. But her long period in office, and Labour's own disillusionment at its inability to defeat Thatcher at the polls, had entrenched demand for constitutional change within the opposition party. When Tony Blair led Labour to victory in 1997, a reform of the British system of government was a key part of the party's program.

Decentralizing Britain: Devolution and Northern Ireland

The most urgent item on Labour's reform agenda was "devolution"—the creation of new tiers of government in Scotland, Wales, and Northern Ireland, all part of the United Kingdom but culturally and politically distinct from England, where the bulk (around 85 percent) of the British population lives. Devolution addressed one of the most potent critiques of the British system of government: its intense centralization of power around the capital city, London, where the executive, civil service, and Parliament are based. Decentralization—bringing government closer to the people—was a prominent feature of Blair's Third Way discourse, and it appeared to offer a response to citizens' growing sense of detachment from the political elite. Labour had long pushed for greater decentralization of power, unsuccessfully proposing devolution to Scotland and Wales in its previous period of government in the 1970s. Reviving this project in the 1990s was consistent with both Labour tradition and the New Labour image.

Understanding the devolution issue requires an understanding of the rather complex history of the United Kingdom.[7] It was argued earlier that the British state has enjoyed remarkable institutional continuity in the past three centuries, but the same cannot be said for the UK's borders. The core of the British state, England, has a long history as a unified nation, dating on some accounts from the tenth century. The history of Britain, however, is marked by a process of expansion and then partial retreat. Wales was definitively annexed by England under King Henry VIII in 1536, and Scotland was absorbed into the British state by the Act of Union in 1707. The island of Ireland, long dominated by its larger neighbor, was integrated into the United Kingdom in 1800. This political unity of the British Isles did not last long. Discontent among the majority Catholic population of Ireland developed into a political movement for Irish independence, and the "Irish question" dominated British political life toward the end of the nineteenth century and the beginning of the twentieth. Faced with constant unrest, the London Parliament decided in 1921 to pull out of most of Ireland, but it retained six counties with a large Protestant population (mostly descendants of Scottish settlers) in the north of the country. This act, known as "partition," allowed for the creation of an independent Irish Republic in the south, while the north remained part of the United Kingdom. Northern Ireland was governed by its own Parliament, based at Stormont Castle outside Belfast, which was dominated by Unionists—mostly Protestant supporters of the union with Britain. This arrangement was relatively stable until the 1960s, when the growing Catholic population of Ulster—largely of Irish Nationalist sympathies—began to protest against discrimination and denial of political rights. This movement, initially a peaceful protest, turned to violence as the Unionist-dominated security forces adopted a repressive line, and the British army was sent over to restore order. After thirteen Catholic protesters were shot by British troops on Bloody Sunday (1973), the situation developed into open conflict, between Nationalist paramilitaries (the Irish Republican Army—IRA) fighting for a united Ireland, Unionist paramilitaries defending the status quo, and the British army, which quickly became identified with the Unionist side. Two decades of sectarian violence followed, including terrorist attacks in London and other British cities.[8]

The situation in Scotland and Wales was very different. Although both countries had a distinctive national identity, expressed through culture, language, and political movements, Scottish and Welsh nationalisms were almost exclusively nonviolent. Political nationalism in the two countries had emerged with some force in the 1974 election, where both the Scottish National Party and Plaid Cymru (the Party of Wales) made spectacular electoral gains, winning substantial parliamentary representation at Westminster. Although the Labour government of the late 1970s failed to push through devolution, Scottish and Welsh nationalism grew in strength in the 1980s and 1990s. This was in part a response to Margaret Thatcher's virulent English nationalism, and in part the result of Scotland and Wales suffering disproportionately from the economic changes resulting from her free-market reforms. Governed by an increasingly unpopular Conservative Party, despite voting overwhelmingly for the Labour opposition, both Scotland and Wales saw big increases in support for more self-government, and Labour adopted devolution as one of its priorities once elected.

Although devolution to Scotland, Wales, and Northern Ireland may have appeared to form part of a coherent package of constitutional reform, there was a clear difference between the Scottish and Welsh situations, on the one hand, and Northern Ireland, on the other.[9] In Scotland and Wales, Labour was keen to shore up its support base by delivering decentralized government. In Northern Ireland, the aim was to resolve a historic problem facing the British state, taking advantage of the shift in mood in Irish nationalism, increasingly favorable to a negotiated solution. By dealing with these very different issues simultaneously, Labour could also attempt to defuse the Northern Ireland situation by pointing to the peaceful nature of territorial reform in the rest of the United Kingdom.

THE GOOD FRIDAY AGREEMENT

Although Tony Blair's government could claim credit for addressing the Northern Ireland problem, it also enjoyed favorable circumstances. Under his Conservative predecessor John Major, the IRA had sent clear signals of a change in strategy, calling a cease-fire in 1994 that held for two years. The Major government was unable to take advantage of the opportunity, in part because of opposition to negotiations among hard-line sectors of the Conservative Party, and in part because his weak government frequently sought the support of Unionist MPs in the House of Commons to pass legislation. Shortly after the 1997 election, the IRA called a new cease-fire, and after several months of negotiations, agreement was reached between the Unionist and Nationalist leaderships in

Northern Ireland, and between the British and Irish governments, with the U.S. administration playing an important mediating role.

The basis of this agreement was that the Northern Ireland Unionists would share power with Nationalists in a new Northern Ireland Assembly and executive, rather than being governed directly from London, which most Unionists preferred. In return, the Nationalists accepted the "principle of consent"—in other words, that Northern Ireland would remain part of the United Kingdom until a majority of its population decided otherwise. Given the Unionists' majority status in the "Six Counties," this locked the province into the UK for the foreseeable future, a major concession for the IRA, dedicated to the creation of a united, independent Ireland. The Irish Republic, as part of the deal, removed its territorial claim on the Six Counties from its constitution. All of this was directed at reassuring the Protestant majority in the north that they would not be swallowed up into a united Ireland as a result of the agreement. Just as importantly, the agreement included a commitment, albeit vaguely worded, from the IRA to disarm and definitively renounce violence, while the British government undertook to reduce significantly its military presence in Northern Ireland.

The power-sharing agreement meant that the Nationalist community would gain a substantial role in the government of Northern Ireland, a role denied them under direct rule from Westminster. The Northern Ireland Assembly was to be elected by proportional representation in order to ensure that each community was adequately represented. Moreover, its procedures were to be based on "cross-community consent": assembly members would have to declare their "community identity"—Unionist, Nationalist, or "other"—and important decisions would require the support of either a majority of the community, or a 60 percent majority with at least 40 percent support in each community. This innovative arrangement forced the two sides into a close working relationship if the province was to be governed effectively, encouraging political leaders to overcome the suspicions of the previous decades. The outcome of the agreement remained uncertain even as the Blair government moved into its third term. On the positive side, an effective cease-fire of all the major paramilitary organizations had remained in place ever since the agreement, a remarkable achievement given the levels of bloodshed of the previous quarter century. Moreover, historical enemies had indeed been involved in joint decision making, with Nationalist leaders for the first time taking on significant executive powers. On the negative side, the newly devolved institutions had to be suspended four times and direct rule reestablished, due to the difficulties involved in verifying the IRA's adherence to the commitment to dismantle its paramilitary structure. Nevertheless, although the future of the agreement cannot be taken for granted, the achievement of almost two decades of effective peace has changed, perhaps irreversibly, the political atmosphere in Northern Ireland.

DEVOLUTION TO SCOTLAND AND WALES

In the context of resolving such a difficult issue as Northern Ireland, the creation of decentralized government institutions in Scotland and Wales appeared rather straightforward. Unlike Northern Ireland, where a majority of the population was at the very least skeptical, and in part openly hostile, to devolution, in Scotland and Wales there was broad support for institutions of self-government. Moreover, in the Scottish case, all the major parties, with the exception of the Conservatives, had been working together to plan devolution for some time. The vast majority of the Scottish political class was therefore broadly in agreement on the path to follow, and the Labour Party in Scotland, itself closely aligned with the national leadership in London, was an enthusiastic proponent. A referendum held in Scotland in September 1997, only four months after the Blair government was elected, showed overwhelming support for devolution, with 74 percent of Scots voting in favor.

The Scotland Act of 1998 established a Scottish Parliament in Edinburgh, which would elect a Scottish executive responsible for a range of policy areas, including education, health care, transport, and local government. The Parliament, elected by proportional representation, has legislative powers and can pass laws on any issue except those "reserved" to Westminster, the most important of which are foreign and defense policy, monetary and fiscal policy, and social security. The Wales Act of 1998 established devolved government for Wales, but with more limited powers. Only a bare majority (50.3 percent) voted in favor of devolution in the Welsh referendum, and the project came within a handful of votes of failing at the first hurdle. The Welsh Assembly, elected on similar principles to the Scottish Parliament, was granted only secondary legislative powers, meaning that it could only develop the detailed implementation of legislation emanating from the Westminster Parliament, rather than making laws of its own. These secondary powers related to similar areas as those devolved to Scotland: mainly education and health. Unlike Scotland, which had minor tax-raising powers, Wales was entirely dependent on the central government in London for its budget.

Devolution made an immediate political impact in these two territories. The first step toward devolution was the election of representatives to sit in the new institutions, and the elections in Scotland and Wales in 1999 suggested a major change in the workings of British politics.[10] Most significantly, the elections took place under a form of proportional representation, making it difficult for Labour—the dominant party in both territories—to win sufficient support to govern alone, and making coalition government almost an inevitability. In Wales, the party fell just short of a majority, forcing it to rely on the support first of the centrist Liberal Democrats, and then that of the nationalist Plaid Cymru. In Scotland, Labour was far short of a majority, and therefore it formed a coalition government with the Liberal Democrats. Coalition government and initially frequent changes of executive leadership marked a departure from the patterns of government stability observed in Westminster.

Devolution, as might be expected, also led to Scotland and Wales adopting different policies from those followed in England. In Scotland, policy differences were partly the result of coalition government: although the Scottish Labour Party was close to the UK party leadership, the demands of coalition government with the Liberal Democrats led to policy decisions that were at odds with those taken at Westminster. The most notable examples of this were over university tuition fees, which were raised in England under Westminster legislation, but were turned into a form of "graduate tax" on the future earnings of university graduates in Scotland. More dramatically, in 2007, after two terms of Labour-Liberal coalitions, the Scottish Parliament elections gave a narrow victory to the Scottish Nationalists (SNP), who became the largest party in the assembly (albeit by the tiniest of margins). Although the SNP leader Alex Salmond was unable to piece together a majority and had to form a minority administration, it is still a hugely symbolic development for the Scottish executive to be in the hands of a party that openly advocates Scottish independence. However, the promised referendum on independence has yet to materialize, and the SNP's period in office has been more significant perhaps for the seamless transition to a nationalist government and the absence of open conflict with London.

Although devolution has not brought about dramatic change, it has opened up the possibility for the two countries to express their distinctiveness through their own institutions and through different patterns of policymaking. It has not been as successful as was hoped in reversing the trend toward citizen disillusionment with democratic politics, and unedifying spectacles such as the spiraling cost of the new Scottish Parliament building in Edinburgh have led to considerable skepticism over the benefits of devolution. However, the popularity of the devolved institutions in their territories is relatively high, and even the initially unenthusiastic Welsh ultimately warmed to devolution, demanding powers comparable to those enjoyed by the Scottish Parliament. The return to power of the Conservatives at the UK level has the potential to complicate the relationship between London and Edinburgh, but the presence of the Liberal Democrats in the UK government attenuates the "Englishness" of the central state. Up to the end of 2010, there was little sign of constitutional crisis with respect to devolution.

The New Politics?

Although devolution and Northern Ireland had by far the highest profile, the Blair government also introduced other significant reforms to the British system of government. As well as reform of the House of Lords, Labour also made a major commitment in its 1997 manifesto to the reform of the House of Commons, the pillar of the British system of government. Most radically, Blair promised an inquiry into the possibility of a reform of the electoral system for the Commons, followed by a referendum on a proposed reform. The inquiry, headed by former Labour chancellor Roy Jenkins, did take place and recommended a form of proportional representation similar to that used in the Federal Republic of Germany.[11] However, this report was simply ignored, and no referendum was held. This outcome was perhaps predictable in light of the enormous difficulties involved in persuading members of an elected institution to change the system that elected them. The Blair government did introduce some changes to modernize the working practices of the Commons, including more family-friendly hours. But the basic workings of the Commons and its role in the constitution remained essentially the same.

The 2010 election, however, threatened to change this. First of all, the 2010 poll saw the departure of one of the most discredited parliaments in recent history. In 2009, the conservative newspaper the *Daily Telegraph* revealed details of expenses claims made by sitting MPs, mostly related to the allowance members receive for the costs of maintaining a second residence in London. The newspaper reported various examples of abuse of the system, with MPs often claiming very large sums to buy expensive items of furniture, and in some embarrassing cases using public money to pay for items such as tree felling, toothbrushes, and lightbulbs, and in perhaps the most memorable case, a floating house for ducks. Uncovered at the height of Britain's economic downturn under an increasingly unpopular prime minister, the effect of these revelations was explosive, particularly for the governing Labour Party (although many Conservatives and others were affected too). In addition to further weakening an already fatally damaged government, the scandal fueled demands for a departure from past practices and a (vaguely defined) "new" approach to politics.

The main beneficiaries of this public mood were the new Conservative leader David Cameron and, particularly, the Liberal Democrat leader Nick Clegg. Gordon Brown, at fifty-eight and with two and a half decades in frontline politics behind him, was unable to dissociate himself from the excesses of his fellow MPs, despite having a relatively clean bill of health in regard to his own expenses. His opposition rivals, both aged forty-three in the election year, belonged to a different generation. Clegg, in particular, sought to present himself as a representative of the "new politics," offering a break with the two-party system of the past and a new coalitional approach to democratic politics. Clegg was a relative unknown to the British public before the election campaign began, but he made a huge impact in the televised debates held between the three main party leaders, briefly boosting the Liberal Democrats to a polling lead. Although the ultimate vote share won by the Liberal Democrats was disappointingly only a marginal improvement on the 2005 result, the failure of the

Conservatives to win an outright majority placed Clegg's centrist party in a commanding position.

The "hung parliament" resulting from the 2010 election left open several possibilities. First, the Conservatives could have formed a minority government, seeking support from other parties for individual pieces of legislation. This option was feasible given that the party was only a few seats short of a majority in the House of Commons, but it had the disadvantage that it would necessitate constant bargaining with minor parties. Second, the Conservatives could form a coalition with the Liberal Democrats, which would provide the new administration with an ample majority, but it would force major policy concessions from both sides given the important political differences between the two parties. Finally, a Labour–Liberal Democrat coalition could have formed a government with support from the Scottish and Welsh nationalist parties. This coalition would have been plausible given the common ground between these parties on many issues, but it was effectively impossible given Nick Clegg's stated refusal to work with sitting prime minister Gordon Brown. The result, after several days of negotiations, was Gordon Brown's resignation and an invitation to Buckingham Palace for Conservative leader David Cameron, who by reaching an agreement with Nick Clegg had secured sufficient parliamentary support to form a government. Although no major constitutional change has yet resulted from this coalitional arrangement, the tradition of two-party politics and single-party governments has suffered a brusque interruption.

Britain in the World: Which Side of the Atlantic?

The last decade has been a controversial one for British foreign policy. In the 1990s, the most pressing problem facing the United Kingdom in international affairs appeared to be its relationship with the European Union, marked by tensions and misunderstandings in the final years of the Thatcher-Major era. Over the following decade or so, a very different set of problems were posed, with the consequences of the September 11 attacks and the resultant changes to U.S. foreign policy. Although foreign and European policies were far from most voters' minds when Labour was elected to government in 1997, the 2000s have been dominated by Britain's international role, particularly its relationship with the United States.

THE BACKGROUND: ATLANTICISM AND EURO-SKEPTICISM

At the end of World War II, the United Kingdom found itself in a contradictory position. On the one hand, it still retained a vast overseas empire, and by virtue of its successful defense of its borders against the Nazi military threat, it was able to take its place at the postwar negotiations between the great powers at Yalta. On the other hand, Britain was exhausted by a conflict that had confirmed the extraordinary military and political weight of the two new superpowers, the United States and the Soviet Union. Britain's status was now clearly that of a "second-rate" world power, while its colonial interests were threatened by economic limitations and the growth of independence movements in various parts of the empire. It is often said that postwar British foreign policy has revolved around "managing decline"—retreating from colonial commitments and recalibrating its international role in recognition of its diminished resources. But this process of managing decline has thrown up a major dilemma. The UK, as a founder member of NATO boasting a "special relationship" with the United States, has seen a close transatlantic alliance as the key to maximizing its influence in the world. But this closeness to the United States, reinforced by a shared language and historical ties, has frequently been viewed with suspicion by Britain's partners in Western Europe, determined to enhance integration between the European democracies, in part to counterbalance U.S. power. British governments since the war have been pulled in different directions by the global perspective inherited from the country's imperial past, and by the European imperative dictated by its geographical position and commercial priorities.

Britain's complex relationship with the rest of Europe began with the historic decision not to participate in the first phase of the process of European integration. Preoccupied with maintaining ties to the former colonies in the Commonwealth, and hoping to "punch above its weight" through the transatlantic "special relationship," the UK stayed out of the European Economic Community (EEC) established in 1957 by the Treaty of Rome. Very quickly, British foreign-policy makers changed their minds, applying for membership in 1963, but the French President de Gaulle, suspicious of Britain's closeness to the United States, vetoed the application. When the UK finally entered the EEC in 1973, the organization's essential characteristics were already entrenched, and the close alliance between the two largest founder members, France and West Germany, left Britain in a marginal position. Britain's ambiguous position was also illustrated by its close military cooperation with the United States and the presence of significant U.S. military installations on British soil.[12]

The essential tension between Atlanticism and Europeanism came to a head during the 1980s under the premiership of Margaret Thatcher. Thatcher was an instinctive Atlanticist, a great admirer of the United States and its economic dynamism, and supportive of the United States' tough approach to communism and the Soviet Union. Conversely, Thatcher was suspicious of France and Germany and had little patience for the intricate negotiations that characterized European policymaking. Although a strong supporter of the European Community's deregulatory drive to create a Single European Market by 1992, she was generally unsympathetic to further integration. Her close personal friendship with Ronald Reagan, and poor relations with European leaders such as Mitterrand and Kohl, pushed her into increasingly Euro-skeptical attitudes at a time when other member states were planning to share sovereignty over an increasing range of policy areas, including monetary policy and home and foreign affairs. The situation came to a head in 1990, when Thatcher marked her clear opposition to proposals made by European Commission president Jacques Delors in the House of Commons, declaring ''No, no, no'' to his vision of Europe.

   Although Thatcher was forced out of office shortly afterward, the situation under John Major improved little, and anti-European Conservative MPs forced

---

Box 2.2   An Awkward Partner: Margaret Thatcher on Europe

Willing and active cooperation between independent sovereign states is the best way to build a successful European Community.

   To try to suppress nationhood and concentrate power at the center of a European conglomerate would be highly damaging and would jeopardize the objectives we seek to achieve.

   Europe will be stronger precisely because it has France as France, Spain as Spain, Britain as Britain, each with its own customs, traditions and identity. It would be folly to try to fit them into some sort of identikit European personality. . . .

   I am the first to say that on many great issues the countries of Europe should try to speak with a single voice. I want to see us work more closely on the things we can do better together than alone. Europe is stronger when we do so, whether it be in trade, in defense, or in our relations with the rest of the world.

   But working more closely together does not require power to be centralized in Brussels or decisions to be taken by an appointed bureaucracy.

   Indeed, it is ironic that just when those countries such as the Soviet Union, which have tried to run everything from the center, are learning that success depends on dispersing power and decisions away from the center, some in the Community seem to want to move in the opposite direction.

   We have not successfully rolled back the frontiers of the state in Britain, only to see them reimposed at a European level, with a European superstate exercising a new dominance from Brussels.

   Certainly we want to see Europe more united and with a greater sense of common purpose. But it must be in a way which preserves the different traditions, parliamentary powers and sense of national pride in one's own country; for these have been the source of Europe's vitality through the centuries.

Excerpt from Margaret Thatcher's speech to the College of Europe, Bruges, September 20, 1988

(*Source:* Reproduced at http://www.brugesgroup.com/mediacentre/index.live?article=92)

Major to adopt a tough line toward the other member states. At one stage, this went so far as to order British representatives to "boycott" all European decision-making processes, in protest against the European ban on British beef during the "mad cow disease" crisis. By the mid-1990s, British relations with its European partners were at a low point, and one of Tony Blair's key promises during the 1997 election campaign was to place Britain "at the heart of Europe." This new pro-European policy included the controversial proposal for Britain to join the new euro currency agreed at the Maastricht summit of 1991.

BLAIR'S EUROPEAN POLICY

Tony Blair's relations with the other European Union (EU) member states got off to a promising start, in part because of the relief felt among other European leaders at no longer having to deal with an instinctively hostile Conservative administration. The honeymoon period in UK-Europe relations was extended because of the election of a number of center-left governments in the EU toward the end of the 1990s. Center-left leaders were eager to associate themselves with a leader who had won the 1997 election so decisively and was enjoying high levels of popularity in his own country. This led to the attempt by Blair and the German Social Democrat leader Gerhard Schröder to develop a close working relationship around Third Way principles, the German party having adopted a similar slogan, the "Neue Mitte" (New Center). However, the apparent conservatism of many of Blair's public statements, and the UK's refusal to commit to joining the euro zone, put a damper on cooperation.

The euro, launched in 1999, was a difficult issue for the Labour government to address. Opinion polls suggested that the British public was overwhelmingly opposed to membership, and the UK's relatively virtuous economic performance in the second half of the 1990s did little to predispose Euro-skeptic Britons toward a currency dominated by apparently sluggish economies such as those in France, Germany, and Italy. Blair appeared strongly committed to membership, while his chancellor, the key figure in determining economic policymaking, was unenthusiastic. A wait-and-see approach was therefore adopted, with the government expressing its intention to join the euro "in principle," but only making a final decision in view of a complex set of five "economic tests" announced in 1997. These tests—such as, for instance, "Would joining the euro promote higher growth, stability, and a lasting increase in jobs?"—were sufficiently ambiguous to allow the government to make a decision on the grounds of short-term realpolitik. The Blair government's failure to join the euro in the first wave has effectively marginalized Britain from economic decision making in the European Union.

However, Blair's government did engage with European policymaking in other ways, most significantly by arguing strongly for structural reforms to liberalize European economies.[13] This pressure on relatively more regulated economies such as France and Germany to adopt an "Anglo-Saxon" model of economic governance was not always popular in European capitals and reminded some Europeans a little too much of the overbearing style of his Conservative predecessors. However, Blair won sufficient support among some other reform-minded governments to launch the so-called Lisbon agenda for economic reform at the European Council in the Portuguese capital in 2000. The aim of the Lisbon process, rather optimistically, was to turn the European Union into the world's foremost knowledge economy within ten years, an aim that a decade later appears laughable. However, the Lisbon objective did amount to a coherent plan for reform, combining liberalization of markets with an emphasis on innovation and technology on the one hand, and sustainability and social justice on the other. Although the process has not been taken as seriously as Blair had hoped, it certainly amounted to an important constructive British intervention in the debate on Europe's future.

More difficult for the Labour government was the constitutional issue arising from the expansion of the EU eastward in 2005. Faced with a further ten member states, the EU's institutions clearly needed updating and reforming, but the proposal to combine this updating with the writing of a European constitution created a serious dilemma for the UK. Britain's tendency toward Euro-skepticism, added to its tradition of constitutional ambiguity and flexibility, made a European constitution an unwelcome proposal and placed Labour in an uncomfortable position. Blair wanted to play an active, constructive role in the debate, but he was wary of how the constitutional issue would play at home and thus he committed the government to holding a popular referendum. Although by most accounts Labour were successful in defending what the government perceived as UK interests in the proposed constitutional text, opinion polls continued to show unremitting hostility. Fortunately for Blair and his government, the "no" votes cast in the French and Dutch referenda in 2005 made the constitutional project unviable, allowing Britain to suspend its referendum and wait for the issue to disappear. The paralysis of the process of European integration since then has defused the issue in the UK, enabling the Euro-skeptical Conservatives and the pro-European Liberal Democrats to work together without Europe emerging as a source of discord, at least as of late 2010.

FOREIGN AND SECURITY POLICY: TONY BLAIR AND THE "WAR ON TERROR"

The last decade in British foreign policy, and Tony Blair's premiership, were ultimately defined by the decision to align Britain wholeheartedly with George W. Bush's "war on terror." Although Blair quickly succeeded in overcoming much of the negative legacy of Euro-skepticism bequeathed by the Conservatives, his relationship with the other European member states was to run into trouble as a result of the dramatic events of September 11, 2001. The response to the challenge of al-Qaeda terrorism drove a wedge between the United States and the most important continental European powers, Germany and France. Britain's difficult position as the transatlantic "bridge" was placed under acute strain by these developments, and the consequences of the choices made by the Labour government have defined the closing phases of Tony Blair's premiership.

Blair's emergence as an ambitious and activist world leader surprised many, as the Labour leader appeared to pay little attention to foreign affairs before his election in 1997.[14] Very quickly, however, he developed a distinctive approach to foreign affairs that contrasted with the flexible pragmatism that had marked British policy toward international affairs in the postwar period. Very quickly, the Blair government found itself involved in military action, first cooperating with the United States in air strikes on Iraq in 1998, and then playing a visible role in the U.S.-led intervention in the Kosovo region of Serbia, where alleged ethnic cleansing was practiced against the Albanian majority population. Indeed, during the Kosovo conflict, Blair made a major statement on foreign affairs in Chicago, in which he laid out an agenda for active commitment on the part of Western powers to intervene against dictatorships and use military action on humanitarian grounds. This speech demonstrates that the choices Blair made after September 11 were actually consistent with his thinking almost from the very beginning of his premiership. The British intervention in Kosovo was facilitated by Blair's close relationship with Bill Clinton, an enthusiast of Third Way thinking and fellow alumnus of Oxford University. What surprised many was Blair's keenness to continue such a close relationship with Clinton's successor, George W. Bush, a very different kind of political figure who appeared to have little in common with the British prime minister.

In the aftermath of September 11, Blair was quick to line up behind the U.S. administration in its response to the atrocities. The British government participated in the attack on Afghanistan, but perhaps most significantly, it also backed the shift in strategy announced by the Bush administration soon after, which opened up the possibility of preemptive military action against potential threats to U.S. security. The Afghanistan operation received almost unanimous backing from shocked European governments, but the next phase of the U.S. "war on terror," military intervention in Iraq, divided the European powers to an unprecedented degree. Although opposition to the invasion of Iraq was weaker in Britain than in countries such as France, Italy, and Spain, public opinion could be described as at best skeptical, and there was deep unease within the Labour Party toward the plan. In these circumstances, Blair was able to exploit the powerful constitutional position of a British prime minister to push ahead with support for, and full participation in, the Iraq operation. Despite losing two members of his cabinet, who resigned in protest, and facing substantial parliamentary opposition from a large number of Labour MPs, Blair pressed ahead. The consequences were far reaching.

As far as European politics were concerned, the Iraq issue divided the UK from the other major European actors on the international stage, with both France and Germany vehemently opposed. Blair was therefore forced to line up with conservative governments in Spain and Italy in supporting the Bush administration. This had consequences for Britain's European policy, with the initial attempts to form alliances with friendly center-left governments in France, and particularly Germany, being definitively shelved. The Lisbon agenda for economic reform was also tainted by association, as Blair's closeness to Bush on foreign policy discredited his center-left credentials on socioeconomic issues. More broadly, British influence over European politics was affected by the increasing perception, especially in the founding member states of the European Community, that Britain was a mere proxy for U.S. power.

The consequences for Blair's domestic standing were if anything far more serious. Determined to roll back U.S. unilateralism, Blair was instrumental in persuading Colin Powell to seek a UN mandate for the invasion of Iraq, regarding suspicions that Saddam Hussein was developing weapons of mass destruction (WMDs) as the most effective rationale for a UN resolution. This move was insufficient to win broad international backing for the war, but it did force Blair into exaggerating the available evidence of the WMD threat in a government document used to win over the British foreign policy community. The misleading suggestion that Iraq could launch WMDs in forty minutes had devastating consequences for Blair's political credibility when, after the invasion, no such capacity could be found.

The political damage suffered by the Labour government over Iraq is difficult to calculate accurately, but it appears substantial. First, even before the war, massive demonstrations took place around Europe, with the turnout of up to 2 million protestors in London constituting perhaps the largest public protest in British history. Second, the war caused deep upset in Britain's large Muslim population. British Muslims, who are mostly of Pakistani or Bangladeshi origins and tend to be concentrated in the less prosperous areas of Britain's largest cities, have traditionally been strong supporters of the Labour Party, perceived as the most effective defender of ethnic minority rights. However, the Iraq war and its aftermath undermined this long-standing relationship. Muslim unease with Labour policy was exploited by George Galloway, a former dissident Labour MP expelled from the party for his close relations with the Saddam Hussein regime. Galloway founded a party called Respect, which mobilized around the Iraq issue and was able to win election in 2005, defeating a Labour MP in one of Labour's safest London constituencies. Many Muslims also abstained or supported the Liberal Democrats, who had opposed the war. The Iraq issue undoubtedly cost Labour in the 2005 election, which saw its majority cut in half and its vote share decline to just 35 percent.

Blair's decision to back Bush's war in Iraq, and subsequent pro-U.S. positions over Israel and Palestine, including the Israeli attack on Lebanon in 2006, became the defining features of British foreign policy in the first decade of the twenty-first century. Any British prime minister would have been placed in a difficult position by world events after September 11, 2001, given the UK's historically close relationship with the United States and ambiguous relationship with the rest of the European Union. But Blair took a big risk in identifying himself so closely and so publicly with the Bush administration, which became

Box 2.3   Blair on Iraq

"Saddam Hussein's regime is despicable, he is developing weapons of mass destruction, and we cannot leave him doing so unchecked. He is a threat to his own people and to the region and, if allowed to develop these weapons, a threat to us also.
      "Doing nothing is not an option."

—House of Commons, April 10, 2002

"[Saddam's] weapons of mass destruction program is active, detailed and growing. The policy of containment is not working. The weapons of mass destruction program is not shut down. It is up and running. . . . The intelligence picture (the intelligence services) paint is one accumulated over the past four years. It is extensive, detailed and authoritative. It concludes that Iraq has chemical and biological weapons, that Saddam has continued to produce them, that he has existing and active military plans for the use of chemical and biological weapons, which could be activated within 45 minutes, including against his own Shia population; and that he is actively trying to acquire nuclear weapons capability."

—House of Commons, September 24, 2002

"We are asked now seriously to accept that in the last few years—contrary to all history, contrary to all intelligence—Saddam decided unilaterally to destroy those weapons. I say that such a claim is palpably absurd."

—House of Commons, March 18, 2003

"We expected, I expected to find actual usable, chemical or biological weapons after we entered Iraq. But I have to accept, as the months have passed, it seems increasingly clear that at the time of invasion, Saddam did not have stockpiles of chemical or biological weapons ready to deploy."

—House of Commons, July 14, 2004

(*Sources:* http://news.bbc.co.uk/1/hi/uk_politics/2847197.stm;
http://news.bbc.co.uk/1/hi/uk_politics/2955632.stm;
http://news.bbc.co.uk/1/hi/uk_politics/3893987.stm;
also at http://www.publications.parliament.uk/pa/pahansard.htm)

extremely unpopular in British and European public opinion. It is difficult to escape the conclusion that the Blair premiership will be remembered more for its foreign policy choices than for anything else.

Foreign policy under Blair's successors has had a far lower profile both internationally and domestically. Gordon Brown had little interest in foreign policy and sought to focus on the economy and social issues, withdrawing British troops from Iraq but with little fanfare. Brown maintained a British presence in Afghanistan, which proved an increasingly unpopular war by the end of his premiership, due to the apparent lack of progress and significant British casualties. But with the collapse of the economy, foreign affairs have moved to the back of British politics, and the new Conservative–Liberal Democrat administration has been concerned with reducing defense spending rather than taking on new foreign policy commitments.

Conclusion

The 2010 election marked the end of an era: a thirteen-year period in which the Labour Party, for the first time in its history, was able to maintain a parliamentary majority for three whole legislatures. This feat, which had eluded every Labour Party leader before 1994, was testament to the remarkable political abilities of Tony Blair, who led the party to victory in three successive elections. Although the 2005 election saw incipient signs of Labour's electoral decline, Blair left office in 2007 undefeated. The task of leading Labour to defeat fell to Gordon Brown, who proved a far less effective prime minister and was unlucky enough to take the reins just as the world financial crisis began. Labour's period in power was a curious mix of unprecedented success and unexpected failure. The usual problems facing Labour governments in Britain in the past—economic problems, pressure from trade unions and other vested interests, small parliamentary majorities—were avoided during Tony Blair's tenure as prime minister as Labour presided over a remarkable period of consistent economic growth and rising living standards. In many respects, Blair's government could be seen as one of the most successful in recent British history, combining economic expansion with strong public investment in popular services such as education and health care, and largely popular constitutional reforms.

However, the financial crisis of 2007–2008 and the deep recession that followed it has blotted Labour's record. Although Tony Blair left office as an unpopular prime minister, due in large part to controversial foreign policy choices surrounding Iraq and the war on terror, in many other respects Labour could point to a largely successful period in government up to 2007. But the financial collapse revealed that the British economy's problems had not, after all, been solved, and the prosperity of the early 2000s was to an extent the product of a financial bubble that has wrought terrible economic destruction. New Labour had claimed credit for the wealth created by a deregulated City of London, so it therefore could not escape blame when the City's appetite for risk blew a hole in the nation's balance sheet. Worse, the collapse in economic output opened up a gaping budget deficit that exposed the limits of Labour's expansion of the public sector. The new Conservative–Liberal Democrat coalition has set about reducing the deficit by slashing government programs, reversing much of the socioeconomic project Labour had painstakingly constructed. Labour's crushing defeat in the 2010 election reflected popular disillusionment with the whole New Labour project.

The 2010 election may prove to be the end of an era in a much more fundamental way. For the first time since the Second World War, no British political party was able to form a government alone, and the centrist Liberal Democrats, excluded from government for the best part of eighty years, found themselves once again in power. This marks a significant change in British politics, which has revolved around a two-party system for decades, and which has little recent experience with the kind of coalition government common in continental Europe. At the very least, the pattern of government formation is likely to change, as the decline of the two main political parties points toward an increasingly "multiparty" politics in Westminster, similar to developments in Scotland, Wales, and Northern Ireland. But further changes could result if the Liberal Democrats' plans for constitutional reform make any headway. One of the Liberal Democrats' conditions for supporting David Cameron as prime minister was the promise of a referendum on electoral reform, in which British voters will have the choice of retaining the current arrangements or opting for elections through the alternative vote (AV). If electoral reform is successful, coalition governments may become more likely, which in turn will facilitate further reforms.

This scenario is by no means certain, and if the Labour Party were to recover under its new leader Ed Miliband, single-party majority government could return in the near future, ushering in a reversion to two-party politics. However, the secular trend is toward greater fragmentation of voter choice and a decline in the strength of the traditional parties. If this trend continues, the British political system will need to change to accommodate the end of the "old politics."

Suggested Readings

Bogdanor, Vernon, *The New British Constitution*, Oxford: Hart, 2009.

Denver, David, *Elections and Voting in Britain*, 2nd ed., Basingstoke: Palgrave, 2006.

Dunleavy, Patrick, Richard Heffernan, Philip Cowley, and Colin Hay (eds.), *Developments in British Politics 8*, Basingstoke: Palgrave, 2006.

Gamble, Andrew, *Between Europe and America: The Future of British Politics*, Basingstoke: Palgrave, 2003.

Geddes, Andrew, *The European Union and British Politics*, Basingstoke: Palgrave, 2003.

Heath, Anthony, Roger Jowell, and John Curtice, *The Rise of New Labour: Party Policies and Voter Choices*, Oxford: Oxford University Press, 2001.

Jenkins, Simon, *Thatcher & Sons: A Revolution in Three Acts*, London: Penguin, 2007.

Seldon, Anthony (ed.), *Blair's Britain, 1997–2007*, Cambridge: Cambridge University Press, 2008.

Williams, Paul, *British Foreign Policy under New Labour*, Basingstoke: Palgrave, 2006.

Websites

Richard Kimber's Political Science Resources: http://www.psr.keele.ac.uk/area/uk.htm.

Constitution Unit, University College London: http://www.ucl.ac.uk/constitution-unit/.

Webpage of the prime minister: http://www.number-10.gov.uk/output/Page1.asp.

UK Parliament: http://www.parliament.uk/.

BBC British Politics Pages: http://news.bbc.co.uk/1/hi/uk_politics/default.stm.

Hansard Society: http://www.hansardsociety.org.uk/.

Conservative Party: http://www.conservatives.com/.

Labour Party: http://www.labour.org.uk/home.

CHAPTER 3

Germany: Two Decades of Passage from Bonn to Berlin

Helga A. Welsh

Germany

Population (million):	81.9
Area in Square Miles:	137,830
Population Density per Square Mile:	594
GDP (in billion dollars, 2009):	$2,969.9
GDP per capita (PPP, 2005):	$32,145
Joined EC/EU:	January 1, 1958

Performance of Key Political Parties in Parliamentary Elections of September 27, 2009

Christian Democratic Union (CDU)/Christian Social Union (CSU)	33.8%
Free Democratic Party (FDP)	14.6%
Alliance 90/The Greens	10.7%
The Left (Die Linke)	11.9%
Social Democratic Party (SPD)	23.0%

Main Office Holders: Chancellor: Angela Merkel—CDU (2005); President: Christian Wulff—CDU (2010).

Owing to Germany's tumultuous history, hardly a year goes by that does not involve commemoration of significant past events. In such an environment, the regularity of religious and the dearth of political holidays, limited to two—Labor Day on May 1 and Day of German Unity on October 3—may be surprising. They are mostly celebrated as work-free days, and German Unity Day does not evoke the spirit of patriotism associated with Fourth of July celebrations in the United States or Bastille Day in France.

However, even by German standards, 2009 was particularly rich in historical memory. In May, Germans honored the sixtieth anniversary of the German Constitution (Basic Law) and the founding of the Federal Republic of Germany. Seventy years earlier, on September 1, Germany had invaded Poland and World War II began. In October and November, attention turned to the revolutionary events that led to the toppling of the Berlin Wall on 9 November 1989, symbolizing the end of the Cold War; the twentieth anniversary of this momentous event attracted worldwide attention and participation by foreign dignitaries. Two days later, Chancellor Angela Merkel traveled to France to honor Remembrance Day together with French president Nicolas Sarkozy—remembering the signing of the armistice between the World War I allies and Germany, thereby adding to the long list of reconciliatory gestures between the two countries.

In other ways as well, 2009 was anything but tranquil: it was another super-election year, with voting to determine the German parliament, the Bundestag; the European Parliament; the federal president (not by popular vote but electoral college); and several regional and communal offices. Political news intermingled with, and was at times overshadowed by, financial shock waves. Just when the markets seemed to have settled after earlier convulsions in 2008–2009, their volatility was exposed again in spring 2010, sooner than expected. While the earlier economic turmoil was widely perceived as having spread from the United States to much of the world, the debt crises in several European countries, first and foremost Greece, questioned the very foundations of the European currency regime. As Europe's preeminent economic power, Germany was called upon both times to play a major role in stabilizing the financial markets. The euro rescue packages were vital but also difficult to sell to a domestic audience that had only reluctantly given up its beloved Deutsche Mark.

Spring 2010 was consumed by the currency crisis and the shaky start of the new coalition government between the Christian Democratic Union/Christian Social Union (CDU/CSU[1]) and the Free Democratic Party (FDP), elected only months earlier. During the summer and fall, the economic news brightened slightly as the German economy rebounded. Looking back at twenty years of unification between the communist-governed German Democratic Republic (GDR) and democratic West Germany in October 1990, pride in achievement mingled with muted concern. Unity, however, remains elusive. For many citizens in the west, the east remains a distant, if not foreign, country, and despite huge transfers of funds from west to east, economic disparity remains.

The Berlin Republic registers both continuity with, and change from, the Bonn Republic (1949–1990). A long-missing sense of normality has returned to German politics. In this chapter, the central role of history and memory informs an analysis of the fundamentals of German politics and policymaking, demonstrating how continuity has meshed with change. It will focus on political parties and elites, elections and coalition governments, the federal system, and the connection between negotiation democracy and policy change before turning to key aspects of foreign and security policy.

History's Legacy
A TUMULTUOUS CENTURY

History is a combination of evidence and interpretation that allows both understanding and illusion. A country's history is particularly difficult to master when, as in Germany's case, the path toward a securely anchored liberal democracy was tortuous and marked by major ruptures. In one short century (1914–1991), to use Eric Hobsbawm's term, Germans experienced the collapse of three forms of dictatorship and one democratic political system. The first major transformation came in 1918–1919. As a result of defeat in World War I and the collapse of the Second Reich (1871–1918), an authoritarian monarchy was overturned and replaced by the democratic parliamentary system of the Weimar Republic. Its beginnings were inauspicious, associated with defeat and humiliation, widespread political violence, and severe economic and social problems. The Constitution's optimistic assumptions about the balance of power among president, chancellor, and parliament were sorely tested by extreme party fragmentation and polarization, and economic deterioration after 1928 added to the sense of instability. Democracy was shallowly rooted in both the public and the elites and was rather quickly abandoned. The National Socialist Party, one of many marginal radical groups in 1928, with 2.6 percent of the vote, received 37.8 percent in the 1932 elections. Once in power, Adolf Hitler ruthlessly and with amazing speed consolidated his leadership. Nazi Germany unleashed World War II to fulfill Hitler's geopolitical goal of building a "Thousand-Year Reich." Germany invaded most of Europe; Nazism's racist claim of "Aryan" superiority and anti-Semitic, homophobic, anticommunist, and eugenic views led to the murder, torture, and enslavement of millions of people across Europe and totalitarian rule at home.

By May 1945, Germans were confronted with utter defeat; to signify both an end and a new beginning, this moment is often referred to as "Zero Hour." Time had not stopped; on the contrary, the past would shape German political institutions, policies, and political culture, yet the future was uncertain and open to different scenarios. The country's division into two states was central to, and an early by-product of, the emerging Cold War between East and West. Out of the ashes, in May 1949, the Federal Republic of Germany was created in the western part. The sleepy town of Bonn was chosen as the temporary capital and seat of government; similarly, the constitution was named the Basic Law to emphasize its transitory character, yet a stable democracy evolved. Soviet and eastern German communists founded the German Democratic Republic (GDR) in October 1949, where, under Soviet tutelage, a communist dictatorship took hold. With the hope of eventual reunification and from a position of strength, Western allies and western Germans sought to secure democracy and to buffer against Soviet expansion. The West promulgated the Federal Republic as the official successor state of the defeated Germany; international recognition of the GDR was denied until the 1970s. The building of the Berlin Wall in August 1961 eliminated the last escape valve for eastern Germans; the ensuing diplomatic ice age between the two German states melted only gradually in the 1970s and 1980s.

Initially, both German states—supported by their respective allies—pursued unification. In response to West German chancellor Willy Brandt's 1969 pronouncement that there are two states but one German nation, eastern leaders developed a policy of strict demarcation and separate identity. For them, unification was no longer on the agenda. In the west, the practicality of unification as a policy goal was increasingly questioned. However, while apparently stable, the communist regime slowly regressed; in 1989, it suddenly collapsed. The promise of unification, kept alive in western Germany as a constitutional prerogative, finally and unexpectedly became reality after four decades of separation.

Article 23 of the Basic Law expeditiously allowed the former GDR to join the constitutional framework of the Federal Republic in October 1990. The more cumbersome approach of renegotiating a new constitution, based on Article 146, was never seriously considered. Unification was a jump into cold water, and its consequences have played out in many ways. Germans in the east and west live in a democratic society whose fundamental beliefs are accepted, but "the growing together of what belongs together," to use the words of former chancellor Willy Brandt, has taken longer than anticipated.

A DIFFICULT FATHERLAND

The past may have made Germany, in the words of poet C. K. Williams, a symbolic nation;[2] Germans are usually defined not by what they are but what they represent. Germany is admired for its cultural and scientific achievements and reviled for horrible crimes. The first eighty years of its history as a nation-state were, in many ways, defined by authoritarianism, militarism, and nationalism.

The lessons of the Weimar Republic's democratic breakdown and the Nazis' smashing of constitutional parliamentary government influenced later politics. "Bonn is not Weimar"—the determination not to repeat the instability that led to Hitler's dictatorship informed the writing of the West German Constitution, the creation of its political parties, and its economic system after World War II. These steps aimed to avoid the mistakes of the past by defending democracy and establishing political, economic, and social conditions that would provide security for individuals and the country as a whole.

The horrors inflicted by the Third Reich forced Germans toward a critical and open confrontation with their past. This process started in 1945 as part of Allied de-Nazification and democratization programs but, after the onset of the Cold War in 1947, swift political and economic consolidation took precedence over historical contemplation. The future seemed more important then, but the past would not go away. Challenged by a new generation, the hush muffling German involvement and collusion with Hitler's regime was shattered in the late 1950s and early 1960s, and step by step, a historical consciousness emerged that informs the public discourse to this day. No interpretation of German history can avoid confronting the horrors of Auschwitz. The legacy of the concentration camps has pervaded debates ranging from abortion and political asylum to reparations of Nazi victims and foreign military involvement. It explains the heightened sensitivity at home and abroad to right-wing activities. After the fall of communism, how to address questions of justice and historical recollection in dealing with victims and perpetrators of the deposed communist regime added another layer of complexity. With the beginning of the twenty-first century, after a long silence, Germans also began once again to discuss their own suffering during and after World War II, including expulsions from their homes, mass rape, and the death and destruction wreaked by Allied bombing.

Predictably, how the past should be remembered often sparks heated debates. While the discourse largely takes place among political and cultural elites, many of its arguments are reflected in newsprint, novels, popular movies, and television documentaries and trickle down into collective consciousness. Germany has joined the many Western European countries setting memories of the Holocaust quite literally "in stone."[3] The new capital of Berlin is home to the Jewish Museum and, after many years of controversy regarding its design and designation, the Holocaust Memorial, officially named the Monument to the Murdered Jews of Europe. Berlin has also become the center of revival for Jewish culture in Germany. At the beginning of the 1930s, about 600,000 Jews lived in Germany; by 1950, the number had dwindled to 15,000 but rose to 25,000 by 1989. Today, the Jewish communities (Jüdische Gemeinden) represent more than 100,000 members, more than two-thirds of whom came from the former Soviet Union and arrived in Germany only after 1990. The large influx of Russian Jews has made the German community the third-largest in Europe and has presented the unique challenge of integrating the newcomers.[4]

The fall of communism ended Germany's division into two separate states, granted the country full sovereignty, and rendered obsolete its role as the front line between hostile ideological camps. The "German question" had finally been resolved peacefully, and Germany's room for political maneuvering in the international arena increased. However, the impact of Germany's history remains a cornerstone of the political discourse, even as new generations of Germans balance the responsibilities and constraints it imposes with national consciousness and pride.[5] For Germans, as British commentator Roger Boyes points out, history and memory are never easy (see box 3.1).

Vigilance remains tied to its difficult past but also to its role in European affairs. Foreign observers are at times quick to question Germany's commitment to European integration and solidarity, as shown in the wake of the euro crisis in spring 2010. When, during the 2006 soccer World Cup, hosted by Germany, younger generations of Germans for the first time waved the national flag and sported the nation's colors, reactions were mixed. Some felt that the fans were expressing loyalty and support for their team, celebrating a joyous athletic event. Others saw the burst of black, red, and gold as one more step toward a new enlightened or cosmopolitan patriotism. Those who argued along these lines also felt that by using the colors in an identity-building but non-threatening way, German soccer fans were preventing the radical right (neo-Nazis) from usurping them for xenophobic purposes. Still others watched the display of national colors with unease, recalling the dark sides of German history. In their view, "normality" should and will forever remain elusive for Germany. Now, routinely every two years, on the occasion of the European or World soccer cups, the national colors are rolled out, only to retreat when the tournaments end, and anxieties have been largely laid to rest.

Governance and Policymaking

Germany's political system is commonly called a party democracy or party state. Both expressions emphasize the central role of political parties in recruitment and selection of career politicians, among other things. Functions and organizational principles for political parties are explicitly set out in Article 21 of the Basic Law, but the extent of party influence goes far beyond representing the will of the people in the legislature and executive. Over the years, party representatives have become an integral part of federal, *Land* (state), and even public institutions, such as the public television stations; the staffing of leadership positions in many sectors of public life is characterized by power sharing among the main political parties.

Through its rulings, the Federal Constitutional Court has reinforced the

Box 3.1   The Nervousness about Facing the Positive Aspects of German History

Roger Boyes (2009)

It is a big anniversary year for Germany. Sixty years since the Berlin airlift and the signing of the constitution, the *Grundgesetz*. And of course 20 years since the crumbling of the Berlin Wall, the collapse of communism and the reunification of the country. So Germany should be celebrating a party all year long, right? Wrong.

The country is agonizing, yet again, over how it should show its joy. Dare I say: "*Typisch deutsch*" [typically German]? The Berlin airlift commemorations, I must admit, went relatively well: thousands of Berliners ate *Wurst* and potato salad in Tempelhof airport; old pilots, American and British, returned and reminisced with old Berliners. True, there was grumbling—this was Berlin, after all, the European capital of grumbling—about the closing of Tempelhof airport. But the Senate may yet rescue its reputation with the older generation by shifting the impressive Allied Museum—with its detailed history of the airlift—to some of the empty buildings in the former airport. So far, so good; a *Volksfest* [fair] was exactly what was required for this anniversary. And the local authorities knew what to do because this was about the history of West Berlin and about the transatlantic relationship, about hardship and the heroism of foreigners.

How to Create a Credible Storyline for the Country

The problem starts as soon as one tries to dream up ways of celebrating something abstract—like the *Grundgesetz*. How do you have a *Volksfest* about a document drawn up by politicians and lawyers, with almost no emotional resonance? The anniversary of the *Grundgesetz* is, of course, simply a way of marking the birth of the Bundesrepublik. But if you talk to Germans who lived through these years, you find out that they were moved by economic development rather than the sudden arrival of political freedoms, rights and duties. "I believe we are more concerned with economic myths, the economic miracle, the D-Mark . . . ," says the political scientist Herfried Münkler. "The *Grundgesetz* did not play such a big role in the collective memory of the Germans." . . . The question then, in the 60th year of the Federal Republic, is how to create a narrative, a credible storyline for the country. . . .

Reluctance to Identify German Heroes

Now, let's be clear about this: Germans know how to party. People in England are still talking about the carnival mood during the 2006 World Cup, when fans literally danced in the streets. Until the German flags were carefully rolled away, everyone talked about a "relaxed patriotism." Now we are back with more customary tense, nail-biting, lip-chewing, look-over-your-shoulder, are-we-doing-anything-wrong patriotism. Part of the challenge, it seems to me, is the reluctance to identify German heroes who can be used as role models and focal points for celebration. . . .

Lack of a Clear Historical Concept

It is this timidity, the nervousness about facing the positive aspects of German history, that so baffles foreigners. A competition was recently launched to find a monument to mark German unity. It is supposed to be unveiled on November 9, 2009, and the competition was thrown open to everybody. Good! No fewer than 532 proposals were submitted. Even better! But then the 19-man jury, overwhelmed by the numbers, by the lack of clarity, decided that none of the designs was good enough. . . . The reason for this debacle was not so much the poor quality—some designs could certainly have been developed into something more interesting—but rather the lack of a clear historical concept. Germany's new monument was supposed to be a "freedom and unity monument," taking in the spirit of past centuries but looking positively to the future. Yet freedom and unity have not always gone together. Bismarck united Germany through war and the crushing of domestic critics; Hitler too led a unified Germany. I talked to British architects about this dilemma, about how to fuse, in a single design, complex and competing versions of history. Their solution was simple: accept that ordinary East German people made a major contribution to German unification by abandoning their fear and taking to the streets. . . .

The irony is that Germany is very good at celebrating its victims. The underground library to mark the Nazi book burning is widely regarded as an enrichment of Berlin. Peter Eisenman's Holocaust memorial remains impressive. Naturally, these constructions also took time and political wrangling. But that was understandable: the designers had to take into account the sensibilities of the victims. The Freedom and Unity monument should not be bound by these inhibitions. It should simply be a brave and interesting tribute to German heroism. Why is this so difficult for Germany?

Copyright: Goethe-Institut e. V., Online-Redaktion, May 2009, http://www.goethe.de/ges/mol/typ/en4608276.htm

central role of political parties and given meaning to the principle of "militant democracy" by banning two parties. In the early days of the Federal Republic, one party on the right, the Socialist Reich Party, and one party on the left, the Communist Party of Germany, were declared illegal on the basis of their antidemocratic ideologies. Since then, attitudes have relaxed, trusting that the electorate will reject extremism, but not to the point of abandoning precautions. The Federal Office for the Protection of the Constitution monitors extremist parties to the left and right; most controversial is observation of the Left Party, which is represented in the Bundestag and many *Land* parliaments. The observation of right-wing parties such as the National Democratic Party of Germany (NPD) and the German People's Union (DVU) generally arouses less controversy. Shunned and criticized by the media and all major political players and hampered by infighting and lack of strong leadership, these parties have not been able to elevate their voice to the national level but rear their heads in some *Land* and municipal constituencies.

As with all parliamentary systems, the head of government—called chancellor in Austria and Germany; prime minister in other countries—is responsible to, and dependent on, his or her party. In Germany, he or she is a member of parliament, elected from its ranks, and can be removed by a positive vote of no confidence; that is, a chancellor can only be voted out of office if, at the same time, the members of parliament can agree on the successor. In replacing chancellors, political parties, not the electorate, are the prime movers and shakers. Only Helmut Kohl's sixteen-year tenure ended with a clear verdict at the voting booth in 1998; in all other cases, the parties' political maneuvering determined the coalition partners that were able to form a new government. In Germany, the president, who acts as head of state, is chosen by an electoral college. The duties are largely ceremonial, but presidents have used their "soft power" effectively to address questions of national significance, such as reform gridlock or disenchantment with politics.

The number of Bundestag and government members born or socialized under the Third Reich has consistently declined. Today, only 10 of the 622 members of the Bundestag were born before 1941, compared to almost one-third in the 1990s. Generational replacement is a continuous process. In 1998, with the advent of a coalition between the Social Democratic Party (SPD) and Alliance 90/The Greens, a new generation of political leaders came to the helm of government. In their youth, many of them had been active in critically examining Germany's past; as members or supporters of the "68ers," the rebellious student movement of the 1960s, their "antifascist" credentials were beyond dispute.

A woman leading a major party and becoming head of government did cause a few headlines in 2005, but no waves; in the 2009 elections, Angela Merkel was the clear leader of the CDU and remains popular among the German public, despite low ratings for the current CDU/CSU-FDP coalition government. Women in German politics have come a long way; the first female cabinet minister was appointed only in 1961, and practice limited women to one or two government positions in "soft" areas, such as health, family, and youth, until the end of the 1980s. Now, routinely more than 30 percent of the members of the federal legislature are women, and women occupy leadership positions in parties and interest groups, including the powerful trade unions.

As in other democracies, the background of the political elite does not reflect that of the population at large. A university degree has become the norm, and lawyers dominate; for sixteen members, at least one parent is not a German citizen, haltingly bringing in some ethnic diversity. East Germans are proportionally represented in the Bundestag but are stunningly underrepresented in leadership positions, Merkel's chancellorship notwithstanding. She has carefully avoided making her eastern roots a matter of political significance; she once remarked that U.S. citizens seem more interested in her background than West Germans.[6]

Beyond her upbringing in communist East Germany, Merkel defies the image of most political leaders. She holds a doctorate in physics and became politically active only in the final days of the GDR as a member of one of the newly emerging parties. When her party dissolved, she joined the CDU; her career under the tutelage of then-chancellor Helmut Kohl involved different posts in the cabinet and the party leadership. In 1998 she became general secretary and in 2000 chair of the CDU. Her scientific background is often cited to explain her systematic approach to, and mastering of, complex policy issues as well as her nonideological approach to politics. Critics see the latter as reluctance to commit to clear policy positions; supporters see it as a desirable pragmatism committed to getting things done. *Forbes* magazine routinely ranks her first among the most powerful women in the world; under her leadership, the international visibility of the chancellor has grown at the expense of the foreign minister.

ELECTIONS AND COALITION GOVERNMENTS

The need to form coalition governments at the national and *Land* levels is a recurring feature of German politics. In national politics, only once, in 1957, was one party, the CDU/CSU, able to garner a majority of the votes, and even then it entered a coalition. In Germany, coalition governments most often form when one major party aligns with a minor party or parties to achieve a majority in the parliament. Under such arrangements, the profile and political clout of smaller parties is elevated. Formal coalition agreements have become the norm; they outline policy priorities and, at times, procedural issues for a four-year term.

Given the centrality of political parties, the gradual shift from the "frozen" three-party system of the postwar era to the five-party system of today has affected coalition arithmetic as well as resource and power allocation, a process that is still unfolding. In the 1970s, CDU/CSU and SPD garnered over 90 percent of the ballots; by 2005, just below 70 percent; in 2009, 66.8 percent, the second worst election result for the CDU/CSU, and for the SPD the worst election result since 1949, the beginning of the Federal Republic of Germany. In turn, Alliance 90/The Greens, the Left Party, and the Free Democratic Party reached all-time high support at the ballot boxes. The national elections mirror voting behavior at the *Land* level; party identification has declined, resulting in greater volatility in electoral outcomes. Though still high compared to the United States and many other democracies, in 2009 voter turnout in the national elections declined to an all-time low of 70.8 percent.

CDU/CSU and SPD vie for voters at the center of the political spectrum and portray themselves as catchall and social welfare parties; that is, parties with wide appeal. After World War II, CDU/CSU and SPD represented clear ideo-

Table 3.1   2009 Parliamentary Election

Party	Second Vote[1]	No. of Seats	Difference 2009–2005 (in percentages)
CDU/CSU	33.8	239	− 1.4
SPD	23.0	146	− 11.2
Alliance 90/The Greens	10.7	68	+ 2.6
FDP	14.6	93	+ 4.7
Left Party	11.9	76	+ 3.2
Other	6.0	0	+ 2.1

[1] Germany uses a personalized proportional representation voting system. Each person casts two votes. The first elects one representative from a district, similar to the single-member district vote in the United States. The number of seats in the *Bundestag*, however, is determined by a vote for a party list (second vote).

Only parties that receive at least 5 percent of valid votes or three constituency mandates can be represented in the federal diet.

Voter turnout in the 2009 election was 70.8 percent, down from 77.7 percent in 2005.

(*Source:* Adapted from Forschungsgruppe Wahlen e.V., *Bundestagswahl. Eine Analyse der Wahl vom 27 September 2009* [Berichte der Forschungsgruppe Wahlen e.V., Mannheim, 138], Mannheim: October 2009.)

logical choices and strategies ranging from economic to military policy. For many years, SPD strength was based on mass membership, whereas the CDU/CSU seemed to have a built-in electoral majority. By the mid-1970s, the ideological positions of the major parties had converged in many areas, including foreign and security policy. The incremental narrowing of the ideological gap contributed to shifts in electoral strength.

For most of the postwar period in West Germany, the FDP, rooted in classic European liberalism, had the luxury of choosing its coalition partner; a small party acted as the power broker. Traditionally, the FDP favors the CDU/CSU, although from 1969 to 1982 it aligned with the SPD. Since the 1980s, two additional parties have been elected to the national parliament. The Greens (officially Alliance 90/The Greens after 1993) have brought "new politics" issues, such as gender, environment, peace, and grassroots participation, to the forefront. Ever since the Red-Green coalition of 1998–2005, the Green Party is seen as the SPD's most likely coalition partner.

Following the fall of the Berlin Wall in November 1989, the former ruling Socialist Unity Party in East Germany changed program and leadership; it renamed itself the Party of Democratic Socialism (PDS). Its considerable electoral success was restricted to the eastern part of the country until disillusioned members of the SPD and trade unionists in the west founded their own party, Labor and Social Justice. The two forged an electoral alliance in 2005, and in 2007 they merged to form the Left Party. This marriage of political expedience aligned western and eastern voters to earn 8.7 percent of the national vote in

2005 and 11.9 percent in 2009; the Left Party is also represented in many *Land* parliaments. In a climate of economic uncertainty, it has established itself as a formidable force on the left, although plagued by factional struggles.

The shifting electoral landscape indicates declining party identification but also a divided electorate. Some favor comprehensive policy changes associated with the globalization of the economy, the growing needs of a knowledge society, and the challenges associated with demographic change. Others feel that recent political moves have led to an unacceptable weakening of the social safety net and social decline for many. Politicians are challenged to introduce changes that are effective yet socially fair. This dilemma affects the people's or catchall parties, CDU/CSU and SPD, while the FDP and the Left Party, for example, use it to present distinct versions of the neoliberal versus socialist policy positions.

Traditional coalition patterns, which favored the combination of either CDU/CSU or SPD with a smaller party, often no longer work. Should CDU/CSU and SPD form grand coalitions, reach out to new coalition partners, or align with two smaller parties instead of just one to garner sufficient votes? All options have been pursued recently at the *Land* level, with one exception: so far, both major parties have ruled out a coalition with the Left Party, excluding Berlin and the *Länder* in the east, where such coalitions exist. The matter is urgent for the SPD; in light of its decline at the voting booth, it cannot ignore the rising Left Party in forging a coalition to the left of the political spectrum.

In Germany, grand coalition governments, that is, governments led by the two major parties CDU/CSU and SPD, arouse different reactions. Supporters emphasize that such coalitions can overcome political hurdles to move the policy agenda from initiation to implementation since they garner sufficient votes in both houses of parliament. Critics lament that in such a political arrangement meaningful parliamentary opposition is limited to minor parties with no power to seriously challenge policy proposals. Others focus on whether such extreme majority coalitions can deliver promised policy changes. Far from innovative, they argue, grand coalitions promote policies that please the least common denominator since party competition continues; the partners have to uphold their programmatic distinctiveness to avoid alienating their voters. Critics and advocates agree that success is not guaranteed. It has to be supported by political will, and leadership is crucial. They also agree that grand coalitions should only be enacted for limited periods in times of duress.

In 2005, the only viable solution turned out to be a grand coalition government. It was not a novelty; a similar, and as regards policy outcomes largely successful, arrangement existed once before between 1966 and 1969. The grand coalition between 2005 and 2009 deserves similar credit. By and large, it kept partisan bickering in check and got things done. In contrast to the first grand coalition government, democratic principles were not devaluated, as opposition parties were stronger compared to the 1960s, and Germany's democracy was

Table 3.2   Federal Elections, Coalition Governments, and Chancellors, 1949–2009

Election Year	Coalition Parties	Chancellor
1949	CDU/CSU, FDP, and DP (German Party)	Konrad Adenauer (CDU)
1953	CDU/CSU, FDP, DP, and GB/BHE (All-German Bloc/Federation of Expellees and Displaced Persons)	Konrad Adenauer (CDU)
1957	CDU/CSU and DP	Konrad Adenauer (CDU)
1961	CDU/CSU and FDP	Konrad Adenauer (CDU) Oct. 1963: Ludwig Erhard (CDU)
1965	CDU/CSU and FDP Dec. 1966: CDU/CSU and SPD	Ludwig Erhard (CDU) Kurt Georg Kiesinger (CDU)
1969	SPD and FDP	Willy Brandt (SPD)
1972	SPD and FDP	Willy Brandt (SPD) May 1974: Helmut Schmidt (SPD)
1976	SPD and FDP	Helmut Schmidt (SPD)
1980	SPD and FDP Sept. 1982: SPD Oct. 1982: CDU/CSU and FDP	Helmut Schmidt (SPD) Helmut Schmidt (SPD) Helmut Kohl (CDU)
1983	CDU/CSU and FDP	Helmut Kohl (CDU)
1987	CDU/CSU and FDP	Helmut Kohl (CDU)
1990	CDU/CSU and FDP	Helmut Kohl (CDU)
1994	CDU/CSU and FDP	Helmut Kohl (CDU)
1998	SPD and Alliance 90/The Greens	Gerhard Schröder (SPD)
2002	SPD and Alliance 90/The Greens	Gerhard Schröder (SPD)
2005	CDU/CSU and SPD	Angela Merkel (CDU)
2009	CDU/CSU and FDP	Angela Merkel (CDU)

(*Source:* Adapted from Forschungsgruppe Wahlen e.V., *Bundestagswahl. Eine Analyse der Wahl vom 27 September 2009* [Berichte der Forschungsgruppe Wahlen e.V., Mannheim, 138], Mannheim: October 2009, 84.)

established. At the end of the four-year period, shifting from cooperation to confrontation proved difficult for its main leaders, Chancellor Angela Merkel (CDU) and Foreign Minister Frank-Walter Steinmeier (SPD). From the vantage point of summer 2010, the much-anticipated new coalition government between CDU/CSU and FDP has found little common ground, demonstrating that aligning parties with ostensibly similar programs can run into difficulties.

The German political system has no primaries; the parties select candidates. Campaigns are generally limited to a few weeks, but the staggering of elections—*Land* and municipal elections often take place between national elections—puts pressure on politicians. When voters cast their ballots in *Land* elections, local and national concerns intermingle, and parties can rebound, stabilize, or fail, with consequences for national politics as the distribution of seats in the second chamber, the Bundesrat, fluctuates directly with electoral fortunes at the *Land* level (see below under "the Federal System"). In recent years, *Land* coalitions have tested uncharted waters. For example, in Hamburg, CDU and the Green Party, and in Saarland, CDU, FDP, and the Greens have combined forces to govern jointly. In 2010, the SPD, battered by the national elections of 2009, recovered part of its electoral strength in North Rhine-Westphalia, by far the most populous *Land* in Germany; it was the CDU's turn to lose big. In the end, CDU and SPD won the same number of seats in the *Land* parliament. The election confirmed the trend of elevating smaller parties to new prominence, inviting "experiments" with novel coalition formations. The standoff between CDU and SPD resulted in a minority coalition between SPD and Alliance 90/The Greens. Minority governments do not have a stable parliamentary majority but have to vie for votes from other parties to pass legislation. Not unusual, this practice is rare in Germany and is viewed with suspicion, as it may endanger government stability.

THE FEDERAL SYSTEM

The capital of Berlin has reemerged as a cultural and scientific hub, and after architectural renovation of the center, its past as a divided city has been erased. New traffic patterns reconnect it with the world, and new architectural venues, including the Reichstag, the seat of the German parliament, have received accolades for innovate design. A major international tourist destination, its special flair was summed up by the principal conductor of its Philharmonic Orchestra, Englishman Sir Simon Rattle, as "60 percent Germany, 38 percent New York, and the rest Wild West."[7] Its increasingly prominent role notwithstanding, federalism engenders competition with other major cities, such as Cologne, Frankfurt, Hamburg, Leipzig, and Munich. The sharing of competencies and power contrasts with unitary states, such as the United Kingdom and France, where London and Paris clearly dominate national cultural, economic, and financial life.

Historically, regionalism has been strong in Germany, and the impact of the regions and their state governments is manifest in, among other things, the *Länder*'s leadership role in asserting regional rights vis-à-vis the European Union, the training and recruitment of national leaders through state offices, the division of labor between the federal government and the individual *Länder*, the reciprocal influence of *Land* and national elections, and the eminent role of the Federal Council in policymaking. The authors of the Basic Law institutionalized *Land* participation and multiple checks and balances in policymaking.

Box 3.2   Berlin: City on the Move

Claudia Wahjudi (2005)

Viewed from the eleventh floor of a block of flats in the middle of the city, Berlin presents itself from its best side—in elegant gray. The plain of stone, asphalt, plaster, concrete, granite, steel and glass extends as far as the horizon, interspersed with the green of parks and the red brick of old factories. Rising up in the center, there are little towers, curved or straight, and a few skyscrapers, some functionally rectangular, others with the sharp angles familiar from computer games. Colors and forms tell of the discontinuities of the city's history: from industrialization, which suddenly made the little residence city a metropolis, to the pomp of the German Empire and the social reforms of the Weimar Republic; from the megalomania of the National Socialists to the bombs and firestorms of the Second World War; from the division of the city into an Eastern European half and a Western European half to the building boom that followed the fall of the Wall. But now you can only sense where the Wall, Berlin's most famous structure, once stood: somewhere over there between the round roof of the Sony Center and the new glass cupola of the Reichstag Building, the seat of the German parliament. . . .

Every time a political system collapses in Germany, its stone witnesses are disposed of in Berlin as an example to others. A practice that is not always free of contradictions. Some people would even like to have a section of the almost completely demolished Wall back: when a private museum recently built a mock-up, locals and tourists flocked to see it.

There is always building, demolition and rebuilding going on. The various currents of German society compete for visible representation in the capital, which in just 100 years has seen five German states and the end of the Second World War in Europe. Now it is like a patchwork quilt full of holes that someone is supposed to be mending. . . .

Berlin is a city of opposites. It has glittering new government buildings, embassies, shopping malls and sport arenas, but a few meters away plaster is peeling from a municipal building and cars are bouncing through potholes. The Love Parade, the famous street procession held to the sound of techno beats, was conceived in Berlin, which also hosts a Carnival of the Cultures, Christopher Street Day celebrations, the annual Berlinale film festival and a Biennale for contemporary art. The 2006 football World Cup final will kick off in its Olympic Stadium. The city has 19 universities and higher education institutions, three opera houses and about 300 galleries, you will hear Turkish, English, Polish and Russian being spoken, and some days more than 120 bands and orchestras perform there. Yet, to the amazement of guests from other major cities, Berlin seems pleasantly empty: such wide pavements, so much sky, so few traffic jams—it is almost as restful as a holiday resort.

Copyright: Goethe-Institut, Online-Redaktion: http://goethe.de/ges/mol/dos/ber/en1543951 .htm

Decentralization is based on a complex division of power; the interests of the initially eleven and, after unification, sixteen *Länder* are represented in the Federal Council. Depending on the size of its population, each *Land* varies in its electoral weight from three to six votes. State governments select their representatives and instruct them how to vote; thus, each *Land* casts its vote as a unit. The interconnectedness of the federal and state levels has reinforced multilevel bargaining in policymaking.

Divided majorities in the two houses of parliament became more frequent from 1972 to 1982, from 1991 to 1998, and from 1999 to 2005. In this scenario, the opposition party in the Federal Parliament has the majority in the Federal Council. Thus the passage of many bills could be blocked or subjected to lengthy negotiations in the mediation committee. A reform of the federal system was deemed essential to get efficient decision making back on track. Called the "mother of all reforms," modernization of the federal system finally passed in July 2006. Discussed for decades and elaborated on for more than two years in a special commission composed of members of both houses of parliament, the revision of the federal system has been the most comprehensive constitutional reform since the founding of the Federal Republic in 1949. It involved numerous changes in the Basic Law, the German Constitution, and federal laws.

One major goal of the reform was to clearly demarcate responsibilities between the federal and regional governments. New boundaries are supposed to increase transparency and to reduce the number of bills requiring approval by the Federal Council. In exchange for a reduction in Federal Council power—the body of the *Land* governments—the *Länder* gained more responsibility for certain policy areas, such as education and civil service. In 2009, a second federalism reform went into effect, setting new constitutional limits on debt borrowing by the federal government and the *Länder* and outlining new strategies for modernizing public administration. However, the asymmetry in population and in particular economic power, as well as enduring center-periphery networks, makes delineating power exceedingly difficult. Despite major constitutional changes, the long-term political implications for policymaking remain unclear.

German federalism is built on sharing the fiscal burden. To reduce economic inequities, funds are transferred from richer to poorer states. Although givers and takers have changed during the life of the Federal Republic, most of the west is more prosperous than the east, and, due to shifts in employment and industrial patterns, the south (in particular Baden Württemberg and Bavaria) is now economically better off than the north (e.g., Mecklenburg-Western Pomerania and Schleswig-Holstein). Until 1994, uniformity (*Einheitlichkeit*) of living conditions in the different parts of Germany had been the constitutionally prescribed goal, but as part of constitutional reform in the aftermath of German unification, the term was replaced with equality (*Gleichwertigkeit*). The superimposition of the east-west divide on the existing north-south gap has added new levels of competition and conflict over the distribution of funds. Today, in the political struggle for influence, who is rich and who is poor matters more than ever.

NEGOTIATION DEMOCRACY AND POLICYMAKING

In all democratic settings, politics is the art of getting things done. It requires bargaining and compromise. In the German "negotiation democracy," a complex system of checks, balances, and conflict-solving mechanisms has emerged. Some features of consensual decision making were intentional; others evolved through cultural preference and political stipulation. Multilevel policymaking combines features of majority government, based on competition, with power-sharing characteristics such as consensus seeking through bargaining and granting autonomy and veto power to important political actors.

Negotiation democracy takes multiple forms; many are tied to the particulars of German federalism, which combines power sharing with strong centralizing tendencies and operates in a political culture in which equality of norms and living standards across the federation is highly valued. The Federal Council and the Federal Constitutional Court both favor competition and have significant potential as tools of the opposition. However, frequent and successful use of the mediation committee between the two houses of parliament points to the critical role of negotiation in Germany's political system. The procedures to appoint judges to the highest federal courts, including the Federal Constitutional Court, are shared by the major political parties and emphasize cooperation. Veto players encompass powerful interest groups, notably the labor unions and employers' associations, but they, along with other groups, are often drawn into "rounds of consensus" in the form of expert commissions. Informal politics, relying on long-standing networks across party aisles and groups, has swelled. Such methods secure high levels of acceptance once new policies are formed, but they also tend to slow down or even block the policymaking process. The challenges associated with such a system became starkly evident in the 1990s.

The German penchant for joining words and coining new ones is well known, and a new "word of the year" is chosen by a jury of experts to capture a national issue of major significance. Some fade away, while others become part of the vocabulary. Pressure for change in the areas of taxes, health care, pensions, the labor market, and immigration built up in the 1980s and boiled over in the 1990s. Decision-making overload, political haggling, and resistance seemed to make reforms impossible. Hence, in 1997, the term *Reformstau* was born.

Economic globalization, accelerating competition, the outsourcing of jobs, the spread of information technologies, and the migration of ideas and people has had profound effects on all Western economies. The forging of a closer union among the member states of the European Union has also exerted pressure for change. Benchmarking—that is, performance comparison within the European Union and the Organization for the Economic Cooperation and Development (OECD)—has become the norm. In an environment of shrinking and aging populations, low economic growth rates, and competition for resources, including knowledge and education, Germans were asked to change their ways. Such a task is not easily accomplished under the best of circumstances, but potential reform dynamics were initially absorbed and blocked by the consequences and the costs of merging East and West Germany in the 1990s.

Like most Europeans, many Germans turn to the government to address problems that affect their well-being. While direct state intervention is circumscribed, governmental institutions play important roles as mediators and set the legal framework for semipublic institutions, such as the Federal Agency for Labor. Economic and social systems, including the social welfare system, rely on a highly regulatory culture and transfer of payments. These systems evolved after World War II and won out over competing ideas of socialism and pure capitalism. Germans prioritized economic and social stability. A high level of employment and social protection, extensive participatory rights for workers, collective bargaining, and close cooperation between labor unions and employer associations, both of which were given privileged access to, and roles in, managing the economy, became central to the "model" Germany. Praised as a social market economy, for many years this model worked extremely well. At least as important, the principles of social justice and solidarity became important reference points in the political discourse and to this day find widespread public approval.

Calls for leadership and decisive action to advance reforms increased after the 2002 election. In March 2003, Chancellor Gerhard Schröder announced a comprehensive policy program, Agenda 2010, to reform the welfare system and labor market policies. However, associated cuts in social benefits aroused strong opposition, especially within the left wing of Schröder's party, the SPD, leading to widespread protests and the creation of a new party, the Labor and Social Justice Party, which later merged with the PDS to form the Left Party. The grand coalition (2005–2009) followed up on numerous reform proposals that had been batted back and forth in parliament and many rounds of informal talks. The lengthy reform impasse has disappeared: in recent years, new policies have been instituted regarding taxes, pensions, immigration, family allowances, child care, health care, the labor market, education, and the federal system, to name the most important.

Reform capacity is linked to economic performance. Germany competes for the role of world export champion, dueling with the United States and, more recently, China for the top spot. Some tax rates have decreased. Relative to economic output, unit labor costs have fallen, labor unions and their workers have shown wage restraint, and work contracts have become more flexible. Unemployment numbers have declined to a level not seen since the mid-1990s, but regional variations are pronounced, and they are still higher in the east than the west. For many years, it has been fashionable to portray a "sickly" German economy; average economic growth between 1995 and 2009 was a paltry 1 percent, including the worst recession since the end of World War II (4.9 percent in 2009). In 2010, recovery glimmered on the horizon, but for how long and how strongly remained unclear.

Problems remain: Birthrates have consistently declined since the 1960s, while life expectancy has increased, challenging the viability of the pension and health-care systems. New immigration and integration acts went into effect, but the practice of allowing immigrants to settle in Germany remains restricted, and immigration policies are emotionally charged. Recalibrating the education system from early child care to higher education has progressed but encounters resistance. Inequality has grown, and regional differences have become more pronounced. Keeping the German economic engine tuned is an ongoing challenge and relies heavily (some say too heavily) on export growth.

The Merging of Old and New: Foreign and Security Policy[8]

In no other policy area is the collective memory of Germany's past more persistent and relevant than foreign and security policy. After World War II, membership in international organizations provided an opportunity to reenter world affairs and to fend off potentially resurgent nationalism. The history of the Federal Republic reflects a network of international cooperation.[9] The Western allies' aspiration to control (West) Germany, while simultaneously integrating it with the international community of democratic nations, contributed to the creation of the North Atlantic Treaty Organization (NATO) in 1949, and after a heated domestic debate regarding remilitarization, Germany joined in 1955. The notion that NATO was formed to keep the Americans in Western Europe, the Russians out, and the Germans down captured prevailing concerns. (West) Germany's membership in the European Coal and Steel Community (1952) proved pivotal in the process of European integration; while containing Germany's power, the organization also granted it a chance to emerge as one of its leaders.

Prior to unification, Germany was widely considered an economic giant but, due to its limited international role, a political dwarf. In 1990, the end of the Cold War allowed it to regain full sovereignty and to unify East and West.

An evaluation of German foreign and security policy since then depends on the source and the questions asked. Are we interested in Germany's influence on concrete foreign policy agendas and outcomes or its role in shaping specific policy environments? Are we concerned with Germany's role in international organizations, such as the European Union or the United Nations? Has Germany been staunchly multilateral in security and military affairs but more self-interested and aggressive in economic policies? Is it moving beyond the European theater to assert global influence?

Power—the ability to influence others to act in ways they otherwise would not—can be measured in terms of population, economy, and military strength. Unified Germany, with its slightly less than 82 million people, clearly surpasses its powerful neighbor France (60.8 million) and the United Kingdom (61.4 million) in population. Measured in GDP, it is by far the largest economy in Europe and the fourth largest in the world, trailing the United States, the People's Republic of China, and Japan. Its military is intentionally weak in certain areas. To this day, Germany renounces possession of nuclear, biological, and chemical weapons, as well as long-range combat aircraft and missiles. It has no general staff apart from NATO troops; its troop strength is down to around 250,000 soldiers, with further cuts on the horizon. Its defense expenditures remain low in comparison to those of France and the United Kingdom, yet it has emerged as an important player in international peacekeeping and humanitarian efforts. Power projection also depends on how a country is perceived by its international environment, which is the result of expectations built on, and influenced by, long memories and conditioned by change. Finally, the extent to which power is translated into influence also depends on the willingness to use economic and other resources, the preferences of domestic and international actors, and more intangible considerations, such as bargaining skills and institutional constraints and possibilities.

No longer is Germany called a "political dwarf" or even a "reluctant power" but the "central power in Europe," the "leading European power," a "global economic power," a "permanently reformed civilian power," or a "re-emerging military power."[10] Beverly Crawford argues that "Germany has become a 'regional hegemon' in Europe and one of the 'great powers' on the international stage." She refers to Germany as a "normative power," relying on civilian power and multilateralism; power remains tied to downplaying power.[11] Placed in an environment where power is at times still measured in traditional terms, such a strategy has been praised as worth emulating or criticized as bypassing international responsibilities and burden sharing. Finding the balance remains a challenge for policymakers.

Germany's evolving international status has been the result of ad hoc responses to changes in the international environment, not the outcome of strategic recalculations. Major characteristics of German foreign and security policy are summarized here and taken up again in the following analysis.

- Germany's foreign and security policy continues to be shaped by the collective memory of the past and interests and institutional arrangements that emphasize multilateral decision making; that is, a team approach to solving international problems within the parameters of international organizations, such as the European Union, NATO, and the United Nations. New leadership roles are embedded in the framework of those organizations; Germany considers itself a partner in leadership.

- The strategic triangle—Berlin, Paris, and Washington—remains the fulcrum of German foreign policy, even if the style of the discourse and the perception of influence have changed. European integration as a prerequisite for peace and prosperity, France as Germany's most important ally in Europe, and the United States as a close partner are postulates that continue to shape German foreign policy.

- Foreign and security policy remains a matter of broad consensus among German elites and the public. Thus changes in leadership and government do not produce any significant policy alterations, although differences in style and nuances arise, even in continuity.

GERMANY AND EUROPE

In recent decades, European integration has extended from economic areas to include, among other things, foreign and defense policies, justice and home affairs, research, education and culture, and the environment. It has significantly changed the dynamics among EU member states; the Europeanization of its members' national politics has evolved as a major trend. European integration is widely seen as a success story, bringing peace and prosperity, yet headlines mostly announce various "crises." They are instigated, first, by individual countries blocking policy proposals regarding, for example, restructuring the Common Agricultural Policy and, more recently, addressing the monetary crisis. Second, the failure to ratify new EU treaties through national referenda has repeatedly shaken the European policy establishment. The failed public referenda in France and the Netherlands for an EU Constitution in 2005 fall into this category. They initiated a "reflection phase" after a decade of multifarious activities that taxed politicians and citizens alike before the watered-down Lisbon Treaty could go into effect in December 2009. Third, a "permanent crisis" relates to the openness of European integration with regard to both its final goal and its territorial expansion.[12]

With unification, Germany became by far the most populous country. Its share of members in the European Parliament is higher than that of other member countries, but its votes in the much more important Council of Ministers have remained equal to those of other "large" countries.[13] Still, Germany's crucial role in shaping European integration is undisputed. For example, it has been very successful in dictating the conditions under which countries can join the European currency and how the euro is managed. It set the tone and pushed for expansion of the European Union into Central and Eastern Europe. It also has played a crucial role in framing and implementing European foreign and military initiatives in the Balkans.

Germany's role in various crises has generally been as problem solver and mediator. It is still the primary net contributor to the EU budget, although accession of the eastern *Länder* has also made it a noteworthy beneficiary of funds. Its crucial role during the 2010 Greek debt crisis proceeded along those lines, although the style was different. Chancellor Angela Merkel's government openly resisted the rescue package for debt-ridden Greece and loan guarantees for countries under similar default pressures, but in the end, Germany acquiesced and assumed a major financial part in stabilizing the euro zone. At the time, Merkel was either credited with taking her time to set the stage for German commitment against domestic resistance and forcing Greece to implement important austerity measures or criticized for indecision that delayed much-needed action. Praise and criticism, also apparent in the handling of public debt and public consumption, reveal clashes in economic philosophies and cultures among Western governments that are not easily resolved.

Some disagreements notwithstanding, the European Union remains central to Germany, and Germany's commitment to European integration continues to be firm. After World War II, German supporters of European integration saw membership as a way to assure reconciliation and lasting peace with rival and former enemy France; now and then, the two countries are considered the "motor" that drives the integration process. More broadly, "Project Europe" provided an avenue for peace, economic prosperity, and international recognition. The German Constitution explicitly authorizes the federation to "transfer sovereign powers to intergovernmental institutions," including a mutual collective security system and the European Union. Political elites recognize the interconnectedness of national and European politics; German and European interests are seen as compatible, if not identical. Commitment to Europe also reflects a strong attachment to multilateralism as an idea and as a means for pursuing national interests. Germany's main parties do not contest European policies, with the partial exception of the Left Party. European integration was hardly debated during recent electoral campaigns, and the changes from one administration to the next have been marked by remarkable continuity in policies toward the European Union.

Continuity is not stagnation. The political profiles and policy styles of chancellors react to an evolving international environment, vary, and leave their imprint. Chancellor Helmut Kohl (1982–1998) considered German and European unity as two sides of the same coin; the promotion of European integration through close Franco-German relations was central to his European policy. Chancellor Gerhard Schröder (1998–2005) came to power with little foreign policy experience, yet he paved the way for a self-confident foreign policy style that paid greater attention to national concerns. Angela Merkel (2005–) started her chancellorship on a high note. During the December 2005 Council summit meeting, she successfully brokered a compromise on the long-standing issue of the EU budget, earning accolades at home and abroad. She took a leading role in salvaging important aspects of the constitutional treaty during her EU presidency in spring 2007; more recently she strongly defended German interests in the recent financial crisis.

German citizens support European integration, though somewhat less enthusiastically than their leaders; most see advantages and disadvantages. Similar to other member states, a more sober attitude toward the integration project has emerged over the last two decades. Compared to other member countries, Germany is not as skeptical as the British or some Scandinavians, or as supportive as some of the smaller countries, particularly in southern Europe. German citizens predominantly associate EU membership with a common currency, the free movement of people, cultural variety, peace, and greater world participation. They widely endorse common security measures, defense policy, and foreign policy. Divisive topics include EU enlargement, but nothing was more opposed by the German electorate than the introduction of the euro. A few months before euro coins and banknotes were officially introduced in January 2002, only 45 percent of western Germans and 27 percent of eastern Germans considered replacing the mark to be a good thing. This skepticism continues and was reinforced in the euro crisis of 2010; the euro remains "unloved but accepted." In contrast, for the political elites, giving up the "sacred cow" of the national currency was unambiguously the price of unification: Germany had to sacrifice its lead financial role in Europe to compensate for its increased population and status. Neither one of the major political parties veered from completing the project.

The European Union affords Germany political and economic clout. To explain the support for European integration, aspects of political culture, political structure, and policy style must be considered. After World War II, European integration provided a vehicle for international recognition; it was also widely seen as contributing to the economic miracle of the 1950s. Germany's complementary institutional structure has also been cited as facilitating its pro-European attitude. The highly decentralized political system, coalition governments, and the principle of delegation to semipublic institutions have made the interaction with European institutions, in the words of one observer, a "warm bath" instead of the "cold shower" that many British elites and citizens may feel.[14] Similarly, a bureaucratic culture of rules and regulations is part of both European and German policymaking. Finally, lengthy negotiation and bargaining that aim at achieving consensus are key elements of both German and European policymaking. In other words, German politicians are at ease with the institutional and policymaking environment of the European Union.

Institutional features may also partially explain why a reluctant or negative attitude toward European integration has remained a "dark matter" in German politics. Charles Lees argues that through the expression of reservations about EU policies and the election of small right-wing parties with an anti-European agenda, the *Länder* have given "soft Euro-skepticism" a limited outlet; it could be articulated and contained at the same time. The adoption of an anti-European attitude by parties on the far right may have discredited Euro-skepticism "by association."[15] Despite pockets of Euro-skeptic attitudes, also shared by members of the Left Party, cross-party consensus in the European Union's favor has remained high.

Since the beginning of European integration, France and Germany set the timing according to which it moved or stalled. The relationship is closely watched, and over the years observers have emphasized either ties that bind or degrees of separation. International developments since German unification have favored a more influential Germany and weakened the special position of France. France's national identity is closely tied to its prominent role in European and world affairs; thus a shift in the balance of power between the two nations is an important reference point for French politicians. Cordial and close relations between French and German leaders covered up recurring bilateral conflicts of interest, reinforced by different policy styles, preferences, and leadership. After being elected, chancellors and French presidents routinely visit each other on their first official state visits abroad, emphasizing the special relationship in a symbolic gesture. The friendships between Konrad Adenauer and Charles de Gaulle, Helmut Schmidt and Valéry Giscard d'Estaing, and Helmut Kohl and François Mitterrand are legendary. The relationship between Angela Merkel and Nicolas Sarkozy has been rockier; they disagree on euro governance, among other things. Tensions are partly due to opposing leadership styles, but mutual interests and shared responsibility for driving EU initiatives and consensus prevail. Franco-German relations still stand as a model of reconciliation; after three German invasions of France between 1870 and 1940 alone, military conflict between the two has become unthinkable. They remain each other's most important trading partners, and thousands of educational exchanges and partnerships between towns and villages reinforce bonds at the grassroots level.

In 2004 and 2007, overall twelve countries joined the European Union, increasing the total number of member states to twenty-seven; ten are located in Central and Eastern Europe. Despite the electorate's critical view, German politicians strongly supported Central and Eastern Europe's inclusion in the European Union and NATO, due in no small part to the wish to be surrounded by peaceful, democratic neighbors. Germany is the region's main source for direct investment and maintains a multifaceted and high level of trading relations. More than any other EU member state, it provided aid, assistance, and a model for institutions ranging from banking to electoral regulations. Incorporating

Western institutions was a way for the Central and Eastern European countries to speed up the process of democratization and to compensate for the price they had to pay when Europe was divided after World War II.

Attention has turned to further expansion, in particular the potential membership of Turkey. Turkish membership is a hotly debated and divisive issue in Europe, especially in Germany, where about 2 million Turks reside. A clear and consistent majority of German citizens disapprove of Turkish membership in the European Union. The question is one of the few to spark partisan differences. CDU/CSU politicians have long said that they prefer a "privileged partnership" to full membership.

Jacques Delors, former French EU Commission president (1985–1994), has joined the chorus of many experts in asserting that the climate in the European Union has changed. The partial renationalization of European politics, according to Delors, owes its origins to domestic pressures created by globalization and generational change that takes Europe for granted. Addressing French concerns that German leaders may have lost their drive to push for greater European integration, he remarked that today "Germans must be convinced . . . that Europe is their future."[16] At least for now, gone are the days of visions, when German politicians like Joschka Fischer and public intellectuals like philosopher Jürgen Habermas, at times with French philosopher Jacques Derrida, advanced European discussions on the role and future of Europe.[17] The politicization of European issues was shown during the debate on the Lisbon Treaty in 2008 and 2009. Several members of the Bundestag, from the left and right, challenged the treaty's constitutionality on different grounds. Some criticized the democratic deficit, and others the transfer of power to European institutions. In summer 2009, judges confirmed the treaty's compliance with the constitution but requested additional safeguards to strengthen the powers of the Bundestag in regard to European legislation; such legislation was subsequently passed, and the treaty was ratified. Germany's commitment to European integration remains steadfast, but after rounds of enlargement, a drawn-out constitutional debate, and financial upheavals, its leaders are content with small steps rather than great leaps.[18]

The "return to Europe" for countries that used to be communist-governed and under Soviet influence also necessitated a reworked relationship with Russia. Germany was in a unique position to assist in the region's stabilization since it could build on a long-standing, close relationship. With the final withdrawal of Russian troops from eastern German territory in 1994, an important chapter in postwar history closed. In the tumultuous decade that followed, German policy was geared toward preventing a collapse of the Russian economy and government. Under the leadership of Vladimir Putin (president, 2000–2008; prime minister since) and President Dmitry Medvedev (2008–), domestic stability has replaced disorder; Russia has reemerged as a player in world politics, albeit with increasing authoritarian tendencies. Between 1998 and 2008, the

Russian economy has boomed, fueled by rising energy prices, but it was particularly hard hit during the worldwide economic crisis of 2008–2009. The two countries have strong mutual economic interests, if not dependencies: Germany is Russia's largest trading partner, while Russia supplies large shares of oil and natural gas to Germany. Their relations are not exclusively based on economic expedience. Germany is uniquely positioned to help anchor Russia, yet, with Western partners, it must do so without ignoring the democratic backlash.

TRANSATLANTIC RELATIONS

After the European Union, the relationship with the United States is the second pillar of German foreign policy. Integration with Europe and close cooperation with the United States have always been interrelated as part of Germany's strong commitment to Western alliances. With the advent of a European foreign and defense policy, they have become even more intertwined. In foreign and security policy, Germany sees itself as the carrier of both national and European interests.

During the Cold War, Western Europe in general and West Germany in particular benefited greatly from U.S. support in military, economic, and political matters. U.S. leadership was crucial in bringing about German unification when the opportunity arose in 1989–1990. The network of cultural, economic, and political exchanges is dense and has reached a level that is normally reserved for countries that are members of regional integration schemes, such as the European Union. With record speed, the occupation power turned into a trusted friend and ally. Americans came to expect German leaders to emphasize friendship and appreciation and to criticize, if at all, subtly and behind closed doors.

The distinct downturn in relations during the debate about how to deal with Iraq in 2002 and 2003 led to intense soul-searching among German elites and the public. To be sure, with joint responsibilities and tasks come competition, and conflicts had emerged in the past as well, yet the level of disharmony and distrust evident during the Iraqi conflict revealed a new and different climate. The adage "all politics is local" may explain Chancellor Schröder's outspoken anti–Iraq war rhetoric during the 2002 electoral campaign. It led to tense, emotional exchanges between him and U.S. president George W. Bush. But soon the policy establishments on both sides of the Atlantic worked diligently at "normalization."

Foreign policy is a matter of pursuing national interests in interaction with other countries. It cannot ignore the importance of personal relationships and the policy styles of politicians at the helm. While good chemistry between the leaders of different countries is no guarantee for the successful pursuit of interests, it can promote closer consultation and a cordial climate of cooperation. A significant step was taken with the election of Angela Merkel, which coincided with greater efforts by the Bush administration to consult with European leaders on matters of international concern. The 2008 election of Barack Obama to the U.S. presidency brought transatlantic relations back on track, as his policy style and major initiatives—for example, his support for multilateral strategies, nuclear disarmament, and environmental concerns—conform with German preferences. Approval ratings for U.S. foreign policy jumped from a low of 30 percent in 2007 to 64 percent in 2009 and only declined by 1 percent in 2010; that President Obama "would do the right thing in world affairs" is believed by about 90 percent of Germans surveyed in the 2010 Pew Global Attitudes Project.[19]

The normalization of transatlantic relations is not a return to the previous status quo. The roles of both Germany and the United States have changed significantly since the end of the Cold War. The discourse is friendly and frank; in the new global international environment, transatlantic relations still matter greatly but clearly less so in the post–Cold War era.

CIVILIAN POWER AND SECURITY POLICY

Nowhere is the change in Germany's international role more apparent than in its security policy. Until the early 1990s, checkbook diplomacy was the preferred way to show international solidarity and responsibility. Based on Article 87a of the Basic Law, Germany shied away from direct involvement in military conflict in "out-of-area" operations and instead provided financial assistance to defray the costs. However, first the Gulf War in 1990–1991 and then the conflicts in the former Yugoslavia rendered this position increasingly untenable. Pressure mounted on the Kohl government to engage members of the armed forces in humanitarian aid and crisis management. The Federal Constitutional Court's 1994 ruling on Article 87a opened the door for out-of-area military deployment, provided that it was part of multilateral operations, had the blessing of the United Nations, and received the approval of the Bundestag. Burning villages and ethnic cleansing in Bosnia-Herzegovina and Kosovo catalyzed a moral policy of "never again" (Auschwitz) and reinforced the prevailing notion of "never alone." In particular, the Green Party has its roots in the peace movement. Joschka Fischer, the respected foreign minister in both cabinets under Chancellor Gerhard Schröder, used his personal and his party's pacifist credentials to legitimize greater engagement in foreign and security policy. Pacifism and antifascism provided the basis for a new self-confidence. Many have argued that the acceptance of Germany's increased role in foreign and security policy at home and abroad owes much to the Red-Green leadership of confirmed pacifists.

In 1999, the postwar taboo on German military involvement was broken when the German air force engaged in the Kosovo conflict. Since then, Germany has rapidly widened the scope of its military operations. In 1998, about

Box 3.3   Speech by Federal Chancellor Angela Merkel before the United States Congress

Tuesday, November 3, 2009

I would like to thank you for the great honor and privilege to address you today, shortly before the 20th anniversary of the fall of the Berlin Wall.

I am the second German Chancellor on whom this honor has been bestowed. The first was Konrad Adenauer when he addressed both Houses of Congress in 1957, albeit one after the other.

Our lives could not have been more different. In 1957 I was just a small child of three years. I lived with my parents in Brandenburg, a region that belonged to the German Democratic Republic (GDR), the part of Germany that was not free. My father was a Protestant pastor. My mother, who had studied English and Latin to become a teacher, was not allowed to work in her chosen profession in the GDR.

In 1957 Konrad Adenauer was already 81 years old. He had lived through the German Empire, the First World War, the Weimar Republic and the Second World War. The National Socialists ousted him from his position as mayor of the city of Cologne. After the war, he was among the men and women who helped build up the free, democratic Federal Republic of Germany.

Nothing is more symbolic of the Federal Republic of Germany than its constitution, the Basic Law, or "Grundgesetz." It was adopted exactly 60 years ago. Article 1 of the Grundgesetz proclaims, and I quote, "Human dignity shall be inviolable." This short, simple sentence—"Human dignity shall be inviolable"—was the answer to the catastrophe that was the Second World War, to the murder of six million Jews in the Holocaust, to the hate, destruction and annihilation that Germany brought upon Europe and the world.

November 9th is just a few days away. It was on November 9, 1989 that the Berlin Wall fell and it was also on November 9 in 1938 that an indelible mark was branded into Germany's memory and Europe's history. On that day the National Socialists destroyed synagogues, setting them on fire, and murdered countless people. It was the beginning of what led to the break with civilization, the Shoah. I cannot stand before you today without remembering the victims of this day and of the Shoah. . . .

Not even in my wildest dreams could I have imagined, twenty years ago before the Wall fell, that this would happen. It was beyond imagination then to even think about traveling to the United States of America let alone standing here today.

The land of unlimited opportunity—for a long time it was impossible for me to reach. The Wall, barbed wire and the order to shoot those who tried to leave limited my access to the free world. So I had to create my own picture of the United States from films and books, some of which were smuggled in from the West by relatives.

What did I see and what did I read? What was I passionate about?

I was passionate about the American dream—the opportunity for everyone to be successful, to make it in life through their own personal effort.

(continued)

Box 3.3   *(Continued)*

I, like many other teenagers, was passionate about a certain brand of jeans that were not available in the GDR and which my aunt in West Germany regularly sent to me.

I was passionate about the vast American landscape which seemed to breathe the very spirit of freedom and independence. Immediately in 1990 my husband and I traveled for the first time in our lives to America, to California. We will never forget our first glimpse of the Pacific Ocean. It was simply gorgeous.

I was passionate about all of these things and much more, even though until 1989 America was simply out of reach for me. And then, on November 9, 1989, the Berlin Wall came down. The border that for decades had divided a nation into two worlds was now open.

And that is why for me today is, first of all, the time to say thank you. . . .

Where there was once only a dark wall, a door suddenly opened and we all walked through it: onto the streets, into the churches, across the borders. Everyone was given the chance to build something new, to make a difference, to venture a new beginning.

I also started anew. I left my job as a physicist at the Academy of Sciences in East Berlin behind me and went into politics. Because I finally had the chance to make a difference. Because I had the impression that now it was possible to change things. It was possible for me to do something. . . .

Ladies and gentlemen, it is true that America and Europe have had their share of disagreements. One may feel the other is sometimes too hesitant and fearful, or from the opposite perspective, too headstrong and pushy. And nevertheless, I am deeply convinced that there is no better partner for Europe than America and no better partner for America than Europe.

Because what brings Europeans and Americans together and keeps them together is not just a shared history. What brings and keeps Europeans and Americans together are not just shared interests and the common global challenges that all regions of the world face. That alone would not be sufficient to explain the very special partnership between Europe and America and make it last. It is more than that. That which brings Europeans and Americans closer together and keeps them close is a common basis of shared values. It is a common idea of the individual and his inviolable dignity. It is a common understanding of freedom in responsibility. This is what we stand for in the unique transatlantic partnership and in the community of shared values that is NATO. This is what fills "Partnership in Leadership" with life, ladies and gentlemen. . . .

I am convinced that, just as we found the strength in the 20th century to tear down a wall made of barbed wire and concrete, today we have the strength to overcome the walls of the 21st century, walls in our minds, walls of short-sighted self-interest, walls between the present and the future.

Ladies and gentlemen, my confidence is inspired by a very special sound— that of the Freedom Bell in the Schöneberg Town Hall in Berlin. Since 1950 a copy of the original American Liberty Bell has hung there. A gift from American citizens, it is a symbol of the promise of freedom, a promise that has been fulfilled. On October 3, 1990 the Freedom Bell rang to mark the reunification of Germany, the greatest moment of joy for the German people. On September 13, 2001, two days after 9/11, it tolled again, to mark America's darkest hour.

The Freedom Bell in Berlin is, like the Liberty Bell in Philadelphia, a symbol which reminds us that freedom does not come about of itself. It must be struggled for and then defended anew every day of our lives. In this endeavor Germany and Europe will also in future remain strong and dependable partners for America. That I promise you. Thank you very much.

Copyright: REGIERUNGonline: The Press and Information Office of the Federal Government.

2,000 soldiers were engaged in humanitarian and peacekeeping operations abroad. At the beginning of the twenty-first century, the number had risen to over 8,000, making Germany one of the major sources of international troops. In mid-2010, about 6,700 German soldiers were deployed in Africa, Asia, and Europe. In line with its security policy, military activities are pursued within the framework of international organizations: NATO, the European Union, the United Nations, and the Organization for Security and Cooperation in Europe.

Germany has successfully shifted from territorial defense to international conflict prevention—including the fight against international terrorism—and crisis management. Its widening military engagement has been accompanied by ongoing reform of the armed forces yet remains hampered by the reluctance to increase military spending to match goals. Personnel and equipment are stretched to their limits, but recent international developments have also driven home the need for action. Despite the constitutionally prescribed compulsory military service for men, among the 250,000 soldiers reported in 2010, only some 32,700 were conscripts, and the time of service continually declines, shifting once again in July 2010 from nine to six months. Most troops are professional members of the armed forces or conscripts who voluntarily sign up for extended service. Most European countries have switched to a professional army; as of July 2011 conscription will be abandoned but not eliminated so that it can be reinstated when needed.

Of the forty-seven countries that contributed troops to the Afghan battlefield in 2010, Germany supplied the third-largest contingent, with close to 4,600 soldiers. Often criticized abroad, they are employed in the safer northern part of the country, where war casualties are lower. Defending German security interests in the "Hindu Kush," taking up the phrase by former defense minister Peter Struck (SPD) to rationalize German involvement in the Afghan conflict, remains a difficult sell for all governments, as involvement is opposed by most Germans. While a cross-party consensus to support German involvement still holds, excepting the Left Party, the German government, like many other governments involved in the Afghanistan war, stands under pressure to set a timetable for withdrawal.

Are We There Yet? The New Germany

In the long view of history, the period of separation into a communist-governed eastern Germany and a democratic western Germany turned out to be a mere interlude, and German politics is most often analyzed as the continuous development of the Federal Republic of Germany. At first, radical transformation of the former GDR seemed the price of continuity in the west. One part of the country was to change according to the parameters set by the other. However, the sense of continuity was deceiving; new transitions, as I suggest here, seized the unified Germany, affecting policies, institutions, and identity.

The country as a whole has settled into its status as a major European power without upsetting the continental balance. The tone and strategies of its political leaders may have become more assertive, but its commitments to European integration and strong ties to the United States and Western alliance structures have not wavered. In domestic affairs, much has changed since unification twenty years ago. Federalism is alive but also altered due to the addition of the former East Germany. The changing party landscape is the result of declining party identification and shifting voter preferences. The combined forces of globalization, Europeanization, and unification have ratcheted up pressure for policy adjustments and, with some delay, have unleashed forces for policy change. Looking back on the history of the Federal Republic, institutional and policy changes have been marked by a distinct preference for piecemeal approaches and consensual conflict-solving mechanisms rather than radical transformations. This tradition continues; most reforms have been incremental and, with few exceptions, refrain from dramatically altering basic structures. Nevertheless, the sum of the small steps can amount to "subterranean shifts";[20] reforming the reforms is an ongoing process.

Challenges remain. The integration of foreign-born residents into society is still hampered by mental and bureaucratic obstacles. Low fertility rates and an aging population not only exert pressures on pension and health-care systems but also expose the need for continued immigration. The influx of foreigners has made society more heterogeneous; so has the addition of 16 million citizens from the former East Germany. Taking stock of twenty years of unification is an exercise in weighing pros and cons; assessments vary depending on the criteria and the benchmarks used. If we are primarily interested in economic and political convergence between east and west and the tearing down of mental barriers, then we must concede that unity between east and west has not been accomplished. However, if we shift the focus and ask whether democratic stability has been maintained; economic transformation, painful as it was, completed; and progress made toward integrating the two parts of the country, then the balance is more impressive. Most importantly, there is no desire to turn back the wheel of history to the period before 1989; in survey after survey, an overwhelming majority of Germans endorse unification.

The simultaneous forces of continuity and change in the last two decades have challenged German political analysts. They have tried to capture the disparate dynamics with terms such as "modified continuity" and "adaptation of existing policies" while stressing the emergence of a new Germany. Is it "older and wiser," as the *Economist* suggested in the title of its special German section in March 2010, or just more at ease and less unique, as many Germany watchers, among them Charles S. Maier, have pointed out?[21] Have Germans become "normal," like their neighbors in Europe? Some say yes. Konrad H. Jarausch asserts that at age sixty, the country has settled into "comfortable middle age . . . exuding a sense of competent normalcy."[22] Almost there, says the *Economist*, referring to it as a "muted normality" in which a future normality is visible on the horizon. According to the author, it includes heeding the lessons of history, assertiveness in international affairs, and greater national pride.[23] Nuances in interpretation notwithstanding, the road on the long journey toward normalcy has become less bumpy, allowing Germany to move ahead.

Suggested Readings

Anderson, Jeffrey J., and Eric Langenbacher (eds.), *From the Bonn to the Berlin Republic: Germany at the Twentieth Anniversary of Unification*, New York and Oxford: Berghahn Books, 2010.

Crawford, Beverly, *Power and German Foreign Policy: Embedded Hegemony in Europe*, Houndsmills: Palgrave Macmillan, 2007.

Crawshaw, Steve, *Easier Fatherland: Germany and the Twenty-first Century*, London and New York: Continuum, 2004.

German History in Documents and Images, http://www.ghi-dc.org (collection of primary source materials documenting Germany's political, social, and cultural history from 1500 to the present).

Green, Simon, and William E. Paterson (eds.), *Governance in Contemporary Germany: The Semisovereign State Revisited*, Cambridge: Cambridge University Press, 2005.

Haftendorn, Helga, *Coming of Age: German Foreign Policy since 1945*, Lanham, MD: Rowman & Littlefield, 2006.

Peck, Jeffrey M., *Being Jewish in the New Germany*, New Brunswick, NJ: Rutgers University Press, 2006.

Sarotte, Mary Elise, *1989: The Struggle to Create Post–Cold War Europe*, Princeton, NJ: Princeton University Press, 2009.

Zelikow, Philip, and Condoleezza Rice, *Germany United and Europe Transformed: A Study in Statecraft*, Cambridge: MIT University Press, 1995.

Specialized Scholarly Journals

German Politics (Routledge).
German Politics and Society (Berghahn Publishers).
Internationale Politik, transatlantic edition (in English; published by the German Council on Foreign Relations).

CHAPTER 4

Italy: Politics in the Age of Berlusconi

Gianfranco Baldini

Italy

Population (million):	60.4
Area in Square Miles:	116,320
Population Density per Square Mile:	519
GDP (in billion dollars, 2009):	$1,921.8
GDP per capita (PPP, 2005):	$26,558
Joined EC/EU:	January 1, 1958

Performance of Key Political Parties in Parliamentary Elections of April 13–14, 2008

Coalition Silvio Berlusconi:	46.8%
People of Liberty	37.4%
Movement for Autonomy	1.1%
Northern League (LN)	8.3%
Coalition Walter Vetroni:	37.5%
Democratic Party	33.2%
Italy of Values	4.4%

Main Office Holders: Prime Minister: Silvio Berlusconi—People of Liberty, formerly Forward Italy (2008, 2001–2006, 1994–1995); Head of State: Giorgio Napolitano—DS (2006).

Seen from the United States, Italian politics has always been problematic. Government instability, corruption, the Mafia, scandals, lack of trust (or "amoral familism")—these are among the words most frequently associated with Italian politics during the so-called First Republic (1946–1992). Things did not change much after 1992, despite the collapse of the old party system. Over the last eighteen years, Italian politics has been dominated by the controversial figure of Silvio Berlusconi. Since his first electoral victory in 1994, he has been prime minister for almost a decade, thus becoming the longest-serving head of government in postwar Italian history. Because of the peculiarities mentioned above, Italy has often been treated as a special case of liberal democracy, thereby emphasizing the political system's many anomalies.[1] This chapter explains why Italy has been a troubled democracy ever since its birth as a republic in 1946, and to some extent a problematic polity ever since the foundation of the modern Italian state in 1861. As this chapter is written during the 150th anniversary of the Italian state, it will take a somewhat longer historical view than the other country studies in this volume.

The Weight of the Past

The most important thing to understand about modern Italy is how much baggage it carries from the past 150 years. Certain influences have emerged at each of the many stages of its development. And like country houses or furniture, they have been passed down from one generation to the next. The following are particularly important: weak governments, unstable majorities, clientelism, low perceptions of legitimacy, poor social capital, and a ubiquitous North-South dichotomy.

Italy was born as a state in 1861, after the Kingdom of Sardinia (but based in Piedmont) managed to unify a territory that had been plagued by rivalries and fragmentation for centuries. The Savoy monarchy led an elitist annexation of the ten existing kingdoms. The result was unsuccessful in centralizing authority, and Italian governments were weak ever since state unification.

The Italian state inherited its basic institutional structure from the Kingdom of Sardinia: the Albertine Statute (1848) set up a parliamentary monarchy, which was replaced exactly a century later by the Italian Constitution (1948). Prime ministers were constrained on the one side by the powers of the monarchy (the king alone had executive power, which meant he alone could appoint and dismiss ministers) and on the other side by scrutiny provided by parliament.

At the parliamentary level, political affiliations were weak. As a result, many deputies of both left and right used to switch sides to pave the way for the succession of the different governments. This practice—called *trasformismo*—meant that coalitions were unstable, and yet no real political alternation took place. In other words, governments were weak, but political leaders were also unaccountable to the electorate. This practice had enduring consequences for the development of the political system.

At the societal level, relations between political elites and the electorate were mainly conducted on the basis of clientelistic exchanges, meaning that "deputies were bribed into supporting the government by the uninhibited use of patronage, both for themselves (honors, cabinet posts) and for their constituencies (railways, bridges, government contracts). It required delicate balancing of personal and local interests, and led to numerous changes of government as cabinets were reshuffled and new interests satisfied."[2]

In such a context, left and right were empty labels. Meanwhile, elected officials tended to develop unhealthy relationships with the civil servants who controlled access to state resources. For example, various liberal notables managed to control their own constituencies thanks to the help they got from the prefects, the "local guardians" of state power. Italy was very fragmented, poor, and illiterate, and its political institutions were mainly framed in order to govern a backward society from the center: more local government autonomy would have probably meant the breakup of the polity. Moreover, Italy's early politicians were well aware of the fragile nature of the Italian state. Hence they incorporated the use of prefects to extend the power of central government and so bind the country together in administrative terms. In effect, they inadvertently created the institutions for centralized patronage as well.[3]

If elites were aware of the fragility of the state, the masses were aware of its intrusiveness. The process of state building never managed to gain full popular consent, let alone mass enthusiasm. In fact, the masses often saw unification as an imposition: the *Risorgimento* (or, more colloquially, the process of Italian unification) was never a popular phenomenon and was viewed with suspicion by both Catholics and communists, who constituted the two most important political groups until the collapse of the First Republic in 1992. This skepticism was linked to conflicting loyalties vis-à-vis the new Italian polity, mainly coming from the Catholic electorate and the southern regions. When Italy was born as a state, the papacy (based in the Vatican, in Rome) did not want to give up its powers; the *non expedit* (1868) meant that Catholics should not take part in politics (being "neither elector nor elected"). Although it was progressively relaxed, the *non expedit* was abrogated only in 1919, the year after the first Catholic party, Don Luigi Sturzo's Italian Popular Party (PPI), came into being. This process was particularly problematic in the South, where higher levels of religious practice were complemented by a violent struggle against the state-building process: brigandage was among the most powerful manifestations of hostility toward unification, to such an extent that it has frequently been likened to a civil war.

In such a context, it is not surprising that the democratization process was both contested and only partially successful. Although Massimo D'Azeglio's famous phrase "We have made Italy, now we must make Italians" has become one of the most cited clichés on Italy, the saying bears more than a grain of truth: making Italians proved to be much more complicated than making Italian institutions. Social inequality and fragmentation were extensive. By the turn of the nineteenth century, Italy had the highest rates of illiteracy in Western Europe, and the second highest percentage of employees in the primary (or agricultural) sector; almost forty years after unification, truancy among school-aged children still reached 80 percent in some southern areas.[4]

Moreover, late extension of the franchise (near universal voting rights, or "suffrage," for men was introduced only in 1913) meant that all of the main political parties were weak and had extraparliamentary origins. The Catholics were an obvious example, because of their roots in the institutions of the church, but this was true also for nonreligious ideological groups such as the socialists and the republicans. The extraparliamentary origins of the major political parties had important implications for the post–World War I period. The liberals, who had always governed during the late nineteenth and early twentieth centuries, lacked a strong institutional structure. The other main political parties were marginally better organized and yet gained access to seats in parliament when proportional representation (PR) was introduced in 1919.

After PR was introduced, the other parties gained more influence over parliament. However, contrary to the experience in many other Western European countries, this change did not lead to democratization as expressed in terms of an abiding and widespread commitment of the electorate to the maintenance of democratic principles. Just a few years after incorporating the masses into the political process through the extension of voting rights, the Italian democratic system was still unprepared to face the combined pressures of a deep economic crisis, revanchist sentiments coming out of the First World War, and a radical mobilization of the workforce.[5] Weak and divided parties were unable to govern such convulsive processes, and their divisions gave way to the rise of Fascism.

The actual experience of Fascism is less important to our understanding of the current situation than the impact this experience had on Italian political attitudes and economic institutions. The Fascist regime left crucial legacies to the (second and more successful) democratization process that took place in the years that surrounded the birth of Italy as a republic in 1946. On the political side, the main legacy was to be found in the peculiar path that led to the fall of Fascism and the subsequent armistice. Indeed, the final two years of the war affected "the whole organism of the Italian state, almost causing—in reality and, most importantly, in the imagination—its virtual disappearance."[6] Hence, the parties that emerged at the end of the Second World War did not share a common idea of the Italian nation; rather, what bound them together was their opposition to Fascism. By implication, popular perceptions of the legitimacy of the Italian state remained weak, and the points of difference both between and within the political parties remained significant. For example, the left-wing resistance movement that emerged during the Second World War was affected by deep ideological divisions between its predominant radical component (led by the Italian Communist Party, PCI) and a minority moderate one. Although the PCI soon developed a more pragmatic position on many issues, it remained committed to the belief that democracy is just a provisional step in the long march toward socialism.[7] The different visions held by the political parties involved in building a new postwar Italy—coupled with the enduring weakness of state legitimacy—meant that Italian democratization was difficult, even when compared to those other south European countries that also experienced authoritarian regimes.

As far as the economy is concerned, Italy inherited from Fascism the second-largest public sector in Europe after the Soviet Union (USSR). Large, state-owned holding companies created in the 1930s, such as IRI (the Industrial Reconstruction Institute) for industry, or IMI (Istituto Mobiliare Italiano) for banking, were not dismantled after the war. Such institutions constituted a whole new arena for unhealthy relations to develop between elected officials and appointed civil servants—this time controlling industries rather than regions. As such, they became critical targets for partisan control.

Finally, it is important to consider the structure of life outside the Italian state—or what is called "civil society." Social institutions and the way they function exert a powerful influence on the attitudes and behavior of ordinary people. Some institutions have a very positive influence; others are more negative. Italy had both sorts. As a consequence, social capital, defined by Robert Putnam as "the features of social organization, such as trust, norms, and networks, that can improve the efficiency of society by facilitating coordinated actions," developed very differently in the North and South of the country.[8] In his study of Italian democracy, Putnam contends that different levels of social capital in different parts of the country gave rise to very different sorts of political outcomes. Robert Putnam's thesis underlines the deep-rooted historical reasons for the difference between North and South.

Putnam's overarching thesis is controversial, and yet few doubt but that there are a wide array of social attitudes and structures that are necessary to explain the North-South divide. Underdeveloped, opposed to unification, resistant to what they perceived as the invaders coming from the North, the South was to provide the greatest socioeconomic challenges to the Italian political and economic system throughout its 150 years of existence. As of 2010, some southern regions still display record-high levels of unemployment and poverty, also as a consequence of an ineffective use of European structural funds. Moreover, the South never completely reconciled with state authority; hence the great success of monarchical parties for as long as two decades after the birth of the republic, and the success of criminal organizations (like the Sicilian Mafia) that still hamper the legitimacy of state institutions in vast areas of the country. The fact that the South has become, after the political crisis of the 1990s, the most volatile area when election time comes, adds further significance to this question.

The Many Pathologies of the Italian First Republic

The defining characteristics of the Italian state during the first decades after unification were the distinguishing features of the First Italian Republic as well. Between the birth of the republic (1946) and the fall of the Berlin Wall (1989), Italian politics was marked by significant continuities with the prewar regimes. Little or no alternation between left and right took place. Governments were weak because of the many constraints aimed at avoiding the resurgence of Fascism. Consensual rules were built in order to tame radicalization. All this, together with the legacies of *trasformismo* and the increasing public resources available with the "economic miracle" of the 1960s meant that the pathologies mentioned at the outset of this chapter came to affect Italian politics even more pervasively once democratization finally took hold.

Changes in government were limited to a restricted alternation between partners of the predominant Christian party (Christian Democrats, henceforth DC), which was *always* in government and which, until 1981, *always* selected the (many) prime ministers from among its ranks. Meanwhile, the political system included antisystem parties ranging from the PCI on the left to the neo-Fascist Italian Social Movement (MSI) on the extreme right. This meant that the DC faced opposition on both sides of the left-right political spectrum seeking to challenge its hegemonic control over the center. It also meant that the ideological distance (or polarization) between left and right was great and that competition for votes was centrifugal and so kept the ideologies apart. Hence Italy was a textbook case of what Italian political scientist Giovanni Sartori described as "polarized pluralism"—pluralist because of the many political movements it included and yet polarized because these movements actively opposed each other as well as the governing majority and so resisted consensus.[9]

The polarization worked within as well as between the left and right of the political spectrum. The left camp was divided between the socialists (PSI, Italian Socialist Party) and the PCI (see table 4.1). Until it condemned the USSR's invasion of Hungary in 1956, the PSI was still an orthodox Marxist party. On the extreme right, the MSI had to contend with the monarchists. As a consequence, the first general elections in the republic saw the antisystem (or antidemocratic) forces win almost as many seats as the prodemocracy moderates. These divisions had a regional dimension to them as well. Data from the 1946 referendum on the form of state (monarchical or republican) reveal that behind an overall 54.3 percent in favor of the republic, as many as 85 percent of the voters supported change in the northern Trento Province as contrasted with as few as 23.5 percent in southern Campania. Finally, there was the overarching context of the

Table 4.1 Italy's First Republic National Election (Votes [v] and seats [s]) for main parties, 1946–1992

	Left Others[a]	PCI[b]	Rad/Gre[c]	PSI[d]	PSDI	DC	PRI	PLI	MSI	Mon/LN[e]	Others
1946 (v)	–	18.9	–	20.7	–	35.2	4.4	6.8	–	8.0	6.0
1946 (s)	–	18.7	–	20.7	–	37.2	4.1	7.4	–	8.3	3.6
1948 (v)	–	31.0	–		7.1	48.5	2.5	2.0	6.6	2.4	
1948 (s)	–	31.9	–		5.7	53.1	1.6	1.0		0.9	
1953 (v)	–	22.6	–	12.7	4.5	40.1	1.6	3.0	5.8	6.8	2.8
1953 (s)	–	24.2	–	12.7	3.2	44.6	0.8	2.2	4.9	6.8	0.5
1958 (v)	–	22.7	–	14.2	4.6	42.4	1.4	3.5	4.8	4.9	1.6
1958 (s)	–	23.5	–	14.1	3.7	45.8	1.3	2.9	4.0	4.2	0.5
1963 (v)	–	25.3	–	13.8	6.1	38.3	1.4	7.0	5.1	1.7	1.3
1963 (s)	–	26.3	–	13.8	5.2	41.3	1.0	6.2	4.3	1.3	0.6
1968 (v)	4.4	26.9	–	14.5		39.1	2.0	5.8	4.4	1.3	1.5
1968 (s)	3.7	28.1	–	14.4		42.2	1.4	4.9	3.8	1.0	0.5
1972 (v)	1.9	27.2	–	9.6	5.1	38.7	2.9	3.9	8.7	–	2.1
1972 (s)	0.0	28.4	–	9.7	4.6	42.2	2.4	3.2	8.9	–	0.6
1976 (v)	1.5	34.4	1.1	9.6	3.4	38.7	3.1	1.3	6.1	–	0.8
1976 (s)	1.0	36.0	0.6	9.0	2.4	41.7	2.2	0.8	5.6	–	0.6
1979 (v)	1.4	30.4	3.4	9.8	3.8	38.3	3.0	1.9	5.3	–	2.6
1979 (s)	1.0	31.9	2.9	9.8	3.2	41.6	2.5	1.4	4.8	–	1.0
1983 (v)	1.5	29.9	2.2	11.4	4.1	32.9	5.1	2.9	6.8	–	3.2
1983 (s)	1.1	31.4	1.7	11.6	3.7	35.7	4.6	2.5	6.7	–	1.0
1987 (v)	1.7	26.6	5.1	14.3	3.0	34.3	3.7	2.1	5.9	0.5	3.0
1987 (s)	1.3	28.1	4.1	14.9	2.7	37.1	3.3	1.7	5.6	0.2	1.0
1992 (v)	5.6	16.1 PDS	5.9	13.6	2.7	29.7	4.4	2.9	5.4	8.7	5.1
1992 (s)	5.6	17.0	5.6	14.6	2.5	32.7	4.3	2.7	5.4	8.7	1.0

a Sin = Vari di sinistra. Nel 1968 Psiup, nel 1976, 1983 e 1987 Dp, nel 1979 Pdup, nel 1992 Prc.

b PDS = Democratic Party of the Left, which was the new name for the PCI after 1992.

c R/V = Radicals until 1983, 1987 Greens + Radicals (separate parties); 1992 same parties plus the Network (la Rete).

d 1968 PSU, where PSI and PSDI had merged.

e 1948 Uomo Qualunque; 1948–1968 Monarchists, different labels; as of 1987 Lega lombarda/Lega Nord.

(Source: Istituto Cattaneo.)

Cold War. After Prime Minister Alcide De Gasperi's visit to the United States in 1947, the PCI was permanently excluded from government—a pattern only partly mitigated by the party's presence in the local government of important towns in the so-called Red Area (such as Florence and Bologna) and, after the late birth of regional institutions in 1970, at the leadership of regional governments in this same area. This Cold War dimension quickly permeated the whole structure of political competition, with the result that a communist-anticommunist cleavage soon overshadowed the more traditional left-right dimension. This can be seen by looking at the very polarized 1948 elections, when the DC and the Popular Front (a coalition of PCI and PSI) fought a harsh battle featuring apocalyptic propaganda.

The institutions of the First Republic took shape before this freezing of political alternatives. As mentioned earlier, the consensus underpinning these new institutions was dominated by (and limited to) the fear of Fascism and the desire to prevent the reemergence of a tyrant like Benito Mussolini. Hence, the Constitution of the Italian Republic included a panoply of liberal mechanisms (such as a broad array of entrenched civil and social rights, a president of the republic with significant powers, and an independent judiciary) aimed at constraining the executive in favor of strengthening the role of parliament. Similar checks and balances operated within the parliament as well, in the form of three broad procedural principles. First, the parliament provided a "parity norm" protecting the relative positions of all political actors based on both their proportional representation of the electorate and very consensual rules of procedure. Second, the parliament placed both the upper and lower chambers (the Senate and the Chamber of Deputies) on equal footing in a form of balanced bicameralism that remains unique among advanced industrial democracies. Third, the parliamentary structures were built on a broader logic of "institutional polycentrism," which creates many different and at times even countervailing positions of power and influence. As a result, the PCI was able to play an active role in Italian political life at the national level despite the fact that it was perpetually excluded from participation in government.[10]

The combination of antifascism and bitter polarization explains why the institutions created during the democratization process became so entrenched. Institutions designed to prevent the emergence of a single powerful political force made it easy for multiple competing parties to protect themselves and so resist destruction. This was particularly the case for the electoral system—a very inclusive form of proportional representation—which, despite being written in statute and thus not part of the actual Constitution, soon became part and parcel of the Italian First Republic. Of course the DC had an interest in changing this situation given its hegemonic control of the political center. The problem was that it did not have the power to do so acting alone. Once the DC failed to nail down its parliamentary majority with a change in the electoral formula in the 1953 elections,[11] all political parties developed vested interests in

Table 4.2 Coalition Governance and Governments in Italy, 1948–2010

Legislative Term	Types/Phases of Coalition	Number of Governments	Average Duration of Governments (Days)	Prime Ministers*
I (1948–1953)	Centrism (golden age) DC, PSDI, PLI, PRI	3	613	De Gasperi
II (1953–1958)	Centrism (crisis, new stabilization)	6	278	De Gasperi; Pella, Fanfani, Scelba, Segni, Zoli
III (1958–1963)	Centrism (new crisis), preparation of center-left	5	341	Fanfani, Segni; Tambroni, Fanfani
IV (1963–1968)	Center-left (golden age: PSI enters)	4	431	Leone, Moro
V (1968–1972)	Center-left (crisis and new stabilization)	6	204	Leone, Rumor; Colombo, Andreotti
VI (1972–1976)	Centre-left (final crisis)	5	256	Andreotti, Rumor, Moro
VII (1976–1979)	National Solidarity	3	308	Andreotti

VIII (1979–1983)	*Preparation of five-party formula (DC, PSI, PRI, PSDI, PLI)*	6	203	Cossiga, Forlani, Spadolini (PRI), Fanfani
IX (1983–1987)	*Five-party (golden age)*	3	429	Craxi (PSI), Fanfani
X (1987–1992)	*Five-party (renegotiation, new stabilization and new crisis)*	4	405	Goria, De Mita, Andreotti
XI (1992–1994)	*End of five-party formula and technocratic government*	2	280	Amato (PSI), Ciampi (technocrat)
XII (1994–1996)	*Centre-right attempt and technocratic government*	2	311	Berlusconi, Dini (technocrat)
XIII (1996–2001)	*Center-left*	4	450	Prodi, D'Alema, Amato
XIV (2001–2006)	*Center-right*	2	1,092	Berlusconi
XV (2006–2008)	*Center-left*	1	722	Prodi
XVI (2008–)	*Center-right*	1	-	Berlusconi

* Until 1992: all DC members unless otherwise indicated
(*Source*: adapted and updated from Cotta and Verzichelli, 2007, pp. 111–112.)

maintaining PR as the status quo. Indeed, PR soon developed as the best guarantee for sharing the spoils in government—which all of the main parties but the PCI and MSI were to enter—as well as gaining access to seats in parliament and control over regional or local executives for the PCI.

The DC may have failed to reshape the electoral arena to ensure a permanent majority, but it nevertheless managed to get a strong hold on the economy. This colonization of state resources by the DC operated first through the holding companies left over from Fascism and then reached its peak in the 1950s, with the creation of ENI (Ente Nazionale Idrocarburi, the state-controlled energy conglomerate); the Cassa per il Mezzogiorno (a development aid agency for the South); and the Ministry of State participation, which the party always kept for itself until the 1980s. At the same time, the DC was able to influence and exploit interest groups and public administration for its own benefit. This meant that the governing parties (meaning the DC and its ever-widening circle of allies) were eager to hold strict control over appointments. Nevertheless, because the lack of alternation weakened lines of accountability, the governing parties maintained a more tenuous control over policymaking (which was often dictated by long-term civil servants).

Political parties controlled the institutions of the First Republic, and they also managed to dominate civil society.[12] In part this was due to the role of the parties as agents of political socialization. In their polarized and clientelistic competition with one another, the parties failed to play any integrative role across society as a whole and thus jeopardized the development of social capital and the recognition of civic responsibilities.[13] Party system stability—and the "unstable stability" format that came to be associated with Italian governments more generally—was also built on very stable patterns of electoral behavior, whose determinants were not easily captured by traditional cleavages such as class or religion.

In fact, territory was very important at least for two of the three categories of voting identified in the mid-1970s as the bases of party-voters' linkages: belonging, exchange, and opinion.[14] In some parts of the country, for example, partisan identification was socially embedded in regional subcultures. This social embeddedness was most obvious in the areas where the two main parties—DC and PCI—managed to aggregate and mediate interests by exploiting cooperative social networks and high levels of social capital. The DC predominated in the northeast with Trentino-Alto Adige, Friuli-Venezia Giulia, and Veneto; the PCI controlled the center-north with Emilia-Romagna, Tuscany, and Umbria, as well as the northern province of Marche. In this way, a "vote of belonging" to the subculture of the region also reflected the voter's long-standing affective loyalty to the party concerned (estimated to still be typical of a majority of voters at the end of the 1980s).

Elsewhere in the country, local ties hindered the politicization of the center-periphery cleavage. This was particularly important in Sicily and across the

South. Hence the few existing regionalist parties developed in the rich northern areas of Valle d'Aosta or Alto Adige and in Sardinia, even though Sardinian nationalism had never presented a problem. Meanwhile, the South developed as a crucial basin for the DC vote, as well as an area where "exchange" voting—meaning votes cast in return for the satisfaction of a need or in return for the meeting of a particular interest—was more developed. By contrast, "opinion" voting, where voters cast their ballots based on a pragmatic evaluation of the competing party platforms, was much less in evidence.

The postelectoral nature of Italian governments was broadly consistent with these patterns of electoral choice. Instead of being determined by results at the polls, the composition of Italian governments soon came to be dictated by factional agreements within the DC or between the DC and its allies. This factional dominance over government composition was only reinforced once PR was introduced as the internal rule in DC party congresses in the early 1960s. The result was a degenerative pathology of spoils divisions among the different *capi-corrente* (chiefs of factions), who numbered twelve at the peak of the factionalization process in the early 1980s. With a system frozen along stable partisan lines and the PCI permanently excluded from power, the first unanticipated election only took place in 1972. Despite Italy's reputation for weak and changeable governments, all previous parliaments had been able to complete their full legislative terms.[15]

The combination of polarization and an absence of left-right alternation affected Italy's international status as well as its political performance throughout the First Republic. Italy has traditionally been described as "the least of the great powers" or "the largest of the smaller powers."[16] This reputation is not for want of ambition. Because of its geographical location, Italy always cultivated a Mediterranean vocation. It also laid claim to an early Atlantic affiliation. Nevertheless, the facts that Italy was always changing its alliances during the wars, that the Iron Curtain had its southwesternmost border in Trieste (where Italy contended with Yugoslavia), and that Italy hosted the largest communist party in Western Europe all meant that the United States never regarded Italy as an easy or reliable ally. Moreover, any American suspicion of Italy was more than reciprocated by Italians looking at the United States. Anti-Americanism was not just strong inside the two antisystem forces, PCI and MSI, but also in the PSI—at least until Hungary's invasion in 1956—and, throughout the First Republic, inside a sizeable component of the Catholic world, including the leadership of the DC itself.

Italy was among the founding signatory countries of both the NATO and EEC treaties (the latter having been launched in Messina in 1955 and signed in Rome in 1957). However, neither choice was noncontentious. In the 1950s, some DC leaders such as Giuseppe Dossetti and Giorgio La Pira were hostile to NATO membership (and president of the republic Giovanni Gronchi arguably cultivated "micro-Gaullist" aspirations at the turn of the 1960s), not to mention the more natural hostility displayed by the PCI until the 1970s. Indeed, when PCI party leader Enrico Berlinguer, on the eve of his party's best-ever electoral result, declared that he felt safe under the NATO umbrella (1976), hostility within the PCI toward Europe had already been significantly reduced. Of course European integration was somewhat easier to accept than NATO because of the spread of Euro-communism in the 1970s—not to mention the fact that one of Europe's founding fathers, Altiero Spinelli, was elected as an independent on the PCI ticket in the first European elections of 1979.

Outside the domain of the communists, attitudes toward Europe were mixed. De Gasperi was a convinced Europeanist, as were most of the members of his centrist governments. For its part, public opinion was distant but positive about EEC membership. Nevertheless, much of the political class was only lukewarm. For them, "Brussels was considered a sort of exile from the delicious intrigues and power-brokering of Montecitorio" (the location of parliament in Rome).[17] Suffice it to mention here the fact that the first Italian to be nominated president of the European Commission, the Christian Democrat Franco Maria Malfatti, in 1970, left his post after less than two years in order to take part in the Italian general elections of 1972.

Despite the mixed emotions shared between Italy and the United States, Italy has long been an American semiprotectorate. The country was protected in its strategic affiliation with NATO during the Cold War, but was also a democracy that enjoyed full sovereignty (despite frequent claims that Italian sovereignty was actually still limited).[18] So if protection meant interference in domestic affairs, this did not affect day-to-day politics in the Italo-American relationship. Indeed, both sides were quickly able to overcome significant moments of tension. Hence, U.S. administrations accepted the PSI's entry into government in the early 1960s. By the same token, the Sigonella incident (1985), when PSI party leader and prime minister Bettino Craxi refused the request of U.S. president Ronald Reagan to extradite the hijackers of the cruise ship *Achille Lauro*, should not be read as a sign of anti-Americanism. Rather, it was part of an attempt to raise Italian international status above its low profile. This episode, at the same time, was just part of a patchwork of Italian ambiguities—from Enrico Mattei's ENI Middle East policy in the late 1950s to the convention that saw for many years the cohabitation of a pro-Israeli and a pro-Palestine politician balancing Italian foreign policy in the Ministry of Foreign Affairs and the Ministry of Defense, or vice versa.

Therefore one can argue that during the Cold War, Italy was at the same time firmly located on the Western side and was perceived as a kind of unfaithful ally, to be watched carefully both for its delicate geopolitical position, for the underlying strength of anti-American sentiments inside both predominant Italian political cultures (Catholic and Marxist), and for some recurrent anomalies like those mentioned above. At the same time, one can argue that both NATO and the EEC, together with the Vatican just a few hundred meters from the loci of power—the office of the prime minister (Palazzo Chigi), the houses of parliament (Montecitorio), and the office of the president (Quirinale)—framed Italian political life during the First Republic. Once the First Republic was over, former president of the republic Francesco Cossiga articulated this point at its best: "[During the First Republic] we had compulsory constraints: our military policy was based on NATO, our economic policy was that of the EEC, our ideology was that of the Church. At most we could take some break, thanks to the strategic security guaranteed from the outside."[19]

To sum up, the First Republic was a dysfunctional system. Political parties dominated the public sphere by exploiting the weakness of the state to their own benefit. This colonization of state institutions by political parties had particularly negative consequences in the South, where distrust vis-à-vis the state was traditionally higher, and where clienteles were built upon state-dependent beneficiaries like public officials and state-subsidized business to such an extent that borders between local control of the "exchange vote" and highly successful criminal organizations such as the Sicilian Mafia, Campania's Camorra, and Calabria's 'Ndrangheta became more and more blurred. Lack of alternation meant also that parties did not compete on substantive programmatic issues. This, combined with factionalized control over government composition—and therefore a substantial lack of direct accountability to the voter—meant that parties in government could use public resources without restraint, thus fueling public debt. Rather, competition was often centered on micropolicies, such as those linked to patronage and the control of preference voting. Indeed, while preference voting gave the appearance of creating more direct popular influence on the political process, it actually became the main mechanism through which party factions could prosper and cultivate their slice of the pie.

Toward a Second Republic?

In the early 1990s, Italy underwent one of the most dramatic transitions that any Western European democracy has experienced in the last sixty years, with the possible exception of France in 1958. Indeed, at its height there was doubt as to whether Italian democracy had the capacity to survive. The crisis was all the more dramatic because it came after the decade during which the five-party formula (*pentapartito*, see table 4.2) saw the extension of *partitocrazia* (or party dominance over state institutions and resources) to its greatest extent. Meanwhile, the political parties ignored important signs of popular discontent and a burgeoning public debt (which would soon reach 100 percent of the country's gross domestic product, or GDP).[20] They also ignored a series of crucial events that set the stage for the transformation of the system (see box 4.1).

And yet, almost twenty years later, many of the problems that brought down the First Republic (and that weakened the Italian state throughout its ex-

> ## Box 4.1   The Crisis of the First Republic (Chronology)
>
> **November 1989:** fall of the Berlin Wall. This event took by surprise the PCI. Party leader Achille Occhetto announced a change in party brand just a few days after the wall fell. But this left the activists puzzled as to where the newly branded Democrats of the Left (PDS, born in 1991) was going, triggering a split of Re-founded Communists and significant electoral backlashes in 1992.
>
> **May 1990:** regional elections. Umberto Bossi's Lombard League, to be merged in the Northern League the following year, becomes the second most voted party in Lombardy, the richest and most populated Italian region.
>
> **June 1991:** referendum on single preference vote. Despite invitations from both governing parties to boycott the poll (especially PSI party leader Bettino Craxi who suggested that voters should go the beaches instead of voting), and the Northern League not to go to the polls, 65 percent of Italians do go, and 91 percent of the voters approve change. By cutting "exchange vote" practices by the different chiefs of party factions, the referendum was meant to be a proxy for a change toward majoritarianism, and popular pressure for reform mounted significantly as a consequence of the referendum's success.
>
> **February 1992:** numerous changes. In Maastricht, Giulio Andreotti signs the new treaty. A week after, the Milanese PSI Mario Chiesa is arrested in Milan: it is the first of a long series of arrests in the judicial investigations of *mani pulite*, "clean hands," which will decapitate the governing parties.

istence) remain unresolved. It is undeniable that Italy has made great strides in the struggle against criminal organizations, that an increase in the apparent stability of the government has come about, and that progress has been made in many other sectors as well. Nevertheless, international agencies such as Transparency International and Freedom House,[21] in their 2009–2010 reports, still express concern about the level of corruption (specifically about Prime Minister Silvio Berlusconi's conflicts of interest). Meanwhile, major newspapers and magazines like the *Financial Times*, the *New York Times*, and the *Economist* editorialize about the poor state of Italian democracy. Why did the removal of the political class (an impressive 44 percent turnover in parliament took place in 1994), which had been responsible for perpetuating many of the pathologies of the First Republic, not usher in a period of more "normal" politics? Why did the reform of electoral institutions fail to foster a stable pattern of left-right competition based on normal alternations of the political parties in power? And why did the exposure of corruption at all levels of government not pave the way for a brand new and more legitimate political system based on transparency and accountability to take its place?

Several intertwined factors are necessary to consider in understanding why it is still difficult to talk today of a "Second Republic." Of these, three deserve particular attention: the nature of the transition, the incomplete process of institutional reform, and the shortcomings of both coalitions, represented on one side by the near total dominance of Silvio Berlusconi and on the other side by the chronic incapacity of the center-left to build a credible alternative.

European pressures significantly helped Italy to build up a more solid economy. As early as 1987, for example, Italians were able to celebrate the fact that their economy had overtaken that of the United Kingdom in size. Even today, when the United Kingdom has regained its position, there are important measures where the Italian economy performs better.[22] That said, the transition was more about politics than economics, and it was driven by domestic rather than European forces. In that context, the changes that were wrought were ambivalent. Hence, while the judicial inquiries of 1992–1993 were mainly driven by the noble aims of tackling unbearable levels of corruption, they also significantly contributed to the reinforcement of antipolitical attitudes within the electorate that would never completely disappear in the following years.

The point here is not that the judicial inquiries should not have taken place. No one can seriously deny the need to put a halt to the endemic system of corruption built during the First Republic. Rather, it is to suggest that they had unintended political consequences as well as intended ones. The depoliticization (or, better, disillusionment) of the electorate was one consequence; the politicization of the judiciary was another. Once the trials started to be televised and some prosecutors made exaggerated use of instruments such as preventive incarceration, the stage was set for the activity of the magistrates to be politicized even further by a master of communication like then media magnate, now prime minister, Silvio Berlusconi. After entering politics by firmly supporting the judges' initiatives—and unsuccessfully courting also one of the most famous of them, Antonio Di Pietro, who later went on to build his own personal party in the center-left camp (Italy of Values)—Berlusconi was able to use his own media empire to turn public opinion against the judges. He was also able to deflect public attention away from the spread of corruption, which was to remain very high throughout the following years.[23] Finally, once his own media empire was made the subject of judicial inquiries, Berlusconi was able to denounce these judicial actions as politically motivated as well. Of course Berlusconi was not the author of this whole state of affairs. The politicization of the judiciary and the spread of corruption after the fall of the First Republic was also a consequence of the lack of intervention by successive governments, which did nothing to shore up the very precarious state of the Italian justice system.[24] Nevertheless, Berlusconi was certainly a willing protagonist.

In other words, judicial investigations, while contributing decisively to the collapse of the old party system, contributed also to the rise of a populist mood, which created the best conditions for Berlusconi's rise and success. The point to note, however, is that Berlusconi was not alone. He was well positioned, particularly given his domination over the media, which ably captured and led the cultural change toward consumerism already present since the 1980s. But he also depended on allies. Berlusconi's populist campaign complemented the Northern League's (LN) federalist message against centralized control by the national government in Rome over the regions, and against the use of public resources (including tax revenues raised in the North) to subsidize the South. Berlusconi was also able to grant legitimacy to right-wing sentiments that had long been confined to a neo-Fascist ghetto. While Umberto Bossi's LN clearly benefited from the collapse of the DC, as the geography of its vote strikingly confirms,[25] Gianfranco Fini's MSI,[26] later renamed the National Alliance (AN), needed Berlusconi's support to escape what remained of the anti-Fascist consensus. Berlusconi, Bossi, and Fini are all new players who have grown to prominence only since the fall of the First Republic (and arguably because of it). This is an undeniable change in Italian politics. Nevertheless, the fact that these same three leaders are still leading their own personal political parties some seventeen years later suggests the emergence of new, unintended, and problematic patterns.

Party System Change, Electoral and Institutional Reforms

Italy is the only European democracy to have voted with three significantly different electoral systems in the past twenty years. Yet discussions on electoral reform still loom large at the end of 2010. Why is this the case? The answer can be found in a combination of ineffective reforms and the absence of instruments that can complement electoral laws in sectors such as rules regarding parliamentary group affiliations and party finance. Moreover, political competition seems now to center on yet another all-Italian cleavage. It is not communist versus anticommunist as it was during much of the Cold War; rather it is Berlusconi, for and against.

Both electoral reforms, which took place in 1993 and 2005, were driven by partisan aims. At the time of the first reform, however, political parties were experiencing the harshest moments of the judicial investigations. In the space of a few months, governing parties were decapitated, and more than half of the MPs were investigated. They also faced the outcome of a popular referendum in April 1993 on the abolition of PR, which showed the extent of support for such a change. Nevertheless, they managed not to lose complete control of the electoral reform process. Instead of moving toward a single-round, first-past-the-post system like that used in the United Kingdom, or a two-round plurality system like that used in France, they set up a mixed-member majoritarian system (MMM), which worked through various and very intricate devices to mitigate the majoritarian effect of the single-member districts. Arguably, either a first-past-the-post system or a two-round plurality system would have done away with the country's tradition for polarized pluralism by forcing the parties into a more clearly bipolar left-right division. Not only would this simplify choices for the voters, but it would ensure some alternation between government and opposition as well. A mixed-member majoritarian system had no such clear-cut implications. In that sense, adoption of MMM conflicted with the referendum movement which, albeit divided between proponents of single- and double-round options, had attracted significant support in its campaign for a change in electoral institutions that could drive Italy closer to other large-state patterns of party-system simplification and bipolar alternation.

This victory of the parties over the reform movement is all the more surprising given that, while almost all political parties of the First Republic disappeared in 1992, the old communist left suddenly found its position improved. The party changed names from the PCI to the Democratic Party of the Left (PDS) just before the judicial earthquake (in 1991 rather than 1992). Moreover, since the old PCI had not been involved in government outside a few regions, it was correspondingly less involved in the judicial investigations into corruption in office. Hence, at the end of 1993, the new PDS could face the prospect of an easy win in the forthcoming 1994 elections, to be fought under the new electoral law. It should have been in the interest of the PDS to embrace and not water down a majoritarian electoral system. Moreover, that interest should have been mirrored on the center-right because it is at this point that Berlusconi entered the field of Italian politics with his Forza Italia (Go Italy) and swept the board.[27] If only the picture were that simple.

In fact, Berlusconi's first victory was built on heterogeneous alliances in different parts of the country. In the North, Berlusconi relied on the Northern League; in the South, he depended on the MSI. Indeed, his dependence on the support of these groups was such that the government he formed lasted less than seven months, as a consequence of the Northern League's defection. In turn, this made it possible for the center-left to achieve victory in the following 1996 elections, with Romano Prodi's Olive Tree coalition. Once again, however, the coalition depended on the goodwill of smaller parties, and as a consequence the Prodi government lasted only two years. At the end of the Prodi government, the Italian political system moved even further from the majoritarian bipolar ideal. For the first (and so far only) time in Italian history, a government fell on a lost-confidence vote, and a new executive was formed, mainly thanks to the defections of some centrist MPs elected in 1996 as part of the center-right. Massimo D'Alema became prime minister in a new PDS-dominated government, not as an expression of alternation, but in a new form of *trasformismo* for a new age.

This episode marked a significant departure from the spirit, if not the letter, of the 1993 electoral law. Although it is not uncommon for a British or French government to change without elections when one prime minister agrees (or

Box 4.2   Silvio Berlusconi: A Very Peculiar Politician

Silvio Berlusconi is no average politician. As of 2010, he is the third richest man in Italy. His personal fortune includes assets in the fields of television, newspapers, publishing, cinema, finance, banking, insurance, and sports. Indeed he became known to the public in the 1980s, when he took over AC Milan, making it one of the most successful football teams in Europe. Craxi's support was instrumental in assuring that his television stations could compete against public TV: in 1984, the so-called Berlusconi decree overcame the Constitutional Court ban on Berlusconi's private broadcasting, which was broadcasting at the national level rather than by using local frequencies, as the law prescribed at the time. "Dear Bettino, my warmest thanks for what you did. I know it's not been easy and that you've had to spend all your authority and credibility to get this through," quoted in G. D'Avanzo, "Il Psi, il governo, Tangentopoli: ecco le carte dell'archivio Craxi," *La Repubblica*, December 6, 2007. In 1990, the Mammì law effectively sanctioned what was to become the Berlusconi-owned Mediaset and public RAI's TV duopoly. Since the RAI has always been politicized, once Berlusconi entered Palazzo Chigi, this meant that most of the media were biased in his favor. Berlusconi's judicial problems included a number of inquiries on embezzlement, tax evasion, false accounting, bribery of judges, and corruption. Some trials were dropped because of statutory limitations for the prosecution of past crimes, he was acquitted for other crimes, and a law proposing his immunity while in power still remains a major bone of contention at the start of 2011.

accepts) to stand down as leader of their party so that another can take his or her place—as with Margaret Thatcher and John Major in 1990 or Tony Blair and Gordon Brown in 2007—D'Alema's replacement of Prodi was nothing of the sort. Although they belonged to the same coalition, D'Alema controlled a political party, and Prodi arguably did not. More importantly, the contest between them had little to do with who was strong within the coalition and much to do with who could be convinced to cross the aisle. In that sense, the change in government was an attempt to restore the primacy of parties over coalitions, as well as a gamble on the idea that a new political center could be created that could monopolize the representation of the Catholic electorate. With hindsight, this political maneuver inadvertently delayed the formation of a party that could effectively compete against Berlusconi. The quest for a new hegemonic center drew attention away from the necessity of merging the remnants of the Catholic and communist cultures in a united party of the center-left and instead perpetuated a climate within which Catholics and communists continue to wrestle with one another for control.

Therefore, the first two elections with the new system saw the repetition of patterns commonly associated with the First Republic: the average cabinet duration was only slightly longer, *trasformismo* continued to be practiced, and the party system remained fragmented. In addition, the failure of two further referenda in 1999 and 2000[28] fostered the idea that electoral reform had failed in rationalizing the political system along a pattern of party system simplification and bipolar alternation. Worse, it may even have fueled the (underlying) idea that it would be better to switch back to PR. This is essentially what happened in the electoral reform of 2005. Although, this being Italy, it happened in a very peculiar way.

Before briefly sketching out the many faults of the current law, it is important to explain how the electoral system used in the 1994, 1996, and 2001 elections diluted the pressure to create a simplified bipolar party system. From a strict majoritarian perspective, the MMM law clearly had many flaws. Among them, the use of cross-party endorsements of candidacies within coalitions inside the single-member districts had the effect of fostering, instead of curbing, the fragmentation of the party system. All small parties had to do was convince the rest of the coalition of their essential worth and then rely on cross-endorsements from their coalition partners to ensure that they held on to a negotiated number of safe seats on the center-left or center-right. Indeed, this practice was carried out to such an extent that a new all-Italian category of "fragmented bipolarism" has been invented to describe the new party system that resulted.[29]

Moreover, this new fragmented bipolar system behaved somewhat differently from the polarized pluralism of the First Republic, during which each party made up its own parliamentary group. Indeed, and oddly given the expressed desire of the electorate to create incentives for simplification, the rules regulating party groups in parliament were not reformed from the First Republic to the Second Republic. Hence, while parties forged coalitions during elections, they operated as free agents once in parliament. This effectively created two different party systems: one operating at the electoral level, which could appear simplified at first sight, but a different one, much more fragmented, operating in parliament. Moreover, party finance regulation was reformed in the opposite direction, in such a way as to facilitate party proliferation by progressively lowering the thresholds for access to reimbursements and refunds. Indeed, party finance regulations make it so easy to gain support that even parties outside parliament, and indeed in some cases barely existing, manage to get funds from the state.[30]

The 2005 reform, in its turn, did not affect these two crucial elements—meaning the independence of parties once in parliament and in terms of party finances. Almost fifteen years after the beginning of efforts to promote a bipolar political arena, popular interest in using electoral rules to help engineer a more simplified party system had faded. Hence, the way was clear for parties to reform the system to their own advantage: the center-right decided to act after their defeat in the 2005 regional elections and facing increasingly negative opinion polls in anticipation of the 2006 general election. The law drafted by the center-right government extended the principle of an "adjusted-bonus" form of proportional representation to the national level. This principle already operated at all the lower territorial levels of government (meaning for the election of the regional, provincial, and municipal councils) in order to provide a seat bonus to the winning list or coalition (subject to complicated thresholds) to ensure that the winning group received a workable majority.[31] The main effect was to create two catchall coalitions, one on the center-right and one on the center-left (see table 4.2). In this context, the return of Romano Prodi in 2006 at the head of a center-left government was mainly due to an anti-Berlusconi appeal rather than to the presence of a coherent coalition capable of governing for a full term.

Arguably, the 2005 electoral reform contained provisions that greatly strengthened the control of the political parties over the whole of the system. Among these, the most important was the introduction of blocked lists through which the party leadership can determine who is likely to receive a seat in parliament and who is not. As an instrument for creating discipline within the party, such lists clearly reinforce the lines of authority from the top down. It is small wonder, therefore, that they have become the object of some of the harshest protests from antipolitics movements such as satirist Beppe Grillo's "five-star movement." Of course, blocked lists are not unique to Italy and can be found in the electoral laws of other countries such as Spain. Nevertheless, in the Italian case, blocked lists meant that parties regained complete freedom of choice in the candidate selection process. In turn, they used this freedom to return to parliament many party professionals, in a very autoreferential pattern.

More generally, the inertia against reforming rules on party finance and parliamentary groups comes from the very nature of party-political competition. As Luciano Bardi explains, it emerges from

> the need of parties to maintain their individual identities and positions between elections so that they can negotiate candidatures for the next elections with coalition partners and, if need be, with the other side—producing individual party behavior that can be very damaging for coalition unity and, in the case of majority parties, for government stability. Such behavior is very difficult to eradicate as it can give strategically well-placed parties a dual advantage: a bonus in terms of seats in the electoral party system and another in the form of committee and cabinet positions in the parliamentary/governmental system.[32]

In other words, the rules for party organization and electoral competition are now mutually reinforcing, and the effects of that reinforcement can be seen in the behavior and preferences of those politicians who must take responsibility for any future reform.

There is a way out of this negative equilibrium. At the end of 2007, the prospects for party system change increased as a consequence of the initiative of the former mayor of Rome, Walter Veltroni. Veltroni became the leader of the newly founded (and much-awaited) Democratic Party toward the end of 2007. This party brought together the two main center-left parties, Left Democrats (DS) and the more centrist Daisy (Margherita). Unfortunately, however, the formation of the Democratic Party had the unintended consequence of undermining the already precarious coalition supporting the Prodi government. The election of Veltroni as the first Democratic Party leader weakened and delegitimated Prodi's leadership of the coalition. And, on the other side of the political spectrum, it triggered an analogous streamlining process among the parties of the center-right, which led to the formation of the People of Freedom (PDL) by Berlusconi (later reluctantly joined by Fini).

The consequences were mixed. Prodi's government fell in 2008, which led to early parliamentary elections. Nevertheless, those elections did bring about a significant simplification of the Italian party system. The radical left was out of parliament, the Union of Center (UDC) barely entered, and Berlusconi had a strong majority and a two-party coalition. Given that this occurred under extremely unfavorable electoral institutions, should we conclude that Italy has finally arrived at a stable bipolar arrangement?

The answer is clearly no. On September 29, 2010, which was also the day of his seventy-fourth birthday, Berlusconi won a confidence vote in the Chamber of Deputies, thanks only to the support of the newly formed group of Future and Freedom, Futuro e Libertà (FLI). This group is led by the president of the chamber, Gianfranco Fini. Fini was Berlusconi's longtime ally and a cofounder of his People of Freedom party. Nevertheless, Fini had been expelled from Berlusconi's party two months earlier (and just over two years into the mandate for Berlusconi's center-right government). Despite the fact that Fini's new FLI supported the government in its confidence vote, the simple fact that the FLI exists suggests that Berlusconi might soon be forced to call early elections. Moreover, while it is likely that Fini hopes to build a new center-right more in line with European standards, which could free itself from the ubiquitous presence of Berlusconi's leadership, it is also obvious that Italian political institutions make it easier to carve out a small political party than to hold together a large one. The simplification apparent in the 2008–2010 government will most likely give way to another long period of fragmentation.

Politics in the Age of Berlusconi

On February 2011, a month before official celebrations of the 150th anniversary of the Italian state take place all over the country, the Northern League, currently the oldest political party—both inside and outside parliament—celebrates its twentieth birthday. All parties have changed, yet the political sys-

Figure 4.1 Parties and Electoral Alliances (1994–2010)

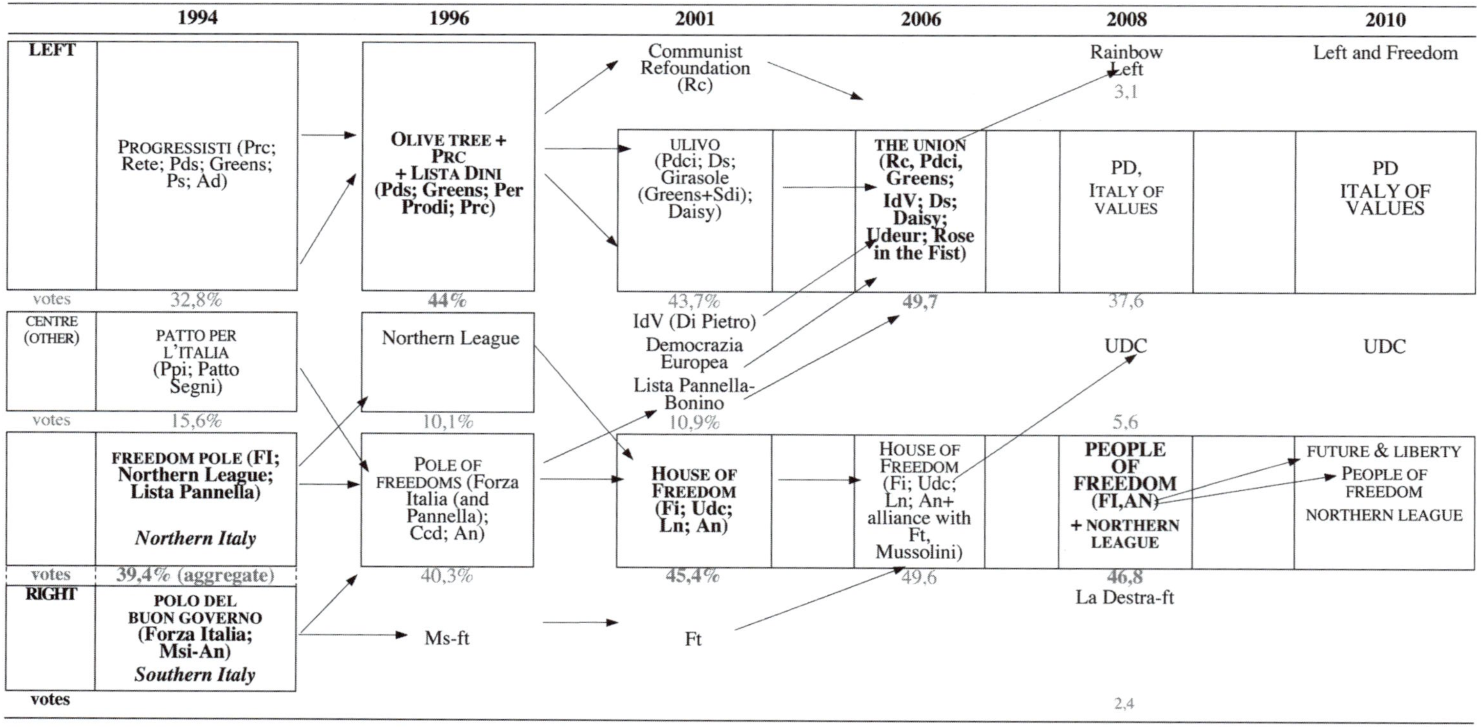

	1994	1996	2001	2006	2008	2010
LEFT	PROGRESSISTI (Prc; Rete; Pds; Greens; Ps; Ad)	**OLIVE TREE + PRC + LISTA DINI (Pds; Greens; Per Prodi; Pre)**	Communist Refoundation (Rc); ULIVO (Pdci; Ds; Girasole (Greens+Sdi); Daisy)	**THE UNION (Rc, Pdci, Greens; IdV; Ds; Daisy; L'deur; Rose in the Fist)**	Rainbow Left 3,1; PD, ITALY OF VALUES	Left and Freedom; PD ITALY OF VALUES
votes	32,8%	44%	43,7%	49,7	37,6	
CENTRE (OTHER)	PATTO PER L'ITALIA (Ppi; Patto Segni)	Northern League	IdV (Di Pietro) Democrazia Europea Lista Pannella-Bonino	UDC	UDC 5,6	UDC
votes	15,6%	10,1%	10,9%			
RIGHT	FREEDOM POLE (FI; Northern League; Lista Pannella) *Northern Italy*; POLO DEL BUON GOVERNO (Forza Italia; Msi-An) *Southern Italy*	Pole of Freedoms (Forza Italia (and Pannella); Ccd; An); Ms-ft	**HOUSE OF FREEDOM (FI; Udc; Ln; An)**; Ft	HOUSE OF FREEDOM (Fi; Udc; Ln; An+ alliance with Ft, Mussolini)	**PEOPLE OF FREEDOM (FI,AN) + NORTHERN LEAGUE**; La Destra-ft	FUTURE & LIBERTY; PEOPLE OF FREEDOM; NORTHERN LEAGUE
votes	39,4% (aggregate)	40,3%	45,4%	49,6	46,8	
votes					2,4	

tem as a whole still displays many continuities, the most important being the centrality of the North-South divide, which in itself explains the birth, success, and longevity of the League itself. Yet there are issues today that were unknown in the First Republic, immigration being a crucial case in point. From a country of emigration, in the last two decades Italy has become among the most common target of (mainly) low-skilled immigration, predominantly coming from Africa's northern shores and Eastern Europe.

One can argue that the League today enjoys a privileged position in the political system. Thanks to its successful campaign against immigration, the party has arguably contributed to a rising xenophobic tide in Italy. It is now more than a decade since accurate research confirmed that crimes such as drug dealing and trafficking, smuggling, and living off prostitution indeed have higher rates among immigrants.[33] However, media distortions have done much to fuel the perception that crime rates in the last decade or two are higher (which is not the case), specifically because of immigration (again, simplifying much more complicated trends). For instance, one should consider that after the murder of a woman by a Romanian citizen in Rome in October 2007, the powerful wave of hostility toward immigrants that followed was mainly goaded by hammering television coverage, unequaled in the months following the 2008 elections, which brought Berlusconi back to power. This is just one example of many that could be provided.[34]

The League's success has also brought about, since the mid-1990s, a new approach to federalism. While the introduction of direct elections for chief executives at all substate levels (starting in 1993 with communes and provinces, then in 1999 with regions) has generally been evaluated positively—despite the fact that the rhetoric of reform in some cases, such as Naples' alleged renaissance with Antonio Bassolino, could mislead public opinion on the real potential of a device like direct election—an enduring cultural shift took place in those same years, which still struggles, however, to find a practical solution. To put it briefly, if federalism was something still inconceivable both in the political class and among the electorate at the beginning of the 1990s, as that decade came to a close, almost all parties were supporting some kind of federalist option for Italy, including the MSI turned National Alliance, which in the First Republic had been the only nationalistic party. Temperate federalism was introduced by the center-left with a constitutional reform in 2001. However, the process was still incomplete and the party could still sustain federalism as its main programmatic point after the controversial 2005 constitutional reform (unilaterally and very controversially elaborated by Berlusconi's coalition) was rejected by a referendum in the wake of the 2006 elections. Today the League aims at introducing fiscal federalism, whose implementation, however, remains problematic, as it touches the still very sensitive pattern of the North-South divide.

The League also has many times displayed anti-EU attitudes, accusing the

EU of being a superstate, of not protecting citizens from the dangers of globalization, and of sponsoring Turkey's entry. Although Berlusconi supports Turkish membership in the EU, he has been much less euro friendly than the center-left, and with his unconditional support for George W. Bush's war against Iraq, he has stood firmly with the prowar axis including the UK, Spain, and some other East European countries, which contributed to important divisions inside the EU. However, despite some claims to the contrary, Italian international and European policies have seen a number of continuities in the pattern of alternation over the last fifteen years. Atlanticism and Europeanism should not be viewed as a zero-sum game.[35]

As of November 2010, the Northern League enjoys high popularity in opinion polls: Bossi, despite having signed, with Fini, the current legislation on immigration back in 2002, has been the staunchest proponent of early elections as a consequence of Fini's departure from the People of Liberty. One can argue that the LN, whose electorate is less educated and more sensitive to losing jobs and privileges from immigration and globalization, still enjoys to this day the privilege of being in power without being perceived as mainly responsible for its actions. The burden of responsibility is left to Berlusconi, the "almighty" leader, and his PDL. Yet the LN matters a lot for Berlusconi's fortunes. They not only support Berlusconi's government, but they also extend its reach into areas where Berlusconi himself cannot go. Bossi and his followers in the League often say things that, for the sake of political correctness, Berlusconi cannot say. Anti-immigrant rhetoric is only one such domain; there are many others. Indeed, it might even be possible to suggest that Berlusconi himself is a kind of *leghista* (or LN loyalist) in disguise.

Meanwhile, the center-left is trapped in the toxic mix created by Berlusconi's personality. In part this is due to the inability of the center-left to construct—and unite around—a credible alternative. Arguably, after forty years of a left divided by poisoned relations between PSI and PCI, with the communists denied power because of the radical nature of their ideology, Berlusconi's opponents are still fighting over the best strategy to follow in removing him from office. The center-left is also wary of promoting strong leaders, and it is slow to recognize the progressive personalization of modern politics. Hence, while Romano Prodi managed to construct coalitions to defeat Berlusconi in both of the elections he contested as leader of the center-left (1996 and 2006), Berlusconi has boasted (in 2010) of having "swallowed" as many as seven leaders of the center-left since 1994. The center-left has also failed to respond to the cultural dominance that Berlusconi has achieved through his control over the media. The solidity of Berlusconi's popularity has (so far) meant that he has been able to survive revelations about his behavior. Even the most damaging, such as allegations that some of his closest collaborators had relations with the Mafia both prior to and during Berlusconi's time as a politician, have left Berlusconi unscathed.

Berlusconi's dominance over the center-right and his splintering of the center-left means that the future of the political system depends in many ways on the future of the man himself. As Fini's departure from the PDL shows, the apparent simplification of Italian politics into a clear choice between right and left may soon come to an end. Indeed, the PDL practically does not exist as a party beyond Berlusconi's personal will, his personal wealth, and his proprietary control. Moreover, if there is no alternative to Berlusconi on the center-left, there is no alternative on the center-right either. Even Gianfranco Fini, who still aspires to be Berlusconi's successor despite having abandoned the PDL, carries a potentially fatal neo-Fascist legacy.[36]

All this means that today, despite the great rupture experienced in Italian politics twenty years ago, Italian problems should still be understood as a result of the combination of ineffective political institutions and a profound lack of civic culture and social capital, as much as fifty years ago—if not one hundred and fifty.[37] Economic progress and—more recently—party system change, have not done much to improve the overall state of the country. In every election but those of 2008, when the global economic crisis started to emerge, Berlusconi had promised a liberal revolution, to free enterprises from a baroque fiscal system, to foster public investment in infrastructure, and to invest in advanced technology. Yet not much has been done to overcome the structural weaknesses of the Italian economy, and long-term burdens, such as its shadow economy, still hamper any effective improvement.[38]

As in many other countries, Italian changes and continuities blend in an often inextricable way. Governments now tend to be stronger, although they are still affected by difficult coalition patterns and incessant parliamentary maneuvering. Italy's political crisis of the early 1990s reflected a cultural failure to develop institutions resting on universalistic values, above all those of efficiency and transparency in public life. The disintegration of this system has brought about new protagonists, but also a rather peculiar blend of old problems (weak identification in the institutions, a weak civic culture, and the enduring strength of the North-South divide) and new divisions, to the extent that today Italy is trapped in a pro-anti Berlusconi cleavage, and the political transition that started as many as twenty years ago still remains incomplete. One can only hope that once Berlusconi stands aside, the clock of politics will not turn back to 1993.

Suggested Readings

Cotta, Maurizio, and Luca Verzichelli, *Political Institutions in Italy*, Oxford: Oxford University Press, 2007.

Ginsborg, Paul, *Italy and Its Discontents, 1980–2001*, New York: Penguin, 2003.

Giuliani, Marco, and Erik Jones (eds.), *Italian Politics 2010: Managing Uncertainty*, New York: Berghahn Books, 2010.

Hine, David, *Governing Italy: The Politics of Bargained Pluralism*, Oxford: Oxford University Press, 1993.

Morlino, Leonardo, *Democracy between Consolidation and Crisis: Parties, Groups, and Citizens in Southern Europe*, Oxford: Oxford University Press, 1998.

Putnam, Robert D. et al., *Making Democracy Work: Civic Traditions in Modern Italy*, Princeton, NJ: Princeton University Press, 1993.

Ziblatt, Daniel, *Structuring the State: The Formation of Italy and Germany and the Puzzle of Federalism*, Princeton, NJ: Princeton University Press, 2006.

CHAPTER 5

Scandinavia: Still the Middle Way?

Eric S. Einhorn and John Logue

Scandinavia

Norway

Population (million):	4.8
Area in Square Miles:	125,050
Population Density per Square Mile:	38
GDP (in billion dollars, 2009):	$266.5
GDP per capita (PPP, 2005):	$47,257
Not a member of EC/EU; joined European Economic Area	1992

Performance of Key Political Parties in Parliamentary Elections of September 14, 2009

Centre [agrarian] Party (SP)	6.2%
Christian People's Party (KrF)	5.5%
Conservative Party (H)	17.2%
Labour Party (DNA)	35.4%
Left Party (V)	3.9%
Progress Party (FrP)	22.9%
Socialist Left Party (SV)	6.2%

Main Office Holders: Prime Minister: Jens Stoltenberg—DNA (2005); Head of State: King Harald V.

Sweden

Population (million):	9.3
Area in Square Miles:	173,730
Population Density per Square Mile:	54
GDP (in billion dollars, 2009):	$352.6
GDP per capita (PPP, 2005):	$32,179
Joined EC/EU	January 1, 1995

Performance of Key Political Parties in Parliamentary Elections of September 19, 2010

Centre [agrarian] Party (C)	6.6%
Christian Democrats (KD)	5.6%
Green Party (MP)	7.2%
Left Party (V)	5.6%
Liberal People's Party (FP)	7.1%
Moderates (M)	30.0%
Social Democrats (SD)	30.9%
Swedish Democrats	5.7%

Main Office Holders: Prime Minister: Fredrik Reinfeldt—M (2006); Head of State: King Carl XVI Gustaf.

Denmark

Population (million):	5.5
Area in Square Miles:	16,637
Population Density per Square Mile:	331
GDP (in billion dollars, 2009):	$203.6
GDP per capita (PPP, 2005):	$32,293
Joined EC/EU	January 1, 1973

Performance of Key Political Parties in Parliamentary Elections of November 13, 2007

Danish People's Party (DF)	13.9%
Unity List-The Red Greens (ERG)	2.2%
Conservative People's Party (KF)	10.4%
Radical Liberal (RV)	5.1%
Social Democracy in Denmark (SD)	25.5%
Socialist People's Party (SF)	13%
Liberal [agrarian] Party of Denmark (VDLP)	26.2%
New Alliance (NA)	2.8%

Main Office Holders: Prime Minister: Lars Løkke Rasmussen—VDLP (2009); Head of State: Queen Margrethe II.

Finland

Population (million):	5.5
Area in Square Miles:	130,560
Population Density per Square Mile:	42
GDP (in billion dollars, 2009):	$185.4
GDP per capita (PPP, 2005):	$30,781
Joined EC/EU	January 1, 1995

Performance of Key Political Parties in Parliamentary Elections of March 18, 2007

Christian Democrats (KD)	4.9%
Finnish Centre [agrarian] Party (Kesk)	23.1%
Finnish Social Democratic Party (SD)	21.4%
Green Party (Vihr)	8.5%
Left Wing Alliance (Vas)	8.8%
Conservative Party (Kok)	22.3%
Swedish People's Party (RKP/SFP)	4.6%
True Finns Party (PS)	4.1%

Main Office Holders: President: Tarja Kaarina Halonen—SD (2000); Prime Minister: Mari Kiviniemi–Kesk (2010).

The Rise and Fall of the Scandinavian "Middle Way"

The Scandinavian "middle way" first attracted international attention in the 1930s at the depths of the Great Depression, coinciding with an era when the fragile foundations of democracy were crumbling across Europe. Industrial capitalism based on "free markets," as well as the still-shallow roots of political democracy, was threatened by a rising fascist tide on the right and a brutal but, for many on the left, attractive communist model in the Soviet Union. President Franklin D. Roosevelt's 1933 perception of "a third of the nation, ill-clothed, ill-fed, and ill-housed" described most of the industrialized world. Out of this chaos came a unique welfare-state model in Denmark, Norway, and Sweden, offering a "middle way" between these extremes. It developed over time and out of an accumulation of experience. But if you have to pick a "birthday," January 30, 1933, is our choice.

Copenhagen was cold and foggy in its midwinter gloom. The political and economic situation was as bleak as the weather. Fully 40 percent of Danish wage earners—two out of five—were out of work in this gray third winter of the Great Depression.

The Danish Employers Federation had announced that it would lock out all union members still working on February 1 to enforce its demand on the unions for a 20 percent wage reduction. Farm mortgage foreclosures, following a general collapse of agricultural prices, cast a long shadow in the countryside. The Danish Social Democratic prime minister, Thorvald Stauning—a former cigar worker who had led the government briefly in the 1920s and formed another government with the center-left Radical Liberals in 1929 on the eve of the Depression—called an extraordinary Sunday-morning parliamentary session. The agenda was legislation to extend the national labor contract under which the unions worked, thus to stave off economic disaster. Behind closed doors, the government negotiated with the Agrarians and Radical Liberals to provide the necessary votes on the bill's third reading the following day. When an acceptable compromise could not be reached, Prime Minister Stauning invited the negotiators home for what turned out to be a historic bargaining session.

The agreement that emerged in the predawn hours of January 30 in Stauning's modest apartment in a city-owned housing block on Kanslergade called for four major actions:

1. an extension of the existing labor agreements without wage reductions,
2. a massive public works program to put the unemployed back to work and to provide winter relief for their families,
3. a devaluation of the currency to stimulate farm exports and agricultural price supports to stabilize farm incomes, and

4. a fundamental restructuring of the Danish patchwork of social insurance and poverty relief measures into a comprehensive program.

The exhausted cabinet members and Agrarian Liberal Party leadership announced the agreement to parliament and struggled through Monday evening to finish putting the deal together. Without realizing it, these Danish politicians were founding what would become known as the Scandinavian middle way.

This was, however, not the only portentous political event of January 30. South of the Danish border that same Monday, the German president, Paul von Hindenburg, facing the Weimar Republic's collapse into economic depression and political extremism, summoned a controversial, untried party leader to form a new government. The recipient of von Hindenburg's confidence was Adolf Hitler.

THE MEANING OF THE MIDDLE WAY

Hitler's Third Reich engulfed Europe in flames during the next decade, but it finally collapsed under its own aggressive and self-destructive impulses. The hard-won Danish "Kanslergade Compromise," by contrast, set the pattern for the modern Scandinavian welfare states that have far outlasted Nazism and Stalinist Communism.

The Kanslergade Compromise called for wide-ranging state intervention to manage the market economy. The government became involved in setting wages and agricultural prices, establishing credit and exchange policy, and putting the unemployed back to work. It created a comprehensive economic security net for the unemployed and for all those out of the labor market. And, as a compromise between Social Democrats, Radical Liberals, and Agrarians, it broadened and cemented the center of the political spectrum.

In a way, events in Germany that day changed the very complexion of democratic politics in Scandinavia. Before Hitler's assumption of power, the Scandinavian Social Democrats—by far the largest party in Denmark, Norway, and Sweden—could reasonably strive to win a majority on their own to enact a socialist program, with the political polarization that would ensue. In Finland, the Social Democrats had emerged from a civil war in a tie with the Agrarians for the largest percentage of the vote. But with Hitler's rise to power in the Weimar Republic, the handwriting was on the wall: compromise among democratic parties was vital.

As Hitler consolidated his power by crushing the German Social Democrats, the Communist Party, and the independent trade unions, in Sweden a new Social Democratic government quickly followed the Danish example by agreeing with center parties on minimum farm prices and a public works program to create jobs for the unemployed. The Norwegian Labor Party struck a similar deal with its Agrarian Party in 1935.

A compromise across the dividing line between socialist and "bourgeois" parties was initially a kind of defeat for the Scandinavian socialist and social democratic parties because it postponed indefinitely the achievement of true socialism. But cooperation did solidify democratic politics in a situation that threatened the very existence of social democracy.

Thereafter, Scandinavian compromise became much more than a tactic; it grew to be seen as virtuous in itself because it solidified a broad national consensus around democracy. The social democratic welfare state, interventionist and protective of the people, became a surrogate for socialism. Its principle was to achieve redistribution and broadly shared prosperity through compromises acceptable to the nonsocialist center parties. Moreover, compromise worked: state intervention in the collapsing market economy began to stabilize farm income, put the unemployed back to work, reduce conflict in the labor market, and offer hope to the Scandinavian peoples in despair over the Depression and the threat of German aggression. Over the ensuing decades, such compromises would become the hallmark of effective parliamentary democracy throughout much of Europe and beyond.

Right and left faced off despite the Nazi threat in countries such as France. But in Scandinavia, a "national democratic compromise" started building what the Swedish Social Democratic prime minister, Per Albin Hansson, called "the people's home": a society that took care of all its citizens.

This Scandinavian model—an interventionist state managing the market economy toward a combination of growth, full employment, and large-scale welfare programs supported by agreement between employers and unions— was widely followed subsequently in Western Europe. In fact, it was the precursor of the Western European "postwar Keynesian consensus" after World War II. In the 1930s, the U.S. journalist Marquis Childs (*Sweden: The Middle Way*, 1936) dubbed the Scandinavian accord "the middle way"—meaning a middle or third way between "savage" capitalism—that is, the failed capitalism of the Depression era in the West—and Stalinist Communism, the totalitarian regime then reigning in Russia.

After the war, the Scandinavian democracies continued to constitute a middle way in the Cold War ideological and geopolitical conflict, both in domestic and foreign policy terms. For many in the West (including the United States), the Scandinavian middle way was extremely attractive. A leading U.S. journalist, William L. Shirer, for example, in *The Challenge of Scandinavia* (1955), updated Childs' account to describe the region's blend of capitalism with a social conscience; private production would support full employment and an expanding social welfare network, and it would reduce social and economic inequalities.

In domestic policy, Denmark, Norway, and Sweden built advanced capitalist market economies in which the state played both a regulatory and a redistributive role. Under predominantly Social Democratic governments, the state's role for a generation was far greater than in almost all of the other Western, capitalist democracies, although policy innovations in Scandinavia often set the pattern for policies elsewhere on the Continent ten or twenty years later.

During the Cold War, the Scandinavians sought a middle way in foreign policy as well. Although strong supporters of the United Nations, they recognized quickly its limitations. Efforts to fashion a Scandinavian defense union that would provide a viable military foundation for neutrality broke down in 1949, and on Scandinavia's western fringes, Denmark, Norway, and Iceland joined the North Atlantic Treaty Organization (NATO), although they often seemed reluctant members. Finland, which had fought World War II on the German side, signed a separate peace agreement with the Soviet Union in 1944; its neutrality was guaranteed by treaty. Sweden continued to pursue a neutrality policy that had kept it out of war since 1815. Defense strategists wrote of a "Nordic balance," in which Swedish neutrality between NATO in the West and the Warsaw Pact in the East guaranteed Finnish neutrality and independence vis-à-vis the Soviet Union and permitted Denmark and Norway to pursue a strategy of lowering tensions on the northern flank of NATO by refusing to allow foreign troops or nuclear weapons on their territory.

In international economic affairs, there was balance as well. Denmark joined the European Community (now the European Union) when Britain did in 1973, albeit reluctantly; the Norwegians, even more reluctant, voted narrowly against joining Europe. Sweden and Finland held that joining the European Community would compromise their neutrality. All four distinguished themselves by supporting international cooperation that reached across the dividing lines between East and West and between north and south.

Finland developed differently between World War I and World War II—primarily because of the bitter civil war between the "Whites" and the "Reds" in 1917–1918 that the conservative Whites won. Yet in the post–World War II period, Finland came increasingly to resemble the rest of the Scandinavian area in the realm of domestic politics, as it caught up in terms of industrialization, welfare, and living standards. Even its peculiar international position gradually assumed a more Scandinavian "balance."

All this changed at the end of the 1980s. With the end of Soviet dominance of Eastern Europe and the collapse of the USSR itself in 1991, the Scandinavian countries found their middle way questioned anew. What was it a middle way between?

The middle way that had served the Scandinavian countries so well domestically and internationally from the 1930s into the 1980s became confused amid economic crises and globalization, along with political discord at home. Sweden and Finland opted for EU membership and closer ties to Europe in 1995. The middle way's extensive public services, high taxes, and state regulation of the market economy were challenged as well by international economic integration and the growing predominance of free-market thinking. New interest groups and social changes, including new roles for women, an aging population, and significant non-European immigration, challenged the consensus.

The rest of this chapter analyzes the rise and fall of the Scandinavian model in domestic politics, in European integration policy, and in foreign policy generally.

A Social Laboratory

The Nordic countries are idiosyncratic in many ways. They are small in terms of population (see the data on the chapter's opening page). With the exception of Iceland (with 307,000 inhabitants), they are roughly comparable to medium-sized U.S. states. When compared to other members of the European Union, Sweden is about the size of Greece or Portugal; Ireland and Luxembourg are smaller than Denmark and Finland.

Denmark, Iceland, Norway, and Sweden share common roots ethnically, linguistically, and culturally; and Finland—despite its distinct ethnic and linguistic origins—shares a common Nordic history and religion with them. Further, Denmark, Iceland, Norway, and Sweden also were distinguished by remarkable internal ethnic, racial, religious, and linguistic homogeneity. This aspect of Scandinavian societies, more than any other, made the development of the solidaristic Scandinavian model possible.

Until they began to receive a substantial flow of immigrants in the 1960s, more than 90 percent of the population of each country shared the same cultural, linguistic, and racial roots. About 95 percent of the population was Lutheran and belonged to the state church. As a consequence, politics and policy in all three countries focused for decades to a unique degree on economic and class issues rather than the religious, linguistic, and ethnic conflicts that often dominate other societies. However, a generation of immigration, much of it from non-European countries, has literally changed the face of Denmark, Norway, and Sweden. Today, more than one in ten Swedish residents is born abroad. For the first time in more than a century, "ethnic" and immigration issues have become a source of political conflict.

Historically, Finland has been substantially more divided domestically than its Scandinavian neighbors. The legacy of Swedish settlement and rule until 1809 and of Russian rule from 1809 to 1917 left a significant Swedish-speaking population on the southwest coast of Finland and a small Russian Orthodox religious minority. Moreover, Finland was torn by a bitter civil war in 1917–1918 between Reds and Whites. The former were radical socialists who sought to emulate Lenin's Bolshevik Revolution; the latter were a coalition of primarily antiradical nationalists. The Finnish Whites, backed by German troops, won the war and interned their opponents in concentration camps for a number of years. Half a century later, the way Finns voted in national elections was still closely tied to which side of the civil war their grandfathers had fought on. Unlike Denmark, Norway, and Sweden—where the communists played a major role only immediately after World War I and World War II—the Finnish labor movement was split down the middle between communists and social democrats, by the civil war and its aftermath. This division prevented the social democratic dominance in Finland that Denmark, Norway, and Sweden witnessed in the 1930s.

Geopolitical proximity to "big brother" Russia shaped the Finns' national political agenda. Finland by itself fought a brave but doomed war against Russia in the winter of 1939–1940. Then, after Germany invaded the Soviet Union in June 1941, Finland reentered the war on the German side, exiting with a separate peace treaty in 1944. Russia held a major naval base on Finnish soil covering the approaches to Helsinki until 1956.

In the postwar period, the decline in the Swedish minority through assimilation and emigration to Sweden has diminished traditional ethnic and linguistic divisions, and memories of the Finnish civil war have faded. Migration into Finland has been much less than that seen in most Western European countries. And, of course, Finland's dangerous situation vis-à-vis Russia changed dramatically with the Soviet Union's collapse. In the last thirty years, Finnish politics has converged increasingly with the general Scandinavian social democratic model.[1]

DOMESTIC POLITICS: HOW DIFFERENT IS SCANDINAVIA?

Its location on the geographical fringe of Europe has meant that the Scandinavian countries have escaped some European developments entirely, while lagging behind on others.

Throughout most of the nineteenth century, the Scandinavians trailed Western Europe in both industrial and political development. Industrialization came late, beginning only in about 1855 in Denmark, 1890 in Sweden, and 1905 in Norway—a full century after England, Germany, Belgium, and France. Viewing nineteenth-century European political development in terms of three central themes—constitutionalism, nationalism, and democracy—the Scandinavians lagged behind in all but the first, with Sweden's strong state and well-established constitutional traditions and Norway's 1814 Constitution remaining the oldest written European constitution still in force. Nationalism first became a major impulse in Denmark following its confrontations with German nationalism along its southern boundary after 1848 and the loss of Denmark's

Box 5.1   Why Do the Scandinavian Welfare States Survive?

One mystery to Americans is how political support for the Scandinavian welfare states survives when ordinary working people have to pay 50 to 60 percent of their earnings in income and other taxes. When their taxes come due, why don't they rise up in anger and overthrow the government? After all, American taxpayers have rebelled at far lower rates.

The answer is, first, that the Scandinavian welfare states rest on the principle of *solidarity*. By contrast, welfare programs in the United States rest on the principle of social insurance (Social Security, Medicare, workers' compensation, unemployment insurance) or altruism (charity to the poor). The limit of social insurance is that we agree to insure ourselves against only those risks that we cannot afford, and altruism is even more circumscribed, limited to keeping the bodies and souls of the poor together. But solidarity—defined as "reciprocal responsibility and mutual obligation"—has permitted the Scandinavians to build far more elaborate structures of mutual support on a consensual basis.

Second, Scandinavian welfare measures are generally *universal* in scope, rather than means-tested. Thus, both transfer payments (such as pensions, sick pay, maternity pay, family allowances) and social services (such as medical and dental care, home assistance for the elderly, free education through college, and day care and after-school care for children) are available to everyone in the category, whether they are poor, working class, or middle class. Transfer payments are usually taxed, so that wealthier recipients keep a smaller share than the truly needy. Fees for some social services, such as day care, also rise with income. But generally speaking, everyone is in the same system and receives the same benefits. Every year, almost every family receives some benefits. As a witty phrase describes the situation, "The richest 90 percent help support the poorest 90 percent."

Such universal programs are costly. Scandinavian public spending on social security transfer payments is 20 percent to 40 percent higher than elsewhere in Europe and the United States.[1] Rising take-up rates for social services such as day care and after-school care have continued to push up social welfare spending despite the financial constraints on public sector spending. More disturbing, the self-restraint of the older generation about utilizing the welfare net is giving way to a culture of "entitlement" among the younger generation. Thus in Denmark, for example, statistics indicate that the young are sicker than the old, even taking into account legitimate reasons, such as taking care of ill children. Sweden, one of the healthiest nations in the world, has more people on sick leave than most wealthy countries.

Still, universal public provision of social services generally provides a higher standard and is cheaper than provision through employer-funded, private insurance schemes. The classic case is medical care, which is both far more costly (by about 70 percent) in the United States as a proportion of gross domestic product and less adequately distributed than in Scandinavia. Consequently, the Scandinavian countries' health statistics (infant mortality, lifespan, etc.) beat the United States by a wide margin. Likewise, the "top 1 percent" in Scandinavia earns three or four times the median income, not ten or more times as in the United States.

Typical middle-class living standards are very similar to the American level, while low-income groups in Scandinavia have a substantially higher living standard than in the United States: after-tax, after-benefit poverty rates in Scandinavia are only about a quarter of the American rate.

Everyone pays, but everyone also benefits.

1. Accounting definitions make exact comparison difficult. Overall social expenditures in Germany, Belgium, and the Netherlands are roughly comparable to Scandinavia, with France not far behind. See William Adema and Maxime Ladaique, "Net Social Expenditure," 2005 ed., *OECD Social, Employment and Migration Working Papers No. 29*, OECD, 2005.

German duchies in 1864.[2] Norway enjoyed a national cultural revival in the 1880s, and its confrontation with Sweden over full independence in 1905 sharpened national feelings in both countries. Political democracy (parliamentary supremacy) came even more slowly: 1884 in Norway, 1901 in Denmark, and 1917 in Sweden and Finland.

Late development in these spheres meant that the economic basis for liberalism developed late. The agrarian and labor movements, which began in Scandinavia as elsewhere in Europe in the latter half of the nineteenth century, swept through the countryside and the new industrial towns like a prairie fire. Organizing in a virtual vacuum, the "popular movements" of family farmers and industrial workers built their own economic and political organizations, which claimed the high ground of an egalitarian response to industrialization and political democracy. Thanks to the high literacy levels encouraged by Lutheranism and by state educational policies in the eighteenth and early nineteenth centuries, the democratic popular movements were led from below, and the tie between the leaders and the led remains close even today.[3]

Even as the Scandinavians lagged behind Europe in many areas in the eighteenth and nineteenth centuries, they led in one: the strong state. The Swedes developed in the sixteenth and seventeenth centuries what was probably the most modern state in Europe in terms of its capacity to govern, and Swedish military prowess from the Thirty Years' War through Charles XII's misadventures in Russia reflected both the state's strength and the success of state-sponsored development of military industries. By the time of the establishment of modern political organizations and democratic institutions in the last part of the nineteenth century, the Scandinavians had a well-established tradition of a strong state and a professional civil service. The right saw the strong state as good in itself; the left, as a tool for reform.

These three factors—relative isolation, powerful popular movements, and a strong state—created the conditions for the Scandinavian middle way in the twentieth century.

Social Democracy and European Development: Success, Then Crisis

More than any other single factor, what set Scandinavian politics and policy apart was the predominant role played by the "popular movements"—farmers and labor—that represented the economically disenfranchised. Organizing from below in a virtual political vacuum in the latter half of the nineteenth century, farm and labor organizations swept the countryside, towns, and cities in an evangelical wave. In addition to the creation of the agrarian and labor parties, which came to be the great bearers of the democratic tradition, they created an immense economic and cultural infrastructure, including producer and consumer cooperatives, colleges, sports clubs, newspapers and publishing houses, theaters, and much else.

Both agrarian and labor movements shared certain central values. These included egalitarianism, a belief in democracy, and a strong commitment to building their own institutions. Allied in the struggle for political democracy, farmers and workers had much that united them even when ideology—private property versus socialization of the means of production—divided them. It is not inconsequential that the Danish Social Democrats adopted land reform and support for small farmers as their agrarian policy in the 1890s, much to the chagrin of the more orthodox German Social Democrats who were otherwise the Danes' mentors.

This massive political organization preceded the establishment of parliamentary democracy everywhere except Norway, where it coincided with the democratic breakthrough. Because numbers had not counted previously in politics, the conservatives had never taken the trouble to organize. Consequently, they found themselves playing catch-up after the agrarian radicals' and labor movement's ideas had already won adherents from their tenants in the countryside and servants in the cities.

Scandinavian popular movements were most remarkable in the degree to which they drew their leadership from the ranks of the movement itself, rather than from the educated elite. The liberal agrarian parties were led predominantly by farmers, and the labor parties by workers—not lawyers, teachers, civil servants, or priests.[4] This kept them honest. Government for the people works best when it is by the people and of the people.

The combination of democracy from below—of leaders sprung from and tied to the organizations of those they lead—with relative ethnic and religious homogeneity, overarching agreement on basic values, and relatively small communities, offers powerful drivers for a cohesive, solidaristic welfare state based, as one turn-of-the-century trade union tract put it, on the principle of "reciprocal obligation or mutual responsibility."

Despite such advantages, nineteenth-century Scandinavia was a poor, class-ridden, and static region, as reflected in the waves of immigration to North America that also contributed to rapid social changes. Millions of Swedes and Norwegians, as well as many Danes and Finns, simply left for new opportunities. At first this removed considerable political and economic pressure, but later it stimulated interest in social, economic, and political reforms even among national conservatives. Knowledge of better economic opportunities abroad and the success of democratic government in North America and later Britain encouraged domestic reformers in both the labor and agrarian movements. Nationalists recoiled at the loss of youthful and energetic citizens.

Out of these conflicts emerged a civil society of the strongest sort. Citizens in the popular movements connected in a myriad of voluntary associations that mediated between them and the state and also provided direct economic, cultural, and social benefits. Organizing successfully around these associations, popular movements ultimately also captured state power. In the last fifty years, the welfare, educational, and regulatory functions of the popular-movement organizations were transferred to public administration, and many of the social and cultural functions previously provided by the popular-movement organizations were taken over by local and national government and provided by public employees instead of movement members. This generalized those social services to all the people, but it removed them from control from below. This also left the popular movements—especially the social democratic labor movement—dependent on control of the state to achieve their objectives.

The existence of a strong state and the tradition of an honest and professional civil service offered the mechanism for building a more egalitarian society. Principles of Keynesian economics advocating job-creating public programs were independently developed by Scandinavian economists during the Depression. Cautiously applied, they offered a route to use the state to improve the performance of capitalist market economies. The combination of the two provided the means to solve the classic problem of industrial capitalism—great and pervasive poverty amid great wealth—without revolution, by a lasting commitment to spread growth more equally than the existing distribution of wealth and income. That commitment lay at the core of the Kanslergade Compromise and the subsequent, similar national compromises in Norway and Sweden. It was driven forward politically by the Social Democrats with what proved to be a virtually unparalleled grasp on power in democratic elections.

Within the lifetime of a single generation, this commitment transformed Scandinavia from a region of great poverty—characterized by the immigrants' "flight to America"—into societies of widely shared affluence. The image of "the fortified poorhouse," as the title of Zeth Höglund's book characterized Sweden in 1913, gave way to Per Albin Hansson's view of Sweden as "the people's home" in the 1930s, as class struggle gave way to national construction under social democratic government. By the 1960s, Sweden and Norway, which had been among the poorest European countries some fifty years earlier, were among the most affluent. The slums and poverty were gone.

The Scandinavian success relied on the use of the state to achieve broad economic goals, and that rested on the assumption that the nation-state was the relevant unit for economic policy. That certainly was true following the collapse of the international trading system in the 1930s, which was anomalous given Scandinavia's long global trading history. It was equally true in the reconstruction after World War II. But by the 1960s and 1970s, as growing national affluence transformed the lives of the working class, the Scandinavian countries once again became fully enmeshed in an interdependent global trading system. This development accelerated prosperity but brought vulnerability to the oil crises of the 1970s and the ever more invasive global business cycles after 1990.[5]

Political Democracy Scandinavian Style

Denmark, Norway, and Sweden share a great deal in terms of political structures and political actors. Finland is different historically, but it has converged on the other three countries in the postwar period.[6] Much of what they have in common stems from their similarities in terms of cohesion, as discussed earlier. Some of it stems from their close ties in the Nordic Council and various European organizations, which facilitates diffusion of political ideas. The Scandinavian labor movements and the Social Democratic parties have interacted especially closely over the years.

POLITICAL INSTITUTIONS

All four countries are parliamentary democracies based on proportional representation. All are clearly democratic in the sense that regular elections determine who holds political office and what policies are made. All are parliamentary systems in the sense that parliament—the legislative body—is the most important branch of government.

Denmark, Norway, and Sweden are pure parliamentary systems. The legislative majority selects the executive (the prime minister and the cabinet) and can force the executive out by a vote of "no confidence." In both cases, parliament is the ultimate arbiter of the constitutionality of its own legislation, although a variety of checks are imposed on parliamentary abuses of power, as we will discuss. Courts rarely review the constitutionality of parliamentary legislation, as the U.S. Supreme Court does, but their membership in the EU has injected substantial portions of EU law into their national legal systems with increasing controversy. EU courts review national legislation and policies, and national courts enforce European laws. Norway is unique in Europe, as its Constitution, dating back to 1814, prevents calling early elections, which is otherwise a standard characteristic of parliamentary government.

Finland has a mixed presidential-parliamentary form of government, not unlike that of France in the Fifth Republic. The president, who heads the executive branch, is directly elected by a popular vote (prior to 1994, Finnish law provided for indirect election) for a six-year term. The president directs foreign policy, commands the armed forces, and can dissolve parliament. A new constitution entered into force in 2000, clarifying and strengthening the primacy of the prime minister and the cabinet, which are selected by the parliament. Together the executive cabinet, led by the prime minister, and parliament share primary responsibility for domestic and EU affairs. Parliament can force the cabinet from office by a vote of "no confidence." In practice this division has made the prime minister the most important actor of the executive branch in terms of policymaking, but there certainly were times during the Cold War when the president's role overshadowed that of his prime minister. There is no national judicial review of the constitutionality of legislation, but again national courts frequently enforce the supremacy of EU law.

Despite the multiparty system—today seven to ten or more parties are represented in the national parliaments—and the rarity of single-party majorities, the Scandinavians have had stable and effective government because they practice what Dankwart Rustow called "the politics of compromise" in his 1955 classic study of that name.[7] Scandinavian government is coalition government, sometimes through multiparty governments and at other times through bargains worked out in parliament between a minority government and other parties whose agreement has been attained on an issue-by-issue basis.

Although Denmark and Sweden maintained an upper house of parliament until 1953 and 1970, respectively, all four now elect a unicameral—single-house—parliament. The Norwegian parliament (Stortinget) divides into two bodies to consider certain types of legislation, although most proceedings take place in the plenary parliament. In all parliaments, much of the detailed legislative and oversight work and most of the necessary multiparty compromises are worked out in standing committees. There are usually parliamentary committees for each governmental ministry, plus some with special competency (constitutional affairs or relations with the European Union). Parties are represented on committees in proportion to their overall strength, but coalitions are usually required for any significant actions. Most proceedings are in secret, precisely to encourage interparty compromises, but occasional hearings are held publicly and there are increasing demands to "open up" the parliamentary processes to greater media scrutiny.

In all four countries, a proportional representation system is used in electing parliament as well as local councils. Thus, all parties of significant size are represented in parliament with approximately the same proportion of seats as they have support among voters. Although proportional representation was introduced in an existing multiparty system and stabilized it for a number of decades, as new lines of division—including those over the European Union, the environment, and immigration—have come to the fore in recent years, this election system has permitted growing fragmentation in parliament.

The basic principle of parliamentary democracy—that the prime minister and the executive branch are responsible to the majority in the house of parliament with the broadest suffrage—was established in 1884 in Norway, while the country was still under Swedish rule; in 1901 in Denmark; and in 1917 in Sweden. Finland established the same principle in 1917 with independence from Russia, but the losing side in the civil war was pretty much excluded from politics during the 1920s.

Denmark, Norway, and Sweden remain constitutional monarchies. Scandinavian monarchs took office within constitutional limits (Karl Johan in Sweden in 1809 and Norway in 1815; Haakon VII in Norway in 1905) or accepted these limits with relative grace (Frederik VII in Denmark in 1849). They proved more resistant to yielding the power to choose the prime minister to the elected parliamentary majority (1884 in Norway, 1901 in Denmark, and 1917 in Sweden), but here, too, they bowed to the winds of change. Although the governmental power of the Scandinavian monarchs is virtually nil today, they remain important symbols of national unity, above the lines of party or division by interest. In times of crisis, this symbolic role has had real political significance.

In Finland, the president has the symbolic role played by the monarchs, as well as a more practical role in foreign policy. Although elected with a partisan affiliation, the Finnish president stands above party lines while in office. For more than fifty years (1939–1991), the presidents assumed a special role in managing relations with the USSR. This also enhanced presidential internal political powers.

All four countries have unitary, rather than federal, governments in the sense that all sovereignty resides in the national government, and the powers of the provinces and other subunits of government are derived from the national government. However, Finland provides far-reaching local autonomy for the Swedish-speaking Åland Islands, and Denmark provides even greater autonomy for Greenland and the Faeroe Islands, which have been granted the status of near independence. The Faeroes never joined the European Community, and Greenland, which acquired autonomy in 1979, quickly used its independence to withdraw from the European Community—the only territory to date to do so. In the past decade, both have grown increasingly impatient with their ties to Denmark, but with no substitute in sight for the large budgetary subsidies that are sent from Copenhagen, the status quo will continue for a while longer.

Although power is clearly concentrated in the hands of the national government, many governmental services have been delegated to municipal and county government. Thus, most social services, including education, medical care, hospitals, and services for children, families, and the elderly are provided by municipalities. Indeed, a higher proportion of governmental spending occurs at the local level in Scandinavia than at the state and local levels in the United States. Thus, within unitary states, the Scandinavians have thoroughly decentralized the provision of governmental services.

In order to make this decentralization effective, Denmark, Norway, and Sweden undertook similar consolidations of local government in the late 1960s and early 1970s. The consequence was to cut the number of local governments by half in Norway, three-fourths in Sweden, and four-fifths in Denmark. Denmark further consolidated local and regional government in 2007. In Finland, a similar consolidation was blocked, and the number of local administrations was reduced only by about a sixth in this period. Generally speaking, these reforms were successful in establishing the capacity to expand social services in smaller towns and rural areas, but they undercut the relationship between citizens and their government in rural districts. Although the density of elected officials remains high in Scandinavia by comparison to most other democracies, it is much diminished in comparison to the past.

Local and regional governments enjoy substantial taxing powers, but their dependence on budgetary transfers from the central government and the standardization of social, educational, and other local services has constrained their autonomy. In Denmark, for example, fourteen counties were consolidated into five "regions" with responsibility primarily limited to health care, but a similar proposal in Norway was withdrawn. One striking aspect of Scandinavian politics is the degree to which government and the civil service are seen as national resources. This is a result of a convergence of causes. Scandinavian conservatives have traditionally supported a strong state as an instrument of national development. Popular movements, including especially the social democratic labor movement, have seen the government as a mechanism for generalizing their egalitarian goals to the entire society. General antigovernment or antistate movements have always been weak. The distrust of government that we see across the political spectrum in the United States has generally been absent in Scandinavia. Furthermore, Scandinavian public administration generally has been deserving of citizen respect: its bureaucrats have been self-effacing, efficient, and honest.

However, that popular belief in the benevolence of public administration does not extend to the transnational public policy dimension. The European Union's multitudinous rules and regulations frequently strike most Scandinavians as downright arcane. For example, the European Union promulgated measures regulating the size of strawberries and the curvature of cucumbers shortly before the 1992 Danish referendum on the Maastricht Treaty; an effort to harmonize the dimensions of condoms, however, foundered on Italian opposition. One acerbic Danish placard during this referendum put it succinctly: "If you think there are already enough idiots running your life, vote no!" As EU regulations become targets for public ridicule and additional policy responsibilities shift from national capitals to distant EU institutions, the problem of the "democratic deficit" will become more acute.

POLITICAL ACTORS

Scandinavian democracy historically has been based on strong, disciplined, mass-membership parties, which organize hundreds of thousands of voters as dues-paying party members. Parties had structured political competition at the local as well as the national level. They provided channels for recruiting political leaders; the career pattern was to start by running for the local municipal council. Municipal office or parliament followed for those who proved themselves. Regular local party meetings ensured close contacts between the elected officials and their party constituency. Because the parties offered different policy choices in the election campaigns, they allowed citizens a means to control not just the people in government but also the policies of government. Problematic for democratic participation has been an accelerating decline in party memberships. Social Democratic parties, which no longer automatically enroll union members, account for much of this decline, but all traditional parties have been hit.

The parties have been complemented by equally strong interest groups that organize workers, farmers, and employers. These groups, which we will look at, have typically been closely linked to individual parties. The unions have traditionally been Social Democratic (except in Finland, where they were hotly contested by the Communists), the farmer organizations have been the mainstays of the agrarian parties, and the employers have typically had a looser association with the Conservatives. Unlike many Western countries, Scandinavian labor unions have maintained their remarkably high memberships (often over 80 percent of blue- and white-collar employees). While most are rather passive members, organized labor remains a strong political actor.

PARTIES AND PARTY SYSTEMS

From the origins of parliamentary democracy at the turn of the twentieth century to the 1970s, the predominant pattern in all four countries was the five- or six-party system. On the right was the Conservative Party, which had been late to organize a mass base because it had wielded the levers of power on behalf of the elites and propertied classes before the democratic breakthrough. In the center were the nineteenth-century proponents of democracy: the Liberals and the Agrarians. To the left of center were the Social Democrats, their junior allies in the nineteenth-century push for democracy. The Social Democrats outgrew the coalition by the mid-1920s and typically polled about 40 to 45 percent of the vote from the 1930s through the 1970s. On the extreme left were the radical socialists—Communists from the 1920s through the late 1950s—and the Socialist People's Parties, which displaced the Communists in the late 1950s and early 1960s in Denmark and Norway. The remaining communists in Sweden and Finland became increasingly independent of the Soviet Union after 1960 and evolved into "radical socialist" parties by the 1980s.

There were also some variants on this general theme, especially in the center of the political spectrum. The accommodating proportional representation system allowed small parties to gain parliamentary seats on issues such as prohibition, land taxation, and cultural distinctions. The Finns had a Swedish People's Party to represent the Swedish-speaking minority. The Norwegians supported a strong Christian People's Party, which was culturally and religiously conservative but centrist in economic terms. It gradually grew into a major force in Norwegian politics. Over the past forty years, similar parties have appeared in the other Nordic countries.

Since the 1920s, the voters have been roughly split between the parties of the right and center (the "bourgeois parties") on the one hand and the left (the "labor" or "socialist" parties) on the other. Until recently, those with bourgeois leanings divided their votes among three or four parties of approximately equal size, while the Social Democrats typically captured the lion's share of the labor vote—40 to 45 percent of the total—with the Communists/Socialist People's Party getting 5 to 10 percent. Numerically, this gave the Social Democrats an obvious edge. Furthermore, because of the deep historical division during the struggle for parliamentary democracy between the Conservatives on the one hand and the Agrarians and Liberals on the other through the 1930s, the Social Democrats were able to form coalitions with the parties of the center once they put state socialism on the back burner after 1933.

Thus, the Social Democrats achieved a degree of hegemony in Denmark, Norway, and Sweden that was unparalleled in democratic elections. Social Democrats led the government of Denmark from 1929 to 1968, with only two breaks totaling four years (and two more during the German occupation); of Norway from 1935 to 1965, with a break of two weeks in 1963 and of five years during the German occupation; and of Sweden from 1932 to 1976, with a break of only a couple of months in the summer of 1936. They were able to use these extraordinary periods in government to reshape society by building an exceptionally strong public sector.

Finland constituted something of an exception. The Finnish labor vote (and trade unions as well) was roughly evenly split between the Communist Party and the Social Democrats, and they were direct political competitors. Consequently, the fulcrum of Finnish party politics was in the center, especially with the well-led agrarian Center Party. After 1960, the Communist-led electoral alliance vote declined, and it has taken a course similar to that of the radical socialists in the other countries and has been integrated into the parliamentary give-and-take.

The culmination of this period of Social Democratic construction of the Scandinavian welfare state was the reforms of the late 1960s and early 1970s, which expanded social services into rural areas and raised income replacement rates for the unemployed, sick, injured, and disabled from 40 to 50 percent of their market income to 70 to 90 percent of the average wage. These reforms came on line just about the time the oil price shock of 1973–1974 set off a period of economic adjustment and economic globalization throughout the West. Social democratic ideas and their carefully constructed tools of public economic management, as we will discuss, offered fewer answers in a global economy.

This relatively stable party system changed dramatically in the 1970s and 1980s. New protest parties arose on the right in protest against high taxes, growing immigrant populations, and the fact that the bourgeois parties that finally took governmental power in the late 1960s and 1970s administered the social democratic system rather than abolishing it; these were the so-called Progress Parties in Denmark and Norway and the short-lived New Democracy Party and later the Sweden Democrats in Sweden. Finland had somewhat similar but weaker protest parties, including the Rural Party (now known as the "True Finns"). There was further subdivision in the center. Denmark saw the development of a Christian People's Party and a Center Democrat split from the right wing of the Social Democrats. In Sweden, the Christian Democrats also broke into parliament. Environmentalist parties won seats in both Sweden and Finland, and the Danes and Norwegians both sent a few members to parliament from groups to the left of the Socialist People's Parties.

The consequence was that the relatively stable five- or six-party model of the 1920–1970 period has given way to a seven- or eight-party model in which the Christian Democrats in the center and a protest party on the right seem to be a permanent part of the parliamentary constellation today. The Scandinavian Christian Democrats have more of a "Sermon on the Mount" orientation than the rightist orientation of U.S. fundamentalists. Although socially conservative (especially on the issues of abortion, drugs, pornography, and alcohol), they are strong supporters of the welfare state, foreign aid, and restrained materialism. They show a remarkable streak of religious tolerance as well: although Christian Democratic voters are overwhelmingly devout, evangelical Lutherans, the Danish party was led for some years by a Catholic, and the Swedish party included a prominent immigrant Jewish physician among its leaders and members of parliament. (They have not, however, taken ecumenicalism to the point of inclusion of Muslims.) Consequently, they have accommodated themselves easily to the give-and-take of parliamentary compromise.

The protest parties of the populist right have been less accommodating, and they were initially kept outside the patterns of parliamentary coalitions. Driven originally by opposition to taxes and bureaucracy, they have in recent years become increasingly strident in their opposition to immigrants, particularly those racially or culturally distinguishable, such as Africans, Asians, and Muslims. For a long time they were "heard" but not "listened to." This began to change in the late 1990s as their electoral advances made them too large to be ignored. Nonsocialist governments in Norway and most recently in Denmark have counted on parliamentary votes from the "New Right." In local government, the pattern is similar; once radical parties draw 10 to 20 percent of the vote, their political influence grows. The rise of the Sweden Democrats since 2000 continues the trend.

Although the division of the voters between the blocs long remained relatively even, there has been an increasing tilt to the right, especially when the rightist protest parties gained a growing share of working-class votes. Further, the Social Democrats were weakened by a seepage of voters to their left, especially over the issue of European Community membership in the 1970s in Denmark and Norway, and European Union membership in 1994 in Sweden. For the current division of parliamentary seats among the parties, see table 5.1.

The cumulative loss of Social Democratic votes since the 1980s has been 5 to 15 percentage points compared to the 1940s–1970s; even with proportional representation, this produces a significant shift in the parliamentary balance. The forty years of Social Democratic hegemony that began during the Depression came to an end. However, despite increased party fragmentation, the loss of part of their voting base, and a certain poverty of ideas, the Social Democrats remained the largest party in parliament in Denmark (until 2001), Norway, and Sweden. The Finnish Social Democrats have also been the largest parliamentary party for most of the post-1945 period. The Social Democrats have ceased to be the normal party of government, but they are perfectly capable of savaging governments of the right that try to cut the welfare state. Just as the nonsocialist parties have largely accepted the universal welfare state, Social Democrats have followed many neoliberal (free market) doctrines over the past quarter century.

One of the major consequences of the fragmented party system and declining Social Democratic hegemony has been the growing prevalence of minority cabinets. If we split the post–World War II period at the 1972 mark—the Danish and Norwegian European Community referenda—the Danes managed majority governments for 25 percent of the period prior to 1972 and 2 percent of the period since. The Norwegians had majority governments for 80 percent of the pre-1972 period and 20 percent of the period since. The Swedes mustered majority governments for 40 percent of the first period and only 11 percent of the most recent period. Finland remains committed to broad majority coalitions, which have accounted for nearly all its governments over the past thirty years. While one might think that this would produce political paralysis, the governments seem to function about as effectively as in the past.

There are three reasons for this. The first is the value, already discussed, placed on compromise, which makes minority government much less frustrating than it otherwise would be. The second is that various "radical" and "protest" parties on the political left and, more tentatively, on the right have become substantially less radical and more interested in participating in shaping legislation through compromise; Social Democratic minority governments can turn to their left as well as to the center for votes, while nonsocialists look to their right. The third is that, by and large, Scandinavian governments of the last twenty years have only undertaken major domestic reforms with broad parliamentary support extending well beyond the governing coalition.

INTEREST GROUPS

The Scandinavian countries are the most thoroughly organized in the world. Practically everybody belongs to his or her economic interest organization. Manufacturers, shopkeepers, renters, farmers, workers, and students are all organized. Overall, 75 to 90 percent of all wage and salaried workers are union members, and farmer and employer organizational percentages are equally impressive. Schoolchildren, university students, priests, and military personnel each have their usually well-ordered group.

As this list suggests, Scandinavian interest organizations are divided primarily along economic lines. This mirrors the lines of political division in these societies. Moreover, the larger of the interest organizations, including both the trade union federation and the employers' organization, are sufficiently inclusive that they have to take broader, societal interests into consideration. Furthermore, until the 1980s they were highly centralized: labor agreements were negotiated nationally between the national employers' organization and the national trade union organization. Recently, collective bargaining has been decentralized by economic sector (e.g., metal industry, public sector employees, etc.). In practice, unions and employers keep a close eye across the labor market, and contract provisions tend to move across it in similar directions. Thus, areas of conflict and cooperation spread across the economy and have immediate societal consequences.

As a result, the Scandinavian countries remain models of a peculiar kind of social democratic corporatism, in which interest organizations as a matter of course are integrated in making and implementing public policy. Some prefer to call the process "the negotiated economy." Interest organizations have highly professional staffs and are constantly involved in governmental commissions for designing policy, including the Swedish "remiss" system of formal consultation on major initiatives with all relevant interest organizations. It remains a process of interest representation very different from Washington lobbying, but such consultations have declined over the past two decades. Governments are now more inclined to take initiatives without corporatist negotiation.

Not only are Scandinavian interest organizations involved in drafting pol-

Table 5.1   Party Parliamentary Strength in October 2010

Country/Party	Seats
Denmark	179
Social Democrats	45
Liberals*	46
Danish People's	24
Conservatives*	17
Socialist People's	23
Radical Liberals	9
Liberal Alliance	5
Leftists	4
Greenland and Faeroe Islands	4
Independents~	2
Christian Democrat~	1
Finland	200
Social Democrats	45
Center (agrarian)*	51
Conservatives*	50
Left Alliance	17
Swedish People's*	10
Greens*	15
Christian Democrats	7
True Finns	5
Norway	169
Labor (Social Democrats)*	64
Conservatives	30
Progress	41
Socialist Left*	11
Christian People's	10
Center (agrarian)*	11
Liberals	2
Sweden	349
Social Democrats	112
Moderates (conservatives)*	107
Liberals*	24
Christian Democrats*	19
Leftists	19
Center (agrarian)*	23
Greens	25
Sweden Democrats	20

* In government as of July 2010.
~ Quit party group.

icy, they implement it. Consider the national labor agreement, for example, in the years that a single overarching national contract for the private sector is negotiated: the unions and the employers, with the government as a third party, hammer out the contract, since the contract essentially determines wage formation for the period. The primary aim of the government, in terms of management of the economy, is to ensure that wage increases are noninflationary.

The practice of corporatism is eased by the small scale of the national political class in the Scandinavian countries. One faces the same people across the table. Working together becomes second nature. Economic globalization, neoliberalism, and perhaps European integration have created stress for this cozy but flexible structure. Structural economic changes, the relative decline of the industrial sector, and the rise in small enterprises also challenge the Scandinavian corporatist model. However, the current international interest in the Scandinavian "flexicurity" (flexible labor markets, active public retraining, and generous social security systems) shows that corporatism has not been static.

RESTRAINING THE GOVERNORS

The concentration of power in unicameral parliaments and the presence of strong, disciplined parties not only permit effective and responsive policymaking but also raise the specter of majority tyranny. What prevents a unified parliamentary majority from running roughshod over all opposition? What prevents systematic abuses of citizen rights? In the United States, the system of government has been carefully designed to avert majority tyranny by the division of powers between the three branches of government—legislative, executive, and judicial—and between the federal and state governments. The court system is engaged in a continual review of governmental acts. The Scandinavians do not have those mechanical checks and balances built into their government institutions. They have developed a different set of checks on abuse of power and majority tyranny.

First, the ombudsman—a Scandinavian concept that has entered the English language and U.S. practice—serves as a standing, independent check on abuses of executive power. This position was created in the Swedish Constitution of 1809 as a parliamentary restraint on abuse of royal executive power; today it serves as a more general check on abuses throughout the executive branch. The Swedish ombudsman is elected by parliament for a four-year term and is empowered both to respond to formal citizen complaints and to initiate investigations on, for example, the basis of press reports. In recent years, the Swedish ombudsman has handled about three thousand cases a year; about 90 percent are citizen initiated. Less prominent but even older is the institution of the chancellor of justice (Justitiekanslern) created in 1713 by King Charles XII. In March 2006, the chancellor's office pressured Foreign Minister Freivalds to resign after she lied about her efforts to censor an anti-Muslim website. The modern media are also watchdogs: just after the change of government in Sweden in October 2006, two new conservative ministers were forced to resign when the press revealed unpaid taxes and radio/TV license fees.

The Finns added an ombudsman in 1919 at the birth of the republic on the Swedish model. The Danes added a parliamentary ombudsman in the Constitution of 1953, and the Norwegians established a similar office in 1962. The formal powers of ombudsmen are amplified by a strong tradition of parliamentary inquiry (both questions to the government and committee hearings) and investigative journalism.

Second, voter referenda have increasingly checked parliamentary majorities. This is most formalized in Denmark, which has held nineteen referenda since 1915; Denmark is second only to Switzerland in direct citizen votes on key legislation, but there are no "initiatives" (citizen-proposed legislation). All constitutional changes go to a citizen vote (after having been approved by two sessions of parliament with an intervening election), any legislation except finance and tax measures can be sent to a vote by one-third of parliament, and any surrender of national sovereignty can be sent to a vote by one-sixth of parliament. Such provisions strengthen the hands of the minority vis-à-vis the majority, but they have been used only once, in 1963. While Finland and Norway lack a constitutional sanction for binding referenda (and Sweden limits it to constitutional changes), governments have always abided by voter decision except in the case of the Swedish referendum concerning which side of the road they should drive on (in 1955, despite the government's recommendation and common sense, Swedes voted to continue driving on the left; in 1967, the government shifted without a referendum). Increasingly, highly divisive issues such as nuclear power (Sweden, 1980); European Community/European Union membership (Denmark, 1972; Norway, 1972 and 1994; Sweden and Finland, 1994); and further EU integration (Denmark, 1986, 1992, 1993, 1998, and 2000; Sweden, 2003) have been decided by the people directly.

Third, two aspects of Scandinavian political culture tend to check parliamentary majorities. One is that facts count in Scandinavian politics. The policy debate, both in the media and the parliament, is couched in empirical terms. Demagoguery discredits the user, except, possibly, on the immigration issue. The other is that a value is placed on broader compromise. All recent governments have been formal or informal coalitions. Moreover, parties involved in compromises will not reverse the policy when they are in government. But another part is the concept that legislation passed by narrow majorities is less legitimate than that passed by broad majorities. Thus there is a tendency to seek broader majorities than are necessary simply to pass legislation.

Finally, as mentioned earlier, Scandinavian corporatism provides an open door in policymaking. Major legislative initiatives are generally preceded by governmental commissions that involve not only the political parties but all the relevant interest groups. Trade unions, employers, and farmers' organizations are involved in practically all of these, and more specialized interest organizations take part in commissions in their spheres of interest. Such political transparency is reinforced by an active and diverse media and is supplemented nowadays by the Internet. If, however, Scandinavian corporatism continues to recede, these democratic safeguards will weaken.

The Welfare State and Economic Stability

The Scandinavian responses to the economic crises of the 1930s marked a sea change in the role of the state. The old "night watchman state" provided national defense, justice, police protection, roads, and elementary education. The new "welfare state" was to regulate the market economy to ensure full employment and growth and to provide social and economic security for those out of the labor market because of old age, sickness, unemployment, and disability and for families whose market income was small and number of children large.[8] This is what political scientists have come to call the "postwar consensus," but in Scandinavia it started before World War II, driven primarily by the predominant popular movements with more of an egalitarian perspective.

Scandinavian welfare states, like those in Europe generally, are not for the poor alone. They are a method of providing universal social services and economic security for the middle class as well as the working class and the marginalized poor. Practically all social welfare expenses are in the public sector. This includes family allowances, day care and after-school care, unemployment, health care, maternity and sick pay, pensions, disability, housing subsidies, and social assistance. In the United States, by contrast, a number of these, including medical and dental care, maternity and sick pay, and the bulk of our pensions, are handled privately through employers. Unlike the U.S. provision of these services, which varies tremendously between occupational groups and among employers, Scandinavians universally receive about the same benefits.

In the postwar period, Scandinavian governments worked to achieve broadly shared affluence by two mechanisms. First, they sought to manage the economy to limit cyclical unemployment and to bring up the standards of the worst-off in the labor market by channeling capital investment and labor from the least efficient firms to the most efficient firms. The trade unions' "solidaristic wage policy" was the most effective mechanism for this purpose. Over time, it raised the wages of the unskilled relative to the skilled and of women relative to men at the same time as it increased the overall efficiency of the economy.

Second, they sought to spread the dividends of economic growth more equally than the existing system distributed income and wealth. Those outside the labor market or in low-income groups gained, but no one lost absolutely.

As a result, the policy enjoyed widespread political support, and social expenditures expanded rapidly.

Between 1960 and 1974, social spending as a share of GDP nearly doubled in the Scandinavian countries. The growth really was a product of substantial improvements in the social security net that included raising income replacement ratios for the unemployed and the disabled, raising pension levels, and expanding some social services from urban areas to include rural areas. With unemployment at a minimal 2 percent level, it cost little to raise the income replacement ratio to 80 or even 90 percent of market wages. All this occurred during a period of prolonged economic growth and, generally speaking, shared the affluence of those in the labor market with those outside and those in the labor market who had low-income families and numerous children (see table 5.2).

By contrast, the decades after 1974 were characterized by the two oil crises, the unpredicted combination of economic stagnation and inflation ("stagflation"), recurring financial crises, and the new challenges of globalization in Scandinavia as in most Western economies. In Denmark, new social expenditures from the end of the good years finished coming on line, and there was also a rapid expansion of countercyclical social expenditures because of the bad times that saw unemployment rise from the frictional level of about 2 percent to 8 percent. Sweden continued to grow the national economy and hold down unemployment by expanding the public sector; this kept unemployment at 3 percent and restrained social spending for countercyclical programs, but it pushed some economic problems forward. Norway, blessed with North Sea oil, initially escaped the hard times. Finland's economy benefited from continuing

Table 5.2   Public Social Security Transfers as a Percentage of GDP, 1960–2008. Average for Period

	1960–1973	1974–1979	1980–1989	1990–1999	2008
Denmark	9.5	14.0	17.1	19.1	14.9
Finland	6.6	11.2	13.9	20.3	15.2
Norway	10.3	12.9	12.7	15.9	11.7
Sweden	10.0	15.9	18.3	20.9	15.1
EU (15) average	11.4	12.3	16.5	17.3	
United States	6.4	10.2	11.0	12.6*	12.3°

* Average 1990–1996.
° 2007.

(Source: Organization for Economic Cooperation and Development, Historical Statistics, 1960–97; Historical Statistics, 1970–99; OECD in Figures, 2009, Paris: OECD, 1999, 2000, and 2009, respectively.)

modernization and substantial trade with Soviet Russia and other Eastern European states until 1990.

Rising social expenditures in a low-growth economy began to squeeze the tax base, private consumption, and capital investment. Increasingly since the 1970s, the Scandinavian countries have struggled with maintaining economic balance. Generous unemployment benefits protected living standards when the economy turned bad, but how long can you sustain using 4 to 5 percent of GDP for that purpose? Denmark did so for two decades (1975–1995), but the cost forced unemployment policy reforms that, like Sweden's long-standing policy, emphasized "activation"—emergency employment or training—rather than passive support. Rising income tax levels yielded increasing tax avoidance strategies until tax reform broadened the tax base by reducing deductions and bringing down marginal rates in the 1980s and early 1990s. All of the Scandinavians except the oil-rich Norwegians repeatedly sought to trim welfare programs at the margins. But despite their best efforts to hold down costs, the secular trends pushing costs up combined with growth in unemployment (particularly long-term unemployment) continued to push spending and taxes up. Governmental expenditures rose roughly 15 percent of GDP between 1974 and 1996 in all Nordic countries except Norway (unchanged thanks to petroleum-fueled prosperity). Structural economic changes finally reversed this negative trend after 1995, and social expenditures declined as unemployment fell and economic growth accelerated until the onset of the global economic crisis in 2008. The Scandinavian states once again face the challenge of effective adjustment to the global economy.

While the welfare state was being constructed—from the 1930s through the early 1970s—increased expenditures were closely correlated with real gains in living standards. Unemployment compensation was enhanced, maternity and paternity leaves were introduced, pensions went up, housing was improved, day-care centers were built, and so on. In recent years, however, expenditures have continued to rise without such clear improvements in welfare.

Today, the cost of social programs is being pushed up in Scandinavia by three other forces: demography, technology, and rising take-up rates. Aging populations—and Scandinavians top the list internationally in terms of life expectancy—require longer pensions and more services. To deal with the former, national pension-funding reforms have raised pension savings and cut unfunded liabilities. The latter is more troublesome. Improved (and expensive) medical technology continues to drive the costs of the health-care system higher; despite the comprehensive and efficient national health systems in the four countries, a health-care cost crisis looms. And take-up rates for social programs have continued to rise among the young, who shape their behavior to conform to the mold of the social-benefit system. The result is that increasing expenditures do not necessarily increase welfare. Medical technology certainly extends life, but much of the costs of that new technology are incurred in the last few months of life, when the quality of life is low.

The costs of Scandinavian social programs burden national economic competitiveness, but strong public sectors can also be a competitive advantage. Global capital mobility means that investment in high-wage areas, such as the Nordic countries, will lag unless productivity (and applied research), or currency devaluations, maintain competitiveness. Fortunately, innovative firms, rising education levels and labor force skills, and cost containment in both the public and private sectors have been successful over the past decade. Some Scandinavian policies, such as the active labor market policy and the solidaristic wage policy, address the competitiveness issue directly. Others, such as national health insurance, spread medical costs generally across society, rather than burdening particular employers.[9] The economic protections provided to families through the social welfare system encourage employees to accept technological innovation. The term "flexicurity"—a flexible economy resting on a secure social security system—has has been coined to describe twenty-first-century Scandinavia.

A different—and troubling—issue in Scandinavia is the rapid increase in a noticeable immigrant population. Today about 6 percent of the population of Sweden, Denmark, and Norway carry foreign passports, as do 2 percent of the population of Finland, and the percentage of the foreign-born is higher, especially in Sweden, where more than 10 percent were born somewhere else.[10] They and their immediate descendants are now citizens, but integration into the social mainstream has been very uneven. To a considerable extent, support for the solidaristic social welfare system rested on the fact that those who benefited and those who paid were very similar. They spoke the same language, worshiped in the same church (at least at Christmas), shared the same culture, and looked very much alike. Under these circumstances, solidarity was easy. It is far from clear that the same solidarity will pertain as immigrant populations grow. Successful integration of non–Western European immigrants has so far eluded the Nordic countries. The result has been higher social costs and the rise of explicitly anti-immigration parties in Denmark and Norway and more recently in Sweden.

In the long run, Scandinavian prosperity in the global economy depends on sustaining the currently successful pattern of high wages and high performance. That requires action in Brussels and Frankfurt, where full employment has not been part of the prevailing ideology of the European Union and especially the European Central Bank. It also requires both anchoring domestic and attracting foreign capital. Pension and tax reforms have encouraged a high rate of savings, bringing mass investment (under professional management) even to Sweden, which in the past has prospered with perhaps the most concentrated ownership of any capitalist country under social democratic economic management.

Box 5.2   Cartoons and Immigrants:
No Laughing Matter

Early in 2006, Denmark faced one of its worst foreign policy crises since World War II. The country's largest newspaper, the liberal *Jyllands-Posten*, had published the previous September a dozen caricatures of the Prophet Muhammad, or other drawings about contemporary Danish perceptions of Islam. For some religious Muslims, any portrayal of their holiest prophet is sacrilegious, and the humorous, derogatory, or satirical drawings offended many, including some non-Muslims. Without imagining the possible global consequences, several editors at the paper had invited numerous Danish cartoonists to submit such drawings to prove that they would not be intimidated by the threat some artists felt at drawing even positive images of the Prophet. For weeks, the issue simmered; Danish prime minister Fogh Rasmussen refused a request by Arab ambassadors to discuss the issue even though he specifically addressed issues of tolerance and mutual respect in his annual New Year address.

Several radical Islamist activists were not content to let the issue fade. Traveling through the Middle East, they complained to several Arab governments about the intolerable insult directed at their faith. To embellish the case, several especially insulting pictures—neither drawn nor published in Denmark—were added to the "collection." Within days, Arab and foreign media spread the "news," and riots erupted in dozens of cities throughout the Muslim world. Danish embassies were attacked and in some cases destroyed (usually with the passive assistance of the "protecting" local government). Danish firms and products faced widespread boycotts. Other Scandinavian and European papers published the caricatures in support of the right to publish freely. Soon talk of a "clash of civilizations" and threats to freedom filled the debate. Recurring threats to the cartoonists and publishers have continued.

Underlying this crisis is the challenge of integrating tens of thousands of recent immigrants into the once homogeneous Scandinavian countries. Accommodating differences has always been a challenge to societies, even when the migrants came from distant Scandinavian regions: Finns moving to Sweden in the 1950s and 1960s or Greenlanders moving to Denmark a decade later often received less than enthusiastic welcomes. The real challenge was adjusting to non-European immigrants who were a trickle in the 1960s but became the majority of immigrants twenty years later. Now even Scandinavian-born children of the immigrants face significant lags in educational and vocational progress. Some social housing estates have largely immigrant populations, with "natives" fleeing the surrounding areas and schools.

Sweden and Iceland have relied on the labor market supplemented by language and other support to promote integration. When immigrants work and become self-supporting, they are more likely to adjust to the culture. Denmark faced its largest wave of immigrants and refugees during a time of high unemployment and tended to support the new residents through generous social benefits. It was not a successful program, and over the past decade the emphasis has been on rapid movement into the labor market, compulsory language and cultural instruction, and reduced social benefits. Norway and Finland have tended more toward the Danish model. In Norway and Denmark and more recently Sweden, rightist populist parties have attracted growing political support from voters who fear and distrust the new multiethnic society in which they live. In response, the main-stream political parties have shed their reluctance to discuss the problem and have reaffirmed the supremacy of traditional Scandinavian values, particularly against violence and in favor of women's rights.

More positively, moderates among the immigrant groups have entered the political process through the traditional political parties and are represented from city councils to national parliaments. A willingness to discuss the problems openly—still a challenge in Sweden—but respectfully may have received a boost from the "cartoon crisis," but the immigration and cultural diversity issues will figure prominently in Scandinavian politics for many years to come.[1]

1. For a scholarly and balanced study of the "cartoon crisis," see Jytte Klausen, *The Cartoons That Shook the World*, New Haven, CT: Yale University Press, 2009.

The past thirty years have been a watershed. The great social democratic project—the comprehensive welfare state supported by state economic intervention to manage the market economy—was completed with the able assistance of the center parties. There was no new, equivalent central thrust for reform. Minority governments of the center-right and center-left could administer this system, but it came under increasing pressure. Accelerating demographic changes—an aging and increasingly "multicultural" population—as well as relentless changes in the European Union and in the global economy ensure that the pressure will continue. Damage from the 2008 "Great Recession" has been less severe in the Scandinavian countries (except Iceland) than elsewhere in Europe, but a prolonged period of economic stagnation in Europe (and beyond) will take its toll on these export-dependent economies. Few in Scandinavia fault the welfare state for the latest crisis, but social policy must adjust to the new realities.

And so the question becomes whether and how the Scandinavian model can continue to be reshaped to meet the challenges of economic globalization while retaining its comprehensive, solidaristic, and humane structure. That is the current challenge.

The Roads to Europe

Europe, including Scandinavia, faced four vital questions in the wake of World War II. Two continental conflicts within a quarter century had threatened to extinguish European civilization. Armed struggle for control of Europe could not be allowed to occur again. At issue was, first, whether cooperation should be regional or global. A closely related second question was whether states should seek to build intensive integrated communities with like-minded states or whether cooperation should be restrained so as to include the largest number of participating countries (so-called "depth" versus "breadth," or "deepening" versus "widening" arguments). Third, should collaboration focus narrowly on specific economic or other policy problems (i.e., functional issues), or should it seek broad federal arrangements in which states would yield sovereignty over a range of policy matters? Finally, should this new international regime reinforce intergovernmental cooperation or should it carefully construct new international organizations with supranational responsibilities?

The Scandinavian states responded cautiously to these questions. Domestic issues were primary, but defensive isolation had failed between 1939 and 1945. The collapse of world trade in the 1930s had hurt their economies. Sweden had narrowly preserved its traditional neutrality during World War II, but only by accommodating the dominant belligerents. Denmark, Norway, and Finland had been invaded and found traditional nonalignment and neutrality largely discredited at the end of war. All had supported the League of Nations after World War I, only to see ruthless power politics and fanatical nationalism return. After 1945 they hoped that the emerging United Nations organization would allow them to preserve their independence while participating in the global community and a revitalized collective security system. Finland's position as a defeated power made its position especially precarious. Hard-liners in the Soviet Union believed that Finland had been a willing ally of Nazi Germany; instead, Finland's "continuation war" against the Soviet Union had been retaliation for Stalin's attack on Finland in 1939 (which had been encouraged by the Nazi-Soviet pact of August 1939 that established spheres of domination over Eastern Europe).

Scandinavia sought security and prosperity through broad European cooperation. All wished to avoid new divisions despite the obvious differences between the Western democracies and Stalin's Soviet Union. The term applied to this policy of reconciliation and constructive diplomacy was "bridge building." Bridges are built over chasms; the Scandinavian states recognized the fundamental conflicts that threatened the postwar order.

It is useful to view Scandinavian foreign policies from four perspectives: Nordic, European, Atlantic, and global. Such geopolitical shorthand is, admittedly, not precise, especially given the many changes since the Cold War.

The Nordic perspective reflects history and culture, but it also implies deliberate choices. We have mentioned the common roots of the Scandinavian states, which are traceable to a loose dynastic entity known as the Kalmar Union (1397–1523).[11] The next four hundred years saw frequent and often bitter rivalry in the Nordic region until the current five independent states emerged in the twentieth century. Sweden and Denmark competed for hegemony throughout the Baltic: first against the Hanseatic League and later against the emerging Slavic powers of Poland-Lithuania and finally Russia. The dominance of Russia from the eighteenth century onward, and later the growth of German power, forced the Scandinavians into an increasingly defensive position. Not until the collapse of the Soviet Union and its sphere of influence after 1990 would the Nordic states take a proactive role (now based on cooperation) in the Baltic.

Yet even as nationalism was shaping five distinct sovereign countries, there were calls for regional cooperation. They followed two lines: a romantic "pan-Scandinavianism" that argued for a federation of the increasingly democratic societies of the north, and pragmatic functional proposals covering a range of public policies common to the industrializing economies of the five states. Although "Scandinavianism" ended historic rivalries, it did not prevent the further division of the region into the five modern nations. The practical policy approach proved most fruitful, starting with a monetary union at the end of the nineteenth century (which collapsed during World War I), an "interparliamentary union" in 1907, and regular meetings between political leaders.

After World War II, the more ambitious goals of advocates for Nordic integration repeatedly ran into two obstacles. First, the interests of the Scandinavian countries were often different and not infrequently competitive. This strengthened historical and nationalist desires in Norway, Finland, and Iceland to maintain full independence from the older Scandinavian states. Second, outside political and economic ties outweighed Scandinavian alternatives. This would be seen most dramatically in security policy after 1948, when Denmark, Norway, and Iceland chose the Atlantic alliance led by the United States; Finland accommodated its foreign relations within the narrow limits demanded by the Soviet Union; and Sweden reaffirmed its historical and successful nonalignment.

Later, economic cooperation followed a similar path, with broader European opportunities outweighing the potential of narrower Nordic proposals. Although intra-Scandinavian trade expanded significantly after 1950, access to European and global markets remained the higher priority. Despite these setbacks, in 1952 the Nordic countries established the Nordic Council—essentially an extension of the interparliamentary union—that would coordinate legislation and encourage Nordic initiatives whenever consensus could be reached. Underlying the development of Nordic policy cooperation was the primacy of Social Democratic and Labor parties during much of the 1945 to 1975 period. Even in Iceland and Finland, where this was not the case, centrist governments adopted much of the Social Democratic agenda on labor, social, and economic issues. This paved the way for regional cooperation.

Nordic cooperation continues on three levels—parliamentary, ministerial, and nongovernmental—but most efforts are now channeled through the European Union. The annual meetings of parliamentary delegations from the five countries (plus the three autonomous regions: Åland, Greenland, and the Faeroes) encourage pragmatic cooperation and foster personal contacts across the region as well as a comparative perspective on policy issues. Ministerial contacts are more intense and continuous. In addition, there are regular ministerial "summits"—routinized since 1971 through the Nordic Council of Ministers—which bring together the top political and administrative people for detailed discussions and planning. A common Nordic political culture that emphasizes consensus, fact-finding, pragmatism, and responsibility helps this process. Common positions on European and international questions can multiply the weight of these small states. Finally, there are the various nongovernmental organizations in the educational, cultural, and scientific area that bring Scandinavians together on specific projects and interests. Again, this invigorates Nordic cooperation at the grass roots but also mobilizes important interests in support of these activities.

"Europe" in the form of "Western Europe" was at first a Cold War concept, but it increasingly gained real political and economic significance. The Nordic countries chose not to be part of the evolving European community that started with the Brussels Pact of 1948, the Schuman Plan of 1950 for a coal and steel community, and especially the Treaty of Rome in 1957, which sparked the development of a European common market. Yet all but Finland participated in the European Recovery Program (the Marshall Plan) and became part of looser institutional structures that were also favored by Great Britain. Likewise, Denmark and Norway found that NATO membership brought them closer to the Western European democracies and expedited reconciliation with the Federal Republic of Germany. By the 1960s, relationships with expanding Western European institutions (notably the Common Market) became a permanent issue on the Scandinavian political agenda.

The Atlantic dimension overlaps considerably with the European, but it has three distinctive facets. After 1940, the Scandinavian states developed sustained and intensive relations with the United States (and to a lesser extent Canada), with which they had previously had important ethnic ties but no intensive diplomatic history. Further, the Atlantic dimension brought particularly the three Scandinavian NATO members into a much wider community in Europe (especially with the Mediterranean NATO members). Finally, it evolved into a broader Western community exemplified by the Organization for Economic Cooperation and Development (OECD), which emerged in 1960 out of the narrower Marshall Plan structure. Even after the end of the Cold War, the Scandinavian states have sought to keep the United States immersed in European affairs and have encouraged NATO's enlargement eastward. Interestingly, neither Sweden nor Finland considered NATO membership but were satisfied with the Partnership for Peace and with the slowly emerging foreign and security cooperation in the European Union and with NATO when authorized by the UN.

Relations with Eastern Europe and the former parts of the Soviet Union represent the legacy of the Cold War, which also dominated Scandinavia for more than forty years. For the past two centuries, Scandinavia's relations with

Eastern Europe have been distant, and Russia was most often seen as a threat. After a period of bridge building between 1944 and 1948, the Scandinavian countries chose different options to cope with the East-West struggle. Common to each was a desire to maintain relatively low tensions in the Nordic region and to develop autonomous Nordic relations. Since 1990, Scandinavia's "Eastern question" has become far more complex. At present, three developments have emerged from the former Eastern bloc. First is the renewed independence of the Baltic states of Estonia, Latvia, and Lithuania. The Scandinavian countries have greeted this unexpected development with sustained economic and political involvement. Second, Russia's instability and uncertain steps toward democracy represent a continuing challenge for the Nordic states. The norm had been an authoritarian, powerful, but often conservative Russia. Finally, as the expanding EU encompasses Central and Eastern Europe, the Nordic countries must adjust to changing institutional and political arrangements while maintaining their influence and independence.

Finally, there is a global perspective that includes Scandinavia's historic commitment to the United Nations and other forms of international cooperation. Scandinavian military units have played a role in many UN peacekeeping missions. The Nordic countries have global economic interests and collectively represent a substantial global economic power. They are among the most generous and steadfast contributors to international economic assistance efforts and often champion the less-developed countries in international organizations. Yet they are far from major actors whose decisions can affect global affairs. Here, too, a strategy of bridge building can be constructive, as illustrated by the role of Norway and its late foreign minister, Johann Jørgen Holst, in facilitating the 1993 Israeli-Palestinian Oslo Accords. Scandinavian diplomats continue to pursue "peacemaking," despite frequent frustration.

POST–WORLD WAR II AND COLD WAR SECURITY OPTIONS

Initially the Nordic countries placed their trust mainly in the new United Nations and its promise of "collective security" and broad global cooperation. The disappointments of the 1930s were balanced by the lessons of appeasement and the leadership promised by the United States, along with hopes for Soviet cooperation in the postwar order. As a defeated power, Finland was initially denied membership in the UN, but the other four Nordic nations were in from the start. Scandinavians could see that their best foreign policy option was continuing great-power cooperation in the UN, and it was here that bridge-building efforts between the emerging Cold War blocs were focused. The appointment of Norwegian statesman Trygve Lie as the first secretary general of the UN (1946–1953) augured well for Scandinavian engagement, and he was followed by Swedish diplomat Dag Hammarskjöld (1953–1961), who expanded the writ of the secretary general.

After 1945, there were two new factors in European and Scandinavian geopolitics: the dominant position of the Soviet Union in Eastern Europe and the Baltic and the global stature of the United States. Soviet forces occupied Finland and kept bases near Helsinki until 1956. With the apparent breakdown of East-West cooperation in 1946–1947, the Scandinavian states sought to play a mediating role. The term "bridge building" was applied to diplomatic efforts to reconcile the two blocs. Had the focus been northern Europe, such pains might have borne results, but Scandinavia was distant from the conflict's center in Central and Eastern Europe. The "Iron Curtain" identified by Winston Churchill in 1946 did not run through Scandinavia, although Finland was vulnerable. All of the Scandinavian countries were handicapped by the weakness of their two main trading partners, Germany and Britain. Hence the Nordic countries were enthusiastic when U.S. Secretary of State George Marshall announced a European Recovery Program in June 1947.

Although the Scandinavian states were reluctant to give up on their bridge-building role, they recognized that by 1948, the East-West divide was a reality. Isolated neutrality had failed in 1940, but for Finland normalizing relations with the Soviet Union was the highest priority. A treaty of "friendship, cooperation, and mutual assistance" was negotiated and became the basis of the next forty years of Finnish-Soviet relations. It required Finland to obtain Moscow's approval for political and economic ties with the West and basically gave Moscow a so-called *droit de regard* (veto right) to scrutinize Finnish foreign policy and in practice, for more than twenty years, Soviet veto power over certain Finnish politicians. Crucially, however, it did not end Finland's recovering parliamentary democracy and capitalist economy.

Neither the United States nor Great Britain focused on Scandinavia after 1945. The United States had northern strategic concerns, but these were mainly the air bases in Iceland and, to a lesser extent, Greenland. Both were essential for U.S. military operations in Europe, and their strategic importance would grow significantly during the Cold War. While Finnish options were sharply limited, the other Scandinavian states agreed to reassess their collective security in 1948–1949. Isolated neutrality was discredited in Denmark and Norway, and even the Swedes seemed willing to consider a regional security arrangement.

The effort to create a nonaligned Scandinavian Defense Union failed basically because Norway sought closer ties with the emerging Western defense alliance that evolved into NATO. As one Norwegian politician put it, "We want to be defended, not liberated." Western (in practice, U.S.) military assistance would be directed at the broader alliance and not at peripheral blocs, and without such assistance, Scandinavian military potential would remain at a level characterized by one contemporary observer as a "$0 + 0 + 0 = 0$" equation. After Norway's choice, Sweden was uninterested in a bilateral arrangement, and

Denmark followed Norway into the North Atlantic Treaty Organization in April 1949. Sweden would preserve its nonalignment in peace and hope for neutrality in war.

For the next forty years, this arrangement prevailed with only marginal adjustments. Norway became initially the most enthusiastic Scandinavian NATO member, although the Norwegians adopted a policy of nonprovocation toward the Soviet Union, with which they shared a border in the far north. Denmark also refused to allow permanent foreign bases on its territory in time of peace, although NATO staff and periodic military exercises were accommodated. Denmark also accepted U.S. bases in Greenland without inquiring too closely about their military activities. Norway made a substantial effort to build up its armed forces; in Denmark, defense expenditures were controversial. Nevertheless, both countries developed and maintained military forces and alliance ties that were without historical precedent.

Sweden's nonalignment initially stimulated a considerable defense effort. Swedes believed that their successful neutrality during World War II came from achieving enough military strength to make invasion too costly. That became their defense policy in the Cold War, although we now know that Sweden cooperated secretly with NATO in the 1950s and 1960s in coordinating a defense against the Soviet Union.

THE NORDIC BALANCE

By the 1960s, Nordic foreign policies had established patterns that, with occasional variations, were maintained until the end of the Cold War in 1990. Each Nordic country had, of course, its own interests and priorities. Despite the lack of a formal common Nordic foreign policy, each country has assessed the impact its foreign policy might have on an overall "Nordic balance." In addition, as the Norwegian analyst Arne O. Brundtland and others noted, each Nordic country generally has assumed that the success of one Nordic country's foreign policy would benefit the entire region and minimize regional tensions. Nordic regional cooperation avoided defense and security policy, although a de facto Nordic bloc emerged in the 1960s in the United Nations and other international organizations. Nordic political leaders continued their tradition of regular informal consultation on issues of common interest.

Traditional small-state discretion gradually gave way to activism; indeed, Finland's expansive president, Urho Kekkonen, pursued "active nonalignment" for twenty-five years in order to maximize his country's options and assure the Soviet Union of Finland's friendly intentions. His preemptive anticipation of Soviet requests elicited domestic and foreign criticism, including the notorious concept of "Finlandization." Coined by West German politicians but broadly used by Western conservatives and critics of détente, it implied a passive regard for Soviet interests in lieu of Western cooperation.

Swedish leader Olof Palme also rejected the discretion of his predecessors and tried to shape a Swedish profile of active nonalignment in international affairs. A prominent global figure, Palme increasingly challenged the superpowers and promoted the development agenda for the so-called Third World until his assassination in 1986. He pushed a distinctive Swedish policy that gave the country international visibility that it had not had before and has not had since. He became the symbol of a strident criticism of U.S. foreign policy in the wake of the Vietnam War. Both Finland and Sweden put pressure on Denmark and Norway to minimize their engagement in NATO and to reconsider a more active Nordic security commitment. There were many in these countries who were tempted to follow such a line, but the choice of 1949—to rely primarily on broader Western defense cooperation—prevailed.

The Nordic balance remained deliberately vague and flexible throughout the Cold War. NATO and particularly the U.S. guarantee to Western Europe formed the foundation of national security policy in Denmark, Iceland, and Norway, and both Finland and Sweden counted on that ultimate source of assistance should things go wrong. All sought to reinforce the reality that northern Europe was not the main axis of East-West tensions.

Despite the different Nordic responses to the Cold War, each country sought to combine credible national security, conflict avoidance with the Soviet Union, and cautious steps toward relaxation of tensions between East and West. From the outset, few Scandinavians believed that the Soviet Union had a timetable for war with the West. War was more likely to occur because of miscalculation or the escalation of conflicts outside of Europe. Hence a policy of "reassurance" and conflict resolution won broad support, although there were genuine arguments about how to carry it out. This was not a policy of "appeasement"; Nordic criticism of Soviet human rights violations and imperialism in Eastern Europe became louder through the 1970s and 1980s. As noted earlier, both the Nordic and global dimensions of foreign policy allowed considerable diplomatic opportunities. Not all were successful, but such negotiations would at least communicate to the superpowers (especially the USSR) that the Nordic countries believed in "peaceful coexistence" combined with full respect for national independence.

While successfully restraining most Cold War tensions in their region, the Nordic countries never succeeded in creating a region truly distinct from the larger European context. In the security sphere, they had insufficient power; in economic matters, their ties to Europe remained supreme. By 1961, however, the dynamic Common Market was a serious issue in Scandinavia. West Germany had become again a vital market for the Scandinavian states, soon surpassing Britain. As security issues waned, economic questions demanded difficult choices: first between competing blocs and models (the European

Economic Community, EEC, versus the looser European Free Trade Association, EFTA), and then over the extent of integration and its political consequences.

BEYOND NORDIC BALANCE

Twenty years after the sudden collapse of communism in Europe and the end of the Cold War, it is hard to recall the passions and tensions of its final phase. Diplomatic, political, economic, as well as military confrontations followed the failure of East-West détente at the end of the 1970s. Then, and almost without warning, the political winds shifted. The accession of Mikhail Gorbachev to leadership in the Soviet Union in 1985 was the key element, but both U.S. president Reagan and especially Britain's Margaret Thatcher were quick to sense an opening with the new regime in the Kremlin. The spontaneous summit meeting in Reykjavik, Iceland, between Reagan and Gorbachev in November 1986 failed to produce a conclusive Euro-missile agreement, but unlike previous diplomatic disappointments, this meeting seemed to intensify negotiations and the spirit of compromise. The Soviet regime proclaimed "new thinking" in both domestic and foreign policy. Washington, London, and Bonn were prepared to give the Gorbachev proposals a full hearing.

In 1989–1991, Scandinavians, along with Europeans and Americans, watched with amazement as forty years of East-West competition ended, a dozen Marxist-Leninist regimes collapsed, and the Soviet Union split into its component republics. More proactively, the Nordic states gave diplomatic and economic support to the emerging independence movements in the Baltic republics (Estonia, Latvia, and Lithuania), which had been forcibly annexed by the Soviet Union fifty years earlier. As in 1918–1920 and 1945–1949, Nordic leaders had to rethink their international position and foreign policy priorities. The challenge would be to balance traditional interests and perspectives with the new opportunities and threats of a changed world. The Nordic balance soon became the "Northern Dimension" to the European Union.[12]

Scandinavia and the European Union

Scandinavia, as noted earlier, remained on the periphery of the European integration project for nearly twenty-five years after World War II. Three factors have repeatedly deterred the Scandinavian states from aggressively pursuing European integration and unity. First was the alternative attraction of Nordic economic cooperation. Although initial attempts to form a Nordic customs union in the 1950s failed, the project was resurrected in new versions until 1970, when Denmark and Norway declared definitively for the European alternative. However, only Denmark joined the EEC in 1973, while Norwegian voters rejected membership and Sweden and Finland never applied. Denmark would preserve its Nordic links and would even promote regional interests in Brussels, but the limits of Nordic cooperation seemed clear. Second, the ultimate goal of a united Europe enjoyed only modest support among the political leadership and the public in these small states, historically unaligned and mistrustful of larger neighbors. Third, with broader free-trade ambitions, the Nordic countries have resisted having to choose sides in economic communities. Until 1973, Britain and Germany belonged to different European trading blocs, while the attractions of global trade (especially with North America and Japan, and even with socialist countries such as the Soviet Union, China, and Eastern Europe) deterred commitment to the European project.

The Scandinavian states favored European cooperation over unity. Cooperation aimed at removing barriers to free trade and investment as well as policy collaboration in areas of common concerns (e.g., environment, refugees, human rights, defense) have come to be regarded as "Europe à la carte." States can pick and choose the collection of projects in which they will participate. The alternative they resisted was more grandiose: a "United States of Europe" with genuinely federal institutions that would move significant portions of public policy into a European entity. National governments would still have residual powers through the principle of "subsidiarity," but like other federal systems, the whole would be more than the sum of its parts. Ancient cultures and states would be unlikely to disappear or become mere provinces, but the four-hundred-year tradition of state sovereignty largely would be ended in principle as well as in practice. This second vision has little support in Scandinavia and has met much vigorous resistance.

ECONOMIC COOPERATION

As trading states, the Scandinavian countries have long been wary of economic isolationism. All suffered from the economic nationalism and mercantilism of the interwar period. In response, domestic protectionism gained a foothold in the agricultural and other primary economic sectors.

The Scandinavian countries did not participate significantly in any of the meetings between 1955 and 1957 that led to the Rome Treaty establishing the EEC. Likewise they had not been involved in the precursors of the Schuman Plan and the European Coal and Steel Community of 1952. The broader trade bloc did raise concerns, especially in Denmark and Sweden, which had important economic ties to the rapidly growing West German economy. British refusal to consider participation, and its establishment of an alternative European Free Trade Association (EFTA) in 1959 confirmed the division of Europe into "sixes and sevens." Generally the Scandinavians favored free trade for industrial goods and international services (e.g., shipping), but only Denmark accepted similar liberalization for the agricultural sector. None of them believed that the integration of all economic sectors, as had begun with the European Coal and Steel Community, was relevant for their economic situation. This distinction between free trade and harmonization would continue.

By 1961, it was clear that the EEC would progress and that the EFTA would be less significant. The ambiguous British decision to apply for EEC membership forced the Scandinavian countries to reconsider their position. French president Charles de Gaulle delayed British entry for a decade, but when in 1969 the issue again became germane, it was clear that the EEC was an economic and political success and that there would be no other significant European alternative. As the European option again appeared promising, the Nordic countries (now including Finland) commenced negotiations on a wider Nordic economic community that would possibly lead to a common Nordic entry into the EEC. This possibility threatened Finland's special regard for Soviet sensibilities, but Sweden too was concerned about its "nonaligned" status (a point already raised in 1963). In short, whenever a wider European option became promising, the Nordic countries found that they each had different perspectives.

The result would be four Scandinavian roads to Europe, with Denmark's entry into the EEC in 1973, Sweden and Finland in 1995, and Norway's two failed entry attempts in 1972 and 1994. Just to complicate matters, the two Danish autonomous North Atlantic territories of Greenland and the Faeroe Islands remained outside of the EEC, with Greenland actually withdrawing in 1982. Following its severe financial crisis in 2008–2009, Iceland commenced negotiations for entry into the EU.

It is notable that joining Europe has been a divisive issue in domestic politics everywhere, even including Finland, where the European Union seemed to offer guarantees against renewed Russian pressure in the future. The referenda results in table 5.3 suggest just how disputed this key decision in fact was. Ironically, the strength of domestic opposition has not slowed Danish integration into European structures in those areas approved by the voters; Denmark has typically ranked among the top countries in the European Union in actually adapting national legislation and regulation to fit European requirements. As late entrants, Sweden and Finland had to accept the developing European Union in 1995, including its extensive rules and regulation (the so-called *acquis communautaire*). The ongoing EU debates and, in the case of Denmark, repeated referenda on Europe disrupted the normal patterns of partisan allegiance in domestic politics.

RELUCTANT EUROPEANS

The European integration project has evolved significantly over the past twenty years, starting with the Maastricht Treaty of 1991 (as amended in Edinburgh

[1992] and further in Amsterdam [1997] and Nice [2001]) and the unsuccessful constitutional treaty (2004) to the Lisbon Treaty (2007), but the Nordic countries remain skeptical participants. Norway is linked through the agreement on a European Economic Area (EEA), which was negotiated in 1990, took effect in 1993, and essentially gives these countries access to the "Single European Market" in all areas excepting agriculture, natural resources, and other issues of vital national interest. This is the "outer ring" of the European orbit, and although EEA countries (there are only three: Iceland, Norway, and Liechtenstein) have essentially full access to European markets, they have no direct influence on the development of the European Union.

Denmark, along with Britain, circles the EU more closely. Both are signatories to the Maastricht Treaty and its successors but have significant, though different, reservations. Denmark has rejected monetary union, although its economy is among the strongest in the EU and its currency has been closely tied to the German mark and now the euro since 1982. It has been cautious about harmonization of police and judicial affairs and participation in key elements of the common foreign and security policy. Every significant change in European policy has sparked a bitter fight in Denmark and resulting national referenda. The 1997 Amsterdam revision of the union treaty was approved by the Danish voters, but in September 2000 they rejected the euro as their national currency. The Danish government accepted the Nice Treaty of 2001, which prepared the EU for a significant expansion to include Eastern and southern European states. Although domestic opponents of the EU have railed against opening the union to hordes of poor Eastern Europeans, others see the expansion as postponing "federalism" for an indefinite period. Anti-EU parties (on the extreme right and left) are well represented in parliament, and a quarter of the delegates elected by the Danes to the European Parliament are anti-EU activists. The EU constitutional treaty would have required a Danish referendum

Table 5.3   European Community/European Union Referenda

	Denmark						Norway		Sweden		Finland
	1972	1986	1992	1993	1998	2000	1972	1994	1994	2003	1994
Yes	63.3	56.2	49.3	56.7	55.1	46.8	46.5	47.8	52.3	41.8	57.0
No	36.7	43.8	50.7	43.5	44.9	53.2	53.5	52.2	46.8	56.1	43.0
Turnout	90.1	75.4	83.1	86.5	74.8	86.7	79.2	88.8	82.4	81.2	70.8

Note: The referenda were as follows: Denmark 1972: Joining the EC; 1986: EC single market; 1992: Maastricht Treaty; 1993: Edinburgh agreement modifying Maastricht; 1998: Amsterdam Treaty; 2000: adopting the euro; Norway 1972 and 1994, Sweden 1994, Finland 1994: Joining the EC/EU; Sweden 2003: common European currency.

(Sources: Danish Folketinget Website: www.ft.dk; Nordic Council, Norden i Tal, 2002. Swedish Riksdag Website: www.riksdagen.se.)

(and possibly referenda in Sweden and Finland), but it was killed by French and Dutch voters in 2005. The Lisbon Treaty has been deemed a "consolidation" of previous treaties and not a further surrender of sovereignty. The pro-EU Liberal-Conservative government has sought to reduce or eliminate the Danish "opt-outs," but the Danish People's Party, their parliamentary supporters, rejects such a move. The economic turmoil since 2008 has postponed further Danish action on their opt-outs.

Norway has debated the EU issue for more than forty years, and twice its voters vetoed membership that had been approved by wide parliamentary majorities. As elsewhere in the region, Norwegian "Euro-skeptics" have bundled political, cultural, and economic issues into their program, but economic factors seem most salient. Although the 1972 rejection predated Norway's current petroleum-fueled prosperity, the continuing boost of oil and gas exports has shielded the country from most of the economic strains of the past thirty years. Most oil revenues are now shunted into a massive "Government Pension Fund–International," which invests globally and whose assets approached $450 billion in fall 2010. Protection of Norway's heavily subsidized agricultural sector and regionally significant coastal fisheries has also been a factor weighing against membership. As a member of the European Economic Area since the early 1990s, the Norwegian industrial, labor, and service sectors are fully integrated with the EU. Policy cooperation extends to justice, education, and other sectors. The main drawback of this "junior membership" is absence from most of the EU policymaking process.

Sweden and Finland became EU members in 1995 after vigorous national debates and referenda. As new members they were forced to swallow the whole EU system, but not without protest and regret. Their EU parliamentary delegations have strong anti-EU contingents, and opinion at home is no less skeptical of the EU project than that of the doubting Danes. Neither is firmly committed to a common European security policy or to federalism. Like the Danes, they have encouraged eastward expansion, especially to the Baltic states and Poland. During their EU presidencies, they have pushed the social and labor agenda as well as budgetary and administrative reforms of EU institutions. Only Finland has fully joined the Economic and Monetary Union, with the euro replacing the Finnish markka as the national currency in 2002, while Sweden rejected the common currency in 2003.

Today the Scandinavian countries still see the EU mainly in pragmatic economic terms. They have been especially cautious about expanded cooperation on foreign and security policy matters despite the turmoil in the Balkans after 1990, the "war on terrorism" after September 2001, and a host of continuing crises in Africa, the Middle East, and elsewhere that suggest that world politics is not only the global economy. They accepted without significant debate the expansion of the EU to include twelve central, Mediterranean, and Eastern European countries, including the Baltic states and near-neighbor Poland, but they maintain various restrictions on labor migration.

All of the Nordic countries supported the U.S. response to the terrorist attack of 9/11. Danish, Finnish, Norwegian, and Swedish troops serve with the UN-sanctioned but NATO-led International Security Assistance Force in Afghanistan. Indeed, Denmark has suffered significant casualties in relation to its size and military contribution to the Afghan campaigns. The reluctant "multi-lateralism" of the Bush administration and its willingness to work within the UN and NATO initially seemed a hopeful sign to those suspicious of the previous raw unilateralism of the U.S. administration. Unfortunately, the invasion and occupation of Iraq in 2003 by U.S. and British troops deepened Nordic concerns and divisions. The Danish government again gave wholehearted support to military action against the Saddam Hussein regime and provided a military contingent for the occupation, while the Swedes, Finns, and Norwegians were critical of the U.S. and British response. It was yet another reminder of the different national perspectives across Scandinavia. The differences were purely governmental; public opinion throughout Scandinavia became increasingly critical of the Bush administration's unilateralist nationalism. Likewise, the election of Barack Obama in 2008 improved the image of the United States throughout Scandinavia. This was reflected by President Obama's Nobel Peace Prize in 2009, which was awarded by the Norwegian Nobel Committee (with some debate across the region and beyond and furious denunciations by American rightists). Its 2010 award to Chinese political dissident and prisoner Liu Xiabo elicited similar hysterics from the Chinese government.

For the Scandinavian Social Democrats in particular, the European Union and economic globalization more generally pose some ironic dilemmas. Although they have always been rhetorically internationalist—and have lived up to the rhetoric in development aid and in direct support for foreign trade unions and labor parties in the Third World and Eastern Europe—their success at home has been premised on the relevance of the nation-state as the unit for making economic policy. The generous and humane provisions of the social democratic welfare states in Scandinavia yielded a truly decent society for all, but they were dependent on strong, carefully managed economies and full employment. It is far from clear that those are at the top of the European Union's economic agenda. If the welfare state was the surrogate for socialism for the Scandinavian Social Democrats from the 1930s through the 1980s, what is to be the surrogate for the welfare state?

The so-called "Great Recession" following the financial crisis of 2008–2009 has challenged the Scandinavian "model" yet again. The impact of the crisis varied from quite mild in petro-Norway to more severe in Sweden and Denmark and harsh in Finland and Iceland. Compared to southern Europe, the Scandinavian economies are in relatively good shape because of cautious fiscal policies during the good years (international debt was low or declining until

2008) and successful interventions to shore up financial and export sectors. Unemployment has risen everywhere, but once again the social policies have protected the average citizen. The fact remains that the export-oriented Nordic economies (and societies) are now deeply embedded with the European and global economy. Recovery depends in large part on the actions of other countries. Interdependence is not new in Scandinavia.

The habits of nonalignment and independence of all Nordic states, along with their still vigorous sense of nationhood and self-confidence, color their view of Europe and the world. They are also a factor in the continuing debate about non-European immigration and the challenges of multiculturalism. Once again, a Nordic "middle way" has emerged toward the regional and global challenges of the new century. Scandinavians are pragmatic skeptics, seeking "just enough Europeanization" to respond to economic, social, and political challenges. As successful states and just societies, they see no need to bury themselves in a federal Europe. The successful reform and reinvigoration of the "Scandinavian model" since 1990 have given them renewed confidence at home and relevance for larger EU countries seeking new ideas. But they are not isolationists; the past century taught them that their fates are intimately tied to their continent and to global developments. The Nordic EU bloc of three is likely to support a reformed "social Europe" in which the principles of "subsidiarity" and pragmatism will make the Scandinavians more comfortable in the European home. Through reforms and innovation—such as "flexicurity"—the Scandinavian countries will challenge their European neighbors to do better.

Suggested Readings

Derry, T. K., *A History of Scandinavia: Norway, Sweden, Denmark, Finland, and Iceland*, Minneapolis: University of Minnesota Press, 1979.

Einhorn, Eric S., and John Logue, *Modern Welfare States: Scandinavian Politics and Policy in the Global Age*, New York: Praeger, 2003.

Einhorn, Eric S., and John Logue, "Can Welfare States Be Sustained in a Global Economy? Lessons from Scandinavia," *Political Science Quarterly*, 125(1), Spring 2010, 1–29.

Heidar, Knut, *Norway: Elites on Trial*, Boulder, CO: Westview, 2001.

Hilson, Mary, *The Nordic Model: Scandinavia since 1945*, London: Reaktion Books, 2008.

Ingebritsen, Christine, *The Nordic States and European Union: From Economic Interdependence to Political Integration*, Ithaca, NY: Cornell University Press, 1998.

Ingebritsen, Christine, *Scandinavia in World Politics*, Boulder, CO: Rowman & Littlefield, 2006.

Jussila, Osmo, Seppo Hentilä, and Jukka Nevakivi, *From Grand Duchy to a Modern State: A Political History of Finland since 1809*, London: Hurst, 1999.

Nordstrom, Byron J., *Scandinavia since 1500*, Minneapolis: University of Minnesota Press, 2000.

Petersson, Olof, *The Government and Politics of the Nordic Countries*, Stockholm: Fritzes, 1994.

Thakur, Subhash et al., *Sweden's Welfare State: Can the Bumblebee Keep Flying?* Washington: International Monetary Fund, 2003.

CHAPTER 6

Russia: European or Not?

Bruce Parrott

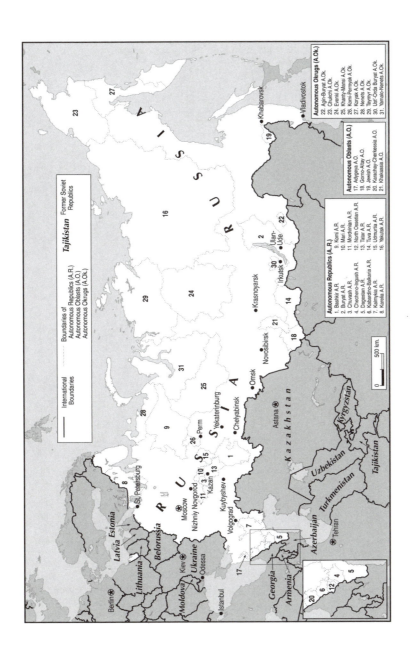

Russian Federation

Population (million):   142
Area in Square Miles: 6,592,819
Population Density per Square Mile: 22
GDP (in billion dollars, 2009): $2,118.6
GDP per capita (PPP, 2005): $14,762
Joined EC/EU: n/a

Performance of Key Political Parties in Parliamentary Elections of December 2, 2007

Agrarian Party of Russia (APR)   2.3%
United Russia (ER)   64.3%
Communist Party of the Russian Federation (KPRF)   11.6%
Liberal Democratic Party of Russia (LDPR)   8.1%
Russian Democratic Party "Yabloko" (RDP)   1.6%
Fair Russia (SR)   7.7%
Civilian Power (GS)   1.0%

Main Office Holders: President: Dmitry Medvedev—ER (2008); Prime Minister: Vladimir Putin—ER (2008).

Is Russia part of Europe? For almost three centuries, observers have debated this question, and their answers have been shaped by the specific conditions in Europe as well as in Russia. During the eighteenth-century era of enlightened absolutism, Russia's dominant elites regarded it as part of Europe, and prominent Europeans agreed. Near the start of the eighteenth century, Peter the Great, one of the most important monarchs in Russian history, traveled extensively in Europe and based his sweeping administrative and economic reforms on the models he found there. A half century later, Voltaire, a leading thinker of the French Enlightenment, wrote an admiring history of Tsarist Russia and corresponded with Catherine the Great, another of Russia's modernizing autocrats.[1] Russia's acquisition of a colonial empire outside Europe strengthened its resemblance to other European imperial states. In the case of countries such as Britain and France, these empires lay overseas. In the Tsarist case, the empire grew primarily through overland expansion into adjacent territories such as the Caucasus and Central Asia. Despite this difference, the Tsars regarded their empire building as a manifestation of their country's "civilizing" European role, and so did many European observers.

However, several changes during the nineteenth and twentieth centuries raised new questions about Russia's relationship to Europe. First, the spread of heterodox political ideas in Europe aroused Russian anxiety and ambivalence about links with the West. Although the Tsars wanted to strengthen Russia through closer economic relations with Europe, they feared that nineteenth-century Europe's increasingly volatile mixture of democratic, nationalist, and Marxist ideas would infect Tsarist society. Fear of such infection nourished the mid-nineteenth-century debate between the Westernizers, a group of political and cultural figures who believed that Russia should emulate trends in the West, and the Slavophiles, a cultural and political group that believed Russia should follow a distinctive non-Western path of development.

In a certain sense, Tsarist fears of ideological infection from Europe came true when the communists seized power in Russia under Lenin's leadership near the end of World War I. However, Lenin and his successors did not intend to remake Russia along conventional Western lines. They sought to transform it according to a communist vision that existed only in the realm of Marxist social theory. They viewed Europe as a theater for communist revolution rather than a model to be imitated, and they expected that communism would ultimately spread to all of Europe and beyond. In other words, they believed that the noncommunist world would increasingly be modeled on the Soviet Union, not the other way around.

Rather than bridging the differences between Russia and Europe at large, the victory of a communist vanguard in Russia deepened them. For seven decades, Russia, as the geographic and demographic core of the Soviet state, was the focus of the Marxist-Leninist drive to create a novel communist order. Launched under the ruthless tyranny of Joseph Stalin, this all-out drive for socioeconomic transformation not only created the world's first planned industrial economy but also killed millions of Soviet citizens through the violent collectivization of agriculture, the creation of a vast network of prison labor camps, and blood purges that decimated the ranks of the Soviet elite itself.

The communist system profoundly altered Russia's social and economic structure, but it did not spread to Europe—at least not to the Western European countries beyond the reach of Stalin's army at the end of World War II. Instead, Western Europe, anchored by the strategic power of the United States, gradually evolved toward a common liberal order antithetical to communism. Due partly to the exhausting effects of World War II, the major European states were also steadily compelled to give up their colonial empires—one of the main features they had earlier shared with Tsarist Russia. In contrast to the USSR, the states of Western Europe no longer had the global ambitions and global reach they had previously possessed.

Toward the end of the twentieth century, the prospects for a new convergence between Europe and Russia improved dramatically. In the mid-1980s, Mikhail Gorbachev, the last Soviet leader, introduced unprecedented internal changes designed to humanize the repressive Soviet political order. These sweeping changes ultimately triggered the collapse of Soviet communism and reversed the vectors of international influence that Soviet officials had long tried to promote. After taking power in Russia and helping enact the final dissolution of the Soviet Union, President Boris Yeltsin and his political allies launched a campaign to make Russia a "normal" state based on liberal-democratic and capitalist principles borrowed from the West. In contrast to a long line of Soviet leaders, they sought to rejoin Europe rather than remake it. However, the workability of their program for Westernizing the country was untested. Moreover, it was unclear whether Russia was ready to disavow the USSR's global role and operate as a regional European power.

The hallmark of this monumental effort to transform Russia has been acute uncertainty for elites and ordinary citizens alike. During the Soviet era, the communist leadership tirelessly promoted the political myth that Marxism-Leninism enabled it to forecast the future. If Soviet citizens learned to discount this claim during the final decades of Soviet power, at least they experienced a large measure of predictability in their personal lives. The form of authoritarianism that evolved after Stalin's death in 1953 offered citizens a substantial measure of socioeconomic security despite heavy restrictions on political freedom. The collapse of the Soviet Union, however, exploded the predictability of daily life along with the ruling myth of communist infallibility. For some Russians, the end of the Soviet system brought freedom and economic opportunity; for others, it brought political disappointment and severe economic hardship. For virtually everyone, it brought great uncertainty and a desire for more stability.

The aftermath of the Soviet collapse also left ordinary Russians unsure of their country's international role. Would Russia establish strong links with Europe, thereby expanding Europe's geographical extent and international influence? Or would it withdraw from Europe and "face east," seeking closer ties with Asian powers such as China in a bid to counterbalance the ascendancy of the United States and its allies in Europe? And what of its relations with the fourteen other former republics of the USSR? Would Moscow accept their gravitation toward Western groupings such as the European Union and NATO, or would it resist these trends, and with what consequences?

Dimensions of Postcommunist Change

To succeed, the reform program for joining the West required fundamental changes in the traditional Soviet order. These included establishing a new territorial state in the heart of the former USSR, creating a democratic political system for choosing leaders and making policy, building a capitalist economy based on private ownership and competitive markets, stimulating civic activism, and creating a system of public administration that could uphold the rule of law in public life.

Considered individually, each of these objectives was daunting. Taken together, they represented a mammoth undertaking. Like individuals, governments have trouble dealing with more than one or two major problems at the same time, due to the limits on their resources and decision-making capacity. For example, the U.S. government struggled unsuccessfully for several decades to enact major health-care reform, and it remains unclear whether the reform passed under President Obama will be economically effective. But reforming U.S. health care is a modest task compared to the sweeping political agenda that has confronted Russian leaders and citizens. The attempt to recast Russia's national identity, political structure, economic order, social life, and system of public administration—*all at the same time*—was bound to produce many unforeseeable consequences.

In deciding how to approach this complex political agenda, Russian leaders and officials have faced perplexing choices about which political tools to use. The consolidation of democracy is sometimes said to depend on a national consensus that "elections are the only game in town"—in other words, that no one can become a major government leader without winning a democratic election. Established democracies rest on the assumption that it is illegitimate to influence the outcome of an election by, for example, urging the armed forces to intervene or using government intelligence agencies to collect confidential information about opposition candidates. Mature democracies allow the leading candidates unfettered access to the news media. They also limit the electoral use of economic resources to, for example, buy votes or divert government funds to favor some candidates over others—although laws limiting the use of private economic resources in political campaigns raise vexing questions of free speech.

Box 6.1   From a Speech by Deputy Head of the Presidential Administration Vladislav Surkov to Workers of the United Russia Political Party

Moscow, February 7, 2006

[A]s President [Vladimir Putin] has indicated in his speeches, on the whole we have followed the same path as other European countries. . . . [A]bsolutism reached its apogee in Russia at about the same time as in France. . . . Russia abolished "dealing in people" [serfdom and slavery] . . . even earlier than . . . the United States of America. Our parliamentarism isn't much younger than that of other countries. As for the fact that we had quite a strange totalitarian state in the twentieth century, it's necessary to remember that we weren't alone, that Nazi Germany, Fascist Italy, and Francoist Spain existed in the same Europe. . . .

The big [Soviet] problem was . . . that such a closed society . . . produced an ineffective elite. . . . [A]t a time when people of the stature of Peter the Great were needed, a group of poorly educated and irresponsible comrades came to power. . . . [Former U.S.] Secretary of State Shultz writes in his memoirs that he was shocked by the incompetence of the Soviet leaders. . . . Rejection of such a society was unavoidable. . . .

[However,] the mass of the country was not prepared . . . for life in conditions of contemporary democracy. . . . [R]ather than move toward democracy, we got . . . an oligarchy. . . . In place of public discussion we got continual court intrigue. Instead of representation we got manipulation. . . . Competition was replaced by corruption. . . . If what I've described is democracy and a free and just society, then what is Sodom and what is Gomorrah? . . . [W]hen people try to convince us that someone [in Russia] is dismantling democracy, that is an absolute distortion. . . . The president is returning the real meaning of the word "democracy" to all democratic institutions. . . .

Russia, without a doubt, must remain in the ranks of the powers that make decisions about . . . the world order. . . . [F]or 500 years ethnic Russians and Russian citizens have been a state-bearing people . . . in contrast to many of our friends from the Soviet Union and many other countries. . . . It's clear that some countries that proclaim entry into the European Union to be their national idea are very happy countries; it is not necessary for them to think much. For them everything is very simple. The "Muscovites" . . . are guilty of everything, now we're running to Brussels and everything there will be all right. It's necessary to remember that these nations were not sovereign for one day of their history. . . . This is normal. They were the province of one country and will become the province of another. . . .

[In Russia] a psychology called "offshore aristocracy" has been established. . . . [Members of this group] see their future and the future of their children as outside Russia. . . . [S]uch people will not stand up for [Russia] or be concerned about it. . . . If our business community is not transformed into a national bourgeoisie, then, of course, we have no future. . . .

A second line of political restorationism . . . is . . . the isolationists. . . . These people are almost Nazis, people who spread the idea that the terrible West is threatening us, that . . . China is stepping on us, . . . that Russia is for Russians,

Tatarstan, apparently, is for Tatars, Yakutia is for Yakuts. . . . [I]f the national-isolationists come to power . . . [this] will lead the nation to a demographic catastrophe and a political crash. . . . [T]o provoke interethnic conflicts in our country is very dangerous. . . . [W]e must strongly oppose this. We stand for a Russia that is for ethnic Russians, Tatars, Mordovians, Ossetians, Chechens, for all of our peoples, for the entire Russia-wide nation.

In postcommunist Russia, elections have certainly acquired heightened importance as a mechanism of elite selection and elite legitimation. However, Russia has inherited many undemocratic tools of coercion and manipulation from the Soviet era, and the competitors for power have frequently resorted to them—sometimes in order to preempt similar action by their political rivals.

The tumultuous attempt to democratize and marketize the public sphere has imposed severe strains on Russian society. Successful cases of capitalist democracy depend on the existence of a vigorous civil society able to foster participatory values in the citizenry and articulate the social interests that feed into government decision making. As used here, the term "civil society" denotes an extensive network of voluntary associations that are active, nonviolent, autonomous from the government, and allow individuals to join or leave on their own initiative. The fact that these civic associations accept the legitimacy of one another's interests, even when those interests diverge, is conducive to social pluralism and political compromise.[2]

In the USSR, the ruling elite, guided by a fundamental hostility to social pluralism, suppressed any tendency toward the development of a civil society. The elite forced society into a straitjacket, extending the party-state apparatus into every corner of daily life and creating a facade of monolithic popular support for communist rule. This Marxist-Leninist formula for state-society relations was boldly rejected by Gorbachev after he became the leader of the USSR. Seeking to tap the population's suppressed initiative and energy, Gorbachev slashed the power of the party-state apparatus and unleashed a surge of spontaneous sociopolitical activism that initially strengthened his campaign to revitalize the Soviet system. The vast upheaval he set in motion has continued in various guises for more than two decades, but its long-term social consequences remain uncertain. Has this torrent of change created the basis of a genuine civil society, or is society destined once again to become a handmaiden of the state?

Knowing a bit about the key turning points in Russia's recent development makes it easier to understand the interaction among these factors. One turning point, of course, was the dissolution of the USSR. The process of political liberalization launched by Gorbachev ultimately escaped his control and generated increasing polarization between anti-Marxist liberals and Leninist conservatives. In 1991, a radical democratic challenge from opponents of the Soviet regime and an unsuccessful last-ditch coup attempt by its supporters intensified the centrifugal forces undermining the Soviet Federation.[3] The outcome was Russia's emergence as an independent state with Boris Yeltsin as president, the promulgation of a program of radical economic reform known as "shock therapy," and a temporary ban on the Communist Party.

Another turning point came in 1993, when President Yeltsin's increasingly bitter political conflict with the Russian parliament finally prompted him to disband the parliament and use the army to crush the opponents who resisted. One result of this confrontation was the adoption of a new Russian constitution with government powers heavily skewed toward the presidency at the expense of the parliament.

A third turning point came in 1995–1996, when the severe economic hardships resulting from shock therapy made it seem likely that Yeltsin would be defeated by a communist candidate in the impending presidential election. Yeltsin seriously considered delaying the election, but in the end a group of new business tycoons who had acquired enormous wealth from the first stages of economic reform rallied around him, enabling him to mount an effective campaign and win the election. These tycoons, commonly known as "oligarchs," deeply feared a possible restoration of communist power.

A fourth turning point came in 1999–2000, when Yeltsin unexpectedly resigned a few months before the end of his term to smooth the way for Vladimir Putin, the politically untested prime minister, to become his successor. Feverish maneuvering in the run-up to the election enabled Putin to defeat better-known presidential candidates who might have prosecuted Yeltsin and his close associates for corruption. Putin, who had spent most of his career in the Soviet security service, began to place security service "alumni" in other state agencies and took steps to rein in the most aggressive oligarchs.

A fifth turning point came in 2003–2005, when Putin's campaign to establish political order and tame the oligarchs culminated in the targeted destruction of Yukos, the country's largest and most efficient oil company. The Yukos affair redefined the relationship between wealth and power in Russia. It marked the ascendancy of political elites determined to reestablish the dominance of the Russian state, and it paved the way for further reductions of electoral competition and freedom in the political arena. These changes were manifested in Putin's landslide victory in the 2004 presidential election against a field of minor political personalities.

In the future, historians may look back on the year 2008 as the start of yet another pivotal juncture. As Putin's second presidential term drew to a close, observers speculated that the struggle over presidential succession might precipitate a major political crisis. Would Putin, they wondered, step down as the constitutional term-limit required, or would he preserve his hold on the presidency by unconstitutional means? In the end, Putin anointed his protégé Dmitry Medvedev as the new president, but he took the post of prime minister, thereby keeping open the option of returning to the presidency once more after Medvedev's term was completed. The onset of a worldwide financial crisis soon compounded uncertainties about the direction of Russia's political evolution. Depending on the ultimate outcome of these developments, observers may look back on the years after 2008 as a further step toward entrenched authoritarianism—or, less likely, as a move away from it.

National Identity and Statehood

Russia's postcommunist experience highlights the complex interaction among national identity, statehood, and democratization. Today, the view that every nation should have its own territorial state, or sovereign political structure, is widely accepted. However, the fit between existing nations and established states is anything but automatic. Most contemporary observers agree that nations are social groupings whose distinguishing characteristics can change over time; they also agree that in the absence of a common understanding about who belongs to a nation—and therefore to the corresponding state—democratization is extremely difficult. Democratic theory rests on the proposition that a nation or a people (the *demos* in the word "democracy") must govern itself.

But what if there is widespread disagreement about which individuals and territories belong to the nation? Democratic theory cannot answer this fundamental question. The problem cannot be resolved by invoking the principle of national self-determination, because conducting a national plebiscite or convening a representative national assembly requires prior agreement on which individuals are entitled to vote or be represented—the very question that the procedure is supposed to solve. Without a shared understanding of national identity, the inhabitants of a territory are likely to clash over whether they should have a single state or separate states. So, any historical situation that requires recasting a nation's identity or a state's structure to make them compatible hobbles the attempt to build democracy.

The Soviet breakup posed the question of which persons and lands belong to the Russian nation. This conundrum was somewhat mitigated by the fact that the Russian republic had been one of the constituent elements of the now-defunct Soviet Federation. Provisional Russian boundaries and a set of rudimentary political institutions already existed; indeed, these institutions were the mechanisms Yeltsin and his allies used to build up power on the eve of the Soviet collapse. Still, independent Russia's emergence from a larger state hampered the construction of a new political system. Many inhabitants of Russia remained ambivalent about the diminution of the state and the apparent shrinkage of the Russian nation.

One problem was whether to "unmix" the multinational populations inherited from the USSR—and if so, how. Many ethnic Russians lived in other former Soviet republics, and many non–ethnic Russians (such as Ukrainians or Georgians) lived in Russia. Should all of these people become citizens of their "ethnic homeland" and "return" to it, even if they were born in another republic and had always lived there? Like most former Soviet republics, Russia dealt with this question by offering national citizenship to all its inhabitants (as well as to the inhabitants of other republics who requested it). Nevertheless, the issue of ethnic Russians living abroad has remained a sensitive topic in Russian domestic politics and foreign policy. This is especially true of Russia's relations with Estonia and Latvia, two former Soviet republics that refused to grant citizenship automatically to the ethnic Russians who put down roots there during the Soviet era. These countries have established stringent criteria for naturalization to emphasize that they were forcibly incorporated into the USSR under Stalin and to fend off any new efforts by Moscow to control them through the local ethnic Russian population. For most ethnic Balts, as well as the citizens of some other former Soviet republics, the end of Moscow's domination represents a deeply satisfying national achievement that must be carefully safeguarded.

Most inhabitants of Russia view the Soviet collapse through a different lens. For many of them, the breakup of the Soviet state came to be perceived as a national loss. Even though the USSR was not a purely Russian state, Russian culture and language enjoyed a privileged position within it, and many Russians regarded the whole of the USSR as their homeland. Hence they regretted the independence of the other constituent republics, especially Belarus and Ukraine, whose main national groups have East Slavic origins in common with ethnic Russians.[4]

Although Moscow has gradually negotiated border agreements with most other former Soviet republics, the problem of ethnically mixed populations remains a source of political anxiety. This is especially true because contemporary Russia itself is a federation consisting partly of regional units that are the nominal homelands of non-Russian ethnic minorities such as the Tatars. The resulting fear that Russia might disintegrate just as the USSR did helps explain why during the past decade and a half Moscow has waged two destructive local wars to prevent Chechnya, a small region in Russia's southwest inhabited primarily by the Chechen ethnic minority, from becoming independent. The brutality of Moscow's military forces has been paralleled by numerous acts of terrorism that Chechen insurgents have committed in other parts of Russia, and Moscow's hold over Chechnya and other small southwestern territories remains uncertain.

Constitutions and Elections

Building reliable political institutions on these uncertain national-territorial foundations has been difficult. In the late 1980s, Gorbachev introduced media freedoms and contested elections as part of his campaign to democratize the Soviet system. But no stable set of democratic institutions crystallized across the USSR, and Russia's achievement of independence at the end of 1991 sharpened the basic contradictions among its own government organs. According to Russia's Soviet-era constitution, the Russian republic's government was parliamentary in form. However, as part of his struggle against Gorbachev, Yeltsin had used a popular referendum to create a new Russian presidency and had won the ensuing election. When the USSR disintegrated soon afterward, independent Russia emerged as an awkward political hybrid. The parliamentary powers enshrined in the constitution conflicted with the powers exercised by the president.

During the brief surge of national enthusiasm following the failed conservative coup and Russia's achievement of independence, the parliament granted Yeltsin authority to make a wide range of decisions by presidential decree, but tensions soon escalated as Yeltsin and his parliamentary critics argued over drafts of a new constitution and traded accusations over the mounting human price of shock therapy. Convinced that Yeltsin was driving the economy to ruin, these critics adopted increasingly confrontational tactics, including a serious threat to impeach the president. Yeltsin finally decided to dissolve the parliament; many of his parliamentary opponents barricaded themselves inside the parliament building and designated their own national president and minister of defense. Yeltsin ended the standoff by ordering the military to shell the parliament building and arrest his parliamentary opponents. Although he reneged on his promise to make early presidential elections part of a crisis settlement, suspicions that he harbored dictatorial ambitions were somewhat allayed by his decision to hold early elections for a new parliament and to conduct a referendum on his proposed new constitution.

The 1993 crisis has exercised a lasting influence on Russia's political development. Successful democratization requires the establishment of a constitutional structure that limits the government's capacity for arbitrary action, and the revamped constitutional structure that emerged from Yeltsin's victory over parliament gives too much power to the presidency. Under the Yeltsin constitution, the parliament lacks the authority to approve the president's selection of ministers for the government cabinet; it can reject his nominee for prime minister, but if it does so three times consecutively, he can dissolve the parliament and call new parliamentary elections. This situation has made it very difficult for the legislature to exercise effective oversight over ministerial behavior and the performance of government agencies, since cabinet ministers are beholden for their posts to the president rather than to the prime minister and other parliamentarians. With one brief exception, none of the prime ministers Yeltsin appointed during his eight years as president came from the party with the largest representation in the parliament.

Almost as serious has been the problem of creating an autonomous judiciary that can interpret the laws dispassionately and ensure that officials and citizens obey them. In 1993, the Constitutional Court was caught in the political cross fire between Yeltsin and the parliament, and Yeltsin showed his displeasure over the court's role by reducing its powers under the new constitution. The Soviet legacy of disdain for courts and the legal rights of individuals has made courts at the lower levels of the judicial system especially weak and susceptible to political pressures. Burdened with a large number of judges selected during the Soviet era for their subservience, the courts must also contend with powerful government investigators and prosecutors who are used to overriding legal safeguards and giving breaks to well-connected individuals. As a result, the judicial branch has generally been unable to counter corruption and other dysfunctional official behavior. In recent years, significant reforms have occurred within the court system, but political and bureaucratic obstacles continue to hinder the implementation of judicial decisions.

Together with a constitutional structure based on checks and balances, competitive elections are the bedrock of a functioning democracy. Although Russia has held national parliamentary and presidential elections at regular intervals since 1993, the conduct of these elections has frequently fallen short of fully democratic standards. This is especially true of elections to the presidency, the most powerful institution in the political system.

On the eve of the 1996 presidential campaign, Yeltsin's single-digit public approval ratings seemed to guarantee that he would be defeated, perhaps by the candidate of the refurbished Communist Party of the Russian Federation (CPRF). Faced with this prospect, Yeltsin made preparations to declare a state of emergency and postpone the election, and some oligarchs signaled that they would favor this step. Significantly, Yeltsin's presidential campaign committee included the head of the Federal Security Service, Russia's main institutional successor of the Soviet Committee for State Security (KGB). It also included the head of the Presidential Security Service, part of a 20,000-strong leadership-protection force that possessed substantial intelligence-gathering capabilities of its own.[5] The chief of the Presidential Security Service, a longtime Yeltsin confidant, repeatedly urged that the election be postponed, and only after he lost a political struggle with other campaign advisers did Yeltsin decide to hold it on time.

Measured by one key yardstick, the election marked the democratic high point of Russia's long political history. The intensity of contestation among the candidates and the closeness of the vote totals were unprecedented.[6] But the election also suffered from serious shortcomings. The media, which were dominated by a handful of new business tycoons who favored Yeltsin's reelection and journalists with a strong aversion to communism, devoted disproportionately large coverage to Yeltsin's campaign and very little to that of his CPRF opponent. Moreover, the media failed to reveal that between the two rounds of voting Yeltsin suffered a heart attack that raised serious questions about his capacity to fulfill the duties of the presidency.

Four years later, the transfer of presidential power from Yeltsin to Putin was marred by more serious political machinations. In parliamentary elections held shortly before the presidential election was to occur, government-owned media outlets launched vicious personal attacks on the two prospective presidential candidates who had the greatest chance of winning the presidency. Deterred by their shrinking popularity ratings, these two candidates ultimately decided not to run, although the CPRF candidate and a few other nationally known politicians stayed in the race. Yeltsin then resigned a few months early, paving the way for Prime Minister Putin, his chosen successor, to become acting president and defeat this less threatening assortment of opponents in early presidential balloting. During the abbreviated electoral contest, Putin did not deign to present a campaign platform; his victory was already virtually certain. On taking office, Putin's first public act was to issue a decree that granted Yeltsin, as a former president, immunity from arrest or prosecution—thereby shielding him from any possible criminal charges connected with the corruption that had flourished during his time in the Kremlin.

Subsequent presidential elections marked a further retreat from democratic standards. Thanks to the Kremlin's tight control of the media, Putin's high public approval ratings, and the possibility of provoking personal retaliation, in 2004 no national politician with a serious political following was willing to enter the race. Instead, Putin faced a small group of second-rank candidates; the contest was like a series of Ralph Naders challenging an incumbent U.S. president.[7] Putin won in a landslide, racking up more than 70 percent of the vote. In 2008, Putin artfully arranged for Medvedev, the first-deputy prime minister he had designated to succeed him in the presidency, to chalk up an equally lopsided victory against a weak field of candidates from which the most serious contenders had been excluded on electoral technicalities.

In addition to fair elections, successful democratization hinges on the creation of a system of political parties that enables voters to hold government leaders responsible for the government's conduct. So far, Russian parties have made little contribution to this democratic objective. During the first post-Soviet decade, they were generally weak and, with a few exceptions, short-lived. Most parties were Moscow-centered factions that lacked firm regional moorings.[8] At the grassroots level, party formation was hampered by widespread public suspicion that anyone who joined a party would face pressures for compulsory political participation and restrictions on personal autonomy like those long imposed on the members of the Communist Party of the Soviet Union (CPSU). Moreover, the rapid changes in new party labels were politically confusing. Many parties sprang up or disappeared, making it almost impossible for voters to hold party politicians responsible for government actions. In 1999, for example, three of the leading parties were all created between two and four months before the parliamentary balloting; in the parliamentary election four years later, 60 percent of the votes for the national party-list seats were cast for parties that had not competed in 1999. The main exception to this pattern was the CPRF, which inherited the grassroots structure and die-hard adherents who previously belonged to the CPSU.

This pattern changed significantly after Putin became president. In 2003, United Russia, a new umbrella party, won slightly less than two-fifths of the party-list vote in the parliamentary elections, but it ultimately obtained control of more than two-thirds of the seats in the lower house of parliament when members elected as independents aligned themselves with the party. Two years later, the government changed the electoral system to make independent candidacies more difficult and to strengthen the party affiliations of legislators. Since then, United Russia has become the dominant party in the electoral landscape. In the 2007 parliamentary elections, it won almost two-thirds of the popular vote, while the CPRF trailed far behind with less than one-eighth of the ballots. Thanks to postelectoral switches of party affiliation by some legislators, United Russia ultimately commanded the loyalty of 70 percent of the lawmakers in the lower house.

These trends in party development have strengthened the Russian government, but their implications for Russian democracy are ambiguous. United Russia has developed a distinct party profile and a considerable public following among ordinary Russians, who accurately perceive it as a center-right party closely identified with Putin and Medvedev, and the party's electoral success has given the two leaders a strong lever for pushing legislation through the parliament.[9] However, there is no opposition party of comparable stature that can serve as an alternative channel for the expression of public dissatisfaction with government policies. Other parties, such as the CPRF and the left-leaning A Just Russia, have won narrow slices of the popular vote and control only a small number of parliamentary seats; the liberal parties that championed radical reform in the Yeltsin era no longer have any parliamentary representatives.[10] The main challenge for United Russia is to consolidate and maintain ties with its social base in the absence of vigorous interparty competition or widespread political debate in the mass media. Under such conditions, a ruling party can easily degenerate into a club for opportunistic office holders unconnected with the electorate. The risk for United Russia—not unlike the fate that befell the CPSU in the post-Stalin years—is that it could become simply another "party of power," devoted entirely to the interests of the ruling elite and cut off from the daily concerns of ordinary citizens.

Paths toward Capitalism

The trauma of shock therapy starkly dramatized the complex relationship between democratization and capitalist economic reform. Although free markets are necessary for the survival of democracy, democracy is not always necessary for the creation of an effective market economy, and the relationship between the *processes* of democratization and marketization is especially problematic.

In Russia, where the government had controlled all enterprises as part of a centrally administered command economy, building capitalism required that reformers carry out three broad types of change: liberalization (paring back government intervention in price setting, distribution, foreign trade, and so forth); stabilization (balancing government budgets and limiting the growth of the money supply to prevent runaway inflation); and privatization (distributing most state property to private owners subject to the economic discipline of competitive markets). In the Soviet era, attempts to introduce much more limited economic reforms in a gradual fashion had been defeated by the foot-dragging tactics of political and bureaucratic opponents. Together with the severity of the economic problems carried over from the final Soviet years, this may be one reason the Yeltsin government tried to introduce its market reforms in a single "big bang."

The political consequences of attempting shock therapy turned out to be different from what many observers expected. The most enthusiastic proponents prophesied that rapid marketization under the auspices of a democratic government would create many "winners"—economic and social groups committed to institutionalizing capitalism and democratic political practices. By contrast, some pessimistic opponents warned that rapid marketization would create so many losers and so much suffering among ordinary citizens that it would trigger an authoritarian popular backlash against democratization as well as economic reform. The outcome fell midway between these forecasts. Attempts to implement shock therapy turned out to be far more difficult and painful than its proponents had anticipated, but the short-term effects were less damaging to electoral democracy than many of the opponents had feared. Nonetheless, shock therapy did damage the quality of Russian political life in ways that became clearer with the passage of time.

Although some reformers tried to ensure that privatization would give ordinary Russians a material stake in shock therapy, the main beneficiaries were officials carried over from the Soviet elite and a significant number of ambitious newcomers willing to seize economic opportunities and exploit them ruthlessly. Bear in mind that the volume of economic resources waiting to be privatized was huge, and that there was no tested body of law and administrative procedure to regulate the scramble for ownership. It was as if the U.S. government owned hundreds of corporations such as Microsoft, Exxon Mobil, du Pont, U.S. Steel, and United Airlines and suddenly had to decide how to distribute them to the public in the midst of a paralyzing constitutional crisis over executive-legislative relations and relations between the federal government and the states. With economic stakes like these up for grabs, Russia's shaky governmental structures came under enormous pressure. To capture and hold these large new sources of wealth, ambitious individuals had compelling motives to manipulate the loose government privatization guidelines and, when necessary, to subvert basic democratic processes.

Paradoxically, the size of the economic stakes also made it harder to carry out shock therapy completely. Some aspiring members of the new economic elite had an interest in freezing economic reform at the halfway point—that is, at a stage where they had become owners but could exploit their personal connections with government officials and the loopholes in the many remaining forms of regulation to reap spectacular gains.[11] For the same reason, government officials in a position to extract bribes had little incentive to reduce or streamline the regulations. Take the example of oil exports. Attempting to avoid a further inflation spike, the government kept energy prices much lower at home than they were on the world market. This in turn required that it limit oil exports to keep adequate supplies inside the country. Hence any businessman able to wangle a government license to export oil was guaranteed an extravagant profit, and any official with the power to grant a license—a power soon acquired by Yeltsin's Presidential Security Service—was in a position to obtain a handsome bribe.

Because privatization was slanted toward individuals with inside connections, it created an economy with an exceptionally high concentration of ownership and a disproportionately large number of rich capitalists by international standards. Today the Russian economy ranks between sixth and twelfth in the world by size of GDP. This puts it in the economic neighborhood of Britain, France, and Brazil. However, Russia ranks near the top of the worldwide list of countries with the most billionaires. It has more billionaires than any other country in Europe, and Moscow is the home of about twice as many billionaires as London. Russia's new rich have benefited from once-in-a-lifetime economic opportunities offered by the cut-rate privatization of state assets and other methods of manipulating government policies. Highly profitable export sectors, such as the oil and gas industries and aluminum production, have become the focus of an especially bitter struggle for ownership and control among business and government elites.

The struggle to acquire valuable properties and economic favors from the state has been ruthless and sometimes deadly. The economic opportunities created by shock therapy were enormous, but so were the risks. Criminal gangs quickly became involved in the quest for property and state favors, and the disputes were often settled by violence. In the "mob war" of the early 1990s, dozens of bankers were assassinated, mostly in Moscow.[12] The career of Boris Berezovsky exemplifies the dangers and opportunities of these years. During the 1990s, Berezovsky became one of the country's most powerful tycoons and wielded great influence over the policies and even the electoral survival of the Yeltsin government. However, achieving this status nearly cost him his life. In 1993, Berezovsky, still a minor economic player with ties to organized crime, fled for several months to Israel to avoid physical threats. The next year, after returning to Russia, he narrowly escaped being killed by a car bomb planted by rivals for control of the bourgeoning automobile market.

Faced with such physical dangers, the oligarchs sought to protect themselves by creating their own security forces. The Yeltsin government's continuing budgetary crisis led to drastic reductions in the funding of government agencies, including the military and security police, and to sharp reductions in personnel. Under these conditions, the oligarchs used their new wealth to buy the services of individuals skilled in the arts of intelligence gathering and physical coercion. These individuals were recruited from the ranks of security agencies, the armed forces, and sports clubs.

Consider the example of the holding company founded by Vladimir Gusinsky, a rising media tycoon during the early Yeltsin years. To protect its property and enforce its agreements with other firms, Gusinsky's company established a 1,000-man private security force. The force was headed by Filipp Bobkov, a former deputy chairman of the KGB who had led the KGB department responsible for monitoring and repressing dissenters critical of the Soviet regime. Many freestanding private security concerns were set up by former government officials with similar backgrounds. By one count, half of these private firms were headed by retired KGB officers, one-quarter by retired officers from the Ministry of Internal Affairs, and the rest by retired officers from military intelligence and other agencies.[13] These trends show that the oligarchs' new wealth gave them the capacity to purchase coercive and intelligence resources that had previously been the sole prerogative of the state. They reflect the oligarchs' search for personal security and commercial advantage in the chaotic political and economic conditions of the 1990s.

During the Yeltsin era, security was much easier for rich businessmen to buy than for entrepreneurs of modest means. In the first two or three years of economic reform, many new businesses were started. Soon, however, the reported growth in the number of small businesses flattened out. There were two main causes of this change. One was a surge in the activities of organized crime, which saw small businesses as easy targets for the extortion of "protection" payments. Another was the growth of predatory behavior by government officials, especially tax officials, who used their posts to squeeze bribes out of small business owners in exchange for allowing them to operate with fewer hindrances. To reduce such harassment, many small entrepreneurs switched their activities to the underground economy; in the late 1990s, government estimates indicated that at least one-quarter of the country's economic activity was in the unofficial sector. Although some of the reported slowdown in establishing new businesses was due to such evasive behavior, much of it was undoubtedly real. The Russian statistics present a striking contrast to other postcommunist countries such as Poland and Hungary, where new businesses were about eight times as numerous in per capita terms and accounted for a substantial share of GDP.[14]

The obstacles to the creation and expansion of small businesses had political implications as well as economic ones. In most countries, the owners of small businesses are an important element of the middle class and one of its main economic underpinnings. In Russia, however, the conditions of shock therapy impeded the growth of this socioeconomic group. The Russian middle class has grown in the post-Soviet period, but it contains disproportionately large numbers of white-collar workers employed at various levels of government. Some evidence suggests that in Russia, small enterprise owners are the business group most favorably disposed toward the election of political leaders and the rule of law, probably because they lack the connections and resources used by big business owners to win special favors from the government.[15] On the other hand, white-collar government employees lack independent sources of legitimate income but do have opportunities for graft that predispose them against reform. The stunted development of the small business sector has therefore narrowed the social foundation for the growth of democracy in Russia.

During the past decade, the forms of elite competition over property have changed significantly. The recourse to physical violence to settle business disputes has declined markedly, but this does not signify that Russian business practices are converging with those of the advanced capitalist countries. By undercutting the resources of some oligarchs, the severe financial crisis of 1998 triggered a new round of struggle in which aggressive new claimants manipulated bankruptcy laws and local "pocket" jurisdictions to wrest holdings from their financially weakened competitors. In other words, a bitter struggle among business magnates continued even after a large amount of property had been transferred from state ownership to private hands. This raised the question of whether privatization had prompted Russian tycoons to put a new emphasis on productive entrepreneurship or had simply perpetuated their past preoccupation with amassing greater quantities of assets, and whether government reformers could promote such a shift by strengthening the curbs on illicit economic activities.[16] Although the answer remained uncertain, in 2006 the gangland-style murder of the deputy chairman of the Russian Central Bank, the leader of a government campaign to eliminate corruption from the commercial banking sector, underlined doubts that reformers could tame the all-out struggle for economic advantage. In any case, the harsh shakeout among Russian billionaires as a result of the global financial meltdown of 2008–2009 reminded them of their heavy dependence on the state in times of crisis.

Public Administration and Federalism

Successful democratization and marketization both depend on basic changes in the operation of government agencies. U.S. observers have often tended to regard good public administration as a natural by-product of political and economic liberalization, but in fact effective bureaucracies are an unusual modern achievement that should not be taken for granted. Under certain conditions, liberalization can actually worsen the functioning of government bureaucracies and heighten the administrative obstacles to successful reform. To achieve a transition to capitalist democracy, government agencies must give up many previous powers connected with the centralized control of society while taking on many new tasks connected with the operation of a market economy. Bureaucrats frequently have a strong incentive not to give up their old prerogatives, especially when these can be used to extract bribes. Moreover, they often lack the capacity to carry out their new responsibilities due to a shortage of the necessary technical skills or guidance from up-to-date laws.

These problems become especially severe when the territorial state is being recast. In the modern world, states are the master institutions of social life. The stability of nearly all other institutions—the worth of the national currency, the rules of property ownership and inheritance, business contracts, court verdicts, the validity of marriages, the certification of professional credentials, and the allocation of the electronic broadcast spectrum, to name just a few—hinges on the integrity of the state. When the state is weakened, other institutions are called into question, and effective governance becomes much more difficult.

Take, for example, the early efforts of the Yeltsin government to establish a modern central bank and manage the national currency (the ruble). When Russia declared independence, it had a central bank of sorts, but the bank had not yet established some key financial tools that are available to central bankers in developed capitalist countries, such as a market in government bonds. Moreover, the man who headed the bank in the mid-1990s believed that its main purpose was to keep industrial firms afloat with heavily subsidized loans, rather than to protect the value of the currency against inflation. This situation was compounded by the nature of the Soviet breakup, which gave the central banks of all the other former republics the authority to issue ruble credits—thereby preventing the Russian Central Bank from controlling the growth of the money supply. Within two or three years, the government solved this problem by abolishing the ruble zone that united most of the former Soviet republics, but not before great economic and human damage had been done in Russia.

Similar and longer-lasting problems plagued the government's effort to collect taxes and balance the budget. During the final stage of Yeltsin's political duel with Gorbachev, the government of the Russian republic waged an economic war against the Soviet central government for the control of fiscal resources and industrial enterprises. The aim was to cripple the central government by encouraging Russian banks and regional administrations to refuse to pay their customary taxes into the federal budget while continuing to draw their regular subsidies from the same budget. In addition, Yeltsin and his allies undermined the central government's control over enterprises located in Russia by offering the enterprise managers lower tax rates and enlarged subsidies if they would shift their allegiance to the Russian government. One effect of this political tactic was to show regional administrators and economic managers that they could avoid or reduce tax burdens by negotiating with higher-level overseers and playing them off against each other.[17] This lesson, which persisted long after the Soviet breakup, contributed to the plunge in the Russian government's own tax receipts, which fell from about one-sixth of GDP in 1992 to less than one-tenth of GDP in 1996.

Russia's problems with public administration have been intensified by the country's geographic immensity and cultural diversity. Even without the rest of the USSR, the territory of the Russian Federation still encompasses eleven time zones and an ethnically diverse population. About one-quarter of Russia's eighty-three territorial units are so-called autonomous republics formally designated as the homelands of particular ethnic minorities such as the Tatars. This feature of Russia's federal structure bears a limited resemblance to the ethnofederal structure of the USSR (where all the constituent republics were designated as the homelands of particular ethnonational groups). As mentioned above, this structural resemblance has contributed to the fears of some observers and officials that Russia, too, might disintegrate, and has played a role in Moscow's policies toward Chechnya and other parts of the increasingly volatile North Caucasus region.

During the Yeltsin years, relations between the federal government and the regions were marked by a dramatic "power deflation." Like the USSR as a whole, Soviet Russia had been a federation in name but a unitary state in fact, and during the 1990s, a large amount of administrative and economic power shifted from Moscow toward various regions. The specific allocation of power between Moscow and individual regions was decided through horse-trading and bilateral power-sharing deals whose terms were generally kept secret. As a result, Russia had no consistent national pattern of center-region relations arrived at through public discussion and legislative action—one of the key features of a genuine federation.[18] Playing on divisions and disorganization inside the federal government, the most assertive regions managed to wrest a great deal of power from Moscow and often ignored its wishes.[19]

For its part, the Yeltsin government needed regional governments to support it, especially by using their so-called administrative resources to mobilize the pro-Yeltsin vote during federal election campaigns. During the 1996 presidential campaign, for example, Yeltsin offered about a dozen regions new agreements that expanded their control over regional natural resources and finances. These circumstances spawned many legal and policy contradictions between the federal and regional governments. One analysis at the end of Yeltsin's presidency found that about one-quarter of regional laws and regulations were incompatible with the federal constitution.[20]

After becoming president, Putin worked hard to eliminate such inconsistencies and to reclaim power for the central government. His gradual consolidation of personal power in the presidency made it much more difficult for the regions to gain concessions by playing off political actors in Moscow against each other, especially during elections. In addition, soon after taking office, Putin established seven administrative "super regions" headed by presidential appointees. The leader of each super region is supposed to supervise about a dozen regional governments and ensure that their policies mesh with those approved in Moscow. Along with a tightening of Moscow's control over appointments, these presidential overseers have curbed local co-optation of the regional representatives of various federal agencies, such as tax collection and law enforcement.

Although this step eliminated many contradictions between regional and federal laws, the subsequent adoption of new regional laws generated fresh contradictions that will be difficult to iron out in the absence of an effective court system with the power to resolve jurisdictional conflicts. This is probably one reason that in 2004–2005 Putin pushed through a federal law replacing the popular election of regional executives with appointment by the president (and pro forma approval by the regional legislature). Although rationalized as a response to a bloody school seizure by Chechen terrorists, the measure was actually an additional attempt to strengthen the leverage of the federal government in the country's far-flung regions. In narrow political terms the measure succeeded, because it helped the central government root out some deeply entrenched governors. However, it also increased the risk that the overcentralization of power in Moscow would make regional governments unresponsive to the needs of the local populations, thereby negating the main benefit of a federal system.[21]

The Depletion of Society

The past two decades of upheaval have taken Russian citizens on a dizzying roller-coaster ride from the heights of optimism to the depths of despair and partway back. Public optimism and political involvement peaked during Gorbachev's campaign for *glasnost* and *perestroika*. At the height of the campaign, the number of subscriptions to liberal newspapers containing real news skyrocketed, while subscriptions to orthodox newspapers stagnated or declined. There was a logical connection between *glasnost* and this surge in popular attention to political affairs, since open news media are a key mechanism through which potential members of civil-society groups learn about one another and articulate their common interests.

The level of direct public participation in politics also soared, even at moments when physical repression was a real danger. Near the climax of the struggle for political liberalization in the spring of 1991, pro-Yeltsin forces staged several Moscow protests that drew as many as 300,000 demonstrators. When Gorbachev declared a ban on public demonstrations and mobilized 50,000 troops to enforce it, Yeltsin countered by calling for another demonstration.

Faced with a massive protest turnout on the streets of Moscow, Gorbachev pulled back from ordering a military assault, and Yeltsin and the demonstrators prevailed.

Since this high point of public enthusiasm and involvement, Russian society has undergone a marked political demobilization. In part, this demobilization was caused by shock therapy. The decision to free many prices caused a huge spike in inflation that wiped out the savings of many ordinary Russians. Although the depositors had banked these savings during the Soviet years partly because they could not find any goods they wanted to buy, slashing the apparent buying power of the accounts had a devastating emotional impact—especially because it was followed by a plunge in the real standard of living for many citizens. In the first three years of shock therapy, Russia's GDP fell by between one-third and one-half, and continued to contract for most of the decade. Sustained growth did not resume for almost eight years, and then only after a severe new financial crisis that drove down real wages by one-third between 1997 and 1998. The plunge impoverished many white-collar employees, technical specialists, and skilled workers, especially those employed in the state sector—in other words, many people who had substantial educational and professional credentials.[22] This dire economic situation was compounded by mounting wage arrears, as cash-starved employers tried to bridge the financial gap by holding back the wages they owed their employees.

These socioeconomic shocks coincided with a broader demographic crisis in Russian society. Since independence, Russia's reported population has declined by about 4 percent, to about 143 million persons. In the 1990s, life expectancy dropped by 2 to 3 years, with the life expectancy of males lagging behind that of females by about thirteen years. Although overall life expectancy has increased somewhat during the past decade, the level for Russian males remains below the worldwide average, which includes Third World countries.[23] The origins of this situation can be traced back to the final three or four decades of Soviet power, but the trauma of shock therapy has made it worse, and Russia's rate of population loss may well speed up due to the influence of high levels of environmental pollution and other severe public health problems.[24]

Although Putin and Medvedev have identified the demographic crisis as one of the most acute problems facing the country, the government's response has been weak, especially with respect to the mounting danger of an AIDS epidemic that could sharply accelerate the population decline. Although other industrialized countries are experiencing sharply reduced or negative rates of domestic population growth, Russia is unique in that the population shrinkage stems largely from diminishing life expectancy due to bad health conditions rather than from declining birth rates. One careful outside analyst has even labeled Russia's situation "a humanitarian catastrophe."[25] Demographers project a total population of somewhere between 122 and 135 million inhabitants in 2030, compared with more than 140 million today.[26] Informed observers predict that the economy will soon be hamstrung by a severe shortage of workers and that the declining number of able-bodied men of draft age may cut the military to less than half its current size.[27]

Trends in the educational and cultural makeup of the population are also worrisome. In the years after the Soviet collapse, Russia's traumatic liberalization and opening to the outside world triggered a dramatic outflow of highly educated professionals in search of better living conditions abroad, thereby depriving the country of many specialists who are needed to promote economic modernization and who generally cannot be replaced through immigration.[28] The situation with less-skilled workers is somewhat different but no less troubling. As in North America and Europe, the Russian demand for labor has contributed to high levels of immigration by unskilled workers, much of it illegal, from Third World regions such as Central Asia. By one reckoning, Russia has one of the largest populations of illegal immigrants in the world—second only to that of the United States. The influx of these non-Slavic immigrants has sparked vigorous public controversy, but it has not been sizable enough to eliminate the negative economic consequences of population decline. Since the Soviet breakup, the inflow has compensated for about half the contraction of the native-born population.

Russia's ethnic diversity has increasingly become a source of social tensions. About 80 percent of the population consists of ethnic Russians. Although this is a much higher level of ethnic homogeneity than the USSR had, some parts of Russia, such as the Northern Caucasus and the Middle Volga regions, have large concentrations of ethnic minorities. The marked increase in friction between ethnic Russians and ethnic groups from the Northern Caucasus has been reflected in a growing Russian tendency to view all inhabitants from the Caucasus as members of a single racial category of untrustworthy "blacks." Ethnic Russians are especially hostile to the Chechens—an attitude that has been reinforced by the wars in Chechnya and dramatic acts of terrorism by Chechen rebels. During Putin's presidency, Russian hate crimes directed against minorities received widespread publicity, and popular sentiment favoring "Russia for the Russians" has gained ground. This outlook has received support from the highly conservative clerics who dominate the Russian Orthodox Church. Some of these churchmen contend that to be a Russian, an individual must have an Orthodox background—a narrow view that relegates the members of non-Orthodox minorities to second-class status.

These trends pose the question of whether Russia is becoming a society that is predominantly "uncivil." In any society, the uncivil and civil sectors have some features in common: both consist of active voluntary associations, and both are autonomous from the state. The key difference is that uncivil groups refuse to acknowledge that other groups' interests are legitimate and deal with them by illicit means that sometimes include violence. Organized crime, networks of corruption, and terrorist groups are all examples of uncivil social elements in Russia. Of course, even solidly democratic countries are home to some uncivil groups. The United States, for instance, has a long tradition of organized crime in big cities such as Chicago and New York, as well as a history of hate groups such as the Ku Klux Klan. The key issue is the relative weight of civil and uncivil groups in a given country.

In Russia, the balance between civil and uncivil groups is unfavorable. The level of citizen membership in voluntary associations is quite low. In postcommunist countries, the level of associational membership is generally lower than in countries emerging from noncommunist authoritarian systems. But Russia's level appears low even by comparison with most other postcommunist countries, and the professional and entrepreneurial elements of society have been slow to organize themselves and protect their interests as groups.[29] The level of membership in trade unions is a partial exception, but most unions were carried over from the Soviet era and have retained members largely because they still exercise control over social welfare benefits.

One barrier to the creation of more voluntary associations is a shortage of trust. Trust is an important part of life for ordinary Russians, but they tend to place their trust in individuals with whom they have long-standing personal ties, not in impersonal civic organizations. Although a substantial number of nongovernmental organizations (NGOs) have been created since the Soviet era, many have lacked broad-based support, and the weakness of domestic philanthropy has made them heavily reliant on foreign donors. The pursuit of outside funding distracts NGOs from developing strong grassroots connections and from focusing on the issues that concern ordinary Russians most; it also makes them vulnerable to the charge that they are the tools of foreign governments. Two thoughtful scholars have cautioned that Russian associational activity may be more extensive than this picture suggests, in part because civil-society initiatives are difficult to measure in the aggregate and are therefore easy to misinterpret.[30] However, even if this is true, civil society in Russia is developing from a low starting point. On the "uncivil" side of the ledger, the level of criminal activity remains high, and corruption continues to expand. Opinion surveys during Putin's second term showed that more than 60 percent of the public believes the governing authorities to be corrupt, up substantially from the level of public skepticism when Putin became president, and surveys of businesspeople suggest that the incidence of corruption in commercial affairs has increased.[31]

The attitudes of the Russian public combine a positive disposition toward democracy with persisting cynicism and ambivalence. Russians recognize and prize the many new personal freedoms they have gained as a result of the end of Soviet power. High on the list are the freedom to start new businesses, to express their personal political views in conversation, and to travel abroad. However, they regard the Russian government as just as unresponsive to public opinion as the Soviet government was, despite the greater measure of electoral competition. In fact, survey respondents believe the Russian government is less likely than the USSR was to treat them fairly, in part because they see it as far more corrupt. Although Russians have an unusually high regard for Putin and Medvedev as leaders, they have very low opinions of the national parliament, the cabinet, the courts, and political parties—levels far lower than those typical of EU citizens.[32]

These feelings of dissatisfaction, however, have not translated into widespread public aversion to democracy. Surveys show that most Russians are opposed to major changes of political structure—such as a military dictatorship—that would amount to a formal repudiation of democratic principles. Moreover, a majority of respondents say that the present-day political system is not a democracy, and even those who think the country must be governed with "a strong hand" turn out mostly to want such rulers to be selected through free and competitive elections.[33] On the other hand, Russian respondents are much less ready to condemn arbitrary official acts, including violations of human rights and press freedoms that citizens in most European countries would regard as undemocratic. Moreover, they show little recognition of the Putin-Medvedev team's manipulation of recent national elections, and the financial meltdown of 2008–2009 has not shaken their faith in the two leaders.[34] Overall, much of this somewhat skeptical and ambivalent worldview might be regarded as rational, given the tumult of the 1990s and the tangible improvement of living standards under the increasingly undemocratic order of the past decade. Nonetheless, without a positive disposition toward civic and political action, ordinary Russians cannot be expected to exert a significant influence on the evolution of the political system.

The evolution of civil society is closely bound up with the fate of the media, which played a pivotal role in activating the public during the *glasnost* era. The Putin-Medvedev team's media policy bears some resemblance to Soviet practice but also differs from it in important respects. Government officials are acutely sensitive to the political impact of the media and work assiduously to shape it. But unlike the Soviet media watchdogs who searched for heresy in every corner of the intellectual world, today's media overseers focus narrowly on the segments of the media that have a large-scale impact on mass attitudes.[35] Above all, this requires close supervision of the political reportage broadcast by the principal television stations. These stations have become the main source of news for most Russians, and they regularly give uncritical image-enhancing coverage of top government officials and favored candidates for office. Media overseers pay less attention than their Soviet predecessors to print outlets, especially small-circulation publications, and the boldest publications still print direct criticism of the country's leaders. The most courageous newspapers also continue to sponsor muckraking investigations of particular cases of crime and corruption, even though this has led to the murder of a large number of journalists.

Perhaps as important as the government's focus on political news is its relaxed attitude toward the media's nonpolitical content. Having abandoned the Soviet ideological determination to transform citizens into morally superior human beings, the government allows television broadcasters free rein to develop nonpolitical shows that are slickly produced and entertaining. One example is a TV show called *The Star Factory*, which resembles *American Idol*. This kind of concession to popular tastes has enabled the Kremlin to avoid the dreariness that made the Soviet media uncommonly boring and contributed to the alienation of many Soviet citizens.

The Quest for a "Strong State"

When Putin became president in 2000, most Russians greeted him as a welcome change from the ailing and erratic Yeltsin. Methodical and low key, the new president spoke frankly about the country's problems and seemed determined to address them. He put a special emphasis on establishing order in Russian public life and strengthening the faltering economy. Putin promised to establish the "dictatorship of law" by requiring consistent compliance from the oligarchs as well as ordinary citizens and by working to make the laws and administrative decisions of various state organs consistent with one another.

Among Putin's early achievements were the introduction of simplified tax laws, which boosted the government's revenues and helped it pay down foreign debts, and an impressive economic revival sustained in large measure by a dramatic rise in the price of Russian oil on global markets. The enthusiastic public response to these changes was easy to understand. Between 2000 and 2005, the average real income of Russians increased by about 75 percent, halving the number of people below the official poverty line. Putin's public approval ratings consistently ranked above 70 percent and sometimes climbed to the low 80s.[36]

Although Putin regularly paid lip service to the goal of further democratization as well as economic liberalization, his acts increasingly belied his words. One straw in the wind was his heavy reliance on personnel with security service backgrounds to fill governmental posts having nothing to do with security issues. Putin had risen rapidly from relative political obscurity during the 1990s and lacked a wide circle of politicians he could trust. A belief that this narrow political base would limit his freedom of action may have been Yeltsin's main motive for choosing him to become the next president.

Putin coped with this paucity of tested political acquaintances by turning to individuals with backgrounds in the security police and the armed forces— the so-called *siloviki* or "force wielders." Individuals with these backgrounds made up about a third of the ministers and deputy ministers appointed in Putin's early years as president, plus about 70 percent of the staffs of the new super regions.[37] Within this pool, former members of the security services were politically more significant than ex-military men because the security services had traditionally penetrated all parts of Russian society and possessed an assortment of manipulative tools that extended well beyond the threat or use of violence.

These staffing decisions bolstered the tendency of the state to play an increasingly assertive role. The initial targets of state pressure were Berezovsky and Gusinsky, the two tycoons who had acquired dominant positions in the media and had used their media clout to advance their own narrow objectives. Under Kremlin-orchestrated harassment from the tax police, the courts, and compliant creditors such as the giant Gazprom energy corporation, the two were stripped of their media empires and driven into foreign exile.

The most important watershed in the Kremlin's relations with the oligarchs was the Khodorkovsky affair of 2003–2005. Mikhail Khodorkovsky, head of Yukos, the richest and best-managed Russian oil company, rejected indirect signals from the government that he should follow these other oligarchs into exile. Instead he plunged deeper into politics and began to underwrite opposition parties in the run-up to the 2003 parliamentary elections. He also worked to reduce the taxation of energy companies—taxation that was essential to maintaining Russia's newfound fiscal health—and challenged the government monopoly on the shipment of energy to foreign buyers.

The trial and imprisonment of Khodorkovsky and his business partners on charges of embezzlement and tax evasion were politically motivated. In the course of privatization, the defendants had undoubtedly engaged in many illegal and corrupt acts, but so had other tycoons who were not put on trial. Moreover, Khodorkovsky had recently taken his company in a new direction, upgrading its corporate governance and transparency in order to attract foreign investment. His real offense was to challenge the Kremlin's growing political dominance. The arrest was well timed to appeal to Russian voters, who had bitter memories of privatization and would soon have an opportunity to vote in the parliamentary and presidential elections. Around this time, one survey revealed that about 90 percent of the population felt that all large fortunes had been built up illegally, nearly 80 percent favored reviewing or revoking the results of the privatization process, and almost 60 percent advocated opening criminal investigations of the rich.[38]

The policies of Putin and Medvedev toward civil society have been more active and restrictive than Yeltsin's policy was. Harassment of civil-society activists by the police and tax authorities has become more pronounced, and the government has begun to sponsor its own "in-house" organizations to compete against civil-society groups perceived as too assertive.[39] For example, the Kremlin founded a youth group called Nashi ("Our Own") to channel the energy of young people into politically acceptable forms of activity. Suspended above this assortment of sponsored organizations is a new, quasi-autonomous "Public Chamber" created by the government. Ostensibly it was set up to facilitate government consultations with society, but critics understandably suspect that its unspoken purpose is to bleed off genuine grassroots energy and initiatives. On the other hand, the government has underscored the need to increase funding for voluntary associations, and it has channeled financial support to some autonomous groups championing such sensitive issues as human rights.[40] Time should clarify how much, or how little, these government measures resemble the state's treatment of society during the Soviet era. At present, they seem to indicate a distinct suspicion of the unregulated expression of social interests, but still nothing like the absolute rejection of autonomous associational life in the Soviet years.

Russia and Europe

In the post-Soviet period, Russians who favor close ties with Europe have faced two fundamental problems that both stem from changes in Europe itself. First, the strategic imperatives that linked Russia to Europe at certain points in the past have disappeared. As long as the major European powers posed military threats to one another, they had a strong security motive to draw Russia into Europe as a counterweight, even when they found its internal politics distasteful. This is what motivated France and Britain to conclude a military alliance with Tsarist Russia against Germany before World War I and to pursue a similar alliance with the USSR on the eve of World War II. After World War II, however, the European powers laid aside their historic military rivalries, partly in order to counter the geopolitical threat from the USSR. Although post-Soviet Russia has changed dramatically and is far weaker militarily than the USSR, some Western observers continue to doubt that the changes have permanently altered Russia's international objectives. This is especially true of observers from Poland and other new EU members that were long trapped inside the Soviet bloc. Thus, to the degree that strategic calculations shape contemporary European attitudes toward Moscow, they make Russian integration into Europe less likely, not more.

Closely related changes within the European states have also made integration a far bigger challenge for Russia than in the past. Two and a half decades ago, Gorbachev evoked an enthusiastic response from Western Europe by proclaiming that the USSR was part of a "Common European Home" that bridged the continent's Cold War divide. Today, however, postcommunist Russia seeks acceptance by a different Europe—one that has reached an unprecedented level of political and economic integration and therefore judges Russia by more exacting criteria. Candidates for EU membership must satisfy demanding EU standards for democratic governance, and under Putin and Medvedev, Russia has arguably moved farther from those standards, not closer to them. The gap separating Russian capitalism from EU economic practices is just as large. To become a realistic EU candidate, Russia would first have to undergo a protracted process of internal change, and even then the EU, whose appetite for enlargement seems nearly exhausted, would probably refuse at the end of the day.

On the Russian side, disenchantment with the idea of joining the West has also grown for several reasons. The Yeltsin government carried out shock therapy under the banner of Westernizing the Russian system. Since the reform effort was actively promoted by the United States and the European Union, the severe socioeconomic hardships that resulted gave many Russians second thoughts about the wisdom of Westernization. For a significant minority of Russians, the word "democracy" became identified with hardship, disorder, and extreme economic inequality. A small proportion of the population even came to believe that the Yeltsin reforms were part of a Western conspiracy to weaken Russia. These sentiments have increased some Russians' receptiveness to the idea that Russian cultural values are fundamentally different from those of the West.

Foreign policy disagreements have contributed to the more distrustful Russian outlook. NATO's decision to extend membership to several of Moscow's former allies in Eastern Europe upset members of the Russian foreign policy establishment, and a further round of NATO enlargement that included the Baltic states vexed them even more. In the interim, NATO's decision to use force against Serbia over Kosovo without UN authorization made the alliance look like a potential threat to Russia, which feared secessionism inside its own borders, especially in Chechnya. Europe and the United States treated Moscow's first war in Chechnya with considerable diplomatic restraint, but they voiced stronger criticism when Moscow renewed the military conflict in the late 1990s and allowed its forces to commit rampant human rights violations against the local population. Many Russians, however, viewed the conflict quite differently. Moscow launched the war following a series of terrorist bombings in the heart of Russia that took several hundred lives and that the government blamed on the Chechens. In these circumstances, a significant proportion of Russians felt that the new war was justified—in contrast to widespread public condemnation of the earlier one.

In addition, during the past half dozen years, Russia has become involved in a heightened competition with the West to influence the direction of change in several other former Soviet republics located on Russia's borders. Two prominent cases are the disputed presidential elections in Ukraine, where the "Orange Revolution" of 2004–2005 sidetracked Moscow's favored candidate, and in Belarus, where Russia successfully backed the fraudulent reelection of the incumbent president. Russian policymakers seem especially determined to block the U.S.-led campaign to win NATO membership for Ukraine, and in recent years their efforts appear to have achieved some success. Whatever the causes of the 2008 war between Russia and Georgia—and the most detailed

Box 6.2   Excerpts from Mikhail Gorbachev, *Perestroika: New Thinking for Our Country and the World* (1988), pp. 180–183, 190–191

This metaphor [of a common European home] came to my mind in one of my discussions. . . . It did not come to me all of a sudden but after much thought and, notably, after meetings with many European leaders. . . . I could no longer accept in the old way the multi-colored, patchwork-quilt-like political map of Europe. The continent has known more than its share of wars and tears. It has had enough. Scanning the panorama of this long suffering land and pondering the common roots of such a multi-form but essentially common European civilization, I felt with growing acuteness the artificiality and temporariness of the bloc-to-bloc confrontation and the archaic nature of the "iron curtain." . . .

Now, about the opportunities the Europeans have . . . to be able to live as dwellers in a "common home."

1. The nations of Europe have the most painful and bitter experience of the two world wars. The awareness of the inadmissibility of a new war has left the deepest of imprints on their historical memory. It is no coincidence that Europe has the largest and the most authoritative antiwar movement. . . .

2. European political tradition as regards the level of conduct in international affairs is the richest in the world. European states' notions of each other are more realistic than in any other region. Their political "acquaintance" is broader, longer, and hence closer.

3. No other continent taken as a whole has such a ramified system of bilateral and multilateral negotiations, consultations, treaties, and contacts at virtually every level. It has to its credit such a unique accomplishment in the history of international relations as the Helsinki process [the Conference on Security and Cooperation in Europe, subsequently renamed the Organization for Security and Cooperation in Europe]. . . . Then the torch was taken up by [an international conference in] Vienna where, we hope, a new step in the development of the Helsinki process will be made. So, the blueprints for the construction of a common European home are all but ready.

4. The economic, scientific, and technical potential of Europe is tremendous. It is dispersed, and the force of repulsion between the East and the West of the continent is greater than that of attraction. However, the . . . prospects are such as to enable some modus to be found for a combination of economic processes in both parts of Europe to the benefit of all. . . .

Europe "from the Atlantic to the Urals" [Russia's Ural Mountains] is a cultural-historical entity united by the common heritage of the Renaissance and the Enlightenment, of the great philosophical and social teachings of the nineteenth and twentieth centuries. . . . A tremendous potential for a policy of peace and neighborliness is inherent in the European cultural heritage. . . .

The building of the "European home" requires a material foundation—constructive cooperation in many different areas. We, in the Soviet Union, are prepared for . . . new forms of cooperation, such as the launching of joint ventures, the implementation of joint projects in third countries, etc. . . .

True, all of this would increase the European states' mutual interdependence, but this would be to the advantage of everyone and would make for greater responsibility and self restraint.

Acting in the spirit of cooperation, a great deal could be done in that vast area which is called "humanitarian" [and includes human rights]. A major landmark on this road would be an international conference on cooperation in the humanitarian field which the Soviet Union proposes for Moscow. At such a conference the sides could discuss all aspects of problems which are of concern to both East and West, including the intricate issue of human rights. That would give a strong new impetus to the Helsinki process.

However, the . . . tangible prospects are such as to reenable some modus [vivendi] to be found for a combination of economic processes in both parts of Europe to the benefit of all.

analysis suggests some responsibility on both sides—one result of the conflict was to reduce the prospect for any further NATO enlargement into the lands of the former USSR. These disagreements reflect a broader divergence of outlooks between Russia and the West. In the Yeltsin and early Putin eras, many Western and Russian leaders appeared to share the assumption that Russia and other former Soviet republics were converging with Western political and economic patterns. There was, in other words, broad-gauged agreement about what progress in the Soviet successor states should look like. Thanks to this shared outlook, leaders from across the continent declared their commitment to the political and human rights standards established under the auspices of the Organization for Security and Cooperation in Europe (OSCE).

However, after several years of Putin's presidency, a "values gap" started to appear between Russia and the West. In particular, the Russian government has begun to champion its own definitions of democracy and democratic practice. It has emphasized the theme of "sovereign democracy," by which it means that outside states should not try to tell Russia or nearby countries how to organize themselves internally or how to behave abroad. And it has worked to make these definitions stick—for example, by blocking efforts by the OSCE to monitor Russian elections and by sending Russian observers who have proclaimed that elections in former Soviet republics such as Belarus were free and fair even when OSCE observers condemned them.

These controversies have spilled over into Russia's economic relations with Europe. By a wide margin, Europe is Russia's largest trade partner and biggest source of direct investment, but European-Russian energy relations have become a focus of tension. Toward the end of the Soviet era, Moscow gradually

Box 6.3   From the Declaration on Human Rights and Dignity of the Tenth World Council of Russian People, Convened by the Russian Orthodox Church, Moscow, April 6, 2006

Aware that the world . . . is facing a threat of conflict between the civilizations with their different understanding of the human being and the human being's calling—the World Russian People's Council, on behalf of the unique Russian civilization, adopts this declaration:

Each person as image of God has singular unalienable worth, which must be respected by every one of us, the society and state. . . .

Rights and liberties are inseparable from human obligations and responsibilities. The individual in pursuit of personal interests is called to relate them to those of the neighbor, family, community, nation and all humanity.

There are values no smaller than human rights. These are faith, morality, the sacred, [and the] motherland. Whenever these values come into conflict with the implementation of human rights, the task of the society, state and law is to bring both to harmony. It is unacceptable, in pursuit of human rights, to oppress faith and moral tradition, insult religious and national feelings, cause harm to revered holy objects and sites, jeopardize the motherland. . . .

We reject the policy of double standards with regard to human rights, as well as attempts to use them for political, ideological, military and economic purposes, for imposition of a particular socio-political system.

We are willing to cooperate with the state and all benevolent forces in ensuring human rights. Particularly important for this cooperation are such endeavors as preserving the rights of nations and ethnic groups to their religion, language and culture, defending the freedom of conscience and the right of believers to their own way of life, combating ethnically and religiously motivated crime, [and] protecting against arbitrary actions by the authorities and employers. . . .

We seek dialogue with people of diverse faiths and views on human rights and their place in the hierarchy of values. Like nothing else, this dialogue today will help avoid the conflict of civilizations and attain a *peaceful diversity of worldviews, cultures, legal and political systems on the globe.*

expanded trade with Europe and built a controversial pipeline to transport natural gas from Russia to Western Europe. The Soviet government took great pains to calm suspicions that it would manipulate the supply of natural gas for political purposes. Since that time, European dependence on Russian gas has grown dramatically, but Moscow's missteps have once again made the energy relationship a matter of Western political debate. In 2006, Russia, attempting to manipulate Ukraine's internal political alignments to suit its own preferences, reduced gas shipments to that country. Because the same pipeline carries gas to Western Europe, this measure caused economic disruptions there and provoked a public outcry, even though Russia quickly resumed full gas shipments.

This episode raised larger questions about the acceptable level of increased Russian investment in European energy distribution systems and the acceptability of Russian curbs on Western investment in energy production and pipelines inside Russia. These issues have become entangled with the concurrent European debate over the terms of ownership and competition among the EU members' own national energy corporations. Given the scope of Europe's energy needs and the importance of energy sales for Russia's economic prosperity, the Russo-European disagreements are likely to be resolved through compromises of some kind. But they show that even limited integration within one key economic sector faces significant obstacles.

Although Russia is highly unlikely to be formally integrated with Europe, it is more likely to remain engaged with Europe than with any other major country or group of countries outside the boundaries of the former USSR. At the elite level, Russian liberal reformers continue to be interested in Europe. Within the citizenry as a whole, Europe enjoys a more favorable reputation and exercises a much stronger attraction than any other region, including the United States and China. A sizable proportion of Russians regard themselves as Europeans; none, of course, regard themselves as North Americans, and few see themselves as East Asians. From time to time, Moscow's leaders may make common diplomatic cause with China in cases of disagreement with the United States, and they will gradually increase their energy exports to growing Asian markets. But Russia's demographic and economic center of gravity remains west of the Ural Mountains, in European Russia, and a significant eastward shift of Russian trade will require two or three decades. Together with Moscow's apprehensions about the long-term security implications of Asia's unprecedented burst of economic dynamism, this structural factor nearly guarantees that Russia will not make a decisive geopolitical "turn" from Europe to Asia.

Conclusion: Russia's Futures

Russia's steady shift toward hypercentralization has given Putin and Medvedev unparalleled preeminence and Russia a renewed semblance of political order. The key question is whether the political structure they have built can deal with the grave problems of economic development and human welfare facing the country. Historically, Russian leaders have often attempted to overcome crises by concentrating power and multiplying the state's administrative controls over society. Under Putin and Medvedev, memories of the severe political conflicts and predatory economic behavior during the Yeltsin era have strengthened the impulse to follow this path. For the most part, ordinary Russians have accepted this formula, even though in principle many would prefer a more democratic political system.

Putin and Medvedev have worked hard to strengthen the Russian state and have achieved some significant successes. For example, their tightening of tax and fiscal discipline enabled the regime to accumulate extensive foreign currency reserves and to withstand the plunge in oil prices during the recent global financial crisis. Although the crisis caused a 10 percent decline in Russian GDP, the regime weathered the storm and emerged intact on the other side.[41] However, it remains unclear whether this formula of state-centered rule can revive Russia socially and economically over the long term. In a domestic context, "state strength" can refer to quite different things. One is the negative capacity of state leaders to defeat actions by social actors they oppose. Another is the positive capacity of leaders to achieve their substantive socioeconomic objectives for the country. A state that is powerful in the negative sense may be quite weak in the positive sense, especially if it attempts to control a wide range of social and economic activities.

To succeed in the contemporary world, states need high levels of active cooperation from their citizens and high levels of information about the internal workings of society. By relying increasingly on direct administrative control, the Russian government will almost certainly thwart essential socioeconomic initiative and shrink both the quality and quantity of information reaching policymakers. The typical result of such restrictive tactics is a state that tries to monopolize the initiative in policymaking but that also lacks the capacity to deal effectively with real societal issues—in other words, a state that combines the appearance of great power with the reality of substantive weakness. Medvedev, in particular, seems to understand this risk, and he has rhetorically embraced the idea of liberal modernization as a means of avoiding it. To date, however, there is little evidence that Putin accepts these ideas, and no indication that Medvedev is prepared to risk a political confrontation with his longtime mentor in order to force their adoption and implementation.

The approach of the 2012 presidential election will sharpen the challenge of agreeing on difficult policy choices and, even more, on a durable division of power. Although both men have asserted that they will reach a mutual accommodation over which of them will run for president, both have also indicated an interest in filling the post again. The political stakes will be high; thanks to a revised law on the presidency, the new president will be elected for a six-year term. In 2008, Putin managed the presidential transition skillfully, balancing rivalries within the elite and containing the factional conflict triggered by succession uncertainties. Whether he and Medvedev will clear the new succession hurdle with equal skill remains to be seen.

Although the person who becomes president in 2012 will receive electoral legitimation, the succession process is virtually certain to be pseudodemocratic rather than genuinely democratic. In Russia, democratic elections have failed to become the "only game in town" for choosing leaders, but competitors for power cannot dispense with elections entirely. Rather, the electoral process is one important political arena that aspirants for power must seek to control. In key instances, the decisive variable is the preelection struggle over who will get onto the ballot, not who will win when citizens go to the polls. Popularity in the eyes of the electorate influences which candidate receives the nomination, but the public exerts no direct influence on the nomination process or the selection of a new president. Under certain conditions the existing electoral procedures might again become the object of real electoral competition, as happened with Soviet elections in the Gorbachev years. But this could occur only if political and economic circumstances inside Russia change fundamentally.

Global economic conditions and the national economy's performance will have a major effect on Russia's political future. Medvedev has recently underscored the need for stepped-up modernization to reduce Russian dependence on energy exports and make the country more competitive with other major powers in high-technology sectors.[42] However, political leaders in Moscow have been sounding this theme for at least five decades without solving the problem. If the energy sector continues to grow rapidly and foreign demand for Russian energy remains strong, this will contribute to domestic political stability but also make the tasks facing the modernizers more difficult. On the other hand, if Russia's wasteful brand of state-dominated capitalism causes energy output to falter, this will create new political tensions that could generate stronger efforts at modernization. Above all, a long-term plunge in energy prices due to a protracted global recession would generate severe economic stresses and could lead to major alterations in the political system.

Whatever the external circumstances, the country's long-term political development will also be influenced by the changing preferences of key social groups. If members of the economic elite choose to pursue greater political and economic security by acting in concert to limit government power, Russia could move in a liberal political direction. If they continue to vie with one another for special favors from the state, as has often occurred in the past, an authoritarian political outcome is more probable. The expansion and political orientation of the middle class will likewise be important. Sustained pressure from an enlarged middle class could facilitate reform of the government bureaucracy and help strengthen the integrity of the judicial system. On the other hand, if the middle class fails to generate this kind of "demand for law," serious reform of the government apparatus is unlikely to succeed. Whether a shrinking society wracked by a severe health crisis can generate this kind of political pressure is uncertain. A dramatic increase in immigration might cushion the demographic decline, but it could easily heighten frictions between ethnic Russians and non-Russians.

Even if Russia ultimately follows a liberal political path, many years are likely to pass before a qualitatively new form of engagement with Europe becomes possible. Closer integration of energy networks and cultural life is quite probable, but political and economic integration along a broader front faces much bigger obstacles. For many years to come, an ambivalent Russia is likely to remain on the periphery of an ambivalent Europe. Internationally as well as domestically, the uncertainty that has pervaded Russia's recent past is likely to shadow its future as well.

Suggested Readings

Åslund, Anders, S. M. Guriev, and Andrew Kuchins (eds.), *Russia after the Global Economic Crisis*, Washington, DC: Peterson Institute for International Economics and Center for Strategic and International Studies, 2010.

Barnes, Andrew, *Owning Russia: The Struggle over Factories, Farms, and Power*, Ithaca, NY: Cornell University Press, 2006.

Brown, Archie, *The Gorbachev Factor*, New York: Oxford University Press, 1996.

Brown, Archie (ed.), *Contemporary Russian Politics: A Reader*, New York: Oxford University Press, 2001.

Brown, Archie, *The Rise and Fall of Communism*, New York: HarperCollins, 2009.

Colton, Timothy J., *Yeltsin: A Life*, New York: Basic Books, 2008.

Eberstadt, Nicholas, *Russia's Peacetime Demographic Crisis: Dimensions, Causes, Implications*, Washington, DC: National Bureau of Asian Research, 2010.

Fish, M. Steven, *Democracy Derailed in Russia: The Failure of Open Politics*, New York: Cambridge University Press, 2005.

Gustafson, Thane, *Capitalism Russian-Style*, New York: Cambridge University Press, 1999.

Hoffman, David E., *The Oligarchs: Wealth and Power in the New Russia*, New York: Public Affairs, 2001.

Knight, Amy W., *Spies without Cloaks: The KGB's Successors*, Princeton, NJ: Princeton University Press, 1996.

Lieven, Anatol, and Dmitri Trenin (eds.), *Ambivalent Neighbors: The EU, NATO and the Price of Membership*, Washington, DC: Carnegie Endowment for International Peace, 2003.

McFaul, Michael, *Russia's Unfinished Revolution: Political Change from Gorbachev to Putin*, Ithaca, NY: Cornell University Press, 2001.

McFaul, Michael, Nikolai Petrov, and Andrei Ryabov (eds.), *Between Dictatorship and Democracy: Russian Postcommunist Political Reform*, Washington, DC: Carnegie Endowment for International Peace, 2004.

Reddaway, Peter, and Dmitri Glinski, *The Tragedy of Russia's Reforms: Market Bolshevism against Democracy*, Washington, DC: United States Institute of Peace Press, 2001.

"Rethinking Russia," special issue, *Journal of International Affairs*, 63(2), Spring/Summer 2010.

Taubman, William, *Khrushchev: The Man and His Era*, New York: Norton, 2003.

Tolz, Vera, *Russia: Inventing the Nation*, New York: Oxford University Press, 2001.

Volkov, Vadim, *Violent Entrepreneurs: The Use of Force in the Making of Russian Capitalism*, Ithaca, NY: Cornell University Press, 2002.

Wegren, Stephen, and Dale Herspring (eds.), *After Putin's Russia: Past Imperfect, Future Unknown*, Lanham, MD: Rowman & Littlefield, 2009.

CHAPTER 7

Poland 20 Years Later: The Long Arm of Transition

Ben Stanley

Poland

Population (million):	38.2
Area in Square Miles:	124,807
Population Density per Square Mile:	306
GDP (in billion dollars, 2009):	$727.2
GDP per capita (PPP, 2005):	$16,703
Joined EC/EU	May 1, 2004

Performance of Key Political Parties in Parliamentary Elections of October 21, 2007

Citizens' Platform (PO)	41.5%
German Minority (MN)	0.2%
Law and Justice (PiS)	32.1%
League of Polish Families (LPR)	1.3%
Polish Peasants' Party (PSL)	8.9%
Self-Defense of the Polish Republic (SRP)	1.5%
Left and Democrats (LiD)	13.1%

Main office holders: President: Bronislaw Komorowski—PO (2010); Prime Minister: Donald Tusk—PO (2007).

The air crash of April 10, 2010, in Smolensk, Russia, claimed the lives of the Polish presidential couple and scores of military, political, and state dignitaries en route to a ceremony honoring the thousands of Polish nationals murdered in the Katyń massacre sixty years previously. In the immediate aftermath, the overwhelming emotion was one of desire for unity in the face of unimaginable tragedy. In moving ceremonies, politicians set aside the aggressive and antagonistic political culture of the Polish parliament to mourn the loss of colleagues from all points of the political spectrum. Journalists struggled to contain their emotions as they related the unfolding of events and attempted to comprehend their implications. A stunned public laid carpets of flowers and candles in scenes of national mourning reminiscent of the reaction to the death of Pope John Paul II almost exactly five years earlier. However, expectations that the enormity of Poland's "second Katyń" would transcend extant divisions and inspire a new unity among elites and within society proved illusory. Both the circumstances of the tragedy and the losses it occasioned were politicized with indecent haste and served only to deepen extant divisions and accelerate their consolidation.

The presidential election that ensued in June saw the reiteration of a discourse of "two Polands," the essence of which resided in an increasingly potent distinction between the "winners" and "losers" of transition. This chapter argues that this "civilizational divide" came to supplant the "regime divide" of the first decade of transition as the "proto-cleavage" of Polish politics. While the party system still remained inchoate and many Poles were not mobilized by any parties, the "long arm" of transition[1] was visible in the bifurcating effects of economic and social reforms. When placed in the comparative context of similar processes of "integration" and "demarcation" under the aegis of globalization in Europe, it seems plausible to expect that the divide over these reforms will deepen into a more durable political cleavage.

The Emergence of a "Liberal Orthodox" Model of Transition

While the ideology of liberalism inspired Poland's postcommunist reform after 1989, Polish liberals were in short supply. Liberal ideas only began to take root during communism, when the opposition movements of the 1970s pursued the development of a pluralistic civil society upholding human and civil rights.[2] These intellectual currents fed into the demands for autonomy and self-organization advanced by the Solidarity movement, which in 1980–1981 numbered some 10 million members. The suppression of Solidarity through the imposition of martial law in 1981 underlined the bankruptcy of communist legitimacy and the exhaustion of zeal for orthodox solutions. Yet the outlawing of the organization and the internment of leading dissidents demonstrated that the coercive powers of the state remained insuperable. During the repressive years of the mid-1980s, opposition intellectuals increasingly turned away from civic, political freedoms and toward notions of freedom through economic liberalization.

After a decade of economic and ideological stagnation, reformers in the Polish United Workers' Party (PZPR) began to change their own attitudes toward the market. Laws on economic activity gave private businesses freedom to hire and promised equality of access to credits and inputs. The renewal of strike activity in the latter half of 1988 impressed on the authorities the need to co-opt Solidarity as a junior partner to ensure the maintenance of social peace.[3] This resulted in the convocation of a Round Table from February to April 1989 that made significant concessions to political freedoms but maintained the principle that the party would remain first among unequals, transferring its executive power to a strong presidency and dominating a legislature in which 65 percent of the seats were reserved for its members.

The semidemocratic elections of June 1989 equipped Poland with a set of bootstraps by which it would haul itself into democracy. Against all expectations, in the first round, Solidarity won 160 of the 161 parliamentary seats they were permitted to contest and 99 out of the 100 freely contested seats in the new Senate. The PZPR and its minor satellite parties did badly in the first round. Their performance was cruelly reflected in the fortunes of prominent governing politicians who were placed on a "national list" of 35 seats to ensure their success. In only two cases did candidates achieve the necessary quota for election. This situation was only resolved through the embarrassing expedient of changing the electoral laws prior to the second round. Effectively, Solidarity won the election. It could not form a government, but after the defection of the satellite United Peasant Party (ZSL), neither could the communists. However, the continued existence of the Soviet Union in 1989 forced Solidarity to accept the communist leader General Wojciech Jaruzelski as president and "guardian" of the Round Table compromise. (A list of the major protagonists in this narrative is given in box 7.1).

In September, Solidarity intellectual Tadeusz Mazowiecki became prime minister of a Grand Coalition, dominated by Solidarity but including ministers from all parties. The rapid fall of communist regimes elsewhere turned thoughts from the selective application of remedial market reforms to the wholesale *transformation* of the economic system. The "Balcerowicz Plan" (named after Leszek Balcerowicz, Mazowiecki's finance minister), an economic package that came into force on January 1, 1990, simultaneously enacted "shock therapy" on the economy and laid the foundations of the new economic order. Balcerowicz emphasized swiftness of action, arguing that the window of opportunity for wholesale reform would rapidly give way to the party and interest-group sclerosis of politics-as-usual.[4]

Box 7.1   Major Personalities

Leszek Balcerowicz: Academic economist. Finance minister in the Mazowiecki government and architect of Poland's "shock therapy" economic reforms; leader of UW from 1995 to 2000.

Wojciech Jaruzelski: Army general and last communist leader of Poland, introduced martial law in December 1981 to suppress the Solidarity movement. First president of the Third Republic of Poland from 1989 to 1990.

Lech Kaczyński: President from 2005 until his death in the 2010 Smolensk tragedy. Previously senator, member of parliament, president of the Supreme Chamber of Control and mayor of Warsaw. Cofounded PiS with his twin brother Jarosław.

Jarosław Kaczyński: Cofounder of PC and PiS. Member of parliament since 1991, except 1993–1997. Prime minister of the PiS-SO-LPR government; currently leader of PiS and chief opposition figure.

Aleksander Kwaśniewski: Reformist member of the PZPR and participant in the Round Table talks. Cofounder of SdPR and member of parliament from 1991 to 1995. President from 1995 to 2005.

Andrzej Lepper: Farmer, founder and unquestioned leader of SO. Led controversial campaigns of direct action during the 1990s. Member of parliament between 2001 and 2007; agriculture minister and deputy prime minister in the PiS-SO-LPR government.

Tadeusz Mazowiecki: Catholic intellectual, author, journalist, and member of parliament from 1961 to 1972 for Znak, a group representing Catholics. Subsequently a prominent Solidarity intellectual and key participant in the Round Table talks. First noncommunist prime minister, serving from 1989 to 1990. Member of parliament from 1991 to 2001, and leader of UD-UW from 1990 to 1995.

Leszek Miller: PZPR activist and participant in the Round Table talks. Cofounder of SdPR and member of parliament from 1991 to 2005. Prime minister in the SLD-UP-PSL government from 2001 to 2004.

Jan Olszewski: Lawyer and Solidarity activist, first prime minister of the first fully democratically elected *Sejm* from 1991 to 1992. Member of parliament from 1991 to 1993 and from 1997 to 2005. Founder and leader of ROP from 1997 to 2001.

Waldemar Pawlak: Member of parliament since 1989. Leader of PSL between 1991 and 1997, and from 2005 to the present. Prime minister of the SLD-PSL government from 1993 to 1995. Deputy prime minister and economy minister in the PO-PSL government from 2007 to the present.

Tadeusz Rydzyk: Redemptorist Catholic priest, proprietor of Radio Maryja and associated Catholic-fundamentalist media outlets.

Donald Tusk: Solidarity activist and cofounder of KLD. Member of parliament for KLD and subsequently UW from 1991 to 2001. Left UW to found PO; leader of PO since 2003. Currently prime minister of the PO-PSL government.

Lech Wałęsa: Shipyard worker who spearheaded the Solidarity movement. President of Poland from 1990 to 1995.

In the new context of transitioning to democracy, the robust individualism advocated by enthusiasts of capitalism assumed a wider relevance. Just as the "proven model" of market capitalism seemed a panacea for economic problems, so the key postulates of liberalism promised remedies for the pathologies of political and cultural existence under communism. Liberalism appeared as "inverted Marxism," offering the opposite of all that was hated in the previous order.[5] As well as establishing a fully functioning capitalist economy, democracy had to be entrenched in accordance with liberal constitutionalist principles. The role of the state was to act as guarantor of the rights and freedoms of the individual and to ensure an open civil society in which free individuals could participate. This required legal protections for individual and minority rights and a decrease in direct state control over areas such as the media and the education system. Social and historical truth was no longer the province of the state but a product of the free market of ideas. Finally, openness in the domestic sphere was complemented by an open, nonantagonistic foreign policy, with an emphasis on cooperation and membership of international organizations.

Whose Poland Is It to Be? From the Round Table to the "War at the Top"

From the outset of transition, Polish liberals feared a backlash against painful reforms. Many had witnessed firsthand the extraordinary political energies unleashed by Solidarity a decade before. Their concern was that in conditions of democratization these might prove destabilizing tendencies. The 1989 elections took part largely in an atmosphere of optimism and goodwill on the part both of political elites and voters. Yet as Balcerowicz had predicted, the period of popular assent was not to last long. The Round Table negotiations quickly became a focal point of resentment for radical opposition groups refusing all negotiation with the communists, a resentment exacerbated by the technocratic political style of the Mazowiecki government and its determination to avoid policies of revenge. The absence of public debate and the strict oversight of parliamentary discussion of the Balcerowicz Plan were easily construed as symptomatic of the unwillingness of the new elite to participate in a dialogue with society.

The deepening of democracy saw a deepening of the rift. Lech Wałęsa supported the drive for "acceleration" of democratic reform, insisting on early presidential elections in which he would run as the Solidarity candidate. Solidarity liberals perceived this stance as a threat to the gradual accretion of democratic gains and supported Mazowiecki's candidacy. Jaruzelski resigned to permit early presidential elections, but the resulting "war at the top" destroyed the unity of Solidarity in the bitter and destructive election campaign of November–December 1990. Liberal fears about the propensity of the electorate to be swayed by demagogic promises were compounded by the success of surprise candidate Stan Tymiński, a conspiracy theory–toting Polish émigré to Canada who attracted a quarter of the vote in the first round, pushing Mazowiecki into third place. Although liberal Solidarity temporarily swung behind Wałęsa to see off the threat of Tymiński, their support was laced with distaste for the lesser evil. (A chronology of major elections and outcomes is given in box 7.2.)

Wałęsa's victory sharpened the appetite for accelerated parliamentary elections, which took place in October 1991. With twenty-nine parties—many of which barely warranted the name—entering the lower house (*Sejm*), the first democratic parliament was incoherent. The two largest parties were the liberal Democratic Union (UD), built around Mazowiecki's milieu, and the successor to the communist PZPR, the Democratic Left Alliance (SLD). Neither was able to form a coalition government: the SLD was politically untouchable, and the UD bore responsibility for Poland's shock therapy. The exclusion of the latter from the eventual five-party minority coalition was testament to the depth of the divide in Solidarity.

As the first government of a fully democratic Poland, this coalition, under the Solidarity lawyer Jan Olszewski, regarded itself as mandated to accelerate transition. Refusing to acknowledge the Round Table compromise as the historical moment of departure from communism, it argued that "lustration" (the exposure of individuals' past collaboration with the communist secret police) was necessary to identify and remove the continuing influence of communists. The coalition's tenure was short and controversial, and its zeal for lustration led to its downfall after a clumsy attempt by Interior Minister Antoni Macierewicz to expose collaborators among the political elite, including Wałęsa himself.[6] In his outgoing speech, Olszewski posed a question that would resonate in the years to come: "From today onwards, the stake in this game is not simply the question of which government will be able to execute the budget to the end of the year; at stake is something more, a certain image of Poland: what sort of Poland it is to be? To put it another way, whose Poland is it to be?"[7]

Olszewski's argument was that in the absence of a clean break with communism, both national identity and autonomy were under threat. However, at a time when many ordinary Poles were suffering the effects of economic reforms, it also raised the question: in whose interests was "shock therapy" working?

Most scholars assumed that politics would revolve around a key economic division between promarket and antimarket parties. This was supplemented by a variety of "cultural" divides such as "religiosity versus secularism," "liberalism versus cosmopolitanism," or "traditionalism versus libertarianism," all of which were in essence about differences between individualist and collectivist conceptions of society.[8] In the Polish case, a "triangle of values" was evident at an early stage: a group of liberal parties (UD and the Liberal-Democratic Con-

Box 7.2   Chronology of Major Elections and Changes in Government

Election to the "Contract Sejm": 6/4/1989 (first round); 6/18/1989 (second round)
Turnout: 62.7% and 25%.
Share of seats: PZPR (38%), ZSL (17%), SD (6%), Catholic (5%), Solidarity (35%).[1]

Government of Tadeusz Mazowiecki (9/12/1989–12/14/1990)[2]
Parties of the governing coalition: OKP, PZPR (SdRP), ZSL (PSL), SD.[3]

Presidential election: 11/25/1990 (first round); 12/9/1990 (second round)
Turnout: 60.6% (first round); 53.4% (second round).
Results (first round): Lech Wałęsa (39.96%), Stanislaw Tymiński (23.10%), Tadeusz Mazowiecki (18.08%).[4]
Results (second round): Lech Wałęsa (74.25%), Stanislaw Tymiński (25.75%).

Government of Jan Krzysztof Bielecki (1/12/1991–12/5/1991)
Significant parties of the governing coalition: KLD, ZChN, PC.[5]

Election to the Sejm: 10/27/1991
Turnout: 43.20%.
Results: UD (12.32%), SLD (11.99%), WAK (8.74%), POC (8.71%), PSL (8.67%), KPN (7.5%), KLD (7.49%).

Government of Jan Olszewski (12/6/1991–6/5/1992)
Significant parties of the governing coalition: PC, ZChN.

Government of Hanna Suchocka (7/8/1992–10/26/1993)
Significant parties of the governing coalition: UD, ZChN, KLD.

Election to the Sejm: 9/19/1993
Turnout: 52.08%.
Results: SLD (20.41%), PSL (15.4%), UD (10.59%), UP (7.28%), KPN (5.77%).

Government of Waldemar Pawlak (10/26/1993–3/1/1995)
Parties of the governing coalition: SLD, PSL.

Government of Józef Oleksy (3/6/1995–1/24/1996)
Parties of the governing coalition: SLD, PSL.

Presidential election: 11/5/1995 (first round); 11/19/1995 (second round)
Turnout: 64.7% (first round); 68.23% (second round).
Results (first round): Aleksander Kwaśniewski (35.11%), Lech Wałęsa (33.11%).
Results (second round): Aleksander Kwaśniewski (51.72%), Lech Wałęsa (48.28%).

Government of Wlodzimierz Cimoszewicz (2/7/1996–10/31/1997)
Parties of the governing coalition: SLD, PSL.

Election to the Sejm: 9/27/1997
Turnout: 47.93%.
Results: AWS (33.83%), SLD (27.13%), UW (13.37%), PSL (7.31%), ROP (5.56%).

Government of Jerzy Buzek (10/31/1997–10/19/2001)
Parties of the governing coalition: AWS, UW (until 6/6/2000).

Presidential election: 10/8/2000
Turnout: 61.08%.
Results: Aleksander Kwaśniewski (53.9%), Marian Krzaklewski (17.3%), Andrzej
    Olechowski (15.57%).

Election to the Sejm: *9/19/2001*
Turnout: 46.18%.
Results: SLD-UP (41.04%), PO (12.68%), SO (10.2%), PiS (9.5%), PSL (8.98%),
    LPR (7.87%).

Government of Leszek Miller (10/19/2001–5/2/2004)
Parties of the governing coalition: SLD, PSL (until 3/3/2003), UP.

Government of Marek Belka (5/5/2004–10/31/2005)
Parties of the governing coalition: SLD, UP, SdPL.

Election to the European Parliament: 6/13/2004
Turnout: 20.87%.
Results: PO (24.10%), LPR (15.92%), PiS (12.67%), SO (10.78%), SLD-UP
    (9.35%), UW (7.33%), PSL (6.34%), SdPL (5.33%).

Presidential election: 10/9/2005 (first round); 10/23/2005 (second round)
Turnout: 49.74% (first round); 50.99% (second round).
Results (first round): Donald Tusk (36.33%), Lech Kaczyński (33.10%), Andrzej
    Lepper (15.11%), Marek Borowski (10.33%).
Results (second round): Lech Kaczyński (54.04%), Donald Tusk (45.96%).

Election to the Sejm: *9/25/2005*
Turnout: 40.57%.
Results: PiS (26.99%), PO (24.14%), SO (11.41%), SLD (11.31%), LPR (7.97%),
    PSL (6.96%).

Government of Kazimierz Marcinkiewicz (10/31/2005–7/14/2006)
Parties of the governing coalition: PiS (plus SO and LPR from 5/5/2006 to 7/14/
    2006).

Government of Jarosław Kaczyński (7/14/2006–11/16/2007)
Parties of the governing coalition: PiS, SO (except 9/21/2006–10/16/2006 and 8/
    6/2007–11/16/2007), LPR (except 10/22/2007–11/16/2007).

Election to the Sejm: *10/21/2007*
Turnout: 53.88%.
Results: PO (41.51%), PiS (32.11%), LiD (13.15%), PSL (8.91%).

Government of Donald Tusk: (11/16/2007–)
Parties of the governing coalition: PO, PSL.

Election to the European Parliament: 6/7/2009
Turnout: 24.53%.
Results: PO (44.43%), PiS (27.40%), SLD-UP (12.34%), PSL (7.01%).

(continued)

Box 7.2   (Continued)

Presidential election: 6/20/2010 (first round); 7/4/2010 (second round)
Turnout: 54.94% (first round); 55.31% (second round).
Results (first round): Bronislaw Komorowski (41.54%), Jarosław Kaczyński
     (36.46%).
Results (second round): Bronislaw Komorowski (53.01%), Jarosław Kaczyński
     (46.99%).

Notes

1. For the 1989 election, seat share is given instead of voter percentages, as Solidarity was only permitted to contest 35 percent of seats.

2. A change in government is registered when the prime minister changes, rather than when the party composition is altered. The endpoint of a government is defined in formal terms as the moment when the next government takes over, rather than the "effective" end that comes with the results of a general election.

3. OKP was the Civic Parliamentary Club, consisting of members of parliament from the election lists of Solidarity's Civic Committees. PZPR was the Polish United Workers' Party, the main party throughout the communist era. ZSL (United Peasant Party) and SD (Democratic Party) were satellite parties of the PZPR.

4. For the sake of relevance, only those presidential candidates gaining more than 10 percent of the vote are included.

5. "Significant parties" are those that proved of relevance to the development of the party "system." See table 7.1 for full names and descriptions of parties.

gress [KLD]) advocated civic rights and rejected socioeconomic rights, the social democratic left (SLD and the Labour Union [UP]) supported both civic and socioeconomic rights, and the conservative-nationalist right (most prominently the Christian-National Union [ZChN]) supported socioeconomic rights but argued for the primacy of the family and the nation over the individual.[9]

The fractious atmosphere of the Olszewski government carried over into the rest of the 1991–1993 term amid growing social discontent with the effects of reforms. Waldemar Pawlak, leader of the agrarian Polish Peasant Party (PSL), failed to assemble a governing coalition, and Hanna Suchocka's post-Solidarity coalition proved too divided and fragile.[10] Both the SLD and the opposition right-wing post-Solidarity parties supported a motion of no confidence, leading to the dissolution of parliament and early elections in September 1993. The SLD won, forming a coalition with the PSL, the only coalition partner to regard them as acceptable. While the UD put up a reasonable showing, the conservative-nationalist element of Solidarity was essentially eliminated from parliament. Around a third of the vote was "wasted" on parties of primarily nonliberal Solidarity provenance that failed to surmount the new 5 percent threshold.

The 1993–1997 parliament was dominated by political forces associated with the negotiated transition. This is not to suggest that consensus reigned undisturbed. The postcommunist "regime divide" still governed popular perceptions of political opposition, and the SLD had campaigned on a platform strongly critical of liberal economic reforms. However, developments over this parliamentary term indicated a more complex ideological configuration underlying the regime divide.

Democratic in Form, Christian in Content? Constituting the New Poland

The early years of transition saw a piecemeal approach to institutional reforms. In April 1989, directly after the conclusion of the Round Table talks, the 1952 Constitution was amended to take account of the changes agreed upon at those talks. The lower house (*Sejm*) still retained its status as the supreme organ of state power, but the directly elected upper house (*Senat*) received limited powers to initiate, review, and delay legislation. The relationship between the two houses was broadly accepted, although periodically the case was made for liquidating the *Senat*.

Unsurprisingly, given the state of geopolitical uncertainty in mid-1989, the presidency was endowed with a number of political powers. As president, Jaruzelski retained many of the competences associated with the communist-era Council of State: he could dissolve parliament and call early elections given certain conditions, he could initiate and veto legislation, and aside from nominating the prime minister, he was also empowered to give his views on ministerial candidates. It was unclear in some cases precisely where the prime minister's sphere of influence ended and that of the president began, with foreign and defense policy areas of particular ambiguity.[11] Jaruzelski displayed restraint in the exercise of his prerogatives, but Wałęsa's tenure was characterized by substantial conflict between the presidency and successive governments, who experienced unpredictable vetoes of legislation and the imposition of ideologically incompatible "presidential ministers" in key portfolios. Initially, it seemed that the presidency would remain strong: the "Little Constitution" of 1992 formalized the president's influence over key ministries, with prime ministers obliged to consult the president over the appointment of the foreign minister, defense minister, and interior minister. The idea of a strong president appealed to some political elites, for whom a powerful nonparliamentary executive could push through necessary reforms in relative freedom from the sectional interests of political parties.[12] However, the experience of the Wałęsa presidency gradually encouraged a mainstream consensus on a presidency set further apart from the day-to-day business of government.

The flourishing of democratic pluralism and President Wałęsa's creative approach to constitutional privilege significantly hindered the vital process of constitution building in the first years of transition. A change of pace occurred with the victory of Aleksander Kwaśniewski, leader of the parliamentary caucus of the SLD, in the presidential elections of November 1995. The eventual promulgation of the 1997 Constitution resolved the issue of executive authority by diminishing the power of the president compared with that of the government. The president, who was no longer able to interfere in ministerial appointments, would be "guarantor of the continuity of state power" (Article 126.1), and the prime minister and his cabinet would be charged with "carry[ing] out the domestic and foreign policies of the Polish Republic" (Article 146). Overall, the Constitution increased the powers of the prime minister, notably with respect to government formation.[13] The structure of the dual executive rested most firmly on the parliamentary pillar. However, the president remained an important political player and far from the largely ceremonial figure preferred by some advocates of the parliamentary model. The ability to veto legislation and delay the countersigning of important documents, as well as wide-ranging competences to make appointments to important state posts, ensured that successive governments would have to take account of presidential opinion.

From the beginning of transition, judicial reform in accordance with liberal legal principles entailed the almost wholesale revision of existing legislation and the promulgation of new laws, establishing the judiciary as independent and separate, and setting up or adapting bodies of oversight. The Little Constitution restored the principle of the division of executive, legislative, and judicial powers: the *Sejm* was no longer the supreme organ of state power.[14] The Constitutional Court, which had been in operation since 1985, became genuinely independent during the first years of transition. The Constitution widened the competences of the court, and most significantly removed the ability of the *Sejm* to overturn its rulings, which now became binding and final. The Constitution provided for independent and apolitical judges protected from political interference and established a judicial system of courts and tribunals with a clear division of competences. A number of institutions of oversight and control were transformed from their communist-era precursors or brought into being, and their scope and competences were outlined in and assured by constitutional articles.

One of the key aims of communist-era opposition movements was the return of real local government. Local government as a subject of legal regulation was liquidated in 1950 and remained so for the rest of the communist era, with local power structures merely instruments of the center, "geared only toward passing commands downward and controlling their fulfilment."[15] Clean, accountable local government was regarded by the reformers as an important element of the establishment of the rule of law and would introduce mechanisms of representation more sensitive to local needs, acting as a counterbalance to central government. In 1990, the commune gained new functions as the basic element of local government, with the principle of administrative dualism revived and attempts made to define the division of competences between central and local government. However, full reform in this sphere was delayed for several years. Eventually, the Constitution articulated the fundamental principle of subsidiarity (that local government should carry out public tasks not reserved to other organs of state), extended legal personality and protection to the commune as the basic unit of local government, and secured for local government "a share of public revenues in accordance with needs."[16] Provincial restructuring aroused much political and public conflict, but it was completed by the beginning of 1999 with the restoration of the county tier of government and the introduction of regional parliaments.

Constitutions do not only define institutions; they also enshrine philosophies of the relationship between individuals and the state, and the process of promulgation brought fundamental ideological differences into conflict. Early in the transition period, the split in Solidarity exposed a significant divide among political elites over attitudes toward *homo post-Sovieticus*. Unsurprisingly, given its close association with Solidarity and the strong identification of most Poles with Catholicism, the years after 1989 saw the reemergence of the Catholic Church as a political actor. Against the civic-individualistic vision espoused by the liberals and social democrats, the Church—and its political allies in the conservative-nationalist bloc—offered a comprehensive collectivist ethical model embracing personal morality, education, gender relations, minority rights, and attitudes toward capitalism and Westernization.

The easy assumption of moral authority by the Church quickly came up against the anticlerical stance of the postcommunists and the determination of liberals to protect individual rights. Education and the media were prominent sites of conflict. Successive ombudsmen complained about violations of the separation of church and state, objecting to prayers and crucifixes in schools, and the insensitivity shown toward religious minorities and nonbelievers during the reintroduction of religious education. The Church left a clear imprint on the 1992 Broadcasting Law, with a clause requiring broadcasters to "respect the Christian value system," and at times enjoyed the indulgence of Catholic politicians in attempts to make media laws more restrictive. Its influence was also evident in the passing of an extremely restrictive abortion law in early 1993 and the subsequent signing of a concordat with the Vatican.

The constitutional debates stimulated a great many issues of controversy, but at the time, the most emotionally heated disagreements revolved around issues of cultural identity and national self-assertion. In debates over the Constitution, clerical input was substantial. The Church demanded that the preamble to the Constitution appeal to God and the principles of natural law and constitute "the Polish Nation," it rejected the principle of separation of church and state, and it demanded the right to life "from conception to natural death." The eventual text attempted to accommodate these sentiments without thwarting the liberal character of the Constitution. The "separation" of church and state was not explicitly articulated, with the state bound instead by "impartiality." The preamble was a masterpiece of pick-and-mix fudging, with "law, justice, good, and beauty" hailed as universal values whether derived from God or elsewhere, acknowledgement of the common culture of Poles "rooted in the Christian heritage of the nation and universal human values," and an invocation of "the Polish Nation—all citizens of the republic . . . responsible to God or to our own conscience." No explicit protection was extended to life "from conception to natural death"; rather, the Constitution referred to the "inborn and inalienable dignity of the individual" (Article 30), which the Polish Republic was bound to defend by legal means (Article 38).

The parliamentary draft document met with strong criticism from those representing the "Solidarity draft," a constitutional project submitted under the auspices of a citizens' initiative. The parliamentary spokesperson for the project echoed the views of other conservative, nationalist, and clerical critics in averring that the final version was "cut off from the values by which the Polish nation abides." In failing to pay tribute to God, legislating for a civic nationalism, and permitting the emergence of an extreme moral relativism, it spurned the "inheritance of history" and "Polish identity."[17] These sentiments reflected a substantial current in public attitudes. Those who favored the Solidarity draft were significantly more likely to agree that the Constitution should contain a preamble invoking God, should be predicated on Catholic social teaching, should contain clauses banning abortion and euthanasia, and should explicitly define postcommunist Poland as the legal and historical continuation of the interwar Second Republic, symbolically cutting it off from the communist Polish People's Republic. Curiously, given the controversy surrounding the issue, both sides declared comparably strong support for an introductory reference to "We, the Polish Nation," rather than a more neutral, civic formulation.[18]

A Poland Richer, but Less Happy

The Polish economy was the first to emerge from recession in postcommunist Europe and was regarded as one of the more successful examples of economic transition. GDP was 35 percent higher in 2005 than in 1989, a significantly greater increase than in neighboring countries.[19] In 2005, 37 percent of households declared that their regular income was insufficient to satisfy current needs; this compared to a figure of 70.6 percent in 1992.[20] However, such positive trends contrasted with the frequent observation that the average Pole was "richer, but unhappy."[21]

Economic policy presented parties with a dilemma. The average Pole was quite supportive of a strong role for the state in the economy. However, serious deviations from macroeconomic orthodoxy risked the wrath of the European Union and the suspicion of foreign investors. The SLD-PSL government of

1993–1997 made more concessions to trade unions than its predecessors but did not substantially depart from the path laid down in the first four years of transition. References to "positive" rights such as full employment and public health care were included in the Constitution at the insistence of the SLD, but these articles were essentially aspirational, with much of the substance relegated to ordinary statute.

Socioeconomic rights were also supported by many in the conservative-nationalist bloc of post-Solidarity parties. Nevertheless, the regime divide again transcended ideological divisions after the elections of September 1997. During the SLD-PSL term, the Solidarity trade union attempted to create a common opposition to the postcommunist resurgence in the form of Solidarity Election Action (AWS), an electoral coalition of some forty parties of largely conservative-nationalist post-Solidarity provenance. The liberals of UD and KLD, meanwhile, banded together as the Freedom Union (UW). AWS and UW formed a post-Solidarity coalition government after the 1997 election, under the premiership of Jerzy Buzek.

The Buzek government faced substantial challenges in the sphere of the economy. If Poland's jump into the market was a swift technocratic exercise, the "deep reforms" of privatization, restructuring of industries, agricultural reform, and the reforms of health care, pensions, and welfare proceeded unevenly. Small-scale privatization was a considerable success, but the privatization of large enterprises was still in an intermediate phase in the second decade of transition; the politically sensitive sectors of mining and energy remained dominated by the state.[22] Agriculture remained largely outside the ambit of the liberal reform process: in addition to tax relief, the state provided credits, financed pensions and welfare, and intervened in the market to purchase products and protect prices.[23] At first, restructuring of the relationship between the state and the individual was more a tale of cuts, with reductions in initially generous unemployment and housing benefits and tightening of eligibility rules, increases in prescription charges, and pensions capped.[24] As part of its programme of "four reforms" (which also included education and the aforementioned changes to local government), the Buzek government attempted to enact significant structural changes to the systems of health care and social security provision, with the intention of injecting an ethos of individual responsibility and choice into both systems.

The changes brought about by economic transition had a profound effect on a society hitherto accustomed to egalitarian ideals and—to a large extent—outcomes. Inequality was relatively low by the standards of Central and Eastern Europe, but significant enough in its own right. Educational capital increasingly mattered: in 1982, only 24 percentage points separated average incomes across the spectrum of educational attainment; in 1987, this stood at 41 percent, and in 2002 at 92 percent.[25] New mechanisms of distribution introduced an inegalitarian logic, with the cutting of subsidies having a differential effect on particular groups and the growth of the private sector seeing greater wage dispersion across professional groups and regions.[26] The liquidation of state-owned farms and factories, the decline of heavy industries, and knock-on effects led to long-term structural unemployment, which was subject to significant regional differentiation on both a macro and a micro scale. Increased inequality and unemployment brought poverty to the fore. This was distinguished by greater physical and social concentration in regions characterized by a prevalence of rural and small-town conditions, and enclaves of poverty in the old centers of industrial cities and in former state farming collectives.[27] Perceptions of inequalities of opportunity and outcome were high and rising.[28]

Reactions to the health-care and social security reforms reflected a generally increasing sense of apprehension that outweighed perceptions of personal economic improvement. People found it more difficult to gain access to a general practitioner, and confusion over the changes led to well-publicized incidents in which individuals were refused medical aid.[29] Public opinion was strongly negative: in 2001, 62 percent of Poles viewed the health-care system as functioning worse than prior to the reforms; only 13 percent asserted that improvements had been made.[30] With social security reforms descending into administrative chaos, 40 percent were unable to say whether they thought it had been a success, and only 13 percent were willing to say that any improvement had occurred.[31]

The coalition, whose structure had lacked integrity from the outset, was shaken apart by these debacles. A frustrated UW departed the coalition in 2000. While economic differences were not the only reason why the coalition and its constituent parties disintegrated, the failure of the post-Solidarity parties to cohere on this dimension had implications whose nature would gradually become apparent over the course of the next decade.

Poland's Political Earthquake: The Return of Transition Anxieties

Szczerbiak (2002) was not alone in opting for a seismic metaphor to describe the September 2001 election, dubbing it an "unexpected political earthquake." One of the tectonic plates remained stable. The victory of the SLD-UP electoral coalition, which gained a hitherto unprecedented 41.04 percent of the vote, was widely expected for many months prior to the election, and a post-communist government coalition was formed with the PSL under the premiership of Leszek Miller. However, on the opposition side, all other parties entered parliament for the first time. This does not mean that they were entirely new. The liberal Civic Platform (PO) was formed in large part by those who had deserted UW after its exit from the coalition, although it was not a continuation

of that party. The core of Law and Justice (PiS), which capitalized on the popularity of hard-line AWS justice minister Lech Kaczyński, consisted of politicians who had cut their teeth in the Olszewski administration. The populist
Self-Defense (SO), and in particular its leader Andrzej Lepper, achieved increasing notoriety throughout the 1990s for protest actions, and had competed
without success in every election from 1991. The League of Polish Families
(LPR) represented the recrudescence of Catholic nationalists like ZChN, with
whom it shared some personnel. (A family history of the major political groupings is given in table 7.1).

The success of SO and LPR was the epicenter of this seismic activity. Both
parties offered abusive critiques of the politics of transition. The LPR gave parliamentary presence to the fundamentalist Catholic social movement centered
around Radio Maryja and its charismatic proprietor Father Tadeusz Rydzyk,
whose tirades against atheist "Judeo-communism" implicated all transition
elites in a conspiracy against "Poles-Catholics." SO, initially formed as an
agrarian protest movement against the effects of economic reforms on small
farmers, broadened its appeal to embrace small-town and urban "transition
losers."

The radicalism of these parties reflected increasing uncertainty among sections of Polish society. The fraught public mood of the early years of transition
gave way to a more optimistic attitude on a number of fronts during the middle
years of the decade, but around the beginning of 1999, it clearly began to turn
negative again. At the start of this year, approximately the same proportion of
Poles viewed the "overall situation of the country" as good as considered it bad
(40 percent); in mid-2001, with elections looming, some 75 percent considered
it bad.[32] Almost exactly the same distributions were in evidence for assessments
of the "economic situation." While successive majorities remained "convinced
of the superiority of the system of democracy over other forms of government," contentment with the way that democracy operated in Poland fluctuated in a 20-to-40 percent band. Persistent minorities remained skeptical of the
significance of democracy in their own lives, with around 40 percent of respondents assenting to the statement that "Sometimes nondemocratic governments
can be more desirable than democratic ones," and "For people like me, it has
no real meaning whether governments are democratic or nondemocratic."[33]

Although dissatisfaction with transition reforms and the democratic system was increasingly widespread in society, there was some evidence that these
sentiments were increasingly concentrated in constituencies of "transition losers" whose economic and social position rendered them less able to take advantage of the new opportunities and who were more likely to be disturbed by the
pace of change and the rise of challenges to traditional values. On the question
of whether post-1989 reforms had succeeded or failed, a higher proportion of
the following groups gave a negative answer: the old, those living in small towns
and villages, those of lower educational attainment, those in the lower income

Table 7.1 Genealogy and Ideology of Major Political Parties/Electoral Coalitions

Name	Origins	Period of Significance	Regime Divide	Economic	Cultural	Attitude to Transition
AWS *Solidarity Election Action*	Coalition of approximately forty post-Solidarity parties	1996–2001	Post-Solidarity	Mixed, both anti- and promarket elements	Conservative, with Catholic-nationalist elements	Broadly positive
KLD *Liberal-Democratic Congress*	Post-Solidarity intellectuals and promarket pioneers	1990–1993	Post-Solidarity	Strongly promarket	Liberal	Positive
KPN *Confederation for an Independent Poland*	Non-Solidarity anticommunist movement (founded in 1979)	1989–1997	Anti-Communist	Mixed, increasingly antimarket	Nationalist	Critical
LiD *Left and Democrats*	Coalition of SLD, SdPL, UP, PD	2006–2008	Mixed	Centrist	Liberal	Positive
LPR *League of Polish Families*	Elements of ZChN, extraparliamentary Catholic nationalist parties	2001–2007	Neither	Mixed, some promarket elements but highly protectionist and autarchic	Strongly nationalist and clerical; moral traditionalism	Negative
PC/POC[1] *Center Accord*	Christian Democratic/conservative Solidarity activists grouped around Jarosław Kaczyński	1990–1993	Post-Solidarity	Mixed, ostensibly promarket but critical of reforms	Moderately conservative	Critical

Party	Origin	Years	Lineage	Economic position	Social position	Attitude
PiS *Law and Justice*	PC, elements of AWS	2001–present	Post-Solidarity	Increasingly statist and antiprivatization	Originally conservative; increasingly nationalist and clerical	Initially critical, then negative
PO *Civic Platform*	UW, KLD, elements of AWS	2001–present	Post-Solidarity	Originally very promarket, more moderately so in recent years	Mixed—both liberal and conservative elements	Positive, although initially critical of transition elites
PSL *Polish Peasant Party*	ZSL (communist-era satellite party)	1989–present	Post-Communist	Centrist	Moderately conservative	Positive
ROP *Movement for the Rebuilding of Poland*	Assorted conservative-nationalist post-Solidarity parties	1997–2001	Post-Solidarity	Mixed, ostensibly promarket but in practice interventionist	Conservative-nationalist	Negative
SdPL *Polish Social Democrats*	Split from SLD	2003–present	Post-Communist	Moderately antimarket	Liberal, anti-clerical	Positive
SLD *Democratic Left Alliance*	Successor to the communist PZPR. Originally a coalition based around Social Democrats of the Polish Republic (SdPR), formally constituted as a party in 1999.	1990–present	Post-Communist	Moderately antimarket	Liberal, anti-clerical	Positive

Table 7.1 (Continued)

Name	Origins	Period of Significance	Regime Divide	Economic	Cultural	Attitude to Transition
SO Self-Defense	Agrarian movement of the early 1990s; constituted as a party in 1992	1992–2007	Neither	Antimarket (especially privatization)	Ambiguous	Negative
UD Democratic Union	Liberal Solidarity intellectuals	1990–1994	Post-Solidarity	Strongly promarket	Liberal, but with a significant conservative faction	Positive
UW/PD Freedom Union / Democratic Party	Formed from the merger of UD and KLD	1994–2004 (UW) 2005–present (PD)	Post-Solidarity	Strongly promarket	Liberal, with conservative elements	Positive
UP Labor Union	Socialist groups from Solidarity; elements of reformist wing of PZPR.	1992–present	Mixed	Moderately antimarket	Liberal, anti-clerical	Positive
ZChN[2] Christian National Union	Clerical and nationalist elements of Solidarity	1989–2001	Post-Solidarity	Ambiguous	Strongly nationalist and clerical; moral traditionalism	Initially positive although increasingly critical

[1] In 1991, PC ran as the main party of the Civic Center Accord (POC).
[2] In 1991, ZChN ran as the main party in Catholic Election Action (WAK).

quartile, the unemployed, the retired, and those receiving invalidity benefits. These patterns were repeated on the question of whether transition had made a positive impact on the life of the respondent, with these groups more likely to indicate that it had not.[34] Transition losers were also more likely to adopt more negative attitudes to democracy.[35]

SO and LPR swiftly exploited their newfound prominence to engage in bouts of direct action both within the *Sejm* and without. They were particularly active in their attacks on the process of Poland's accession to the European Union. While no serious domestic opposition was raised to Poland's accession to NATO in 1999, EU accession proved more troublesome. Nearly ten years of hard negotiation and diminishing patience passed between formal submission to join the union and eventual accession in May 2004. The comprehensive system of monitoring and reporting that characterized the accession process dampened the pro-European ardor of some politicians and heightened fears of the effects accession might have on Poland's agricultural sector and areas of industry such as mining and shipbuilding. Support for European integration always outweighed opposition, but from a high point of 80 percent in 1996, it declined to the mid-50s by the middle of 1999, rising fitfully and moderately to approximately 65 percent just prior to accession.[36] SO and LPR exploited the complicated accession process, aggressively criticizing the SLD-UP-PSL coalition for alleged weak negotiation in areas such as the foreign purchase of Polish land and the level of agricultural subsidies offered to Polish farmers, and generally deploring the loss of sovereignty occasioned by accession. While their efforts were ultimately thwarted by the success of the referendum on EU membership, the startling performance of LPR's candidates in the June 2004 European Parliament elections, gaining ten of Poland's fifty-four seats and coming in second to PO, gave notice that public attitudes remained ambivalent, as did the very low voter turnout of 20.9 percent.

These parties' blanket criticisms of the transition period drew on a number of other prominent areas of discontent, from SO's focus on irregularities in the privatization process to LPR's renewal of the assault on cultural liberalism. Lacking either post-Solidarity or postcommunist pedigrees, both parties claimed to be genuinely antiestablishment forces. However, while SO and LPR caused substantial problems for the ruling parties throughout the parliamentary term, the real challenge to the Third Republic was to emerge from a different source. In late 2002, Polish politics experienced another earthquake in the form of the "Rywingate" scandal, which centered around allegations that the government had attempted to extract a bribe from the owners of the prominent newspaper *Gazeta Wyborcza* in return for potentially lucrative amendments to a media bill. A controversial opposition report, which suggested the existence of a shadowy, extragovernmental "group holding power" and implicated premier Miller in the conspiracy, was accepted by parliament as the official version of events. This, and subsequent *Sejm* investigative commissions on other allegations of corruption, nourished the narrative of "transition gone wrong."

The Miller administration never recovered from the blow of Rywingate, and Miller resigned in May 2004. His successor, phlegmatic social-liberal technocrat Marek Belka, attempted to drain a little of the color from politics. Yet the facts and rumors around Rywin were conducive to the revival of arguments about the "afterlife" of communism. Law and Justice (PiS) was particularly active in this regard. The party's leader, Jarosław Kaczyński, had long advanced a theory of transition in which real power was held by a network comprised of the old communist apparatus—the *nomenklatura*—and liberal elements of Solidarity. Having negotiated the transition in protection of their mutual interests, these actors engaged in covert cooperation to ensure the stability of the new arrangement, systematically excluding patriotic and traditional values and seeking to delegitimize alternative political actors. The promulgation of the 1997 Constitution saw this system reach maturity, crystallizing unequal access to state institutions, the media, and the market and pushing dissenting political formations into more radical stances. The Miller administration witnessed the hubristic overstretching and collapse of the system.[37] Although EU accession in many respects marked the end of the "launch stage" of Polish transition, and the economy began to return to health, the long campaign for the September 2005 elections was dominated by the question of whether there was not something seriously amiss with Polish democracy.

The Short "Fourth Republic": Poland's Populist Moment

The decline of the SLD over its term in office was spectacular. In March 2004, a number of deputies broke away to form Polish Social Democracy (SdPL), citing the party's failure to come to grips with the questionable activities of some of its members. The party entered the dual presidential-parliamentary election campaign of September–October 2005 in a disoriented state, lacking experienced leadership and a clear political appeal. In contrast, both PiS and PO appeared to be credible advocates of the drive to clean up politics and were expected to form a coalition government, the only question being which would be the major partner.

The concurrent presidential race was less clear cut, and the manner in which its shifting dynamics intertwined with those of the parliamentary election had a strong influence on subsequent developments. The three main candidates were PiS's Lech Kaczyński, PO leader Donald Tusk, and former SLD premier Włodzimierz Cimoszewicz. Cimoszewicz initially led the polls, which pitched the presidential election as a choice between representatives of a chastened and repentant postcommunism or radical post-Solidarity. However, a scandal surrounding his alleged nondeclaration of shares to a parliamentary commission led him to withdraw prior to the parliamentary elections. This caused a significant change in the terms of competition. With Kaczyński falling behind Tusk in the polls, the period immediately prior to the parliamentary election saw PiS recast both plebiscites as a choice between the "liberal" ethos of PO and PiS's more "social" or "solidaristic" leanings. The party's efficient public relations department set to work producing demagogic but effective television broadcasts focusing on the potential impact of PO's proposed flat tax on the lives of ordinary Poles. This socially sensitive rhetoric fed into a wider appeal to the losers of transition. The shift toward "social" Poland sharpened PiS's electoral appeal against the background of all other parties at a crucial moment in the campaign. In the parliamentary election, PiS gained marginally more votes than PO. Both SO and LPR improved only slightly on their previous performance, and the SLD was humiliated. PiS's victory cast a shadow over the ongoing presidential campaign. With Tusk having a slight advantage in the first round, both sides escalated their rhetoric, and with it their enmity. After the narrow victory of Lech Kaczyński in the second round, the PO-PiS coalition talks collapsed amid mutual distrust, with PiS left to form a minority government helmed by the largely unknown Kazimierz Marcinkiewicz.

This left PiS with a problem: they had clear ideas about what needed to be done and a president who would support them, but opportunities to effect substantial changes would be hugely inhibited by having to rule as a minority. With the divide between PO and PiS apparently insuperable, PiS cast around for different solutions. After tentative attempts at informal and then more formal cooperation, PiS invited SO and LPR to form a coalition government in May 2006. It was widely assumed that an unwritten taboo existed against coalition partnerships with these radicals, and the liberal elite were horrified at this "exotic threesome."[38] PiS depicted the coalition as a regrettable by-product of legislative mathematics, yet the short and turbulent period that followed saw the party absorb many of the features of its partners.

The term "Fourth Republic" was at first largely a metaphor for decommunization, but it swiftly assumed a more literal meaning. The overriding priority of PiS was the removal of the "network" from institutions it considered to be particularly afflicted by the blight of informal connections and corruption: the justice system, the civil service, military intelligence, and public media. The first major legislative act of the Marcinkiewicz government altered the powers, responsibilities, and personnel of the National Council of Radio and Television (KRRiT), transforming it from an institution in which the parliamentary opposition had representation into one peopled entirely by candidates of the ruling coalition. PiS vigorously pursued a new law on lustration that would significantly widen its scope—notably to embrace media owners, editors, journalists, and academics—and introduce sanctions for failure to submit affidavits. Justice Minister (and simultaneously prosecutor general) Zbigniew Ziobro introduced a raft of reforms, increasing his oversight of the prosecution service and judges and attempting to break open the corporate structures of the legal profession. A Central Anticorruption Bureau (CBA) was set up with the specific remit of fighting corruption and extensive, if ill-defined, powers to detain and search. The Military Information Service (WSI) was liquidated.

Foreign policy was informed by deep-seated grievances about Poland's maltreatment by major European powers during the twentieth century. This posture resulted in tension between Poland and other EU member states and the Polish use or threat of the veto on a number of occasions, most notably over negotiations regarding the European Reform Treaty, that is, the Lisbon Treaty. For the national interest to be pursued, it needed to be defined and inculcated. A vital part of PiS's agenda, and one that chimed deeply with LPR's concerns, was the cultivation of a "politics of history" in which the state took a leading role in the dissemination of national, patriotic, and state traditions, with schools a particular site for the inculcation of such values. As minister of education, LPR leader Roman Giertych was tasked with implementing these policies. The party's flagship policy of "patriotic instruction" as a separate school subject never materialized, but the imprint of the coalition's moral traditionalism was evident throughout Giertych's controversial tenure.

Generally, the coalition trod warily in economic matters; such effects as it had were largely a product of inaction rather than action. The coalition's socially solidaristic rhetoric was tested by a wave of public sector strikes to which it responded in rather antagonistic fashion. Privatization slowed to a crawl as the government concentrated on consolidating state-held industries into strategic conglomerates, particularly in the energy sector. The ministries of Agriculture and Labour and Social Policy, headed by SO nominees, were stymied by incompetent administration and patronage.

The chief outcome of the period was not reform of the Third Republic, but realignment of the terms of political competition.[39] PiS's increasing radicalism saw it adopt and even transcend the populist rhetoric of its coalition partners. "Populism" is one of the most abused words in the political lexicon, but if it is understood as an ideology that is employed to cultivate an antagonistic relationship between an authentic, legitimate, and morally superior "people" against an illegitimate, usurping, and morally compromised elite, then the PiS-SO-LPR government was quintessentially populist. The language of political discourse reached new heights of aggression. PiS surpassed its coalition partners in the art of the damning epithet: Poland became a country in which "mendacious elites" and "pseudointellectuals" were arrayed against "ordinary" or "real" Poles. Politics was increasingly defined not as the clash of competing interests but as a battle of good versus evil. This conflict came to a head in the tense and emotional public debate over the lustration law in the spring of 2007. The Constitutional Tribunal dealt a crushing verdict on the lustration law, ruling many of its provisions unconstitutional and rendering it inoperable. PiS viewed the outraged reaction of the tribunal and those who supported its accusations of political partiality as evidence that the "network" was defending itself, and as justification for redoubling the assault. This pattern was repeated in similar conflicts, such as that over PiS's confrontational approach to foreign policy, which at one point led all hitherto serving foreign ministers of the Third Republic to sign a public letter of rebuke. Political satire and media polemic flourished, but the most vivid expressions of the polarization of public life were the multiple acts of public protest—both against and in support of the government.

Outbreaks of populism tend to describe a steep parabola, and several factors conspired to bring the parliamentary term to a premature end. The turbulent internal life of the coalition increasingly militated against coordinated political action. SO's political and personal indiscipline was a persistent irritation to PiS, culminating in a "sex for jobs" scandal that implicated Lepper and seriously compromised the already shaky credibility of the coalition's claim to be engaged in a "moral revolution." Attempting to regain lost ground on the radical right, LPR made virulent homophobia an ever more prominent feature of the party's public face. Fissures even emerged in PiS's hitherto impregnable inner sanctum over the lack of internal democracy. After a bizarre series of events in which the CBA attempted to entrap Lepper into accepting a bribe to reclassify agricultural land for development, the coalition crumbled over the summer of 2007. The hoped-for flow of SO and LPR deputies to PiS failed to materialize, and with both PO and SLD pressing hard for early elections, PiS had little choice but to support a vote to dissolve parliament.

The election of October 2007 was "a plebiscite on a polarizing and controversial government."[40] This was as much a result of PiS's determination to defend its record as of the attacks conducted by the opposition. In contrast to 2005, PO found the appropriate response. Rowing back from its economic liberalism, it secured the support of many of those public sector workers PiS had alienated, and landed effective blows on PiS's style of government. The role of SO and LPR in the election was minimal; neither party appeared to have much idea how to retain their electorate, much less broaden it. With a high—by Polish standards—voter turnout of 53.8 percent, both major parties benefited. Exit poll figures showed that PO and PiS captured comparable percentages of newly mobilized voters as a proportion of their overall vote share.[41] However, PO's overall gains substantially exceeded those of PiS, and it won in convincing style, forming a coalition with the PSL, now firmly established as a centrist party of perennial coalitionability.

"Poland A versus Poland B": The Proto-Cleavage of Transition Politics

The postcommunist/post-Solidarity regime divide was a natural locus of competition for political elites in the immediate aftermath of transition, and during the first decade of transition it resonated with group identity and cultural attitudes, with those of a nonreligious and anticlerical persuasion more likely to vote for postcommunists.[42] Yet it was premature to hail this as Central and Eastern Europe's contribution to the collection of classic cleavages. Some expected that class politics would grow in relevance as a result of the impact of further privatization and growing inequality;[43] others linked the emergence of economic differentiation to wider processes of Westernization, arguing that "[l]ogically, those who fear Western cultural and, particularly, economic dominance will assume a more protectionist, or even anti-market, position."[44]

After 2005, attitudes toward the communist regime still constituted "a significant point of orientation for a substantial number of voters."[45] Yet the stances of political elites during and after the 2005–2007 parliamentary term suggested that these attitudes were no longer directly relevant to the postcommunist regime divide. Indeed, PiS proved inventive in adapting the symbolism of that divide to current political needs, repeatedly drawing equivalences between the actions of the liberal opposition and those of the communist regime and consciously effacing the difference between liberal Solidarity and the postcommunists. Deepening antagonisms within the post-Solidarity elite seemed to be more of a priority for PiS than maintaining the postcommunist divide. After the 2007 elections, PiS moderates made overtures to the SLD on the grounds of ideological compatibility on the economic dimension, a move unthinkable as recently as 2005.

Evaluations of voter attitudes and behavior with respect to the new dimension were varied. In two studies following the 2005 and 2007 elections, Markowski identified a deepening sociodemographic divide between PO and PiS voters along the lines of the transition winner/loser dichotomy, and evidence of their increasing attitudinal differentiation—albeit in a relative sense—on the economic divide as well as the cultural one.[46] In 2007, flows of voters between parties reflected the division between those who contested the Third Republic and those who upheld it: PiS attracted disproportionally large numbers of those who had previously voted for SO and LPR, while PO attracted in even greater disproportion those who had voted for parties of the postcommunist left.[47] Sociodemographic variables and affinities for parties reflected clear divisions between, on the one hand, those preferring PiS, and, on the other, those preferring PO, PSL, and Left and Democrats (LiD).[48] In 1997, political affinities were firmly oriented around the postcommunist divide and its attendant ideological correlates; by 2007, the main pattern of affinities clearly distinguished between PO and PiS and echoed the "politics of transition" divide. However, the evidence of voter behavior indicated that only limited progress was made in turning these patterns of affinity into the kind of voting behavior that justifies talk of cleavage mobilization. The sociodemographic transition loser/winner divide was present in part, but not strong as a whole. The distribution of voters on both attitudinal dimensions did not indicate a strong attitudinal division between protransition and antitransition cohorts. The most significant finding was not that antiliberals and populists were mobilizing transition losers to vote for them, but that parties were not mobilizing significant proportions of these groups to vote at all.[49]

Against rational-choice accounts which predicted a relatively swift consolidation of cleavage structures in Central and Eastern Europe, developments in the region supported more open-ended theories of cleavage formation in which political agents were influential—often decisively so—in the emergence of patterns of party competition.[50] Where a degree of consistency obtained between party platforms, cohorts of voters, and voter attitudes, the qualified term "proto-cleavage" was more appropriate. The elections of 2007 furnished sufficient evidence to suggest that the distinction of "Poland A" and "Poland B" had overtaken the postcommunist divide as the proto-cleavage of Polish politics. It remained too early to rule on the future electoral efficacy of this division; "[l]eadership volatility, party volatility and electoral volatility created whirlpools of continuing uncertainty."[51] Greater attitudinal bifurcation, sociodemographic penetration, and voter mobilization were all required in order to entrench what remained an inchoate configuration of parties rather than a closed and predictable party system.

Yet there were grounds to expect that these processes would continue. A divide over the politics of transition was more relevant to conditions of rapid, socially disorienting, and still-ongoing modernization than the historical and biographical concerns of the regime divide. Although after 2007 politics took place in a less frenetic register, divergence over the politics of modernization was still in evidence. *Poland 2030*, a strategy document published under the auspices of the office of the prime minister, sought to define the scope of developmental challenges facing Poland and identify policies to tackle them. It advocated the adoption of a "polarization and diffusion" model of growth, by which the development of Poland's metropolitan centers would result in associated benefits for the peripheral regions, and it stressed the need for more thoroughgoing reforms to the social security system and the rationalization of agriculture as elements of a comprehensive reform of public finances.[52]

PO failed to make significant progress with this agenda during the first three years of its term in office. President Kaczyński vetoed key reforms of the PO-PSL government such as health care and public media and provided a strong negative incentive against further liberalizing measures in areas such as state funding for in vitro fertilization (although this excuse was overused by a government increasingly aware that their poll ratings were not affected unduly by inactivity). He also sought to interpret his prerogatives as widely as possible, particularly in the sphere of foreign policy. With both the office of the presidency and the PiS-dominated state broadcaster TVP ensuring that PiS's alternative concepts of economic, cultural, and political order were kept prominent, the Fourth Republic project was, if currently in abeyance, by no means moribund. The government—whose liberal zeal was also tempered by having to share power with the centrist PSL—oscillated between the brave new horizon of *Poland 2030* and the rather more proximate vista of the upcoming presidential and parliamentary elections, with Tusk declaring, "I am not going to give PiS any electoral presents" by attempting to undertake controversial reforms with no certainty of their successful promulgation.[53]

At the electoral level, an increasingly clear geographical distribution of support emerged after 2007. Regional voting patterns at the 2009 European Parliament election and the 2010 presidential elections indicated that PO was increasingly popular in the western and northern regions of Poland, with PiS consolidating its lead in the regions of the southeast and along the eastern border. Observers had long commented on the congruence between patterns of voter behavior and the historical borders along which Poland was partitioned prior to 1918. Some argued that these historical divides were obsolete and that sociodemographic and attitudinal "modernization criteria" were more important determinants of the vote, with PO boasting a better-educated and more affluent promodernization electorate and thus mobilizing the more economically prosperous regions of western Poland. However, divergent patterns of development were in part a legacy of the politics of partition; if Poland was indeed increasingly divided, it reflected both historical and proximate factors. The strength of the divide should not be exaggerated. Color-coded maps tended to obscure the gradations of difference, and nonvoting still blighted Polish democracy.

The Smolensk tragedy and the presidential elections helped further to consolidate the social/liberal proto-cleavage. While Jarosław Kaczyński's decision to run ensured that the campaign for the first round was relatively subdued, the unexpected closeness of the result (see box 7.2 above) prompted both sides to appeal to the 13.6 percent of the electorate who voted for SLD candidate Grzegorz Napieralski.

Kaczyński rushed to downplay his past anticommunist rhetoric and to express the rhetoric of social sensitivity, and Komorowski raised the specter of the potential for a return to the Fourth Republic should Kaczyński emerge victorious. This dynamic was in keeping with the tripolar distribution of ideological positions identified by Kurczewski, but with the SLD now a minor party whose voters might be wooed on different dimensions by (somewhat) culturally progressive liberals or by socially sensitive conservative-nationalists. The fact that Napieralski's small share of the first-round vote was greeted with talk of the party's renaissance was testament to how far its stock had fallen with the public. Meanwhile, PSL candidate Waldemar Pawlak came fifth, trailing behind Janusz Korwin-Mikke, a libertarian generally regarded as one of the perennial novelty candidates. Although presidential elections were rarely a good measure of PSL's strength, PiS's increasing rural popularity threatened the future parliamentary existence of this party.

The aftermath of the election did not see a decline in hostilities but their escalation. PiS moved quickly to harness the emotional and political capital of Smolensk, setting up a parliamentary group to study the causes of the crash, which increasingly embraced conspiracy-theory and anti-Russian rhetoric. PiS also supported various symbolic measures to honor the memory of the late president, some of which were controversial. The decision to bury the presidential couple in the crypt of the Wawel Cathedral proved immediately divisive, and both PiS and the church hierarchy faced criticism for exploiting tragic circumstances for symbolic purposes. Protests against the removal of a large cross that had been erected outside the presidential palace in the days following the crash became a focal point for angry exchanges over the divisions both of church and state and of Catholicism and Polishness. Moderate voices in PiS were again sidelined, with Kaczyński blaming his party's "liberals" for an ineffective election strategy. PO, meanwhile, faced the difficult task of making good on their plans for liberal reforms in the absence of the get-out clause afforded by the promise of President Kaczyński's veto, with a coalition partner wary of being outflanked on its own territory by PiS, and with a parliamentary election scheduled for the autumn of 2011. Both the economic and cultural facets of transition's civilizational divide were certain to play significant roles, both in the campaign to come and in the years beyond.

Conclusion

Twenty years later, in 2010, Poland had in most respects completed the tasks of transition. It was firmly established as a member of the comity of liberal democratic states, with an economy that weathered the economic crisis rather better than many of its European contemporaries and with institutions that proved resistant to illiberal backsliding. It still faced significant problems with corruption and the efficiency of the state, yet these were the problems of a young democracy rather than factors that might imperil the continued existence of democracy in Poland. However, the *politics* of transition were still dominant, both in terms of personnel and policies. While democracy was not contested, its liberal variant was, with the two major parties divided on economic and—to a lesser extent—cultural issues and on the metapolitical divide of "imitative modernization" versus the pursuit of national-particularist paths of development.

In this respect, Poland was hardly an exception. After the entrenchment of democracy following the travails of Mečiarism, Slovakia experienced a similar political division between parties broadly accepting of the liberal orthodoxy and the idiosyncratic politics of the nationalist-populist coalition of 2006–2010, and these were not phenomena restricted to Central and Eastern Europe. A recent study of political change in six Western European democracies contends that processes of globalization have given rise to a bifurcation between the economic and cultural winners and losers of these processes, with the metapolitics of "integration" and "demarcation" becoming increasingly influential determinants of political appeals and voter mobilization.[54] While the strength of traditional political divides has slowed the progress of this bifurcation in some Western European polities, there is potential for those Central and Eastern European countries whose transition models were imported from the West, who have become increasingly exposed to the same pressures of globalization, and whose "inherited" cleavage structures are comparatively weaker, to be in the vanguard of these new cleavage alignments.

It is still too early to judge whether Poland's populist moment was a brief spasm of antiliberal discontent in Poland or the harbinger of more lasting divides. It is also yet unclear whether it has bequeathed to Poland a relatively stable party system or simply a temporary state of arrested instability. However, as this discussion has shown, there is much to support the expectation that if cleavages are to emerge in postcommunist democracies as they emerged in their Western counterparts, the proto-cleavage of transition winners and losers will provide the basis for this. The results of the 2011 parliamentary election will tell us much about its further prospects.

Suggested Readings

Balcerowicz, Leszek, *Socialism, Capitalism, Transformation*, Budapest: Central European University Press, 1995.

Jasiewicz, Krysztof, "The Past Is Never Dead: Identity, Class, and Voting Behavior in Contemporary Poland," *East European Politics and Societies*, 23(4), 2009, 491–508.

Kemp-Welch, Anthony, *Poland under Communism: A Cold War History*, Cambridge: Cambridge University Press, 2008.

Kolodko, Grzegorz W., *From Shock to Therapy: The Political Economy of Postsocialist Transformation*, Oxford: Oxford University Press, 2000.

Kostelecky, Tomas, *Political Parties after Communism*, Baltimore, MD: Johns Hopkins University Press, 2002.

Markowski, Radoslaw, "The Polish Elections of 2005: Pure Chaos or a Restructuring of the Party System?" *West European Politics*, 29(4), 2006, 814–832.

Markowski, Radoslaw, "The 2007 Polish Parliamentary Election: Some Structuring, Still a Lot of Chaos," *West European Politics*, 31(5), 2008, 1055–1068.

Millard, Frances, *The Anatomy of the New Poland: Post-Communist Politics in Its First Phase*, Aldershot: Edward Elgar, 1994.

Millard, Frances, *Polish Politics and Society*, London: Routledge, 1999.

Millard, Frances, "Poland's Politics and the Travails of Transition after 2001: The 2005 Elections," *Europe-Asia Studies*, 58(7), 2006, 1007–1031.

Millard, Frances, "Poland: Parties without a Party System, 1991–2008," *Politics & Policy*, 37(4), 2009, 781–798.

Paczynska, Agnieszka, "Inequality, Political Participation, and Democratic Deepening in Poland," *East European Politics and Societies*, 19(4), 2005, 573–613.

Slomczyński, Kazimierz M., and Goldie Shabad, "Systemic Transformation and the Salience of Class Structure in East Central Europe," *East European Politics and Societies*, 11(1), 1997, 155–189.

Szacki, Jerzy, *Liberalism after Communism*, Budapest: Central European University Press, 1995.

Szczerbiak, Aleks, "Poland's Unexpected Political Earthquake: The September 2001 Parliamentary Election," *Journal of Communist Studies and Transition Politics*, 18(3), 2002, 41–76.

Szczerbiak, Aleks, " 'Social Poland' Defeats 'Liberal Poland'? The September–October 2005 Polish Parliamentary and Presidential Elections," *Journal of Communist Studies and Transition Politics*, 23(2), 2007, 203–232.

Szczerbiak, Aleks, and Sean Hanley, "Introduction: Understanding the Politics of the Right in Contemporary East-Central Europe," *Journal of Communist Studies and Transition Politics*, 20(3), 2004, 1–8.

Zarycki, Tomasz, "Politics in the Periphery: Political Cleavages in Poland Interpreted in Their Historical and International Context," *Europe-Asia Studies*, 52(5), 2000, 851–873.

PART TWO

THEMATIC CHAPTERS

CHAPTER 8

European Integration: Progress and Uncertainty

John Van Oudenaren

After World War II, European political leaders looked to unity as a way to prevent another destructive war in Europe and to promote economic recovery after the depression of the 1930s and the wartime losses of 1939 to 1945. In 1948, Belgium, the Netherlands, and Luxembourg formed the Benelux customs union. That same year, France, Britain, and the three Benelux countries concluded the Treaty of Brussels in which they pledged to come to each other's defense in the event of external attack, hold regular consultations among their foreign ministers, and cooperate in the economic, social, and cultural spheres. The treaty also established the organization that later became the Western European Union (WEU).

Early steps toward European integration received a major boost from the U.S.-backed Marshall Plan, which Secretary of State George C. Marshall proposed in a speech at Harvard University in June 1947. Concerned about the danger of communist subversion in a postwar Europe still wracked by poverty and shortages of food and fuel, Marshall proposed a program in which the United States would provide Europe with money and goods, on the condition that the Europeans came up with a joint program for using this aid effectively. In April 1948, sixteen European states founded the Organization for European Economic Cooperation (OEEC), a Paris-based body that helped to administer Marshall aid and provided a forum in which the member states negotiated arrangements to lower intra-European trade and currency barriers.

The Brussels pact and the OEEC were modest steps toward European cooperation, but they fell short of a full-fledged United States of Europe, the ambitious objective then being advocated by political activists known as federalists. Looking to the United States as a model, they believed that integration had to move beyond treaties among governments and be based directly on the will of the people. The federalists called for the convening of a European assembly, whose members would not be chosen or controlled by national governments. Instead, it would constitute a new organization to unite the peoples of Europe. The federalists convinced the five signatories of the Brussels pact to convene a ten-power conference in London in early 1949 to discuss their ideas. The conference led to the creation of the Council of Europe, a Strasbourg-based organization charged with harmonizing laws and promoting human rights. Although useful in its own way, the Council of Europe was not a truly federal institution. Governments in key countries retained their sovereign powers, setting strict political and legal limits to how far integration could proceed.

The other major development of this period was the creation of the North Atlantic Alliance. In April 1949, the United States, Canada, and nine European states signed the North Atlantic Treaty, in which they pledged to come to each other's assistance in the event of external attack. The treaty was followed by the creation of the North Atlantic Treaty Organization (NATO). Like the Marshall Plan, NATO was an important U.S. contribution to the postwar revival of Europe. It allowed the European countries to concentrate on economic cooperation, leaving sensitive and contentious matters of defense to the Atlantic organization.

Establishing the Community: Coal, Steel, and Supranationalism

The precursor to today's European Union (EU) was the European Coal and Steel Community (ECSC), which was the brainchild of Jean Monnet, a French businessman who had spent the war years in the United States and who had devoted much thought to the problem of bringing about European unity. Like the federalists, Monnet believed that European integration had to go beyond the traditional methods of diplomacy in which governments agreed to cooperate with each other. Governments could easily renege on such commitments and return to old patterns of isolation and mutual hostility. On the other hand, Monnet believed that it was naive to think that Europe could form a federation by a simple act of political will. Too much tradition, too many vested national interests, and direct opposition from Britain, which had no interest in losing its identity in a continental federation, stood in the way.

Monnet concluded that the way to start the process of integration was to achieve concrete results in specific sectors, establish permanent institutions to consolidate those results, and then achieve new results that would generate additional political support and enthusiasm for a united Europe. As a first step, Monnet conceived a plan for France and Germany to combine their coal and steel industries under a joint authority. This authority was to be independent of the governments of the two countries and would guarantee each country full and equal access to a common pool of resources. The significance of this proposal was both political and economic. With the production of coal and steel—the very sinews of modern military capability—subject to a joint authority, war between these two traditional enemies would become unthinkable.

On May 9, 1950, French foreign minister Robert Schuman formally proposed Monnet's plan to the French cabinet. France, West Germany, Belgium, Luxembourg, the Netherlands, and Italy all agreed to join the new community. The treaty establishing the ECSC was negotiated in the months following Schuman's dramatic declaration and was signed in Paris in April 1951, and the ECSC became operational in July 1952. For the commodities covered—coal, coke, iron ore, steel, and scrap—the ECSC created a common market in which all tariff barriers and restrictions on trade among the six member countries were banned. The treaty provided for the establishment of four institutions, roughly corresponding to the executive, legislative, and judicial branches of government, with extensive legal and administrative powers.

The High Authority was established as a nine-member commission with executive powers to administer the market in coal and steel. The members of the authority (two each from France, Germany, and Italy; one each from Belgium, Luxembourg, and the Netherlands) were to be "completely independent in the performance of their duties." They were to decide what was best for the ECSC as a whole, rather than represent the views of the member countries. The High Authority was empowered to issue decisions, recommendations, and opinions prohibiting subsidies and aids to industry that distorted trade, to block mergers and acquisitions, and under certain circumstances to control prices. It could impose fines to ensure compliance with its decisions. Monnet was named the first head of the High Authority.

The Council of Ministers consisted of ministers from the national governments of the member states, with each state represented by one minister. For some policy actions, the Council of Ministers had to endorse the decisions of the High Authority. Some decisions were taken by unanimity, others by majority voting. Thus, even within the Council of Ministers, member states could not always exercise a veto over collective decision making. This was quite different from organizations such as NATO, where decisions were taken only by consensus and where a single state could always block adoption of a decision to which it was opposed.

The Common Assembly introduced an element of legislative participation in the ECSC. Its members were not directly elected by the people but were chosen by the national legislatures. Its power, moreover, was to advise rather than to pass legislation. Still, the principle of parliamentary participation was established, and the powers of what later was to become the European Parliament were to expand greatly in subsequent decades. The European Court of Justice (ECJ) was set up to settle conflicts between member states of the Community or between member states and the ECSC itself.

These institutions were the first genuinely supranational bodies in Europe. They could exercise authority—in their limited areas of competence—over the national governments of the member states. Establishment of the ECSC thus entailed a transfer of sovereignty from the national level to the central institutions, which were to be located in Luxembourg. Along with steps already under way in the OEEC, the elimination of barriers to trade in the coal and steel sectors contributed to the European economic renaissance of the early 1950s. Politically, the Community also began the process of reconciliation between France and West Germany.

THE EUROPEAN ECONOMIC COMMUNITY

The ECSC's scope of activity was by definition quite limited. Seeking to build upon the successes of the ECSC, the six member states began looking for ways to broaden the scope of integration. They turned initially to defense. In May 1952, the six ECSC countries signed a treaty establishing a European Defense Community (EDC) in which decisions over defense and a jointly commanded European army were to be made by supranational institutions patterned on those of the ECSC. However, in August 1954, the French National Assembly rejected the EDC treaty. Whereas national governments and parliaments were willing to surrender sovereignty in some key economic areas, the EDC experience showed that defense was too sensitive—too close to core issues of national identity—to be treated the same way. The emphasis thus shifted back to economics.

Following the EDC setback, the foreign ministers of the six ECSC states met in Messina, Italy, in June 1955 to consider ways to energize the integration process. Two courses of action were discussed: a further stage of *sectoral* integration based on a proposed atomic energy community, and a plan for *market* integration through the elimination of barriers to trade and the eventual creation of a common market. Those who saw integration primarily as a process of building up shared institutions and accomplishing common projects stressed the importance of the atomic energy community. Others saw European integration more as a process of tearing down intra-European barriers and emphasized the common market. These two approaches came to be known as "positive" and "negative" integration, and both have played a role in the development of Europe.

The ministers agreed to establish a committee to study these options and to formulate proposals. The Spaak Committee (named for its chairman, Belgian foreign minister Paul-Henri Spaak) presented its report to the May 1956 Venice meeting of foreign ministers. It struck a balance between the two approaches to integration and proposed that the ECSC states create both a European Atomic Energy Agency (Euratom) and a European Economic Community (EEC). Following arduous negotiations, leaders of the six countries met in Rome on March 25, 1957, to sign two treaties creating these new entities.

Of the two institutions created in 1957, the EEC—or Common Market as it was widely known—was by far the more important. The agreement establishing the EEC became known as the Treaty of Rome and remains in many ways the core constitutional document of today's European Union. The basic objective of the EEC was simple in principle but sweeping in its implications: to create an internal market characterized by the free movement of goods, services, persons, and capital. Initially, the emphasis was on eliminating obstacles to trade in goods. The treaty provided for the phasing out, in stages, of all tariffs and quantitative restrictions on trade among the member states. The common internal market also necessitated the establishment of a common external tariff and a common commercial policy. Since goods that entered one member state could travel freely throughout the EEC, member countries needed to adopt the same tariffs toward third countries, lest goods simply be diverted to ports in countries with the lowest tariff for a given import. The EEC thus was empowered to speak with one voice in international negotiations within the framework of the General Agreement on Tariffs and Trade (GATT).

The Treaty of Rome used the basic institutional framework established for the ECSC. The High Authority for the EEC, called simply the European Commission, was endowed with broad executive powers, including the sole right to initiate Community legislation. The member states were responsible for selecting the commissioners, who were chosen for four-year terms (five-year terms since 1979). The Commission president, also provided for under the treaty and selected by the member states, soon emerged as the most visible champion of and spokesperson for the Community.

A Council of Ministers was to be the main decision-making body of the EEC, in which representatives of the member states would vote on proposals put forward by the Commission. Votes could be made on the basis of unanimity or by qualified majority—a weighted system that assigns votes in rough proportion to the population sizes of the member states and that requires a certain critical mass of votes to pass a measure. France, Italy, and West Germany each had four votes, Belgium and the Netherlands two, and Luxembourg one. Twelve of the seventeen votes were considered a qualified majority. In practice, qualified majority voting was disliked by some member state political leaders, especially in France, as too supranational and was little used until the 1980s. As in the ECSC, the chairmanship of the Council rotated, with each member state serving as Council president for a six-month period.

In addition, the member states agreed that the three communities—the ECSC, Euratom, and the EEC—would share the same Common Assembly and Court of Justice. The ECSC High Authority remained in Luxembourg, but the new European Commission was established in Brussels, which became the de facto capital of uniting Europe. The Common Assembly was situated in Strasbourg, France. The treaty also provided for the establishment of two other institutions, the Economic and Social Committee and the European Investment Bank, that were to play much lesser roles in Community decision making.

Operating under a concept that became known as "functionalism," promoters of European federalism believed that the gradual expansion of economic ties and of cooperation in various practical spheres such as atomic energy eventually would "spill over" into the political realm, as governments, parliaments, and national electorates yielded sovereignty in small but politically manageable steps. This aspiration to go beyond economic cooperation was expressed in the very first sentence of the Treaty of Rome, in which the signatories declared their determination "to lay the foundations of an ever closer union among the peoples of Europe."[1]

Although the focus of the EEC was on the creation of a common market through the elimination of barriers, the Treaty of Rome also provided for the establishment of common policies in other areas. Agriculture was the most important, but others included transport, competition (antitrust), and policies toward colonies and former colonies in Africa and the Caribbean. Over time, the EEC was to assume a role in a growing range of policy areas, some, like telecommunications and industry, closely linked to the internal market, but others, such as the environment, much broader in scope.

Completion of the common market for goods took place between 1958 and 1968, a period of rapid economic growth and rising prosperity. Businesses became more efficient and productive as they were able to sell to a larger market and were forced to invest to meet competition from firms in other countries. The Common Agricultural Policy (CAP) was established in 1962 in accordance with general goals laid down in the Treaty of Rome based on a system of subsidies and protective tariffs designed to benefit European farmers. This system worked in sustaining farmers' incomes and ensuring stability of supplies, but it also led to higher food prices for consumers, overproduction, and disputes with trading partners who were being progressively squeezed out of the protected EEC market.

Despite its initial successes, the EEC went through a crisis in the mid-1960s. President Charles de Gaulle of France was suspicious of what he saw as a power grab by unelected bureaucrats in Brussels that threatened French sovereignty. He thus resisted efforts to strengthen the Community's central institutions and insisted that all decisions be made on the basis of unanimity among the member states, even though this was not the intent of the Treaty of Rome. De Gaulle also vetoed Britain's application to join the EEC. Britain had been a founding member of the WEU, the OEEC, NATO, and the Council of Europe, but it had declined to join the ECSC and the Common Market, which British politicians believed went too far in limiting Britain's national sovereignty. The British economy at that time was still larger than those of the continental European powers, and Britain retained strong links with its colonies, the Commonwealth, and the United States, with which it had a "special relationship" growing out of World War II. It thus was unwilling to surrender sovereignty to a fledgling enterprise based in Brussels.

By the 1960s, however, the empire was dissolving, and Britain's ties with the Commonwealth and the United States were diminishing in importance. British economic growth was lagging that in continental Europe, where British industry saw new and growing markets. Thus, in the summer of 1961, Britain, joined by Denmark and Ireland, applied to become an EEC member.[2] The British government received a rude shock when, at a news conference in January 1963, de Gaulle announced that he would veto Britain's application. This decision was rooted in de Gaulle's distrust of the "Anglo-Saxon powers" and his view that Britain would be a stalking horse for the United States, whose influence in Europe he wanted to diminish. The same three countries subsequently reapplied for membership in May 1967, but de Gaulle would not lift his opposition to British membership.

Despite these many problems, by the end of the 1960s the Common Market was largely complete, and the economic results were positive. Franco-German reconciliation was a reality. De Gaulle relinquished his post in April 1969 to his successor, Georges Pompidou, who was more open to European integration. Pompidou announced, in July 1969, that France no longer would oppose Britain's admission to the Community. The time thus seemed right for bold new initiatives. At the Hague summit in December 1969, the leaders of the six agreed to explore ways to strengthen the EEC's institutions, to establish an "economic and monetary union" by 1980, and to begin cooperation in the foreign policy sphere.

DEVELOPMENTS IN THE 1970s

The 1970s saw a number of milestones in European integration. Cooperation in foreign policy, or European Political Cooperation (EPC), was launched in 1970. The member states agreed to "consult on all questions of foreign policy" and where possible to undertake "common actions" on international problems. EPC was to take place outside the federal structures of the Community. The European Commission and the European Court of Justice did not have competence or jurisdiction in foreign policy matters, making EPC a much weaker form of cooperation than that established in the economic sphere by the Treaty of Rome.

On January 1, 1973, the first enlargement of the Community took place, as Denmark, Ireland, and Britain became members. This was the first of six enlargements (see table 8.1), each of which has required complex negotiations on such matters as payments into and from the Community budget, transition periods for phasing in Community rules, and the weight of each member state in the Community's institutions.

Despite these achievements, the optimistic expectations of the late 1950s and the 1960s were disappointed in the 1970s as the integration process was slowed by unfavorable external economic and political conditions. Economic

Table 8.1   Rounds of EU Enlargement

Founding members: Belgium, France, Germany, Italy, Luxembourg, the Netherlands	1958
Denmark, Greece, Ireland	1973
Greece	1981
Portugal, Spain	1986
Austria, Finland, Sweden	1995
Cyprus, Czech Republic, Estonia, Hungary, Latvia, Lithuania, Malta, Poland, Slovakia, Slovenia	2004
Bulgaria, Romania	2007

policymakers worldwide became preoccupied with the problems of the U.S. dollar and the breakdown of the Bretton Woods monetary system. In August 1971, the United States suspended the convertibility of dollars into gold. This was followed by devaluation of the dollar and a worldwide shift to floating exchange rates. EEC finance ministers and central bankers tried to maintain a "joint float" of their currencies against the dollar, but in the absence of a stable and predictable global monetary system, European plans to achieve economic and monetary union by 1980 were put on hold.[3]

The oil crisis of 1973–1974 delivered another external shock to the integration process. When war broke out in October 1973 between Israel and its Arab neighbors, the Arab countries cut off the export of oil. Importing countries scrambled to find supplies to keep their economies going. In Europe, divergent national responses to the embargo strained the new EPC. Even after the embargo ended, oil prices had shot up to four times their 1970 level. One result was the economic recession of 1974–1975, the most severe since the 1930s. Governments looked to national solutions to combat rising unemployment. The Treaty of Rome prohibited the reimposition of tariffs and import quotas, but governments increased many open and hidden subsidies to industry, imposing nontariff barriers to trade that undermined the single market. The European economies eventually recovered, but for the remainder of the decade, the industrialized world was plagued by "stagflation," the devastating combination of low growth and high inflation.

Among the few positive developments of the 1970s was the strengthening of the Franco-German relationship under French president Valéry Giscard d'Estaing and German chancellor Helmut Schmidt, and the founding, at their urging, of the European Council. At the December 1974 Paris summit, the leaders of the member states agreed to hold summit meetings three times (later changed to twice) each year. These regular gatherings constituted a new institution, the European Council. Unlike the Council of Ministers, which was assigned extensive legislative responsibilities under the Treaty of Rome, the European Council was to operate more informally. It was a forum in which leaders could gather behind closed doors for discussion and bargaining. It became the preferred means by which European leaders reached compromises on deadlocked issues and launched new initiatives relating to the future of the Community. Actual policy implementation still took place in and through the existing treaty-based institutions—the Commission, the Council of Ministers, and the European Parliament—but the European Council became the "motor" behind the integration process.

Giscard d'Estaing and Schmidt also were instrumental in founding, in March 1979, the European Monetary System (EMS), a system of fixed but adjustable currency rates built around a central unit of account, the European Currency Unit (ECU). The latter was an artificial currency whose value was set by a weighted basket of EEC member country currencies. In the EMS, each national currency had a fixed rate against the ECU. The central rates in ECUs then were used to establish a grid of bilateral exchange rates. Countries were responsible for ensuring that this rate fluctuated by no more than 2.25 percent (6 percent in the case of Italy). The central rates could only be changed with the consent of the other members of the EMS. The EMS thus provided a high degree of intra-European monetary stability and paved the way for a still more ambitious project, Economic and Monetary Union (EMU), at the end of the decade.

The first direct elections to the European Parliament took place in June 1979, bringing to Strasbourg a popularly elected body of men and women who could claim to speak for Europe on behalf of the electorate. The Community also began accession negotiations with the three Mediterranean countries, Greece, Portugal, and Spain. These countries were much poorer than the EEC average, and all three were emerging from authoritarian rule and were attempting to establish democratic systems. While many in Europe questioned whether the Community could afford to absorb these applicants, European leaders saw an overriding political imperative for Mediterranean enlargement. The Community thus began accession negotiations in 1976–1979, although membership was only achieved for Greece in 1981 and Portugal and Spain in 1986.

RELAUNCHING THE COMMUNITY: THE SINGLE EUROPEAN ACT

EMS, direct elections to the European Parliament, and enlargement negotiations with the Mediterranean countries were all stirrings of a new dynamism in European integration that was to take hold in the next decade. In the early 1980s, the Community remained bogged down by economic and political problems. The 1979 revolution in Iran produced a second oil shock and another deep recession. The terms "Euro-pessimism" and "Euro-sclerosis" were coined to sum up a sense that Europe's internal structures—businesses, the welfare state, the educational system—were resistant to change and were unable to respond to increased competition from Japan, the United States, and the newly industrializing countries.

Margaret Thatcher, who was elected prime minister of Britain in 1979, was known for her skepticism about European integration.[4] Thatcher was determined to redress the imbalance in Britain's financial relations with the Community that resulted from the fact that Britain imported large amounts of food and industrial goods from outside the EEC on which it paid customs duties and agricultural levies to Brussels, while it received far less back from the CAP, owing to the small size of its farming sector relative to those in other Community countries. By 1979, this imbalance was well over $1 billion per year. For five years, Thatcher pressed her counterparts in the European Council for a rebate, all but crippling political decision making in the Community. The British budgetary question finally was resolved at the Fontainebleau summit in June 1984, where the heads of government agreed to cut Britain's contribution as well as to undertake a wider budgetary reform. Responding to concerns in the European Parliament and the business community about the seeming drift in the Community, the leaders also agreed to a proposal by French president François Mitterrand to establish a committee to explore ways to improve the functioning of the Community and of EPC.

Discussion about the internal market had intensified in the early 1980s among government officials and the leaders of large European corporations who were increasingly concerned about Europe's lackluster economic performance. The Treaty of Rome stated that the EEC was *supposed* to be an internal market characterized by the free flow of goods, services, persons, and capital. As a practical matter, only a free market in goods had been established, and even this was riddled with exceptions. Differing national standards and technical regulations hindered the import of products from other EEC countries. Paperwork at the borders and disparate national policies on taxation, health and safety, company law, and subsidies to industry all fragmented the European market. Markets for services, capital, and labor were still largely national. Businesses had limited ability to compete across borders in industries such as banking, insurance, and construction. Governments and central banks retained controls on capital, making it difficult, for example, for savers to deposit funds in banks outside their country of residence. And citizens of one EEC country seeking to work in another were hampered by rules on residency and working permits and by national pension and insurance schemes.

Jacques Delors, a former French minister of finance, became Commission president on January 1, 1985, and immediately launched a program to complete the single market. The Commission drafted a detailed plan with approximately three hundred proposals to be turned into Community law to complete the internal market. Each proposal was assigned a target date so that the whole program would be implemented by December 31, 1992. The report identified physical, technical, and fiscal barriers to the internal market, all of which it proposed to dismantle. Physical barriers included customs posts and paperwork and inspections at borders. Technical barriers included national standards and regulations that had the effect of impeding commerce among EEC member states. Fiscal barriers included types and levels of taxation that varied from one EEC country to another.

Delors and his advisers realized that many of the plan's specific measures would be difficult to turn into law. Much Community legislation takes the form of directives, which lay out general guidelines as to "the result to be achieved" but leave it to the member states to enact appropriate national legislation. With each of several hundred proposed measures requiring unanimous approval by twelve governments, there was little chance that the ambitious single-market program could be implemented. Institutional reform, meaning change in the way the Community made decisions, thus was needed.

The committee on institutional reform established at Fontainebleau presented its final report to the Brussels summit in March 1985. The report called for a broadening of the EEC's objectives and areas of responsibility and for selected institutional reforms that would strengthen the Community and speed up decision making. It recommended convening an Intergovernmental Conference (IGC) among the member states that would draw up a new treaty of European Union. The general thrust of the report was toward significant changes in the Treaty of Rome as a way of restarting the integration process and ensuring that the single-market program would be implemented.

Under the Treaty of Rome, the member states were empowered to call at any time, by simple majority vote, an IGC to negotiate treaty revisions. This provision had never been invoked, in part because there was limited interest in such revisions, but also because governments invariably took major decisions by consensus, even when the treaties allowed for majority or qualified majority voting. But at the June 1985 session of the European Council in Milan, the member states voted seven to three (Britain, Denmark, and Greece opposed) to convene an IGC.

The IGC began in September 1985 and culminated in an intense round of bargaining among the Community leaders at the December 1985 Luxembourg summit. The result was a new treaty, the Single European Act (SEA), formally signed on February 17, 1986, and which came into effect on July 1, 1987, after all of the member states had ratified. The SEA broadened the Community's areas of responsibility and made changes in Community decision-making processes. New policy areas not mentioned in the Treaty of Rome but added to Community competence included environment, research and technology, and "economic and social cohesion" (meaning regional policy aimed at narrowing income disparities between different parts of the Community). The SEA also inserted a new article in the Treaty of Rome that mandated completion of the internal market by the end of 1992. The SEA specified that for certain policy areas the Council was empowered to take decisions by qualified majority vote.

These areas included some social policy matters, implementation of decisions relating to regional funds and Community research and development programs, and, most importantly, most measures "which have as their object the establishment and functioning of the internal market." This last amendment was the crucial change that allowed the completion of the single-market program by the deadline.

The SEA also increased the power of the European Parliament. Whereas the Treaty of Rome required only that the parliament be consulted on legislation before its adoption or rejection by the Council of Ministers, the SEA introduced a cooperation procedure under which the parliament could demand from the Council an explanation as to why its proposed amendments had not been adopted. The treaty also introduced an assent procedure under which the parliament was required to approve certain legislative actions, including the Community budget and association agreements with countries outside the EEC. These changes expanded the power of the European Parliament and marked a new stage in its transition from a consultative to a genuinely legislative body.

Finally, the Single European Act introduced an important change in the foreign policy sphere by creating a legal basis for EPC. Under the terms of the act, the signatories henceforth were bound by legal agreement, rather than just a political commitment, to consult and cooperate with each other in foreign policy. However, the EPC itself was not (unlike, for example, such new policy areas as environment or regional policy) incorporated into the Treaty of Rome. There thus was no such thing as a Community foreign policy, but rather only an agreement among the member states that they would forge a common foreign policy. This meant that foreign policy would remain a matter for intergovernmental cooperation rather than supranational coordination. Community institutions such as the Commission would not have a role in EPC, and foreign policy decisions would not be subject to the jurisdiction of the European Court of Justice.

The SEA was a compromise between those in Europe who wanted progress toward political union and those, like the British and the Danes, who would have preferred not to convene an IGC at all. It introduced important reforms in the Community's founding treaty and demonstrated that the member states could use the mechanism of an intergovernmental conference to push the integration process forward. Above all, it elevated to the level of a legal principle the key goal—a single market by the end of 1992—that was to become synonymous with the "relaunch" that Delors had sought to achieve and provided added means to achieve that goal through expanded use of qualified majority voting.

The Treaty on European Union

The 1992 Treaty on European Union, or the Maastricht Treaty as it was commonly known after the Dutch city in which it was signed, was by far the most extensive revision of Community treaties ever attempted. Many of the changes wrought by Maastricht had been under discussion for decades, and some likely would have come about under any circumstances, but the sweeping changes that occurred in Central and Eastern Europe in 1989–1991—the fall of the Berlin Wall, the unification of Germany, and the collapse of communism—gave a powerful external push to reform.

EMU had been on the Community agenda since 1969 but was all but forgotten in the 1970s and was only slowly revived as an issue in the 1980s. By 1988, talk of EMU again was becoming fashionable. The EMS had been operating for nearly a decade, and had succeeded in its original goal of insulating intra-European trade from turbulence in global currency markets. As the EMS evolved toward a de facto fixed-rate regime, a growing number of economists and political leaders argued that Europe should take the next logical step and move to full EMU.

The single-market program also strengthened the case for EMU. Proponents argued that there was an inconsistency between the single market and the maintenance of separate currencies, since changes in the value of these currencies affected the prices of goods and services traded in the internal market and thus constituted a barrier to trade. National currencies also imposed transactions costs on businesses and consumers. A second factor strengthening the case for EMU was the elimination, under the single-market program, of all national controls on capital. Economists warned that it would be very difficult to sustain the EMS—a system that retained different national currencies but that tightly regulated variations in the value of these currencies relative to each other—in circumstances in which investors were free to move money across borders to seek the highest rate of return.

Responding to the growing interest in EMU, at the June 1988 Hanover summit the European Council agreed to establish, under the chairmanship of Delors, a committee to propose steps leading to economic and monetary union. Composed mainly of the central bank heads from the member states, the Delors Committee developed a detailed three-stage plan for the establishment of EMU. It proposed that in stage three exchange rate parities be "irrevocably fixed" and full authority for determining economic and monetary policy be transferred to EEC institutions. At the June 1989 summit, the European Council approved the Delors Committee's approach and declared that stage one of EMU should begin on July 1, 1990, with the closer coordination of member state economic policies and completion of plans to free the movement of capital. European leaders further agreed that another IGC would be held to consider moving to stages two and three, which unlike stage one required amendment of the EEC treaty.

EMU most likely would have gone ahead in any case, but developments in Eastern and Central Europe lent new urgency to this project. The opening of the Berlin Wall in November 1989 led to the virtual collapse of the East German communist regime and a fast-moving set of negotiations involving the governments of the two German states, along with the Soviet Union, Britain, France, and the United States (the four victor powers of World War II), that resulted in the reunification of Germany in October 1990. The five states of the former East Germany, with some 16 million inhabitants, automatically became part of the Community. Although leaders such as Mitterrand accepted German reunification as inevitable, they were concerned that creation of a larger and more eastward-oriented Germany could damage the process of European integration. Mitterrand was determined to push forward with plans to "deepen" the Community, and thereby to ensure that the new Germany remained firmly anchored in the West. He was supported in this by the Germans themselves, especially by Chancellor Kohl.

In December 1989, the European Council agreed to convene an IGC on EMU by the end of 1990 and to adopt a social charter—a Community-wide agreement on labor standards that the trade unions had pressed for as a concomitant to the single European market. Alongside these developments in the economic sphere, the changing international situation gave new momentum to the old project for European Political Union (EPU). In April 1990, Kohl and Mitterrand jointly called for steps to realize the aspirations toward EPU expressed in the Single European Act. The Kohl-Mitterrand proposal set the agenda for an extraordinary session of the European Council in Dublin in April 1990, at which the twelve leaders reaffirmed their commitment to political union. Meeting in the same city two months later, the European Council agreed to convene an IGC on political union to begin at the same time as the IGC on EMU and to run in parallel with it. Both IGCs formally opened at the Rome summit in December 1990. Thus, after not holding a single such conference in the three decades after 1955, the Community was to have three IGCs in five years, two of which would run concurrently. This extraordinary situation reflected the extent to which, as Delors had phrased it, history was "accelerating," forcing the Community to respond.

NEGOTIATING THE MAASTRICHT TREATY

The focus of the IGCs was on strengthening the decision-making process in areas in which the EEC already had competence and on extending the range of issues subject to common policymaking. The negotiations lasted a year and concluded at the December 1991 European Council with agreement on the Treaty on European Union, which was agreed after last-minute negotiations in which Britain and Denmark secured the right to "opt out" of certain of the treaty's provisions. The treaty was signed in Maastricht in February 1992.

As its official name indicated, the treaty brought into being a new entity called the European Union—a complicated structure of three "pillars" dealing with different policy areas using different decision-making processes. The first pillar consisted of the three existing communities—the EEC (renamed the European Community [EC] to reflect its broadened and no longer strictly economic areas of responsibility), the ECSC, and Euratom—in which the member states pooled sovereignty and transferred decision-making powers to the Commission, the Council of Ministers, the European Parliament, and the European Court of Justice, with a powerful guiding role also assigned to the European Council.

The second pillar, the Common Foreign and Security Policy (CFSP), replaced and was based upon EPC. Decisions in the second pillar were to remain largely intergovernmental in character, with only a limited role for Community institutions. Such decisions would not be subject to the jurisdiction of the Court of Justice. The European Commission could suggest actions under CFSP, but it was not given the sole right of initiative in this area, as the member states could also initiate policy actions under CFSP. The Maastricht treaty specified certain foreign policy goals that were to be pursued under CFSP, such as safeguarding the common values, fundamental interests, and independence of the EU, strengthening its security, and promoting peace and respect for human rights. These objectives were to be pursued through "common positions" and "joint actions" by the member states, with decisions on these matters taken primarily by unanimity. CFSP also provided for the "eventual framing of a common defense policy" and assigned implementation of EU defense decisions to an existing body, the Western European Union, previously not linked to the structures of the European Communities.

The third pillar consisted of cooperation in the fields of Justice and Home Affairs (JHA), including asylum policy, control of external borders and immigration from outside the EU, and combating drug addiction and international crime. The completion of the single European market and the abolition of controls on the movement of people and capital had made EU-level cooperation on cross-border problems increasingly necessary, but the member states with their different legal traditions and approaches to such sensitive internal matters were reluctant to surrender sovereignty to Brussels in these areas. The twelve thus agreed to establish the third pillar on an intergovernmental basis, with decision-making procedures similar to those used in CFSP. The treaty also established a European citizenship, to supplement rather than replace national citizenship, and which brings with it certain rights, such as the right of an EU citizen to be represented by the consulate of another member state while overseas or to vote in local elections while resident in another member state.

The Maastricht Treaty strengthened the European Parliament by adding a new procedure, called co-decision, under which the parliament for the first time could block legislation introduced by the Commission and passed by the Council of Ministers. Co-decision was prescribed only for a limited number of policy areas, although one of these—the internal market—was quite important.

The parliament was also given a say in the appointment of the Commission and the Commission president, hitherto a matter of exclusive concern for the Council of Ministers. The treaty also established a new institution, the Committee of the Regions, to provide a means whereby regional entities in Europe—states and provinces—can give direct input to policymaking in Brussels.

The most significant achievement of the Maastricht Treaty was EMU. Building on the Delors Committee report and the experience of EMS, the treaty established a detailed timetable and institutional provisions for the phasing out of national currencies and the introduction of a European money, initially called the ECU and later renamed the euro. Stage two of EMU was to begin on January 1, 1994. The member states were to meet certain economic convergence criteria relating to inflation, national debt and deficits, currency stability in the EMS, and long-term interest rates to ensure that the economies entering the economic and monetary union would have broadly similar performance.

Stage three would begin no later than January 1, 1999, and would entail the "irrevocable locking" of the value of the European currencies against each other and their eventual phasing out by July 2002. The treaty provided for the establishment of a European Central Bank and a European System of Central Banks responsible for conducting monetary policy at the EU level. Britain and Denmark, both traditional skeptics of EMU, secured "opt-outs" from the main provisions of EMU and were not required to surrender their national currencies if they chose not to do so.

BEYOND MAASTRICHT: AMSTERDAM AND NICE

After nearly a decade of rapid change, it was perhaps inevitable that the pace would slow and that a reaction to further integration would set in. With Western Europe racing toward union and the old order in Eastern Europe rapidly disintegrating, people needed time to digest these changes. After a short-lived economic boom, the costs of German reunification helped to precipitate another recession in Europe, bringing to an end the job growth of the late 1980s. The 1991 Iraq war and the outbreak of civil war in the former Yugoslavia caused added uncertainty. The mood in Europe became introspective, focused on national concerns such as crime, immigration, and unemployment and more skeptical of the headlong rush to union.

Ratification of the Maastricht Treaty proved unexpectedly difficult. In June 1992, voters in Denmark narrowly rejected the treaty in the referendum that was required under the Danish Constitution. In September, French voters approved the treaty, but only by the narrow margin of 51 to 49 percent. In Germany, the treaty was challenged in the Supreme Court, where opponents argued that it contravened the German Constitution by transferring powers of the

German states to Brussels. Political uncertainty triggered a crisis in the financial markets, which concluded that EMU might not come into effect as pledged in the treaty and speculated heavily against weaker currencies in the EMS system. In the end, the treaty was ratified. The European Council negotiated additional opt-outs for Denmark, and in May 1993, the Danish voters approved the treaty by a healthy margin in a second referendum. Legislatures in the other countries approved the treaty, as did the German federal court. Maastricht thus went into effect on November 1, 1993, some ten months later than originally planned.

On January 1, 1995, the membership of the European Union expanded to fifteen, with the accession of Austria, Finland, and Sweden. This was a mere prelude to the more extensive enlargement that had been placed on the agenda following the collapse of communism in Central and Eastern Europe in 1989–1991. The leaders of these newly democratic countries pressed for admission to the EU and NATO. Many in Western Europe were uncertain about the feasibility of absorbing a relatively poor region with over 100 million inhabitants, but EU leaders soon concluded that they had little choice but to welcome these new democracies into the fold. At the June 1993 Copenhagen summit, the European Council agreed that these countries could become members provided they went through a period of transition in which they prepared their economies and established working democracies.

The prospect of enlargement drew heightened attention to what many observers saw as the shortcomings and unfinished business of the Maastricht Treaty. In many areas, disagreements among the member states had led to vague compromises and statements of intent that could be interpreted in different ways. For example, the article that introduced defense into the EU structure stated, "The common foreign and security policy shall include all questions related to the security of the Union, including the eventual framing of a common defense policy, which might in time lead to a common defense." But how were terms like "eventual" and "might in time" to be interpreted and translated into action? Many of the decision-making procedures provided for in the treaty were slow and cumbersome, and threatened to become more so with the addition of ten or more new member states.

Recognizing that the treaty would need to be revised at some point, the twelve had agreed, in the Maastricht Treaty, to hold another IGC in 1996 to review the workings of the treaty and to introduce such amendments as were necessary. The scheduled IGC convened in Turin in March 1996 and concluded in June 1997 with the adoption of a treaty amending the Maastricht arrangements. Called the Treaty of Amsterdam after the city in which it was signed, the agreement provided for some strengthening of CFSP, for example by creating the post of a high representative for CFSP and by introducing the mechanism of "common strategies" toward third countries and regions. It also mandated closer cooperation in third-pillar matters such as immigration and asylum policies, in large part through a phased shift of these responsibilities from the third to the first pillar. As in past revisions, the powers of the European Parliament were expanded.

Meanwhile, the two ambitious projects of the 1990s—the euro and enlargement—steadily advanced. The euro was introduced as scheduled on January 1, 1999, with eleven EU members (all but the United Kingdom, Denmark, Sweden, and Greece) adopting the common currency and forming their own grouping of economic and financial ministers to coordinate euro-related policy matters. The technical switchover to the euro over the long New Year's holiday went surprisingly well, without computer crashes or increased volatility in financial markets. The European Council decided that accession negotiations with six leading candidate countries—the Czech Republic, Cyprus, Estonia, Hungary, Poland, and Slovenia—could begin in March 1998. At Helsinki in December 1999, the member states further declared that all of the Central and East European candidate countries and Malta (although not yet Turkey) had made sufficient progress in bringing their political and economic situations up to EU levels to begin accession negotiations.

In March 2000, the member states launched yet another IGC, the fourth to take place in less than a decade. With enlargement to another ten countries looming, the focus of the IGC was on streamlining and strengthening EU decision making, goals that were to have been pursued in the previous IGC but which the member states, focused on the transition to the euro, had not seriously tackled. The overriding need was to ensure that an organization with an institutional setup originally designed for six relatively homogeneous members could function with a more diverse membership of twenty-five or more members. As a practical matter, it was also necessary to decide the relative weight—in terms of votes in the Council of Ministers, representatives in the European Parliament, and so forth—each member state of the enlarged union would have.

The most sensitive issue was the reweighting of votes in the Council of Ministers. Qualified majority voting was designed to ensure efficiency through use of majority voting but to preserve some of the safeguards associated with the unanimity procedure. Legislation could not be blocked by one or two recalcitrant member states, but neither could it be passed, as in most national parliamentary systems, by a narrow numerical majority. This system generally had worked quite well. However, as many more small countries joined the Union, France and the other large member states were increasingly concerned about the declining relative weight of the bigger countries. Whereas the original Community of the 1950s had had three large and three small member states, an enlarged Union would have only six large member states (France, Germany, Italy, Poland, Spain, and the UK) and eventually more than twenty smaller members. Concerned about the diminution of its relative influence, France pressed for a reweighting of votes in favor of the large member countries (although not, somewhat inconsistently, an increase in Germany's weight relative to France to reflect its increased postreunification population).[5]

In the end, the fifteen approved, at the December 2000 European Council, a new agreement that became known as the Treaty of Nice. The treaty decided how many seats in the European Parliament and weighted votes in the Council of Ministers each current and projected member would have after enlargement. To reduce the size and thereby preserve the cohesion and effectiveness of the Commission, the "big five" gave up their second commissioner. The treaty further stipulated that after membership reached twenty-seven, the EU would shift to a rotation system in which the number of commissioners would be less than the number of member states. The relative weighting of the big states was increased, but France (along with Italy and the UK) continued to have the same number of votes in the Council of Ministers as Germany. To give somewhat greater weight to population and to defuse German complaints of unfairness, a complex "triple majority" was put in place, under which a qualified majority vote had to have not only the required number of Council votes, but also be formed by countries representing at least 62 percent of the EU's population.

Although Nice technically cleared the way to enlargement by deciding the distribution of decision-making power in an enlarged European Union, the treaty was hardly the simplification and streamlining that many European commentators thought was essential. Its provisions were more complicated than ever. At the insistence of the member states, policy decisions in such key areas as taxation, social policy, cohesion policy, asylum and immigration, and above all such constitutional issues as reform of the treaties remained subject to unanimity rather than qualified majority voting. Most tellingly, the treaty was long, complicated, and difficult for the average citizen to understand and support, a circumstance that was underscored dramatically in June 2001 when the traditionally pro-Europe Irish electorate voted down the treaty. Nice finally went into effect after the Irish voters approved the treaty in a second referendum in October 2002.

ENLARGEMENT AND THE CONSTITUTION

The perceived shortcomings of the Nice Treaty led to renewed efforts at institutional reform. Even before the treaty had been concluded, a number of political leaders were calling for a debate about the envisioned endpoint of the integration process ("finality") and the need for radical reforms going beyond institutional tinkering. In December 2001, the European Council agreed to launch a European Convention to draw up a European Constitution. Chaired by former French president Giscard d'Estaing, the convention was to be composed of representatives of member state governments, members of national parliaments, Commission representatives, and representatives of the European Parliament.

The call for a constitution reflected the emerging sense in Europe that after more than fifty years of integration, the EU needed a basic set of rules that would not be subject to change at frequent IGCs and that could be understood by and serve as a rallying point for the European citizenry.

The convention began work in March 2002 with great enthusiasm, its members conscious that they were embarking on a constitution-building exercise that in some ways paralleled the one that had taken place in the United States in the 1780s. After sixteen months of intense deliberations, the Convention adopted a draft constitutional treaty and forwarded it to the European Council for consideration by the member states. The treaty was to supersede the 1957 Treaty of Rome and all subsequent amendments and additions to the EU's founding treaties. The three-pillar structure was to be abolished and replaced by a single European Union that would have legal personality and the ability to conclude binding agreements with other countries and international organizations. The treaty would preserve the five key EU institutions, but make changes in how they operated, including by providing for a European Council president to be elected by the member states for a two-and-a-half-year term (to replace the rotating six-month presidency in chairing European Council meetings) and a new EU foreign minister. The powers of the European Parliament were to be extended to new (although still not all) policy areas, and the complicated triple majority system enshrined in the Nice Treaty was to be abolished. In place of the system of national weights used since qualified majority voting was established in the Treaty of Rome, the new system would require that for legislation to be adopted, it must be supported by a majority of member states representing at least 60 percent of the EU population.

When the IGC convened in Rome in October 2003 to consider the draft constitutional treaty, key member states led by France and Germany hoped for its rapid approval without significant amendment. This did not happen, however. Spain and Poland (the latter already participating in the IGC as a prospective member state) were unhappy with the diminution from the Nice formula of their relative voting power in the new treaty and blocked its adoption at the European Council. The member states finally approved the treaty in June 2004, after adjustments were made in the formula for qualified majority voting to satisfy the two holdouts. Under the new compromise, passage of legislation would require the support of at least 55 percent of the member states representing 65 percent of the EU's population; in cases where states representing 35 percent or more of the EU population chose to block legislation, at least four member states had to comprise the blocking group. Ratification by the member states was to take place in 2004 and 2005, and the treaty was to go into effect by 2006.

Amid the endless haggling over institutional reform, the EU managed to complete both EMU and enlargement. Euro notes and coins came into circulation in January 2002, successfully completing the transition to EMU and giving the European Union tangible proof of its cohesion and its ability to accomplish ambitious, long-term goals. On May 1, 2004, ten new member states were admitted to the EU. Bulgaria and Romania were making slower progress in meeting the criteria for membership, and their accession was put off to 2007. Some transitional arrangements remained in effect. The old member states were allowed to keep restrictions on the free movement of labor from the acceding countries, and the new member states were not expected to adopt the euro until they had further strengthened their economies. For the most part, however, the new member states were full participants in all of the policies and programs of the Union, beginning, most prominently, with the single market (apart from the restrictions on movement of labor).

CRISIS AND DRIFT

The wrangling over the provisions of the constitutional treaty reflected the difficult political environment in Europe in the first decade of the twenty-first century. Voters were worried about further expansion of the EU, especially to Turkey, which was pressing to become a member. The Iraq war in early 2003 badly split the EU, as France and Germany took the lead in opposing the U.S. effort to topple Saddam Hussein, while leaders in other member states—especially Britain but also Spain, Italy, and the accession countries—were more supportive of U.S. policy. Europe itself was caught up in the post–September 11 conflict between Islamic radicalism and the West, as was seen most dramatically in the March 2004 bombings in Madrid that killed almost two hundred people.

In May 2005, voters in France rejected the constitutional treaty by a stunning margin of 55 percent "no" and 45 percent "yes." A few days later, voters in the Netherlands delivered a similar verdict. The rejection of the treaty in two founding member states of the EU came as a shock to political leaders across the continent and reflected the degree to which public perceptions of the integration project had diverged from the views of the prointegration elites. Whereas the latter saw a larger and more cohesive EU as the key to enhancing Europe's role in the world and to solving the economic and political challenges raised by globalization, the former were no longer so sure about the benefits that integration offered to the average citizen.

Following the votes in France and the Netherlands, European leaders declared a "pause for reflection" while they figured out what to do about the constitutional treaty and the by-now perennial question of institutional reform.[6] This pause lasted until July 2007, when representatives of the member states, meeting in Lisbon, opened another IGC to amend the EU treaties. The plan was to abandon the constitutional treaty as too ambitious and too controversial, and instead to follow the tested path of making incremental changes to the existing treaties, but to try to preserve as much of the substance of the institutional changes that had been agreed in the constitutional treaty. This was in fact achieved over the summer and fall of 2007, with the adoption and signature on December 13, 2007, of the Lisbon Treaty.

The treaty strengthened the powers of the European Parliament and provided for greater involvement by national parliaments in EU affairs, both measures intended to address the widely perceived "democratic deficit" in the EU. On the thorny question of balancing the rights of large and small states in EU decision making, the treaty established a new system of qualified majority voting in the Council of Ministers. From 2014, passage of legislation is to require a new double majority, which will be achieved when 55 percent of member states representing at least 65 percent of the EU's population vote for a measure. The treaty also established two new posts, a president of the European Council, to be elected to a two-and-a-half-year term, and a high representative for the Union in Foreign Affairs and Security Policy (a de facto EU foreign minister), both of which were intended to raise the external profile of the EU. To assist the high representative, a new European External Action Service, or diplomatic corps, was established. In addition, the Lisbon Treaty conferred legal personality on the EU, so that it can now conclude treaties and negotiate directly with third parties on the international stage.

The Lisbon Treaty entered into force on December 1, 2009, after another unanticipated delay caused by the rejection of the treaty by voters in Ireland in June 2008, which was reversed by a second referendum approving the treaty in October 2009. The member states elected former Belgian prime minister Herman Van Rompuy to the post of European Council president, and selected British politician and trade commissioner Catherine Ashton as high representative. The fact that both individuals were rather low-key figures suggested to many observers that the member states, while they in principle favored giving the EU a higher international profile and a means to speak with a single voice, were wary of turning over power and the spotlight to a higher-profile figure such as former British prime minister Tony Blair.

Amid the vast amount of attention the EU member states devoted to institutional reform, the EU struggled to make itself relevant to a number of pressing domestic and international policy problems. Turkey was still formally a candidate for EU membership and was engaged in membership negotiations, but governments in key countries, France and Germany in particular, were opposed to full membership for Turkey, preferring instead a "privileged partnership" with Ankara. The domestic sensitivity with regard to membership for Turkey reflected both the complex state of Europe's relationship with the Muslim world and rising fears among EU voters concerning the problems of immigration, unemployment, and loss of national identity in a globalizing world.

The euro was an apparent success of European integration, as confirmed by the adoption of the currency, in 2008 and 2009, by four new member states—Slovenia, Cyprus, Malta, and Slovakia—and by the euro's status as the world's second most widely used reserve currency, after the dollar. But the worldwide financial crisis that erupted in September 2008 cast new shadows over Europe's financial stability. At first the EU seemed to weather the crisis, which originated in the U.S. subprime mortgage crisis, rather better than the United States, but as the crisis dragged on and spread to Europe, it exposed economic disparities within the EU and within the narrower euro zone that potentially threatened the future of the euro.

Since the introduction of the common currency in 1999, Germany had improved its competitiveness, both within the EU and globally, and enjoyed rising exports and generally sound national finances. However, in Eastern and southern Europe, as well as in Ireland, the situation was far different. These countries were running large fiscal and current account deficits, and their industries had lost competitiveness over the past decade, raising questions about how they would repay their international debts and produce economic recovery. The situation was particularly acute in Greece, where investors feared that the government, unable to restore its finances by sufficiently raising taxes and cutting expenditures (a large part of which were accounted for by wages and benefits to public sector employees, who were resisting cuts), might be forced to default on its bonds.

The EU eventually came to Greece's rescue with a financial support package, and in May 2010 set up a new European Financial Stability Facility intended to provide financing to indebted EU member states no longer able to raise funds on private markets. But the fact that support for Greece was strongly opposed by voters and politicians in Germany and other more affluent member states raised doubts about the future of EU cohesion and solidarity. The German government also insisted that the International Monetary Fund be brought into the potential rescue packages for EU member countries and provide both economic advice and additional financing. IMF involvement in Europe's internal affairs was an especially bitter pill for federalists such as Delors, who had always argued that the whole point of the euro was to increase the EU's international financial power and autonomy.

The international financial crisis also raised new questions about Europe's position in the world. The speed with which China and the other "BRICs" (Brazil, Russia, India, and China) recovered from the crisis was widely seen as marking a shift in relative power from the West—Europe and the United States—to the emerging markets of the developing world. Europe's plans to build an effective and autonomous European Security and Defense Policy were called into question by deep cuts in defense spending in many countries, Britain in particular, necessitated by the economic crisis. Since the early 2000s, the EU had promulgated "effective multilateralism" as the guiding light of EU foreign policy. As articulated in the European Security Strategy of 2003, this concept meant that the EU would lead the way in building a system of global governance, more or less patterned after intra-EU norms of adherence to law and sharing of sovereignty, in which the international community would collectively address such problems as climate change, international terrorism, and the proliferation of weapons of mass destruction. Effective multilateralism was an implicit rebuke to the United States under the Bush administration, which the EU accused of taking a "unilateral" approach to addressing international problems, and an invitation to powers such as China, India, and Russia to follow the EU's lead in addressing shared problems.

By the second half of the decade, however, it was becoming increasingly clear that rising, assertive powers elsewhere in the world were more interested in ruthlessly pursuing their own narrow economic and political interests than in following the EU's lead in building a new system of global governance. Russia reimposed authoritarian rule at home, invaded neighboring Georgia in 2008, and ignored many trade and other agreements it had signed. China clamped down on dissidents at home, sought to lock up natural resources in Africa, and manipulated the value of its currency to maintain a competitive advantage. Iran showed few signs of abandoning its drive toward possession of nuclear weapons.

Europeans were for the most part gratified by the election, in November 2008, of Barack Obama to the U.S. presidency, whom they saw as favoring a more "European" approach to dealing with international problems. But enthusiasm for the Obama administration was counterbalanced by a growing awareness of the challenges from China and elsewhere, and by Obama's own seeming indifference to a Europe that was seen in the United States as in relative decline, and in any case not able to provide Obama with solutions to his own domestic and foreign policy problems. These international trends contributed to a new realism in the EU, at times bordering on pessimism, at the end of the first decade of the 2000s, but they also made European governments, and the EU's central institutions, more convinced than ever that European unity was needed to ensure that Europe's voice could still be heard in an increasingly multipolar world, and that the EU could maintain its economic competitiveness and standards of living.

As the new decade began, European governments, for all their jockeying for national advantage and complaints about interference from "Brussels," were preparing to use the possibilities offered by the new Lisbon Treaty to continue on the path of building a more united Europe that had begun sixty years earlier with the coal and steel pool. To what extent the proverbial European man and woman "in the street" viewed the world through the same lenses and was prepared to go along with continued progress toward integration remained, however, very much an open question.

Suggested Readings

Dinan, Desmond, *Ever Closer Union: An Introduction to European Integration*, 4th ed., New York: Palgrave Macmillan, 2010.

Grant, Charles, *Delors: Inside the House that Jacques Built*, London: Nicholas Brealey, 1994.

Kenen, Peter B., *Economic and Monetary Union in Europe: Moving beyond Maastricht*, New York: Cambridge University Press, 1995.

Monnet, Jean, *Memoirs*, Garden City: Doubleday, 1978.

Moravcsik, Andrew, *The Choice for Europe: Social Purpose and State Power from Messina to Maastricht*, Ithaca, NY: Cornell University Press, 1998.

Nugent, Neill, *The Government and Politics of the European Union*, 7th ed., New York: Palgrave Macmillan, 2010.

Tiersky, Ronald, and John Van Oudenaren (eds.), *European Foreign Policies: Does Europe Still Matter?* Lanham, MD: Rowman & Littlefield, 2010.

Van Oudenaren, John, *Uniting Europe: An Introduction to the European Union*, Lanham, MD: Rowman & Littlefield, 2004.

CHAPTER 9

Economic Governance and Varieties of Capitalism

Benedicta Marzinotto

The recent global financial and economic crisis sparked a vast debate about the relative merits of different models of capitalism, defined as "ways of organizing a market economy." The initial reaction to the crisis was to blame the Anglo-Saxon model for allowing excessive liberty in financial markets. According to this view, the subprime crisis was in fact largely due to excessive financial innovations, poor regulation, and insufficient supervision of financial markets. Despite its U.S. origins, however, it did not take long for the crisis to affect the euro zone as well, where there was less financial innovation and stronger reliance on normally more regulated bank credit. There was nevertheless an important difference between developments in the United States and in Europe. In the euro zone, unlike in the United States, the crisis soon translated into a sovereign debt crisis where it affected a range of different countries—like Greece, Ireland, Portugal, and Spain—each for different reasons.

The purpose of this chapter is to analyze the process of European economic integration and the crisis phenomenon in light of the debate on different varieties of capitalism. It deals with the contentions about member state predominance and national distinctiveness but does not fail to recognize that European integration has forced adjustment from within its numerous member states, especially following the completion of the Single European Market (SEM) and the introduction of the single currency. At the same time, the 2007–2009 crisis questions the notion that one model of capitalism is superior to another and calls for a rethinking of the borders as well as the distribution of competences and responsibilities between European Union (EU) institutions and national governments. The discussion builds on four contentions:

- First, the United States and Europe represent two distinct models of capitalism. They mainly differ in the level of competition on products, labor, and financial markets, and over time their macroeconomic performances have also diverged. However, it is probably inappropriate to compare such distinct ways of organizing a market economy. Any recipe that works well for the

United States may be unable to solve the same problem in Europe, and any change to the organization of production in Europe is deemed to compromise the region's strong record in the delivery and preservation of some degree of income equality.

- Second, in Europe itself, there are different models of capitalism. European integration inevitably poses a challenge to national forms of capitalism, their organization of production, and their management of aggregate demand through monetary and fiscal policy tools. Still, economic integration in Europe and the protection of national specificities and institutions have not always been in contraposition. The postwar period is considered to be the heyday of European integration, not least because greater trade liberalization served the purpose of sustaining the growth of national economies. The contrast emerged thereafter, when full economic integration and Economic and Monetary Union (EMU) membership required that member governments lost portions of power over product market regulation, monetary policy, and fiscal policy.

- Third, the constant tension between the EU and national prerogatives since the 1980s is responsible for the complex structure of EU economic governance, in which multiple state and nonstate actors are simultaneously involved with shared or at times confusingly overlapping competences.

- Fourth, the crisis of 2007–2009 questioned the need to impose one single model of capitalism and highlighted weaknesses in the structures of economic governance. Some adjustments to the EMU architecture will most probably be introduced, but they will not offer an alternative to the complex multilevel governance structure we have been seeing so far, considering that the appetite for political union is not there in Europe.

This chapter has five sections. The first sketches both the strengths and the limitations of any argument that builds on the notion of varieties of capitalism. The second describes key institutional differences between the Anglo-Saxon model, as epitomized by the United States, and the European continental model of capitalism, explaining the extent to which differences in institutional settings between these two regions have led to differences in economic performance at different points in time. The third probes more deeply into the varieties of capitalism that have been identified in the literature along selected institutional domains, namely skills regimes, labor markets, financial systems, and macroeconomic regimes. The fifth links this discussion to the broader structure of EU economic governance, and by doing so, it looks at the areas in which the impact of the European integration process was mostly felt. The fifth focuses on the new challenges posed by the 2007–2009 crisis to the notion of a single successful model of capitalism and to the management of newly emerged EMU-related problems.

What's on the Menu?

The crisis of 2007–2009 reopened the debate about which of the two models of capitalism is superior. But it should be obvious to everyone that there is no single superior model of capitalism. Free markets in the Anglo-Saxon world may have been responsible for the financial exuberance that led to the subprime crisis, but more bank-based systems in Europe did not perform any better; they, too, relied on lax monetary policy during the previous years, which resulted in a vast expansion of credit including a high volume of nonperforming loans at the outbreak of the crisis, eventually forcing disrupted banks to cut lending or increase lending spreads for customers. In some instances, the national financial sector of different European countries not only had liquidity problems but was actually insolvent, as in the case of Ireland, where the government had to step in to bail out the country's largest banks, with the result that Ireland's deficit and debt jumped to historically unprecedented levels.

Not only is there no single superior model, but it is also probably misleading to compare different varieties of capitalism to each other, especially the United States and Europe, which differ substantially in their institutions and in the institutional frameworks under which they operate. Hence, despite the stimulus package passed by the Obama administration in the early months of 2009, the crisis in the United States never created a realistic concern that the federal government would go bankrupt. On the contrary, many economists believe the stimulus package was too small and the Obama administration too timid. In Europe, by contrast, financial markets started betting in favor of a default by one or the other troubled member states because it was clear that, in the absence of some kind of mechanism to share fiscal resources across countries, the European Union did not have the means to intervene systematically in support of member countries under stress by means of top-down transfers. At the very last minute, the EU had to decide in favor of a one-off loan to Greece and put together an emergency rescue package to support possible future victims. These ad hoc solutions to the problem of government default posed a number of interlinked challenges that have been unique to the euro area, such as the role and efficacy of fiscal policy coordination, the role of the independent European Central Bank (ECB), and indeed the need for crisis management tools.

Despite these more idiosyncratic differences, however, there are some patterns that suggest the need for comparison. For example, the crisis caused more unemployment in the United States, on average, than it did among those countries that use the euro as their currency (the euro zone). Nevertheless, the unemployment created in Europe will probably be more persistent than in the United States, especially in countries like Italy or Spain, which already had a history of high levels of long-term unemployment. The reason the U.S. unemployment rate has increased disproportionally during the crisis but is likely to have a shorter duration has to do with the way in which their market economy is organized. The U.S. labor market is more flexible in the sense that workers move quite freely from one part of the country to the next, and wages are often determined individually rather than through collective bargaining, so they end up reflecting the characteristics of individual workers, such as their level of education and training, seniority, and so forth. This is what makes U.S. wages competitive from an economic perspective. It implies that employers will increase demand for labor whenever in need, as when the economic cycle is improving, and it implies that the wage employers will have to pay new employees is fair from their perspective, meaning that it reflects the worker's relative productivity and so is unlikely to generate losses that could push the firm out of the market. Moreover, relatively weak employment protection legislation allows employers to hire new workers in good times and to eliminate redundancies whenever the cycle turns negative. In a nutshell, labor demand in the United States is very much dependent on economic cycles so that negative shocks increase unemployment, and positive shocks decrease it. As the U.S. economy comes out of the recession, it is probable, even if obviously not assured, that more employment will be naturally created, limiting the need for the government to rely on fiscal policy to create jobs.

The European labor market, with the possible exception of the UK, is much less flexible than in the United States. Labor mobility has increased in Europe over the last decade, but it remains relatively low. In addition, it is common in Europe for wages to be agreed collectively by trade unions and employers and then extended to all workers in one particular sector, or even to the entire economy in some cases. This implies that wages do not always reflect the specific characteristics of individual workers. They might be too high or too low relative to actual productivity. Employers are careful when it comes to hiring because they worry that worker productivity will be too low to cover the cost of collectively agreed wages. They also worry that strict employment protection legislation will make it difficult or expensive to lay off workers should economic conditions take a turn for the worse. Unemployment in Europe has surged in the crisis, even if not to the same extent across all European countries and overall not as much as in the United States. But it has been held down because strict employment protection legislation has impeded layoffs. The same kind of stickiness will operate on the upside as well. Market forces alone are unlikely to offer a substantial contribution to employment creation in the recovery, and so government will come under pressure to create jobs. This is the debate about supply-side reform in Europe: it concerns how quickly and how comprehensively governments should pass legislation to make labor markets more flexible through individual wage bargaining and weaker employment protection.

Such patterns in labor market performance do lend themselves to analysis using the notion of varieties of capitalism. The comparative political economy literature distinguishes between two ideal types: liberal market economies (LMEs) or the Anglo-Saxon model, and coordinated market economies (CMEs) coinciding closely with the Continental European model.[1] Crucial to the distinction is the level and role of market competition. LMEs are characterized by strong competition on goods, labor, and financial markets. Price mechanisms allow the efficient allocation of resources; namely, prices of whatever type—be it goods' prices, wages, or asset prices—send signals about what products, employees, or financial investments are worthwhile. The key feature of coordinated market economies is by contrast the high level of protection on goods, labor, and financial markets and the fact that it is up to institutional actors such as organized employers, employees, or management boards to allocate resources (that is, raw materials, labor, and capital) in a strategically efficient fashion.

The theoretical framework is useful, but it should be used with caution. In this debate, the United States and Europe are often portrayed as the ideal types of a liberal and a coordinated market economy, respectively, even though Europe is in fact a group of very heterogeneous countries, and all the more so after the enlargement of the European Union to Central and Eastern European countries. Put simply, there are important differences in the ways the national economic systems are organized. Germany is close to the ideal type for a coordinated market economy. Government regulation imposes important barriers to entry on product markets; unions negotiate wages with their employers for the entire sector, with the result that there is limited wage differentiation across types of workers and almost no differentiation at all across firms in the same sector; firms rely on patient long-term credit from banks and are less dependent on equities and thus on external pressures about their short-run sales and profits performance. By contrast, the UK is clearly more liberal than coordinated. British product markets are intensely competitive, wages are negotiated individually in many sectors of the economy, and large firms get their finances not from banks but directly from the markets. Moreover, Germany and the UK are hardly the only alternatives. The Mediterranean countries represent a third category characterized by high product market regulation and bank-based financial systems, as in coordinated market economies, but less centralized wage setting than in Germany or the Scandinavian countries. Finally, the new member states of Central and Eastern Europe went from being transition economies to liberal market economies, but they still have features distinct from the rest of the European Union.

While there is no easy way to determine whether one model is superior to the others in guaranteeing long-term economic growth, there are certainly differences concerning other dimensions of performance, particularly in terms of the distribution of income, patterns of innovation—whether radical or incre-

mental—and, for some, the relative efficiency with which they use scarce resources (like labor, but also energy and other inputs to production). Hence, for
example, Belgian economist André Sapir classifies models of capitalism along
the dimensions of efficiency and equity. In Sapir's classification, efficient economic systems are those in which labor markets are flexible and quick, meaning
that it is easy both to find a job and to switch from one job to the other, mainly
because employment protection legislation is not so strict that it would hinder
labor mobility. The opposite holds for inefficient economic systems, where
strict employment legislation is the main reason that it is difficult for outsiders
to access the labor market and why insiders on the other hand can preserve
their position over time. The contrast here is similar to the one made between
liberal economies and coordinated economies, but the emphasis is much more
on outcomes than on institutions per se. Sapir defines equity in terms of the
distribution of income and the level of poverty in each system. More equitable
systems have a more even distribution of income and a low incidence of poverty; less equitable systems have a skewed distribution of income—meaning the
rich have much more than anyone else—and a high incidence of poverty.

European countries can be found to illustrate any possible combination of
efficiency and equity as Sapir describes those traits. The extremes are easy to
identify. The Scandinavian countries score high on both dimensions. They tend
to have very high rates of employment, low unemployment, an even distribution of income, and very few people below the poverty line. The Mediterranean
countries underperform in terms of both efficiency and equity. Employment is
low, unemployment is high, income is unevenly distributed, and many people
are poor. The mixed types are also present. For example, the UK is more efficient than equitable. It has relatively high employment and low unemployment,
but income is distributed inequitably and many are poor. Meanwhile, the continental countries such as France and Germany are more equitable than efficient.[2]
They have equitably distributed income and a low incidence of poverty, but
employment rates are low and unemployment is persistently high.

The fact that all these countries participate in the same European Union
does not eliminate the importance of the differences between them. On the contrary, given the diversity across European countries, it is hardly surprising that
different member states would at times perceive the process of European integration as a threat to their own economic well-being or autonomy. This was
not so evident in the early days after World War II when European integration
was mainly about the liberalization of trade, an objective that was largely consistent with the preservation of national specificities. However, as the EU progressed to ever deeper levels of economic integration, from the further liberalization of goods, services, capital, and labor movements in the late 1980s to the
creation of the EMU in the late 1990s, virtually every country was forced to
adapt. Repeated stops and starts in the process of European integration and
member state oscillation between the desire for integration and the will to pre-

serve national sovereignty have also had an effect. Hence, the more Europe has grown to resemble the United States as a large integrated economy, the less the European Union has come to resemble anything like the U.S. government. Today the EU is a complex system of governance in which some decisions are sponsored by the EU Commission and then voted by a majority of the member countries, while others are fully initiated by the national governments and voted by unanimity only.

The U.S. versus the European Model and Their Performance

Having worked through the necessary qualifications, it is necessary to admit that the contrast between Europe and the United States nevertheless frames much of the contemporary debate. Indeed, the United States and Europe are often portrayed as the ideal types of a liberal market economy (U.S.) and a co-ordinated market economy (EU), respectively. The contrast between the two models became especially prominent in the 1980s. The United States was perceived as flourishing under the influence of Reaganomics and, compared to Europe, had freer product markets; American labor markets were weakly regulated, with trade unions having very limited bargaining power; and equity markets were efficient in punishing underperforming firms and rewarding profitable ones. In the same period, in West European economies, product market regulation was intense and public ownership of enterprises was widespread; labor markets remained very rigid and equity markets were not sufficiently developed; in addition, EU economies were showing signs of fatigue, suffering from significant fiscal imbalances, high interest rates, and accelerating inflation; welfare states had clearly reached the limits of their expansion and were believed to operate as a constraint on potential growth.

It did not take long for observers to conclude that the Anglo-Saxon model was more successful in terms of macroeconomic performance than the European model. This situation created the myth of a superior model of capitalism, that of the United States, to which the old Continental Europe should have aspired. An important contribution to this debate came from the economics profession, where the consensus had shifted from Keynesianism and its strong focus on the role of the state in the economy toward the new orthodoxy and its appreciation of monetary and fiscal discipline as means to liberate resources that had been captured by the state, allowing for the full operation of private markets.

The 1980s were an era in which European economies went through important transformations under different pressures ranging from the example of the successful U.S. economy, to the changed ideational context in which policy decisions were taken, to the parallel strength of autonomous global forces. It is no coincidence that the European project for the full liberalization of trade and the free movement of capital and labor took root in these years. Starting with the late 1980s, European economies entered a period of strong liberalization. Soon after, in the early 1990s, candidates for Europe's economic and monetary union had to start preparing for accession into the new single currency. The reform process in the run-up to EMU was extensive for most candidates, with the possible exception of Germany. Especially the Mediterranean countries had to go through a vast macroeconomic stabilization program to bring interest rates, inflation, deficit, and debt down to levels comparable to those of the other EU countries, most notably Germany. The so-called Maastricht fiscal criteria required, for example, that candidate countries' deficit and debt levels not exceed 3 and 60 percent of gross domestic product (GDP), respectively. Such a requirement implied that the large majority of EU countries had to implement massive fiscal consolidation measures, either by raising taxes or by cutting expenditures. It was often not sufficient to opt for one-off tax increases or expenditure restraints, but instead it became necessary to put in place structural measures to reform the welfare state so as to make it sustainable over time.

The reform process initiated in the late 1980s and in the run-up to EMU was viewed by many as an effort to impose a more liberal economy. In particular, product market reform and the privatization of numerous state-owned companies enhanced product market competition in all European countries. But any convergence toward a common model of capitalism probably stops there. Notwithstanding the project for the completion of the internal market, progress in the liberalization of the service sector—from insurance and general financial services to the liberal professions, like law, medicine, or architecture—has been much more modest than in the goods sector, held back by the persistence of protectionist national regulations. Labor markets have not reached levels of flexibility comparable to those of the United States. In some cases, employment protection legislation has been softened, but there was no evident movement toward greater decentralization in wage bargaining, which is normally associated with greater wage flexibility. If anything, the trend toward the decentralization of wage bargaining that started in the 1980s in many European countries was reversed. With the emergence of a few social pacts across the EU from 1991 to 1997 (e.g., Belgium, the Netherlands, Ireland, Italy), collective wage bargaining became more and more centralized, with trade unions preferring national wages over firm-level negotiations. The reason centralization in wage bargaining was so popular at the time also had to do with how the process of convergence in preparation for monetary union was organized. The Maastricht Treaty required that EMU candidates fulfill a series of criteria in addition to the fiscal consolidation mentioned earlier in order to qualify for participation in the single currency. One of the most important of these was the requirement to achieve a moderate rate of price inflation—within 1.5 percent of the three best performers in Europe. By negotiating wages at the national level, trade unions were better able to offer a direct and tangible contribution to controlling inflation while obtaining in return some social benefits or at least the preservation of the status quo. The new social pacts of the 1990s were thus political exchanges between unions and governments, in which the former offered their help to control inflation and the latter limited welfare retrenchment or at least accepted that any labor market reform was collectively discussed.

If compared to the United States in terms of macroeconomic performance, Europe continued to disappoint expectations in the 1990s and 2000s, and that despite any putative progress toward American-style liberalization. Just before the onset of the global economic and financial crisis, output per capita was still much higher in the United States than in Europe. Measured in dollars and corrected for relative purchasing power, output per capita was about $30,000 on average in 2007 across the twenty-seven member countries of the European Union (EU-27)—which means including the original member states as well as Central and Eastern European countries—and it was just above $34,000 in Germany. Meanwhile, output per capita was $45,500 in the United States. Remarkable differences stand out also in labor markets. The unemployment rate in EU-27 was 7.1 percent of the active labor population in 2007 and 8.4 percent in Germany, while the corresponding U.S. figure was only 4.6 percent. In the same year, the employment rate in EU-27 was 65.4 percent and 71.8 percent in the United States. Again, even a newly invigorated German labor market—with 69 percent of working-age people holding a job—could not match American performance. Differences in the average participation rate were mostly driven by the modest employment activities of women in Europe, with only 58.3 percent of working-age females having a job in EU-27, against a much higher percentage of 65.9 in the United States.[3]

Differences in macroeconomic outcomes have also been evident in the current crisis. True, the detonator was the subprime mortgage market in the United States, and North America was the first region to be hit by lower growth and higher unemployment, but the signs of recovery in 2010 have been much more evident there than in Europe. The explanation is twofold. First, Europe is still affected by labor market rigidities. Where the crisis has forced employers to lay off workers, these are unlikely to find a job in the short term because tight employment protection legislation discourages firms from employing new people in times of uncertainty. They may well remain unemployed for a while, and the long-term unfavorable scenario may be that their unused skills will gradually deteriorate or, worse, become obsolete. Second, an accompanying factor that may have contributed to different rebound dynamics is the size of the fiscal stimulus packages conceived in reaction to the crisis. The U.S. government injected resources into the system at an amount that was about three times the sum of the fiscal efforts by individual European governments. If the U.S. stimulus package was too timid for many economists, the European version hardly had an impact. At the same time, however, and linked to the relative size of the stimulus packages, the fiscal position of the United States is worse than that of the euro zone taken as a whole. The United States is unlikely to go bankrupt—and some euro-zone countries may well face default—but on average it has gone considerably deeper into debt. Moreover, that difference looks set to widen. The U.S. fiscal deficit is higher than the euro area average, and the U.S. debt is expected to grow more than in Europe over the next twenty years. Against this scenario, it is paradoxical that, in the aftermath of the crisis, Europe has been more explicit about the need to go back to fiscal rigor than the United States.

Overall, it is difficult to establish what accounts for Europe's incapacity to mimic the macroeconomic performance of North America, especially in terms of productivity and hence long-term economic growth. The reform process Europe went through in the late 1980s and 1990s is not yet complete. But then, should it be? The United States and Europe represent very different models of capitalism, and it is not necessarily true that full liberalization in Europe will succeed in delivering a macroeconomic performance similar to that of the United States. Also, European countries have a much better record in guaranteeing and preserving income equality, and any dramatic reform process risks jeopardizing this dimension of performance. The section that follows looks specifically at the institutional domains along which varieties of capitalism differ from each other.

The Varieties of Capitalism

The varieties of capitalism (VoC) literature has provided instruments for grouping national economies into distinct models of capitalism. There are two key ideas behind this literature. First, it is possible to classify economies into distinct varieties with regard to the degree of regulation in product markets, labor markets, welfare regimes, and financial and corporate governance. Second, the institutions of one variety of capitalism are complementary to each other, meaning that one institution works better if the other one is present, or only the two together can lead to efficient economic outcomes. This notion of "institutional complementarity" is at the heart of the VoC approach.

In their book *Varieties of Capitalism*, Peter Hall and David Soskice (2001) set out the characteristic features of liberal market economies and coordinated market economies. Product market competition is pivotal to their distinction between the two ideal types. The core idea is that liberal market economies mimic the functioning of perfectly competitive markets in which equilibrium outcomes are dictated by relative prices and market signals, as in neoclassical economic models. They are thus characterized by deregulated product and financial markets, flexible labor markets, and systems of corporate governance that encourage firms to pay almost exclusive attention to actual earnings and to the price of their shares. A typical example is that of the UK in Europe or of the United States. By contrast, coordinated market economies are governed by imperfectly competitive markets in which coordination between all the relevant economic agents is of a nonmarket nature. In the coordinated market economies, product and credit markets are highly regulated, labor markets are fairly rigid, and systems of corporate governance are such that companies are not necessarily dependent upon current returns but can rely on patient capital from banks, as in the case of Germany.

Table 9.1 provides a description of the most exploited institutional domains along which varieties of capitalism have been defined and highlights key differences between the two ideal types. The VoC approach is originally an institutional theory of the supply side. Its most original feature is in fact the orientation of the firm at the center of the analysis. Firms are socializing agencies, centers of power and institutions that build sanctions and incentives that generate other actions. By exploiting these potentials, they affect a country's macroeconomic performance in important ways. It follows that the institutional domains that have been identified by the literature concern supply conditions in one way or another and include the availability of certain types of skills (i.e., whether general or specific), their cost (i.e., wage levels), outside options (i.e., employment protection legislation), and the availability of credit (i.e., whether coming from banks or equity markets). Only recently has the VoC literature been enriched with an explicit account of the demand side, having incorporated a reference to the fact that liberal market economies and coordinated market economies also have distinct macroeconomic regimes, as will be explained below.

Labor is a key input to production. The availability and the quality of labor importantly direct production decisions by firms. The VoC literature has been mainly concerned with the contents of the skills of one country's labor force and has distinguished between general and specific skills. The reference framework is Nobel Prize–winner Gary Becker's theory of human capital. General

Table 9.1 Institutional Features of LMEs and CMEs

		LMEs	*CMEs*
Supply-side	Content of skills	General	Sector or firm-specific
	Level of skills	Low–high	Average–high
	Wage bargaining	Individual (decentralization)	Collective (centralization)
	Labor markets	Low EPL	High EPL
	Financial systems	Market-based	Bank-based
Demand-side	Macroeconomic regime	Flexible/discretionary	Rigid/rule-based

skills are portable in the sense that they are useful with other employers. A worker that has general skills can move quite easily from one job to another. Specific skills are not portable and can be used with one employer only. Hall and Soskice further distinguish between firm- and sector-specific assets, where the firm-specific assets are useful in one company only and sector-specific assets are useful across a whole sector. A worker that has long worked in a very specialized firm and has accumulated knowledge of both the products and the organizational structure of that particular firm would find it difficult to move to a different company while being equally productive. Similarly, workers that have been trained to work in the automotive industry can probably use their skills in any company of the same sector but are unlikely to need the same skills should they have to move to the service sector, for example.

The literature associates liberal market economies with general skills and coordinated market economies with sector- or firm-specific skills. Why would freer markets be associated with general skills, and more regulated ones with specific skills? The impressionistic argument developed by David Soskice, both independently and in collaboration with Peter Hall, is that neither employers nor employees have an incentive to invest in specific nonportable skills in highly competitive product markets, where in fact the firm survival probability is low. Specific training is an investment that employers are unlikely to recoup, while employees would be left unemployed if the firm is indeed pushed out of the market. For the same reason, employers and employees have an incentive to develop firm-specific skills in the presence of tight regulatory regimes. Employers can afford to invest in training because limited competition in product markets implies that they have high chances of remaining in the market, thus having sufficient time to benefit from the returns of their investment. Employees themselves feel protected from highly volatile market dynamics and are guaranteed that they will make use of their skills as long as the firm that employs them is not pushed out of the market. In coordinated market economies, strong vocational training institutions contribute to the supply of firm- or sector-specific skills.

Besides the effect of product market competition on the content of skills, skill levels are also affected. When markets are competitive, as they are in liberal market economies, the worker's wage equals her productivity so that there is no incentive for employers to invest in skill formation, of whatever type,[4] because workers are still paid proportionally with their skills, and employers do not get a profit from paying workers less than they should. Under these premises, the key investor is the employee only. Whether she obtains high-level skills or not depends on her capacity to pay for it. In turn, two distinct equilibriums can emerge depending on the relative efficiency of credit markets. If credit-constrained, workers will give up investing in their own education. However, in the presence of efficient loan markets, employees are expected to have a strong interest in funding their own education, considering that their wage rises proportionally with their productivity.[5] The situation is reversed in coordinated market economies. Product markets are not fully competitive. There are high-to-average entry costs for firms, and employers can exercise power by controlling positions of employment, implying that they are the only ones or among the few that demand labor in the markets. Under these circumstances, the very few employers that are in the market will be able to extract rents out of the employment relationship and to use these rents to support on-the-job training. They do have an interest in doing so, as stronger skills will further increase the size of rents to employers, if wage levels remain unchanged. The end result is the high-skill equilibrium that has been detected, for example, in the case of Germany.[6]

Another important dimension of labor markets is the way that wages are determined. Wage bargaining in liberal market economies is decentralized, meaning that wages are negotiated individually by the employee and the employer. This results in high levels of wage flexibility. In the case of a boom, full flexibility means that individual wage earners can easily ask and obtain higher wages since labor is scarce in good times by definition. By the same token, they are also more likely to accept wage cuts in bad times because liberal market economies tend to be less unionized. As noted above, an important notion in the VoC literature is that institutions complement one another. For example, wage determination modes are complementary to the existing skill regime. Decentralized wage bargaining is the preferred option in liberal market economies. Here, as skills tend to be general and their level is determined by the amount of private investment each individual puts into her own education, highly educated workers will be able to arbitrage between different employers to obtain individual wages that maximize returns on their private investment in education. Employers themselves embrace decentralization as a mechanism that allows them to acquire educated employees. In coordinated market economies, by contrast, wages are determined collectively by industrial unions and then are extended to all employees in the same sector or even in the entire economy, as happened in some Scandinavian countries until the 1980s (e.g., Sweden). This form of wage bargaining is called "centralized," meaning that wage formation takes place at the sectoral or even at the national level. Employers in coordinated market economies have a strong interest in centralized wage bargaining because equal wages across the same sector prevent poaching of highly skilled workers by other firms in the same sector. Indeed a worker with sector-specific skills could move freely from one firm to the other but is unlikely to do so unless she is promised a higher wage. Again, there is an important and visible complementary relationship between wage and skill-formation institutions.

An additional feature of labor markets is the level of employment protection legislation—which is to say, the extent to which it is easy to access or exit the labor market. Liberal market economies typically have low levels of employment protection. Easy access to and exit from labor markets implies that job tenure is generally short, with employees moving freely from one job to another. This also enhances the cyclical component of unemployment, meaning that in bad times employers will have no institutional constraint that prevents them from firing unnecessary workers. Unemployment will rise in recession but also fall in good times, when employers are easy about hiring new employees because they can lay them off at any time. In coordinated market economies, labor markets are highly regulated, and strong employment protection creates a divide between labor market insiders (those who have a permanent job) and outsiders (those who are seeking work or who are employed part time or in temporary contracts). The insiders are likely to stay where they are, resulting in long job tenure and incentivizing the development of sector- or firm-specific skills. On the other hand, outsiders will find it very difficult to find a permanent place in the labor market and may remain long-term unemployed.

One factor that importantly affects the level and quality of production by firms is access to credit. Financial systems are classified into market based and bank based.[7] Market-based systems are typical of most liberal market economies, where companies are financed through equity markets and are thus obliged to keep a firm eye on short-term returns and profitability. Bank-based systems prevail in coordinated market economies. Here, banks have responsibility for mobilizing savings, allocating capital, and monitoring decisions made by corporate managers. Firms in coordinated market economies are thus mainly financed through bank credit, and it is access to patient capital of this kind that allows them to focus on long-term objectives, such as investment in research and development and incremental innovation.

The explicit interest of the VoC literature in macroeconomics and in demand-side conditions is quite recent. In a comprehensive overview of the relationship between varieties of capitalism and aggregate demand management, David Soskice (2007) observes that liberal market economies tend to be characterized by flexible and discretionary macroeconomic regimes, while coordinated market economies are more rigid and mostly rule based.

Monetary and fiscal policies make a macroeconomic regime. They both determine demand conditions in one economic system. Historically, central banks have been responsible for monetary policy, either in association with governments or autonomously (i.e., central bank independence). Practically, this means that central banks set official interest rates for the economy as a whole. By fixing the price of money, they impact on aggregate demand and, more precisely, on two components of aggregate demand, investment in machinery and equipment, which is very much sensitive to interest rate levels and changes, and consumption in all those cases in which consumers need to borrow money in order to buy goods (i.e., credit consumption). This is how monetary policy determines aggregate demand.

The channels through which fiscal policy operates are different, but fiscal policy also conditions aggregate demand. Fiscal policy is a government's responsibility and concerns all the decisions about tax systems and public expenditures. National governments influence the level of disposable income, for example, to the extent that they decide on income taxes. They also determine the spending capacity of specific social groups such as pensioners or the unemployed when they make decisions on how to distribute public resources across spending programs like pensions and unemployment benefits.

Saying that liberal market economies are characterized by flexible and discretionary macroeconomic regimes is much the same as saying that national monetary and fiscal authorities react flexibly when it comes to offsetting unfavorable cyclical fluctuations and do so with full discretion. The evidence is that, in the case of a recession, the central banks of Anglo-Saxon countries are prompt in reducing interest rates to support investment and (credit) consumption. Similarly, fiscal authorities allow for some deficit spending until the business cycle turns favorable. In coordinated market economies, macroeconomic regimes are instead rigid and are founded on rules rather than discretion. Monetary and fiscal authorities typically refrain from responding to exogenous shocks by using, respectively, monetary or fiscal leverage. Central banks are often independent and are subjected to an inflation-targeting regime. Historically, they have reduced interest rates only moderately and progressively to boost demand in a recession and immediately reacted to inflationary booms by raising interest rates. Most coordinated market economies also have formal or informal fiscal rules that limit their room to maneuver in the management of business cycles. Successive German governments have been historically devoted to the objective of fiscal discipline, for example. The Merkel government has recently agreed to introduce a constitutional rule that requires the government to achieve a balanced fiscal position over the medium term. The sovereign debt crisis will probably also force other EU member states to adopt fiscal rules as a means of strengthening their national fiscal frameworks.

The liberal and coordinated market economies responded differently to the crisis, and in line with expectations for the two different types of regime. The average fiscal effort over 2009–2010 was 1.7 percent of GDP in Europe, if one takes as a reference the policies of the three largest euro-zone countries, Germany, France, and Italy, but it was a much more generous 4.7 percent of GDP in the United States,[8] confirming that liberal market economies react more flexibly to poor demand conditions than coordinated market economies do.

EU Economic Governance Structure and Varieties of Capitalism

Throughout the history of European integration, it has been clear that a unified Europe could only be governed by a multiplicity of actors, national (e.g., the

Council of Ministers of the EU) and supranational (e.g., the EU Commission), state (e.g., the Council of Ministers of the EU) and nonstate actors (e.g., the Economic and Social Committee and the ECB). The end result is a complex structure of multilevel governance in which hard and soft forms of power are shared among EU institutions, national governments, parliaments, regions, and social partners. At present, all of these actors are involved in one way or another in the legislative process at the EU level. The standard procedure, known as the "Community" method, prescribes that the supranational EU Commission initiates a piece of legislation. This then is passed on to the Council of Ministers, which gathers all the national ministers of the EU member states and is asked to vote on the proposal in co-decision with the European Parliament. In most instances, the Economic and Social Committee and the Committee of the Regions are consulted in the process but do not have veto power.

While the Community method is the standard procedure, it is not the only one. Moreover, the Community method applies only to specific policy sectors, most notably all the regulations concerning the main aspects of the single European market and the liberalization of product markets in Europe. In other policy areas, however, the Council of Ministers becomes de facto the only body with decision-making powers, the EU Commission plays no role, and the European Parliament is merely consulted. This is notably the case when at stake are discussions regarding the Common Foreign and Security Policy (CFSP) and Justice and Home Affairs (JHA).

The main reason for the complex multilevel governance that is now in place is that, over time, national governments have been differently inclined to devolve portions of national sovereignty so that the current governance architecture is the result of successive stratifications of decisions taken by governments with different attitudes toward European integration. The EU moved from relatively soft forms of economic integration in the postwar period to ever deeper ones, culminating in the adoption of the single currency in 1999. Initially the process of economic integration posed little challenge to national models of capitalism, but over time the EU has become progressively more intrusive, forcing governments to adjust their ways of organizing the national market economy to the new EU rules.

When the heads of government and state gathered to discuss European integration at the end of World War II, the strong message that came through and that seemed to be acceptable to most of them was that full political integration of Europe would have been too ambitious for a start, but economic integration—mainly through the removal of barriers to trade—would serve the same purpose if the desire for further integration spilled over to other policy areas and levels. So, in the early days from the Treaty of Rome (1957) to the actual completion of the common market (1968), the members of the European Economic Community accepted the abolition of tariffs, quotas, and other tangible barriers to trade as the first step toward a future common political union. The process at the time foresaw the creation of a customs union, which implied the abolition of internal barriers to trade, but also the adoption of a common external tariff vis-à-vis third countries that the EEC would trade with. This was as far as the loss of sovereignty was going, and it explains, for example, the initial refusal by the United Kingdom to take part in the foundation of the EEC due to the fear that it would in fact lose preferential trade agreements with Commonwealth countries.

The six founding member states, Germany, France, Italy, Belgium, the Netherlands, and Luxembourg, in fact did not perceive the project as a threat to their national authority. Stronger international competition following the elimination of barriers to trade supported industrial exports and, indirectly, the growth of national economies. This form of European integration is what theorists call "negative integration," which consists of the elimination of existing obstacles to integration but does not require large adjustment efforts from within, let alone the devolution of key policy competences and the creation of new institutions.

Still, the convergence of national interests and European integration was only a fortunate coincidence and thus was deemed to be short lived. The 1970s marked a weakening of integrationist forces in the midst of the collapse of the Bretton Woods system and the two successive oil shocks. The Bretton Woods system was a mechanism for allowing international payments by making international currencies convertible with each other. It implied that national governments and central banks in Europe had to make monetary policy decisions with an eye to the impact that changes in money supply would exercise on the declared parity between the national currency and other European currencies. It became unsustainable at a time when national economic interests started diverging and the first oil shock shifted policy priorities away from the preservation of the exchange rate parity toward the fight against inflation and poor growth.

The creation of the European Monetary System (EMS) in 1979 relaunched the European project. The EMS was meant to replace the collapsed Bretton Woods system. It was a currency regime in which bilateral parities were fixed between European currencies. Exchange rates were thus fixed, but they were adjustable. Participation in the EMS implied some loss of control over monetary policy because any change in the official interest rate by national central banks also had to serve the purpose of respecting the parity declared within the EMS agreement, but the fact that the fixed exchange rate could actually be changed under some circumstances gave national governments the impression that autonomy in monetary policymaking could have been taken back at any time.

Starting in the 1980s, it became evident that any progress in European integration would have forced individual member states to devolve portions of their national sovereignty and to adapt their distinct models of capitalism to ever-developing new challenges. This was a time in which economic integration stopped being an instrument and started being considered an end in itself, not least because full political integration was not a realistic target anymore. Projects such as the completion of the European internal market and EMU in the 1990s fall under this category. They both represent examples of what theorists call "positive integration." Neither project was about the elimination of existing constraints on integration. Instead, they required the devolution of sovereignty in the areas of product market regulation and monetary policy, respectively, and they culminated, in the case of monetary union, in the creation of the new independent European Central Bank.

The project launched in 1985 to complete the internal market thus marked a structural break from the past. It extended liberalization to nontariff barriers to trade in goods and services and devised measures to allow the free movement of capital and people. It was more than just eliminating taxes on imports, which had been the very first objective of the EEC. By imposing stronger competition on product markets and by improving the efficiency of European financial markets through capital mobility, the internal market required that changes be made to the national organization of production. Producers in the export-oriented sectors were forced to cut profit margins to preserve market shares. It required changing national regulatory frameworks and recognizing other member states' regulations, for example, in the area of technical standards. In this respect, the completion of the internal market implied a deeper level of economic integration.

At the same time, the internal market project granted the European Commission with exclusive responsibility over competition policy, meaning that it is now the responsibility of that institution to monitor the functioning of the internal market and make sure that the European market does not suffer from anticompetitive practices, whether these take the form of state aid, international mergers that generate dominant positions, cartels, or monopolies. In the area of finance, consumers and investors in Germany, Austria, and France continued to use bank credit more than any other financing tool (e.g., equities and bonds), but capital markets certainly did gain greater importance, also increasing managers' sensitivity to short-term returns and performances. As a result, all European countries were under much less regulation on financial markets than in the past, a development that to some extent brought typical coordinated market economies such as Germany much closer to the Anglo-Saxon model.

The monetary union, whose operations started officially in 1999, represented the final step toward the completion of the internal market and full economic integration. Not only can goods, services, capital, and people currently move freely within the internal market, but a common currency further facilitates trade and free movement by allowing cost and price comparability. Seen this way, EMU is about the supply side, much like the completion of the internal market. It fosters the mobility of production inputs and promotes the fight against anticompetitive practices. Its impact falls largely on producers and the conditions under which they operate, whether these concern the cost of their inputs or the factors they need to take into account when determining output prices (i.e., the role of competitors). But the supply side is only one dimension of EMU. In fact, the most revolutionary change that came about with the introduction of the euro concerns the demand side: EMU indeed represents a new macroeconomic regime for Europe.

Monetary unification involved more than just the creation of a single European currency. It also depended on fiscal policy coordination between the member states through a collection of rules and procedures called the "Stability and Growth Pact" (SGP). As part of this pact, euro-zone member states have accepted limits on the conduct of their fiscal policies by committing not to run deficits greater than 3 percent of gross domestic product. Thus, in the case of fiscal policy, national governments continue to be responsible for decisions on tax systems and welfare spending, but they are constrained in their aggregate figures. Such coordination challenges the organization of individual forms of capitalism to a much greater extent than previous forms of European integration.

Monetary policy is now an exclusive competence of the European Central Bank. The new common central bank is in charge of setting official interest rates for the monetary union as a whole and is fully independent in the exercise of this policy function. The ECB operates in a so-called inflation targeting regime. This means that it has committed to an average inflation of 2 percent and manages monetary policy, in full independence from the member states, with the final objective of preserving price stability. So, in boom periods, when prices start growing excessively under demand pressures until they risk overshooting the formal inflation target, the ECB would intervene by increasing interest rates. In periods of recession, the common central bank would do the opposite, but with caution. During the recent crisis, for example, the ECB reacted much later than the U.S. Federal Reserve did to lower interest rates.

Overall, EMU is a relatively rigid macroeconomic regime with a nonaccommodating central bank and a strong emphasis on fiscal rigor that largely resembles the German macroeconomic regime before the introduction of the single currency. The success of this new regime has been mixed. The introduction of a single currency for such a vast and diverse regional area is by all means a political success; in practice, EMU was also able to deliver price stability and some convergence in real growth. Yet two important challenges remain and would have been visible even if the crisis had not happened. First, the ECB is conducting a single monetary policy for a group of sixteen different countries. It is not an easy task when the member states find themselves in different positions in the business cycle. By way of example, countries in deep recession would need a lower interest rate than countries that are not in recession, as low interest rates would help stimulate demand for consumption and investment.

By contrast, they risk producing inflation where economic growth is already sustained. If euro-zone member countries find themselves in relatively different business cycle positions, as has happened over the last few years, then the ECB cannot be optimal for each of them. Second, the stability and growth pact imposes fiscal policy coordination across EMU in the sense that all member states need to have similarly low deficit levels. The recent crisis has demonstrated the difficulty associated with fiscal surveillance and its enforcement. The Greek case shows how public budgets can easily go out of order even in the presence of a formally binding commitment such as the SGP, and cases like Spain and Ireland show how quickly fiscal positions can in fact deteriorate once the government is obliged to step in either to support the national economy in recession or, more specifically, to rescue the financial sector. These are the main reasons that have forced EU institutions to rethink European economic governance after the crisis, a process that is still ongoing.

But economic policy coordination in Europe is not only about the demand side. It can also concern structural reform. The need to combine the creation of the new aggregate demand management regime of EMU with supply-side measures had emerged already in the 1990s. At the time, EMU candidates were preparing for access into the monetary union with draconian measures that aimed to control inflation and cut public deficits and debts. There was a risk that the rigid and severe macroeconomic regime that was coming into place was detrimental to growth. Fiscal consolidation in particular required candidate countries to either increase fiscal pressure to improve budget positions or to cut spending, or both. In this climate, the attention of EU institutions shifted to the need to counterbalance possible negative growth effects with measures that, on the supply side, would support employment creation. The renewed interest in the supply side took the form of the so-called Lisbon strategy, a policy initiative launched in 2000 whose primary objective was to make of Europe "the most competitive and dynamic knowledge-based economy in the world capable of sustainable economic growth with more and better jobs and greater social cohesion" by 2010.[9] At the time, the focus was on the need to promote spending in research and development and to support innovation, skill formation, and education. The Lisbon strategy disappointed expectations and was relaunched in 2005 with the objective of achieving "more and better jobs."

The success of the 2005 Lisbon strategy was compromised by the outbreak of the financial and economic crisis in 2007. It is now being substituted by "EU2020," a new policy initiative that, different from the older Lisbon strategies, places greater emphasis on human capital accumulation and skills, and less on technology and innovation. The Brussels European Council summit conclusion of June 17, 2010, indicates that "the new strategy responds to the challenges of reorienting policies away from crisis management towards the introduction of medium- to longer-term reforms that promote growth and employment and ensure the sustainability of public finances, *inter alia* through the reform of pension systems."[10] EU2020 imposes new headline targets regarding employment, the conditions for innovation, research and development, climate change and energy objectives, education and social inclusion, and poverty. As for the governance of the new strategy, there is a much stronger emphasis on national ownership of the reform process compared to the past, and extraordinary weight is given to the long-term national reform plans each EU member state is obliged to submit to EU institutions.

The European Council is explicit about the fact that

> Member States must now act to implement these policy priorities at their level. They should, in close dialogue with the Commission, rapidly finalise their national targets, taking account of their relative starting positions and national circumstances, and according to their national decision-making procedures. They should also identify the main bottlenecks to growth and indicate, in their National Reform Programmes, how they intend to tackle them. Progress towards the headline targets will be regularly reviewed.[11]

The Crisis and the Reform of EU Economic Governance

European integration has been an ambitious project, with important political and economic elements to it. Still, no one can deny that the economic dimension has prevailed at many points in time, either as the primary instrument for integration or as the final objective of an integrationist project, or as the signal of profound weaknesses in the governance structure of the EU and an expedient for rethinking the EU architecture, as demonstrated in the financial and economic crisis of 2007–2009. Indeed, the crisis further strengthened the perception that the EU is primarily an economic project that is fragile and strong at the same time. On the one hand, the economic and the ensuing sovereign debt crisis revealed the failure of fiscal surveillance and the lack of attention devoted to other macroeconomic imbalances (i.e., private sector debt). On the other hand, however, the political response was prompt—all considered—and some of the reform proposals were sufficiently innovative to calm financial markets for some time.

In Europe, the financial and economic crisis transformed rapidly into a sovereign debt crisis, questioning the fiscal governance structure of the EU but also the little attention devoted to imbalances other than fiscal ones. Greece had accumulated excessive deficits and debts over a long period of time, and its fiscal problems well preceded the economic crisis. In the European scenario, it represents a special case, one of weak budget institutions and maybe of technical incompetence. Still, the existing Stability and Growth Pact was insufficient to induce successive reforms. As the crisis dragged on, financial markets began to worry about the prospect of a Greek default. They also began to consider whether other economies were on shaky foundations. The costs of servicing public debt also rose for Spain, Portugal, and Ireland. Spain, for example, did not have the same severe fiscal problems that Greece had. However, the country had been accumulating high private debts over the previous decade. Both consumption and investment were buoyant, but national savings were not sufficient to finance them. They were eventually financed by foreigners in the form of capital inflows, which turned into a growing current account deficit. Market participants generally feared that the Spanish government would intervene to rescue debtors, thus transforming large private liabilities into public ones. Whereas surveillance on fiscal positions was weak in EMU, surveillance on private sector imbalances was completely missing.[12]

The extensiveness of the crisis and the awareness that there were flaws in the structure and governance of EMU induced the EU, in particular the Council of Ministers, and the European Council to make special provisions to face the emergency and put forward proposals to improve economic governance. The March European Council in 2010 oversaw the creation of the "Van Rompuy Task Force" with the responsibility of producing recommendations to enhance governance. In May 2010, the EU Commission conceived a series of proposals to strengthen surveillance on fiscal positions as well as to extend it to other macroeconomic imbalances, such as high levels of private debt and large trade deficits, a proposal endorsed by the June European Council (see box 9.1).

In September 2010, the EU Commission officially published a set of recommendations to tackle weaknesses in EMU economic governance. The Commission proposes to strengthen the Stability and Growth Pact by encouraging euro-zone members to maintain fiscal discipline in good times, creating buffers that would be useful in bad times. The proposal makes the Stability and Growth Pact even more stringent by tightening the constraints on the debt level, which should not exceed 60 percent of GDP, and by strengthening the application of sanctions in the case of noncompliance. More needs to be done at the national level too. Not all member states have efficient national fiscal frameworks. Not all of them have a practice of medium- to long-term financial planning; many of them still concede to parliament's extensive amendment powers on government budget proposals, which inevitably end up altering the aggregates of public finance. The EU Commission states that greater economic policy coordination across countries is needed and that the best way to achieve this result is through a "European semester" every spring, in which finance ministers of the EU would meet to anticipate the main contents of their budget law proposals. Finally, for private sector imbalances, the EU Commission proposes a strict monitoring exercise of countries' current accounts, competitiveness developments, and financial sector indicators as a means of controlling the buildup of macroeconomic imbalances other than fiscal ones. Where these im-

Box 9.1   European Council Conclusions, Brussels, June 17, 2010

Enhancing economic governance

1. The crisis has revealed clear weaknesses in our economic governance, in particular as regards budgetary and broader macroeconomic surveillance. Reinforcing economic policy coordination therefore constitutes a crucial and urgent priority.

2. The European Council welcomes the progress report of the President of the Task Force on economic governance and agrees on a first set of orientations.

3. The present rules on budgetary discipline must be fully implemented. As regards their strengthening, the European Council agrees on the following orientations:

    a) strengthening both the preventive and corrective arms of the Stability and Growth Pact, with sanctions attached to the consolidation path towards the medium term objective; these will be reviewed so as to have a coherent and progressive system, ensuring a level playing field across Member States. Due account will be taken of the particular situation of Member States which are members of the euro area and Member States' respective obligations under the Treaties will be fully respected;

    b) giving, in budgetary surveillance, a much more prominent role to levels and evolutions of debt and overall sustainability, as originally foreseen in the Stability and Growth Pact;

    c) from 2011 onwards, in the context of a "European semester," presenting to the Commission in the spring Stability and Convergence Programmes for the upcoming years, taking account of national budgetary procedures;

    d) ensuring that all Member States have national budgetary rules and medium term budgetary frameworks in line with the Stability and Growth Pact; their effects should be assessed by the Commission and the Council;

    e) ensuring the quality of statistical data, essential for a sound budgetary policy and budgetary surveillance; statistical offices should be fully independent for data provision.

4. As regards macro-economic surveillance, it agrees on the following orientations:

    a) developing a scoreboard to better assess competitiveness developments and imbalances and allow for an early detection of unsustainable or dangerous trends;

    b) developing an effective surveillance framework, reflecting the particular situation of euro area Member States.

5. The European Council invites the Task Force and the Commission to rapidly develop further and make operational these orientations. It looks forward to the final report of the Task Force, covering the full scope of its mandate, for its meeting in October 2010.

Source: The full text of the European Council Conclusions can be downloaded from http://www.consilium.europa.eu/uedocs/cms_data/docs/pressdata/e n/ec/115346.pdf

balances have been identified but not corrected, the EU foresees a system of sanctions similar to that of the SGP.[13]

Whatever shape the reform of EU economic governance takes, there is no reason to believe that the resulting EU will be different from the complex multilevel governance that characterizes it at present, mainly because there is no appetite for any change that would move Europe toward a closer political union.

Suggested Readings

Acemoglu, Daron, and Jorn Steffen Pischke, "Beyond Becker: Training in Imperfect Labor Markets," *Economic Policy*, 109, 1999.

Allen, Franklin, and Douglas Gale, *Comparing Financial Systems*, Cambridge, MA: MIT Press, 2000.

Altomonte, C., and Benedicta Marzinotto, "Monitoring Macroeconomic Imbalances: Proposal for a Refined Analytical Framework," Monetary and Economic Affairs Committee, European Parliament, 2010.

Culpepper, Pepper D., "The Future of the High-Skill Equilibrium in Germany," *Oxford Review of Economic Policy*, 15, 1999, 43–59.

Hall, Peter A., and David Soskice (eds.), *Varieties of Capitalism: The Institutional Foundations of Comparative Advantage*, Oxford: Oxford University Press, 2001.

International Monetary Fund, "Fiscal Monitor: Navigating the Fiscal Challenges Ahead," May 14, 2010.

Marzinotto, Benedicta, Jean Pisani-Ferry, and André Sapir, "Two Crises, Two Responses," *Bruegel Policy Brief*, March 2010.

Sapir, André, "Globalization and the Reform of European Social Models," *Journal of Common Market Studies*, 44(2), 1996, 369–390.

Soskice, David, "Macroeconomics and Varieties of Capitalism," in R. Hanckè (ed.), *Beyond Varieties of Capitalism*, Oxford: Oxford University Press, 2007, pp. 86–125.

CHAPTER 10

Europe and the Global Economic Crisis

Erik Jones

At an extraordinary meeting of the Council of Economics and Finance Ministers on the weekend of May 8 and 9, 2010, the heads of state and government of the European Union (EU) agreed to allocate €500 billion in special assistance to help member states that no longer have access to market-based financing to meet their balance of payments and fiscal obligations. They also negotiated with the International Monetary Fund (IMF) to "provide at least half as much as the EU contribution through its usual facilities"—bringing the total volume of financial assistance to €750 billion.[1] This support was worth just over $968 billion, meaning $200 billion more than the "troubled asset relief funds" requested by the outgoing George W. Bush administration and authorized by Congress in 2008 during the market turmoil that followed the failure of the Lehman Brothers investment bank.[2] Meanwhile, the Governing Council of the European Central Bank (ECB) decided over the same weekend to intervene directly in "dysfunctional" public and private debt security markets in order to ensure that they remain both liquid and deep, buying up distressed bonds and holding them on its own balance sheet.[3] This may sound reassuringly technical to anyone unfamiliar with the arcana of central banking, but for those who follow European central banking practices, it was as though the world turned upside down.

The purpose of this chapter is to explain how the EU got into such a dire situation—one that many have described as the most important challenge yet to the stability of the single European currency. The chapter has six sections. The first looks at the proximate problem of Greek indebtedness. The second explains how this problem extends well beyond Greece. The third sketches Europe's halting attempts to address this situation before it evolved into a crisis. The fourth suggests why those efforts were not more successful. The fifth offers a short narrative of Europe's last-ditch effort to stabilize the Greek situation and explains how Ireland (and other countries like Portugal and Spain) became swept up in the events that followed. The sixth concludes with speculation as to how things are likely to develop from here.

Greek Public Finances[4]

For much of the world, the crisis in European sovereign debt markets traces back to the Greek national parliamentary elections that were held on October 4, 2010. These elections were called early due to a combination of social unrest and corruption scandals—the previous elections were held only in 2007—and they were fought primarily along economic lines.[5] The incumbent New Democracy (ND) party sought a mandate for austerity. Although the government reported only a relatively modest fiscal deficit—estimated at 3.7 percent of gross domestic product (GDP) for 2009—the party leadership was well aware of the need to rebalance government finances in light of the global economic downturn. The opposition Panhellenic Socialist (Pasok) Party took the opposite view and campaigned on a platform of increased government spending to restart the economy. Given these alternatives, the voters opted for a Keynesian-style reflation; ND's vote share fell by more than 8.3 percentage points, Pasok's increased by 5.8 percentage points, and Pasok leader George Papandreou was allowed to form the government with control of over 160 out of 300 seats.[6]

Once in power, Papandreou necessarily changed course on his economic proposals. Although he remained committed to some kind of stimulus package to mitigate the downturn, he revealed that the prospects for a Keynesian-style spending increase were limited by the unexpected magnitude of the country's fiscal deficit. On October 21, his government sent revised data to the EU's statistical reporting agency, Eurostat, indicating that the deficit for 2008 would come in at 7.7 percent of GDP rather than the 5.0 percent reported the previous April by his predecessor, and revising the 2009 estimate from 3.7 percent of GDP to 12.5 percent. Moreover, most of this difference was due to a misreporting of the fiscal data rather than a mistaken estimation of the underlying GDP. When Eurostat announced this to the financial community the following day, it included a footnote in the press release signaling its reservations "due to significant uncertainties over the figures notified by Greek statistical authorities."[7]

The Pasok government may have hoped to demonstrate that it had more integrity than its predecessor; instead, what it underscored was the scope of the country's statistical and fiscal mismanagement. With each successive news story, confidence in Greek self-reported data diminished and concern about the country's "true" fiscal situation grew. This dynamic took root because Pasok had confirmed what most financial actors already suspected, rather than surprising them with something that nobody knew. The ND government was forced to revise its fiscal estimates upward in October 2008 as well.[8] Moreover, the significance of this move was not lost on the markets. The Standard & Poor's rating agency downgraded Greece's creditworthiness in January 2009, citing concern over the structural weakness of the country's fiscal practices.[9]

This set off a round of speculation that sent Greek sovereign debt yields (or effective interest rates) to their highest levels compared to Germany since Greece joined the euro. This speculation only calmed down when the then German finance minister, Peer Steinbrück, made it clear that his country would not stand by and allow another euro-zone member state to go into default.[10]

The fact is that Greece has a long history of poor accounting practices dating back at least to the mid-1990s, if not earlier. Eurostat has always had difficulties getting reliable data from the Greek government, and it was an ND government that first conducted a major restatement of public accounts in 2004.[11] Nevertheless, European bond traders hoped that participation in the euro zone would create both the opportunity and the incentive for Greece to get its fiscal house in order. At a minimum, they assumed that someone would bail them out if they got into serious trouble. The gradual decline in the country's debt-to-GDP ratio since the early 2000s seemed to suggest that Greece was making headway on its fiscal consolidation, at least until the current crisis began to take its toll. As a result, the difference between Greek and German bond yields from early 2003 until March 2008 was less than fifty basis points, or one-half of 1 percent.[12]

As the crisis set in, interest rates between Greece and Germany diverged as investors worried about Greece's fiscal prospects. Once reassured by German finance minister Steinbrück, however, the focus of market attention shifted from the incentives for fiscal consolidation to the prospect that any losses could be avoided through a bailout. Interest rate differentials between Greece and Germany peaked at over three percentage points on February 17, 2009, but then fell back by more than sixty basis points (or six-tenths of a percent) by early April. The point to note here is that Greek interest rates began to converge again on German norms during the late spring and summer of 2009, even as concern about Greece's fiscal practices continued to mount. Well before Pasok won the October elections, the International Monetary Fund published the results of its annual Article IV consultations—which made it very clear not only that "Greece needs a coherent fiscal adjustment path, based on durable measures," but also that "staff is concerned that large and growing data discrepancies . . . could harbor a worse underlying deficit than currently reported."[13] All Pasok did with its data revisions was underscore that such IMF concerns were justified. The markets were very slow to react. According to data from Global Insight, Greek ten-year government bonds yielded 4.66 percent on October 19, just days before the Pasok government submitted its revised deficit forecasts, and they yielded 4.63 percent on the day that those revised estimates were announced. It would be almost a month before Greek ten-year bonds crossed the 5 percent yield threshold, and it was only in December that market movements became severe. These data are reproduced in figure 10.1. The figure also includes references to events that are discussed in greater detail later and so is worth keeping in mind as the narrative progresses.

Figure 10.1   Greek-German Interest Rate Differential

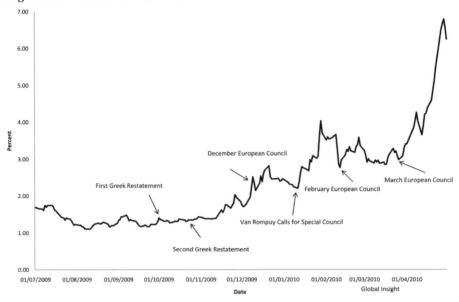

Macroeconomic Imbalances

To understand why the markets took such a sanguine view of the Pasok government's Greek deficit revisions—and the poor state of Greek fiscal accounting more generally—it is necessary to look at how the euro-zone member states have become financially interdependent as a consequence of their monetary integration. To begin with, countries that share a common currency are no longer constrained by international payments requirements—only the monetary union as a whole must worry about matching its assets and liabilities in relation to the rest of the world. Hence, if Greece or any other country wants to import more than it exports, it can always borrow the money—in euros—from other countries in the euro zone. Similarly, if Germany or any other country wants to export more than it imports, it can always lend the excess money it receives—again, in euros—to other countries in the euro zone.

This notion of "excess money" is the only confusing part. It is easy to see that a country that wants to consume more than it makes must borrow from abroad. If a country's income is limited to its output and yet it wants to consume more than it produces, it obviously does not have the income, and so the money to purchase that excess consumption must come from somewhere else. The idea of "excess money" on the net exporting side of the relationship comes from looking at things the other way around. If a country wants to export some of its output, then it must consume less than what it produces and therefore also less than what it earns. Indeed, that only makes sense because it must be earning money on those goods that it produces and yet sells abroad (rather than at home). The problem is that this money cannot be used at home; otherwise it would raise consumption (or physical investment) to match the level of output and so eventually would eliminate the trade surplus. Therefore that money must be sent (invested, lent) abroad.

The link between foreign lending and net exports is important because it makes it possible to tell the story starting with capital accounts rather than trade accounts. For this to make sense, however, it is necessary to dispense with the fiction that countries trade and to focus on firms and individuals. Suppose German firms or individuals decide to lend some of their savings—such as retained earnings or financial investments to be used later for education, health care, pensions, and so forth—abroad. The motivation for doing this is simply that they know they can get a higher rate of interest in other countries than they can get at home. Moreover, they believe that the excess rate of return more than exceeds the risk of putting their money in another country. This seems a particularly reasonable assumption when the other country uses the same currency as Germans do at home, so no matter what the rate of inflation over there, Germans know they will get the money back in euros that they can use at face value, without any exchange rate risk, for domestic consumption in their own low-inflation market (where the value of the currency has been protected). This kind of thinking explains why the gap between German and Greek interest rates on long-term government debt collapsed from more than twenty percentage points in the early 1990s to less than one-half of one percentage point in the early 2000s.

A consequence of this type of investment behavior—where Germans send some of their savings to chase higher interest rates in Greece—is that these same Germans are going to have to look for export markets to absorb some of their excess output. The reason they have to export more than they import is that the money they sent abroad was earned by generating output at home and yet not spent on consuming that output either directly or in making a physical investment. Germany ran current account deficits in the 1990s when the gap between German and Greek interest rates was very high, and Germany ran current account surpluses in the 2000s after changing investment patterns, with Germans investing in Greek assets, thereby pushing interest rates in Greece to very low levels. Meanwhile, firms and individuals in countries like Greece were willing to pay higher rates of interest than in Germany because they have historically had much less access to credit and because they paid more in terms of premiums to cover the cost of inflation or exchange rate risk associated with their domestic currency. But once Greek firms and individuals began to borrow from abroad above and beyond their income, they also needed to buy goods from abroad because this new inflow of credit had to be spent on something that the Greeks themselves did not produce.

The argument about capital markets and goods markets is best illustrated through the data. Since this story is mostly about Greece, we will start there. The crucial data concerns the nominal interest rate on long-term government bonds and the balance on current transactions (meaning the trade in goods and services, but also net transfers and the income from net lending). The argument is that bond investors abroad began to put their money in Greek bonds. This not only meant that the interest rate on those bonds declined, but it also ensured that more money would be available for lending and investment within the Greek economy, and so interest rates declined for Greek private sector borrowers as well. All things being equal, those private sector borrowers responded to lower interest rates by increasing their spending on investment and consumption. Some of this money fell on domestically produced goods, but some of it was spent on imports as well. Hence, as low interest rates spread throughout the Greek economy and began to affect decisions made in the private sector, the country began to experience a deficit on its current accounts. This can be seen in figure 10.2, which provides both the nominal interest rates on long-term government bonds and the balance on current accounts as a share of GDP. The figure is drawn with two different vertical axes (y-axes) to make it easier to compare movements in the two lines of data. The story starts with high nominal interest rates and a balanced current account position (equal to zero). First, interest rates on government bonds begin to fall, and then—as these lower interest rates spread through the Greek economy—the current account position begins to decline as well.

Figure 10.2   Long-term Interest Rates and Current Account Balances in Greece

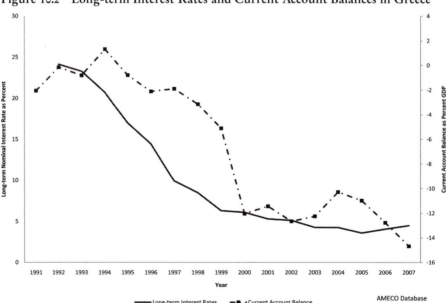

The influence of these decisions about where to save money and where to invest money can also be seen in the data for gross fixed capital formation, which is a very crude measure of the level of physical investment in the economy. During the 1990s, for example, the German economy grew in real (meaning price-deflated) terms by about 16 percent—not annually, but over the whole period. Real gross fixed capital formation accounted for just over 22 percent of that real growth, or 3.6 percentage points in the total headline figure. The story in Greece during the same period is slightly more impressive because the Greek economy is less developed and so has to invest and grow at a higher level in order to catch up. Hence the Greek economy grew in real terms in the 1990s by just over 20 percent, of which real gross fixed capital formation accounted for 31 percent, or 6.3 percentage points of the total. Once the two countries joined in the same currency, the difference became much more striking. From 2000 to 2007, German growth collapsed to just 9 percent (again, not annually but over the whole of the period), and gross fixed capital formation accounted for only 3 percent of that growth, or 0.3 percentage points of the total. In other words, investment in Germany increased very little, if at all. Meanwhile, the Greek economy expanded by more than 20 percent in real terms over the same period, and gross fixed capital formation accounted for 27 percent (or 7.7 percentage points) of that expansion. Germans sent their savings to Greece, and the Greeks borrowed that money to invest in the growth of their domestic economy.[14]

Actually, the story is not entirely complete. Some of the money borrowed at lower interest rates—meaning some of the excess credit available to Greeks by Germans (and others)—was used to purchase services that cannot be traded internationally. As the demand for these services increased beyond Greek ability to supply them, inflation in Greece accelerated as well. The reverse is true for Germany. Money sent abroad could not be used at home, and so demand for everything—not just tradable manufactured goods but also services—declined. Inflation in Germany slowed down as a result. The price effects here are perhaps only marginal. Nevertheless, an increase in one year adds to the base level for the next, and so the implications are cumulatively important. The longer these divergent patterns of relative inflation rates continue, the more prices in Greece and Germany will appear to diverge.

For the present argument, though, the important point is that monetary integration brought German lenders and Greek borrowers together by lowering the risk associated with Germans lending to Greeks, while at the same time lowering the cost associated with Greeks borrowing from Germans. Moreover, the same is true across the euro zone, with the consequence that numerous Austrian, Belgian, Dutch, German, and French banks ended up lending vast amounts of money to governments, firms, and individuals in Greece, Ireland, Italy, Spain, and Portugal. Some of that money went to firms and individuals directly in the form of corporate borrowing or interbank lending; some went indirectly in the form of sovereign debts to finance government expenditures that otherwise would have to be paid for out of tax receipts.

The symptoms of this exchange showed up in the form of current account balances and relative inflation rates. The borrowing countries had relatively large current account deficits and high rates of inflation (because domestic demand outstripped domestic supply); the lending countries showed relatively large current account surpluses and low rates of inflation (because domestic supply exceeded domestic demand). The effects here can be seen in figure 10.3, which shows the dispersion (or standard deviation) of interest rates and current account performance across the euro zone as a whole. The downward movement in the dispersion of interest rates represents a convergence of borrowing costs across the euro zone as a whole. At the end of the story, there is essentially only one interest rate within the single currency, plus or minus about one-half of 1 percent. The upward movement in the dispersion of current account performance represents a divergence in positions from one country to the next. Some countries, like Greece and Ireland, run significant deficits; others, like Germany and the Netherlands, run surpluses.

Nevertheless, the euro zone as a whole worked almost as though it were a closed system with a balanced position on its current account transactions with the outside world and a relatively low rate of aggregate price inflation. In this sense, the lenders and borrowers in the euro zone were two sides of the same coin. To give a sense of the symmetry, consider the respective current account positions of Germany, on the one hand, and Greece, Spain, Italy, Ireland, and

Figure 10.3   Interest Rate Convergence and Macroeconomic Imbalances

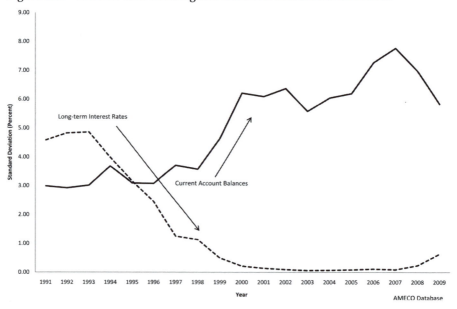

Portugal on the other hand. In 2007, Germany recorded a surplus of €192.1 billion; taken together, the smaller and more peripheral euro-zone economies showed a deficit of €192.8 billion. The point here is not to suggest that there is a strict bilateral relationship between Germany and the rest. Rather it is to suggest that both sides are out of balance. The relative exposure is more complicated because there are many more actors involved in European bond markets than just the Europeans themselves, and many European countries in addition to those highlighted in this analysis. Nevertheless, the level of exposure is significant, as the Bank for International Settlements made clear in its June 2010 quarterly review:

> As of 31 December 2009, banks headquartered in the eurozone accounted for almost two thirds (62 percent) of all internationally active banks' exposures to the residents of the euro area countries facing market pressures (Greece, Ireland, Portugal and Spain). Together, they had $727 billion of exposures to Spain, $402 billion to Ireland, $244 billion to Portugal and $206 billion to Greece. French and German banks were particularly exposed to the residents of Greece, Ireland, Portugal and Spain. At the end of 2009, they had $958 billion of combined exposures ($493 billion and $465 billion, respectively) to the residents of these countries. This amounted to 61 percent of all reported euro area banks' exposures to those economies.[15]

No wonder the lenders would expect the borrowers to be bailed out. If Greek borrowers defaulted on their debts, German lenders would suffer the losses. It only stands to reason, therefore, that the German government would have an interest in ensuring that did not happen. So long as everyone participated in the system and everyone continued to benefit, everyone had a reason to keep the system intact.

Halting Responses

The problem with this logic is that the response of the euro-zone governments to the Greek crisis failed to live up to market expectations. This is where we return to the events indicated in figure 10.1. Everyone in the bond markets knew that there was a problem with Greek fiscal accounting, and few were surprised when the incoming Papandreou government announced that it would have to restate Greek accounts. That is why secondary markets for Greek long-term debt instruments were so slow to respond. Unsurprised is not unconcerned, however, and so market actors looked to political leaders in the euro zone to see how they would address the problem and whether, if necessary, Greece would be bailed out. What they saw was less than reassuring. A number of creditor countries, Germany foremost among them, expressed dismay that the Greeks had been so profligate. They criticized the Greeks for failing to abide by the rules for fiscal stability in the euro zone and even more so for having failed to reorganize and rationalize control over their national statistics. Rather than embrace the new estimates provided by the Papandreou government, they questioned whether the Greeks could ever provide reliable fiscal data. And rather than accept Papandreou's admission that he would have to follow a policy of fiscal austerity rather than Keynesian reflation, they criticized Greece for failing to do enough.

This criticism of Greece gathered momentum in November and early December of 2009. When the European Council met on 10 and 11 December, the Greek crisis was not on the official agenda. Nevertheless, it was clear that the issue would be raised in the margins of the meeting. The results were disappointing for the markets. German chancellor Angela Merkel came out of the meeting and made it clear that assistance for Greece was not on the table. Instead, she insisted, the Greek government would have to accept its responsibility for making sweeping structural reforms.[16] The bond markets were unimpressed. The more voices expressed criticism of Greece and the less likely it became that anyone would bail the Greeks out, the harder it became to find buyers for Greek debt instruments in secondary markets. Greek ten-year bonds had a yield of just 5 percent in early December; by the twenty-first of the month, the yield on those bonds broke through 6 percent.

The situation stabilized in late December and early January but then darkened again about three weeks into the new year. Greek ten-year bond yields hit 6.23 percent on January 20 and then soared to 7.26 percent on the twenty-eighth. Already in early January, the European Council had agreed to address the issue in a special summit called by the newly installed Council president Herman Van Rompuy. Given the obvious turmoil in the bond markets, this summit took on a much higher significance. Nevertheless, the results were again less than hoped for by the markets. Although there were many expressions of solidarity with the Greeks, it was clear that the other countries continued to hold the Greek government responsible and also that there was no firm commitment of support on offer.[17]

Confusion over how much the other countries of the euro zone were willing to do to help Greece simmered through February and into March, although the stabilization of bond prices during this period suggests that, on balance, bondholders were reassured. Moreover, whenever the Greek government went into the markets to issue new debt as part of its regular refinancing operations, it found much more demand than it expected. This experience was replicated elsewhere in the euro zone, with the consequence that net exposure of banks in Germany and France to lending in Greece, Spain, Portugal, and Ireland only increased.[18] Nevertheless, by the time of the spring European Council summit, the situation changed suddenly as the solidarity that had been expressed on 11 February unraveled. In its place, Chancellor Merkel provided a clear statement of her conditions. Greece would only receive support in the event that financing via private capital markets was unavailable, and even then only on condition that the IMF participate as well.[19]

These conditions injected real concern into the bond markets. If euro-zone support would only be available after private financing had collapsed, then bond prices could have a long way to fall. And if the IMF would be brought in, there was a very real chance that Greece could default. Greek ten-year bond yields stood at 6.14 percent when the March summit finished on the twenty-sixth. Those yields increased as Greek bond prices fell almost consistently from one day to the next, and by April 28, Greek bond yields had risen to almost 10 percent. Investors would rather take a certain loss in the present than face and accept the uncertainty of what might come in the future. The Greek government finally threw in the towel and called for euro-zone support because it feared that private sector financing for the new debt issues it had to post in May would not be available.

Political Constraints

If the lack of political support explains the turmoil in Greek bond markets, it is worth considering why politicians were not more forthcoming in their commitment to come to the aid of Greece. This is particularly true considering that much of the debt issued by Greece was held by other countries' banks, France and Germany foremost among them. There are many good arguments to explain the situation. Four of the most commonly held positions concern trade competitiveness, moral hazard, populist politics, and constitutional courts.

The competitiveness argument builds on the relative price movements that have been described above. Put simply, price inflation was higher in Greece than it was in Germany. As a result, or so the argument runs, the Greeks have priced themselves out of foreign markets. Hence any correction of Greek current account balances should come as a result of efforts to slow down (and even reverse) the inflation of prices and wages in Greece. Attempts by countries like Germany to bail out the Greek government would not solve the underlying competitiveness problem and might even make it worse. So long as Greeks are able to borrow money in order to live beyond their means, they will have little incentive to accept the austerity measures necessary to bring their trade accounts back into balance.

This competitiveness issue is a serious one that has attracted a lot of attention from important economists (particularly in the United States) who believe that Greece was wrong to enter into a monetary union with Germany in the first place—or, more generally, that European monetary integration was a folly. These economists claim they also knew that two such different economies could not survive the discipline of having a common monetary policy, that some countries will experience competitiveness problems that would impose long-term adjustment costs on the society as a whole, and that only a devaluation of the currency—supported by fiscal austerity measures and effective wage restraints—can bring the pain of that adjustment down to acceptable levels.[20]

The problem with this competitiveness argument is that it does not fit the data very well. While it is true that inflation rates have differed between Germany and Greece, there is little sign that this has had a negative impact on Greek exports. Indeed, Greece's external market share is roughly unchanged throughout its participation in Europe's economic and monetary union. Much the same is true for countries like Italy, Ireland, Spain, and Portugal as well. Indeed, if we look across the whole period of monetary unification—starting with the 1991 Maastricht Treaty and ending with the onset of the global economic crisis in 2007—the combined export market shares of these five peripheral countries hold up better than the market share for Germany itself. Manufacturing employment in the peripheral countries has done better still. Both Germany, on the one hand, and the peripheral countries, on the other hand, had about 10 million manufacturing workers at the start of the 1990s. By 2007, the peripheral countries still had about 10 million manufacturing workers, and Germany had about 7.6 million. If Greece and the other countries were suffering from competitiveness problems before the onset of the crisis, this level of manufacturing employment should not be sustainable alongside a relatively constant export market share. Something just does not add up.

The problems with the competitiveness argument get even worse when we compare Greece's situation within the euro zone with its situation before monetary integration. The simple fact of the matter is that Greece lost more competitiveness under the fixed but adjustable exchange rate regime embedded in the European Monetary System (EMS) than it lost while in the single currency—at least when we measure competitiveness in terms of relative movements in the relative real effective exchange rate. Meanwhile, the cumulative deficit on Greece's current account was almost four times worse under the euro than during the EMS period that preceded it. Again, something just does not add up here. If relative movements in competitiveness were behind Greece's foreign indebtedness, we would expect the situation to be the other way around and the EMS period would show more Greek borrowing than took place under the euro.[21]

The moral hazard argument is more straightforward. If Germany bails out Greece for becoming so heavily indebted this time, what is to prevent Greece or some other country from doing it again? Worse, as more and more countries take advantage of Germany's largesse, the result will be to increase government expenditures across the euro zone as a whole and so run the risk of accelerating price inflation. This is why the European Union included a no-bailout clause in its provisions for economic and monetary union in the first place. It is also why it included a prohibition against excessive deficits, to which Germany insisted that the EU member states add a Stability and Growth Pact (SGP). Of course, the fact that Germany itself was responsible for suspending the excessive deficit procedure in 2003 and reforming the Stability and Growth Pact in 2005 does create some confusion. The perils of moral hazard are not limited to the Greeks. Nevertheless, it is clear that some rules need to be in place (and enforced) if the Greek crisis is not to be a harbinger of more widespread profligacy in the future. The precise wording of the no-bailout clause in the Treaty on the Functioning of the European Union is reproduced in box 10.1. The point to note is that while the treaty does provide for exceptional circumstances, it also sets out fairly starkly worded restrictions.

The populist argument is unambiguous as well. Like it or not, there is much prejudice among northern Europeans toward southern Europeans, particularly toward the Greeks. According to this prejudice, the south is lazy and corrupt while the north is hardworking and virtuous. Hence, any north European politician seen to be bailing out the south risks being portrayed as rewarding indolence and abetting corruption. Examples of this tendency are not limited to the German tabloid *Bild-Zeitung* but can be found across euro-zone member states from the Netherlands to Slovakia and all points in between. Again, there is a problem with the data. If we stick to a comparison between Greece and Germany, it is easy to show that the Greeks work longer hours on an annual basis and that they tend to work longer during their lifetimes as well. Of course the data for these comparisons are hardly perfect. Nevertheless, two factors stand out. One is the magnitude of the difference in average annual hours worked. In 2008, for example, the average Greek worked 2,120 hours, while the average German worked just 1,432. The other feature that stands out is the fact that while Greeks tend to work beyond their statutory retirement age, Germans tend to retire before they even qualify for full benefits.[22]

These data never entered into the popular debate in Germany, and it is unlikely they would have been accepted had anyone tried to introduce them.[23] Instead, the public embraced stereotypes about lazy southern Europeans and so moved staunchly against any spending of their hard-earned tax receipts to bail them out. According to this line of argument, Chancellor Merkel was most concerned about the consequences of aiding Greece for her party's performance in the regional election held on May 9 in North-Rhine Westphalia. This election was crucial to her control over the upper house of the German federal parliament; any bailout of Greece was wildly unpopular with the voters, so the chancellor had to appear tough on the Greeks to stand a chance at the polls. There is, no doubt, some truth to this argument—not least because the 2005 elections in that same region signaled the demise of the previous German chancellor on the center-left—but it is hard to see it as the principal factor.[24] In any event, when the votes were cast on May 9, the German chancellor's Christian Democrats lost more than ten percentage points in support.

The constitutional argument is arguably more important.[25] In October

Box 10.1   Treaty Provisions Pertaining to the "No-Bailout Clause"

Consolidated Version of the Treaty on the Functioning of the European Union

Published May 9, 2008
(emphasis added)

Article 122 (ex Article 100 TEC)

1. Without prejudice to any other procedures provided for in the Treaties, the Council, on a proposal from the Commission, may decide, in a spirit of solidarity between Member States, upon the measures appropriate to the economic situation, in particular if severe difficulties arise in the supply of certain products, notably in the area of energy.

2. *Where a Member State is in difficulties or is seriously threatened with severe difficulties caused by natural disasters or exceptional occurrences beyond its control, the Council, on a proposal from the Commission, may grant, under certain conditions, Union financial assistance to the Member State concerned.* The President of the Council shall inform the European Parliament of the decision taken.

Article 123 (ex Article 101 TEC)

1. *Overdraft facilities or any other type of credit facility with the European Central Bank* or with the central banks of the Member States (hereinafter referred to as "national central banks") in favour of Union institutions, bodies, offices or agencies, central governments, regional, local or other public authorities, other bodies governed by public law, or public undertakings of Member States *shall be prohibited, as shall the purchase directly from them by the European Central Bank or national central banks of debt instruments.*

2. Paragraph 1 shall not apply to publicly owned credit institutions which, in the context of the supply of reserves by central banks, shall be given the same treatment by national central banks and the European Central Bank as private credit institutions.

Article 124 (ex Article 102 TEC)

Any measure, not based on prudential considerations, *establishing privileged access* by Union institutions, bodies, offices or agencies, central governments, regional, local or other public authorities, other bodies governed by public law, or public undertakings of Member States *to financial institutions, shall be prohibited.*

Article 125 (ex Article 103 TEC)

1. *The Union shall not be liable for or assume the commitments of central governments,* regional, local or other public authorities, other bodies governed by public law, or public undertakings of any Member State, without prejudice to mutual financial guarantees for the joint execution of a specific project. *A Member State shall not be liable for or assume the*

> commitments of central governments, regional, local or other public authorities, other bodies governed by public law, or public undertakings *of another Member State*, without prejudice to mutual financial guarantees for the joint execution of a specific project.
> 2. The Council, on a proposal from the Commission and after consulting the European Parliament, may, as required, specify definitions for the application of the prohibitions referred to in Articles 123 and 124 and in this Article.

1993 and March 1998, the German high court rendered decisions about the constitutionality of Germany's participation in the euro zone. The first decision made it clear that the European Union is a union of states—not of peoples—and so established that German constitutional law has priority over European treaty obligations (including those related to monetary union). That decision also underscored that any international monetary union must guarantee the same level of protection as the German currency. By implication, the euro must be as solid as the Deutsch Mark that it replaced. The 1998 decision reinforced these performance considerations. Germany could enter the euro zone, the court ruled, but only because strong guarantees for the price-stability of the euro remain in place. The prohibition of excessive deficits and the no-bailout clause are among the most important of those guarantees. Should Chancellor Merkel show little regard for these restrictions by bailing out a profligate Greece, she would invite a challenge in the high court—and there were many people queued up, including prominent economists, petitioning to make the case against her. An unfavourable decision by the German high court would cast the euro zone into turmoil. Chancellor Merkel's decision to set firm conditions for supporting Greece was designed to ensure that would not take place.

This constitutional threat is debatable because it is reasonable to believe that the German high court would be very reluctant to pass a ruling with such wide implications. Moreover, it would be even more reluctant to be seen as usurping the sovereignty of the German parliament and, by implication, of the people who elected those representatives in the first place. To understand why this is so, it is worth considering the bases upon which plaintiffs have argued against Germany's participation in the euro. Essentially, they claim that a weak international currency would undermine the value of their property, which the German constitution promises to defend. They argue that a weak currency would interfere with their personal freedom in the marketplace because it would complicate relationships between buyers and sellers. And they argue that a weak multinational currency would violate the sanctity of the relationship between representatives and voters because the German parliament would have no recourse through which it could make the currency strong again.

Of these arguments, the German high court has only given serious consideration to the sanctity of parliament. That is why the court refused to accept an automatic entry into the euro in its 1993 ruling—because the German parliament should retain the right to decide. That is also why it placed such emphasis on institutional guarantees in its 1998 ruling—because these guarantees were an important part of what the German parliament accepted to join. The implication of this line of argument is clear. The German high court is unlikely to interfere with the single currency so long as the German government maintains parliamentary support for its actions. If Merkel was slow to respond to the Greek crisis, it was most likely because she doubted whether she could maintain that support.

Stabilization and Contagion

The euro-zone finance ministers met to respond to Greece's calls for financial assistance on May 2. What they agreed was to provide the country with up to €110 billion over a three-year period, €30 billion of which would come from the IMF. They also set firm conditions for the fiscal consolidation that Greece would have to put in place. In the meantime, the European Central Bank agreed to lift any credit-rating requirements for the use of Greek debt instruments as collateral in central banking operations. By implication, not only should the Greek government be able to remain outside the financial markets for new debt instruments, but the secondary market for existing Greek debt should remain liquid as well. The price tag was very high both financially and in terms of ECB commitments. Nevertheless, it was enough to hold the Greece crisis at bay.[26]

The only problem was that the crisis was never limited to Greece. Every part of the euro zone played a role in the redistribution of capital, and all were implicated in the macroeconomic imbalances that were the result. Greece was heavily indebted in its fiscal accounts, but Spain and Portugal were indebted in the private sector. Hence few actors in the financial markets viewed the European solution to the Greek crisis as a credible solution for the system as a whole. And as they worried about precisely which institutions were going to lose financially because of the wider implications, they began to panic. In this sense, Greece was very much like a European "Lehman Brothers"—it was small in the greater scheme of things but yet still "too big to fail."

The trillion-dollar bailout announced on May 11 was the consequence. The German government supported the creation of a "special purpose vehicle" to raise money in order to lend to governments in need. As with the Greek bailout, this arrangement would last only three years, until 2013. In the meantime, governments would have to use its resources sparingly because, as indicated above, the total exposure to troubled economies was many times greater than the financing available for a bailout. The new financial stabilization arrangement could survive another small country like Greece, but it would struggle with Ireland or Portugal and could never handle something larger like Spain, Italy, or Belgium. Hence, while Europe's political leaders sought to use their stabilization resources sparingly, they would also have to make considerable efforts to ensure that no other countries faced such dire needs. Traders in the bond markets looked for evidence that the European political will was sufficient to stop the crisis at this point. They also looked for a clear indication that European politicians would do whatever was necessary to prevent a similar crisis from recurring in the future.

Virtually everyone acknowledged that the European financial stabilization mechanism treated the symptoms of the crisis but not the underlying problem. To go any further would require a substantial reform of the European Union's system for macroeconomic governance. That is the clear implication of the crisis in sovereign debt markets that developed in the spring of 2010. What was less clear was where the emphasis should lie in reforming European institutions, who should direct the process, and how wide the remit for reform should be. These elements depend on a number of different factors related to what actors believe about how the crisis occurred in the first place, who is to blame, and who should be responsible for ensuring that it does not happen again. The European Union is deeply divided on these questions, both among the member states and between the member states and the principal institutions.

The tension between German chancellor Angela Merkel and European Commission president José Manuel Barroso has been particularly pronounced. When the Commission published its communication on "reinforcing economic policy coordination," Merkel gave it a cold reception.[27] She admitted that much of what the Commission proposed makes sense but argued that the Commission did not go far enough. When Merkel released her government's counterproposal to strengthen fiscal discipline, Barroso denounced it as "naive."[28]

These two proposals were poles apart in the debate about reforming European macroeconomic governance. The Commission proposal was comprehensive and supranational. It included provisions to improve the coordination of macroeconomic policy in general, not just fiscal policy. It stressed the importance of monitoring competitiveness, matching fiscal positions to economic conditions and forecasts, and strengthening crisis management procedures. By contrast, the German proposal focused more narrowly on the importance of fiscal prudence and emphasized the role of national responsibility. It included tougher sanctions on those countries that violate the rules for fiscal coordination, such as automatic sanctions and the withdrawal of voting rights. And it suggested that provisions be made for putting overextended member states into a form of managed insolvency (echoing earlier calls by Germany to expel errant countries from the euro).[29] By implication, private sector bondholders would have to share some of the cost of rectifying the overindebtedness of peripheral states.

The principal forum for this debate was supposed to be taking place within the special task force on economic governance reform that was chartered by the European Council during its March 2010 economic summit. That task force was chaired by European Council president Herman Van Rompuy and included representatives from all member states, not just those that had adopted the euro. It also included representation from the rotating presidency (which was Spain in the first half of 2010 and Belgium from July 1 of that year) and from the Europe Central Bank.[30]

Unfortunately, such representation did not reflect the true balance of power among the member states. During the first three meetings of the task force, it was clear that the consensus of views lay closer to the Commission than to the German proposals. After the first meeting of the task force on May 21 (which was also when the German proposals were first officially presented), Van Rompuy announced that it would pursue four main objectives: improved fiscal discipline, strengthened macroeconomic competitiveness, more robust crisis management, and more effective economic governance.[31] When it met again on June 6, the task force emphasized the importance of broad macroeconomic surveillance and the use of graduated sanctions to attract attention both to fiscal policy and to macroeconomic competitiveness at an early stage, rather than waiting until things got out of hand.[32] And at its third meeting on July 12, the task force reiterated its desire to establish an effective early-warning procedure and added that it would strengthen fiscal policy coordination by focusing more attention on outstanding public debts.[33]

In part, the success of this broader agenda was due to the remit that was given both to the Commission and to the task force. When the European Council called for the Commission to issue its communication as part of the decisions taken at the March 2010 summit, it asked not only for a solution to the current crisis in the euro zone, but also for mechanisms to push its "Europe 2020 Agenda," which is a revised attempt to promote economic competitiveness along the lines first drawn at the Lisbon European Council summit in March 2000. Hence, while there is agreement on the need for fiscal discipline, that agreement was always going to be couched in a broader context at the European level than might be preferred by Angela Merkel's government in Berlin.[34] More specifically, however, there was little acceptance of the need to structure a managed sovereign default (and far less for the implicit prospect of de facto expulsion from the single currency).

For their part, the Germans were not willing to come away empty-handed. Although the Commission made some headway with its proposals for more effective and tightly coordinated supervision of economic policies, this fell far short of the "economic governance" long favored by the French. As the Van Rompuy task force's deliberations progressed, it became clear that the European Union would not create a separate secretariat for the countries of the euro zone, and neither would it engage in another round of sweeping treaty revisions. Any changes made to the treaty would take place only in order to ensure that disciplinary and support actions were grounded in strong legal foundations. Hence, while the substantive agenda may have been wider than the Germans would have preferred, the institutional agenda was not.[35]

At the time, some observers believed that this combination of factors represented a shift in the balance of power between France and Germany, with Germany finally graduating from partnership to leadership. If so, there was little reason to anticipate that the situation would be reversed or that the Council of the European Union would take up a more ambitious agenda for institution building or institutional reform.[36] More importantly, it suggested that the European Union would not be able to agree on a first-best resolution to the crisis. The rules governing fiscal policy coordination may be strengthened and the Stability and Growth Pact may be reinforced, but the euro zone will remain vulnerable nonetheless.

Here it is useful to recall that Germany insisted on the Stability and Growth Pact in the mid-1990s as a means of shoring up and strengthening the excessive deficit procedure set down in the 1992 Maastricht Treaty. Then, as now, the emphasis lay on generating a clear sense of timing for European-level supervision and intervention, an early-warning mechanism to ensure that member states could make a timely policy response, and a solemn commitment to exceed the already rigorous constraints on fiscal policy in the short term but to strive to achieve a structural position close to balance or in surplus over the longer term. At the time, many overestimated the success of this strengthened commitment; they complained about the stringency of the Stability and Growth Pact, and they worried about whether the threat of sanctions—including financial penalties—would push Europe toward a near-permanent state of fiscal austerity. Almost no one anticipated that Germany would find itself in violation of the injunction against excessive deficits, and few imagined that the member states would arrange to have the excessive deficit procedure set aside.[37]

German chancellor Angela Merkel has made it clear that her country's role in setting aside the excessive deficit procedure and subsequently reforming the Stability and Growth Pact was a mistake. Her efforts to strengthen fiscal discipline within the euro zone by adding harsher penalties and automatic sanctions have been an attempt to redress the balance. The big question is whether it is really worth the effort. That big question can only be answered by addressing four smaller ones first.

To begin with, could stricter controls on fiscal policy have prevented the Greek crisis? It is difficult to give a positive answer to this question, not least because of clear evidence that Greece sought to hide the extent of its overindebtedness. It sold off (or hypothecated) future income streams from user fees and other forms of taxation. It systematically understated its expenditures and overestimated its revenues. And it was able to do all this while under special supervisory regimes that were in many ways more intrusive than for any other country in the euro zone. European Commission proposals—since adopted by the task force—to emphasize debts over deficits may help to uncover some of these practices in the future. Greek commitments to protect the political independence of its statistical agencies may go even further. But there is nothing in this story to suggest that either a more intrusive regime or a more credible threat of sanctions would have made much of a difference. Unless there is a clear positive incentive to comply with European requirements for statistical collection and budgetary reporting, some circumvention is almost sure to occur.

For the sake of argument, though, it is possible to assume that a new and more vigorous system for fiscal discipline could be more effective than the one it replaces. A second question is thus whether tight controls on public borrowing would eliminate the problem. Here again, there is little reason to be sanguine. Countries like Spain and Portugal did not have obvious fiscal problems on the scale of Greece, and yet nevertheless they fell into difficulty. Meanwhile, countries like Belgium and Italy were much more heavily indebted in their public accounts than Spain and Portugal, yet they fared better once the financial market turmoil hit. The explanation lies in the macroeconomic balance between savings and investment rather than in the level of public indebtedness per se. Private savings in Belgium and Italy offset much of the borrowing on the public side in those countries; public savings in Spain and Portugal comes nowhere close to offsetting private sector indebtedness. This is why the European Commission called for greater attention to be paid to macroeconomic imbalances and national current account positions within the euro zone. The problem is that these imbalances are symmetrical; German current account surpluses are offset by southern deficits just as German excess savings is paired with southern indebtedness. Constraints on fiscal deficits only address one small part of the larger issue. Even efforts to ensure competitiveness among the deficit countries will do little to address the imbalances generated by those countries that run persistent surpluses. Hence, as Wolfgang Münchau quips, politicians who believe in the success of the German-sponsored reform proposals have clearly forgotten how to add up to zero.[38]

The comparison between Italy and Spain raises an interesting consideration that runs perpendicular to the current economic governance reform debate and brings us to the third question: Is the solution macroeconomic, regulatory, or some combination of the two? Recent musings by IMF chief economist Olivier Blanchard suggest that some effort on the regulatory side might be necessary alongside any macroeconomic rebalancing of savings and investment. The logic of his argument follows from the dynamics of asset market bubbles. As savings flows from one country to the next, it tends to channel into asset markets (stocks, bonds, real estate), where it sets off a vicious cycle of rising prices and further investment. Hence it is necessary to combine macroeconomic policy with regulatory policy that can stabilize the growth of asset prices.[39] Italy has tight restrictions on its housing market that Spain does not have; Spain suffered more than Italy as a consequence.

The member states are primarily responsible for asset market regulation. They are responsible for export-led growth strategies, national wage bargains, statistical collection, and fiscal policy as well. Hence any solution to the problem must be designed with a focus on creating positive incentives for national compliance. Governments have to want to achieve a savings-investment balance; given that the member states are ultimately responsible for enforcement, it is not enough to hope they will worry about what happens if they get caught. Chancellor Merkel may prefer to embrace austerity. As easily, one of her successors may not. Hence, the fourth question is, what is the best way to shape incentives? It is unlikely that a supranationally monitored and yet intergovernmentally implemented institutional framework is the answer.

On the very day that the Van Rompuy task force was due to announce its preliminary recommendations, Chancellor Merkel decided to preempt the debate. In a joint declaration with French president Nicolas Sarkozy in Deauville, she announced that institutional reform would concentrate on fiscal discipline and that private sector investors would have to share in the cost of any future debt restructuring. The text of this announcement is reproduced in box 10.2. From the wording of the text, it is clear that Merkel's interests in avoiding moral hazard and punishing fiscal profligacy were paramount. So too was her strong conviction that German taxpayers should not have to pay for irresponsible borrowing elsewhere.

Unfortunately, Merkel's actions showed a poor understanding of how traders in the bond market discount future events. Even if it is true that the cost to the private sector will be borne only from 2013 onward, that is no reason why the cost of those future expected losses cannot be priced into government bond purchases today. The principal victim was not Greece, however, but Ireland. Once Merkel and Sarkozy made their Deauville declaration, the Irish bond market went into a rout. As can be seen in figure 10.4, the effect was not unlike what happened to Greek bonds after the March 2010 European Council summit. The consequences were similar as well. Within weeks of the Deauville declaration, the Irish government became the second in the single currency to make a formal request for financial help.[40]

Not a Conclusion but a Transition: To Ireland and Beyond

The Irish case is a good place to end this analysis because the situation in Ireland is so different from the situation in Greece. To begin with, excessive government borrowing was never a problem in Ireland. On the contrary, Irish fis-

Box 10.2   Franco-German Declaration
Statement for the France-Germany-Russia Summit
Deauville—Monday, October 18, 2010
(emphasis added)

France and Germany agree that the economic governance needs to be reinforced. To this aim they have agreed on the following points:

1. France and Germany emphasize that budgetary surveillance and economic policy coordination procedures should be strengthened and accelerated. This includes the following issues:
   a. *A wider range of sanctions should be applied* progressively in both the preventive and corrective arm of the Pact. *These sanctions should be more automatic*, while respecting the role of the different institutions and the institutional balance. In enforcing the preventive arm of the Pact, the Council should be empowered to decide, acting by QMV to impose progressively sanctions in the form of interest-bearing deposits on any Member State whose fiscal consolidation path deviates particularly significantly from the adjustment path foreseen in the Stability and Growth Pact.
   b. As to the corrective arm, *whenever the Council decides to open an excessive deficit procedure, there should be automatic sanctions for any Member States found by the Council, acting by QMV, to have failed to implement the necessary corrective measures within a 6-month time limit.*
   c. Complementing the new legislative framework for the surveillance of economic imbalances, the case of any Member State with persistent imbalances under surveillance by the Council will be referred to the European Council for discussion.

2. France and Germany consider that an amendment of the Treaties is needed and that the President of the European Council should be asked to present, in close contact with the Members of the European Council, concrete options allowing the establishment of a robust crisis resolution framework before its meeting in March 2011. The amendment of the Treaties will be restricted to the following issues:
   a. The establishment of a permanent and robust framework to ensure orderly crisis management in the future, *providing the necessary arrangements for an adequate participation of private creditors* and allowing Member States to take appropriate coordinated measures to safeguard financial stability of the Euro area as a whole.
   b. In case of a serious violation of basic principles of Economic and Monetary Union, and following appropriate procedures, *suspension of the voting rights* of the Member State concerned. The necessary amendment to the Treaties should be adopted and ratified by Member States in accordance with their respective constitutional requirements in due time before 2013.

Figure 10.4   Irish Long-term Sovereign Yield Differentials with Germany

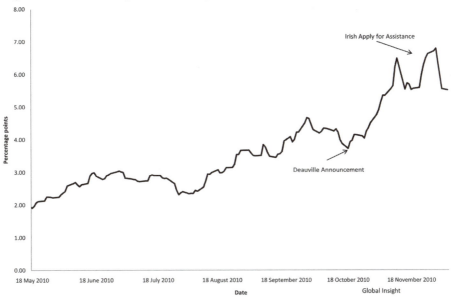

cal consolidation was one of the European Union's greatest success stories. When it peaked in 1987, Irish public debt amounted to almost 113 percent of the country's gross domestic product. Ireland's debt-to-GDP ratio was just 48.5 percent at the start of the single currency in 1999. By 2007, Irish public debt amounted to just 25 percent of GDP. It is hard to find a comparable case of a country reducing its public debt so much in just twenty years. It is even harder to imagine what the Irish must be feeling to see their situation go so rapidly into reverse. According to November 2010 estimates of the European Commission, Ireland's debt-to-GDP ratio will cross the 100 percent marker again early in 2011; by the end of 2012, it is expected to be back up around 114 percent of GDP.[41]

The explanation lies in the guarantees given by the Irish government to the Irish banking sector. If Greece is an illustration of public profligacy, Ireland exemplifies the free-market version. Irish banks bet badly on U.S. mortgage markets, they pumped money into their country's own residential and commercial real estate, and they borrowed heavily from abroad. As these banks ran into trouble during the autumn of 2008, the Irish government suddenly realized that the size of their asset books was many times larger than the whole of the economy. In order to prevent a run on the banks, the government stepped in to guarantee deposits and then to underwrite bank liabilities more generally. The effect was to transfer the bad debts of the banking system onto the government's own balance sheets. The state became excessively indebted so that the banks could be kept whole. The situation was never well accepted in the markets. Indeed, for much of 2009, Irish sovereign debt was cheaper to buy than Greek paper. Hence, when the Greek situation began to deteriorate in the spring of 2010, most actors in the bond markets realized that an Irish crisis was only a matter of time.

The Deauville declaration did not cause the crisis for Ireland; it just brought the time forward. What caused the crisis was the unintended consequence of financial integration between countries that traditionally have very different rates of interest. Moreover, this pattern of causality extends far beyond Ireland and Greece. The question now is whether Portugal and Spain will go the same way as well. Given the pace of events, it is very likely that this question will find an answer before this chapter goes to press. What is less likely is that we will have any indication as to how this problem can be solved. Europe's leaders have shown little willingness to accept the logic of their interdependence. They recognize that it would be folly to break up the single currency, but they do not agree on how it should be held together. They accepted a reform process in the December 2010 European Council summit, but it bears little relation to the underlying problem and so has little prospect for success. The global economic crisis has left an enduring legacy in Europe. Indeed it is still developing. Watch this space.

Suggested Readings

As will be obvious both from the text of this chapter and from the references given in the notes, this is a fast-moving topic. The suggested readings indicated here give more of a background on the economic and financial crisis than a close coverage of the European sovereign debt crisis. They are important for understanding current developments in Europe nonetheless.

Blanchard, Olivier, and Francesco Giavazzi, "Current Account Deficits in the Euro Area: The End of the Feldstein-Horioka Puzzle?" *Brookings Papers on Economic Activity*, 2002, pp. 147–209.

Caballero, Ricardo J., Emmanuel Farhi, and Pierre-Olivier Gourinchas, "Financial Crash, Commodity Prices, and Global Imbalances," *Brookings Papers on Economic Activity*, 2008, pp. 1–55.

Decressin, Jörg, and Emil Stavrev, "Current Accounts in a Currency Union," IMF Working Paper WP/09/127, Washington, DC: IMF, June 2009.

Fagan, Gabriel, and Vítor Gaspar, "Macroeconomic Adjustment to Monetary Union," *ECB Working Paper No. 946*, Frankfurt: European Central Bank, October 2008.

Jones, Erik, "Liberalized Capital Markets, State Autonomy, and European Monetary Union," *European Journal of Political Research*, 42(2), March 2003, 111–136.

Jones, Erik, "Shifting the Focus: The New Political Economy of Global Macroeconomic Imbalances," *SAIS Review*, 29(2), Summer/Fall 2009, 61–73.

Jones, Erik, "Merkel's Folly," *Survival*, 52(3), June/July 2010, 21–38.

Wolf, Martin, *Fixing Global Finance*, New Haven, CT: Yale University Press, 2009.

CHAPTER 11

European Law and Politics

R. Daniel Kelemen

Since the end of World War II, across Europe the power of courts has expanded dramatically. Many scholars refer to this trend as the "judicialization of politics." The judicialization of politics in Europe takes many forms—national constitutional courts declaring acts of parliaments unconstitutional, administrative courts challenging state actions, aggressive prosecutors using the courts to stamp out corruption and topple politicians at the highest levels of government, the European Court of Justice asserting legal doctrines that erode national sovereignty, or the European Court of Human Rights issuing rulings that challenge national practices on highly controversial social and cultural issues. In the broadest sense, the judicialization of politics involves "[greater] reliance on courts and judicial means for addressing core moral predicaments, public policy questions and political controversies."[1]

While the judicialization of politics is a global phenomenon, it is nowhere more pronounced than in Europe.[2] In Europe, judicialization has occurred at both the national level and the regional or supranational level. At the national level, constitutional courts have increasingly asserted the power of judicial review, and other courts have become more significant actors in a variety of policy processes. Above the level of the nation-state, the European Court of Justice (ECJ) and the European Court of Human Rights (ECHR) have emerged as the most powerful supranational courts in world history. Developments at these two levels have been tightly linked, with supranational and national courts often relying on one another as allies in expanding judicial power.

This chapter examines the causes, the scope, and the consequences of the judicialization of politics in Europe. First, we explore why courts have gained so much power in recent decades. Next, we survey the reach of judicial power. What fields of politics and policy do national and supranational courts influence at the moment? Finally, we ask, "What difference does judicialization make?" If democratically elected parliaments have lost power relative to courts, does this mean that judicialization has undermined democracy? Or are courts providing vital safeguards for individual rights? Ultimately, is judicialization a positive development to be celebrated or a worrying trend that needs to be reined in?

Causes of Judicialization

The growth of judicial power in Europe cannot be attributed to a single explanation. A confluence of trends at the national, supranational, and global levels has led courts to take on an unprecedented degree of political power.

THE AGE OF RIGHTS

The aftermath of World War II saw the spread of a rights discourse and a rights ideology across advanced industrialized countries. With the United Nations' adoption of the Universal Declaration of Human Rights in 1948 and the near universal acceptance of the idea of human rights in subsequent decades, we entered what Louis Henkin termed "the age of rights."[3] Across Europe and the world, democracies placed greater emphasis on the protection of individual human rights. In part, this was a reaction to the crimes committed by the Nazis and other fascist regimes in Europe. The rise of fascism discredited the model of unrestricted parliamentary democracy that had prevailed in most European democracies. Unlike in the United States, where the doctrine of separation of powers and the practice of judicial review were already deeply entrenched, most European democracies had been based on the concept of parliamentary sovereignty. Parliamentary sovereignty suggests that the parliament, as the elected body representing the will of the people, is sovereign and has supremacy over all other organs of government. However, fascist parties had used the democratic process to gain power in parliaments and then used that power to extinguish individual rights. The lesson drawn by postwar leaders was that the power to govern could not simply be left to parliamentary majorities. Government power would need to be checked by powerful courts that could protect individual rights, even against the wishes of powerful parliamentary majorities. Thus it is no surprise that some of the most powerful constitutional courts in Europe were created in countries with some of the darkest wartime legacies.

The postwar architects of democracy in West Germany, Italy, and Austria all opted to create powerful constitutional courts, dedicated to the protection of individual rights.[4] After the collapse of their authoritarian regimes in the 1970s, Spain and Portugal followed suit. These courts were given extraordinary powers of judicial review. In Germany, individuals were guaranteed direct access to the constitutional court (the *Bundesverfassungsgericht*). In Italy, any court that doubted the constitutionality of a statute at issue in a case under its consideration was given the power to refer the case to the Italian Constitutional Court (*Corte costituzionale*) for an opinion on the constitutionality of the statute.

In expanding the protection of fundamental human rights, national constitutional courts were not acting alone. They received significant encouragement from the supranational level through the work of the European Court of Human Rights. The European Court of Human Rights (not to be confused with the European Court of Justice, which we discuss below) is a judicial body attached to the Council of Europe. Established in 1949, the Council of Europe aimed to promote democracy, human rights, the rule of law, and European integration. A year later, the Council of Europe drafted a European Convention on Human Rights, a treaty that required all Council of Europe member countries to protect the human rights of their citizens and that established a court (the European Court of Human Rights) to hear cases brought by citizens who claimed that their rights had been violated. As Andrew Moravcsik has argued, the European Convention on Human Rights served as a kind of commitment device, enabling governments to credibly signal their commitment to human rights norms and to assure neighbors that they could not abandon liberal democracy.[5] By submitting themselves to the jurisdiction of the supranational European Court of Human Rights, European governments put an external check on themselves, tying their own hands.

ECONOMIC LIBERALIZATION AND THE CHANGING ROLE OF THE STATE

Over the past thirty years, European countries have profoundly liberalized their economies. To a large extent, this process of economic liberalization has been linked to the process of European integration and the construction of a common market, as we discuss below. But even if we leave aside for a moment the EU dimension, it is clear that at the national level the state has retreated from many of its traditional roles in economic management and has liberalized previously restricted markets. This economic liberalization has encouraged judicialization across a wide range of areas of economic regulation.

The connection between economic liberalization and judicialization is not self-evident. Economic liberalization is widely understood as a process that relies on deregulation—the removal of legal restrictions on free enterprise. In fact, scholars from Karl Polanyi to Steven Vogel have explained that deregulation of one kind is often followed by reregulation of another, and the establishment of freer markets may paradoxically require the adoption of even more rules.[6] Why? In part, the explanation is political, as the public demands new rules to add a social component to the process of market making and to protect them against the vagaries of free markets. In part, the explanation is functional. When economic liberalization lifts restrictions on entry into economic markets, it allows a far greater number of economic actors to enter the marketplace. In these circumstances, policymakers tasked with pursuing public policy goals—such as protecting consumer safety or policing fraud of various sorts—cannot easily rely on the sorts of informal, flexible approaches to regulation that are

354 R. DANIEL KELEMEN

effective in relatively closed markets with a limited number of familiar players. Instead, they find it more effective to rely on more formal, transparent, and "juridical" rules that assure that all market players are treated equally.

One related aspect of this phenomenon concerns privatization of state-owned enterprises. When governments privatize state-owned monopolies in areas such as transportation, energy, and telecommunications (as European countries did throughout the 1980s and 1990s), they set up systems of regulation to ensure fair competition in the new markets and to ensure that providers meet minimal safety standards and public service obligations. While the enterprises were state owned, the government could achieve most of its policy aims by pressuring management; once they are privatized, it sets up enforceable rules and invites the courts to keep a watchful eye on new entrants to these markets.

EUROPEAN INTEGRATION

The process of European integration—the term scholars use for the ongoing transfer of authority from national governments to the European Union—has played a major role in encouraging the judicialization of politics across all the EU's member states. Courts have both helped to drive forward the process of European integration while they have also been empowered by European integration. The European Union's legal system is unprecedented in world history. Over time, the European Court of Justice has emerged as the supreme court of the European Union, with jurisdiction—and supremacy—over the many areas of law in which the EU is active. It is the EU's legal system more than anything that distinguishes the EU from other international organizations and gives it the character of a quasi-federal political system.

European integration has encouraged judicialization for two main reasons. First, it is the very political structure of the EU that encourages the process. The EU has a weak and highly fragmented institutional structure that stimulates lawmakers to rely on courts to pursue their policy objectives. With little more than 20,000 civil servants working for EU institutions, the EU has extremely limited capacities to administer its own policies. The EU adopts policies that affect nearly half a billion citizens, but they must attempt to do so with the same number of employees as a typical midsized European city. Instead of implementing its own policies, the EU relies primarily on national governments for implementation. But EU lawmakers do not trust national governments to implement EU laws faithfully. They have good reasons to be skeptical, as many EU rules impose substantial costs on national governments and industries. Not only do policymakers in the European Commission and European Parliament distrust member states, but the governments represented in the EU's Council of Ministers may also distrust one another's commitment to implementing EU law.

Given the EU's weakness and the desire of EU lawmakers to ensure that EU laws are implemented in all member states, lawmakers draft laws in a way that invites the European Court of Justice and national courts to play an active role in monitoring implementation. Lawmakers do this by framing many policies in terms of rights, such as rights for employees, rights for shareholders, rights for consumers, rights for women, and economic rights for firms. The EU's strategy is to encourage the individuals and companies that enjoy these rights to enforce them before national and EU courts. Moreover, despite the fact that national leaders frequently protest that the ECJ is engaging in judicial activism and illegitimately extending its own powers, leaders have nevertheless repeatedly introduced institutional reforms designed to strengthen the ECJ. For instance, in the 1992 Maastricht Treaty, member governments gave the ECJ the authority to impose penalty payments on member states that fail to comply with previous ECJ rulings. Through a series of treaty revisions over the past thirty years, the member states have steadily expanded the ECJ's jurisdiction. Most recently, with the Lisbon Treaty, they extended the jurisdiction of the ECJ to all EU matters except for foreign policy.

While EU policymakers in the Council of Ministers, the European Parliament, and the European Commission clearly play an important role in encouraging judicialization, the European Court of Justice has hardly been a passive player in this process.

The ECJ has not simply accepted policymakers' invitation to become involved in the policy process; the court has played an indispensible role in extending its own power far beyond what many EU lawmakers had envisioned. Over the years, the ECJ's expansive interpretations of European Community law transformed a set of international treaties into a constitution in all but name. In landmark rulings in the early 1960s, the ECJ asserted the revolutionary legal doctrines of direct effect (*Van Gend en Loos*[7]) and supremacy (*Costa v. ENEL*[8]), establishing the bedrock of the Community legal order.

The combination of direct effect and supremacy created a situation in which individuals could go before their national courts and invoke their rights under European Community law, even where these conflicted with national law. Certainly these highly controversial doctrines were not accepted overnight. But over the course of the next two decades, national courts and national governments across Europe did come to accept direct effect and supremacy—along with a variety of other bold ECJ doctrines.[9] The puzzling question is how the ECJ managed to assert these bold doctrines and strip so much away from national sovereignty without national governments slapping the court down. In other words, how did the ECJ defy the laws of political gravity and lift itself by its own bootstraps to a position of supremacy?

One key to the ECJ's success has been its ability to build partnerships with and attract the support of judges across Europe. The ECJ did not cloister itself away in Luxembourg but actively reached out to judges in the EU member

Box 11.1   The European Court of Justice

The European Court of Justice is the supreme court of the European Union. Located in Luxembourg City, the court is composed of twenty-seven judges, one appointed by each member state for a six-year, renewable term. The plenary of twenty-seven judges very rarely hears a case together. Rather, the ECJ organizes itself into a system of chambers, and chambers of three or five judges hear most cases. Very significant cases are heard by the "Grand Chamber" of thirteen judges. Though various combinations of judges decide cases, the decisions are always published and treated as the consensus ruling of the ECJ. No minority opinions are drafted, and no records of internal deliberations are published. To protect the independence of individual judges—for instance, to shield them from pressure from their home government—the deliberations of the court are kept secret.

To help the ECJ cope with its burgeoning case load, the 1986 Single European Act called for the establishment of a lower court beneath the ECJ. This "Court of First Instance" commenced operations in 1989, and with the adoption of the Lisbon Treaty in 2010, its name changed to the "General Court." Like the ECJ, the General Court is composed of twenty-seven judges, who divide themselves into chambers, deliberate in secret, and issue their opinions as the consensus of the court. Much of the General Court's jurisdiction focuses on cases brought directly by private parties—such as firms—that claim they have been harmed by actions or omissions by the European Commission or other EU institutions. The General Court's rulings can be appealed to the ECJ.

states, encouraging them to embrace Community law and to refer cases to the ECJ through the preliminary ruling procedure. If national courts have been the ECJ's indispensable partners in contracting the EU's legal order, then the preliminary ruling procedure has been the key channel of communication through which they developed their relationship.

The preliminary ruling procedure had a modest birth as a clause of little note included in the Treaty of Rome, with little thought given to its potential consequences. The procedure was included in the treaty as a way to allow individuals to challenge European law and to help national courts interpret it. But this little procedure took on a big life as it enabled national courts—not just courts but even the most obscure tribunals—that were faced with cases that hinged on questions of Community law to send references to the ECJ to ask for its interpretation of Community law. In other words, national courts could order a stay in their proceedings and send a reference to the ECJ asking for its interpretation of the legal questions of European Community law that would determine the outcome of the case. The ECJ did not simply wait for the cases to arrive in its mailbox. The court actively cultivated and trained a network of national judges committed to European law who might send them cases through the preliminary ruling procedure.[10]

Box 11.2 Direct Effect and Supremacy

The principle of direct effect held that Community law was, under some conditions, capable of conferring rights on individuals which those individuals could invoke in legal proceedings before national courts. This marked a profound departure from traditional approaches to international law. Normally, international law is binding upon states: the states that sign treaties are obliged (at least in principle) to fulfill their treaty obligations. But international treaties do not confer rights directly on individuals. However, in *Van Gend*, the ECJ ruled that the Treaty of Rome was not an ordinary treaty between states, but instead that the treaty established a Community that comprised both the states and their citizens. Thus, as the court explained, "the Community constitutes a new legal order of international law for the benefit of which the states have limited their sovereign rights, albeit within limited fields, and the subjects of which comprise not only Member States but also their nationals. Independently of the legislation of Member States, Community law therefore not only imposes obligations on individuals but is also intended to confer upon them rights which become part of their legal heritage."[1]

In its 1964 *Costa v. ENEL* ruling, the ECJ took the next landmark step by asserting the principle of supremacy. Supremacy means that in cases where national law and Community law conflict, Community law must take supremacy. Again, this was a radical doctrine that departed from traditional norms of international law and certainly from what many governments had in mind when they signed the Treaty of Rome in 1957. As it clarified and developed the concept of supremacy in subsequent rulings, the ECJ asserted that national courts were legally bound to set aside any provisions of national law that were incompatible with requirements of European Community law.

1. *Van Gend en Loos*, [1963] ECR 13.

This procedure had a number of profound effects. First, it established a channel for direct dialogue between the ECJ and national courts not mediated by national governments. This eventually allowed the ECJ to enlist national courts as its partners in the construction of the European legal order in a way that national governments could scarcely impede. When a national court used a ruling from the ECJ as the basis for its own domestic judgment, this ruling became part of domestic law, which governments could only resist by ignoring their own courts. In the 1960s and 1970s, national governments did attempt to pressure their courts to ignore the ECJ's supremacy claims.[11] However, given the value placed on judicial independence and the rule of law in European democracies, governments were loath to defy their own courts when—as became increasingly common—those courts relied on ECJ jurisprudence.

Second, the preliminary ruling procedure helped trigger a dynamic of intercourt competition, whereby many judges at lower-level courts within national judicial systems saw references to the ECJ as a way to circumvent supe-

Box 11.3   The Preliminary Ruling Procedure

Article 267 of the Treaty on the Functioning of the European Union ("The Lisbon Treaty")

The Court of Justice of the European Union shall have jurisdiction to give preliminary rulings concerning:

(a) the interpretation of the Treaties;
(b) the validity and interpretation of acts of the institutions, bodies, offices or agencies of the Union;

Where such a question is raised before any court or tribunal of a Member State, that court or tribunal may, if it considers that a decision on the question is necessary to enable it to give judgment, request the Court to give a ruling thereon.

Where any such question is raised in a case pending before a court or tribunal of a Member State against whose decisions there is no judicial remedy under national law, that court or tribunal shall bring the matter before the Court.

If such a question is raised in a case pending before a court or tribunal of a Member State with regard to a person in custody, the Court of Justice of the European Union shall act with the minimum of delay.

rior courts or rival courts within their own judicial hierarchy.[12] Lower-court judges who feared having their rulings quashed by higher courts in their national judicial hierarchies could skip over these higher courts and request a preliminary ruling directly from the European Court of Justice. In other words, the ECJ became the judicial trump card in national intercourt disputes. More generally, many courts across Europe came to see the ECJ as their ally in the cause of empowering the judiciary vis-à-vis other branches of government.[13]

Finally, by opening up a channel for cases brought by private litigants to reach the ECJ, the preliminary ruling procedure democratized European law and dramatically increased the potential volume of cases the ECJ could hear. To be vibrant and powerful, courts need cases. A steady volume of cases unleashes a self-reinforcing cycle of institutionalization in which rulings establish legal doctrines that then provide the legal basis for judging subsequent disputes. A steady volume of cases also enhances the legitimacy of a court as the authoritative forum in which disputes are resolved within a political system. The European Commission did (and still does) bring many enforcement cases (so-called "infringement proceedings") before the ECJ. However, given the Commission's limited capacities, it was vital to open up the legal system to private parties.

The combination of doctrines such as direct effect and supremacy with the channel afforded by the preliminary ruling procedure meant that private actors with an interest in enforcing their EU rights could at least have indirect access to the ECJ through their national courts. And litigants took advantage of that channel in large numbers.[14] To be sure, access to European justice has been very uneven, with privileged litigants (such as large corporations) enjoying better access than individuals of modest means. Individuals contemplating litigation to enforce their rights under European law face extremely high hurdles, in terms of the cost and time involved in the legal process. Therefore, for all but the most privileged litigants, litigation support structures, such as legal aid services, are crucial.[15] Nevertheless, it is clear that a variety of groups have mobilized to help their members benefit from their rights under European law.[16]

The fragmentation of political power in the EU discussed above also opened up space for ECJ activism. Many ECJ decisions have sparked denunciations from the individual national governments directly touched by those decisions. Some ECJ decisions have proven controversial enough to spark outcries from multiple member state governments. But very few decisions have ever led member states to act collectively to rein in the ECJ.[17] To overturn ECJ interpretations of European law, the member states either have to pass new laws (which typically involves supermajority voting and the support of the European Parliament) or revise treaties (which requires unanimous agreement of all member states). Given the diversity of preferences among member state governments, they will rarely take the same view of controversial ECJ decisions or be able to agree on how to respond. This political division allows the ECJ to assert its interpretations of EU law with little fear of political backlash. Moreover, there is considerable evidence that the ECJ tends to engage in what Miguel Maduro (1998) has called "majoritarian activism," meaning that they make rulings that strike down national laws and practices differing from those that prevail in the majority of member states. In other words, many ECJ decisions essentially impose the will of the majority of member states, which clearly makes it unlikely that that majority would seek to reverse those decisions.

Thus far we have focused on how the institutional structure of the EU and the activism of the ECJ encouraged judicialization, but European integration has encouraged judicialization through another pathway as well—by promoting economic liberalization. As discussed in general terms above, economic liberalization tends to enhance judicialization. The EU has played an important role in driving forward this dynamic in recent decades. Since its founding, one of the EU's central aims has been to construct a single European market in which goods, services, capital, and labor can move freely. The project gained new momentum in the mid-1980s when Commission president Jacques Delors relaunched the stalled effort to complete the single market. One might assume (and many have) that creating a single market simply requires lawmakers to eliminate tariffs and dismantle nontariff barriers to trade (such as national regulations that discriminate against foreign products, services, and workers) through deregulation. But completing Europe's single market has in fact also required reregulation.

In areas where national rules that distorted trade were dismantled, new EU-level regulations have been put in place to create a level playing field for economic actors. For example, in many areas where national consumer safety and environmental protection standards distorted trade, these have been replaced with uniform EU regulations. Or likewise in the field of financial regulation, many traditional national regulations were dismantled and replaced with EU regulations that aimed to establish an integrated European financial market. Compared to the national regulatory systems they replaced, the new EU regulations rely far more on courts and litigation. So the creation of a single market has sparked a cycle of deregulation and judicialized reregulation.[18]

The Scope of Judicialization

Just how far has judicialization in Europe gone? Which areas of policy are affected by the growing power of courts? The judicialization of politics in Europe has led courts to become involved in nearly every sort of major political and policy dispute imaginable. The words of Aharon Barak, former chief justice of the Supreme Court of Israel and noted legal scholar, capture the broad scope of the law's impact in contemporary Europe. As he put it, "Nothing falls beyond the purview of judicial review; the world is filled with law; anything and everything is justiciable."[19] Commenting on the distinctive features of the American legal system and legal culture in the 1830s, Alexis de Tocqueville wrote, "Scarcely any political question arises in the United States which is not resolved, sooner or later, into a judicial question."[20] Much the same could be said of Europe today.

At the national level, constitutional courts across Europe have intervened decisively in most major areas of political life. From governing the economy; to determining the relations between different branches and levels of government; to setting the terms of immigration, asylum, and citizenship policies; to combating discrimination; to setting the terms of church-state relations; to protecting civil liberties in the context of the struggle against terrorism, again and again we can observe national high courts asserting themselves in the midst of some of the most heated political controversies.

Germany's constitution (the Basic Law, or *Grundgesetz*) enables citizens who allege that public authorities have violated their fundamental rights to file a constitutional complaint directly with the Constitutional Court. Thousands of such individual complaints are filed every year, generating the main source of the Constitutional Court's caseload and the basis on which it has issued many of its most significant judgments. The Constitutional Court has declared hundreds of federal and state statutes to be unconstitutional, and its rulings have shaped German policy on major issues including abortion, criminal sentencing, education, nuclear power, divorce, and taxation.[21] As a result, German lawmakers take into account the anticipated reactions of the Constitutional Court when crafting legislation.[22]

The Italian Constitutional Court has shaped policy in areas as diverse as pensions, divorce, sexual identity, executive-legislative relations, civil liberties, and church-state relations.[23] Beyond the impact of the Constitutional Court, the judiciary has transformed politics in even more fundamental ways. Aggressive public prosecutors worked through the courts in the *mani pulite* (clean hands) investigations to expose the *Tangentopoli* (Bribeville) scandal that helped to topple the Italian political establishment.[24]

France too has experienced a dramatic expansion of judicial power in recent decades.[25] Under the Constitution of France's Fifth Republic introduced in 1958 (with reforms introduced in 1974), a group of lawmakers from the legislative minority (a minimum of sixty deputies in the National Assembly or sixty senators) can challenge the constitutionality of a statute before it goes into effect. Through this "abstract review" procedure, minority lawmakers can and do use the Constitutional Council (*Conseil Constitutionnel*) to place a check on the legislative majority, striking down unconstitutional laws before they ever go into effect. As Alec Stone explains, "Since the late 1970s, virtually every major bill, and every budget since 1974, has been referred [to the Constitutional Council] by parliamentary minorities. Their efforts have been rewarded: since 1981 more than half of all referrals have resulted in annulments." In 1982, the Constitutional Council blocked the centerpiece of the new Socialist government's economic plan. The council ruled that a bill to nationalize major industrial conglomerates, banks, and financial services firms was unconstitutional because it failed to provide adequate compensation to those (i.e., shareholders) whose property was nationalized. To satisfy the Constitutional Council, the Socialist government later passed a new version of the bill that provided for more compensation to shareholders, and which substantially increased the cost of the privatization program. As Alec Stone (later Stone Sweet) has demonstrated, as a result of such assertions of judicial power, French lawmakers regularly shape their legislative proposals in order to guard against censure by the Constitutional Council.[26] Nevertheless, rulings by the Constitutional Council annulling government bills have decisively shaped policy in a host of areas, including media pluralism, electoral rules, and education.

In the United Kingdom (UK), this process has been driven to a significant degree by the introduction of the Human Rights Act of 1998. The Human Rights Act sought to strengthen British compliance with the European Convention on Human Rights. It did so by enabling individuals to invoke rights contained in the European Convention on Human Rights before British courts and by demanding that those courts seek to interpret UK law in a manner compatible with the charter. Where UK law clearly violates the charter, British courts can issue a "declaration of incompatibility," which, while not formally voiding the legislation, places immense pressure on Parliament to amend the legislation such that it will comply with the charter.

In the UK, the Appellate Committee of the House of Lords (until recently the highest judicial authority in the UK) declared the UK's post-9/11 state-of-emergency legislation unconstitutional (*Belmarsh*[27]) and ruled on whether the government had to take action on behalf of Guantanamo detainees who might be tortured by U.S. authorities (*Al Rawi*[28]). Even more dramatically, the UK reorganized its judiciary by establishing a new Supreme Court in October 2009. The Supreme Court replaced the Appellate Committee of the House of Lords as the highest court in the United Kingdom. The fact that the highest court of the UK had in fact been an organ of its (undemocratic) upper legislative chamber (the House of Lords), and that the lord chancellor was in fact a member of the cabinet (in other words, the executive), violated prevailing norms concerning judicial independence across Europe—and potentially violated the European Convention on Human Rights (Article 6) requirement that states provide for a fair trial before an "independent" court. The establishment of an independent Supreme Court sets the stage for an even greater judicialization of British politics in the future.

At the European level, the EU and the ECJ have encouraged judicialization across a broad spectrum of policy areas. European law has had a profound impact on the fight against discrimination in Europe. The judicialization of anti-discrimination policy arose first in the field of gender equality. The Treaty of Rome included a provision that prohibited discrimination in employment on the basis of sex. This provision was not included due to a deep commitment to gender equality on the part of the EU's founders, but rather because some member states feared that others would gain a competitive advantage by relying on lower-wage female workers. Nevertheless, on the basis of this treaty article and subsequent directives on gender equality enacted by EU lawmakers, the ECJ dramatically expanded gender equality rights in Europe.

The process began in the 1970s, when a Belgian labor lawyer, Elaine Vogel-Polsky, working together with a Belgian flight attendant, Gabrielle Defrenne, brought a series of test cases asserting that the Treaty of Rome's prohibition on sex discrimination in employment (in what was then Article 141) constituted an individual right with direct effect. The court agreed that the sex equality rule did have direct effect, setting the stage for other women's organizations and activists to wage strategic litigation campaigns based on European rights in later years. Proponents of gender equality in a number of member states leveraged women's rights under European law in order to generate pressure for policy reform in their countries.[29] Over the years, the ECJ has extended the prohibition on gender discrimination to protect against discrimination on the basis of pregnancy, to demand gender equality in pensions, and to declare that unequal treatment of part-time workers (in terms of not offering them the same benefits as full-time workers) amounted to indirect sex discrimination, since the majority of part-time workers were women.

More recently, the EU's adoption of the Employment Equality and Racial Equality directives (directives 2000/78/EC and 2000/43/EC, respectively) in 2000 has set the stage for extending the model developed in the gender discrimination field to fight other forms of discrimination. The Racial Equality Directive prohibits discrimination on the basis of race in employment, education, social protection, and access to goods and services. The Employment Equality Directive prohibits discrimination in employment on the basis of age, disability, religion, and sexual orientation. Already national courts have experienced an upsurge of discrimination claims in some fields, such as age discrimination, and important cases have reached the ECJ.[30] With the adoption of the Lisbon Treaty, which gives legal force to the EU's Charter of Fundamental Rights, more rights-based litigation can be expected.

We can observe significant judicialization in a wide range of areas of economic policymaking. The field of antitrust—or as it is known in Europe, competition policy—has become thoroughly juridified. Traditionally, European approaches to competition policy were based on an approach that granted regulators great flexibility and involved little litigation or judicial review. Government regulators had the flexibility to balance the promotion of competition against other policy goals such as maintaining employment or encouraging industrial cooperation to foster technological innovation. However, over the past twenty years, as the European Commission became more aggressive in enforcing competition policy and penalizing violators, the European Court of Justice and the Court of First Instance (now called the General Court) have pressed European regulators to adhere to strict procedures and to provide legally defensible justifications for its actions. The Commission now regularly imposes multimillion-euro fines on companies, only to see those fines challenged by the firms before European courts. Since 2004, as part of the so-called modernization of competition policy, the EU has pushed to encourage private parties to play a more active role in enforcing competition policy by taking legal action before national courts against competitors who violate EU competition law.[31]

In the field of securities regulation, EU legislation has established a host of shareholders' rights that have provided a legal basis for the emergence of shareholder litigation in countries across the EU—a phenomenon that had been almost unheard of before the EU became involved in the field. Before the mid 1980s, stock exchanges across Europe were largely self-regulating. Generally, governments imposed few disclosure requirements and did little to protect investors; instead, they relied on the notion that the established, trusted players in their sheltered financial markets would self-regulate in the interest of maintaining their reputations. But as the EU has worked to open up national markets and create a truly pan-European market for trading stocks, bonds, and other financial instruments, it has simultaneously encouraged the judicialization of regulation. The EU has established an enormous body of law that establishes legally enforceable disclosure rules and various investor rights.[32] This in turn has triggered the emergence of forms of shareholder litigation that were previously unknown in Europe, as investors seek to enforce their EU rights (and recoup their losses) in court.

The ECJ has developed a body of jurisprudence that significantly influences national health-care systems.[33] The health-care sector was long thought to be immune to the influence of European law. However, in recent years, ECJ rulings have affected patients, doctors, and other major players in the health-care sector. The ECJ has applied the Working Time Directive to health care, issuing rulings on maximum allowable working hours for doctors. Beginning with its 1998 *Kohll*[34] and *Decker*[35] decisions, the court has issued a string of judgments on patients' rights, in particular the right to seek nonemergency medical care across borders.

One landmark decision involved the case of a British woman who was suffering extreme pain while lingering on a National Health Service (NHS) waiting list for hip replacement surgery. She decided to go to France to have the hip replacement surgery done and then asked her local NHS health-care trust to reimburse her for the costs—which they refused to do. She challenged that decision in the British courts, and the case was eventually referred to the ECJ through the preliminary ruling procedure. In its *Watts*[36] judgment, the ECJ ruled that the NHS must reimburse patients for treatments in other member states if the waiting time for treatment in the UK exceeds "the period which is acceptable in the light of an objective medical assessment of the clinical needs of the person concerned" (pars. 68 and 149[4]). The court said that the NHS must allow clinical experts to assess the acceptable waiting time for the individual—depending on their case and their level of pain—and patients must be able to challenge refusals to grant authorization for treatment abroad in "judicial or quasi-judicial proceedings" (pars. 116–117). Beyond patients and doctors, other economic actors in the health-care sector, such as health service providers and insurers, have been affected as the court has extended EU rules on competition, state aid, and public procurement to the health sector in some instances.[37]

The ECJ's highly controversial rulings in *Viking*,[38] *Laval*,[39] and *Rüffert*[40] demonstrate the significant—and potentially destabilizing—impact that European law is having on systems of industrial relations. These rulings center on the conflict between the right to free movement of services in the common market, on the one hand, and national systems of industrial relations, on the other. The details of each case differ, though in essence the conflicts involve service providers (in fields such as construction) from lower-wage jurisdictions that wish to provide their services in higher-wage member states.

Should firms from lower-wage countries who win contracts in higher-wage countries be able to pay the workers that they send there to do the work with the lower wages that prevail in their home country, or with the higher wages that prevail in the country where the job is being done? Should unions in the host country be able to strike to block the lower-wage workers from completing the job? The ECJ has held that where national law provides for a legal minimum wage, foreign workers must be paid that wage. However, where wages and other working conditions are set through collective bargaining between employers and unions—rather than through statutes—the terms of those collective bargains cannot be applied to foreign companies. In other words, the ECJ rulings could force countries that wish to defend their minimum wages and working conditions to transform their systems of industrial relations—setting minimum wages and working conditions by statute rather than through collective bargaining if they want to apply them to foreign operators.

While this might sound like a technicality, it would actually involve a profound transformation of systems of industrial relations that are deeply rooted in the distinctive national "styles of capitalism" that prevail in each EU member country.[41] So far, the ECJ has held that while unions have a right to take collective action, this can only interfere with the freedom to provide services where it is "justified, proportionate and necessary." The ECJ's rulings in this field have sparked an outcry from trade unions across Europe who argue that the ECJ will encourage a race to the bottom in wages and working conditions.

Historically, the ECJ's role in the field of protecting fundamental human rights has been more limited, as human rights protection fell to the jurisdiction of the European Court of Human Rights, which as mentioned above is a judicial body attached to an entirely separate international organization—the Council of Europe. The division in jurisdiction between the ECJ and the ECHR has its roots in the early postwar decades and the distinct approaches to European integration taken by the European Economic Community (the predecessor of today's EU) and the Council of Europe. As its name suggests, the European Economic Community (EEC) focused on economic integration—aiming to create a common market. While many of its founders hoped the EEC would eventually encourage far-reaching political integration of Europe, initially the scope of the EEC's activities was limited to matters of economic regulation relevant to the construction of a common market. In this context, questions of human rights did not seem particularly relevant, and the ECJ initially ruled that it did not have the power to review acts of Community institutions to ensure respect for fundamental human rights.[42] Though the ECJ later affirmed that it would uphold fundamental human rights as general principles of Community law,[43] international human rights adjudication remained for the most part in the jurisdiction of the European Court of Human Rights.

The power of the ECHR has developed more slowly and inconsistently than that of the ECJ. Nevertheless, the ECHR has had a profound impact in many areas. The ECHR has impacted national practices in highly sensitive areas such as rights of prisoners, gay rights, the display of religious symbols, and abortion. In an early landmark ruling, the ECHR ruled that a number of interrogation techniques practiced by the United Kingdom in the context of the conflict in Northern Ireland amounted to "inhuman and degrading treatment" prohibited by the European Convention on Human Rights.[44] In a 1981 judgment, the ECHR ruled that the criminalization of homosexuality in Northern Ireland violated the convention.[45]

The ECHR has heard a series of cases challenging national restrictions on the wearing of Islamic veils in various contexts. Generally, the court has upheld governments' rights—under certain conditions—to impose such restrictions.[46] In 2009, a panel of the ECHR ruled on a case, *Lautsi v. Italy*,[47] in which a parent argued that her right under the convention to educate her children in keeping with her convictions and her children's right to freedom of religion were violated by Italy's practice of affixing crucifixes in Italian public schools. The ECHR ruled unanimously that her rights had been violated and ordered Italy to pay her 5,000 in damages. The Italian government denounced the decision, and nineteen other governments have joined the Italian government in opposing it. The case has been referred to the ECHR's Grand Chamber on appeal. In December 2009, the ECHR heard yet another highly controversial case, *A., B. and C. v. Ireland*,[48] as three Irish women challenged, under the convention, the legality of Ireland's ban on abortion.

The ECHR has also worked to empower national courts directly. Article 6 of the European Convention on Human Rights guarantees a right to a fair trial, which entails a hearing before an independent tribunal in a reasonable time. Article 6 has been by far the most frequent basis for legal action before the ECHR. Thousands of litigants dissatisfied with the pace of domestic civil, criminal, and administrative proceedings; their rights of defense; or their access to courts more generally have resorted to the ECHR.

Stepping back from individual cases and looking at aggregate trends in litigation before the ECHR, we can observe a judicial body that is clearly gaining momentum—in some ways too much for its own good. Prior to 1998, cases brought to the ECHR by individuals were screened by a gatekeeping body (the European Commission on Human Rights), which severely restricted the flow of cases to the ECHR. However, the structure of the ECHR was transformed in 1998. Reforms instituted that year abolished the European Commission on Human Rights and opened up direct access to the court for residents of all forty-seven member states of the Council of Europe—approximately 800 million people.

The result of this opening has been a flood of cases; in recent years, the ECHR has regularly faced a backlog of roughly 100,000 cases. And while the court declares many cases inadmissible on various technical grounds, it has issued rulings on thousands of cases in recent years, finding states to be in violation of the European Convention on Human Rights in approximately 70 percent of the cases.[49] Though the ECHR has clearly gained strength over the years and had remarkable success in securing compliance with its rulings, today the court is having difficulty coping with the huge volume of cases it receives every year.

Normative Implications of Judicialization

How should we assess the implications of the judicialization of politics in Europe? Is it a destructive trend, or a healthy development? Some critics argue that the growing power of judges undermines democracy. Other critics warn of the spread of an "American disease" of excessive reliance on lawyers and litigation in the policy process. Defenders of judicialization may argue that the trend brings with it greater legal certainty, transparency, and access to justice for European citizens. Let us examine these views.

How much government or governance by judges should we accept in a democracy? Does the fact that courts regularly annul the legislative acts and administrative decisions of democratically elected officials threaten democracy? Is it legitimate for courts to block elected representatives from enacting laws pursuant to their electoral mandate? Is it legitimate for courts tasked with interpreting and applying the law to interpret it in an expansive way, creating new rights and effectively "legislating from the bench"? To evaluate such activities, we must begin by recalling, as was mentioned earlier in this chapter, that after World War II European democracies largely discarded the concept of unlimited parliamentary sovereignty. The UK was an exception in this regard, but even the venerable Parliament in Westminster has to a large extent bowed to the supremacy of the European courts in Strasbourg and Luxembourg City. Contemporary European democracies are liberal democracies under the rule of law; in other words, they are democracies in which elected majorities are restrained by the requirement that their actions respect individual rights—even the rights of unpopular minorities. And it is courts that protect those rights. National constitutional courts—and even more so the European Court of Justice and the European Court of Human Rights—have surely extended their powers further than their founders intended, but in a broader sense, courts in Europe are doing what the political systems in which they are embedded have asked them to do.

In assessing the impact of judicialization on democracy, we must not ignore the democratic dimensions of courts and legal processes. The fact that judges are not elected does not make courts and the judicial process entirely undemocratic. First, while national constitutional courts and European courts (the ECJ and ECHR) may be a step removed from the democratic process, they are formed with democratic input. Democratically elected national governments appoint the judges who sit on the ECJ and ECHR. The processes for appointing judges to national constitutional courts vary, but in all cases, democratically elected officials play a central role. Second, the judicial process itself creates opportunities for democratic participation. The process of judicialization has brought with it new opportunities for "access to justice" as the expansion of rights and the reform of legal procedures to encourage enforcement of those rights has created new opportunities for previously marginalized groups to influence policy through the courts.[50] More generally, courts can serve as a powerful tool that citizens can use to hold their governments accountable, thus ultimately enhancing the quality of democracy in Europe.

The judicialization of politics encourages policymakers to frame policies in the language of rights. By framing policies as rights, policymakers can essentially privatize some of the work of governance—encouraging individuals to enforce their own rights in court so that the state does not have to. Framing policies in the language of rights also has strong rhetorical appeal, as the defense of individual rights is a fundamental value of all modern European democracies. For the EU, developing a "rights-based" model of citizenship is particularly appealing, given that the EU cannot ground its citizenship on any unifying sense of national identity. But, in another sense, framing policies in terms of rights and engaging in rights discourse creates tensions with central aspects of the prevailing models of democracy in Europe. As Arend Lijphart (1999) has explained, most European democracies are based on a consensus model of democracy that emphasizes not simply following the will of the majority but building consensus and compromise among a broad range of stakeholders. The increasing focus on the judicial enforcement of individual rights may undermine the political culture of compromise and the emphasis on policies that serve general public interests that is central to European democracies.[51]

Finally, it is important to recognize that judicialization will bring with it certain economic costs. The judicialization of politics has encouraged a dramatic increase in the number of lawyers in Europe and in the size of the legal services industry.[52] Compared to the more flexible, informal approaches to regulation that traditionally prevailed in Europe, the highly judicialized approaches that are taking root in many fields today often operate more slowly and are far more costly. In many economic sectors affected by the rise of judicialization, business groups have warned against the dangers of moving toward American-style litigiousness.

The judicialization of politics in Europe entails costs and benefits. Regulatory processes may become slower and more expensive, while providing ample employment opportunities for lawyers. And unelected judges may substitute their decisions for those taken by elected representatives. At the same time, these trends will enhance the transparency and accountability of government and ensure greater access to justice and the protection of individual rights.

Suggested Readings

Alter, Karen, *Establishing the Supremacy of European Law: The Making of an International Rule of Law in Europe*, Oxford: Oxford University Press, 2001.

Burley, Anne-Marie, and Walter Mattli, "Europe before the Court: A Political Theory of Legal Integration," *International Organization*, 47, 1993, 41–76.

Cichowski, Rachel, *The European Court and Civil Society*, New York: Cambridge University Press, 2007.

Conant, Lisa, *Justice Contained: Law and Politics in the European Union*, Ithaca, NY: Cornell University Press, 2002.

Kelemen, R. Daniel, *Eurolegalism: The Transformation of Law and Regulation in the European Union*, Cambridge, MA: Harvard University Press, 2011.

Lijphart, Arend, *Patterns of Democracy: Government Forms and Performance in Thirty-Six Countries*, New Haven: Yale University Press, 1999.

Maduro, Miguel, *We, the Court: The European Court of Justice and the European Economic Constitution*, Oxford: Hart Publishing, 1998.

Slaughter, Anne-Marie, Alec Stone Sweet, and Joseph Weiler (eds.), *The European Courts and National Courts: Doctrine and Jurisprudence*, Oxford: Hart Publishing, 1998.

Stone Sweet, Alec. *The Judicial Construction of Europe*. Oxford: Oxford University Press, 2004.

Weiler, Joseph H. H., "The Transformation of Europe," *Yale Law Journal*, 100, 1991, 2403–2483.

CHAPTER 12

Migration in Europe

Jonathon W. Moses

The history of Europe is one of massive movements of people, either across Europe, beyond Europe, or (increasingly) into Europe. While these long-term trends provide an important backdrop, this chapter focuses on the nature of these flows today and on some of their most evident consequences.

To do this, we need to untangle the complex political and institutional weave that influences migration patterns in Europe today. In the process, we can learn of the two important roles that migration plays in the larger European project. The first of these is functional, in that free labor mobility plays a central role in the establishment of a common European market. The second role is more ideational, in that migration facilitates the creation of a common European identity. When German workers move to France, they gain perspective on their own national identities; they begin to see themselves less as Germans, and more as Europeans.

But there is a backside to the face of European identity, one more visible in recent years. Europe is scarred by a growing xenophobia, and many Europeans see their own identities and communities being threatened by foreigners. This fear is reflected in the rise of Europe's radical right and its calls to restrict immigration. In short, the European project both depends upon and is threatened by the foreigner at its doorstep.

This chapter aims to shine some light on Europe's inconvenient truth. It begins with a short introduction to the history of European migration patterns before offering a brief description of the nature of contemporary migration trends in Europe. The bulk of the chapter is then used to describe the complex and overlapping political geometry that regulates and channels these diverse flows. In this depiction, the European Union is just one of several relevant actors—but it is one that is playing an increasingly visible and important role. The third section considers the difficulty of integrating Europe's sundry faces into a common identity, while the forth section concludes.

Europeans on the Move

We begin by sketching out a historical backdrop. This backdrop can help us see how Europe's relationship with migration has changed over time and how that relationship is neither particularly unique nor special. In fact, when we manage to wrestle a little distance between ourselves and the current context, we can see that the history of European migration follows a familiar pattern: over the course of 150 years, Europe has gone from a region that experienced net emigration to one that is now characterized by net immigration.

The history of Europe is full of migrant stories. From the middle of the sixteenth century until the French Revolution, Europe experienced a number of major population shifts, whether it was the repopulation of the German territories after the Thirty Years' War, the flow of migrants that followed the retreat of the Ottomans under Hapsburg rule, the opening up of the southern Russian plains for settlement, or the Baltic migration system that followed in the wake of the Hanseatic League.

The continent was also animated by more temporary migration flows, as rural populations moved around in search of better farmland, to follow the harvests, or to settle in towns and cities. Merchants and skilled artisans moved from town to town selling their wares and skills—or they were tempted to settle in new areas following the incentives offered by enterprising political elites. To give you an idea of the size of these flows, consider the growth of a major European city. From 1600 to 1650, Amsterdam is said to have grown from 60,000 to 175,000 people! This expansion could not have occurred by natural population growth alone—the town was filling up with the likes of German workers, Norwegian sailors, French refugees, and Spanish traders. With industrialization, the opportunity for temporary migration increased along with the ease of transport. Large industrial projects—such as the digging of canals or the construction of railway and road networks—required workers to travel, often to faraway places.

With time, these local and regional migration patterns became increasingly international. In the last quarter of the nineteenth century, before World War I, millions of Europeans left the continent in search of a better life. As a percentage of population, the Irish, Norwegians, and Italians were most prone to intercontinental emigration, but their examples were followed by many across Europe. In the century after 1820, it is estimated that about 55 million people left Europe to settle in the New World.

This story of Europe, as a source of emigration, is well told and understood—but this period of the Great Atlantic Migration tells another story, less often heard. While large numbers of Europeans left for the New World, even larger numbers stayed in Europe but moved within the continent. Small landowners moved into towns, skilled artisans and workers moved to markets that still appreciated their skills, and unskilled workers of all sorts moved to Europe's growing industrial centers in search of employment. Given the nature of this emigration, its size is more difficult to trace: the migrants were not collected in large, oceangoing vessels, with clear and explicit destinations. But we know that intra-European migration was large and varied: England attracted workers from Ireland, Switzerland from Italy, Germany from Poland and Italy, and France from wherever she could find them. Indeed, France was already a major importer of labor before World War I and was a country of immigration when the rest of Europe was experiencing net emigration. Whatever the reason, we find it convenient to remember the exodus from Europe to the New World while forgetting about the even larger migration streams that crisscrossed Europe at the same time.

After World War II, the same sort of bias in perspective is evident: our attention is drawn to the immigrant experience in Europe. We know that Europe has turned from exporting to importing its workers, and this transition introduces significant challenges. But we must not forget that Europe maintains a heavy ballast of internal migrants, of Europeans moving from one state or region to another. While the external balance may have changed over time, pan-European migration has remained an important and relatively constant feature on the face of European politics.

State of the Union

Before exploring the tricky politics of European migration, we can begin with a simple demographic snapshot. This picture gives us a glimpse of the nature and scope of migration in Europe, lending a backdrop for the discussion that follows.

In 2006, about 3.5 million people moved to a new country within the EU-27.[1] This is a remarkably large number of people—but what does the figure actually capture, and how has it changed in recent years? Of these 3.5 million people, a slight majority (52 percent) came from non-EU countries (roughly distributed across world regions), 34 percent came from other EU member states, and the remaining 14 percent were people returning home after living abroad. Across the EU-27, the rate of immigration is about 7 per mill (‰), that is, 7 immigrants per 1,000 inhabitants.

Of course, people are leaving Europe as well, so if we look at the net migration level in the EU-27, we see more sobering numbers: slightly less than 2 million people (net) entered EU member states from a foreign country. This constitutes much less than 1 percent (actually 0.39 percent) of the total number of inhabitants in the EU-27 that year (2007). As is evident in figure 12.1, this trend jumped around the turn of the millennium, but it now seems to have stabilized.

In 2007, most of these immigrants ended up entering Spain, Italy, and the United Kingdom. But the heaviest hit states (in terms of the size of the immigrant flow relative to the population) were in Cyprus, Spain, Ireland, and Luxembourg, as seen in figure 12.2. These countries experienced immigrant inflows that represented about 1.5 percent of their respective populations. Outside of

Figure 12.1 Net Migration, EU-27

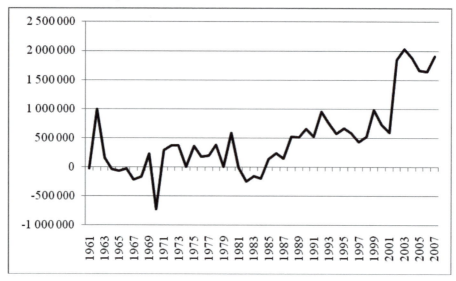

Source: Eurostat Yearbook 2009 (Brussels: EU): 168.

the EU, Iceland, Switzerland, and Norway were also exposed to significant immigration.

Figures 12.1 and 12.2 capture the foreigner's most common means of entry
into European states: worker migration, family reunion, and as students. These
figures reveal a very broad measure of immigration, but there are two additional
categories of migrants that fall outside these statistics: refugees and irregular
migrants.

Figure 12.2 Net Migration in 2007, by Country

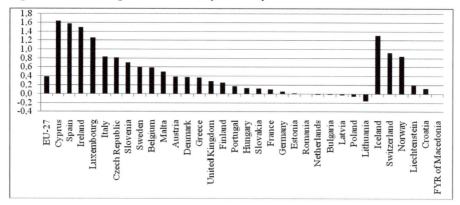

Source: Eurostat Yearbook 2009 (Brussels: EU): 169.

A refugee is someone who has been granted a right to live in a country because the authorities suspect that he or she will suffer persecution at home (e.g., on account of race, religion, nationality, class, group, or even political opinion). This right is granted under the 1951 UN Convention Relating to the Status of Refugees. States that have signed this convention—including all states in Europe—are obliged to take in refugees: this is not something they are allowed to steer for political gain. But signatory states do evaluate asylum claims to see whether they are legitimate. To gain access, then, a person must first apply for asylum, and the host state is obliged to grant asylum if the applicant can show that she or he meets the convention's criteria. As a result of this process, there is a wide spectrum of different types of immigrant status that fall under the refugee rubric.[2]

The size of the asylum stream into Europe is surprisingly small when compared to the more general migration figures shown in figures 12.1 and 12.2. In 2006, the EU-27 received just less than 200,000 asylum applicants, with France, the UK, Sweden, and Germany receiving the largest numbers. This compares to the EU's 3.5 million total immigrants (or roughly 2 million net immigrants). On top of this, about 60 percent of asylum applications are rejected by EU-27 member states. Thus, while the number of asylum seekers is relatively small to start with, an even smaller number of them makes it through the verification process: only about 55,000 refugees were granted protection by EU member states in 2006. This is a remarkably small number of refugees, from a world mired in political conflict, for an area whose total population exceeds 500 million people! Nonetheless, as refugees tend to receive much critical media attention, the public's perception of their numbers is almost always larger than they actually are.

The third remaining source of foreigners is more difficult to measure: this is the stream of undocumented immigrants to Europe. While some rough flow counts are available, attempts at measuring irregular migrant stocks are somewhat more reliable. To take one example, the Hamburg Institute of International Economics estimates that there were between 1.9 and 3.8 million irregular foreigners living in the EU-27 in 2008.[3] This represents somewhere between 0.39 and 0.77 percent of the total population. To get a feel for the size of this irregular stock, Eurostat's estimate of the share of the (regular) foreign-born population in the EU-27 was about 8 percent in that year.

When we combine these three different sources of immigration, we realize that a lot of people are moving around Europe today. A very rough count (including both regular and irregular immigrants and refugees) puts the total (gross) number at around 4.5 million people a year. Roughly 1.7 million of these are people moving within Europe, from one European country to another. This means that a substantial number of foreigners have been arriving in Europe for some time, and we can expect their numbers to accumulate. For this reason, it is important to be familiar with the size of Europe's foreign population stock.

Figure 12.3 presents the share of foreign residents, by state, across Europe in 2009. On average, for the twenty-five member states included in the dataset (for unknown reasons, Belgium and Romania are not included), foreigners make up about 8 percent of the total European population. This average was spread across Europe, with small states such as Luxembourg, Latvia, Cyprus, and Estonia (and non-EU member, Switzerland) reaping the largest shares. This handful of states at the deep end of integration suggests that the distribution of the share of foreigners across Europe reflects the history (the foreign populations of Latvia and Estonia are predominantly Russian) and size of these countries, as much as any evidence of a move toward greater labor market harmonization.

In fact, Europe's share of foreigners is not all that large by international standards. Compared to other world regions, such as North America and Oceania, the broader European migrant stock was relatively small, at 9.5 percent of the population (see table 12.1). This level is especially low when one realizes that the European figures include migrants from other member states of the European Union. On the other hand, compared to Africa, Asia, and Latin America, Europeans do host many foreigners.

There is a substantial amount of migration within and across Europe. Most of this movement comes from beyond Europe's common borders—in the form of broad-based immigrants, refugees, and irregulars. But a significant share consists of fellow Europeans moving around within the EU. The next section

Figure 12.3   Share of Foreign Population by State, 2009

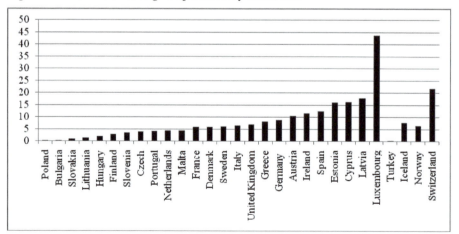

Source: Eurostat 2010.

Table 12.1   International Migration Stocks by World Region, 2010

	Number of Migrants	*Migrant Share (% of Population)*
L. America & Caribbean	7,480,267	1.3
Asia	61,323,979	1.5
Africa	19,263,183	1.9
Europe	69,819,282	9.5
N. America	50,042,408	14.2
Oceania	6,014,693	16.8

Source: United Nations, *Trends in International Migrant Stock: The 2008 Revision*, United Nations database, POP/DB/MIG/Stock/Rev.2008, Department of Economic and Social Affairs, Population Division, 2009, online at http://esa.un.org/migration/index.asp?panel = 1.

seeks to unravel the complex political constellations that channel these migration flows in, and around, Europe.

Levels of Difference

The challenge of understanding European migration patterns lies in the fact that there is no one political authority, or no single set of rules, that applies to each type of migrant. Thus the rules affecting migration between EU member states are different from the rules affecting migration between nonmember states and member states. Worse, those rules can change from member state to member state, and from one type of migration to another. For this reason, it is rather optimistic, even misleading, to speak of an EU migration regime. What we have is a complex, multilevel geometry of political authority governing European migration. The task of this section is to make sense of this confusion.

The easiest way to do this is to break the migrant stream down into three component types: European migration, international migration, and asylum. At this level of generality, one can begin to see the different rules, and constellations of power, that are relevant for understanding the size and nature of the component flows.

EUROPEAN MIGRATION

European migration refers to migrant streams within Europe, but across national borders.[4] This realm is usually seen as the domain of EU politics, as it was one of the fundamental rights secured in the 1957 Treaty of Rome. As such, worker mobility is understood to be an integral part of the logic of Europe's market integration: workers need to be able to move across national borders as freely as do capital, goods, and services.

But this interpretation privileges the European Community. Mobility is a right that is also enjoyed by other workers, whether they originate in nonmember EU states or from further abroad. Already in 1953, the Organization for European Economic Cooperation (OEEC, subsequently the OECD) adopted a rule that facilitated movement across member states: when a job opened up, native workers were given priority for a specified period of time (usually four weeks), after which foreign workers were allowed to compete on an equal footing with native workers. In the following year (1954), the Nordic countries entered into a formal agreement that secured a common labor market across signatory states (Denmark, Finland, Iceland, Norway, and Sweden). Also, several individual states in Europe had remarkably liberal immigration laws in the immediate postwar period (e.g., Switzerland and the UK). In short, worker mobility is not some sort of gift from the European Union—it is an ambition that precedes the Treaty of Rome and one that has found a home in several multinational organizations across Europe.

Still, the Treaty of Rome is often used as a road sign to mark the advent of a European common labor market, and the EU is clearly the most important political mover on this front today. The 1957 treaty embraced the free movement of labor within Europe, and—just as importantly—it provided mobility rights for workers from other member states.

Immediately after World War II, the Treaty of Rome and the OEEC agreement proved insufficient for meeting the labor needs of Europe's growing economy. For this reason, member states found it necessary to open their labor markets by way of a number of bilateral guest-worker agreements, which extended these mobility rights to workers from other countries. Individual states in Europe signed agreements with other states (both within Europe and across the Maghreb) to facilitate temporary migration.

Since then, there has been much progress (and resistance!) in securing a borderless labor market for European workers, and a more secure and fortified border for keeping low-skilled foreign workers at bay. (As we shall soon see, these are two sides of the same coin.) Today, European legislation grants all EU citizens the right to move and settle with their family to any other member state, so long as they are able to support themselves.

The problem is that this EU-wide system applies to more than just EU member states. Actually, when speaking about European-wide labor markets, it is more accurate to refer to the European Economic Area (EEA), created in 1994, and which includes EU member states plus EFTA member states (Iceland, Liechtenstein, and Norway).[5] Add to this the fact that Swiss voters passed a referendum in 2005 that allowed them to participate in this common labor market (effective December 2008). Finally, several non-EU microstates (such as Monaco, Lichtenstein, San Marino, and the Vatican City) participate de facto in the European labor market, as they enjoy open borders with neighboring states that are already integrated into the broader EEA area. Thus, when we speak about a European migration regime, we refer to the mobility rights that exist between most of the EU member states (more on this later), plus the EFTA states, plus Switzerland and the microstates. For this reason, it is more accurate to refer to this area as the EEA+.

Locating the political center of gravity for this variable geometry of European migration issues is anything but straightforward. It tends to shift with the issue space: sometimes it is located in the EU, sometimes it is not. The heterogeneity and institutional rigidities of the EU make it difficult to secure consensus on contentious issues—even when they reflect the core values agreed to in the Treaty of Rome. For this reason, EU member states sometimes find it more convenient to work outside the EU's political framework.

This sort of difficulty is clearly evident in the history of the Schengen Agreement—the original pilot project for today's borderless Europe. In the mid-1980s, the EC's ten member states could not agree among themselves about how to further liberalize the borders that separated them. Five of these states—Belgium, France, Luxembourg, the Netherlands, and West Germany—became impatient with the lack of progress and set out on their own path to a borderless Europe. In 1985, these states met to sign an agreement on a riverboat in Schengen, Luxembourg—an agreement that would remove physical border controls among signatory states. In 1990, this agreement was made into a convention, and other states (both EU member states and not) began to join the club. In 1991, Italy signed the convention, followed by Spain (1992), Portugal (1992), Greece (1995), Austria (1995), and in 1996 the Nordic countries—including the nonmember states Iceland and Norway. It was only with the Amsterdam Treaty in 1999—fourteen years later—that the Schengen Convention was integrated into the EU framework, introducing the Schengen *acquis*.

Since 1999, most of the remaining EU member states have embraced the Schengen idea, if not all its glory. Indeed, most of the subsequent signatory states have only agreed to certain aspects of the larger dream. The original Schengen Agreement was about abolishing border controls and checks among signatory states and creating a unified external border where common rules of entry into the Schengen Area were to be carried out. To facilitate this common border control, signatory states needed to pool and share information in what is now known as the Schengen Information System (SIS) and its supporting network of Supplementary Information Request at the National Entry (SIRENE) offices. (EU bureaucrats have an odd affinity for unwieldy names, so long as they produce sexy acronyms.) This framework, in effect, instituted a system for sharing relevant political and legal information among signatory states.

After the Amsterdam Treaty, most new signatory states to Schengen have only agreed to the police- and judicial-cooperation elements of the treaty—they have not yet agreed to drop their border guards. In other words, one could argue that the police forces of new member states have gained more than their ordinary workers. This is true of the UK (2000), Ireland (2002), and each of the ten new member states in 2004. Since the Amsterdam Treaty, only Switzerland (a non-EU member state) has agreed to full membership in the Schengen Agreement (in 2004, pulling Lichtenstein in with it).[6]

Neither does this area of free mobility apply to workers in all states equally. Old members of the European club have always treated new members with equal doses of caution and suspicion, and the EU has allowed states to employ restrictions on migrants coming from new member states. Thus workers from Greece, Spain, and Portugal were not allowed access to the whole of the European labor market until six years after joining (i.e., Greece in 1987, Spain and Portugal in 1992). The argument for limiting these member state rights was the need to ensure that labor migration from poorer states did not have a sudden and inverse impact on older member state economies. In practice, these concerns proved to be overblown, but that has not stopped today's member states from exploiting the precedent.

Two of the new member states in 2004 managed to avoid this fate. Malta and Cyprus secured immediate access for their workers in the European labor market. But the other eight new members, the A8,[7] met a colder reception (like Greece, Spain, and Portugal before them). A number of protectionist measures were allowed by the EU, as it did not require existing member states to open their labor markets to A8 workers until seven years after their joining (i.e., 2011). In effect, the new member states were not granted full access to EEA+ labor markets unless individual member states granted them dispensation.

Several EEA+ states have done just that. Ireland, Norway, Sweden, and the UK allowed immediate access to workers from the ten new member states. Other states agreed to a variable timeline: some member states agreed to a two-year moratorium (Finland, Greece, Portugal, Spain, and Italy); others to three years (the Netherlands, Luxembourg); four years (France); or five years (Belgium and Denmark); while still others chose to protect their domestic labor markets until the entire grace period had expired (Germany and Austria). Thus EU membership for these eight countries did not offer immediate or full access for their workers, only the promise to secure that access over time.

In theory, worker mobility rights in the EEA+ are impressive. And it is important not to belittle this remarkable and admirable achievement: the opportunities available to millions of workers and their families have been expanded significantly. In practice, however, these rights are too often curtailed by a number of factors. Migrants must be able to prove that they have sufficient means to support themselves (and their families), and member states retain the prerogative to determine nationality and citizenship laws. These constraints, in addition to the barriers of culture and bureaucratic/legal entanglement, mean that the European labor market remains very rigid.

To understand the nature of these constraints, we might look at them from the perspective of a fictional worker. Imagine that you are an unemployed real estate agent from Portugal in search of work in Germany. As an EEA+ citizen, you have a right to enter any other EEA+ member state (including Germany) on presenting a valid form of identification. You can then stay there for six months. At the end of this period, you will need to apply for permission to stay, and that permission will depend on your ability to show one of the following four things: (1) that you are working or self-employed; (2) that you are not a drain on Germany's resources (i.e., that you have enough resources, including health insurance); (3) that you are enrolled in a vocational school (and have the financial support necessary to continue); or (4) that you are a family member of someone who meets one of the three previous requirements. If you meet these criteria and stay for five years, you can then gain a right to permanent residency.

But the constraints do not end here. There are a whole slew of informal constraints that are difficult to overcome. The most striking of these is the formidable language barrier that separates Portuguese from German. And before you move, you will need to check to see if your Portuguese realtors' license is valid in Germany, and you'll have to learn the very different ways that the German real estate market works compared to the Portuguese market. You will need to consider the difficulty of transferring your pension credits and social security benefits, and the very different tax regimes in both countries.

To put this in a comparative perspective, I'll make this personal. Several years ago, I moved from Seattle to Los Angeles to pursue my graduate career. I found the move difficult, not only because I missed the rain. Everything from the traffic rules to the tax code seemed to be different in these two states. Despite these challenges, I was still speaking the same language, still paying taxes to the same federal government, and I didn't even need to change my television news provider (or, more importantly, my brewer). The nature of the constraints facing a Portuguese migrant to Germany is of a whole different order of magnitude.

The European Union is completely aware of these difficulties and how they limit the options available to workers (and the degree of mobility that they can hope to entice). Europe cannot expect to experience the same level of mobility found in the United States—not to mention the degree of mobility we find for capital, goods, and services. But the EU has worked hard for several years (if not decades) to try and minimize these barriers. Already in 1996, the Commission set up a High-Level Panel on the Free Movement of Persons, which identified a number of barriers to mobility and produced eighty (!) recommendations, many of which were included in the Commission's 1997 Action Plan for the Free Movement of Workers. This action plan has been succeeded by others, but the barriers to free mobility across the EEA+ area—although shrinking—remain formidable.

382 JONATHON W. MOSES

But the level of migration across European states remains remarkably low. This is especially problematic for a region where many of these states share a common currency, the euro, as labor mobility and wage flexibility are important means for regional economic adjustment within a common currency area. Labor market integration is a necessary and integral part of the attempt to create a common European-wide market. The asymmetries in this market allow European firms and capital much more freedom of mobility compared to European workers. Compared to the United States, for example, EU citizens are about half as mobile: over the last ten years, 38 percent of EU citizens changed residence, but only about 4 percent of these moved to another member state.[8]

As mentioned briefly in the introduction, the creation of a common labor market plays an important role in the larger European project. The lack of real mobility in Europe is a symbol of the difficulty in creating a common sense of identity and trust across nation-states with deep and conflict-filled histories. While much progress has been made, we still refer to Polish and Portuguese workers—not to European workers—even in an increasingly integrated European labor market.

NON-EUROPEAN IMMIGRATION

Europe's regulatory attitude toward immigrants from beyond the EEA +, so-called third-country nationals (or TCNs), is even more chaotic. One reason for this is that the Treaty of Rome failed to mention external border controls. Another reason is that member states have long histories, some of which include colonialist pasts, and have several good reasons for maintaining special relationships with some third-country nationals. Not to be left out is the recognition that states are often leery of seceding political authority, and physical control of the border is seen by many as a core sovereign right.

It is for these reasons that the regulation of TCN immigration has been located mostly outside of the EU's legal framework: member states jealously guard this area of authority. But it is to this area—the effort to create a common immigration, asylum, and family-reunion policy with respect to TCNs—that the EU is devoting much of its current attention.

Despite these intentions and much supporting rhetoric, there remains remarkable variation across states in Europe with respect to their TCN immigration policies. To illustrate this variation, consider the immigration policies of two neighboring countries in northern Europe, both of which are EU member states: Sweden and Denmark.

Sweden has a remarkably liberal immigration policy with respect to TCNs. Indeed, as we saw in the discussion about Schengen, Sweden has embraced immigrant labor from the new member states as well. In December 2008, the Swedish government introduced new laws and regulations that allow Swedish employers to hire TCN workers directly, if they are not able to find suitable workers in the EEA+ labor pool.

In effect, the Swedish government is giving its employers a free hand to decide which workers are best qualified to do the required work. These employers—not the state—are then put in charge of processing the necessary residence and work permits based on their own assessment of needs. The Swedish Migration Board then ensures that the terms being offered (e.g., salary, insurance protection, and other terms of employment) are in accordance with the rules and standards applied to employees who are already in Sweden. As part of the reform, it has become easier to attend job interviews in Sweden, and permit periods are more easily extended to help match the supply and demand for labor in Sweden.

Just a stone's throw away, across the Kattegat, sits a state whose immigration policy has a much more colored reputation: Denmark. In practice, Danish immigration policy, with respect to skilled TCN workers, is not as restrictive as its reputation would have it. Indeed, the Danish authorities are very active in trying to attract highly skilled workers from outside of Europe, so long as they meet a number of specific criteria, collected under three rubrics: the Danish green-card system, which allocates temporary permits on the basis of age, education, work experience, and language skills; a "positive list," where certain occupations are fast-tracked; and a "pay limit scheme," which provides access to high-salaried foreign employees. But, in contrast to Sweden, the state is a very central actor (and gatekeeper) in this heavily-regulated system.

Denmark's isolationist reputation is earned not from its attitude toward foreign (and skilled) workers, but for its restrictive position with respect to family reunification. In particular, Danish immigration laws block family reunification for non-EU citizens residing in Denmark illegally and in cases where one of the spouses is under the age of twenty-four. Denmark also requires that family reunion applicants sign a declaration of integration before they are granted a right of entry.

In fact, a 2008 ruling of the European Court of Justice (ECJ) challenged this law, to the annoyance of Denmark's authorities. The court's decision prompted Denmark's prime minister, Anders Fogh Rasmussen, to declare, "Denmark determines its own immigration policy and it remains unchanged. . . . The government will not tolerate having its family reunification rules hijacked."[9] Fogh Rasmussen's rebuttal to the ECJ illustrates the challenges facing European Union authorities as they try to streamline and coordinate member state immigration policies. Immigration is a very high-profile and sensitive political issue, and elected national officials are hesitant to secede authority to the European Union, unless this secession brings with it a more restrictive policy that they can defend in front of skeptical constituents.

Despite the resistance of many member state governments, the EU has made much progress in coordinating member state policies and assuming greater authority over wider areas of immigration policy. This evolving role is traced in table 12.2, where we can see immigration and asylum issues being increasingly consolidated under the EU's political mandate.

Given this rapidly changing distribution of authority and responsibility, it makes little sense to focus on the particular institutions involved in forming and implementing Europe's immigration policy. Needless to say, there is a dense network of committees, permanent representatives, and working groups—most of which are associated with the Justice and Home Affairs (JHA) Council—producing a series of five-year action plans: Tampere (1999–2004), The Hague (2005–2009), and Stockholm (2010–2014).

For most Europeans, however, the authority of the European Union in these matters is most evident in its issuing of regulations, directives, decisions, and recommendations. It is important to note that these actions apply to both EU and EFTA states, even if the latter do not have any formal say as to how they are formulated. To illustrate the breadth of this reach, and its controversial nature, we can take a brief glimpse at three important directives, each on an important source of migration: European migration, family reunification, and irregular migration.

- The Services Directive (2004) is one of the most controversial directives to come down the European pipeline. The biggest magnet of controversy was a reference in the original draft to the so-called country-of-origin principle, under which companies registered in any member state could provide services abroad, but under the laws and regulations of the country in which they are registered. This destined the directive to become a focal point in a larger debate about social dumping in Europe. While the "country-of-origin" reference was dropped from the text of the revised directive, its political sting lingered, as it provoked intense debate and mass protests in several countries, including France, Belgium, Sweden, and Denmark. Indeed, the directive became a flashpoint for European integration; it was perceived as a critical test for the Commission's (liberalizing) agenda and a threat to the power of organized labor in Europe.
- The Directive on Family Reunion (2003) came to life only after a rather lengthy and controversial period of negotiation, as it concerns the right to family reunification for TCNs who reside lawfully in the EEA+. The directive sets out the conditions for entry and residence in the EEA+ area, the sort of demands that these states can make on TCNs, and the specific rights that family members have once reunification is granted (e.g., with respect to education and training). The controversial nature of the directive is underscored by the fact that it doesn't apply to all EEA states: Denmark, Ireland, the UK, and Switzerland are not subject to its provisions.
- The Returns Directive (2008) underwent three years of negotiations following the original Commission proposal before final adoption by the European

Table 12.2   Evolving EU Control over Immigration Issues

1976	Council of Ministers' Resolution encouraging member states to develop common immigration policies, in consultation with the Commission.
1985	The Commission issues a series of "Guidelines for a Common Policy on Migration." • But emphasis is on free mobility for EU citizens and equal treatment for all migrants (EU-citizen or not). Commission decision requiring member states to signal in advance future decisions relating to TCNs. • But member states challenged the decision in the ECJ, which delivers a compromise opinion.
1986	With the introduction of the Single European Act and its four freedoms, the Commission interprets "freedom of persons" to mean legally resident people. • But member states issue a declaration affirming their right to control immigration policy.
1992	The Maastricht Treaty attempts to introduce a common migration policy, based on a common asylum and immigration policy and control over a common external border (Art. K.1 EUV). • But the resulting institutional setup, with a third (intergovernmental) "pillar" to deal with Justice and Home Affairs (JHA), effectively prevented this. Decisions needed to be unanimous, and were largely made outside EU institutions.
1999	The Amsterdam Treaty pushes immigration cooperation back to center stage, by incorporating the Schengen Agreement into the EU framework, and taking migration and asylum out of the JHA pillar (and away from intergovernmental cooperation) and into a new Title IV TEC* (concerning visas, asylum, immigration, and other policies related to the free movement of persons). The explicit competences were laid out in articles 62 through 64 and included things like responsibility for assessing asylum claims, action against undocumented migrants, procedures for granting/withdrawing refugee status, and the like. The ECJ was given jurisdiction over immigration issues (but only on referrals from high courts). • But UK, Ireland, and Denmark opt out.
2001	The Nice Treaty places visa, asylum, and immigration policy under the co-decision principle (where the Commission presents proposals, and the text is adopted if it secures the approval of the European Parliament and the Council, where member states vote by qualified majority, QMV). In particular, Article 61 was amended to put a deadline on adopting measures aimed at ensuring free

Table 12.2   (Continued)

	movement within Europe and flanking measures with respect to external border controls, asylum, and immigration. • But the right of member states to determine access to their labor markets by (and integration of) TCNs remains unaffected by the treaty.
2004	FRONTEX, or the Agency for the Management of Operational Cooperation at the External Borders of the Member States of the EU, is created by a Council Regulation to coordinate the border security measures of member states.
2005	Commission green paper on the "EU Approach to Managing Economic Migration" aims to establish a common framework for economic immigration. For example, it proposes to adopt common admission criteria for TCNs, simplify entry procedures, and clarify the rights and legal status of the different types of migrants. It also emphasizes the importance of accompanying measures for ensuring the control of immigration.
2008	Commission creates a European Border Surveillance System (EUROSUR) to prevent unauthorized border crossings, to reduce the number of deaths associated with irregular immigration, and to prevent cross-border crime.
2009	The Lisbon Treaty further increases consolidation: migration and asylum become, in effect, "normal" EU issues, with QMV in the Council, co-decision with the European Parliament, and the ECJ given complete jurisdiction (with referrals now from any-level court). In relation to specific measures, articles 77 through 80 set out provisions on borders, asylum, and migration. • But member states maintain an exclusive right to determine the number of foreign nationals admitted to their territory. Also, cooperation on integration is supplementary and not about the harmonization of laws. EU Blue Card is introduced. The Council adopts a directive to facilitate the entry and residence of TCNs with desired skills for employment in Europe. In effect, it introduces a fast-track procedure for issuing a special residence and work permit. • But UK, Ireland, and DK opt out.

* *TEC refers to the Consolidated Treaty establishing the European Community, i.e., the revised Treaty of Rome.*

Parliament. Its purpose is to lay down EU-wide rules and procedures on the return of irregular immigrants. It covers periods of custody, reentry bans, and a number of legal safeguards. EEA + states are banned from applying harsher rules to irregular immigrants, but they are allowed to keep or adopt more generous rules. In any case, this legislation applies only after a decision has been taken by the national authorities to deport an illegal immigrant: that is, each state retains the authority to decide whether it wishes to regularize or deport the immigrant.

As in the realm of European migration, considerable progress has been made toward establishing a legislative foundation and the institutions necessary to formulate and implement a common immigration policy for TCNs. Immigration and asylum issues have been taken out of an institutional setting that allowed states a veto over sensitive outcomes, and moved into a new institutional setting that is determined mostly by qualified majority voting. While substantial areas of national policy autonomy remain, and national politicians loathe ceding any more authority, the institutional framework now in place ensures that the EU can advance its common immigration policy.

ASYLUM

Europe believes that it must erect imposing and common barriers toward the outside world if its internal market is to work as planned. A common internal market implies a common external front. Given the political history of Europe's component states, it has proven quite difficult to secure consensus over the rules governing family reunion and immigration from TCNs. These sorts of constraints do not hinder Europe's common asylum policy, at least not to the same degree. It is for this reason that we see most progress on developing a common front in the area of Europe's asylum policy.

The willingness of states to cooperate has resulted in an ambitious attempt to standardize national approaches, processes, applications, and recognition of status for protection. The end result of this collaboration has been a generally more restrictive policy with respect to asylum across Europe—if only because the number of potential asylum havens has diminished, thereby limiting the opportunities available to asylum seekers.

Since the Amsterdam Treaty, one European agreement after the other has signaled an interest in creating a common European asylum policy. In particular, the Nice Treaty moved asylum issues from the third to the first pillar of European governance, allowing asylum decisions to be carried out by majority voting. This means that member states lost their right to veto policies that they oppose, accelerating the development of a common policy in this area. In short, the EU intends to create a common EEA-wide asylum system. This system would rely on a single procedure, mutual recognition of member state decisions, and the creation of an institutional hub at the European Asylum Support Office. So far, a European-wide asylum system rests on four important components:

- The first of these is known as the Dublin Regulation from 2003, the objective of which is to identify (as quickly as possible) the member state responsible for examining an asylum application, to establish reasonable time limits for each of the phases of determining the member state responsible, and to prevent abuse of asylum procedures in the form of multiple applications. In effect, this regulation creates a one-stop asylum procedure, where asylum applicants are forced to make a claim in the first EEA+ state that they enter or pass through. The system is designed to prevent "asylum shopping" and, at the same time, to ensure that each asylum applicant's case is processed by only one member state. Thus, if you enter the EEA+ space through Italy but settle in Denmark, your application for asylum needs to be filed in Italy, and Italy alone.

- The second component of a European-wide asylum system is anchored in the Reception Conditions Directive (2003), which introduced minimum standards for reception and detention (e.g., access to information, labor markets, health care, etc.). The motivation behind the directive was to ensure that asylum applicants received a dignified standard of living, wherever they settled in the EEA+ area. This is especially important now that asylum seekers have lost their ability to choose the state that will examine their application (due to the Dublin Regulation, above).

- The third component lies in the Asylum Procedures Directive of 2005, where states are obliged to agree on minimum standards for processing asylum claims. In particular, the directive grants certain basic procedural guarantees (e.g., the right to a lawyer and interpreter, access to the United Nations High Commissioner for Refugees [UNHCR], and the right to appeal).

- Finally, the Qualifications Directive (2004) establishes minimum standards for granting and withdrawing refugee status. The objective of this directive is to establish common criteria for identifying persons who need international protection (and to ensure that they are granted a minimum level of benefits). In particular, the directive provides minimum standards for protection from "refoulement" (the forced return of a person to a country where he or she faces persecution); maintaining family unity; and access to employment, education, health care, and so forth.

These four legislative steps have brought the European Union much closer to a common asylum policy, and the future will surely bring even more harmonization and streamlining. But there is still a very long way to go before Europe's asylum policies and practices are completely harmonized. National governments continue to wield significant power, and national practices are remarkably diverse.

This diversity can be seen in the different rates by which member states still reject (or, inversely, recognize) asylum claims. For example, in 2007, the rejection rate ranged from a low of just under 30 percent (in Poland) to 98.6 percent (in Greece). National differences are also evident in the very different ways that member states responded to recent asylum streams from Afghanistan, Iraq, and

Chechnya. In short, states interpret common regulations in different ways and employ derogation clauses that allow them to maintain national policies and interests. The end result is a lack of harmonization, both in terms of recognition and reception conditions.

Shades of Difference

Thus far I have aimed to paint a face of European immigration that is varied but not threateningly different. As we have seen, European immigration levels are not especially high in a global perspective, Europeans have been on the move for centuries, and a significant share of European migration comes from other European states.

My intent with this depiction is to temper a more common perception of Europe—a picture of Europe full to the gills with foreigners (mostly draped in burkas and turbans), and going quickly to hell in a handbasket. Foreigners are seen as a growing threat to romanticized images of the European polity, bringing with them values and social practices that threaten the essence of European traditions. This picture is familiar to anybody following European politics in recent years, and I would like to close this chapter by reflecting on some of the integration challenges facing Europe today.

THE RISE OF THE RIGHT

In recent decades, the radical right has gained significant political support in Europe. In almost every European country, it is possible to find a nationalist party that is poised to exploit voter dissatisfaction and alienation. The radical right has gained enough support to enter government coalitions in Austria, Denmark, Italy, the Netherlands, and Switzerland. Vehement national parties can also be found in Belgium, Bulgaria, France, Finland, Greece, Hungary, Latvia, Romania, and Slovakia (though they are not yet strong enough to enter government).

This political landscape is marked by a number of important and influential political figures, whose political successes have rippled across Europe. In France, Jean-Marie Le Pen's National Front has been the third-largest party for most of the millennium, and he was runner-up in the 2002 French presidential elections. In 2000, Jörg Haider—then leader of the FPÖ (Freedom Party of Austria)—joined a coalition government that sent the European Union into a political frenzy. In the Austrian elections of 2008, far-right parties captured 30 percent of the vote, and in the Netherlands, Geert Wilders' Partij voor de Vrijheid (Party for Freedom, PVV) finished as the third-biggest party in the country's 2010 elections.

The nationalist right is rising at the European level as well. In the June 2009 European Parliament (EP) elections, almost a million Brits voted for the British National Party (BNP), giving the party its first two seats in the EP. In the Netherlands, Geert Wilders' PVV won second place. Similar parties managed to gain around 15 percent of the European vote in Austria, Denmark, Hungary, and Slovakia.

These are complex and varied political movements, responding mostly to local conditions in each country. This makes it difficult to generalize about them. But they do share some common features, the most common of which are a very critical view of the current state of affairs and a strong and explicit distrust of foreigners, especially Muslims.

From an outsider's perspective, Europeans seem intent on provoking conflict. Danish newspaper editors gloated in their stubborn determination to publish offensive caricatures of the Prophet Muhammad in 2005. Voters in a 2009 referendum in Switzerland accepted a constitutional amendment banning the construction of new minarets. Across Europe, politicians debate whether and how to regulate the religious attire of their increasingly diverse populations (in an effort to liberate women from what they see as the tyranny of the veil). Clearly, something is amiss in Europe—and its problems seem to be connected to immigration.

WHERE'S THE BEEF?

The rhetoric of the radical right links its rise to increasing immigration to Europe. The net numbers lend some credence to this claim. As we saw in figure 12.1, net immigration to the EU-27 countries increased dramatically, more than doubling, at the turn of the millennium (although it has since leveled off). It could be that the intensity and pace of this immigration surge is driving European xenophobia. But this interpretation should be tempered by the realization that Europe's share of foreigners, as a percentage of population, is not particularly high from a global perspective, as we saw in table 12.1.

Neither is the size of Europe's Muslim population particularly high. Figure 12.4 ranks European countries by the share of their Muslim population. Here we see a very significant variation separating Ireland (0.01 percent) and Slovakia (0.02 percent) from France (10 percent) and Bulgaria (11.9 percent). On average, however, the percentage of the EEA+ population that is Muslim is only about 2.2 percent.[10] This is very close to the 2.19 percent we find in North America and is not especially high or threatening in its own right. Given the remarkably small size of the Muslim population in Europe (2.2 percent!), it draws an inordinate amount of critical attention.

Whatever the reason, foreigners in Europe are treated differently. Evidence of this is seen in the variance in unemployment levels between foreigners and

Figure 12.4   Muslim Population

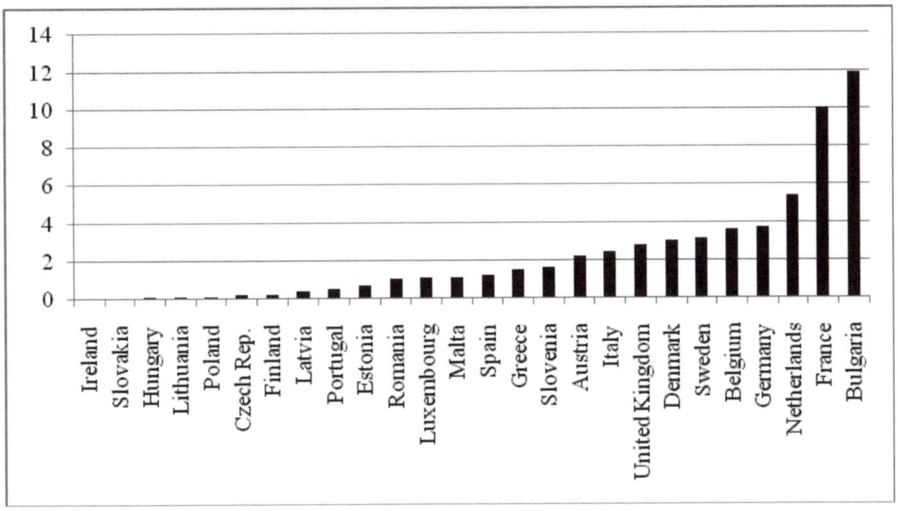

Source: Islamicpopulation.com (2008)

nationals across European labor markets. Figure 12.5 compares these unemployment spreads. Here we see that foreigners in the EU-27 average have an unemployment rate that is more than double that of EU-27 nationals (14.4 percent compared to 6.7 percent for nationals), but the spread differs remarkably across Europe, with Luxembourg and Belgium hosting the largest spread, whereas foreigners in Cyprus and Greece enjoy a lower unemployment rate than the natives (!), or the rates are indistinguishable.

In short, it would seem that Europeans have a difficult time integrating their foreigners—even in the labor market, where most of the EU's legal and political attention has been focused. To understand this difficulty, we need to glance back on the history of nationalism in Europe, and at the competing perceptions of how to control membership in Europe's national communities.

NATIONALISM AND INTEGRATION

Immigration has a long history of challenging traditional conceptions of community. This history is complicated, in that its effect works in two opposing directions. On the one hand, migrants provide a convenient benchmark for defining "the other." On the other hand, immigration forces communities to consider ways by which newcomers can (or cannot) be incorporated into that community.

The first lesson is clearly seen in the long history of European migration, as briefly traced in the introduction to this chapter. It is a history that has al-

Figure 12.5   Unemployment Spreads in Europe, by Country, 2008

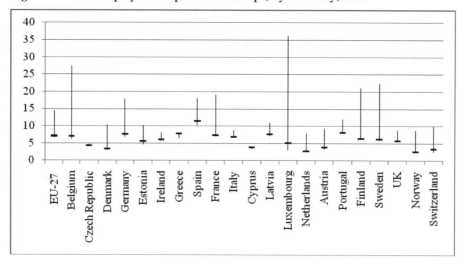

Source: Eurostat 2010.

ways brought communities into contact with foreigners—whether they are from across the valley, the continent, or the globe.

Today we think of the foreigner in terms of religion or skin color, but differences can be spun out of almost anything (or nothing at all). Indeed, during earlier periods of (intra-European) migration, the migrant in question did not look or act any differently from his or her host: they often shared the same religion, diets, music, and traditions—but host communities still excluded the migrants as outsiders, as foreign. We have a remarkable capacity to find (and to generate) the differences we use to separate ourselves.

This primitive sentiment was exacerbated by a system of nation-states built on national myths. The modern nation-state system was born in northern Europe with the Treaty of Westphalia in 1648. Its modern forms of citizenship were the result of a very European debate about the source of nationhood (and membership in the national community) and competing conceptions of how new members should be integrated into those national communities.

While these traditions are slowly eroding, they continue to influence the way that many Europeans think about membership and inclusion in the political community. These attitudes also hamper attempts by Europe's political elites to create a new common identity for all Europeans.

- *Citizenship.* There have been two main traditions by which membership in the political community was determined in Europe: *jus sanguinis* and *jus soli*. *Jus sanguinis* grants citizenship on the basis of ethnicity (it is Latin, meaning "right of blood"), so that a person gains access to citizenship by being born of parents who are already citizens of the state. Traditionally, this has been the most common means of allocating citizenship in continental Europe, and Germany is usually seen as the archetype. The alternative source of citizenship, *jus soli* ("right of soil"), provides citizenship to any individual born in the territory of the state, even if the child's parents were ethnically foreign. The archetype for this source of citizenship is republican France. As it becomes easier to migrate and settle across Europe, we might expect Europeans to abandon *sanguini* traditions of citizenship. After all, the birthright (*soli*) tradition of citizenship facilitates immigrant inclusion (as immigrants cannot choose the ethnicity of their parents). Instead, we find a convergence of citizenship traditions in Europe, as states such as Germany soften up their *sanguini* positions, while countries such as France have scuttled important *soli* components.

- *Integration.* On top of these competing conceptions of citizenship lies another relevant cleavage. States in Europe have maintained different traditions for incorporating or integrating new members into the political community. While the first (citizenship) cleavage concerns an individual's access to rights, obligations, and privileges, the second cleavage concerns the character or nature of the resulting community. Here, too, we can distinguish between two main variants: assimilationist and multiculturalist integration strategies. Assimilationists believe that immigrants benefit most if they become part and parcel of the new community. In effect, immigrants are expected to grow into the host culture, adopting its norms and values. This assimilation is directed by a number of host culture institutions (e.g., schools, local communities, state officials, etc.), but also by families and civic-society organizations. In Europe, the archetypical state in this tradition is France, where immigrants are not encouraged to embrace their ethnic or national background or to describe themselves as Algerian-French (as Norwegian-Americans do in the United States, for example). Rather, a Frenchman is a Frenchman is a Frenchman. Multiculturalists, by contrast, celebrate difference; they are less concerned about the need to fuse immigrant and host communities together. Instead, the emphasis is on encouraging tolerance and pluralism so that different immigrant communities can coexist with, without feeling threatened by, the host community. In this approach, the host community's efforts are directed at ensuring that immigrant groups are not disadvantaged with respect to established groups, and at creating social conditions that encourage tolerance. From the EU's perspective, it makes sense to encourage member states to embrace multiculturalist approaches: the creation of a common European identity cannot be facilitated by a mushrooming of twenty-seven competing assimilationist responses!

Some of Europe's growing xenophobia may be explained by the way that increased integration challenges attitudes borne of these competing conceptions of citizenship and integration. More to the point, these competing conceptions represent a serious challenge to the effort by Europe's political elites to create a new, and common, *European* identity.

This challenge is particularly difficult in Europe, if only because the modern nation-state was born there, and the concept of (and debate about) nationhood has deep roots in European soil. It is, after all, this strong sense of nationalism that is often blamed for Europe's affinity for war and conflict; and it is this sort of nationalist history that the European Union is designed to overcome. The point of creating a pan-European identity is not just to create a common European market so that producers can sell more products. One of the driving logics of the European project has been to create a common sense of identity in order to overcome national identities, which have too often led to war and conflict.

To bridge these competing conceptions of nationhood, citizenship, and integration, Europe needs to create a common political space where different nationalities can meet and meld. Somehow it needs to navigate the treacherous waters that separate *jus soli* from *jus sanguinis*, and assimilationists from multiculturalists. It is this tricky navigational task that the next section considers.

POLITICAL EFFORTS AT INTEGRATION

Like everything else in Europe, competing integration policies can be seen at different levels of government. At the member state level, vestiges of earlier traditions continue to linger, but more European states seem to be embracing assimilationist strategies.

In particular, a growing number of European states now require potential TCN immigrants to take an exam that tests their capacity to integrate. Best known of these, perhaps, is the "Civic Integration Examination Abroad" given to non-EU immigrants to the Netherlands at the Dutch embassy of the sending country in question. This examination consists of a half-hour-long film, some questions (in Dutch) about the film, and a more general test of the potential immigrant's Dutch-language skills. But there is nothing unique about the Netherlands in this regard: other countries conduct similar tests (including the UK, Denmark, France, and Germany).

Increasingly, European states expect TCN immigrants to assimilate into the distinct national cultures of the host country. These states expect immigrants to bear the costs of integration; by implication, they do not see a need to facilitate integration by changing national attitudes or institutions. At the national level, the effort of integration is aimed at minimizing the original distance separating the foreigner (on arrival) from the host culture.

The strategy at the European level is somewhat different, if not fully developed. The EU is obviously concerned about the problem, but it can hardly support twenty-seven different assimilation policies, where each new TCN immigrant is turned into a new mininationalist! Instead, the EU's legislative efforts have aimed to secure immigrants' equal treatment and protection from discrimination after they arrive. While member states lean in the direction of more assimilationist policies, the EU's thrust has been in a more multiculturalist direction.

In particular, the EU's focus is trained on deterring abuses and discrimination in member states. By implication, the problem of integration lies in national frameworks that require correction. This concern is long lasting, and we can see it early on in the EC's desire to make jobs available to foreign workers from other EU states, or by TCNs already working in Europe.

Indeed, the treatment of TCNs has been a hot-potato issue for several years between the EU and its member states. Already in 1986, with the Single European Act's (SEA's) commitment to the four freedoms, the Commission was anxious to interpret the freedom of persons to include legally resident TCNs—but member states wanted this freedom to be restricted to EU citizens only. In 1999, the Tampere European Council emphasized the need to harmonize national legislation on the conditions for admission and residence of TCNs.

In 2003, the Commission introduced a directive (2003/109/EC) that created a single status for long-term TCN residents to ensure their equal treatment across the EU, regardless of state residence. While the original ambitions were admirable, the resulting legislation was watered down by a number of national requirements, including a German demand for favoring the treatment of nationals over TCNs. Member states were also allowed to set numerical quotas on TCNs and to require them to comply with integration measures (such as taking the sort of language classes referenced above).

On a parallel front, Europe is developing a common antidiscrimination policy. The seeds of this policy were planted in the 1997 Treaty of Amsterdam, where the Community gained new powers in Article 13 to combat discrimination. These seeds have begun to bear fruit in the form of three directives. The first two of these were enacted in 2000. The Race Discrimination Directive (2000/43) guarantees equal treatment of people, irrespective of racial or ethnic origin, while the Equal Treatment Framework Directive (2000/78) provides a framework for equal treatment at the job (or training) site. As these directives were limited to the sphere of employment, the Commission has more recently (July 2, 2008) issued a new draft directive on antidiscrimination, which is intended to extend antidiscrimination protections into areas that go beyond employment.

Mostly the EU has talked about the need for action but has accomplished very little. Since 2002, the EU has issued annual reports on migration and integration, which basically review trends in member state integration policies and identify common barriers; it has published a handbook on integration (2004), which lists a number of best practices; and EU leaders have adopted several (mostly common-sense) principles for immigrant integration policy. It has established the European Union Agency for Fundamental Rights (FRA) and the European Commission against Racism and Intolerance (ECRI) to document and advise on these sorts of issues. In the same year (2004), the Commission proposed a "Common Agenda for Integration," which included some very concrete proposals (such as boosting participation of immigrant women in the workplace, promoting interfaith dialogue, etc.), but—like all the measures noted in this paragraph—none of its proposals were binding.

More promising is the European Fund for the Integration of TCNs—an €825-million fund (covering the 2007–2013 period) to help member states enable TCNs in their attempt to integrate into their host countries. Tellingly, Denmark is the only member state to have opted out.

Conclusion

Even though Europe has a long relationship and much experience with migration, it has not been able to develop a coordinated response to the challenges of migration, whether the migrants are workers from other member states or TCNs from abroad. Europe's difficulty is evident in the relatively low levels of internal (European) migration and the frighteningly high levels of support for the xenophobic parties of the radical right.

The European Union has worked hard to try and overcome these difficulties, and recent developments have clearly shifted more responsibility for migration issues from member states up to the EU level. But the unwillingness of member states to consistently adopt European policies that apply to issues of mobility, immigration, and integration has meant that the European policy space with respect to migration issues is remarkably complex.

To provide some order to these overlapping ambitions, policies, and outcomes, I have divided immigration issues up into three main areas: European migration, international immigration, and asylum. Within each of these areas, I have shown how different states interpret and respond to EU proposals, and this variance makes it difficult to refer to any common EU policy platform with respect to migration issues.

This variance is also evident in the ways in which member states and the EU respond to the growing challenges of integration. With the growth of nationalist sentiment and the radical right, we see a plethora of attempts to require foreigners to assimilate into diverse national political cultures. The EU's response to this development has been a rather feeble attempt to discourage discrimination.

Suggested Readings

Bauböck, Rainer (ed.), *Migration and Citizenship: Legal Status, Rights and Political Participation*, Amsterdam: Amsterdam University Press, 2006.

Boswell, Christina, and Andrew Geddes, *Migration and Mobility in the European Union*, Palgrave, 2011.

Luedtke, Adam, "The European Union Dimension: Supranational Integration, Free Movement of Persons, and Immigration Politics," in Craig A. Parsons and Timothy M. Smeeding (eds.), *Immigration and the Transformation of Europe*, Cambridge: Cambridge University Press, 2006, pp. 419–441.

Papademetrious, Demetrios, *Coming Together or Pulling Apart? The European Union's Struggle with Immigration and Asylum*, Washington, DC: Carnegie Endowment for International Peace, 1996.

CHAPTER 13

Still at the Crossroads: Europe, the United States, and NATO

Simon Duke and Roberta Haar

In spite of NATO's apparent longevity, it remains at a critical juncture. On the one hand, NATO has confounded numerous detractors who postulated that with the end of the Cold War the glue had disappeared from the alliance, and it would, inexorably, come undone.[1] On the other hand, NATO's future survival continues to depend on whether it can meet the security challenges of the post–Cold War world. As Richard Lugar pointed out, the future of the alliance depends on its ability to meet "the challenge of going out of area, or out of business."[2] This process of adaptation or even reinvention continues in the form of a New Strategic Concept for the alliance, unveiled in November 2010.

NATO's secretary general, Anders Fogh Rasmussen, has further outlined four principal challenges for the alliance. First, NATO must build relations with Russia, as it is a major security partner on a wide spectrum of issues ranging from Afghanistan, counterterrorism, and nonproliferation of weapons of mass destruction (WMDs) to the fight against organized crime. Second, NATO must evidence a willingness to adopt longer-term roles in Afghanistan, especially supervising the process of transition to a full Afghan lead. Third, NATO must clarify its relations with the European Union (EU), since the alliance's metamorphosis from a collective-defense alliance to a broader-based security organization means that there is the potential for considerable overlap in terms of mission. Fourth, the launch of the New Strategic Concept mandates that NATO must demonstrate value for money to NATO taxpayers in what Rasmussen describes as "a process of continual reform."[3]

This chapter will explore the nature of NATO's crossroads by first examining the journey from collective defense, the original purpose of the alliance, to what we have termed its existential crisis. The chapter then briefly looks at the pros and cons of NATO's enlargement to twenty-eight members, including a consideration of the general implications of enlargement for the alliance. The next four sections consider Rasmussen's themes mentioned above, commencing with the future of NATO's relations with Russia. We then consider NATO's involvement in Afghanistan, in particular the idea that Afghanistan is a litmus test for the alliance's ability to meet new global security challenges. The fifth section considers Rasmussen's observations on the complicated relationship between NATO and the EU. This relationship is based on the assumption that NATO and the EU display facets of both cooperative as well as competitive behavior. The sixth part looks beyond the crossroads by considering the New Strategic Concept and the extent to which it is likely to reinvigorate the alliance. The final section, as befitting an organization in its sixtieth decade, considers the possible future directions that the alliance could take. Two polar positions are considered, that of NATO's eminent demise, due to irrelevance, and the possibility that the alliance will enjoy a rebirth and prove its enduring significance. A third default scenario assumes that NATO continues to survive, albeit with a number of fundamental questions about its longer-term health left unanswered.

From Collective Defense to Existential Crisis

NATO is a product of the early Cold War period, and so NATO's formation must be understood within the overall postwar goals of securing and integrating Europe. Postwar security concerns centered first on the Soviet-communist threat that became apparent not long after the Soviet Union refused to observe its election promises in Eastern Europe while at the same time it supported subversive communist groups in Greece and Turkey and put pressure on Iran. A communist coup in Czechoslovakia and the Berlin blockade in 1948 reinforced the realization that the Soviet Union was a potent physical threat to Europe. The Western response to this threat was to form NATO with the signing of the Washington Treaty on April 4, 1949. The preamble to the treaty sets forth the general aims of membership of the alliance as being to "promote stability and well-being in the North Atlantic area. [The members] are resolved to unite their efforts for collective defense and for the preservation of peace and security."[4] The danger of the emerging Cold War turning hot was considered the greatest threat in the early 1950s in the aftermath of North Korea's invasion of South Korea. The first chancellor of the Federal Republic of Germany, Konrad Adenauer, reflected this fear when he recorded in his memoirs that "Stalin was planning the same procedure for West Germany as had been used for Korea."[5]

Throughout the Cold War, NATO was the cornerstone of the Western alliance. The protection offered by NATO allowed some of the European allies to move ahead with various types of economic and, eventually, political integration. During the evolution of the European Coal and Steel Community, to the creation of the European Economic Community (EEC) in 1957, to the attachment of the foreign and security aspects of the newly formed union at the tail end of the Cold War, NATO provided the framework for high-level foreign and security policy discussions to take place. In essence, NATO and its close ties to the United States provided a security environment in which the EEC, the European Community, and then the European Union could take shape. The Western European Union (WEU), created in 1954, extended an existing self-defense treaty, signed by Belgium, France, the Netherlands, Luxembourg, and the United Kingdom, to include Italy and the Federal Republic of Germany.[6] The WEU would spend much of its life in the shadow first of NATO and, more recently, that of the EU as it handed over its collection of defense-related tasks, known as the Petersberg tasks after the picturesque German town where they were agreed upon, to the EU.

The overwhelming military and political weight of the United States during this period, symbolized by 326,000 American military personnel based in various European countries, meant that it was an American-dominated alliance. As such, NATO was often subject to buffeting by variations in political barometric pressures within the alliance. Indeed each decade starting from the 1950s had an alliance crisis, with NATO often acting as the conduit for the expression of transatlantic discontent. The Suez crisis of 1956 saw Britain and France at variance with the United States and was followed, a mere decade later, by the demands of General Charles de Gaulle for all U.S. military installations to be withdrawn from French soil. Other debates, such as those surrounding the controversial placement of Pershing II or ground-launched cruise missiles in Europe in the 1980s, also proved highly divisive across the Atlantic, as well as within the members themselves. Some of the winds came the other way across the Atlantic, such as the divisive burden-sharing debates, sparked by Senator Mike Mansfield in the 1970s, which alleged free riding by the allies. NATO was therefore no stranger to differences between its members, but in the context of the Cold War, there was always the glue of the common external threat posed by the Soviet Union and the Warsaw Pact to keep any centrifugal forces in check.

The end of the Cold War and the lack of any obvious enemy against whom NATO could concentrate its energies gave rise to fundamental questions about the direction and the utility of the alliance. Doctrinally, NATO was quick to adapt to the changing circumstances of the post–Cold War world. In practice, however, NATO was slower to adapt, and as will be examined later, there are diverging opinions on the extent to which it has really adapted at all. Even post–Cold War operations, such as Operation Deliberate Force in Bosnia-Herzegovina in 1995 and Operation Allied Force against the Federal Republic of Yugoslavia in 1999, while nominally successful, raised as many questions about the future of the alliance as they apparently answered.

Two different lessons were gleaned from these operations that would have the overall effect of weakening the standing of the alliance. First, the obvious reliance upon not only American military power but also diplomatic influence spurred the ambitions of some European allies for more foreign and security policy autonomy as an integral part of wider European integration. Second, the

Table 13.1   Timeline of NATO, the European Union, and the West European Union

Year	North Atlantic Treaty Organization (NATO)	European Community / European Union	West European Union
1948–1949	Washington Treaty		Brussels Treaty
1954–1955	Warsaw Pact created	European Defense Community fails	Modified Brussels Treaty
1957		Rome Treaty (European Economic Community)	
1966	France withdraws from integrated military command		
1970		European Political Cooperation	
1986		Single European Act	
1989	Warsaw Pact dissolves		
1992–1993	First Gulf War	Maastricht Treaty (Common Foreign and Security Policy)	Petersberg Tasks
1997		Amsterdam Treaty	
1999–2001	New Strategic Concept	Nice Treaty	Marseille Declaration
2003		European Security Strategy	
2009		Lisbon Treaty	
2010	New Strategic Concept		Treaty Terminated

technical, logistical, and even political inability (as well as a measure of unwillingness) of a number of the European allies to work with American forces strengthened Washington's determination to avoid planning and running operations through the North Atlantic Council (NAC), NATO's highest civilian-level body. Instead, Washington's preference would be for handpicked allies, or "coalitions of the willing," to collaborate in geostrategic locations, with the United States as the dominant partner. This preference explains why, when the European members of NATO invoked for the first (and only) time the collective defense commitment (in Article 5) of the North Atlantic Treaty in the immediate aftermath of the 9/11 attacks, the Pentagon rebuffed them.[7] This snub would subsequently have influence on European political debates about the desirable level of association or autonomy from NATO and the United States.

The growing American preference to work with coalitions of the willing undermined the utility of the alliance as a discussion forum for the security issues of the day and as a base upon which future consensual action could be built. Nowhere was this more true than in the case of the multinational force (MNF) in Iraq, arguably one of the biggest foreign and security policy actions of the decade and one in which both NATO and the EU were essentially bypassed. The net result of the successive use of coalitions is that NATO has become less of an alliance and more of a toolbox out of which the necessary coalitions can be assembled.

The NATO Response Force (NRF), first suggested by U.S. secretary of defense Donald Rumsfeld in 2002, was designed in part to allay the growing concerns about reliance on coalitions of the willing. The NRF is intended for worldwide missions addressing many different types of scenarios, but with the primary purpose of acting as a short-term stabilization or bridgehead force preparing the way, if need be, for larger follow-on missions. The NRF is composed of land, sea, and air components made available by NATO members on a rotating six-month basis. The response force can number up to 25,000 troops, can commence deployment after five days' notice, and can be sustained for up to thirty days or longer.

In spite of the potential of the NRF on paper, it has been activated for duties that were arguably not envisaged as core missions. In August 2004, the NRF was used for protection duties at the Summer Olympics in Athens, and from September to October 2005 it was deployed to assist in Hurricane Katrina disaster relief. From October 2005 until February 2006, the NRF was deployed in earthquake relief in Pakistan. Despite the police and humanitarian nature of these deployments, the NRF remains, according to NATO's own website, "the driving engine of NATO's military transformation."[8] Such statements add to the confusion concerning the direction of the alliance as well as its relations with the EU, which has also created a more modest version of the NRF under the Battlegroup concept, with a similarly broad range of missions in mind.[9]

Alongside the creation of the NRF, new threats have been promoted as potential sources of alliance solidarity. Ivo Daalder, before he became the U.S. ambassador to NATO for the Barack Obama administration, argued that Washington viewed its European NATO allies as crucial partners in "trying to defeat the terrible trinity of terrorists, tyrants and technologies of mass destruction." However, Daalder also emphasized that in the wake of 9/11, Washington viewed Europe as a partner only when it supported "the fundamental course that Washington is embarked upon."[10] The perspectives of the European allies do not necessarily match the clear perception of NATO's mission from an American perspective. This would explain part of the evident frustration expressed by the allies when faced with American demands for military transformation, especially if any such efforts are not reciprocated by a corresponding share in allied decision making. But more importantly, in spite of the apparently compelling nature of the threat posed by the "terrible trinity," none has demonstrated the sticking power of the Cold War threat of massive tank and troop movements coming through the Hof Corridor or the Fulda Gap. Disagreements exist across the Atlantic as well as among the alliance members about how pressing these threats are as well as the best means to address them. To NATO's critics, there is no inherent reason why NATO should meet such threats or challenges specifically, thus denying the alliance a compelling future raison d'être. Unlike the Cold War era, where NATO and the Warsaw Pact were the primary security actors and antagonists, the current era has many more actors, ranging from the United Nations (UN) to the Organization for Security and Cooperation in Europe (OSCE) and the EU, that also have a role to play in addressing new security challenges.

NATO continues to be buffeted by conflicting opinions about its usefulness, the extent to which it can and should be modified, and more practical issues concerning the preparedness and interoperability of its members. Politically, the alliance remains caught between the transatlantic upheavals during the eight years of George W. Bush's presidency and the question of whether any discernable "Obama bounce" will repair divisive transatlantic (and intra-Europe) differences over Iraq and Afghanistan. Although the arrival of the Obama administration in January 2009 was highly popular in Europe, it is evident that some of the shine has rubbed off and that many of the difficulties in transatlantic relations, which were so readily ascribed to the Bush administration, remain.[11] A new, and possibly uncomfortable, truth has emerged in which European and American priorities and perspectives are changing, perhaps with longer-term implications for NATO. One of the tests of the vitality of an organization is often its ability to attract new members.[12] NATO has enlarged over the years to twenty-eight members, but there are important questions about the alliance's power of attraction, as well as the wisdom of further enlargement, which are addressed in the following portion of this chapter.

Now We Are at Twenty-Eight

NATO has enlarged seven times since it was founded in 1949. The last two members, Albania and Croatia, joined in NATO's sixtieth year. There are currently twenty-eight members, with another twenty-two engaged in the Partnership for Peace (PfP). The latter enables countries to enter into an individually tailored partnership program (IPAP) that, in some cases, will be the precursor to a membership action plan (MAP) with eventual membership. The value of the PfP lies in its ability to extend military integration and interoperability beyond current NATO members, which in turn can serve as the basis for NATO's adaptability to its political and military nonthreat security missions.[13]

Nation-states that might in the future become members of NATO are located to the east and the south of current members. Any expansion of membership to the east, however, is conditioned by NATO/U.S.-Russia relations, which remain exceedingly divisive. For example, the 2008 alliance summit in Bucharest proved highly discordant when, based on strong American support for Ukrainian membership and close military cooperation with Georgia, a political commitment to eventual Ukrainian and Georgian membership was made. But an actual MAP was not offered because of European resistance, especially Franco-German, to Ukrainian membership. European opposition was based on reluctance to further antagonize relations with Russia, which were already strained by plans to install a missile defense system in Poland and the Czech Republic. The current official position on Ukraine and Georgia, reiterated at the Strasbourg-Kehl summit of April 2009, is that they will at some point become NATO members.[14] For the immediate future, any potential eastern candidates will remain caught between what Russian president Dmitry Medvedev refers to as Russia's "sphere of influence" and NATO's (and the EU's) attempts to define its eastern boundaries.[15]

Other future NATO members are more likely to be from the south rather than the east. For instance, the former Yugoslav Republic of Macedonia has started a MAP. However, its eventual membership remains paralyzed due to disputes with Greece over the use of the name Republic of Macedonia. In December 2009, Montenegro also embarked upon a MAP, while Bosnia-Herzegovina anticipates one, subject to prior reforms, and Serbia has initiated an IPAP. Membership to the south, especially on the part of the Western Balkans, can be aided and abetted by their applications to the EU. Although the membership processes for NATO and the EU are distinct, the insistence upon similar principles and standards of behavior are obviously mutually reinforcing.

The classical justification for enlarging the alliance is that it increases NATO's general deterrent effect. In the post–Cold War context, such arguments are, however, weakened both by the lack of any immediate and plausible armed threat to NATO's members, as well as by the fact that many of the potential enlargement countries bring little to the table in terms of resources and capabilities. This has led some, like Julian Lindley-French, to observe that NATO enlargement is paradoxical because, "while embracing states in a security regime is normally deemed to reinforce its strength, this is by no means automatically the case, either in the context of European security or in the case of NATO."[16] For the aspiring members, the question is whether they wish to join the alliance because of what it *was* or, at a time of continual reform, for what it might be? The response to this question and the willingness or ability of any new members to bring resources to the table will have important consequences for the alliance.

The second justification for NATO's growth is that it is part and parcel of the strengthening of democratic institutions and practices. The alliance's 1991 strategic concept observes that one of NATO's fundamental tasks is to "provide one of the indispensable foundations for a stable security environment in Europe, based on the growth of democratic institutions and commitment to the peaceful resolution of disputes."[17] The idea of NATO membership as a means to spread democracy finds willing ears, especially in the United States. The advantages of spreading democracy are based on the prevailing notion that democracies are less likely to engage in conflict with other democracies.[18] Whether NATO membership has fostered democratic institutions and practices is debatable and ultimately difficult to determine, especially since many of those seeking NATO membership have also been subject to the more rigorous preparations for EU membership. Further NATO membership is nevertheless anticipated, especially with regard to the western Balkan countries. Enlargement to the east is altogether more problematic and will largely be determined by developments in NATO-Russia relations—the next subject to be considered.

NATO-Russia Relations

NATO must engage in a difficult balancing act with Russia and potential member states (and anxious current member states)—an act that keeps the diplomatic channels open to Moscow while also reassuring worried member states who question NATO's resolve to live up to its Article 5 commitments. The key vehicle for NATO-Russian collaboration is the NATO-Russia Council (NRC), established at the NATO-Russia summit in Rome on May 28, 2002. The NRC replaced the Permanent Joint Council (PJC), a forum for consultation and cooperation created by the 1997 NATO-Russia Founding Act on Mutual Relations, Cooperation and Security, which continues to be the formal basis for NATO-Russia relations.[19] In general, relations with Russia have been strained since the August 2008 military intervention in Georgia. Russian conduct in Georgia led to the immediate conclusion from the NATO foreign ministers that it was no longer possible to conduct "business as usual."[20] In spite of the fact that some meetings of the NRC were suspended, there was evidence as early as September 2008 that relations in key areas of common interest, such as counterterrorism, Afghanistan, the Treaty on Conventional Armed Forces in Europe, and nuclear weapons, were gradually normalizing. At a meeting of NATO foreign ministers in December 2008, it was agreed to reengage with Russia while maintaining that the alliance could not accept the take-over of Abkhazia and South Ossetia. NATO foreign ministers decided at their March 2009 meeting to resume formal meetings and practical cooperation under the NRC, even though Russia had evidently not complied fully with the terms of the August 12, 2008, armistice plan (which included the withdrawal of its forces).

NATO's historic sixtieth-anniversary Strasbourg-Kehl summit in April 2009 maintained the difficult dual approach of firmness on the one hand regarding the Southern Caucasus and cooperation on issues of common interest on the other. A few months later, in December, the first formal NRC since the Georgian crisis produced agreement on the need to reinvigorate NATO-Russia defense cooperation and to launch a joint review of twenty-first-century common security challenges. The NRC met for the first time in political advisory format in June 2010 to discuss how the council could become more of a "substance-based forum."[21]

Although there are numerous examples of NATO-Russia cooperation in areas of joint concern (like counterterrorism, narcotics, nonproliferation, arms control, and the fight against piracy), any genuine breakthrough in relations remains stymied by two factors. First, Russia's excessive fears regarding NATO and the United States hamper collaboration. Second, Russophobia in Europe, which is based on suspicions that Moscow wishes to create new forms of subjugation and thus control over the former Soviet republics, also impedes relations.[22] These fears are heightened by Russian approaches to regional security. Rather than enhance NATO-Russia cooperation, Russia wants to promote an entirely new security architecture for Europe. On June 5, 2008, Medvedev first unveiled the idea of developing a pan-European security treaty.[23] The proposal involves overriding the OSCE and NATO in favor of a new comprehensive and indivisible European security architecture, the intention being to create a "common undivided space" that would finally end the Cold War legacy of which NATO, in Russian eyes, is a part. Such a treaty would, according to Russian foreign minister Sergei Lavrov, be more appropriate to the unfolding "polycentric international system."[24] Medvedev also subsequently suggested formalizing in international law the principle of indivisible security for the Euro-Atlantic region. Eventually, according to the Russian vision, the new treaty and the Platform for Cooperative Security could assume the (outdated) tasks of the OSCE, NATO, the EU, the Commonwealth of Independent States (CIS), and the Collective Security Treaty Organization (CSTO).[25]

In reality, Russia's European Security Treaty is unlikely to challenge the

OSCE, NATO, or EU security mandates in any substantive manner in the near future.[26] It does, nevertheless, pose a dilemma: How should NATO members address the Russian proposal, bearing in mind that it could involve usefully tying Russia to the stipulation that the "use of force or the threat of force against the territorial integrity or political independence of any state, or in any other way inconsistent with the goals and principles of the Charter of the United Nations is inadmissible in their mutual relations?"[27] Whether the adoption of any such commitment by Russia, with future Georgia-type scenarios in mind, would make a substantive difference is open to debate. The decision by the United States to cancel the planned deployment of long-range missile defense interceptors and equipment in Poland and the Czech Republic in September 2009 has created a more fertile ground for the development of mutual relations from the Russian point of view, as has the new Strategic Arms Control Reduction (START) agreement of April 2010 (replacing the original START I agreement, which expired at the end of December 2009). Topics that might prove constructive for deepening the NATO-Russia relationship include energy security and Afghanistan (with a possible CSTO role).

Afghanistan—Pass the Hot Potato

A second indicator that is applied to NATO as a sign of its relevance, or lack thereof, is its ability to help address the shorter and longer-term challenges in Afghanistan. NATO's involvement in Afghanistan was intended to unequivocally demonstrate its relevance to new global security challenges. It is for this reason that Afghanistan is commonly presented as NATO's first real litmus test. Joshua Walker is representative of those who hold this position when he states that "Afghanistan is the first out of Europe deployment operation for NATO in its entire history. Thus success in Afghanistan is not only crucial for any future hopes of a globally engaged and active NATO, but for the very existence and credibility of NATO."[28]

Put simply, the perceived failure of NATO in Afghanistan will severely weaken the alliance and end any out-of-area adventurism, if not the alliance itself. Approval of President Obama's handling of the situation in Afghanistan (and Iran) is lower across the EU than it is in the United States.[29] The Europeans are uniformly more skeptical about stabilizing Afghanistan compared to their American counterparts. The question remains open about whether any perceived failure would be viewed as NATO's or whether it would be attributed primarily to the United States itself. At the end of the day, this may be an academic point, since America so clearly dominates the alliance, and any loss of confidence in the United States and its willingness to engage in complex overseas operations would have profound effects on NATO. From the American point of view, conclusions about NATO's vigor and relevance will be based on the allies' ability to engage in a mission that commands ever-dwindling public support and where cost considerations are also at the fore.

NATO's participation in Afghanistan began in 2001 when the International Security Assistance Force (ISAF) was first deployed under the aegis of the UN Security Council.[30] The mandate of the force was to assist the authorities in Kabul to maintain security in the capital and environs. This was obviously of extreme importance for the safety of the UN and numerous other agencies operating in the area. Interestingly, ISAF did not have an explicit counterterrorism mission, although fighting the Taliban and the narcotics trade was viewed as a means of preventing the return of al-Qaeda or other radical Islamic groups "inimical to western interests."[31] The operation was transferred to NATO in full in August 2003, based on a request by the government of the Islamic Republic of Afghanistan. Although NATO's initial mandate was restricted to Kabul, it was extended to include the rest of Afghanistan in October 2003.

As of June 2010, there were forty-six nations contributing to ISAF's twenty-seven provincial reconstruction teams (PRTs), with a total strength of 119,500 troops.[32] It should be noted, though, that some contributors imposed restrictions, or national caveats, on participation that led to demands for the removal of such restrictions at the November 2006 NATO Riga summit. The existence of national caveats was deeply contentious since it was seen as tying the hands of the commanders on the ground and putting some soldiers in danger while others were relatively sheltered. The United States accounted for under half of the military in 2006, but by 2010 it accounted for over two-thirds. The U.S. portion will probably climb as allies reduce their commitments further. By coincidence, June 2010 was also one of the deadliest months to date, as well as the month in which the length of U.S. involvement exceeded that in Vietnam.[33] These grim statistics, in part a result of the surge of 30,000 troops agreed to in December 2009, reflect a deeper concern that campaigns in Afghanistan are unwinnable and that it is now primarily a matter of extraction and saving face. NATO's own efforts, up until the military and parallel civilian surges, were characterized by "complacency and drift."[34] It is little wonder that the Atlantic Council, and those promoting the pre–New Strategic Concept debates (as discussed below), such as former U.S. secretary of state Madeline Albright, insist that "NATO is about much more than Afghanistan," while Supreme Allied Commander Admiral Jim Stravidis claims that "Afghanistan is not a GO/NO GO litmus test."[35]

While Americans may be underplaying the litmus test, most of the European allies tend to see the importance of Afghanistan as having far more to do with transatlantic relations than NATO per se. In this context, Jeremy Shapiro and Nick Witney note that "European politicians have often done little to make the case, framed in terms of European interests, that Afghanistan is worth the effort Europe is putting in." One result of their vague statements of commitment is that most European NATO members have ignored frequent requests that more troops and greater flexibility are required for success. The implication, according to Shapiro and Witney, "is that most European governments see Afghanistan as a problem that should be left to the Americans to solve."[36] The European tendency to promote Afghanistan as a NATO/American problem is further reflected in European endeavors to concentrate their efforts on the European Police Mission in Afghanistan (EUPOL), which commenced in May 2007. As of June 2010, the mission included 265 international staff and 163 local staff.[37] European promotion of EUPOL contrasts with the fact that the EU has committed over €8 billion to Afghanistan since 2002, making it one of the largest donors. But the pretence by some of the European allies that Afghanistan is a NATO problem, or more specifically an American one, could backfire and although their dwindling support may eventually land failure predominantly in America's lap, it will have highly negative consequences for alliance solidarity. The fact that a number of allies, such as the Netherlands, Poland, and Spain, have had controversial public debates about their involvement in Afghanistan that eventually ended in decisions to withdraw is further symptomatic of growing public unease with operations in Afghanistan as well as with dependence on the United States.

Even if Albright insists that Afghanistan is not NATO's litmus test, the developments in that country will nevertheless shape the atmosphere immediately before and after the adoption of the New Strategic Concept. Engaging in the blame game will be counterproductive. There are elements of this already, with frequent complaints against America's allies for their reluctance or inability to produce the required manpower and resources. EUPOL has also met with derision as an example of the EU's "shambolic performance in Afghanistan," forgetting that police missions are a vital part of nation building.[38]

If Afghanistan is a test of alliance solidarity from the American perspective, from a European standpoint it is also about the United States' ability and commitment to lead NATO. Moreover, the obvious split between the military and civilian planners in the United States, exemplified by General Stanley McChrystal's remarks to *Rolling Stone Magazine*, which cost him his job and added to the confusion over the "political" goal of withdrawing American forces by July 2011, indicates wider discontent among the American public with the cumulative casualty rates.[39] NATO's involvement in Afghanistan has become a classic example of mission drift in circumstances where alliance members (notably the United States) have little experience in nation building, which is further complicated by the difficult scale and difficult circumstances. The allies are increasingly reluctant to deal with the dilemma of "breaking down suspected insurgents' doors in the morning [only to] build bridges in the afternoon."[40]

Afghanistan may yet prove useful to NATO (and the EU) if it provides the opportunity to fundamentally refocus the alliance. However, the timetable for the launch of NATO's New Strategic Concept in November 2010 and the drawdown of American forces in Afghanistan suggests that few of the fundamental issues will be solved. In a somewhat similar manner to the EU, which faced the abyss in March 2003 after bitter disagreements over the wisdom of military intervention in Iraq, it may take a dramatic situation such as that in Afghanistan to put issues into sharp relief. This is unlikely to come about as the result of any carefully worded and nuanced strategic concept, but it may well be prompted by Afghanistan itself. Albright may well be correct after all; it is not NATO's litmus test, but a far wider one about the nature and direction of transatlantic relations.

A False Alternative: NATO and the European Option?

NATO's relations with the EU remain largely undefined and underdeveloped. The increasing overlap between the various security organizations is also becoming more noticeable, hence Rasmussen's prescient observation that the future of EU-NATO relations is at a critical stage. It is unclear whether NATO and the EU are developing as partners or, increasingly, as competitors.

To give a quick practical example of how NATO-EU relations overlap, consider their mutual relations with Russia. The EU's dialogue with Russia is organized around four euphemistically named "common spaces" (covering economic issues and the environment; freedom, security, and justice; external security; and research and education, including cultural aspects). The discourse on external security is by far the most challenging, largely because of the sensitivities surrounding South Ossetia and Abkhazia in Georgia and the disputes over the (Russian-backed) separatists in the Transnistria region of Moldova. However, the EU's European Neighborhood Policy, which reaches out to neighbors to the east and south, means that the EU and Russia are destined to be dialogue partners in these regions whether they like it or not, and for many years to come. The EU-Russian discourse includes many aspects that NATO also professes an interest in: counterterrorism, organized crime, migration, nonproliferation, human trafficking, and human rights. The increasingly expansive definition of security (or the "securitization" of issues areas) further contributes to the overlap of their issues. In the case of the EU, its considerable economic leverage is an important supplement to its ability to address a variety of security issues.

It was argued in an earlier section that the post-9/11 environment left NATO largely as a toolbox out of which "coalitions of the willing" could be assembled in pursuit of predominantly American goals. This left other members of the alliance with two basic choices, to either prove that they were good allies by supporting the United States or to put more energy and resources into other international actors, in particular to tighten the ties linking them together in the EU. In fact, the European allies have tried to do both. Some have made highly conspicuous (and domestically costly) demonstrations of support for the United States. For example, eight heads of government forcefully supported the American interpretation of UN Security Council Resolution 1441, which was subsequently used as the underpinning legal justification for the military intervention in Iraq.[41] However, the deep unpopularity of the George W. Bush administrations (especially the first) was instrumental in pushing those allies that are also EU members toward the option of working closer together.

Historically, the EU began to coordinate its general approaches to questions of international relations as early as 1970, but it was only in the early 1990s that the Common Foreign and Security Policy (CFSP) emerged as a more formal way of routinely coordinating matters of general interest. CFSP was created largely as a result of the EU's inability at the time to present the full range of foreign policy tools, from the diplomatic and the use of economic leverage to the threat of the use of force and, if necessary, the ability to actually use it. However, the EU conspicuously lacked the latter—the ability to use force—and with the hard lessons from the Western Balkans in mind, the European Security and Defense Policy (ESDP) was developed. The first military operation in the ESDP area took place in 2003 in the Democratic Republic of the Congo. This action was spearheaded by France, which in particular viewed the operation as a means of visibly demonstrating the EU's autonomy from NATO and as an alternative to indefinite reliance on the United States. The importance of such an autonomous capacity was underscored by the disagreements over Iraq in 2003. As Sven Biscop commented, "An autonomous capacity instead of relying exclusively on an American-led Alliance and on the U.S. itself becomes a necessity when U.S. intervention is no longer automatically considered legitimate and opportune."[42]

Since 2003, ESDP has developed rapidly, with the EU embarking on a number of civilian crisis-management and military operations.[43] The EU also developed the Battlegroup concept, which consists of two groups of 1,500 combat personnel on standby for a six-month period. Additionally, a number of agreements with NATO established the circumstances in which the EU borrows resources[44] and exchanges classified information.[45] The problem of a lack of resources was also tackled through the creation of a European Defense Agency (EDA), which began operating in 2004.[46] The EDA's efforts aim to coax EU member states to more joint procurement of military equipment, to conduct joint research and development, and wherever possible to develop common platforms in order to promote interoperability.

An important turning point in the EU and NATO relationship took place in December 1998 at Saint Malo, France, where a meeting between French and British leaders produced a clear intent to develop EU capacities. The St. Malo declaration states that the EU shall have "the capacity for autonomous action, backed up by credible military forces, the means to decide to use them and a readiness to do so, in order to respond to international crises."[47] Nevertheless, it left sufficient latitude to interpret the precise relationship with NATO in diverging ways. The declaration includes the following stipulations: In order for the European Union to take decisions and approve military action where the alliance as a whole is not engaged, the union must be given appropriate structures and a capacity for analysis of situations, sources of intelligence, and a capability for relevant strategic planning, without unnecessary duplication, taking account of the existing assets of the WEU and the evolution of its relations with the EU. In this regard, the European Union will also need to have recourse to suitable military means (European capabilities predesignated within NATO's European pillar or national or multinational European means outside the NATO framework).

Five notable factors emerge from these provisions. First, although the "capacity for autonomous action" is mentioned, it is conditioned by the caveat that "the Alliance [NATO] as a whole is not engaged" in the possible operation. This qualification satisfied French concerns about overreliance on NATO while also safeguarding British fears that the statement should not be misinterpreted in Washington (which was not entirely successful). This stipulation also created divergent opinions on whether or not NATO enjoyed a right of first refusal.

The second factor relates to the Western European Union, which was responsible for the defense-related aspects of the EU's work. The WEU's role and mandate made it difficult for the EU itself to assume the full gamut of security and defense responsibilities. Indeed, it was not long before the development of military crisis-management tools in the EU context, and the lack of any overt territorial threat, presented the WEU with a stark choice: either transform or transfer responsibilities. The decision to hand over crisis-management responsibilities to the EU was made in the 2000 Marseille Declaration,[48] which in effect condemned the WEU to a minor role in regional security. The ratification of the Lisbon Treaty by EU members in December 2009 spelled the end of the road for the WEU, since Article 42(7) of the treaty states, "If a Member State is the victim of armed aggression on its territory, the other Member States shall have towards it an obligation of aid and assistance by all the means in their power, in accordance with Article 51 of the United Nations Charter." Since this clause effectively ended the need for the WEU, a decision was made to cease its activities by June 2011.

The third factor concerns what capacities the EU should build, while at the same time avoiding Albright's infamous three Ds—the duplication of NATO assets, the decoupling of the transatlantic alliance, and discrimination against non-EU members. None of the strictures proved easy to follow, and serious clashes were provoked by an April 2003 proposal by Belgium, France, Germany, and Luxembourg to create a permanent and autonomous operations headquarters within shouting distance of the official residence of the United States ambassador to NATO. The United States and the United Kingdom re-

Figure 13.1   European Security Organizations

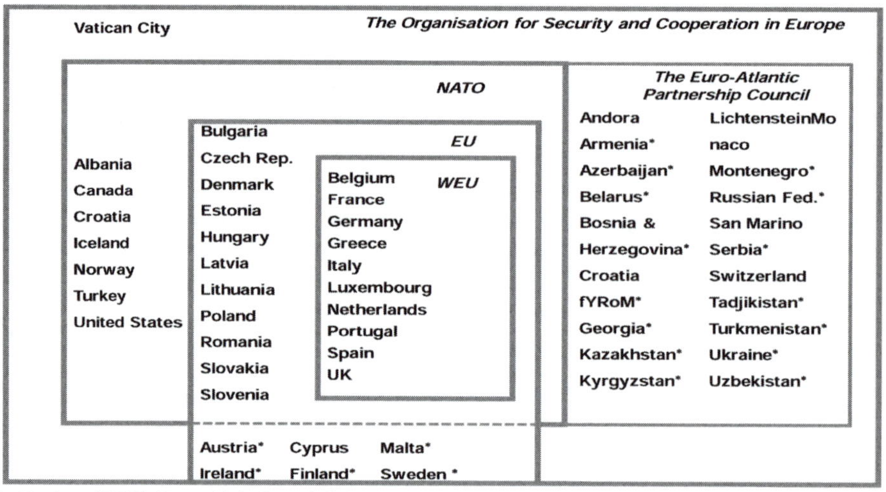

Vatican City				The Organisation for Security and Cooperation in Europe	
			NATO		**The Euro-Atlantic Partnership Council**
Albania	Bulgaria		*EU*	Andora	LichtensteinMo
Canada	Czech Rep.	Belgium	*WEU*	Armenia*	naco
Croatia	Denmark	France		Azerbaijan*	Montenegro*
Iceland	Estonia	Germany		Belarus*	Russian Fed.*
Norway	Hungary	Greece		Bosnia &	San Marino
Turkey	Latvia	Italy		Herzegovina*	Serbia*
United States	Lithuania	Luxembourg		Croatia	Switzerland
	Poland	Netherlands		fYRoM*	Tadjikistan*
	Romania	Portugal		Georgia*	Turkmenistan*
	Slovakia	Spain		Kazakhstan*	Ukraine*
	Slovenia	UK		Kyrgyzstan*	Uzbekistan*
	Austria* Cyprus Malta*				
	Ireland* Finland* Sweden *				

* = Members of NATO's Partnership for Peace (+ Switzerland)

acted negatively, with a State Department spokesman making a derogatory reference to the "chocolate summit."[49] Interestingly, this incident paved the way for the eventual creation of a civilian-military cell in the EU military staff as well as an operations center, both announced with a minimum of fanfare or reaction.

The fourth factor of note is that there are many links between the EU and NATO, both in terms of agreements and personnel. The NATO-EU declaration on ESDP, agreed on December 16, 2002, sets forth the political parameters for cooperation between the two organizations, while the March 17, 2003, Berlin Plus arrangements specify the basis for NATO-EU cooperation in crisis management. The documents contain framework agreements for several areas of cooperation, including mutual crisis consultation, security and exchange of information, assured access to NATO planning, the availability of NATO assets and capabilities, and a NATO European command option for those operations using NATO assets under the EU's aegis. The importance of the Berlin Plus arrangements is further emphasized by their rather grand portrayal as establishing a "framework for permanent relations."[50] Since 2003, these agreements have occasionally been invoked. Operation Concordia (2003) in the former Yugoslav Republic of Macedonia is one example in which NATO assets were used and where the EU operations commander was the deputy supreme allied commander Europe (DSACEUR). In December 2004, the EU launched Operation Althea, taking over from NATO's stabilization force (SFOR) in Bosnia-Herzegovina. Operation Althea drew upon NATO planning assets, and again the DSACEUR assumed command of the operation. EU-NATO cooperation is also close in Kosovo, where the EU's Rule of Law Mission (EULEX), which deployed fully in December 2008, and NATO's peacekeeping force (KFOR) work hand in hand. On the personnel side, there are formal links between the respective civilian and military bodies in the EU and NATO. At the highest civilian level, discussions take place between the North Atlantic Council and, on the EU side, the Political and Security Committee. A NATO permanent liaison team has been operating at the EU military staff since November 2005, and an EU cell was set up in March 2006 at SHAPE (Supreme Headquarters Allied Powers Europe, NATO's strategic command for operations, in Mons, Belgium).

Finally, the fifth factor of note concerns the lack of military capacity on the part of NATO's European members. As discussed above, the European Defense Agency was created to address this problem. The EU has further introduced the "European Capabilities Action Plan" and "permanent structured cooperation" in the Lisbon Treaty to resolve this matter. Article 42(6) of the Lisbon Treaty states that "those Member States whose military capabilities fulfill higher criteria and which have made more binding commitments to one another in this area with a view to the most demanding missions shall establish permanent structured cooperation within the Union framework."[51] The latter can be viewed primarily as an incentive mechanism to encourage members to fulfill the "higher criteria" as well as to introduce an element of flexibility for those that wish to move faster and further. NATO has also made efforts to address the military capacity problem. In the Prague summit of November 2002, a "Prague Capabilities Commitment" (PCC) was approved, which represented a more ambitious and focused version of the earlier 1999 Defense Capabilities Initiative (DCI).

In the context of ESDP, the EU has also developed substantial civilian capabilities for crisis management. These include a 5,000-strong police force available for international missions (of which 1,000 should be deployable within thirty days). The creation of this police force is a significant step since most of the EU's twenty-three missions to date have been police missions. There are also 200 national rule-of-law experts who may be called upon (including a rapid-response team capable of deployment within a month). National civilian administrators can also be summoned, as can two to three national civil-protection assessment teams and up to 2,000 civilian-protection intervention personnel. A European Gendarmerie Force (EGF), agreed upon in September 2004 by France, Italy, Portugal, the Netherlands, and Spain, is also available to the EU and other international organizations, including NATO. The EGF consists of 900 police officers that can be deployed within thirty days. To supplement these measures, the EU has both civilian and military "headline" goals for 2010, which are designed to give the members targets for improvement.[52]

For NATO's European allies, the resource issue is also complicated by political will and competing priorities. As Paul Cornish points out, "In terms of both economics and personnel, European states enjoy more than adequate resources upon which to build security and defense cooperation, if they chose to do so."[53] Since CFSP is an intergovernmental part of the EU, spending priorities tend to reflect national priorities. The lack of a transatlantic defense marketplace also contributes to the resource problem. Currently, the United States zealously safeguards its technological prowess, normally under the rubric of avoiding "technology transfers" (with the partial exception of sharing with the United Kingdom). The EU has shown that it is not afraid to compete head to head with the United States in some defense industrial areas, notably aerospace. But in this context, "Europe" is dominated by France and the United Kingdom (with Germany, Italy, Spain, and Sweden as the only other countries with appreciable defense sectors).

In practice, the EU-NATO arrangements are a good deal more complicated than the agreements on paper might suggest. For instance, both the EU *and* NATO have a rhetoric-resources gap.[54] Their ability to function is also significantly complicated by the unsolved Cyprus problem, since Turkey is a NATO member but not an EU member, and Cyprus is an EU member but not a NATO member (and not even in the Partnership for Peace program). The reality is that the political ramifications of the Cyprus problem stymie much of the practical cooperation other than on Bosnia-Herzegovina. Additionally, the alleged lack of allied capabilities has provided the United States with an incentive for going it alone or cherry-picking from the more able (and compliant) allies. The extent to which this remains a viable option for the United States, both politically and economically, is an open question and indeed may have more to do with differing perspectives on power than on actual resources.

In fact, the most complex part of the EU-NATO relationship is at the strategic level, with the resource dilemma resulting in part from differing viewpoints on the utility of hard and soft power.[55] NATO is often portrayed as an example of hard power, since it is backed primarily by the United States, whereas the EU is often seen as predominantly a soft power—or a civilian power, as Europeans prefer. Such terms are misleading and risk producing Kaganesque stereotypes that, while immensely fun, oversimplify.[56] The EU has chosen to promote the rule of law, effective multilateralism and negotiation, and, as a result of the latter, contracts or agreements. Yet it is not without its hard(er) aspects, since those agreements, even if nonsecurity in nature, will help structure the relations of third parties with the contractual partners and thus condition their behavior (Russia's relations with the Baltic states being a case in point).

The Kaganesque stereotype also falls apart in its depiction of the United States as having a preference for hard power. Since 9/11, the United States is more inclined to link the use of military force with other aspects of power. However, by doing so it may trade off one form of influence for another, as is being shown in Afghanistan where it is notoriously difficult to combine the elements of power into a nation-building effort (see above). NATO itself is, arguably, a soft power, since its greatest achievement was to allow a pacified Western Europe to develop and flourish. The different historical experiences, whereby two world wars were fought largely on European soil alongside the fact that 9/11 occurred in America, have led to different conclusions about the use of force and the utility of other forms of power and persuasion. Nowhere was this better illustrated than in the global war on terrorism (GWOT), a label that was never used by the European allies since they saw the nature of the threat as demanding predominantly intelligence, financial, and police assets as a response. Their view was that it was far from a war and more of a struggle to which, unfortunately, many European countries were accustomed. The growth of the EU is gradually leading its members to the realization that soft power is not enough. As a result, the union is slowly developing complementary crisis-management capabilities with the intention of becoming a more complete international actor. In a similar fashion, the United States has realized that hard power needs to be complemented by soft power to ensure longer-term stability, particularly if it continues engaging in nation-building operations in postconflict scenarios.

The picture that emerges is thus a complex one where stereotypes of hard and soft power should be laid aside. It is not true that the EU is only a civilian power par excellence, or that NATO only stands for the exercise of hard power. Any efforts to rejuvenate NATO must therefore be set in the wider context of U.S.-EU relations and a new strategic direction for the alliance.[57]

The New Strategic Concept—Putting Vitality Back into NATO?

The focus of current efforts to reassert the vitality of the alliance is NATO's 2010 New Strategic Concept. The previous concept was drafted in 1999, in the shadow of NATO's military involvement in the Western Balkans, and in particular Kosovo. Since this earlier document was written prior to 9/11, it did not reflect the changed security circumstances of the first decade of the twenty-first century. To rectify this situation, the strategy was updated at the Prague summit in 2002, the Riga summit in 2006, and the Strasbourg-Kehl summit in 2009. The adaptations at these summits underlined the growing importance of crisis management to the alliance's mission. According to NATO's own Web portal, a crisis "can be political, military or humanitarian and can be caused by political or armed conflict, technological incidents or natural disasters." In such instances, crisis management consists of "the different means of dealing with these different forms of crises."[58] This growing emphasis on crisis management, as opposed to traditional defense preoccupations, underpinned the rationale for the creation of the Allied Command Transformation (ACT) and the NATO Response Force (discussed above).

ACT was responsible for developing a Multiple Futures Project (MFP) in 2008–2009. The MFP ascertained broad threats facing alliance members until 2030 and paved the way for a new NATO department dealing with emerging security challenges.[59] In meeting these new dangers, the MFP argues that "the Alliance will have to transform itself from a predominantly defense-based military alliance into a comprehensive political and military security community."[60] The project presented four possible futures and a variety of responses, with the broad conclusion that it is more likely the alliance will be threatened by instability and the weakness of others than by invading conventional forces. Inter-state conflicts in different regions of the world will remain likely, and while they may not threaten NATO directly, the consequences of such conflicts may have a significant impact on the security of the alliance.[61]

The MFP gives the overall impression that the center of gravity within NATO will move to Article 4 since the principal future challenges (ballistic missile attacks perpetuated by a terrorist group, the proliferation of weapons of mass destruction, cyberattacks, and energy security) fall under its catchall provisions. The report makes it clear that the alliance may have to decide "whether to act outside the traditional Alliance areas of engagement, in response to growing resource competition; the increased exploitation of space, cyberspace, and the maritime commons; as well as the spill-over of regional conflicts."[62] The Article 5 mission is not, however, neglected, since this is portrayed as still "the core" charge. However, the nature of the challenges that might invoke activation of Article 5 is likely to change. Good examples of this transformation are the January 2007 cyberattack on Estonia, which crippled most of the central government's computer systems, or Russia's August 2008 invasion of Georgia. These new challenges mean that the core mission, in doctrinal terms, has moved to a "comprehensive approach" toward security.

The MFP did lead to questions regarding NATO's "open-door" policy for membership, since emphasis is now placed on enhanced "strategic partnerships" with key international actors. The EU is included in the MFP's reference to "strategic partnerships," with the overall goal of implementing "fully NATO's partnership with the EU at the strategic, operational and tactical levels."[63] The broad state of NATO-EU relations has already been reflected upon, but the move toward comprehensive security on the part of the alliance will emphasize the nonmilitary aspects of security, which, in the civilian realm, is one area where the EU has considerable expertise and resources. Indeed, only seven of the twenty-four past or ongoing ESDP/CSDP missions have been military in nature. The fact that the EU has experience in civilian security only reinforces the need for a closer relationship between NATO and the EU, notwithstanding the obvious problems relating to Cyprus or French concerns about the development of the alliance's civilian capabilities.

The MFP further addressed the key challenge of resource questions and the perceived opportunity costs of defense expenditures for NATO's members.

The MFP proposes that "an increasing number of states refocus their budgets to cope with domestic challenges. Significant defense spending in the absence of an identifiable threat becomes less justifiable. Subsequently, the ability for a state to anticipate, sense, and shape the external security environment is severely degraded."[64] Any recommendations regarding the affordability of responding to a wider set of challenges will raise serious questions about how realistic this may be, especially when the alliance members cannot live up to their existing commitment to conduct up to two larger operations and six smaller ones.

The MFP and the various summits did not address the larger questions surrounding the future of the alliance. In 2009, it became clear that no matter how many summits attempted to modify or adapt NATO's mission, a new strategic concept was required. The path leading to the new document began in July 2009 with a series of consultations with experts, academics, and interest groups. The consultation process itself became helpful in the sense that it clearly illustrated the diversity of opinion about what can be realistically expected from the new concept, ranging from the optimistic to the skeptical.[65] On the optimistic side, the recommendation of a group of twelve experts, chaired by Albright, is found in their report *NATO 2020: Assured Security; Dynamic Engagement* and unsurprisingly reinforces the idea that the alliance continues to be relevant. The group concluded that NATO remains an "essential source of stability in an uncertain and unpredictable world," and that "between now and 2020, it will be tested by the emergence of new dangers, the many-sided demands of complex operations, and the challenge of organizing itself efficiently in an era where rapid responses are vital, versatility critical, and resources tight."[66] The group of experts ultimately established the general political message for the New Strategic Concept to follow. However, making the case for NATO's relevance also took the form of an online "Security Jam," which, in spite of its MTV-oriented title, pulled together an impressive array of well-established security practitioners and analysts in a variety of forums and gave the wider public a chance to circulate new ideas.[67]

The discussions leading up to the New Strategic Concept also exposed serious differences between the so-called Article 5 coalition and those in favor of a more comprehensive and global orientation for the alliance. The Article 5 coalition members favor a more fundamental and restricted interpretation of the Washington Treaty, with a strong emphasis on its collective self-defense mission. Indeed, the assertion of this as the primary role of the alliance was very much at the fore in the declaration following NATO's anniversary summit in Strasbourg-Kehl in April 2009.[68] Most of the coalition members emphasized territorial defense based on NATO structures, and in some cases, such as Poland and the Baltic states, a relatively tough line with Russia was included, although it was not directly mentioned as a potential aggressor. The three Baltic states, Estonia, Latvia, and Lithuania are prominent members of this group. In particular, the Russian military intervention in Georgia prompted a vigorous discussion regarding the credibility of NATO's defense commitments toward them. The absence of any significant NATO infrastructure in the Baltic states, alongside frequent Russian violations of their airspace, has deepened such concerns.

The Article 5 coalition members include a number of older NATO (and EU) states, like Belgium and Luxembourg, as well as newer members, like the Czech Republic and Slovakia. These four states favor emphasizing NATO's Article 5 mission over any broadening of NATO's charge, for fear that it could dilute the basic purpose of the alliance. France could be included in this group, although there is acknowledgement that the likelihood of territorial aggression against a NATO country is low. Still, the French agree that there may be specific circumstances when intervention beyond the treaty area is justified (as in, for instance, the response to an extraordinary 9/11-type event). Germany, which has closely coordinated its defense and security policies with France since 1963, also falls into this group. However, in Germany's case, the emphasis on Article 5 does not negate the possibility of out-of-area operations if there is a proven external threat to the well-being of one or more NATO allies. Like France, there is opposition to the idea of a "global NATO" and support for the idea of defining NATO's area of interest more precisely. The latter goal is intended to obviate distant roles under an American global policeman, for which there is little popular support in Germany (prompted both by traditional historical reservations as well as by popular opposition to America's military intervention in Iraq).

Italy has come closest to fusing the Article 5 coalition position with that of the advocates of a comprehensive approach. In the Italian rendition, Article 5 continues as the bedrock of the alliance, but it remains the duty of the alliance to protect its members from threats, even if such threats emanate from out-of-area sources. According to the Italians, "Article 5 should be treated as an obligation to ensure comprehensive security."[69] Spain, by way of contrast, prefers to see NATO actions limited to the Euro-Atlantic area, as defined in NATO's founding treaty. This does not, however, preclude nonterritorial defense activities. In most of the above cases, an additional caveat is the strong preference for a binding UN mandate as a precondition for involvement in military operations.

Others, like Bulgaria, the Netherlands, and the United Kingdom, have embraced a more comprehensive approach to NATO's future role. All are linked by the belief that the alliance needs to have more effective ways of engaging external threats to NATO members, but they differ on priorities. A common thread is that NATO should play an active part in discussions on global security issues like nonproliferation of WMDs, climate change, and energy security. Indeed, all members of this group aspire to have these facets reflected in the New Strategic Concept, with, however, an acknowledgement that only in extremely unlikely circumstances will these issues call for the use of military force. The use of NATO as a consensus-building alliance, which can support other partners and organizations, would reflect the broader-based mandate envisaged by these countries but would not go as far as the original (American) notion of a global alliance or a league of democracies. For this reason, more emphasis tends to be placed on the Partnership for Peace and the Euro-Atlantic Partnership Council as extensions of NATO's mission and as forums for encouraging defense reform.

Most of those in favor of a comprehensive approach are also united in their discomfort with the tough position vis-à-vis Russia implied in some of the Article 5 coalition positions, especially on enlargement-related questions. A comprehensive approach would instead reassure Russia that an antagonistic NATO is not emerging at its "inner abroad."[70] For those in favor of a comprehensive approach, President Medvedev's June 2008 proposal for a new European security architecture remains on the table; it would frame NATO's future in terms of a wider security architecture drawing in the Council of Europe, the EU, and the OSCE. Although the group of experts led by Albright did recommend strengthening the NATO-Russia Council with more frequent consultations, it failed to address Medvedev's plans.

Any differences between Article 5 coalition members and those who favor a comprehensive approach may well be obviated by the fact that the meaning of this central article is open to reinterpretation. Does an attack have to be an "armed" attack, or might a concerted cyberattack, or actions by nonstate actors possibly against NATO citizens outside the transatlantic area, be considered as falling into the latter-day remit of this article? The fact that all NATO members are vulnerable beyond their territories needs to be acknowledged, but at the same time, the risk is that attempts to move toward a comprehensive approach may leave NATO without focus and a compelling raison d'être.

It is also essential that any transformation on NATO's part should not be seen as a purely elite-driven process. The small circle of Washington or Brussels aficionados, who really understand NATO (or the EU), will have to find ways of sharpening their public diplomacy since publics remain ambivalent. Stefanie Babst, who is herself engaged in NATO's public diplomacy, makes the interesting observation that the alliance "has changed faster than its image has."[71] Indeed, NATO's image, as illustrated by the *Transatlantic Trends* series from the German Marshall Fund, paints a picture of an alliance with fading support. In 2010, the view that NATO is essential was supported by 60 percent of both the Americans and the French polled, while only 30 percent of Turks held that view—by far the lowest of any European country polled. Americans and French who viewed NATO as no longer essential were 29 percent and 34 percent, respectively, with 43 percent of Turks agreeing (approached only by Germany with 41 percent). Also of interest was the fact that far more Turks (27 percent) had no opinion or did not respond when asked about the importance of NATO.[72] Significant discrepancies are also found with American handling of the situation in Afghanistan (again with 42 percent in Turkey disapproving "very much," along with an average of 18 percent in the other European countries polled). Turks and Germans are also pessimistic about whether the situation in Afghanistan can be stabilized (tied at 33 percent).[73]

Poll data are notoriously difficult to interpret. Nevertheless, the data do suggest that the New Strategic Concept must be accompanied by persuasive public diplomacy. NATO needs to demonstrate its relevance to publics in the transatlantic space, especially Turkey, whose role in Europe generally, but more specifically in NATO, appears increasingly at variance. In this regard, the question of whether Washington (and Brussels) can engage with Ankara will become one of the key questions for the health of NATO. The future of NATO operations in Afghanistan will also have a decisive influence on efforts to revitalize the alliance, since there is an apparent clash between the efforts to promote NATO's relevance and the increasingly negative public reactions to further involvement in Afghanistan.

NATO at Sixty and Beyond—Three Scenarios

Thus far we have established that NATO's role will be decisively influenced by NATO-Russia relations, by the situation in Afghanistan, by NATO-EU relations, and finally by attempts to redirect it strategically in the form of the New Strategic Concept. None of this, however, tells us which road the alliance may take. Although substantial attempts have been made at reinvention, including taking on missions well out of the traditional transatlantic area, enlarging to twenty-eight, and engaging in active public diplomacy, the alliance's mission and vitality remain in question.

The prognostications for NATO's life beyond sixty vary enormously, and for the sake of simplicity, three possibilities will be explored. The first two are polar positions that posit either that NATO is in its last throes (and thus will soon slide into obsolescence) or that it is experiencing a global rebirth that proves its vitality for the future. In the second scenario, NATO finds a new lease on life, fresh inspiration, and new missions. The third option lies between the poles, suggesting that NATO will continue on default mode, not in danger of immediate demise but also showing no particular signs of vitality.

A. THE END OF LIFE

The detractor's position is that NATO is in its last throes, its weaknesses having been exposed by internal hollowing out and growing differences between the members of the alliance over fundamentals, principally those between the European allies and the United States. In this context, the New Strategic Concept represents a lowest-common-denominator position, and while it may paper over cracks at the elite level, it ultimately fails to give the alliance the necessary direction for its future. Stephen Walt, who asked whether anyone would notice if NATO disappeared, expressed this most provocatively. In his evaluation, "the bad news, in short, is that one of the cornerstones of the global security architecture is likely to erode in the years ahead. The good news, however, is that it won't matter very much if it does."[74] In this scenario, fundamental questions of changing geopolitics, economic priorities, issues of effective multilateralism and global governance, and the rule of law, as well as those pertaining to general values and perceptions surrounding the use of force (like liberty, democracy, and the respect for human rights) all exert centrifugal forces on the alliance. In spite of the fact that in terms of missions NATO sees itself as more in demand than ever before,[75] it is seen as peripheral to some of the key security challenges facing its members, and where it is engaged, the results are often ambiguous. The ongoing operations in Afghanistan, in particular, are viewed by this group as a litmus test of NATO's future. Alliance detractors are fond of observing that NATO is beginning to stand for "No Alternative to Obsolescence."[76]

The key arguments that suggest NATO will disappear are based around realist-inspired arguments that alliances are formed in response to one or more threats, and with the disappearance of those threats, the alliance no longer has any utility and will therefore wither and disappear.[77] In support of this notion, Robert Rauchhaus observed that many of the allies did not wait until July 1990 for the announcement of new NATO force plans to complement the changes in Europe, but instead instituted their own unilateral cuts, thus ending even the "pretence of continuing to act as an alliance."[78] The continued existence of NATO, however, confounded post–Cold War realist scholars, since it obviously did not disappear. Instead, the alliance underwent a metamorphosis and emerged principally as a means for America to retain its grip on foreign and military policy among its European allies. In a sense, "old" NATO died, apparently only to resurface as an extension of American foreign and security policy. If this is correct, it still leaves broad questions concerning the future of the alliance, especially if the allies do not share this version of NATO's fundamental purpose and orientation.[79]

The end-of-life position is also based upon a wider set of questions that pertain not only to NATO but, more specifically, to issues of global governance and legitimacy. If we follow the logic of the realist arguments for NATO's endurance, the question is whether a "warrior state," in the form of the United States, can continue to dominate an alliance of predominantly "trade states."[80] This argument goes beyond the familiar Kaganesque cliché of Mars and Venus to postulate that the fundamentals of the alliance will eventually be challenged by the incompatibility of underlying perspectives and views within the alliance over issues of global governance. The eventual collapse or replacement of

Box 13.1   Extracts from the North Atlantic Treaty, Adopted in Washington, D.C., April 4, 1949

Article 1

The Parties undertake, as set forth in the Charter of the United Nations, to settle any international dispute in which they may be involved by peaceful means in such a manner that international peace and security and justice are not endangered, and to refrain in their international relations from the threat or use of force in any manner inconsistent with the purposes of the United Nations.

Article 2

The Parties will contribute toward the further development of peaceful and friendly international relations by strengthening their free institutions, by bringing about a better understanding of the principles upon which these institutions are founded, and by promoting conditions of stability and well-being. They will seek to eliminate conflict in their international economic policies and will encourage economic collaboration between any or all of them.

Article 3

In order more effectively to achieve the objectives of this Treaty, the Parties, separately and jointly, by means of continuous and effective self-help and mutual aid, will maintain and develop their individual and collective capacity to resist armed attack.

The Parties will consult together whenever, in the opinion of any of them, the territorial integrity, political independence or security of any of the Parties is threatened.

Article 5

The Parties agree that an armed attack against one or more of them in Europe or North America shall be considered an attack against them all and consequently they agree that, if such an armed attack occurs, each of them, in exercise of the right of individual or collective self-defence recognised by Article 51 of the Charter of the United Nations, will assist the Party or Parties so attacked by taking forthwith, individually and in concert with the other Parties, such action as it deems necessary, including the use of armed force, to restore and maintain the security of the North Atlantic area.

Any such armed attack and all measures taken as a result thereof shall immediately be reported to the Security Council. Such measures shall be terminated when the Security Council has taken the measures necessary to restore and maintain international peace and security.

Article 10

The Parties may, by unanimous agreement, invite any other European State in a position to further the principles of this Treaty and to contribute to the security of the North Atlantic area to accede to this Treaty. Any State so invited may become a Party to the Treaty by depositing its instrument of accession with the Government of the United States of America. The Government of the United States of America will inform each of the Parties of the deposit of each act of accession.

NATO might result not only because of differences in perception about the post–Cold War world, but through competition to sell or establish vying models of economic or political organization.[81] Differences may not only be transatlantic in nature but intra-European as well. Nor is there any particular time frame associated with these deeply held discrepancies. Provided that there is no major eruption (especially a simultaneous one in two or more regions or nonadjacent countries), NATO could conceivably continue to exist indefinitely. Nevertheless, its continued existence may be at the price of a gradual hollowing out of the alliance, until a point when it becomes a mere facade behind which its members say supportive things but act differently.

The fact that NATO has historically been an American-dominated organization also invites questions concerning the legitimacy of the alliance. The willingness to follow, by persuasion or duress, American leadership has changed over the last decade or so. Anne-Marie Le Gloannec summarizes the essence of this argument when she writes that "2010 could not be more different from 1999 when the previous concept was devised: the U.S. was still the 'hyperpower.' The West now is declining. In the future it is far from sure that NATO will have the legitimacy—endowed by the UN e.g.—and the means to act."[82]

Even if events do not get the better of NATO, more structural factors, such as the Cyprus problem, could also stymie any long-term prospects for the alliance or its ability to form synergies with the EU. The question of the orientation and direction of Turkey, which possesses NATO's second-largest military after the United States and which is an influential actor in the Western Balkans and increasingly Tehran, is of profound concern. Turks hold the lowest approval of President Obama's foreign policies, and their views on the likelihood of the United States exerting strong leadership in the next five years are notably lower than in the EU.[83] Public perceptions of the United States as well as those relating to Iran are also noticeably divergent from the other allies. Turkey further evidences a greater interest in acting alone rather than with EU countries or the United States.[84] Ankara is also highly critical of American-led attempts to broker peace in the Middle East. These viewpoints, combined with the EU's profound reluctance to welcome Turkey into the union, accompanied by mounting disinterest over the last five years by Turks to join it, paint a picture of a key NATO member that is increasingly adrift. The lack of serious EU membership prospects also leaves little incentive for Turkey to resolve the Cyprus problem. This is why NATO's Secretary General Rasmussen has mounted rather late in the day diplomatic pressure to conclude a security agreement with Turkey. At present, the only joint EU-NATO topic that can be openly discussed is Bosnia-Herzegovina.

In the end-of-life scenario, NATO's demise would not be followed by any direct replacement, but by the gradual emergence of a more complex international order marked by increasing region-to-region contacts and the challenge of how to deal with the growing number of nonstate actors in security terms.

B. GLOBAL REBIRTH

The well-crafted report *Shoulder to Shoulder: Forging a Strategic U.S.-EU Part-nership* starts with the premise that the "Atlantic partnership, while indispens-able, is also insufficient to many of the challenges we face. Only by banding together with others are we likely to advance our values, protect our interests, and extend our influence."[85] The authors, who are largely but not exclusively American, see the potential for NATO to form the nucleus of a far wider range of collaborative transatlantic ties on a wide range of security and foreign policy issues.

The logic of this argument is grounded in neoliberal concepts that point to the ability of institutions to adapt and assume new roles and duties.[86] This par-ticular school of thought promotes both the external role of NATO as well as an internal one—that of stability *within* the alliance. While the internal role is neglected in the realist-inspired approaches, it is central to the neoliberal school, since it explains how NATO has survived successive internal crises, ranging from the Anglo-French disputes with the United States over Suez in 1956, General Charles de Gaulle's decision to remove all American forces from France a decade later, the disputes over *Ostpolitik* and ground-launched cruise missiles in the 1980s, and even Anglo-French concerns over the unification of Germany. Thus NATO's mission continues to be relevant within the alliance, while externally the emphasis has moved from collective defense (Article 5) to a more general promotion of political stability and free institutions (Article 2).

The essence of *Shoulder to Shoulder* was reflected in the report by the group of twelve experts who were charged with the responsibility of making recommendations for the 2010 New Strategic Concept. The twelve experts in-sisted that the alliance had clearly adapted to a changed world and had proven that it remains an "essential source of stability in an uncertain and unpredict-able world."[87] In their view, NATO has been able to adjust to the challenges of crisis management, postconflict stabilization, and a wide variety of softer secur-ity challenges (proliferation of WMDs, counterterrorism, and good governance practices). Moreover, they argue that NATO has gone beyond its original trans-atlantic area, and thus it should form the foundations of a wider transatlantic partnership.

The need for NATO's rejuvenation is also built around the observation that there is no other obvious political forum for dialogue on transatlantic se-curity issues. This lack of any obvious alternative, along with the international nature of many of the challenges faced by NATO's membership, led to expan-sive versions of the alliance's future, including that of a "global NATO."[88] Ac-cording to this concept, the renewed alliance would expand its protection to all democracies (including Australia, India, Japan, New Zealand, and South Korea), transforming NATO into a quasi league of democracies. A second strand of global NATO involves offering membership and partnership as a means of spreading democracy and prosperity. Article 2 of NATO's founding treaty is viewed as the legal justification for such a course (see box 13.1). The idea of an "alliance of democracies" actually predates the 2006 Daalder and Goldgeier *Foreign Affairs* article, which is often taken as the reference point. For example, Nicholas Burns, then ambassador of the United States to NATO, referred to the idea in a 2004 speech. It was further popularized by his successor, Victoria Nuland, who "combined the desire for a new, global partnership forum with the necessity of reforming the existing partnership forums and appealed openly for the dissolution of the EAPC [Euro-Atlantic Partnership Council]."[89] The EAPC, first established in 1997 and which now has twenty-two partner countries and twenty-eight full members, provides a platform for the regular exchange of views on a variety of security issues at the ambassadorial level. Nuland viewed EAPC's original mission to strengthen democracy in Central and Eastern Europe as no longer relevant, thus leading her to push to disband it. Critics were quick to point to the apparent tension between the expansive global mission of the alliance and the 1999 NATO Strategic Concept, which states that NATO's main mission is to provide the "indispensable foundations for a stable Euro-Atlantic security environment."[90]

Although very much an American-inspired concept, global partnership or a wider transatlantic partnership has some resonance with a number of allies, including Canada, Denmark, Greece, Romania, and the United Kingdom, and to an extent the Netherlands (although this has to be qualified in light of the fall of the Dutch government over disputes regarding Dutch military contributions to Afghanistan).[91] The failure to communicate what was behind the concept of global partnership led to confusion and general opposition on the part of the other European allies. The lack of any details about the basis upon which the new partners might be selected, and indeed who would select them, fueled by suspicions toward the Bush administration in many European capitals, polarized positions rather than offering a potential rallying point for a reinvigorated NATO.

Even among those member states that are nominally sympathetic to the idea of a global partnership, there are significant differences. Greek perspectives on NATO remain shaped by its fractious triangular relations with Cyprus and Turkey. As a result, Greece has an obvious interest in an international role for NATO and one in which the United States retains strong interest in a strategic role in Europe. Others, like Iceland, Norway, and Turkey, have specific positions based on their membership in NATO and their nonmembership in the EU. For these states, NATO's promotion to the principal transatlantic security forum is crucial, since if the EU assumed this role they would lose influence.

In the case of Canada, the lack of any obvious territorial threat has led to an emphasis on the expeditionary aspects of NATO's mission, which complements Canada's traditional international participation in peacekeeping operations (PKO) and its advocacy of a greater emphasis on NATO's Article 2 role.[92]

With this in mind, the clear Canadian preference is to transform the alliance into a crisis-response organization while at the same time supporting the EU's efforts to this same end (where the Canadians have contributed to several missions). Canada also has a particular interest in the Arctic. However, the Arctic is unlikely to become a key geopolitical focus for NATO given the existence of disputes with other NATO members (Denmark, Iceland, Norway, and the United States) and the strong Russian interests in the region.

The Netherlands' particular vision for NATO's future is connected to its historic association with the United Kingdom and the United States and a preference for stressing alliance cohesion. The question of allied involvement in out-of-area operations is thus not only an issue of external interests having possible ramifications on the security of alliance members; it is also a political question of demonstrating support for the United States and other allies through involvement in combat operations. The Netherlands has also been extremely active in advocating and involving itself in nontraditional security roles, such as those associated with climate change, since it is of such obvious concern for the future well-being of the country. In this context, the Netherlands has also lobbied for an active NATO role since climate change throws up a number of security-related issues, including competition for scarce water resources in sensitive regions of the world such as the "AfPak" region where the Netherlands has been heavily involved. The situation in Romania is somewhat similar, where there is pressure for NATO to play a more active role in energy security issues based on the observation that such a role would link together the various participants in the energy cycle, from providers to upstream distributors, all of whom are represented in the EAPC.

For other European allies, most notably France, the idea of a vague global partnership built around NATO introduced tension with the EU's advocacy of multilateralism, implemented principally through the UN Security Council. This is in contrast to the United States' notion of multilateralism. America continues to see NATO as the "pre-eminent security alliance in the world today," and it "will continue to anchor [its] commitment in Article V, which is fundamental to our collective security."[93] However, the current U.S. National Security Strategy admits that, "In recent years America's frustration with international institutions has led us at times to engage the United Nations (U.N.) system on an ad hoc basis."[94] This statement suggests a clear preference for working through those institutions in which the United States has more leverage, while at the same time it is not beyond advocating the adjustment of European representation in international forums (like the G20, the G8, or the IMF) where it sees Europe as overrepresented.

The promotion of a comprehensive approach to security as part of NATO's rebirth is not unique. It was undertaken by the OSCE under its Lisbon approach in 1996[95] and by the EU since at least 2004.[96] In this sense, NATO may find that the adoption of new mandates will not carve out a new niche for the alliance but may increase the overlap and competition with other organizations. There is also the risk that NATO will be diluted in the name of political expediency, resulting in the loss of both its identity and its mission. Moreover, since the global NATO advocates were primarily American, their arguments were open to allied charges of thinly veiled attempts to buttress American global interests and power into the twenty-first century. Indeed, many of the arguments surrounding the essential nature of NATO are built on the fact that the alliance continues to be dominated by the United States, which underpins it in terms of defense expenditure, research and development, technology, and combat-ready forces. The ability to project power on a global level is also facilitated by America's extensive network of overseas military bases. This remains a unique American capacity within NATO. No other power has the capabilities to project military force on such a scale and to support them with extensive logistical lines running through key bases in Europe, Asia, and significantly, Central Asia.

The key to "rebirth" is thus consensus around a hegemonic power leading the alliance—just as it was with NATO's birth. The presence of a hegemon will, to realists, inevitably lead to competition and balance-of-power behavior, and eventually to a challenge of that hegemon. Yet the reverse logic applies to the rebirth argument. In this scenario, American hegemony will remain broadly acceptable if only to stop the unspoken alternative, which is the reemergence of balance-of-power politics in Europe. This is a reason for the alliance to continue, but it is hardly a ringing endorsement.

C. THE DEFAULT ORGANIZATION

Reflecting on the alliance in its sixtieth year, Jan Petersen suggests that "the key to NATO's longevity is precisely that it has proven to be an adaptable organization that maintains its relevance."[97] This popular explanation is partially true, but the nature of what NATO is transforming *to* is unclear—at times the process appears to be more important than identifying the endpoint.

In this scenario, NATO is neither in imminent danger of expiry, nor will it notably flourish. Instead, it will remain indefinitely in default mode. The essence of this argument is that NATO continues to be backed by one major sponsor, the United States, which continues to view the alliance as relevant to meeting today's security challenges. Unlike the realist-inspired arguments, the dominance of the United States is essential to the continuation of NATO. However, NATO's actual relevance is decreasingly pertinent to the changing environment, which means that NATO is often one step behind, trying to put out potential or actual fires in the Western Balkans or Afghanistan (when Pakistan and Iran are actually burning). Attempts by NATO to prove its relevance, such as by maintaining its open door to membership, may in fact have a negative impact if the new members bring little to the table in terms of substantive capacities and resources. The default mode may also include elements of bureaucratic inertia, especially if the mantra that Europe and America have built "the most successful alliance in history" is repeated often enough.[98]

Shapiro and Witney argue that NATO will remain in the default mode when they observe that the European allies continue to promote the idea of the United States as the guarantor of peace, not necessarily because they believe it but because it is a claim that agrees with them. In their words, "This continued sense of dependence suits Europeans. It absolves them from responsibility and lets the U.S. take the hard decisions, run the risks and incur the costs."[99] Shapiro and Witney further suggest that there may be internal political reasons among the allies for supporting this position that has little to do with the alliance per se. These include an Italian desire to keep Germany off the UN Security Council, a German wish to ignore the French *force de frappe* (nuclear deterrent) by stressing American guarantees, and both Danish and Dutch historical concerns with keeping Germany and France in check.

If this explanation of allied behavior is correct, it suggests that the alliance will not go out of business, but by the same token, there will be no major initiatives that will move NATO forward. Beata Górka-Winter and Marek Madej propose an interesting hypothesis that underscores this predicament. They maintain that rather than polar positions along the lines suggested above, the alliance is dominated by the "passive, undecided and the silent," which they give the acronym PUS.[100] The PUS allies are not anti-NATO, but they tend to view their situation in terms of military threats and are as a rule more inclined to concentrate on their particular security interests. They do not necessarily "view NATO as the sole—or even the principal—instrument" by which their security needs are satisfied.[101] Instead, the PUS, more than other allies, are interested in limiting their costs (both material and nonmaterial) of NATO membership. Górka-Winter and Madej suggest that the PUS countries include Germany, Greece, Portugal, and Spain.

The numbers of PUS may expand, or even become "passive, decided and silent" (PDS), which is far more threatening to the alliance, due to the financial crisis besetting key NATO members. As a result of drastic cuts in budgets, tough choices have to be made about funding social entitlement programs, especially in a graying Europe. Now, more than ever, the political grounds for arguing that defense expenditure needs to be retained in real terms are weak, especially when there is widespread consensus that the allies face no direct security threat. In most of the European NATO countries, defense expenditure is already at or under 2 percent of the gross domestic product, and a number of major allies, such as the United Kingdom, are facing cuts of up to 20 percent as part of more general austerity measures.[102] In the four primary European defense industrial producers, the appeal to uphold or even increase defense budgets is being made not upon strategic grounds, or even expressions of solidarity within the alliance, but on the need to uphold strong and competitive defense industries.[103]

The final variant on the default theme is that since there is no apparent alternative, the Western states are stuck with NATO for the indefinite future. This is basically a reductionist argument whereby no one has demonstrated NATO's irrelevance by demonstrating that something else is more relevant. The normal stream of thought that accompanies this line of reasoning is that the EU's Common Security and Defense Policy (CSDP) remains modest, and even if construed as a challenge to NATO, it will be a long time before it poses any fundamental alternative. This version leaves NATO as the default organization for the indefinite future, but in an enfeebled form. Default NATO may continue to exist as a political expression of shared concerns, but it would remain a shadow of its former self. The eventual demise of the WEU suggests that organizations can be sustained as essentially political facades for a while, but not indefinitely.

CONCLUSION

This chapter has explored the nature of the current crossroads at which NATO finds itself. As we look to the future, the New Strategic Concept may convince elites of the alliance's continuing vitality, but it also needs to appeal to the wider NATO publics who are increasingly anxious about their own economic concerns. The European allies, for the most part, also remain preoccupied with their ongoing (and troubled) integration project and are increasingly unlikely to put the energy required into new arrangements that solidify America's position as *primus inter pares*. It is also easy to forget that although the European allies in NATO may share the same basic values and principles and collaborate on security issues, they are also competitors in many other fields, such as trade.[104]

It is clear that the debates surrounding NATO's future will invoke a broader set of questions about the direction of transatlantic relations. Part of the dialogue will involve impressing upon American audiences the fundamental importance of European integration to the EU members and their publics, and, conversely, it is just as important for the European allies to understand the value of NATO to the United States. Proponents of Euro-Atlanticism will have to convince the skeptics that any "rebirth" of NATO will not prove detrimental to the EU and its interests—especially if, as Pascal Vennesson observes, it "alienates the EU's neighbors, the Islamic world (within and outside Europe), Russia and China."[105]

The broad political discourse provoked by the New Strategic Concept still leaves the European allies the fundamental challenge of how to improve their collective capacities and effectiveness. However, if the allies do so, it will have to be accompanied by a new transatlantic bargain since it is illusory to anticipate that "trilateral arrangements," whereby EU and American civilian assets complement NATO's military efforts, will be acceptable to the allies. There are dangers in a new transatlantic bargain for many of the European allies who, on the whole, give priority to the European integration project, which includes the ambition to address a far wider range of security challenges than NATO. For the European allies, there is the danger that prolonged navel-gazing will only encourage the further shifting of American strategic priorities away from Europe and toward Asia.

The danger for the United States is that the promotion of NATO may encourage European tendencies to free ride as the price for continuing American influence over the alliance. Conversely, if there is a genuine attempt to redress manpower and resource shortcomings among the allies, it may well come with the expectation that the United States would act within the constraints of multilateral institutions and the rule of law—both of which may be difficult to swallow. The adoption of NATO's New Strategic Concept is likely to give the alliance a temporary boost of vigor and purpose. It is, though, a consensual document intended to promote the relevance of the alliance, not to question it. The utility of a strategic vision should not be underestimated, but if the object of the exercise is merely to promote a strategy that is of sufficiently vague content to keep the alliance going, it will have failed.

Suggested Readings

Aybet, Gulnur, and Rebecca R. Moore (eds.), *NATO: In Search of a Vision*, Washington, DC: Georgetown University Press, 2010.

Braun, Aurel, *NATO-Russia Relations in the Twenty-first Century*, Abingdon, Oxon: Routledge, 2008.

Douglas, Frank R., *The United States, NATO, and a New Multilateral Relationship*, Westport, CT: Praeger, 2008.

Goldgeier, James M., *The Future of NATO*, New York: Council on Foreign Relations Press, 2010.

Kaplan, Lawrence, *NATO 1948: The Birth of the Transatlantic Alliance*, Lanham, MD: Rowman & Littlefield, 2007.

Larrabee, F. Stephen, *Turkey as a U.S. Security Partner*, Santa Monica, CA: RAND Corporation, 2008.

Pouliot, Vincent, *International Security in Practice: The Politics of NATO-Russia*, Cambridge: Cambridge University Press, 2010.

Thies, Wallace J., *Why NATO Endures*, New York: Cambridge University Press, 2009.

Toje, Asle, *America, the EU and Strategic Culture: Renegotiating the Transatlantic Bargain*, Abingdon, Oxon: Routledge, 2008.

Sloan, Stanley R., *Permanent Alliance? NATO and the Transatlantic Bargain from Truman to Obama*, London: Continuum, 2010.

Notes

Introduction: The European Outlook

1. See, for example, Robert Kagan, *The Return of History and the End of Dreams*, London: Atlantic Books, 2008; Christopher Caldwell, *Reflections on the Revolution in Europe: Immigration, Islam, and the West*, New York: Doubleday, 2009.

2. Here see T. R. Reid, *The United States of Europe: The New Superpower and the End of American Supremacy*, New York: Penguin, 2005; Jeremy Rifkin, *European Dream: How Europe's Vision of the Future Is Quietly Eclipsing the American Dream*, New York: Tarcher, 2005; Steven Hill, *Europe's Promise: Why the European Way Is the Best Hope in an Insecure Age*, Berkeley: University of California Press, 2010.

3. Astute observers will note that our three examples are all from the United Kingdom. The reality is that it would be just as easy to find representative volumes in each and every EU member state. See Mark Leonard, *Why Europe Will Run the 21st Century*, New York: Public Affairs, 2006; Anand Menon, *Europe: The State of the Union*, London: Atlantic, 2008; Simon Hix, *What's Wrong with the European Union and How to Fix It*, London: Polity, 2008.

4. Chris Patten, "What Is Europe to Do?" *New York Review of Books*, 57(4), March 11, 2010–March 24, 2010, 11–12.

5. See, for example, the conference proceedings published by the European Commission called *Mapping the Future of the EU-US Partnership: Policy and Research Perspectives*, Brussels: European Commission, 2010.

6. *National Security Strategy: May 2010*, Washington, DC: White House, 2010, p. 41. The same language appeared in an editorial signed by President Obama shortly before the November 2010 NATO summit in Lisbon. See "Europe and America, Aligned for the Future," *International Herald Tribune*, November 19, 2010.

7. UN report, "The World at 6 Billion," available online at http://www.un.org/esa/population/publications/sixbillion/sixbilpart1.pdf.

8. See Sonia Lucarelli (ed.), "Beyond Self-Perception: The Others' View of the European Union," special issue, *European Foreign Affairs Review*, 12(3), Autumn 2007.

9. See John van Oudenaren, *Uniting Europe: An Introduction to the European Union*, 2nd ed., Lanham, MD: Rowman & Littlefield, 2004; Roy H. Ginsberg, *Demystifying the European Union: The Enduring Logic of Regional Integration*, 2nd ed., Lanham, MD: Rowman & Littlefield, 2010.

10. For this early European experience in the crisis, see Laura Beke and Erik Jones (eds.), *European Responses to the Global Economic Crisis*, Bologna: Clueb, 2009.

11. See Dermot Hodson and Lucia Quglia (eds.), "European Perspectives on the Global Financial Crisis," special issue, *Journal of Common Market Studies*, 47(5), December 2009.

12. With the entrance of Estonia on January 1, 2011, seventeen out of the twenty-seven EU countries now use the euro, altogether making for the second largest economy in the world.

13. Most of the major quality papers have pulled together online dossiers of their articles on the European sovereign debt crisis. Among those that are freely accessible, the dossier offered by the *New York Times* is the most comprehensive and insightful. See http://topics.nytimes.com/top/reference/timestopics/subjects/e/european_sovereign_debt_crisis/index.html.

14. Again, this kind of information will be found in the online archives of any quality paper. Another source of thoughtful commentary is available from *Financial Times* columnist Wolfgang Münchau through his "eurointelligence" blog. Access to that blog was free throughout most of the crisis, but starting in 2011, readers have to pay a modest monthly charge. See http://www.eurointelligence.com.

15. Martin Feldstein, "EMU and International Conflict," *Foreign Affairs*, 76(6), November–December 1997, 61–62.

16. Paul De Grauwe, "Monetary Integration since the Maastricht Treaty," *Journal of Common Market Studies*, 44(4), November 2006, 711–730.

17. See, for example, Ludger Kühnhardt (ed.), *Crises in European Integration: Challenges and Responses, 1945–2005*, New York: Berghahn Books, 2009. For an argument about NATO along these lines, see Wallace J. Thies, *Why NATO Endures*, Cambridge: Cambridge University Press, 2009.

18. The books by Reid, Rifkin, and Leonard cited above all fall into this category. See also Jan Zielonka, *Europe as Empire: The Nature of the Enlarged European Union*, Oxford: Oxford University Press, 2006; John McCormick, *The European Superpower*, Basingstoke: Palgrave, 2007.

19. The process for ratifying the European constitutional treaty was stopped at this point, but if other referenda had been held, the likelihood that all of them would have passed was small. For more on the crisis in public opinion, see the Menon and Hix volumes cited above. See also Paul Taylor, *The End of European Integration: Anti-Europeanism Examined*, London: Routledge, 2008.

20. As Jolyon Howarth puts it, "Like it or not, the European Union, in the wake of Lisbon, has become an international actor." See Jolyon Howarth, "The EU as a Global Actor: Grand Strategy for a Global Grand Bargain?" *Journal of Common Market Studies*, 48(3), June 2010, 455.

21. Bastian Giegerich, "Military and Civilian Capabilities for EU-led Crisis Management Operations," in Bastian Giegerich (ed.), *Europe and Global Security*, London: Routledge for IISS, 2010, pp. 41–57.

22. See Peter Ludlow, "In the Last Resort: The European Council and the Euro Crisis, Spring 2010," *Eurocomment Briefing Note*, 7(7–8), June 2010.

23. See *BIS Quarterly Review: International Banking and Financial Market Developments*, Basle: Bank for International Settlements, December 2010, p. 11.

24. This line of argument is also suggested by Patten, cited above. See also François Heisbourg, "The European Union and the Major Powers," in Bastian Giegerich (ed.), *Europe and Global Security*, London: Routledge for IISS, 2010, pp. 17–39.

25. See, for example, Jeffrey Mankoff, *Russian Foreign Policy: The Return of Great Power Politics*, Lanham, MD: Rowman & Littlefield, 2009.

26. Michael Stürmer, *Putin and the Rise of Russia*, London: Weidenfeld & Nicholson, 2008.

27. See, for example, Meltem Müftüler-Baç and Yannis A. Stivachtis (eds.), *Turkey-European Union Relations: Dilemmas, Opportunities, and Constraints*, Lanham, MD: Lexington Books, 2008.

28. For a careful analysis of this problem, see Ray Taras, *Europe Old and New: Transnationalism, Belonging, Xenophobia*, Lanham, MD: Rowman & Littlefield, 2009. See also the essays in Roland Hsiu (ed.), *Ethnic Europe: Mobility, Identity, and Conflict in a Globalized World*, Stanford: Stanford University Press, 2010.

29. For contrasting views of this development, see M. Hakan Yavuz, *Secularism and Muslim Democracy in Turkey*, Cambridge: Cambridge University Press, 2009; Gareth Jenkins, *Political Islam in Turkey: Running West, Heading East?* New York: Palgrave Macmillan, 2008.

30. F. Steven Larrabee, "Turkey's New Geopolitics," *Survival*, 52(2), April–May, 157–181.

31. For an assessment of the proposal and the alternatives, see Mark Fitzpatrick, "Iran: The Fragile Promise of the Fuel-Swap Plan," *Survival*, 52(3), June–July 2010, 67–94.

32. For an overview, see Nigel Inkster, "Terrorism in Europe," in Bastian Giegerich (ed.), *Europe and Global Security*, London: Routledge for IISS, 2010, pp. 79–101.

33. Richard J. Aldrich, "Transatlantic Intelligence and Security Cooperation," *International Affairs*, 80(4), July 2004, 731–753.

34. Herbert Kitschelt and Anthony J. McGann, *The Radical Right in Western Europe: A Comparative Analysis*, Ann Arbor: University of Michigan Press, 1997.

35. See Cas Mudde, "The Single Issue Party Thesis: Extreme Right Parties and the Immigration Issue," *West European Politics*, 22(3), July 1999, 182–197; Cas Mudde, *Populist Radical Right Parties in Europe*, Cambridge: Cambridge University Press, 2007.

36. Thilo Sarrazin, *Deutschland schafft sich ab: Wie wir unser Land aufs Spiel setzen*, München: Deutscher Verlags-Anstalt, 2010.

37. Tony Judt, "What Is Living and What Is Dead in Social Democracy," *New York Review of Books*, 56(20), December 17, 2009–January 13, 2010, 86–96. The citations are taken from p. 92.

38. For an excellent overview of Thatcher's legacy in British politics, see Simon Jenkins, *Thatcher and Sons: A Revolution in Three Acts*, London: Penguin, 2007.

39. Here see again the book by Taras cited above. See also Malise Ruthven, "The Big Muslim Problem!" *New York Review of Books*, 56(20), December 17, 2009–January 13, 2010, 62–65.

Chapter 1: France: The Sarkozy Presidency in Historical Perspective

1. Cf., for example, Christopher Caldwell, *Reflections on the Revolution in Europe: Immigration, Islam and the West*, New York: Doubleday, 2009.

2. Deriving its name from the model of industrial organization conceived by Henry

Ford during the 1920s, Fordism represented a self-enclosed economic system based on large-scale rationalized productive units that achieved self-sustenance by fueling internal demand for its own goods through a virtuous cycle of cheaper prices made possible by the increasingly efficient organization of production and the integration of labor-saving technology on the one hand, and consistently rising wage levels imputable to higher worker productivity on the other.

3. Cf. "Redeploying the State: Liberalization and Social Policy in France," in W. Streeck and K. Thelen (eds.), *Beyond Continuity: Institutional Change in Advanced Political Economies*, New York: Oxford University Press, 2005, pp. 103–126.

4. Tim Smith, *France in Crisis: Welfare, Inequality, and Globalization since 1980*, Cambridge, UK: Cambridge University Press, 2004, pp. 102–103.

5. Perhaps the most notorious example of such a program was the Villepin government's ill-fated *Contrat première embauche* (First-time Hires Contract), which dispensed employers from having to pay social security taxes for three years on recently hired unemployed young workers, while giving them the latitude to dismiss these workers at any time. This latter clause provoked the ire of the trade unions and students, leading to a wave of protests against the measure which resulted in its withdrawal in April 2006.

6. Jean-Marie Monnier, "Politique fiscale: Une mise en perspective," in E. Lau (ed.), *L'état de la France, 2009–2010*, Paris: La Découverte, 2009, p. 182.

7. In this last case, the overwhelming proportion of ETA (Euskadi ta Askatasuna, or Basque Homeland and Freedom) violence has been confined to the Spanish side of the border, although a number of ETA activists and safe houses have been uncovered in France.

8. Although the overall size of the immigrant population has not increased that much over the past thirty years—it accounted for 8.1 percent of the total population in 2004—its composition has changed due to the replacement of immigrants from Southern and Eastern Europe by immigrants from North and Sub-Saharan Arica. This has not only made the immigrant presence more visible but has also resulted in France developing the largest Muslim minority in Western Europe.

9. In an unexpected ruling, in October 2010 the Constitutional Court upheld the legality of the law, claiming that it struck "a reasonable balance" between personal liberty and the safeguarding of women's rights and public order. The ruling was a surprise since the Council of State, another government watchdog on legislative affairs, had twice recommended against banning the burka and niqab on the grounds that this would be an unconstitutional infringement of individuals' freedom of religion under French and European law. See John Lichfield, "France's Highest Legal Authority Removes Last Obstacle to Ban on Burka," *The Independent*, available at http://www.independent .co.uk/news/world/europe/frances-highest-legal-authority-removes-last-obstacle-to -ban-on-burka-2101002.html, accessed October 2010.

10. Cf. Rémy Leveau, "Change and Continuity in French Islam," in R. Leveau, K. Mohsen-Finan, and C. Wihtol de Wenden (eds.), *New European Identity and Citizenship*, Aldershot, UK: Ashgate, 2002, pp. 91–99.

11. Jonathan Laurence and Justin Vaïsse, "Understanding the Urban Riots in France," Brookings Institution, available at http://www.brookings.edu/articles/2005/1201france_ laurence.aspx, accessed September 2010.

12. A particularly telling indicator of this discrimination is that young people of immigrant background who hold a university degree are still three times more likely to be unemployed than nonimmigrants with the same degree.

13. Laurence and Vaïsse, "Understanding the Urban Riots in France," p. 3. In belated recognition of this problem, the government has begun to dismantle the *cités*, but this is proving extremely slow and costly.

14. Most legal experts believe these proposals, which have provoked disquiet not only on the Left but also within the ruling UMP, to be unconstitutional under French law.

15. Colette Ysmal, "L'évolution des systèmes de partis: Émiettement, regroupement et alliances," in E. Lau (ed.), *L'état de la France, 2009–2010*, Paris: La Découverte, 2009, p. 214.

16. The reality of Sarkozy's political career has been much more prosaic. For over thirty years, he served as an apparatchik in the RPR, seconding a succession of party "elephants" including Charles Pasqua, Jacques Chirac, and Édouard Balladur before making his way to the top of the party leadership and recasting it as the UMP.

17. Cf. Gérard Grunberg and Florence Haegel, *La France vers le bipartisme? La présidentialisation du PS et de l'UMP*, Paris: Presses de Sciences Po, 2007.

18. Quoted in Chloé Durand-Parenti, "L'état passe un 'pacte' avec les constructeurs automobiles," *Le Point*, available at http://www.lepoint.fr/actualites-economie/l-etat-passe-un-pacte-avec-les-constructeurs-automobiles/916/0/315468, accessed September 2010.

19. Cf. "Nicolas Sarkozy's Foreign Policy: Gaullist by Another Name," Brookings Institution, available at http://www.brookings.edu/articles/2008/04_sarkozy_vaisse.aspx, accessed September 2010.

20. Less successful has been Sarkozy's Union of the Mediterranean, whose promotion of economic and political cooperation in the region was compromised from the start by his refusal to countenance Turkish accession to the EU as well as by the ongoing Israeli-Palestinian conflict. Likewise, the presidency failed to revive ESDP as a prelude to France rejoining NATO's integrated military command, highlighting the persistent wariness of her EU partners with regard to her motivations in this area.

Chapter 2: Great Britain: From New Labour to New Politics?

1. Carl Emmerson et al., *The Government's Fiscal Rules*, Institute of Fiscal Studies Briefing Note 16, http://www.ifs.org.uk/bns/bn16.pdf#search=%22public%20borrowing%22.

2. Anthony Giddens, *The Third Way*, Cambridge: Polity Press, 1998.

3. Andrew Glyn and Stewart Wood, "New Labour's Economic Policy," in Andrew Glyn (ed.), *Social Democracy in Neoliberal Times*, Oxford: Oxford University Press, 2001, ch. 8.

4. Jonathan Hopkin and Daniel Wincott, "New Labour, Economic Reform, and the European Social Model," *British Journal of Politics and International Relations*, 8(1), January 2006, 50–68.

5. Hilaire Barnett, *Britain Unwrapped: Government and Constitution Explained*, London: Penguin, 2002, p. 52.

6. For a powerful denunciation of the risks inherent in this constitutional vagueness, see F. F. Ridley, "There Is No British Constitution: A Dangerous Case of the Emperor's Clothes," *Parliamentary Affairs*, 41(3), July 1988, 340–361.

7. For an extensive discussion of the history of the "territorial question" in modern British politics, see Vernon Bogdanor, *Devolution in the United Kingdom*, Oxford: Oxford University Press, 1998.

8. For an extensive account of the "Irish question," see John McGarry and Brendan O'Leary (eds.), *The Northern Ireland Conflict*, Oxford: Oxford University Press, 2005.

9. Charlie Jeffery, "Devolution and the Lopsided State," in Patrick Dunleavy, Richard Heffernan, Philip Cowley, and Colin Hay (eds.), *Developments in British Politics 8*, Basingstoke: Palgrave, 2006, pp. 138–158.

10. For an analysis of how the major British parties adapted to devolution, see Jonathan Hopkin and Jonathan Bradbury, "British Parties and Multilevel Politics," *Publius: The Journal of Federalism*, 36(1), January 2006, 135–152.

11. "Jenkins Commission" (Independent Commission on the Voting System), report presented to Parliament by the Secretary of State for the Home Department by command of Her Majesty, October 1998, available online at http://www.archive.official-documents.co.uk/document/cm40/4090/4090.htm.

12. See Stephen George, *An Awkward Partner: Britain in the European Community*, Oxford: Oxford University Press, 1998.

13. See Jonathan Hopkin and Daniel Wincott, "New Labour, Economic Reform and the European Social Model," *British Journal of Politics and International Relations*, 8(1), January 2006, 50–68.

14. For an analysis of Blair's foreign policy thinking, see Michael Cox and Tim Oliver, "Security Policy in an Insecure World," in Patrick Dunleavy, Richard Heffernan, Philip Cowley, and Colin Hay (eds.), *Developments in British Politics 8*, Basingstoke: Palgrave, 2006, pp. 174–192.

Chapter 3: Germany: Two Decades of Passage from Bonn to Berlin

1. Various Christian-based political groups organized in 1945, but party consolidation across zones of occupation soon led to the emergence of the Christian Democratic Party of Germany (CDU). Political leaders of the Christian Social Union (CSU) in Bavaria decided to remain separate; the anomaly of two conservative parties, with many programmatic similarities but divided by region, persists. The CDU is the main center-right party in all parts of Germany except Bavaria; its so-called sister party, the CSU, exists only as a Bavarian regional party. This chapter treats the two as one since they almost always act in unison at the federal level, occasional tensions notwithstanding.

2. C. K. Williams, "Das symbolische Volk der Täter," *Die Zeit*, 46, 2002, http://www.zeit.de/2002/46/Symbol (accessed July 20, 2006).

3. Tony Judt, *Postwar: A History of Europe since 1945*, New York: Penguin Press, 2005, p. 826.

4. For more detail, see Jeffrey M. Peck, *Being Jewish in the New Germany*, New Brunswick, NJ: Rutgers University Press, 2006.

5. For a very readable account of Germany's road to normality, see Steve Crawshaw, *Easier Fatherland: Germany and the Twenty-first Century*, London: Continuum, 2004.

6. Interview with Angela Merkel, "Es ist noch viel Arbeit zu erledigen," *Süddeutsche Zeitung*, September 11, 2009, http://www.sueddeutsche.de/politik/972/487380/text/print.html.

7. Quoted in *Deutschland Magazine*, 6(4), 2007. The special issue on Berlin is available at http://www.magazine-deutschland.de/nc/de/heftarchiv/heftdetail/mdissue/076.html.

8. For further elaboration, see Helga A. Welsh, "Germany: Ascent to Middle Power," in Ronald Tiersky and John Van Oudenaren (eds.), *European Foreign Policies: Does Europe Still Matter?* Lanham, MD: Rowman & Littlefield, 2010, pp. 211–234.

9. Beate Kohler-Koch, "Europäisierung: Plädoyer für eine Horizonterweiterung," in Michèle Knodt and Beate Kohler-Koch (eds.), *Deutschland zwischen Europäisierung und Selbstbehauptung*, Frankfurt and New York: Campus Verlag, 2000, p. 11.

10. The list is partially taken from Gunther Hellmann, "Precarious Power: Germany at the Dawn of the Twenty-first Century," in Wolf-Dieter Eberwein and Karl Kaiser (eds.), *Germany's New Foreign Policy: Decision-Making in an Interdependent World*, New York: Palgrave, 2001, p. 293.

11. Beverly Crawford, "The Normative Power of a Normal State: Power and Revolutionary Vision in Germany's Post-Wall Foreign Policy," *German Politics and Society*, 28(2), Summer 2010, pp. 169–170.

12. The typology of crises is taken from Andreas Maurer, "Die Europäische Union zwischen Dauerkrise und Dauerreform," *Ausblick: Deutsche Außenpolitik nach Christoph Bertram*, Berlin: Stiftung Wissenschaft und Politik, September 2005, pp. 26–29.

13. Elisabeth Noelle-Neumann and Thomas Petersen, "Die Bürger in Deutschland," in Werner Weidenfeld (ed.), *Europa-Handbuch*, vol. 2, *Die Staatenwelt Europas*, 3rd rev. ed., Gütersloh: Verlag Bertelsmann Stiftung, 2004, pp. 43–55.

14. Simon J. Bulmer, "Shaping the Rules? The Constitutive Politics of the European Union and German Power," in Peter J. Katzenstein (ed.), *Tamed Power: Germany in Europe*, Ithaca, NY: Cornell University Press, 1997, p. 50.

15. Charles Lees, "'Dark Matter': Institutional Constraints and the Failure of Party-Based Euroscepticism in Germany," *Political Studies*, 50(2), 2002, pp. 244–267.

16. Jacques Delors et al., "Heute muss man die Deutschen von Europa überzeugen. Ein Gespräch mit Jacques Delors," *Leviathan*, 38, 2010, pp. 1–21 (author's translation).

17. Speech by Joschka Fischer at Humboldt University in Berlin, "From Confederacy to Federalism—Thoughts on the Finality of European Integration," May 12, 2000, http://www.ena.lu?lang=2&doc=18824 (accessed July 30, 2006); on Habermas and Derrida, see Daniel Levy et al., *Old Europe, New Europe, Core Europe: Transatlantic Relations after the Iraq War*, London and New York: Verso, 2005.

18. Martin Große Hüttmann and Matthias Chardon, "Bundesrepublik Deutschland," in Werner Weidenfeld and Wolfgang Wessels (eds.), *Jahrbuch der Europäischen Integration 2009*, Baden-Baden: Nomos, 2010, pp. 342–343.

19. "Obama More Popular Abroad than at Home, Global Image of U.S. Continues to Benefit," Twenty-two-Nation Pew Global Attitudes Survey, June 17, 2010, http://pewresearch.org/pubs/1630/obama-more-popular-abroad-global-american-image-benefit-22-nation-global-survey (accessed August 9, 2010).

20. Perry Anderson, "A New Germany?" *New Left Review*, 57, May–June 2009, pp. 5–40.

21. Charles S. Maier, "'Als wär' es ein Stück von uns . . .' German Politics and Society Traverses Twenty Years of United Germany," *German Politics and Society*, 28(2), Summer 2010, pp. 1–16.

22. Konrad A. Jarausch, "The Federal Republic at Sixty: Popular Myths, Actual Accomplishments and Competing Interpretations," *German Politics and Society*, 28(1), Spring 2010, p. 25.

23. "A Muted Normalcy," in "Older and Wiser: A Special Report on Germany," *Economist*, March 13, 2010, pp. 15–16.

Chapter 4: Italy: Politics in the Age of Berlusconi

1. See Fabio Luca Cavazza and Stephen R. Graubard (eds.), *Il caso italiano*, Milan: Rizzoli, 1974; Tommaso Padoa Schioppa and Stephen R. Graubard (eds.), *Il caso italiano 2: dove sta andando il nostro paese?* Milan: Rizzoli, 2001; both first published as special issues of the American Journal *Daedalus*.

2. David Hine, *Governing Italy: The Politics of Bargained Pluralism*, Oxford: Oxford University Press, 1993, p. 15.

3. Prefectures are a typical French (Napoleonic) institution, which Italy inherited from Piedmont. The prefects who control them represent the authority of the centralized state at the local level. These prefects were a key element in the state structure that Italy adopted at unification. Moreover, they were kept with only incremental changes (i.e., regional elective institutions introduced after World War II) until a federalization process started in the mid-1990s. A recent study on the rise of the Italian and German states, while confirming that the federal option was not dismissed as impossible at the outset, plausibly argues that the preunitary states lacked sufficient infrastructural capacity to build a federation similar to the one that Prussia was about to create in Germany. See Daniel Ziblatt, *Structuring the State: The Formation of Italy and Germany and the Puzzle of Federalism*, Princeton, NJ: Princeton University Press, 2006; but see also Carlo Tullio Altan, "Except for Piedmont, Lombardy, Emilia-Romagna and Tuscany, at the time no other Italian region was prepared to be governed with an Anglo Saxon self-government system," *La nostra Italia, Clientelismo, Trasformismo e Ribellismo dall'Unità al 2000*, Milan: Egea, 2000, p. 47.

4. See Stefano Bartolini, *The Political Mobilization of the European Left, 1860–1980*, Cambridge: Cambridge University Press, 2000, pp. 132 and 195, respectively. Italy also displayed a high level of economic inequality (as it still does to this day), a factor often considered critical in democratization processes.

5. In other words, and borrowing Stein Rokkan's terminology, the threshold of representation was significantly lowered too soon after the threshold of incorporation (i.e., the extension of suffrage) had been passed, thus decisively jeopardizing the democratization process.

6. Ernesto Galli della Loggia, *La morte della patria*, Rome: Laterza, 1996, pp. 4–5.

7. The PCI was a Janus-faced party. The official face, well after the death of its leader Palmiro Togliatti 1964, held Moscow as a key reference point. A pragmatic face is

apparent when one looks at the fact that, under the same leadership of Togliatti, the party approved almost three-fourths of the laws passed by parliament in the first four legislative terms.

8. Robert D. Putnam et al., *Making Democracy Work: Civic Traditions in Modern Italy*, Princeton: Princeton University Press, 1993, p. 167.

9. See Giovanni Sartori, *Parties and Party Systems*, Colchester: ECPR Press, 2005.

10. See Maurizio Cotta and Luca Verzichelli, *Political Institutions in Italy*, Oxford: Oxford University Press, 2007, pp. 144, 149.

11. The reform was aimed at fostering DC's governing coalitions and soon was dubbed a "swindle" (*legge truffa*) by the main oppositions as it prescribed a consistent majority bonus (64.4 percent of the seats in the Chamber of Deputies to be assigned to the party or coalition securing 50 percent of the vote). The left's campaign was successful, as it played on the memories of the 1923 Acerbo Law, which gave 60 percent of the seats to the Fascist party. That device, however, was different, as the seat bonus was awarded to the list gaining a plurality of votes; see Gianfranco Baldini, "The Different Trajectories of Italian Electoral Reforms," *West European Politics*, 34(3), 2011, 644–663.

12. Leonardo Morlino, *Democracy between Consolidation and Crisis: Parties, Groups, and Citizens in Southern Europe*, Oxford: Oxford University Press, 1998.

13. See James G. March and Johan P. Olsen, *Rediscovering Institutions: The Organizational Basis of Politics*, New York: Free Press, 1989; and for an application of these concepts to Italy, see Roberto Cartocci, *Fra Lega e Chiesa: L'Italia in cerca di integrazione*, Bologna: Il Mulino, 1994.

14. Arturo Parisi and Gianfranco Pasquino, "Changes in Italian Electoral Behaviour: The Relationships between Parties and Voters," *West European Politics*, 2(3), 1979, 6–30.

15. Incidentally, this was the first year when a paradigmatic figure such as Giulio Andreotti first became prime minister. Andreotti was to lead seven governments, being also always a minister from 1948 to 1992 (and of course sitting in every parliament to this day—now as life senator—being elected the first time at the age of twenty-seven, in 1946). Governments were formed and dismissed by partisan (or factional) agreements in smoked-filled rooms, and ratified in parliament. Factionalism also brought about the very Italian species of *"governi balneari"* (literally "beach government," to last less than a summer).

16. See Carlo Maria Santoro, *La politica estera di una media Potenza*, Bologna: Il Mulino, 1991, and Filippo Andreatta, "Italian Foreign Policy: Domestic Politics, International Requirements and the European Dimension," in Erik Jones and Saskia van Genugten (eds.), "The Future of European Foreign Policy," special issue, *Journal of European Integration*, 30(1), 2008, 169–181.

17. See Paul Ginsborg, *Italy and Its Discontents, 1980–2001*, London: Penguin Books, 2003, p. 240.

18. See Lucio Caracciolo, "L'Italia alla ricerca di se stessa," in Giovanni Sabbatucci and Vittorio Vidotto (eds.), *Storia d'Italia*, vol. 6, *L'Italia contemporanea*, Rome: Laterza, 1999, pp. 541–604.

19. Caracciolo, "L'Italia alla ricerca di se stessa," p. 545.

20. Signs of growing popular discontent included a sharp decrease in interest in politics; the success of antiestablishment movements and parties (such as the Greens and the Radicals); increasing recourse to referenda, after the 1974 referendum on divorce had for

the first time shown that parties were losing voters' confidence; and increasing popular dissatisfaction vis-à-vis the performance of Italian democracy, as documented by several Eurobarometer surveys.

21. Italy was ranked 63 out of 180 countries surveyed in Transparency International's 2009 Corruption Perceptions Index, the second lowest rating for Western Europe.

22. One might argue that the Italian economy, despite high levels of unemployment, reacted well to the crisis that began in 2008. See Erik Jones, "Italy and the Euro in the Global Economic Crisis," *International Spectator*, 44(4), 2009, 93–103. This also meant that in the commonly used PIGS acronym—indicating the weak European (all Mediterranean) economies of Portugal, Italy, Greece, and Spain—Italy recently has often been replaced by Ireland.

23. Arguably corruption levels also remained high because, despite the removal of facilitating factors such as lack of alternation, and despite reforms in public administration transparency, corruption "has been shown to be—and presumably still is—a *system*, not the mere aggregation of many dispersed, isolated illegal acts. It has become a market, which, as in the case of every functioning market, has developed internal rules and codes of behaviour—a *regulated* market, in which the exercise of public authority in many crucial areas—public contracting procedures, licensing, urban planning, etc.—is governed by the laws of supply and demand." Alberto Vannucci, "The Controversial Legacy of '*Mani Pulite*': A Critical Analysis of Italian Corruption and Anti-Corruption Policies," *Bulletin of Italian Politics*, 1(2), 2009, p. 244.

24. In a comparison made in 2009 between the fifteen member states of the European Union (i.e., before the "Great Enlargement"), the data shows that in Italy, it takes 450 days to evict a tenant who has not paid rent—a staggering 426 days more than in Holland, a country characterized by one of the highest levels of judicial efficiency in the world, but even 83 days more than in Austria, which has the second-least-efficient judiciary system. The picture is even more dire if one seeks an injunction for a bounced check: in Italy it takes an average of 415 days—that is, 115 days more than the second slowest, Portugal, and 395 days more than the most efficient country of the EU, Belgium. Justin Frosini, "The Same Old Film: The Never-ending Woes of Italy's Justice System," in Marco Giuliani and Erik Jones (eds.), *Italian Politics 2009: Managing Uncertainty*, New York: Berghahn Books, 2010, pp. 168–183.

25. See Ilvo Diamanti, *Mappe dell'Italia politica*, Bologna: Il Mulino, 2008.

26. See Piero Ignazi, *Il polo escluso*, Bologna: Il Mulino, 1989.

27. As local elections had showed in spring and autumn 1993, DC and PSI, as well as the minor forces of the *pentapartito*, were all gone by the end of the year.

28. Many party leaders (of both coalitions, including Berlusconi himself) continued to pursue particularistic aims and did not support the two referenda, a fact that was instrumental in their defeat due to the lack of a quorum.

29. Roberto D'Alimonte, "Italy: A Case of Fragmented Bipolarism," in Michael Gallagher and Paul Mitchell (eds.), *The Politics of Electoral Systems*, Oxford: Oxford University Press, 2005, pp. 253–277.

30. Maria Chiara Pacini, "Public Funding of Political Parties in Italy," *Modern Italy*, 14(2), 2009, 183–202.

31. For a detailed explanation see Gianfranco Baldini and Adiano Pappalardo, *Elections, Electoral Systems and Volatile Voters*, Basingstoke: Palgrave, 2009, p. 71.

32. Luciano Bardi, "Electoral Change and Its Impact on the Party System in Italy," *West European Politics*, 30(4), 2007, 711–732.

33. See Marzio Barbagli, *Immigrazione e criminalità in Italia*, Bologna: Il Mulino, 1998.

34. See *La sicurezza in Italia. Significati, immagine e realtà. Seconda indagine sulla rappresentazione sociale e mediatica della sicurezza*, report by Demos-Osservatorio di Pavia Media Research, edited by Ilvo Diamanti, partially commented in *Il venerdì di Repubblica*, December 12, 2008.

35. See Osvaldo Croci, "Not a Zero-Sum Game: Atlanticism and Europeanism in Italian Foreign Policy," *International Spectator*, 43(4), 2008, 137–155.

36. See Ernesto Galli della Loggia, "La successione a Berlusconi," *Il Corriere della Sera*, October 18, 2010.

37. See Edward C. Banfield, *The Moral Basis of a Backward Society*, New York: Free Press, 1967 (1958), and Gabriel A. Almond and Sidney Verba, *The Civic Culture: Political Attitudes and Democracy in Five Nations*, London: Sage, 1989 (1965), where Italian culture is defined as "parochial."

38. Italy is twenty-second out of twenty-five OECD countries in the size of its shadow economy, with an increase from 21.2 percent of GNP in 1996 to 23.1 percent in 2006; see Friedrich Schneider and Andreas Buehn, *Shadow Economies and Corruption All Over the World: Revised Estimates for 120 Countries*, www.economics-ejournal.org, 2009, p. 28.

Chapter 5: Scandinavia: Still the Middle Way?

1. For an excellent survey of Scandinavian history, see Derry (1979); more concise and up-to-date is Nordstrom (2000) and Hilson (2008). For full citations, see "Suggested Readings" below.

2. Until the war of 1864, the German-speaking duchies of Schleswig, Holstein, and Lauenburg were part of the Danish realm under an exceedingly complex constitutional arrangement. Schleswig had a substantial Danish population that was denied rights under German rule between 1864 and 1918. Following the German defeat in 1918, the Allies supervised a referendum that returned the northern third of Schleswig to Denmark. Since 1920, the Danish-German border has been fixed, and since the 1950s, the two nationalities have seen greatly improved local relations.

3. Denmark and Norway were under the same monarch from 1380 to 1814. Starting in 1737 in rural Norway, the country was the first in the world to institute universal, compulsory education, culminating in the Danish education act of 1814. Sweden followed with a similar law in 1842. By the second half of the nineteenth century, literacy was nearly universal in Scandinavia, and secondary and adult education was advanced by the "folk colleges" and workers' education movements.

4. An exception was K. Hjalmar Branting (1860–1925), one of the founders of the Swedish Social Democratic Workers Party. Branting was of a middle-class academic background and was university educated. A tireless reformer, he set the Swedish Social Democrats on a moderate path to power. In 1920, he became Europe's first democratically elected Social Democratic prime minister.

5. There are many excellent studies of the global economy. See especially Robert O. Keohane and Joseph S. Nye, *Power and Interdependence*, 3rd ed., Boston: Addison-Wesley, 2000; and for the smaller European states, Peter J. Katzenstein, *Small States in World Markets: Industrial Policy in Europe*, Ithaca, NY: Cornell University Press, 1985.

6. There is a rich literature on Scandinavian political institutions and political actors. For good surveys with copious bibliographies, see the volumes by Olof Petersson and by Eric S. Einhorn and John Logue in "Suggested Readings."

7. D. Rustow, *The Politics of Compromise: A Study of Parties and Cabinet Government in Sweden*, Princeton, NJ: Princeton University Press, 1955.

8. For a more comprehensive discussion of the Scandinavian welfare programs and their impact, see Einhorn and Logue, chapters 6–10.

9. Economic policy issues in the Nordic countries are discussed in detail in the economic surveys published every year or two by the Organization of Economic Cooperation and Development as *Economic Surveys: Denmark*, etc. Sweden's economic problems and especially its welfare received much international attention in the 1990s. The harshest critique may be found in the writings of Assar Lindbeck, most recently in "The Swedish Experiment," *Journal of Economic Literature*, 35, September 1997, 1273–1319. A more technical and less pessimistic survey is Richard B. Freeman, Robert Topel, and Brigitta Swedenborg, *The Welfare State in Transition: Reforming the Swedish Model*, Chicago: University of Chicago Press, 1997. Both the *Financial Times* and the *Economist* regularly survey the Nordic economies, the latter most recently in June 2003.

10. The Nordic countries vary in how they define "immigrants." Including naturalized citizens and second-generation populations inflates the numbers (to about 10–11 percent of the population in Denmark and Norway in 2010) but does reflect the socio-economic challenges of migration.

11. At the end of the fourteenth century, all three Scandinavian crowns passed to Danish Queen Margrethe I. In 1397, this union was formalized by a treaty drafted in Kalmar, Sweden. Although the Kalmar Union survived until 1523, it was constantly challenged. Norway remained united with Denmark until 1814, and then with Sweden until 1905. Iceland was part of the Danish realm until 1944. The Swedish province of Finland became a Russian grand duchy in 1809 and declared its independence in 1917.

12. A concise summary of the Nordic region during the Cold War may be found in "The Nordic Region: Changing Perspectives in International Relations," *The Annals of the American Academy of Political and Social Science*, Martin O. Heisler, special edition, vol. 512, November 1990; and in the books by Stephen J. Blank, *Finnish Security and European Security Policy*, Carlisle Barracks, PA: U.S. Army War College, 1996, and by Don Snidal and Arne Brundtland, *Nordic-Baltic Security*, Washington, DC: Center for Strategic and International Studies, 1993. For the more recent period, see Hilson (2008) and Ingebritsen (2006) in the "Suggested Readings" for chapter 5.

Chapter 6: Russia: European or Not?

1. Martin E. Malia, *Russia under Western Eyes: From the Bronze Horseman to the Lenin Mausoleum*, Cambridge, MA: Belknap Press of Harvard University Press, 1999, pp. 4–12, 43–60.

2. Ernest Gellner, *Conditions of Liberty: Civil Society and Its Rivals*, New York: Allen Lane Penguin Press, 1994, pp. 1–12, 88–96; Richard Rose, "Toward a Civil Economy," *Journal of Democracy*, 3(2), April 1992, 13–26.

3. The coup plotters were conservative leaders from the political police (KGB), the military, and the central organs of the Communist Party and the government. The state of emergency they declared soon collapsed due to their lack of political determination and paralyzing splits inside the military and police agencies. By discrediting the conservatives, the failed coup attempt boosted the centrifugal forces in the country. Equally important, it enabled Boris Yeltsin to eclipse Gorbachev. Yeltsin led public opposition to the coup, while the plotters held Gorbachev in seclusion until the attempt collapsed.

4. Vera Tolz, "Conflicting 'Homeland Myths' and Nation-State Building in Post-Communist Russia," *Slavic Review*, 57(2), Summer 1998, pp. 267–294.

5. Amy Knight, *The Security Services and the Decline of Democracy in Russia, 1996–1999*, Donald W. Treadgold Papers, 23, Seattle: University of Washington, 1999, pp. 14–16.

6. Timothy J. Colton, "Putin and the Attenuation of Russian Democracy," in Alex Pravda (ed.), *Leading Russia: Putin in Perspective; Essays in Honour of Archie Brown*, New York: Oxford University Press, 2005, pp. 103–118.

7. This analogy is taken from Colton, "Putin and the Attenuation of Russian Democracy."

8. Richard Rose, "How Floating Parties Frustrate Democratic Accountability: A Supply-Side View of Russia's Elections," in Archie Brown (ed.), *Contemporary Russian Politics: A Reader,* New York: Oxford University Press, 2001, p. 217; Stephen White, "The Political Parties," in Stephen White, Zvi Gitelman, and Richard Sakwa (eds.), *Developments in Russian Politics*, 6th ed., Durham, NC: Duke University Press, 2005, p. 90.

9. Henry E. Hale and Timothy J. Colton, "What Makes Dominant Parties Dominant in Hybrid Regimes? The Surprising Importance of Ideas in the Case of United Russia," revised version of a paper presented at the Annual Meeting of the American Association for the Advancement of Slavic Studies, Boston, November 12–15, 2009.

10. After the 2007 election, the Communists controlled about 13 percent of the seats in the lower house; A Just Russia controlled about 8 percent.

11. Joel S. Hellman, "Winners Take All: The Politics of Partial Reform in Postcommunist Transitions," *World Politics*, 50(2), January 1998, 203–234.

12. Paul Klebnikov, *Godfather of the Kremlin: Boris Berezovsky and the Looting of Russia*, New York: Harcourt, 2000, pp. 21, 31–32.

13. Vadim Volkov, *Violent Entrepreneurs: The Use of Force in the Making of Russian Capitalism*, Ithaca, NY: Cornell University Press, 2002, pp. 77, 133.

14. Calculated from Harley Balzer, "Routinization of the New Russians?" *Russian Review*, 62(1), January 2003, 23.

15. Timothy Frye, "Markets, Democracy, and New Private Business in Russia," *Post-Soviet Affairs*, 19(1), January–March 2003, 24–45.

16. Andrew Barnes, *Owning Russia: The Struggle over Factories, Farms, and Power*, Ithaca, NY: Cornell University Press, 2006, pp. 1–10.

17. Piroska Mohacsi Nagy, *The Meltdown of the Russian State: The Deformation and Collapse of the State in Russia*, Northampton, MA: Edward Elgar, 2000, pp. 64–66.

18. Alfred Stepan, "Russian Federalism in Comparative Perspective," *Post-Soviet Affairs*, 16(2), April–June 2000, 144.

19. Timothy Frye, "Corruption and Rule of Law," in Anders Åslund, S. M. Guriev, and Andrew Kuchins (eds.), *Russia after the Global Economic Crisis*, Washington, DC: Peterson Institute for International Economics and Center for Strategic and International Studies, 2010, pp. 66–68.

20. Cameron Ross, "Putin's Federal Reforms," in Cameron Ross (ed.), *Russian Politics under Putin*, New York: Manchester University Press, 2004, p. 166.

21. Ekaterina Zhuravskaya, "Federalism in Russia," in Åslund, Guriev, and Kuchins (eds.), *Russia after the Global Economic Crisis*, pp. 59–78.

22. Bertram Silverman and Murray Yanowitch, *New Rich, New Poor, New Russia: Winners and Losers on the Russian Road to Capitalism*, expanded ed., Armonk, NY: Sharpe, 2000, pp. 51–54, 153.

23. The demographic data in this paragraph are from the Population Reference Bureau, http://www.prb.org/Template.cfm?Section = PRB&template = /ContentManagement/ContentDisplay.cfm&ContenID = 6506, accessed July 10, 2006, and October 26, 2010; and the U.S. Census Bureau, http://www.census.gov/cgi-bin/ipc/idbsum.pl?cty = RS, accessed July 10, 2006.

24. Murray Feshbach, "Russia's Population Meltdown," *The Wilson Quarterly*, 25(1), Winter 2001, pp. 12–21; Nicholas Eberstadt, "The Future of AIDS: Grim Toll in Russia, China, and India," *Foreign Affairs*, 81(6), 2002, 22–45.

25. Nicholas Eberstadt, *Russia's Peacetime Demographic Crisis: Dimensions, Causes, Implications*, Washington, DC: National Bureau of Asian Research, 2010, pp. 2, 281–301.

26. Eberstadt, *Russia's Peacetime Demographic Crisis*, p. 30.

27. G. Ioffe and Z. Zayonchkovskaya, "Immigration to Russia: Inevitability and Prospective Inflows," *Eurasian Geography and Economics*, 51(1), 2010, 104–125.

28. Maria Repnikova and Harley Balzer, *Chinese Migration to Russia: Missed Opportunities*, Eurasian Migration Paper No. 3, Washington, DC: Kennan Institute, Woodrow Wilson International Center for Scholars, 2009.

29. Marc Morje Howard, *The Weakness of Civil Society in Postcommunist Europe*, New York: Cambridge University Press, 2003; Michael McFaul and Elina Treyger, "Civil Society," in Michael McFaul, Nikolai Petrov, and Andrei Ryabov (eds.), *Between Dictatorship and Democracy: Russian Post-Communist Political Reform*, Washington, DC: Carnegie Endowment for International Peace, 2004, pp. 140–141; Balzer, "Routinization of the New Russians?" p. 25.

30. Debra Javeline and Sarah Lindemann-Komarova, "A Balanced Assessment of Russian Civil Society," *Journal of International Affairs*, 63(2), 2010, 171–188.

31. The Levada Center (Russian-language version), http://www.levada.ru/files/1142009322.doc, accessed July 11, 2006; Frye, "Corruption and Rule of Law," pp. 83–86.

32. Stephen White, "Russia's Disempowered Electorate," in Cameron Ross (ed.), *Russian Politics under Putin*, New York: Manchester University Press, 2004, pp. 76–78.

33. Vladimir Petukhov and Andrei Ryabov, "Public Attitudes toward Democracy," in Michael McFaul, Nikolai Petrov, and Andrei Ryabov (eds.), *Between Dictatorship and Democracy: Russian Post-Communist Political Reform*, Washington, DC: Carnegie En-

dowment for International Peace, 2004, pp. 269, 290; Henry E. Hale, "The Myth of Mass Russian Authoritarianism: Public Opinion Foundations of a Hybrid Regime," NCEEER Working Paper, September 8, 2009, available at http://www.ucis.pitt.edu/nceeer/2009_823-03_Hale.pdf. A minority of respondents, young as well as old, also have ambivalent or positive feelings about Stalin as a leader (Sarah E. Mendelson and Theodore P. Gerber, "Soviet Nostalgia: An Impediment to Democratization," *Washington Quarterly*, 29(1), Winter 2005–2006, pp. 83–96).

34. Richard Rose and William Mishler, "How Do Electors Respond to an 'Unfair' Election? The Experience of Russians," *Post-Soviet Affairs*, 25(2), 2009, pp. 118–136; Rose and Mishler, "The Impact of Macro-Economic Shock on Russians," *Post-Soviet Affairs*, 26(1), 2010, pp. 38–57.

35. Scott Gehlbach, "Reflections on Putin and the Media," *Post-Soviet Affairs*, 26(1), 2010, pp. 77–87.

36. The Levada Center (Russian-language version), http://www.levada.ru/prezident .html, accessed July 11, 2006.

37. Julie Anderson, "The Chekist Takeover of the Russian State," *International Journal of Intelligence and Counter Intelligence*, 19(2), Summer 2006, pp. 239–240; Stephen White and Olga Kryshtanovskaya, "Putin's Militocracy," *Post-Soviet Affairs*, 19(4), 2003, p. 294.

38. Sergei Guriev and Andrei Rachinsky, "The Role of Oligarchs in Russian Capitalism," *Economic Perspectives*, 19(1), 2005, p. 140.

39. McFaul and Treyger, "Civil Society," pp. 159–166.

40. For example, under a 2010 law designed to provide government financing for "socially oriented NGOs," the Moscow Helsinki Group, an NGO that has been a vigorous defender of human rights inside Russia, received a grant of approximately $100,000. (Javeline and Lindemann-Komarova, "A Balanced Assessment of Russian Civil Society," pp. 177–178.)

41. Padma Desai, "Russia's Financial Crisis: Economic Setbacks and Policy Responses," *Journal of International Affairs*, 63(2), 2010, pp. 141–151.

42. See especially Medvedev's major statement translated as "Go, Russia!" at http://eng.kremlin.ru/news/298.

Chapter 7: Poland 20 Years Later: The Long Arm of Transition

1. Frances Millard, "Poland's Politics and the Travails of Transition after 2001: The 2005 Elections," *Europe-Asia Studies*, 58(7), 2006, 1007.

2. Jerzy Szacki, *Liberalism after Communism*, Budapest: Central European University Press, 1995, p. 100.

3. Anthony Kemp-Welch, *Poland under Communism: A Cold War History*, Cambridge: Cambridge University Press, 2008, pp. 395–396.

4. Leszek Balcerowicz, *Socialism, Capitalism, Transformation*. Budapest: Central European University Press, 1995, pp. 311–312.

5. Szacki, *Liberalism after Communism*, p. 6.

6. For an account of this event, see Frances Millard, *The Anatomy of the New Poland: Post-Communist Politics in Its First Phase*, Aldershot: Edward Elgar, 1994, pp. 99–104.

7. Jan Olszewski, stenographic transcript from the session of the *Sejm* on June 4, 1992, http://orka2.sejm.gov.pl/, accessed October 18, 2009.

8. Tomas Kostelecky, *Political Parties after Communism*, Baltimore, MD: Johns Hopkins University Press, 2002, pp. 171–172.

9. Jacek Kurczewski, *Ścieżki emancypacji: Osobista teoria transformacji ustrojowej w Polsce*, Warszawa: Trio, 2009, pp. 85–88.

10. This government was separated from that of Olszewski by a brief interlude in which Waldemar Pawlak, leader of the PSL, tried and failed to form a government.

11. Millard, "Poland's Politics," p. 149.

12. Joanna Dzwończyk, *Populistyczne tendencje w spoleczeństwie postsocjalistycznym (na przykladzie Polski)*, Torun: Wydawnictwo Adam Marszalek, 2000, p. 82.

13. Marian Kallas, *Historia ustroju Polski*, Warszawa: Wydawnictwo Naukowe PWN, 2005, p. 372.

14. Kallas, *Historia ustroju Polski*, p. 363.

15. Jerzy Regulski, *Samorzadna Polska*, Warszawa: Rosner i Wspólnicy, 2005, p. 18.

16. Kallas, *Historia ustroju Polski*, p. 400.

17. Alicja Grześkowiak, stenographic transcript from the session of the National Assembly on February 24, 1997, http://orka2.sejm.gov.pl/, accessed April 17, 2009.

18. OBOP, "Tresc przyszlej konstytucji w opinii Polaków," tables 4 and 5, 1997, www.obop.com.pl, accessed May 6, 2009.

19. Justyna Grażyna Otto, "Polak bogatszy, ale nieszczęśliwy—portret obywatela po 16 latach transformacji," *Studia Politologiczne 10*, Warszawa: Instytut Nauk Politycznych Uniwersytetu Warszawskiego, 2006.

20. Tomasz Panek, Janusz Czapiński, and Irena E. Kotowska, "Strategie radzenia sobie z trudnościami finansowymi, pomoc spoleczna i doplaty bezpośrednie dla rolników," in Janusz Czapiński and Tomasz Panek (eds.), *Diagnoza Spoleczna 2005: warunki i jakość życia Polaków*, Warszawa: Wyższa Szkola Finansów i Zarzadzania w Warszawie, 2006, p. 48.

21. Otto, "Polak bogatszy," 2006.

22. Maciej Baltowski and Maciej Miszewski, *Transformacja gospodarcza w Polsce*, Warszawa: Wydawnictwo Naukowe PAN, 2006, p. 252.

23. Frances Millard, *Polish Politics and Society*, London: Routledge, 1999, p. 175.

24. Millard, *Polish Politics and Society*, p. 150.

25. Henryk Domański, "Jedna struktura spoleczna," *Polska jedna czy wiele?* Warszawa: Wydawnictwo TRIO, 2005, p. 23.

26. Grzegorz W. Kolodko, *From Shock to Therapy: The Political Economy of Postsocialist Transformation*, Oxford: Oxford University Press, 2000, p. 208.

27. Elżbieta Tarkowska, "Ubóstwo i wykluczenie spoleczne. Koncepcje i polskie problemy," in Jacek Wasilewski (ed.), *Wspólczesne spoleczeństwo polskie: Dynamika zmian*, Warszawa: Wydawnictwo Naukowe Scholar, 2006, p. 352.

28. Barbara Badora, Wlodzimierz Derczyński, and Macieja Falkowska, "Nierównosci spoleczne," in Krysztof Zagorski and Michal Strzeszewski (eds.), *Polska, Europa, Świat: Opinia publiczna w okresie integracji*, Warszawa: Wydawnictwo Naukowe

Scholar, 2005, p. 202; Bogna Wciórka and Michal Wenzel, "Bezrobocie i bezrobotni," in Krysztof Zagorski and Michal Strzeszewski (eds.), *Polska, Europa, Świat: Opinia publiczna w okresie integracji*, Warszawa: Wydawnictwo Naukowe Scholar, 2005, p. 303.

29. Antoni Dudek, *Historia Polityczna Polski, 1989–2005*, Kraków: Wydawnictwo ARCANA, 2007, p. 368.

30. CBOS, "Cztery reformy w opinii spolecznej," BS/14/2001, Warszawa: Centrum Badania Opinii Spolecznej, 2001, table 1.

31. CBOS, "Cztery reformy w opinii spolecznej," table 1.

32. See http://www.cbos.pl/PL/trendy/trendy.php for the trends cited here.

33. CBOS, "Krytyczni demokraci: akceptacja demokracji a ocena jej funkcjonowania w Polsce," BS/7/2007, Warszawa: Centrum Badania Opinii Spolecznej, 2007, tables 1, 3, and 4.

34. Janusz Czapiński, "Stosunek do przemian systemowych i ocena ich wplywu na życie badanych," in Janusz Czapiński and Tomasz Panek (eds.), *Diagnoza Spoleczna 2005: warunki i jakość życia Polaków*, Warszawa: Wyższa Szkola Finansów i Zarzadzania w Warszawie, 2006.

35. Agnieszka Paczynska, "Inequality, Political Participation, and Democratic Deepening in Poland," *East European Politics and Societies*, 19(4), 2005, 598–600.

36. See trend data at http://www.cbos.pl/PL/trendy/trend_06.php.

37. Jarosław Kaczyński, "The Fall of Post-Communism: Transformation in Central and Eastern Europe," 2006, http://www.heritage.org/Press/TheFallofPostCommunism.cfm, accessed September 26, 2006.

38. Janina Paradowska, "Tercet egzotyczny," *Polityka*, 19(2553), 2006, 20–24.

39. Two-thirds of the legislative proposals of the coalition agreement were not realized, either as the result of the failure of the coalition to address these policies in the time available or because legislation had been struck down by the Constitutional Tribunal; see Krzysztof Burnetko and Mariusz Janicki, "Raport specjalny: Duże wierzby, male gruszki, czyli rozliczamy PiS z jego obietnic," *Polityka* 42(2625), 2007, pp. 102–115.

40. Aleks Szczerbiak, "The Birth of a Bi-polar Party System or a Referendum on a Polarizing Government? The October 2007 Polish Parliamentary Election," SEI Working Paper No. 100, University of Sussex: Sussex European Institute, 2008, p. 27.

41. Radoslaw Markowski, "The 2007 Polish Parliamentary Election: Some Structuring, Still a Lot of Chaos," *West European Politics*, 31(5), 2008, 1055–1068.

42. Miroslawa Grabowska, *Podzial postkomunistyczny: Spoleczne podstawy polityki w Polsce po 1989 roku*, Warszawa: Wydawnictwo Naukowe Scholar, 2004, pp. 358–360.

43. Kazimierz M. Slomczyński and Goldie Shabad, "Systemic Transformation and the Salience of Class Structure in East Central Europe," *East European Politics and Societies*, 11(1), 1997, 187.

44. Tomasz Zarycki, "Politics in the Periphery: Political Cleavages in Poland Interpreted in Their Historical and International Context," Europe-Asia Studies, 52(5), 2000, 864–865.

45. Aleks Szczerbiak, "'Social Poland' Defeats 'Liberal Poland'? The September–October 2005 Polish Parliamentary and Presidential Elections," *Journal of Communist Studies and Transition Politics*, 23(2), 2007, 207.

46. Radoslaw Markowski, "The Polish Elections of 2005: Pure Chaos or a Restructuring of the Party System?" *West European Politics*, 29(4), 2006, 826–829; Markowski, "The 2007 Polish Parliamentary Election," p. 1065.

47. Markowski, "The 2007 Polish Parliamentary Election," p. 1060.

48. Krzysztof Jasiewicz, "The Past is Never Dead: Identity, Class, and Voting Behavior in Contemporary Poland," *East European Politics and Societies*, 23(4), 2009, pp. 491–508, tables 1–5, pp. 11–13.

49. Ben Stanley, "Populism in the Polish Party System: Party Appeals and Voter Mobilisation," unpublished Ph.D. manuscript, University of Essex, 2010, pp. 327–330.

50. Aleks Szczerbiak and Sean Hanley, "Introduction: Understanding the Politics of the Right in Contemporary East–Central Europe," *Journal of Communist Studies and Transition Politics*, 20(3), 2004, 4.

51. Frances Millard, "Poland: Parties without a Party System, 1991–2008," *Politics & Policy*, 37(4), 2009, p. 795.

52. Board of Strategic Advisers to the Prime Minister of Poland, *Polska 2030: Development Challenges, Introduction and Final Recommendations*, 2010, 30–35, http://www.zds.kprm.gov.pl/indexen.php?id = 289&id2 = 283, accessed August 2, 2010.

53. Janina Paradowska, "Omamy i wizje," *Polityka*, 48(2733), November 28, 2009.

54. Hanspeter Kriesi et al., "Globalization and Its Impact on National Spaces of Competition," in *West European Politics in the Age of Globalization*, Cambridge: Cambridge University Press, 2008, p. 4.

Chapter 8: European Integration: Progress and Uncertainty

1. European Commission, *European Union: Selected Instruments from the Treaties*, Luxembourg: Office for Official Publications of the European Communities, 1995. The treaties also can be found on http://europa.eu.int.

2. Hugo Young, *This Blessed Plot: Britain and Europe from Churchill to Blair*, Woodstock, NY: Overlook Press, 1999.

3. For the monetary turmoil of the 1970s, see Paul Volcker and Toyoo Gyohten, *Changing Fortunes: The World's Money and the Threat to American Leadership*, New York: Times Books, 1992.

4. For Thatcher's views on Europe, see her memoirs, *Downing Street Years*, New York: HarperCollins, 1993.

5. For a more detailed analysis of the issues, see Youri Devuyst, *The European Union at the Crossroads: An Introduction to the EU's Institutional Evolution*, Brussels: PIE-Peter Lang, 2002.

6. *Brussels European Council, June 15–16, 2006: Presidency Conclusions*, Brussels: Council of the European Union, June 16, 2006.

Chapter 9: Economic Governance and Varieties of Capitalism

1. See Peter A. Hall and David Soskice (eds.), *Varieties of Capitalism: The Institutional Foundations of Comparative Advantage*, Oxford: Oxford University Press, 2001.

2. See André Sapir, "Globalization and the Reform of European Social Models," *Journal of Common Market Studies*, 44(2), 1996, 369–390.

3. Unless otherwise stated, the data are taken from the 2009 edition of the *OECD Factbook*, which is available online at www.oecd.org.

4. See Daron Acemoglu and Jorn Steffen Pischke, "Beyond Becker: Training in Imperfect Labor Markets," *Economic Policy*, 109, 1999.

5. See Benedicta Marzinotto, "Assessing Complementarities between Product and Labor Markets," SASE Annual Conference, Paris, mimeo, 2009.

6. See Pepper D. Culpepper, "The Future of the High-Skill Equilibrium in Germany," *Oxford Review of Economic Policy*, 15, 1999, 43–59.

7. Franklin Allen and Douglas Gale, *Comparing Financial Systems*, Cambridge, MA: MIT Press, 2000.

8. These data are taken from the International Monetary Fund, *Fiscal Monitor: Navigating the Fiscal Challenges Ahead*, May 14, 2010, pp. 54–55.

9. See Lisbon European Council, March 23 and 24, presidency conclusions.

10. The full text of the European Council conclusions can be downloaded from http://www.consilium.europa.eu/uedocs/cms_data/docs/pressdata/en/ec/115346.pdf.

11. European Council conclusions.

12. For a discussion of the different facets of the crisis in Europe, see Benedicta Marzinotto, Jean Pisani-Ferry, and André Sapir, "Two Crises, Two Responses," *Bruegel Policy Brief*, March 2010.

13. See Carlo Altomonte and Benedicta Marzinotto, "Monitoring Macroeconomic Imbalances: Proposal for a Refined Analytical Framework," Monetary and Economic Affairs Committee, European Parliament, 2010.

Chapter 10: Europe and the Global Economic Crisis

1. "Press Release: Extraordinary Council Meeting, Economic and Financial Affairs, 9/10 May 2010," Brussels: Council of the European Union, 9596/10 (Presse 108) Provisional Version, May 10, 2010.

2. This is calculated at interbank exchange rates on the first market day after the policy was announced, May 11. The exchange rate data is taken from www.oanda.com for May 11. The euro strengthened against the dollar that day by two cents, only to fall back once questions began to arise about the details of the rescue package.

3. "Press Release: 10 May 2010—ECB Decides on Measures to Address Severe Tensions in Financial Markets," http://www.ecb.int/press/pr/date/2010/html/pr100510.en .html.

4. Parts of this chapter were published in preliminary form as briefing notes on the website of the University of North Carolina at Chapel Hill's European Union Center of Excellence and are reproduced here with permission. For more briefings on related subjects, please go to http://www.unc.edu/depts/europe/business_media/business.htm.

5. "Greece PM Confirms Election Date," http://news.bbc.co.uk/2/hi/europe/ 8234843.stm.

6. The electoral and seat allocation data come from Adam Carr's electoral archive, http://psephos.adam-carr.net/countries/g/greece/greece2009.txt.

7. "Provision of Deficit and Debt Data for 2008—Second Notification," *Eurostat Newsrelease: Euroindicators*, 149(2009), October 22, 2009, http://epp.eurostat.ec.europa .eu/cache/ITY_PUBLIC/2-22102009-AP/EN/2-22102009-AP-EN.PDF.

8. Dermot Hodson, "The Euro Area in 2009: The Financial Crisis Gets Real," *JCMS Annual Review of the EU in 2009*, 48(supp. 1), September 2010, 225–242.

9. Sam Jones, "S&P Downgrades Greece," *FTAlphaville*, January 14, 2009, http:// ftalphaville.ft.com/blog/2009/01/14/51146/sp-downgrades-greece.

10. Bertrand Benoit and Tony Barber, "Germany Ready to Help Eurozone Members," *Financial Times*, February 19, 2009.

11. "Report on Greek Government Statistics," Brussels: European Commission, COM(2010) 1 final, January 8, 2010.

12. The bond yield data in this and the following paragraph is based on ten-year bid rates taken from Global Insight.

13. "International Monetary Fund: Greece, Staff Report for the 2009 Article IV Consultation," Washington, DC: International Monetary Fund, June 30, 2009, pp. 1, 20.

14. This data is taken from the AMECO database of the European Commission. The relevant data lines are OVGD for real gross domestic product and CVGD2 for the contribution of gross fixed capital formation to real GDP growth. The spreadsheets are easy to compile using the online AMECO database but can also be had on request from the author.

15. Bank for International Settlements, *BIS Quarterly Review*, June 2010, pp. 18–19.

16. "Pressekonferenz der Bundeskanzlerin nach dem Europäischen Rat," December 11, 2009, http://www.bundeskanzlerin.de/nn_683698/Content/DE/Mitschrift/Presse konferenzen/2009/12/2009-12-12-pk-bk-bruessel.html.

17. Sean O'Grady and Vaness Mock, "Cracks Appear in Europe's Response to Greek Crisis," *The Independent*, February 12, 2010.

18. Bank for International Settlements, *BIS Quarterly Review*, September 2010, p. 14.

19. "Pressekonferenz der Bundeskanzlerin nach dem Europäischen Rat," March 26, 2010, http://www.bundeskanzlerin.de/nn_683698/Content/DE/Mitschrift/Pressekon ferenzen/2010/03/2010-03-26-pk-bk-bruessel.html.

20. For a recent review of this literature, see Lars Jonung and Eoin Drea, "It Can't Happen, It's a Bad Idea, It Won't Last: U.S. Economists on the EMU and the Euro, 1989–2002," *Econ Journal Watch*, 7(1), January 2010, 4–52. That article drew considerable criticism from many quarters. The authors' reply to their critics was published as Lars Jonung and Eoin Drea, "The Euro: It Happened, It's Not Reversible, So . . . Make It Work," *Econ Journal Watch*, 7(2), May 2010, pp. 113–118.

21. This data on relative movements in real effective exchange rates and cumulative current account balances is available from the AMECO database of the European Commission. A copy of my calculations is available on request.

22. Erik Jones, "Merkel's Folly," *Survival*, 52(3), June–July 2010, pp. 29–30.

23. The most common reaction I have had to my article ("Merkel's Folly") is to say that no data from Greece can be trusted. I find such a blanket assertion difficult to accept. While we have had consistent indications that the Greeks have problems in their fiscal accounting, the same is not true with respect to their labor market statistics.

24. Klaus-Jürgen Nagel, "North Rhine Westphalia: The *Land* Election that Dismissed a Federal Government," *Regional and Federal Studies*, 16(3), September 2006, 347–354.

25. This paragraph is adapted from Peter Ludlow, "In the Last Resort: The European Council and the Euro Crisis, Spring 2010," *Eurocomment Briefing Note*, 7(7–8), June 2010.

26. It was sufficient to hold the German high court at bay as well. When plaintiffs sought a preliminary injunction to stop the German government from participating in the bailout of Greece, the court accepted that the German government acted in order to prevent even greater damage from arising due to financial instability. And when it ruled on the constitutionality of the broader stabilization mechanism later that summer, the court argued that it was the government's responsibility to forecast economic events and to act accordingly in the country's interest.

27. "Communication from the Commission to the European Parliament, the European Council, the Council, the European Central Bank, the Economic and Social Committee and the Committee of Regions," Brussels: European Commission, COM(2010) 250 final, May 12, 2010.

28. The original German nine-point plan can be found in English here: http://files .droplr.com.s3.amazonaws.com/files/15728807/12QVc1.KeyProposalsEuroArea.pdf. See also Valentina Pop, "Euro Is Facing 'Existential Crisis,' Merkel Says," *Euobserver .com*, May 19, 2010, http://euobserver.com/9/30103. For the European Commission's reaction, see Ian Traynor, "Angela Merkel 'Naive' over Euro, Claims European Commission Chief," *Guardian*, May 25, 2010, http://www.guardian.co.uk/world/2010/may/ 25/merkel-naive-euro-barosso-eu.

29. Jack Ewing, "Merkel Urges Tougher Rules for Eurozone," *New York Times*, March 17, 2010.

30. "European Council, 25/26 March 2010, Conclusions," Brussels: General Secretariat of the Council, EUCO 7/10, CO EUR 4, CONCL 1, March 26, 2010, p. 6.

31. "Remarks by Herman Van Rompuy, President of the European Council, Following the First Meeting of the Task Force on Economic Governance," Brussels: European Council, The President, PCE 102/10, May 21, 2010.

32. "Remarks by Herman Van Rompuy, President of the European Council, Following the Second Meeting of the Task Force on Economic Governance," Brussels: European Council, The President, PCE 118/10, June 7, 2010.

33. "Communiqué from Herman Van Rompuy, President of the European Council, Following the Meeting of the Task Force on Economic Governance," Brussels: European Council, The President, PCE 161/10, July 12, 2010.

34. This wider context is also analyzed in the chapter by Benedicta Marzinotto.

35. Ben Hall and Quentin Peel, "Europe: Adrift amid the Rift," *Financial Times*, June 23, 2010, http://www.ft.com/cms/s/0/18115178-7f0c-11df-84a3-00144feabdc0.html.

36. Wolfgang Proisl, "Why Germany Fell out of Love with Europe," *Bruegel Essay and Lecture Series*, Brussels: Bruegel, June 2010, pp. 36–37.

37. An exception can be found in the concluding chapter to my book on *The Politics of Economic and Monetary Union*. There I argue that it was likely that the excessive deficit procedure would be ignored if it proved to be inconvenient. Just over a year after the book was published, that turned out to be the case. See Erik Jones, *The Politics of Economic and Monetary Union: Integration and Idiosyncrasy*, Lanham, MD: Rowman & Littlefield, 2002.

38. Wolfgang Münchau, "Even Eurozone Optimists Are Not Optimistic," *Financial Times*, July 11, 2010, http://www.ft.com/cms/s/0/833134c6-8d14-11df-bad7-00144feab 49a.html.

39. Olivier Blanchard, Giovanni Dell'Ariccia, and Paolo Mauro, "Rethinking Macro-economic Policy," *IMF Staff Position Note*, Washington, DC: IMF, SPN/10/03, February 12, 2010.

40. Even the Bank for International Settlements agrees that the Deauville declaration constituted the start of the Irish sovereign debt crisis. See Bank for International Settlements, *BIS Quarterly Review*, December 2010, pp. 11–12.

41. This data is available from the AMECO database of the European Commission, data series UDGGL.

Chapter 11: European Law and Politics

1. Ran Hirschl, "The Judicialization of Politics," in K. Whittington and G. Calderia (eds.), *The Oxford Handbook of Law and Politics*, Oxford: Oxford University Press, 2008, p. 119.

2. C. Neal Tate and Torbjörn Vallinder (eds.), *The Global Expansion of Judicial Power*, New York: New York University Press, 1997.

3. Louis Henkin, *The Age of Rights*, New York: Columbia University Press, 1990.

4. It is important to note that the constitutional courts that have become so powerful in postwar Europe were not modeled on the U.S. Supreme Court. Many observers assume that since the judicial review was so well established in the United States, the U.S. model must have guided the construction of the judiciaries in postwar European democracies. However, the courts established in Europe followed the Kelsenian model, which had been established in Austria after World War I (Alec Stone Sweet, *Governing with Judges*, p. 165). In the U.S. system, ordinary judges can declare legislative acts to be unconstitutional, and these decisions can then be appealed up to the U.S. Supreme Court. In the Kelsenian model, developed by Austrian legal theorist (and later University of California, Berkeley, professor) Hans Kelsen, constitutional review could not be exercised by ordinary courts but was the exclusive task of a specialized constitutional court. These Kelsenian constitutional courts were separated from the rest of the judicial system.

5. Andrew Moravcsik, "The Origins of Human Rights Regimes: Democratic Delegation in Postwar Europe," *International Organization*, 54(2), 2000, pp. 217–252.

6. Steven Vogel, *Freer Markets, More Rules: Regulatory Reform in Advanced Industrialized Countries*, Ithaca, NY: Cornell University Press, 1996; Steven Vogel, "Why Freer Markets Need More Rules," in Mark Landy, Martin Levin, and Martin Shapiro (eds.), *Creating Competitive Markets: The Politics of Regulatory Reform*, Washington, DC: Brookings Institution Press, 2007, pp. 25–42.

7. Case 26/62, *Van Gend en Loos v. Nederlandse Administratie der Belastingen* (1963) ECR 1.

8. Case 6/64, *Flaminio Costa v. Ente Nationale per L'Energia Elettrica (ENEL)* (1964) ECR 585, 593.

9. Anne-Marie Slaughter, Alec Stone Sweet, and Joseph Weiler (eds.), *The European*

Courts and National Courts: Doctrine and Jurisprudence, Oxford: Hart Publishing, 1998; Karen Alter, *Establishing the Supremacy of European Law: The Making of an International Rule of Law in Europe*, Oxford: Oxford University Press, 2001; Alec Stone Sweet, *Governing with Judges: Constitutional Politics in Europe*, Oxford: Oxford University Press, 2000.

10. Anne-Marie Burley and Walter Mattli, "Europe before the Court: A Political Theory of Legal Integration," *International Organization*, 47, 1993, 41–76.

11. Karen Alter, "The European Court's Political Power," *West European Politics*, 19(3), 1996, 458–487; and Karen Alter, *Establishing the Supremacy*.

12. Karen Alter, *Establishing the Supremacy*.

13. Stone Sweet 2000, p. 165; Joseph H. H. Weiler, "The Transformation of Europe," *Yale Law Journal*, 100, 1991, 2403–2483; Eric Stein, "Lawyers, Judges and the Making of a Transnational Constitution," *American Journal of International Law*, 75, 1981, 1–27.

14. Burley and Mattli, "Europe before the Court"; Stone Sweet, *Governing with Judges*; Alec Stone Sweet and Thomas Brunell, "Constructing a Supranational Constitution," *American Political Science Review*, 92, 1998, 63–81.

15. Lisa Conant, *Justice Contained: Law and Politics in the European Union*, Ithaca, NY: Cornell University Press, 2002.

16. Rachel Cichowski, *The European Court and Civil Society*, New York: Cambridge University Press, 2007.

17. Geoffrey Garrett, R. Daniel Kelemen, and Heiner Schulz, "The European Court of Justice, National Governments and Legal Integration in the European Union," *International Organization*, 52(1), 1998, 149–176; Mark Pollack, *The Engines of European Integration*, Oxford: Oxford University Press, 2003.

18. Steven Vogel, "Why Freer Markets Need More Rules," in Mark Landy, Martin Levin, and Martin Shapiro (eds.), *Creating Competitive Markets: The Politics of Regulatory Reform*, Washington, DC: Brookings Institution Press, 2007, pp. 25–42; R. Daniel Kelemen, "Suing for Europe: Adversarial Legalism and European Governance," *Comparative Political Studies*, 39(1), 2006, 101–127.

19. Ran Hirschl, *Towards Juristocracy: The Origins and Consequences of the New Constitutionalism*, Cambridge, MA: Harvard University Press, 2004, p. 169.

20. Alexis De Tocqueville, *Democracy in America*, edited and abridged by Richard Heffner, New York: Mentor Books, 1835/1984, p. 126.

21. Donald Kommers, *The Constitutional Jurisprudence of the Federal Republic of Germany*, 2nd ed., Durham, NC: Duke University Press, 1997; Stone Sweet, *Governing with Judges*.

22. C. Landfried, "Judicial Policy-making in Germany: The Federal Constitutional Court," *West European Politics*, 15, 1992, pp. 50–67.

23. Mary Volcansek, "Political Power and Judicial Review in Italy," *Comparative Political Studies*, 26(4), 1994, pp. 492–509; Mary Volcansek, *Constitutional Politics in Italy: The Constitutional Court*, New York: St. Martin's Press, 1999; Mary Volcansek, "Constitutional Courts as Veto Players: Divorce and Decrees in Italy," *European Journal of Political Research*, 39, 2001, 347–372; Maria Elisabetta De Franciscis and Rosella Zannini, "Judicial Policy-making in Italy," *West European Politics*, 15(3), 1992, 68–79; Stone Sweet, *Governing with Judges*.

24. Patrizia Pederzoli and Carlo Guarnieri, "The Judicialization of Politics, Italian

Style," *Journal of Modern Italian Studies*, 2(3), 1997, 321–336; Carlo Guarnieri and Patrizia Pederzoli, *The Power of Judges: A Comparative Study of Courts and Democracy*, Oxford: Oxford University Press, 2001.

25. Alec Stone Sweet, *The Birth of Judicial Politics in France*, New York: Oxford University Press, 1992.

26. Stone Sweet, *The Birth of Judicial Politics in France*.

27. *A (FC) and others (FC) v. Secretary of State for the Home Department* (2004) UKHL 56.

28. *R (Al Rawi) v. Secretary of State for Foreign and Commonwealth Affairs* (2006) EWCA Civ 1279.

29. Karen Alter and Jeannette Vargas, "Explaining Variation in the Use of European Litigation Strategies," *Comparative Political Studies*, 33(4), 2002, 452–482; Cichowski, *The European Court*.

30. See, for instance, Case C-144/04 *Werner Mangold v. Rüdiger Helm* (2005) ECR I-9981; Case C 411/05 *Félix Palacios de la Villa v. Cortefiel Servicios SA* (2007) ECR I-8531; *Case C-13/05 Chacón Navas v. Eurest Colectividades SA* (2006) *ECR* I-6467; *Coleman v. Attridge Law* (2008) ECR I-5603.

31. Alan Riley, "EC Antitrust Modernisation: The Commission Does Very Nicely—Thank You! Part 1: Regulation 1 and the Notification Burden; Part 2: Between the Idea and the Reality: Decentralisation under Regulation 1," *European Competition Law Review*, 24(604–615), 2003, 57–72; Angela Wigger and Andreas Nölke, "Enhanced Roles of Private Actors in the EU Business Regulation and the Erosion of the Rhenish Model of Capitalism: The Case of Antitrust Enforcement," *Journal of Common Market Studies*, 45(2), 2007, 487–513; R. Daniel Kelemen, *Eurolegalism: The Transformation of Law and Regulation in the European Union*, Cambridge, MA: Harvard University Press, 2011.

32. R. D. Kelemen and E. C. Sibbitt, "The Globalization of American Law," *International Organization*, 58(1), 2004, 103–136; Kelemen, *Eurolegalism*.

33. Tamara K. Hervey and Jean Vanessa McHale, *Health Law and the European Union*, New York: Cambridge University Press, 2004; Scott Greer, *The Politics of European Union Health Policies*, Berkshire, England: Open University Press, 2009.

34. Case C-158/96, *Kohll v. Union des Caisses de Maladie* (1998) ECR I-1931.

35. Case C-120/95, *Decker v. Caissede Maladie des Employés Privés* (1998) ECR I-1831.

36. Case C-372/04, *Yvonne Watts v. Bedford Primary Care Trust, Secretary of State for Health* (2006) ECR I-4325.

37. Kelemen, *Eurolegalism*.

38. Case C-438/05, *International Transport Workers' Federation and Finnish Seamen's Union v Viking Line ABP and OÜ Viking Line Eesti (Viking)* (2007) ECR I-10779.

39. Case C-341/05, *Laval un Partneri Ltd v Svenska Byggnadsarbetareförbundet, Svenska Byggnadsarbetareförbundets avdelning 1, Byggettan and Svenska Elektrikerförbundet (Laval)* (2007) ECR I-11767.

40. Case C-346/06, *Rüffert v. Land Niedersachsen* (2008) ECR I-1989.

41. See chapter 9 by Benedicta Marzinotto in this volume.

42. Case 1/58, *Stork v High Authority*, ECR 1959, p. 43.

43. For overviews, see Paul Craig and Gráinne De Búrca, *EU Law: Text, Cases and Materials*, 4th ed., Oxford: Oxford University Press, 2008, pp. 379–389. Early landmark cases include, for instance, Case 29/69 *Stauder* v. *City of Ulm*, (1969) ECR 419 and Case 11/70, *Internationale Handelsgesellschaft* (1970) ECR 1125.

44. *Ireland v. United Kingdom* (1978) ECHR (5310/71).

45. *Dudgeon v. United Kingdom* (1981) ECHR (7525/76).

46. See, for instance, *Leyla Şahin v. Turkey* (2005) ECHR (4474/98); *Dogru v. France* (2008) ECHR (27058/05); *Kervanci v. France* (2008) ECHR (31645/04); *Dahlab v. Switzerland* (2001) ECHR (42393/98).

47. *Lautsi v. Italy* (2009) ECHR (30814/06), referral to the Grand Chamber on March 1, 2010.

48. *A., B. and C. v. Ireland* (application no. 25579/05).

49. Rachel Cichowski, "Courts, Rights and Democratic Participation," *Comparative Political Studies*, 39, 2006, 50–75, 62.

50. Cichowski, "Courts, Rights"; Cichowski, *The European Court*.

51. Stuart Scheingold, *The Politics of Rights: Lawyers, Public Policy and Political Change*, New Haven, CT: Yale University Press, 1974; Mary Ann Glendon, *Rights Talk*, New York: Free Press, 1991.

52. Kelemen, *Eurolegalism*; Kelemen and Sibbitt, "Globalization of American Law."

Chapter 12: Migration in Europe

1. The figures in this section come from Eurostat, *Statistics in Focus*, 98/2008, 2–4, and the *Eurostat Yearbook 2009*. Unless otherwise noted, the rest of the statistics used in this chapter were downloaded from Eurostat's online database: http://epp.eurostat .ec.europa.eu/portal/page/portal/statistics/search_database (henceforth, Eurostat 2010).

2. For example, one region in the United Kingdom (Yorkshire and Humber) lists thirteen distinct categories of refugees/asylum seekers, under three broad headings: refugee (includes refugee status, humanitarian protection, discretionary leave, exception leave to remain, and indefinite leave to remain); asylum seeker (includes induction asylum seeker, dispersed asylum seeker, subs' only asylum seeker, unsupported asylum seeker, and detained asylum seeker); and refused asylum seeker (which includes section 4 refused asylum seeker, destitute refused asylum seeker, and detained refused asylum seeker).

3. Hamburg Institute of International Economics, "Stock Estimates for the EU," 2008, online at http://irregular-migration.hwwi.net/index.php?id=6170, accessed April 20, 2010.

4. European Union officials like to refer to these streams as "mobility," in contrast to "migration," which comes from outside Europe. But it is very difficult to use this politicized terminology in any consistent fashion, so I will leave it to the politicians.

5. EFTA refers to the European Free Trade Association. The EEA is based on the same freedoms of mobility as agreed to in the Treaty of Rome (free movement of goods, persons, services, and capital), and EEA member states enjoy free trade with the European Union in return for adopting parts of European law and contributing significant sums of money to the larger project (in the form of "EEA and Norway grants").

6. In 2008, the Czech Republic, Poland, Slovenia, Slovakia, Hungary, Lithuania, Latvia, Estonia, and Malta have agreed to lift internal air border controls.

7. The A8 countries are Poland, Lithuania, Estonia, Latvia, Slovakia, Slovenia, Hungary, and the Czech Republic.

8. European Commission, "High Level Task Force on Skills and Mobility: Final Report," Directorate-General for Employment and Social Affairs, Unit EMPL/A.3., December 2001.

9. EUBusiness, "EU Court Ruling Threatens Denmark's Immigration Policy," September 1, 2008, online at http://www.eubusiness.com/news-eu/1220245322.26.

10. Europe's continental average is higher—7 percent—but this includes countries such as Russia, with significantly larger Muslim populations. See Islamicpopulation.com, "European Muslim Population," 2008, http://www.islamicpopulation.com/Europe/europe_general.html, accessed April 20, 2010.

Chapter 13: Still at the Crossroads: Europe, the United States, and NATO

1. See John Mearsheimer, "Back to the Future: Instability in Europe after the Cold War," *International Security*, 15(1), 1990, 5–56.

2. Richard Lugar, "NATO: Out of Area or Out of Business: A Call for U.S. Leadership to Revive and Redefine the Alliance," Presentation to the Open Forum of the U.S. Department of State, August 2, 1993.

3. Anders Fogh Rasmussen, "Secretary General Previews Preparations for Lisbon Summit," speech, September 15, 2010, http://www.nato.int/cps/en/natolive/news_66221.htm.

4. North Atlantic Treaty, Washington, DC, April 4, 1949, http://www.nato.int/cps/en/natolive/official_texts_17120.htm.

5. Konrad Adenauer, *Memoirs, 1945–1953*, Chicago: Henry Regnery, 1966, p. 273.

6. The Western European Union (WEU) was created in 1954, when the 1948 Brussels Treaty was modified. It was a collective self-defense organization that until recently had ten EU members among its full members, and if all forms of membership were included, twenty-eight. Like NATO, the WEU also had Article 5 commitments, although in the case of the latter the actual commitment to come to one another's assistance was stronger than in the NATO variant (which only commits the members to take such action as is deemed necessary).

7. Although, in a largely symbolic gesture, NATO AWACs surveillance aircraft were deployed to the United States in order to provide air cover.

8. At http://www.nato.int/cps/en/natolive/topics_49755.htm.

9. The EU's far more modest and younger version of the NRF, the so-called Battlegroups of around 1,500 combat personnel, has never been deployed since it reached full operational capacity in January 2007.

10. Ivo Daalder, "The End of Atlanticism," *Survival*, 45(2), Summer 2003, 150.

11. It should be noted, however, that approval of Obama's leadership and foreign policies remains higher in Europe than in the United States. *Transatlantic Trends: Key Findings 2010*, German Marshall Fund of the United States, 2010.

12. See NATO's secretary general's speech, "NATO: Securing our Future," The Hague, July 6, 2009.

13. Celeste Wallender, "Institutional Assets and Adaptability: NATO after the Cold War," *International Organization*, 54(4), Autumn 2000, 729.

14. *Strasbourg/Kehl Summit Declaration*, issued by the heads of state and government participating in the meeting of the North Atlantic Council in Strasbourg (France)/ Kehl (Germany), April 4, 2009, press release: (2009) 044, par. 29.

15. Vessela Tcherneva, *Where Does Russia's "Sphere of Influence" End?* European Council on Foreign Relations, September 23, 2008, http://www.ecfr.eu/content/entry/ commentary_tcherneva_where_does_russias_sphere_of_influence_end.

16. Julian Lindley-French, "Dilemmas of NATO Enlargement," in Jolyon Howorth and John T. S. Keeler (eds.), *Defending Europe: The EU, NATO and the Quest for European Autonomy*, Basingstoke: Palgrave, 2003, p. 172.

17. The Alliance's New Strategic Concept, agreed by the heads of state and government participating in the meeting of the North Atlantic Council, July 1990, art. 20(i).

18. Although this notion can be traced back to Immanuel Kant, one of the most persuasive modern exponents of democratic peace theory is Bruce Russett, *Grasping the Democratic Peace: Principles for a Post-Cold War World*, Princeton, NJ: Princeton University Press, 1993.

19. For more information on the NRC, see http://www.nato.int/issues/nrc/index .html, and for more information on the 1997 NATO-Russia Founding Act on Mutual Relations, Cooperation and Security, see http://www.nato.int/cps/en/natolive/official_ texts_25468.htm.

20. Statement, meeting of the North Atlantic Council at the level of foreign ministers held at NATO Headquarters, Brussels, August 19, 2008.

21. See http://www.nato.int/cps/en/SID-4C3C1920-10F70D0F/natolive/news_64844 .htm.

22. This point is made by Dimitri Trenin, "Russia's New Place in NATO," *Moscow Times*, April 16, 2010, at http://www.carnegie.ru/publications/?fa=40630.

23. For the text of the speech as well as the draft European Security Treaty, see http:// archive.kremlin.ru/eng/text/themes/2009/11/291600_223080.shtml.

24. Transcript of address by Sergei Lavrov, minister for foreign affairs of the Russian Federation, at the spring part of the 61st Parliamentary Assembly Session, Strasbourg, April 29, 2010, http://en.interaffairs.ru/read.php?item=84.

25. The presidents of Armenia, Belarus, Kazakhstan, Kyrgyzstan, Russia, and Tajikistan signed a charter in Tashkent on October 7, 2002, founding the Collective Security Treaty Organization (CSTO), or the Tashkent Treaty. Georgia and Azerbaijan were members of the former Collective Security Treaty of the CIS but did not join the CSTO.

26. For a discussion of the European Security Treaty, see Patrick Nopens, *A New Security Architecture for Europe? Russian Proposal and Western Reactions*, security policy brief no. 3, Royal Institute for International Relations, Belgium, November 2009.

27. For the text of the draft treaty, see http://eng.kremlin.ru/news/275.

28. Joshua Walker, "NATO's Litmus Test: Prioritizing Afghanistan," *Journal of Military and Strategic Studies*, 9(1), Fall 2006, 2.

29. *Transatlantic Trends: Key Findings 2010*, German Marshall Fund of the United States, pp. 8–9, 15.

30. See http://www.isaf.nato.int.

31. Paul Gallis, "NATO in Afghanistan: A Test of Transatlantic Alliance," *CRS Report for Congress*, January 7, 2008, p. 22.

32. Official ISAF data at http://www.isaf.nato.int/images/stories/File/Placemats/FINAL%20100621%20PLACEMAT.pdf%20-%20Adobe%20Acrobat%20Pro.pdf.

33. Dan Murphy, "Afghanistan: General Petraeus Rethinking Rules of Engagement," *Christian Science Monitor*, June 29, 2010.

34. "The gaffes that cost General Stanley McChrystal his job are symptoms of a far deeper trouble–a war that is being lost," *Economist*, June 24, 2010, http://www.economist.com/node/16425992?story_id=16425992.

35. James Joyner, "Albright: NATO Is Much More Than Afghanistan," May 20, 2010, at http://www.acus.org/new_atlanticist/albright-nato-much-more-afghanistan.

36. Jeremy Shapiro and Nick Witney, *Towards a Post-American Europe: A Power Audit of EU-US Relations*, European Council on Foreign Relations, November 2009, p. 52.

37. EU Brief, EU Police Mission in Afghanistan (EUPOL Afghanistan), Common Security and Defense Policy, Afghanistan/19, June 2010.

38. Sally McNamara, "EU Foreign Policymaking Post-Lisbon: Confused and Contrived," *Backgrounder*, No. 2388, March 16, 2010, p. 9.

39. Michael Hastings, "The Runaway General," *Rolling Stone Magazine*, June 22, 2010, at http://www.rollingstone.com/politics/news/17390/119236?RS_show_page=0.

40. Quoted in Gallis, *CRS Report for Congress*, p. 23.

41. Jose Maria Aznar et al., "United We Stand," *Wall Street Journal*, January 30, 2003, p. A14.

42. Sven Biscop, *NATO, ESDP and the Riga Summit: No Transformation without Reequilibration*, Egmont Papers No. 11, Brussels: Royal Institute for International Relations IRRI-KIIB/Academic Press, p. 3.

43. From January 2003 to July 2010, the EU launched twenty-three operations and missions under the European Security and Defense Policy. Five civilian missions have been completed, and eleven are ongoing. Five military missions have been completed, and three are ongoing. The operation in Sudan/Darfur (Amis II) 2005–2006 was a joint civilian-military operation. For details, see http://www.consilium.europa.eu/showPage.aspx?id=268&lang=EN.

44. When a crisis gives rise to an EU-led operation making use of NATO assets and capabilities, the EU and NATO will draw on the so-called "Berlin Plus arrangements." These arrangements cover three main elements that are directly connected to operations and which can be combined. The elements pertain to EU access to NATO planning, to NATO European command options, and use of NATO assets and capabilities. Council of the European Union, "EU-NATO: The Framework for Permanent Relations and Berlin Plus," November 2003, http://www.consilium.europa.eu/uedocs/cmsUpload/03-11-11%20Berlin%20Plus%20press%20note%20BL.pdf.

45. In order to foster crisis consultations, the EU and NATO have concluded in March 2003 an agreement on the security of information, guaranteeing a secure physical environment and enabling the exchange of classified documents and information.

46. See the website of the European Defense Agency, http://www.eda.europa.eu/genericitem.aspx?area=Background&id=122.

47. Franco-British summit, Joint Declaration on European Defense, Saint Malo, December 4, 1998.

48. Western European Union, Marseille Declaration, WEU Council of Ministers, Marseille, November 13, 2000.

49. François Heisbourg, "The French-German Duo and the Search for a New European Security Model," *International Spectator*, 3, 2004, 62.

50. Council of the European Union, "EU-NATO: The Framework for Permanent Relations and Berlin Plus," November 2003, http://www.consilium.europa.eu/uedocs/cmsUpload/03-11-11%20Berlin%20Plus%20press%20note%20BL.pdf.

51. Treaty on European Union (as amended in the Lisbon Treaty), Article 42.

52. Declaration on Strengthening Capabilities, Council of the European Union, Brussels, December 11, 2008, http://www.consilium.europa.eu/ueDocs/cms_Data/docs/pressData/en/esdp/104676.pdf.

53. Paul Cornish, "NATO: The Practice and Politics of Transformation," *International Affairs*, 80(1), 2004, 70.

54. Simon Duke, "The Rhetoric-Resources Gap in EU Crisis Management," *EIPA-SCOPE*, 2002(3), 1–7.

55. Joseph S. Nye Jr., *Bound to Lead: The Changing Nature of American Power*, New York: Basic Books, 1990.

56. Robert Kagan, "The U.S.-Europe Divide," *Washington Post*, May 26, 2002, and Robert Kagan, *Of Paradise and Power: America and Europe in the New World Order*, New York: Knopf, 2003. In both works, Kagan argues that "Americans are from Mars and Europeans are from Venus." Kagan writes,

> The fact is Europeans and Americans no longer share a common view of the world. On the all-important question of power—the utility of power, the morality of power—they have parted ways. Europeans believe they are moving beyond power into a self-contained world of laws and rules and transnational negotiation and cooperation. Europe itself has entered a post-historical paradise, the realization of Immanuel Kant's "Perpetual Peace." The United States, meanwhile, remains mired in history, exercising power in the anarchic Hobbesian world where international rules are unreliable and where security and the promotion of a liberal order still depend on the possession and use of military might. This is why, on major strategic and international questions today, Americans are from Mars and Europeans are from Venus: They agree on little and understand one another less and less.

57. Daniel S. Hamilton and Frances G. Burwell, *Shoulder to Shoulder: Forging a Strategic U.S.-EU Partnership*, Atlantic Council of the United States, December 2009.

58. See http://www.nato.int/cps/en/natolive/topics_49192.htm.

59. See *Multiple Futures Project Report: Navigating towards 2030*, April 2009, at http://www.act.nato.int/multiplefutures.

60. *Multiple Futures Project Report*, p. 39.

61. *Multiple Futures Project Report*, p. 53.

62. *Multiple Futures Project Report*, p. 54.

63. *Multiple Futures Project Report*, p. 60.

64. MFP, Annex D, *Futures and Strategic Surprises*, p. 107.

65. For a range of opinions, see http://www.nato.int/strategic-concept/strategic-con cept-bibliograpy.html#strategic_concept_recent_articles.

66. *NATO 2020: Assured Security; Dynamic Engagement*, May 17, 2010, NATO Public Diplomacy Division, p. 5.

67. Jonathan Holslag and David Henry Doyle (eds.), *The New Global Security Landscape: 10 New Recommendations from the 2010 Security Jam*, Security and Defense Agenda, 2010.

68. *Declaration on Alliance Security*, issued by the heads of state and government participating in the meeting of the North Atlantic Council in Strasbourg/Kehl, April 4, 2009, press release: (2009) 043.

69. Beata Górka-Winter and Marek Madej (eds.), *NATO Member States and the New Strategic Concept: An Overview*, Warsaw: Polski Instytut Spraw Miêdzynarodowych, 2010, p. 64.

70. Beata Górka-Winter and Marek Madej, p. 7.

71. Stefanie Babst, "Reinventing NATO's Public Diplomacy," research paper no. 41, Rome: NATO Defense College, November 2008, p. 3.

72. *Transatlantic Trends, Topline Data 2010*, German Marshall Fund of the United States, p. 37, http://www.gmfus.org/trends/doc/2010_English_Top.pdf.

73. *Transatlantic Trends, Topline Data 2010*, p. 39.

74. Stephen Walt, "Is NATO Irrelevant?" *Foreign Policy*, October 1, 2010, http://walt.foreignpolicy.com/posts/2010/09/24/is_nato_irrelevant.

75. According to NATO's website, since 1995, NATO has been involved in ten operations and missions. Among them, four have been terminated, and six are currently ongoing.

76. See Douglas Stuart, "NATO'S Future as a Pan-European Security Institution," *NATO Review*, 41(4), August 1993, 15–19, http://www.nato.int/docu/review/1993/9304-4.htm.

77. John J. Mearsheimer, "Back to the Future: Instability in Europe after the Cold War," *International Security*, 15(1), 1990, 5–56.

78. Robert W. Rauchhaus (ed.), *Explaining NATO Enlargement*, London: Frank Cass, 2001, p. 27.

79. For a detailed overview of the realist perspectives on NATO at the end of the Cold War, see Kenneth Walz, "Structural Realism after the Cold War," *International Security*, 25(1), Summer 2000, 5–41.

80. Steven McGuire and Michael Smith, *The European Union and the United States: Competition and Convergence in the Global Arena*, Basingstoke: Palgrave, 2008, p. 259.

81. McGuire and Smith, *The European Union*, p. 259.

82. Anne-Marie Le Gloannec, "The EU and NATO's New Strategic Concept," CERI, SciencesPo, May 2010, http://www.ceri-sciencespo.com/archive/2010/mai/art_amlg.pdf.

83. See *Transatlantic Trends: Key Findings 2010*, German Marshall Fund of the United States, pp. 8, 19, http://www.gmfus.org/trends/2010.

84. *Transatlantic Trends: Key Findings 2010*, p. 23.

85. Daniel S. Hamilton and Frances G. Burwell, *Shoulder to Shoulder: Forging a Strategic U.S.-EU Partnership*, Atlantic Council of the United States, December 2009.

86. See introduction in Helga Haftendorn, Robert Keohane, and Celeste Wallander

(eds.), *Imperfect Unions: Security Institutions over Time and Space*, London, UK: Oxford University Press, 1999.

87. *NATO 2020: Assured Security, Dynamic Engagement, Analysis and Recommendations of the Group of Experts on a New Strategic Concept for NATO*, May 17, 2010, http://www.nato.int/strategic-concept/expertsreport.pdf.

88. Ivo Daalder and James Goldgeier, "Global NATO," *Foreign Affairs*, 85(2), September–October 2006, pp. 105–113.

89. Karl-Heinz Kamp, "'Global Partnership': A New Conflict within NATO?" *Analysen und Argumente der Konrad-Adenauer-Stiftung*, 29, 2006, p. 3.

90. 1999 NATO, New Strategic Concept, http://www.nato.int/cps/en/natolive/topics_56626.htm#1.

91. Beata Górka-Winter and Marek Madej, *NATO Member States and the New Strategic Concept: An Overview*, Warsaw: Polish Institute of International Affairs, May 2010, p. 7.

92. It could be argued that Canada's stance is conditioned by the fact that there is no specific mention of NATO's role vis-à-vis the defense of Canada.

93. National Security Strategy, May 2010, White House, pp. 41–42.

94. National Security Strategy, p. 13.

95. *Lisbon Declaration on a Common and Comprehensive Security Model for Europe for the Twenty-first Century*, Lisbon Document, DOC.S/1/96, OSCE, December 3, 1996.

96. See *A Human Security Doctrine for Europe: The Barcelona Report of the Study Group on Europe's Security Capabilities*, Presented to EU High Representative for Common Foreign and Security Policy, Javier Solana, Barcelona, September 15, 2004.

97. Jan Petersen, "NATO's New Strategic Concept: A Parliamentary View," *NATO Review*, at http://www.nato.int/docu/review/2009/0902/090203/EN/index.htm.

98. Joseph Biden, "Advancing Europe's Security," *International Herald Tribune*, May 6, 2010.

99. Shapiro and Witney, November 2009, p. 21.

100. Beata Górka-Winter and Marek Madej, p. 8.

101. Beata Górka-Winter and Marek Madej, p. 8.

102. Nick Butler and Jeffrey Sterling, "Defence Cuts Will Hit the UK's Industrial Capacity," *Financial Times*, September 29, 2010.

103. See Daniel Keohane and Charlotte Blommestijn, *Strength in Numbers? Comparing EU Military Capabilities in 2009 with 1999*, ISS Policy Brief, Paris: European Institute for Security Studies.

104. Joseph R. Biden Jr., "Advancing Europe's Security," White House, Office of the Vice President, May 5, 2010, reproduced verbatim in the *International Herald Tribune* and the *New York Times*, http://www.nytimes.com/2010/05/06/opinion/06iht-edbiden.html.

105. Pascal Vennesson, "Competing Visions for European Grand Strategy," *European Foreign Affairs Review*, 15, 2010, 68–69.

Glossary

acquis communautaire: A French term denoting the sum total of EU treaties, regulations, and laws developed since the 1950s; must be accepted by new member states as it exists at the time of accession.

Barcelona Process: Initial framework to manage bilateral and regional relations between the European member states and fourteen partners in the Greater Middle East. Its key goals are to establish an area of peace and security in the Mediterranean, to implement a free-trade agreement, and to bolster institutional contacts between the EU and Middle Eastern countries. It was negotiated in 1995, is currently known as the Euro-Mediterranean Partnership, and was relaunched as the Union for the Mediterranean in 2008. See also European Neighborhood Policy.

Bretton Woods system: The international monetary system created at the end of World War II in Bretton Woods, New Hampshire. It was designed to establish international management of the global economy and to provide for the cross-convertibility of national currencies through a fixed exchange rate with gold or with currencies backed by gold (such as the U.S. dollar). The exchange rate system was terminated in 1973, but other key foundations remained in place: the General Agreement on Tariffs and Trade, the International Monetary Fund, and the International Bank for Reconstruction and Development, which in 1956 was merged with other institutions to form the World Bank.

Common Agricultural Policy (CAP): A controversial subsidy and price support system established under the Treaty of Rome to increase agricultural productivity and sustain farm incomes in the European Community. For a long time, it has represented almost half of the EU budget, but it is to decrease substantially by 2013. The main criticism is that it benefits wealthy European farmers and damages developing countries' agricultural exports.

Common Assembly: The parliamentary arm of the European Coal and Steel Community (ECSC). It was the precursor to the European Parliament, existing between 1952 and 1958.

Common Foreign and Security Policy (CFSP): From the Maastricht Treaty to the Lisbon Treaty, the "second pillar" of the European Union. In 1991, it replaced the European Political Cooperation. It establishes the broad foreign policy objectives of the EU and requires member states and the EU institutions to cooperate in promoting these objectives. The Lisbon Treaty created a high representative of the Union for Foreign Affairs and Security Policy as well as an EU diplomatic corps, the European External Action Service.

Common Security and Defense Policy (CSDP): Since the Lisbon Treaty, the successor of the European Security and Defense Policy (ESDP) and part of the Common Foreign and Security Policy. See also European Security and Defense Identity.

Conference on Security and Cooperation in Europe (CSCE): A process designed to promote European cooperation on trade and human rights. Its members include the United States, Canada, Russia, the former Soviet republics, and all of Europe—constituting fifty-six member states. It was renamed the Organization for Security and Cooperation in Europe (OSCE) in 1995.

constitutional monarchies: Monarchy in which the monarch accepts limits on his or her power imposed by a constitution, often keeping mainly ceremonial roles and remaining a safety net for when national politics break down entirely.

consumer price inflation: The rate of increase of the prices for goods and services weighted according to their share in a standard consumption bundle.

Copenhagen criteria: The Copenhagen criteria are the rules that define whether a nation is eligible to join the European Union. The criteria require a state to have the institutions to preserve democratic governance and human rights, to have a functioning market economy, and to accept the *acquis communautaire* (see *acquis communautaire*). These membership criteria were laid down at the June 1993 European Council in Copenhagen, Denmark.

corporatism: Democratic corporatism provides for the representation of organized economic interest groups in the policymaking process. Most often such interests include business, labor, agriculture, and the like. In practice, representation may be formal, such as in the EU Economic and Social Council and in many national commissions (health, environmental protection, etc.), but most often it is informal through lobby groups that have access to the policymaking process.

Council of Europe: Organization established in 1949 to promote European stability through democracy, human rights, and the rule of law. It currently counts forty-seven members, operates the European Court of Human Rights, and is located in Strasbourg. It is not to be confused with the European Council (see European Council).

Council of Ministers: The decision-making institution of the EU, comprising ministerial-level representatives from each of the member states. It differs according to the policy field. In cooperation with the European Parliament, it has the power to adopt or reject EU legislation, but it remains subordinate to the European Council's (heads of state or government) overall authority.

Council for Mutual Economic Assistance (CMEA): Economic organization established by the Soviet Union in 1949 to coordinate trade among the communist countries of Central and Eastern Europe. It was disbanded in 1991 after the breakup of the Soviet Union.

debt-to-GDP ratio: The ratio of gross public debt to gross domestic product (GDP) across all levels of government. The EU threshold for sustainability is formally put at 60 percent and as such is incorporated in the Stability and Growth Pact.

euro: The single European currency, introduced in financial market accounting in 1999. Coins and banknotes replaced national currencies in circulation on January 1, 2002.

EUROCORPS: A multinational military corps comprised of troops from France, Germany, Spain, Belgium, and Italy. It operated within the framework of the West European Union.

Eurogroup: The ministers of finance of the euro-zone member states.

European Atomic Energy Agency (Euratom): One of the three European communities set up in the 1950s, established simultaneously with the European Economic Community (EEC) in 1958 to promote the peaceful use of atomic energy. Since 1967, it has shared common institutions with the EEC and the ECSC.

European Bank for Reconstruction and Development (EBRD): A London-based international development bank established in 1991 to promote economic development and political reform in Central and Eastern Europe. The main shareholders are the EU member states and EU institutions, along with the United States and Japan.

European Central Bank (ECB): The European Central Bank is located in Frankfurt, Germany, and is responsible for the control over—and stability of—the euro. It sets the interstate monetary policy for the whole of Europe's Economic and Monetary Union, though it has, different from the Federal Reserve, no outspoken mandate for economic targets other than currency stability.

European Coal and Steel Community (ECSC): The first institution attempting European integration, created under the 1951 Treaty of Paris. It established a common pool for coal and steel products and strong institutions to regulate the coal and steel industries on a supranational basis, especially to make Germany's and France's economies more interdependent.

European Commission: The executive body of the European Union. It initiates legislation, executes EU policies, negotiates on behalf of the EU in international trade forums, and monitors compliance with EU law and treaties by member states.

European Community (EC): Term used informally before 1993 for what the Maastricht Treaty named the European Union (EU).

European Constitution: Also known as the Treaty Establishing a Constitution for Europe, it was agreed by the European Council in October 2004. It was designed to provide a constitution for the EU that would allow the institution to function effectively with twenty-seven members following the CEEC enlargement. The treaty was rejected by the French and Dutch electorates in national referenda held in 2005. In 2007, negotiations were relaunched and resulted in the adoption of the Lisbon Treaty, the text of which was only slightly different.

European Convention: Also known as the Convention on the Future of Europe. The body was established by the European Council in December 2001 following the Laeken Declaration. Headed by Valéry Giscard d'Estaing, it produced a draft EU constitution. The convention finished its work in July 2003. The draft treaty established a constitution for Europe that later failed ratification.

European Council: The EU institution comprising the heads of state or government of the member states and the president of the European Commission. It meets at least twice each year and sets broad guidelines and directions for the development of the EU, as worked out in the Council of Ministers. The Lisbon Treaty provided the European Council with a more permanent presidency (with a 2.5-year mandate) next to the rotating one.

European Court of Justice (ECJ): The judicial arm of the European Union, which may decide cases brought by EU member states, EU institutions, companies, and, in some cases, individuals. It ensures uniform interpretation of EU law by decisions that are binding upon the member states.

European Currency Unit (ECU): Artificial unit of account established to operate the exchange rate mechanism of the European Monetary System; it consisted of a basket of member states' currencies. It was replaced by the euro on January 1, 1999.

European Economic Area (EEA): Members of the European Economic Area have full access to the European Union's single market in most areas of trade (agriculture and fisheries are exceptions) but do not have influence on the policy decisions of the European Union. The European Economic Area comprises the EU countries and Iceland, Norway, and Liechtenstein.

European Economic Community (EEC): The most important of the original European communities, set up under the 1957 Treaty of Rome to promote an "ever closer union" among the peoples of Europe through the development of a common market, a common external tariff, and common policies in agriculture, transport, and other fields. It was renamed the European Community (EC) in the Maastricht Treaty.

European External Action Service (EEAS): The *corps diplomatique* of the European Union. It has been created by the Lisbon Treaty and will report to the high representative for Foreign Affairs and Security Policy. Its staff comes from both the European Commission, the European Council, and the national diplomatic corps.

European Free Trade Association (EFTA): Organization formed in 1960 under British leadership to promote economic cooperation among European states not wishing to become members of the EC. Unlike the EC, it did not have strong supranational institutions or a mandate to promote political union. It lost importance as most of its members decided to join the EC.

European Monetary System (EMS): Exchange rate regime, established in 1979, to limit currency fluctuations within the European Community. It operated an exchange rate mechanism (ERM) under which member states were required to maintain the value of their currencies relative to those of other member states. It laid the groundwork for monetary union and the single currency (euro), established in January 1999.

European Neighborhood Policy (ENP): Policy aimed at providing Europe with stable and peaceful borders and neighbors. The vision is that of a ring of countries, drawn into further integration, but without necessarily becoming full members of the European Union. The policy was first outlined by the European Commission in March 2003 and was adopted in 2004. The countries covered include the Mediterranean coastal states of Africa and Asia, as well as the European members of the Commonwealth of Independent States (with the exception of Russia and Kazakhstan) in the Caucasus and Eastern Europe.

European Political Cooperation (EPC): Foreign policy cooperation among the member states of the EC, established in 1970 and conducted on an intergovernmental basis by foreign ministries. It was officially included in the Single European Act (1986) and was replaced by the Common Foreign and Security Policy in the Maastricht Treaty.

European Rapid Reaction Force (ERRF): The European Union Rapid Reaction Force is a transnational military force of 60,000 soldiers available for EU missions. Formal agreement to found the ERRF was reached in November 2004.

European Security and Defense Identity (ESDI): The ESDI was first established by the Western European Union as a means of creating a European pillar within

NATO that could fulfill "Petersberg tasks": rescue and relief, peacekeeping, and peacemaking. Following the Anglo-French meeting at St. Malo in December 1998, responsibility for ESDI was transferred to the EU and renamed ESDP. With the Lisbon Treaty, it was renamed once again, to Common Security and Defense Policy (CSDP). It is supported by a number of institutional bodies, including the Political and Security Committee (PSC) of the European Council, an EU Military Committee (EUMC), an EU Military Staff (EUMS), and the European Defense Agency (EDA).

European Security Strategy (ESS): Entitled "A Secure Europe in a Better World," the ESS was drafted by Javier Solana in response to the controversial 2002 National Security Strategy of the United States. Approved by the European Council in December 2003, the ESS identifies a string of key threats that Europe needs to deal with: terrorism, proliferation of weapons of mass destruction, regional conflict, failed states, and organized crime. The 2008 report "Providing Security in a Changing World" reinforces the ESS.

euro zone: The group of countries having adopted the euro; also known as the euro area.

exchange rate mechanism (ERM): A multilateral framework for the joint management of exchange-rate movements between participating countries within set tolerance margins.

General Agreement on Tariffs and Trade (GATT): Multilateral trade treaty signed in 1947 establishing rules for international trade. It was a forum for eight rounds of tariff reductions culminating in the 1994 Uruguay Round agreements and the establishment of the World Trade Organization (WTO) as successor to the GATT.

GDP (gross domestic product): Annual value of goods and services produced in a country.

High Authority: The executive body of the ECSC. It ceased to exist in July 1967 with the entering into effect of the merger treaty establishing a single commission for the ECSC, Euratom, and the EEC.

intergovernmentalism: Approach to integration in which national governments retain their sovereign powers and cooperate with each other by interstate bargaining and agreement. It is opposed to federalism and supranationalism.

Lisbon strategy: Also known as the Lisbon agenda, this is an EU action and development plan adopted for a ten-year period in 2000 in Lisbon, Portugal, by the European Council. The Lisbon strategy intends to deal with the low productivity and stagnation of economic growth in the EU through the formulation of various policy initiatives to be taken by all EU member states. The long-term goal is to make the EU "the world's most dynamic and competitive knowledge-based economy" by 2010. In June 2010, the strategy was replaced by the Europe 2020 strategy.

Lisbon Treaty: Treaty signed in December 2007 but, due to a difficult ratification process, entered into force only in December 2009. Lisbon became plan B after the constitutional treaty failed ratification in 2005. Lisbon provides for, among other things, an EU Council president, a diplomatic corps, and a "high representative of Foreign Affairs and Security Policy." It also boosted the European Parliament with more powers and emphasized the practice of subsidiarity.

Maastricht Treaty: The Treaty on European Union (TEU), known as the Maastricht

Treaty, was signed at Maastricht, the Netherlands, on February 7, 1992. It constituted by far the most sweeping revision of Community treaties ever attempted. The TEU created the entity called the European Union (EU), a complicated structure of three pillars profoundly redefining European economic and political governance and the start of a more organized common foreign policy.

Marshall Plan: Officially known as the European Recovery Program, this plan was proposed in 1947 by U.S. secretary of state George C. Marshall to foster postwar European economic revival through extensive U.S. aid. It is seen as the economic arm of the Truman Doctrine.

nominal long-term interest rate: The rate of return on benchmark government bonds of a set maturity (usually equal to or greater than ten years).

North Atlantic Cooperation Council (NACC): Created by NATO at the Rome summit in November 1991. A U.S. initiative, the NACC was a new institutional relationship of consultation and cooperation on political and security issues open to all of the former, newly independent members of the Warsaw Pact. In July 1997, it was replaced by the Euro-Atlantic Partnership Council (EAPC).

North Atlantic Council: NATO's decision-making body.

North Atlantic Treaty Organization (NATO): A political-military institution founded in 1949 for the collective defense of its member states, which include the United States, Canada, and fourteen European countries. Initially designed against the Soviet threat, the end of the Cold War made NATO enlarge in Central and Eastern European countries and redefine its mission.

Organization for Economic Cooperation and Development (OECD): An international organization established in 1961 comprising mainly industrialized market economy countries of North America, Western Europe, Japan, Australia, and New Zealand. It was the successor to the OEEC and is based in Paris.

Organization for European Economic Cooperation (OEEC): Organization of European Marshall Plan aid recipients, created at the behest of the United States to administer the aid and to serve as a forum for negotiating reductions in intra-European barriers to trade.

Organization for Security and Cooperation in Europe (OSCE): See Conference on Security and Cooperation in Europe.

parliamentary democracy: The form of democracy in which the composition of the executive branch is determined by the legislative majority, which may also dismiss the executive. The legislative branch of government is elected by the people.

Partnership for Peace (PFP): Framework agreements for non-NATO states to have a military relationship with the alliance.

purchasing power parity (PPP): Adjusts foreign currencies for dollar equivalents in purchasing power.

Schengen Agreement: The 1985 Schengen Agreement is an agreement among European states harmonizing visa requirements and external border controls. It includes all European Union states except the Republic of Ireland and the United Kingdom, and includes non-EU members Iceland, Norway, and Switzerland. Border posts and checks have been removed between Schengen countries, and a common "Schengen visa" allows tourist or visitor access to the area.

Single European Act (SEA): First major revision of the founding treaties of the European Community; went into effect in 1987. It increased the powers of the European Parliament, broadened the policy responsibilities of the EC, and, above all, scheduled the completion of a single economic market by December 31, 1992, as a member-state treaty commitment.

Stability and Growth Pact (SGP): Adopted in 1997, member states promised to keep to certain fiscal statistics so as to support the stability of the euro zone. These include limits to inflation differentials, budget deficits, and debt-to-GDP ratios. The pact lacks a punishment mechanism.

Stability Pact for South Eastern Europe: The stability pact was created by the EU on June 10, 1999, to provide a comprehensive, long-term conflict prevention and peace-building strategy for the Balkans. The stability pact is not an organization itself; rather, it offers a political commitment and a framework agreement to develop a shared international approach to enhance stability and growth in the region.

subsidiarity: The practice of handling and deciding issues at the lowest level possible. By applying subsidiarity, a clearer division of labor between the European and the national level is envisioned.

supranationalism: Approach to integration in which participating states transfer sovereign powers and policymaking responsibilities to transnational institutions whose decisions are binding on those states. This is, for example, the case regarding the common market of the EU.

Treaty of Nice: A treaty approved in December 2000 at the European Council amending the Maastricht Treaty to prepare the EU institutions for large-scale enlargement. Nice was widely regarded as an awkward set of compromises, and dissatisfaction with the treaty led to the European Convention of 2002–2003.

The Treaty on European Union (TEU): See Maastricht Treaty.

unicameral parliament: A legislative body consisting of a single house.

unitary government: The form of government in which the national government is the only repository of sovereign power and in which the powers of subordinate levels of government are determined by the national government.

Warsaw Pact: A military alliance founded by the Soviet Union in 1955 in response to West Germany's entry into NATO. Its membership included the USSR and the countries of Central and Eastern Europe.

Western European Union (WEU): An exclusively Western European mutual defense organization established in 1954. It was moribund through much of the Cold War, revived in 1984 as a vehicle to develop European defense cooperation, and designated the defense arm of the EU in the Maastricht Treaty.

Index

9/11. *See* September 11, 2001

A., B. and C. v. Ireland, 366
Åland Islands, 176, 193
Abkhazia. *See* Russo-Georgian war
Act of Union, 82
Action Directe (AD), 18
Action Plan for the Free Movement of
  Workers, 381
acquis communautaire, 201, 379, 465–66
Adenauer, Konrad, *112*, 123, *127*, 400
Afghanistan: war in, 3, 11–12, 17, 59, 93,
  96, 129–30, 204, 399–400, 404, 408–11,
  416, 421–22
Ahmadinejad, Mahmoud, 60
AIDS, 228
Airbus, 55
Albania, 93, 405, *414*
Albright, Madeline, 409–10, 413, 419, 421
Algeria, 18, 47, 60
Alsthom, 55
Al-Qaeda, 409. *See also* September 11,
  2001
Amato, Giuliano, *143*
Amsterdam Treaty, 11, 202, 292–94, 379–
  80, 395
Andreotti, Giulio, *142–43*, 148, 441n15
Anglo-Saxon economic model. *See* Liberal
  Market Economy
anti-Americanism, 3, 145–46
anti-Semitism, 102
appeasement, 195, 198
appellations controlées, 41
Arcelor, 55
AREVA, 60
Ashton, Catherine, 12, 298
Asylum Procedures Directive, 388
Atlanticism, 27, 55, 59–60, 88–89, 158, 431
Aubry, Martine, 35, 64
Austria, 108, 293, 320, 442n24; and EU ac-
  cession, 293; and immigration, 380; and

the radical right, 389–91; and Turkey,
  15. *See also* financial and economic crisis in Austria

Balcerowicz, Leszek, 246–48
Balkans: and EU accession, 405; and
  NATO membership, 405–6; and con-
  flict, 4, 121, 126, 203, 292, 401, 412, 417,
  429
Balladur, Édouard, *30*
Bank of England, 72–73, 76
Barcelona Process, 465. *See also* European
  Neighborhood Policy (ENP)
Barroso, José Manuel, 343
Basic law (Germany), 101, 103, 105, 113,
  115, 126, *127*, 360
Bassolino, Antonio, 157
Basque country, 18, 40, 436n7
Belarus, 216, 235, 237, *414*
Belgium, 284, 310, 389; and European
  Council presidency, 344; and European
  integration, 281, 319, 379; and immigra-
  tion, 380, 384; and NATO, 413, 415,
  420; and the radical right, 389. *See also*
  financial and economic crisis in Belgium
Belka, Marek, *251*, 264
Benelux customs union, 277
Berezovsky, Boris, 222, 233
Berlin, 3, 101, 103–4, *106–7*, 111, *114*
Berlin blockade, *106*, 400
Berlin Plus, *414*, 460n44
Berlin Wall, 101, 103, *106*, 110, *127–28*,
  139, 289
Berlusconi, Silvio, 14, *134–35*, *143*, 148–
  52, 154–55, 157–59
Bettencourt affair, 53
Blair, Tony, 69–73, 75–78, 81–87, 91–96,
  152, 298
Bobkov, Filip, 223
Bosnia-Herzegovina, 126, 401, 405, 416,
  425. *See also* Balkans

473

Bossi, Umberto, *148*, 150, 158

Bové, Jose, 41

Brandt, Willy, 103, *112*

Brazil, 17, 60, 222, 299

Bretton Woods system, 41, 284, 319, 465

Brigate Rosse (BR), 18

Britain. *See* United Kingdom

Brown, Gordon, 69–74, 76–78, 87–88, 96, 152

Brussels Pact. *See* West European Union

Brussels, 146, 281–82, 421

Brussels summit (1985), 287

Brussels summit (March 2010), 322, *325*, 336, 344, 347

Brussels summit (December 2010), 350

Bucharest summit, 405

Bulgaria, 14, 284, 297, 389–90, *414*, 420

Bundesbank, 7

Burns, Nicholas, 427

Bush, George W., 3, 70, 92–95, 125–26, 158, 204, 300, 327, 404, 412, 427

Buzek, Jerzy, *251*, 257

Cameron, David, 16, *68–70, 72*, 87–88, 97

CAP. *See* Common Agricultural Policy

Cassa per il Mezzogiorno, 144

Catherine the Great, 209

Caucasus, 209, 226, 229, 235, 407, 468

Central Anticorruption Bureau (CBA), 266–67

Central and Eastern Europe, 19, 257, 289, 311; demography of, 121; and immigration, 157, 202; and Germany, 123–24; political cleavages in, 268–69, 271–72; and Russia, 13–14, 192; and Scandinavia, 194–96. *See also* European Union and enlargement, North Atlantic Treaty Organization and enlargement

CFSP. *See* Common Foreign and Security Policy

Chad, 56, 62

Charles XII (Sweden), 171

Charter of Fundamental Rights, 363

China, 200, 239, 299–300; and the EU, 431; and the G8, 60; rise of, 2–3, 13, 58, 62, 118–19, 299–300; and Russia, 211–12

Chirac, Jacques, 14, 27, *30*, 32, 34, 50, 51, 54, 56, 58–59

Churchill, Winston, *72*, 196

Christian Democracy (DC, Italy), 139–41, 144

Christian Democratic Union (CDU, Germany), *100*–101, 108–13, 339, 438n1; Christian Social Union (CSU, Germany). *See* Christian Democratic Union

Ciampi, Carlo Azeglio, *143*

Cimoszewicz, Wlodzimierz, *250*, 264

City of London, 73–74, 77, 97

Civic Platform (PO, Poland), 258, *261*, 264–65, 267–71

Clegg, Nick, 69, 87–88

climate change, 59–60, 300, 323, 420, 428

Clinton, Bill, 93

cohabitation, 28, 30, 50–51

Cold War, 14, 194, 234, 400, 404; end of, 4, 13, 289, 401; and France, 58, 60, 62–63, 401, 426; and Germany, 103, 118, 125, *127–28*; and Italy, 141, 145–46, 150; and the post–Cold War era, 58, 60, 126, 192, 399, 405, 423–25; and the USSR, 56, 89, 118, 139, 166, 401 and Scandinavia, 166–167, 175, 194–99

Committee of the Regions, 292, 318

Common Agenda for Integration, 396

Common Agricultural Policy (CAP), 41, 120, 282, 286, 465

Common Assembly, 279, 281, 465. *See also* European Coal and Steel Community

Common Foreign and Security Policy (CFSP), 318, 416, 465, 468; development of 10–12, 56, 412; high representative for, 11–12, 293, 298, 465, 468. *See also* Treaty of Amsterdam, Treaty of Maastricht

Common Security and Defense Policy (CSDP), 299, 412, 437n20, 465, 469; development of, 10–12, 412; operations, 418. *See also* North Atlantic Treaty Organization and the EU

Communist Party of France (PCF), 26, 32–33, 39, 50

Communist Party of the Russian Federation, 218–20

competitiveness, 2, 28, 36, 189, 299–300, 324–25, 337–38, 343–44, 346

Conference on Security and Cooperation in Europe (CSCE). *See* Organization for Security and Cooperation in Europe (OSCE)

Conservative Party (UK), *68*–69, 73, 78, 81, 83, 85–88, 92, 97; Constitutional Court (Austria), 352

Constitutional Court (Germany), 105, 116, 126, 341–42, 352, 360–61

Constitutional Court (Italy), *152*, 352, 361

Constitutional Court (Poland), 254

Constitutional Court (Russia), 218

Conventional Forces in Europe (CFE) Treaty, 14

Coordinated Market Economy, 307, 309, 312–17, 320

Copenhagen criteria, 466

Copenhagen summit (1993), 293

corporatism, 31, 182, 184–86, 466

Corsican National Liberation Front (FLNC), 40

Cossiga, Francesco, *143*, 147

Costa v. ENEL, 355, *357*

Council for Mutual Economic Assistance (CMEA), 466

Council of Europe, 278, 282, 353, 365–66, 421, 466

Court of First Instance. *See* General Court

Craxi, Bettino, *143*, 146, 148, *152*

Croatia, 9, 405. *See also* Balkans.

Cyprus, 294, 298, 380, 418; and Turkey, 416, 425, 427

Czech Republic, 294, 405, 408, 458nn6–7

Czechoslovakia, 400. *See also* Czech Republic, Slovakia

Daalder, Ivo, 404, 427

D'Alema, Massimo, *143*, 151–52

Dati, Rachida, 48

Davutaglu, Ahmet, 16

De Gasperi, Alcide, 141–42, 146

Deauville summit, 347–48, 350, 354n40

Deby, Idriss, 62

Defense Capabilities Initiative (DCI), 415

Defrenne, Gabrielle, 362

Delors Committee, 289, 292

Delors, Jacques, 33, 90, 124, 286–90, 292, 299, 359

democratic deficit, 10, 124, 178, 298

Democratic Left Alliance (SLD, Poland), *247*, 249–54, 256–58, *260–61*, 263–65, 267–68, 270

Democratic Party (Italy), 134, 155

Democratic Party of the Left (PDS, Italy), 148, 151

Democratic Republic of Congo, 12, 412.

Denmark, *161*, *163*–64, 169, 171, 443n2, 444nn10–11; during World War II, 192. economy of, 166, 187–88; and the European Union 185, 199–204, 283–84, 287, 290, 292–94; and homogeneity, 168; and immigration, 189–91, 378, 380, 382–85, 394, 396; and NATO, 167, 204, 193–94, 197–98, 427–28; political parties of, 165, 179–181, *183*, 389–90; political system of, *163*, 174–177, 185; welfare state of, *170*, 187–89. *See also* North Atlantic Treaty Organization and Denmark, Scandinavian social model

Derrida, Jacques, 124

Di Pietro, Antonio, 149

Dini, Lamberto, *143*

direct effect, 355, *357*, 358, 362

Directive on Family Reunion, 384

dirigisme, 33, 35, 54

Dossetti, Giuseppe, 145

droit de regard, 196

EAPC. *See* Euro-Atlantic Partnership Council

East Germany. *See* German Democratic Republic (GDR)

East Timor, 11

Eastern Europe. *See* Central and Eastern Europe

EBRD. *See* European Bank for Reconstruction and Development

ECB. *See* European Central Bank

ECJ. *See* European Court of Justice

Economic and Monetary Union (EMU), 296, 304, 308; criticism of, 337–38; development of, 285, 289–90, 292–93, 310, 320–23; and Germany, 341; reform of, 13, 304, 324–26, 343–44, 346, *348*. *See also* euro

economic governance. *See* Economic and Monetary Union (EMU), reform of

Economic and Social Committee, 281, 318

ECSC. *See* European Coal and Steel Community

ECU. *See* European Monetary System

EDC. *See* European Defense Community

EEA. *See* European Economic Area

EEC. *See* European Economic Community

EFTA. *See* European Free Trade Association

EIB. *See* European Investment Bank

Electricité de France, 36

Employment Equality Directive, 363

EMS. *See* European Monetary System

EMU. *See* Economic and Monetary Union

Ente Nazionale Idrocarburi (ENI), 144, 146

EP. *See* European Parliament

EPC. *See* European Political Cooperation

environmental policy, 41, 61, 110, 120, 176, 180, 200, 228, 282, 287–88, 360

Equal Treatment Framework Directive, 395

Erdogan, Recep Tayyip, 16

Érignac, Claude, 40

ERM. *See* Exchange Rate Mechanism

ESCB. *See* European System of Central Banks

ESDP. *See* Common Security and Defense Policy

Estonia: and European integration, 294, 434n12, 458n7; independence of, 195, 199; and NATO, 418–20; and Russia, 216

ethnic cleansing, 93, 126

EU. *See* European Union

Euratom. *See* European Atomic Energy Authority

euro, 1–2, 5–7, 466; and the euro zone, 121, 299, 469, 471; introduction of, 122, 294, 296, 310, 318. *See also* Economic and Monetary Union, European Central Bank, financial and economic crisis

Euro-Atlantic Partnership Council (EAPC), 427–28, 470

EUROCORPS, 466

Eurogroup, 466

Euro-missiles, 56, 199, 401, 426

Europe 2020, 322–23, 344, 469

Europe à la carte, 200

European Atomic Energy Community (Euratom), 280–81, 291, 466, 469

European Bank for Reconstruction and Development (EBRD), 467

European Border Surveillance System, *386*

European Central Bank (ECB), 318, 467; role of, 7, 189, 305, 321–22, *340*; establishment of, 292, 320. *See also* euro

European Coal and Steel Community (ECSC), 118, 194, 200–201, 278–281, 291, 465, 467, 469

European Commission, 285–86, 467–68; formation of, 281; reform of, 9, 295; powers of, 12, 60–61, 283, 288, 291–92, 309, 318, 320, 323, *340*–41; and legal action, 49, 354–55, 358, 363, 366

European Commission against Racism and Intolerance, 396

European Community (EC). *See* European Union (EU)

European Constitution, 8, 60, 467, 469, 471; development of, 295–97; referenda on, 9, 27, 92, 120, 202–03, 434n19

European Convention. *See* European Constitution

European Convention on Human Rights, 353, 361–62, 366

European Council, 318, *330*, 345, *348*, 354–55, 466–69, 471; creation of, 284–85; powers *vis à vis* European Commission, 60, 291, *340*–41; powers *vis à vis* European Parliament, 288, 291; presidency of, 12, 296, 298, *340*, 344; reform of, 9, 295–96. *See also* qualified majority voting

European Court of Human Rights (EHCR), 351, 353, 365–67, 466

European Court of Justice (ECJ), 279, 291, 353–59, 362–65, 367, 383, 467

European Currency Unit (ECU). *See* European Monetary System (EMS)

European Defense Agency (EDA), 412, 415, 469. *See also* Common Security and Defense Policy (CSDP)

European Defense Community (EDC), 10, 280

European Economic Area (EEA), 202, 378–82, 384, *386*–88, 390, 457n5, 468

European Economic Community (EEC), 201, 280–87, 318–19, 365

European External Action Service (EEAS), 12, 298, 465, 468

European Financial Stability Facility (EFSF), 6, 299, 342–*43*

European Free Trade Agreement (EFTA), 199–201, 378–79, 384, *386*, 468

European Fund for the Integration of Third Country Nationals, 396

European Gendarmerie Force (EGF), 415

European identity, 371, 393–94

European Investment Bank (EIB), 281

European Monetary System (EMS), 285, 289, 292–93, 319, 338, 467–468. *See also* Economic and Monetary Union (EMU)

European Neighborhood Policy (ENP), 12, 411, 465, 468. *See also* Common Foreign and Security Policy (CFSP)

European Parliament (EP), 354–55; and the "democratic deficit," 10, 298; development of, 9–10, 285, 288, 291, 294–96, 298, 469; powers of, 318, 341, 359, 466; and radical right parties, 202, 390; representation in, 120. *See also* European Council powers *vis à vis* European Parliament

European Police Mission in Afghanistan (EUPOL), 410

European Political Cooperation (EPC), 283–84, 286, 288, 291, *402*, 468

European Political Union, 10, 290

European Rapid Reaction Force (ERRF), 468

European Reform Treaty. *See* Lisbon Treaty

European Security and Defense Identity (ESDI), 468–69. *See also* Common Security and Defense Policy (CSDP)

European Security and Defense Policy (ESDP). *See* Common Security and Defense Policy (CSDP)

European Security Strategy (ESS), 299, *402*, 469

European Security Treaty, 407–08

European System of Central Banks, 292

European Union (EU), 278, 290–91, 308–9, 368, *402*; and economic liberalization, 92, 304, 308, 310–12, 318, 320, 353–54, 359–60, 384; economy of, 303–12, 317; and enlargement, 4, 122–24, 201, 283–85, 293–94, 307, 379; and European integration, 2, 318, 354–56; global role of, 3–4, 299–300; post-Maastricht reforms, 296–98; relations with member states, 303–4; and Scandi-navia, 174–77, 199–200. *See also* Denmark and the European Union, financial and economic crisis in the European Union, France and the European Union, Germany and the European Union, immigration in the European Union, Italy and the European Union, North Atlantic Treaty Organization and the European Union

European Union Agency for Fundamental Rights, 396

European Union Military Committee (EUMC), 469

European Union Military Staff (EUMS), 469

Euro-pessimism, 3, 285

Euro-sclerosis, 285

Euro-skepticism, 90–93, 123, 203

Euskadi Ta Askatasuna, 18

excessive deficit procedure, 339, 345, *348*, 453n37

Exchange Rate Mechanism (ERM), 70, 468. *See also* Economic and Monetary Union, European Monetary System

Fabius, Laurent, 34

Faero Islands, 176, 198, 201

Fanfani, Amintore, *142–43*

Federal Council (Germany), 113, 115–116

Federal Republic of Germany. *See* Germany

Fillon, François, 37, 45

financial and economic crisis, 1, 4–7, 12–13, 58, 303–4; in Austria, 333; in Belgium, 5, 333, 343, 346; and the euro, 101, 121, 299, 312, 329–30, 334–338, 342, 345–46; in the European Union, 303–5, 322–24, 327, 342–46; in France, 5, 12, 38, 55, 333, 336, *348*; in Germany, 5–6, 12, 61, 101, 329–31, 333–39, 343–48; in Greece, 5–6, 61, 121, 299, 303, 322–24, 327–39, 341–47, 349–50, 442n22, 452n23, 453n26; in Iceland, 4–5, 191; in Ireland, 4–6, 12, 303, 305, 322, 327, 333–36, 338, 343, 347, 442n22; in Italy, 5–6, 333–34, 338, 343, 346–47, 349–50, 442n22; in the Netherlands, 5, 333–34; in Poland, 5; in Portugal, 5–6, 303, 324, 327, 333–36, 338, 342–*43*, 346, 442n22, 442n24; in Spain, 5–6, 303, 322,

324, 327, 333–36, 338, 342–43, 346–47, 442n22; in the United Kingdom, 4–5, 76–78, 96; in the United States, 5, 38, 303, 305, 349

financial crisis. *See* financial and economic crisis

Fini, Gianfranco, 150, 155, 158–59

Finland, *161, 163,* 444n11; civil war in, 167–69; and the European Union, 167, 200–04, 284; Cold War foreign policy of, 192–98; political parties of, *163,* 165, 178–181, *183,* 389; political system of, 171, 174–177, 185; social model of, 187–89; and immigration, 189–91, 378, 380

Finlandization, 197

first oil shock, 284

Fischer, Joschka, 124, 126

flexicurity, 184, 189, 205

Fontainebleau summit (1984), 286

Forza Italia, 151

France, *25–26;* economy of, 28–39, 42–43, 54–55, 308, 320; and the European Union, 60–61, 279, 281, 284, 294–97, 319; and fifth republic institutions, *28, 30,* 50–51, 361; and the *frappe de force,* 430; and Germany, 4, 7, 12, 57, 60, 101, 120–21, 123, 280, 420; global influence of, 58; and globalization, 39, 41, 43, 54–55; and the *grandes écoles,* 46, 51, 53; and immigration, 43–49, 380, 393–94, 436n8, 437n20; and the Iraq war, 93–94; and Islam, 43–45, 47, 49, 390–91; and *la France profonde,* 40; and the Middle East, 59–60; and NATO, 56, 59, 413, 437n20; and the November 2005 riots, 29, 44, 46–48; third republic of, 40, 43; and welfare state reform, 31–39, 54–55. *See also* Cold War and France, financial and economic crisis in France, North Atlantic Treaty Organization and France, United States and France

francophonie, 57, 62

Frederik VII (Denmark), 176

Free Democratic Party (FDP, Germany), *100*–101, 108–13

functionalism, 281

G-8, 60, 428

Galloway, George, 94

de Gaulle, Charles, *28, 30,* 50, 56–*57,* 59, 62, 89, 123, 201, 282–83, 401, 426. *See also* Gaullism

Gaullism, 27, 55–58. *See also* Charles de Gaulle

Gaz de France (GDF), 36

General Agreement on Tariffs and Trade (GATT), 281, 465, 469

General Court, 356, 363

Georgia, 11, 216, 405, 411. *See also* Russo-Georgian war

German Democratic Republic, 101, 103, 109, *127*–28. *See also* Germany

Germany, *99–100,* 440n3; economy of, 117–18, 299, 307–8, 317, 320, 333; and the European Union, 4, 120–25, 279, 281, 284, 292–96, 319; foreign policy of, 118–20, 124–30, 401, 413, 416, 420–21, 430; and immigration, 373, *374, 375, 376,* 379–81, *391–92,* 393–94; and the Iraq War, 93–94; and NATO, 118–120, 123, 128–29, 413; political system of, 105, 107–8, 113, 115–16; reunification of, 101, 103, *106*–07, 115, 120, 122–23, 125, 128, 130–31, 289–90, 292, 295, 426; and the UN, 60; and welfare state reform, 117–18; and the Weimar Republic, 102, 104, *114, 127,* 165; and World War II, 102. *See also* Central and Eastern Europe and Germany, Cold War and Germany, financial and economic crisis in Germany, France and Germany, North Atlantic Treaty Organization and Germany, Russia/USSR and Germany, United States and Germany

Giertych, Roman, 266

Giscard d'Estaing, Valéry, *30,* 56, 123, 284–85, 295, 467

glasnost, 227, 231

global financial crisis. *See* financial and economic crisis

global warming. *See* climate change

Good Friday Agreement, 83

Gorbachev, Mikhail, 199, 210, 213, 216–17, 225, 227–28, 234, *236–37,* 241, 445n3

Goria, Giovanni, *143*

Greece: asylum policies of, 388; the Cold War in, 400; and EU accession, 4, 285, 379–80; and NATO, 427, 430; and the Macedonia name issue, 405; and the radical right, 389. *See also* financial and economic crisis in Greece

Green Party (Germany), *100*, 108–11, 113, 126

Greenland, 176, *190*, 193, 197, 201

Grillo, Bepe, 154

Gronchi, Giovanni, 145

Gül, Abdullah,16

Gusinsky, Vladimir, 223, 233

Haakon VII (Norway), 176

Habermas, Jürgen, 124

Hague summit (1969), 283

Haider, Jörg, 389

Hanover summit (1988), 289

Hanseatic League, 192, 372

Hammarskjöld, Dag, 196

Hansson, Per Albin, 166, 173

Helsinki process. *See* Organization for Security and Cooperation in Europe

Helsinki summit (1999), 294

Henry VIII (England), 82

Hezbollah, 59

High Authority of the European Coal and Steel Community, 279, 281, 469

High Authority for the Struggle against Discrimination for Equality (HALDE), 46

von Hindenburg, Paul, 165

Hitler, Adolf, 102, 104, 107, 165

Höglund, Zeth, 173

Holocaust, 20, 104, *107, 127*

Holst, Johann Jørgen, 195

House of Commons, 69, 79–81, 83, 87–88, 90

House of Lords, 80–81, 86; Appellate Committee of, 362

Human Rights Act of 1998, 361

Hungary, 139, 145, 223, 284, 294, 389, 390

Hussein, Saddam, 94–5, 204, 297. *See also* Iraq war

Iceland, 167–68, 191, 199, 202, 204; foreign policy of, 192–93, 196, 198. *See also* economic and financial crisis in Iceland

immigration, 2, 20, 229, 371–73; and asylum, 61, 291, 293, 295, 360, 375, *385*, 387–89; in the European Union, 61, 373–82, 384–96; and Islam, 390, *391–92*, 458n10. *See also* Islam and Muslims

India, 3, 49, 58, 60, 299–300, 426

inflation, 7, 32–33, 61, 71–72, 74, 76, 184, 187, 221–22, 225, 228, 284, 292, 309–11, 317, 319, 321–22, 331, 333–34, 337–38, 466

interest rates, 33, 72, 297, 309–10, 316–17, 321, 329, 331–34, 470

Intergovernmental Conferences (IGC), 287–290, 293–94, 296–97

intergovernmentalism, 60, 469

international law, *357*, 407

International Monetary Fund (IMF), 5, 299, 327, 329, 337, 342, 346, *414*, 428

International Security Assistance Force (ISAF). *See* Afghanistan, war in

IMF. *See* International Monetary Fund

Iran, 16–17, 59–60, 240, 285, 300, 400, 408, 425, 429,

Iraq War, 11, 17, 27, 56–57, 70, 93–96, 125, 158, 204, 292, 297, 388, 403–04, 411–12, 420

Ireland: economy of, 299, 349; and EU accession, 283; and EU referenda, 295, 298; and immigration, 373, 380, 384; and the UK, 82, 366. *See also* financial and economic crisis in Ireland

Irish Republican Army (IRA), 18, 82–84

Islam and Muslims, 15–18, 94, 180–81, *190*, 297, 366, 390, *391–92*, 409, 431; anti-Islamism, 18, 185, 390. *See also* immigration and Islam, France and Islam

Israel-Palestine conflict, 16, 62

Italian Communist Party (PCI), 138–41, 144–46, 148, 151, 158

Italian Popular Party (PPI), 136

Italian Social Movement (MSI), 139–*40*, 144–45, 150–51, 157

Italian Socialist Party (PSI), 139–*43*, 145–46, *148*, 158, 166

Italy, *133–34*, 440n3, 442n21, 443n38; and the Catholic church, 136–37, 146–47, 152, 366; economy of, 91, 149, 305–6; election results and resulting governments, *140, 142–143, 156*; and the European Union, 158, 279, 281, 284, 319, 466; fascism in, 137–38; during the First Republic, 135–36, 139–50, 152–53; and immigration, 157–58, 373–74, 380, 388; and the Iraq War, 93–94; and Italy, 145–47; North-South divide in, 135, 138, 156–57, 159; political system of,

150–54, 157; and the *Risorgimento*, 135–36. *See also* Cold War and Italy, financial and economic crisis in Italy, North Atlantic Treaty Organization and Italy, United States and Italy

Japan, 10, 60, 119, 200, 286, 426, 467, 470
Jaruzelsky, Wojciech, 246–48, 253
Jenkins, Roy, 87
Jospin, Lionel, *30*, 35–37, 50
Juppé, Alain, 37, 54
Justice and Home Affairs (JHA), 291, 293, 318, 384–85
Jyllands-Posten cartoon controversy, *190*, 390

Kaczyński, Jarosław, *247*, 252, 264, 270–71
Kaczyński, Lech, *247*, *251*, 259, 264–65, 269, 271
Kalmar Union, 192, 444n11
Kanslergade Compromise, 164–65, 173. *See also* Scandinavian social model
Karl Johan, 176
Kekkonen, Urho, 197
Kemal, Mustafa, 16
Keynesian economics, 19, 35, 166, 173, 309, 328, 336
Khodorkovsky, Mikhail, 233
Kohl, Helmut, 56, 90, 108, *112*, 121, 123, 126, 290
Kok, Wim, 19, *163*
Komorowski, Bronislaw, *244*, 252, 270
Korean war, 400
Korwin-Mikke, Janusz, 270
Kosovo, 11, 93, 126, 235, *414*, 417. *See also* Balkans conflicts.
Kouchner, Bernard, 56
Kwaśniewski, Aleksander, *247*, *250–251*, 254

la malbouffe, 41
La Pira, Giorgio, 145
Labour Party (UK), *68*–78, 81, 83, 85–88, 91–94, 96–97
Laeken Declaration, 467
Latvia, 458nn6–7; independence of, 195, 199, 419; and the radical right, 389; and Russia, 216, 419
Lautsi v. Italy, 366
Lavrov, Sergei, 407

Law and Justice (PiS, Poland), *244*, 259, *261*, 264–71
Le Pen, Jean-Marie, 27, 50, 52, 389. *See also* France and the National Front (FN)
League of Nations, 192
League of Polish Families (LPR), *244*, 259, *260*, 263, 265–68
Lebanon, 59, 62, 95
Left Party (Germany), *100*, 107, 109–11, 117, 121, 123, 129
Lega Nord. See Northern League
Lenin, Vladimir Ilyich, 168, 209
Lepper, Andrzej, *247*, *251*, 259, 267
Liberal Democrats (UK), *68*–69, 85–88, 92, 97
Liberal Market Economy, 307, 309, 312–17, 320
Libya, 56, 60
Lie, Trygve, 195
Liechtenstein, 202, 378, 468
Lisbon summit (2000). *See* Lisbon strategy
Lisbon strategy, 92, 322, 344
Lisbon Treaty, 6, 60–61, 465, 467–69; contents of, 9–10, 12–13, 300, *340*, 355, *358*, 413, 415; development of, 124, 297–98; ratification of, 202, 266. *See also* European Constitution
Lithuania, 14, 192, 195, 199, 284, 419–420
Luxembourg, 277, 279–81, 319, 379, 413–14, 420

Maastricht criteria, 310
Maastricht summit (1991), 91
Maastricht Treaty, 11, 177, 201–202, 355, 465, 467–69, 71; Danish referendum on, 9, 177; development of, 288–93; and the ECJ, 355; French referendum on, 9
Macedonia, 11, 405
mafia, 135, 147, 158
Maghreb, 45, 62, 378
Magna Charta, 79
Major, John, *72*, 74, 83, 88, 90, 152
Malfatti, Franco Maria, 146
Malta, 284, 294, 298, 380, 458n6
Mandelson, Peter, 73
mani pulite, *148*, 361
Mansfield, Mike, 401
Marcinkiewicz, Kazmierz, *251*, 265
Marshall Plan, 194, 196, 277–78, 470

Marxism-Leninism, 166, 199, 209–10, 213
Mattei, Enrico, 146
Mazowiecki, Tadeusz, 246–50
McChrystal, Stanley, 410
Mečiar, Vladimir, 271
Medvedev, Dmitry, 14, 124, *208*, 215, 219–20, 228, 231, 233–34, 239–41, 405, 407, 421
Merkel, Angela, 6, 13, 16, 61, *100*–101, 108–9, *112*, 121–23, 125–29, 317, 336, 339, 341–45, 347
Mexico, 60
Middle East, 58–59, 62–63, *190*, 203, 425, 465
Milan European Council (1985), 287
Miliband, Ed, 97
Miller, Leszek, *247, 251*, 258, 263–64
missile defense system, 405, 408
Mitterrand, François, 27, *30*, 32–33, 36, 39, 51, 56, 58, 90, 123, 286, 290
Moldova, 411
Monnet, Jean, 278–79
Montenegro, 405, *414*
Morocco, 60
Muslims. *See* Islam and Muslims
Mussolini, Benito, 141

Napieralksi, Grzegorz, 270
Nashi, 233
National Alliance (AN, Italy), 150, 157
National Front (FN, France), 26–27, 48, 50–52, 389
National Security Strategy (United States), 428
National Socialist Party (Germany). *See* Nazi Party
nationalism, 13, 83, 104, 118, 145, 169, 192–93, 200, 204, 256, 391, 394
NATO. *See* North Atlantic Treaty Organization
Nazi Party, 89, 102, 104–05, 107, 165–66, 192, *212*, 352
neoliberalism, 111, 181, 184, 426
Netherlands, 154, 277, 319; and immigration, 379–80, 394; and NATO, 410, 420, 427–28, 430; and the radical right, 389–90; and its referendum on European Constitution, 9, 203, 297. *See also* financial and economic crisis in the Netherlands

Neue Mitte, 91
New Labour. *See* Labour Party (UK)
NGO. *See* nongovernmental organizations
Nice Treaty, 8–9, 202, 295–96, 387, 471
nongovernmental organizations, 194, 230
Nordic balance, 197–99. *See also* North Atlantic Treaty Organization and Scandinavia
Nordic Council of Ministers, 194
Nordic customs union, 199
North Atlantic Cooperation Council (NACC), 470
North Atlantic Council, 403, 415, 470
North Atlantic Treaty, 278, 403, *424*
North Atlantic Treaty Organization (NATO), 8, 11, 13–14, 167, 278–79, 282, 293, *402*–403, *414*–415, *420*, 422–*432*, 470; and enlargement, 235, 263, 293, 399, 404–06; and the European Union, 399–401, 410–17, 431–32, 460n44, 469; and the Multiple Futures Project, 418–19; and the New Strategic Concept, 399–400, *402*, 409–10, 417, 419–20, 422–23, 26, 431; and Scandinavia, 194–98. *See also* Afghanistan War, Cold War
Northern Ireland. *See* United Kingdom and Northern Ireland
Northern League (LN, Italy), *134, 148*, 150–51, 155–58
Norway, 154, *161–62*, 443n3, 468, 470; during World War II, 192; economy of, 187–89; and the European Union, 199–204; foreign policy of, 192–98, 427–28; homogeneity of, 168; and immigration, 189–91, 378–80, 444n10; political development of, 171–72; political parties of, *162*, 179–181, *183*; political system of, 174–177, 185. *See also* North Atlantic Treaty Organization and Scandinavia, Scandinavian social model
nuclear disarmament, 126
nuclear power, 28, 60, 185, 361
nuclear weapons, 17, 56, 119, 167, 300, 407

Obama, Barack, 3, 126, 204, 211, 300, 305, 404, 408, 425, 433n6, 458n11
OECD. *See* Organization for Economic Cooperation and Development
OEEC. *See* Organization for Economic Cooperation and Development

Olive Tree coalition (Italy), 151

Olszewski, Jan, *247*, 249–50, 252, 259, 448n10

ombudsman, 184–85

Operation Allied Force, 401. *See also* Yugoslavia

Operation Deliberate Force, 401. *See also* Bosnia-Herzegovina.

Orange Revolution, 14, 235. *See also* Ukraine

Organization for Economic Cooperation and Development (OECD), 117, 129, 194, 237, 277, 280, 282, 378, 470

Organization for European Economic Cooperation (OEEC). *See* Organization for Economic Cooperation and Development (OECD)

Organization for Security and Cooperation in Europe (OSCE), 237, 404, 407–08, *414*, 421, 428, 466, 470

OSCE. *See* Organization for Security and Cooperation in Europe

Oslo Accords, 195

Ostpolitik, 426

Palme, Olof, 198

Papandreou, George, 328, 335–36

Paris summit (1974), 284

Partnership for Peace(PfP), 194, 405, 416, 421, 470

Party for Freedom (PVV, Netherlands), 389

Pasqua, Charles, 51

Pawlak, Waldemar, *247*, *250*, 252, 270, 448n10

peacekeeping, 10–11, 119, 129, 195, 415, 427, 469

Pentagon, 403

People of Freedom (PDL, Italy), 155, 158–59

perestroika, 227, *236–37*

Petersburg tasks, 11, 401–*402*, 469

Plaid Cymru, *68*, 83, 85

Poland, 101, *243–44*; and the Catholic church, 255–256, 271; economy of, 223, 256–258; and the European Union, 263, 266, 284, 294, 296; and immigration, 373, 388, 458n6; and NATO, 405, 410; political cleavages and parties of, *244*, 245–47, 249–53, 256–72; political system of, 253, 264; and Russia, 14, 234, 419; and Scandinavia, 192, 203–4; and shock therapy, 246, 248–49; social policy in, 258–59. *See also* financial and economic crisis in Poland

Political and Security Committee of the European Council (PSC), 469

Pompidou, Georges, *30*, 56, 283

Pope John Paul II, 245

Portugal: and EU accession, 4, 385, 352; and immigration, 379–81; and NATO, 430. *See also* financial and economic crisis in Portugal

Powell, Colin, 94

Prague Capabilities Commitment (PCC), 415

Prague summit (2002), 415, 417

preemptive war, 93

price stability, 321, 341

privileged partnership, 16, 124, 298

Prodi, Romano, 14, *143*, 151–52, 154–55, 158

Putin, Vladimir, 13–14, 124, *208*, *212*, 214, 219–20, 226–34, 237, 239–40

Qualifications Directive, 388

qualified majority voting (QMV), 281, 287–88, 294–96, 298, *348*;

Racial Equality Directive, 363, 395

Radio Maryja, *247*, 259

Raffarin, Jean-Pierre, 36–37, 47, 51

Rasmussen, Anders Fogh, *190*, 399, 411, 425

Reagan, Ronald, 90, 146, 199, 309

Reception Conditions Directive, 388–89

Returns Directive, 384–85

Reykjavic summit (1986), 199

Riga summit (2006), 409, 417

Rocard, Michel, 34

Romania, 4, 284, 297, 389, 427–28

Rome summit (1990), 290

Rome summit (2002), 406

Rome Treaty, 89, 145, 194, 200, 280–82, 284, 286–88, 296, 318, 356–57, 362, 377–79, 382, 457n5, 465, 468

Roosevelt, Franklin Delano, 164

Rote Armee Fraktion (RAF), 18

Rumsfeld, Donald, 403

Russia/USSR, *207–08*, 299–300; and the breakup of the USSR, 2, 10, 215; civil society in, 229–230, 234; and demographic crisis, 19, 228–229; economy of, 220–26, 228, 232–33, 239–41; and the European Union, 4, 13–16, 234–35, 237–39, 241–42; and Germany, 124–25; multinationalism in, 216, 226–27, 229; and NATO, 235, 237, 399, 405–08, 419–421; political and economic liberalization in, 211–221, 224–25, 227, 229, 232; political parties of, 208, 218–20; political system of, 216–18, 240–41; and Scandinavia, 167–169, 192–198; Soviet Committee for State Security (KGB), 218; under the Tsars, 209–10; and World War I, 209. See also Cold War and the USSR, NATO and Russia

Russian Central Bank, 224–25

Russo-Georgian war, 14, 60–61, 235, 300, 406–08, 418–20

Rydzyk, Tadeusz, 247, 259

Rywingate, 263–64

Sarkozy, Nicholas, 6, 13, 16, 26–30, 32, 37–38, 43, 48–49, 51–53, 55, 58–64, 101, 123, 347, 437n16, 437n20

Scandinavian Defense Union, 167, 196

Scandinavian social model, 164–65, 170–71, 186–89

Scelba, Mario, 142

Schengen Agreement, 379–380, 382, 385, 470

Schengen Information System, 379

Schmidt, Helmut, 112, 123, 284–85

Schröder, Gerhard, 14, 91, 112, 117, 121, 125–26

Schuman Plan. See European Coal and Steel Community (ECSC)

Schuman, Robert, 279

Scotland. See United Kingdom and Scotland

SEA. See Single European Act

Sejm, 247, 249, 250–51, 253–54, 264,

September 11, 2001, 129, 204, 403–04, 417, 420.

Serbia, 9, 56, 93, 235, 405. See also Balkans conflicts, Kosovo

Services Directive, 384

SGP. See Stability and Growth Pact

SHAPE. See Supreme Headquarters Allied Powers Europe

Single European Act (SEA), 287–88, 290, 356, 395, 468

single market, 94, 198, 280, 282–83, 286–87, 289, 291, 303, 318, 320, 359

Slavophiles, 209

Slovakia, 271, 298, 339, 389–91, 420, 458n6

Slovenia, 294, 298, 458nn6–7

Smolensk crash, 245, 247, 271

social Europe, 205

Social Democratic Party (SPD, Germany), 90, 100, 108–13, 117

Socialist Party (PS, France), 26, 32–33, 35, 50, 54, 56, 64

Solana, Javier, 11, 469

Solidarity, 245–49, 252

Somalia, 17

South Africa, 60

South Ossetia. See Russo-Georgian war

sovereign debt crisis. See financial and economic crisis

Soviet Union. See Russia/USSR

Spaak, Paul-Henri, 280

Spain, 154, 158, 212, 415–16; economy of, 305–6; and EU accession, 4, 285, 296–97, 352; and immigration, 373–74, 380; and the Iraq War, 93–94, 158; and NATO, 410, 420, 430. See also financial and economic crisis in Spain

Spinelli, Altiero, 146

St. Malo declaration, 11, 412, 469. See also Common Security and Defense Policy (CSDP)

St. Petersberg summit (1992), 11. See also Petersberg tasks

Stability and Growth Pact, 36, 321–26, 339, 345, 348, 466, 471

Stability Pact for South Eastern Europe, 470. See also Balkans conflicts.

stagflation, 187, 284. See also inflation, unemployment

Stalin, Joseph, 165–66, 192, 209–10, 216, 400, 447n33

Stauning, Thorvald, 164

Steinbrück, Peer, 6, 329

Steinmeier, Frank-Walter, 112

Stormont Castle, 82

Stortinget, 175

Strasbourg-Kehl summit, 405, 407, 417, 419

Strategic Arms Control Reduction, 408
Strauss-Kahn, Dominique, 64
Stravidis, Jim, 409
Struck, Peter, 129
structural funds, 138
Sturzo, Don Luigi, 136
subsidiarity, 200, 255, 469, 471
Suchocka, Hanna, *250*, 252
Suez crisis, 401, 426
Supreme Headquarters Allied Powers Europe (SHAPE), 415
Surkov, Vladislav, *212–213*
Sweden, *161–62*, 171, 192, 443n3, 444n11; economy of, 187, 444n9; and the European Union, 200–04, 284, 293–94; and immigration, 189–91, 378, 380, 382–84; military of, 416; and NATO, 204; neutrality of, 167, 192–93, 196–98; political parties of, *162*, 179–181, *183*; political system of, 174–177, 184–85. *See also* North Atlantic Treaty Organization and Scandinavia, Scandinavian social model
Switzerland, 185, 373–74, 376, 378–80, 384, 389–90, 470
Syria, 16, 62

Taliban, 409
Tatars, *213*, 216, 226
terrorism, 4, 17–18, 47, 93, 129, 203, 216, 229, 297, 300, 360, 399, 407, 409, 411, 417, 426. *See also* 9/11 terrorist attacks, United States and the war on terror
Thatcher, Margaret, 19, 70, *72*–74, 81, 83, 88–*90*, 152, 199, 286
Third Way, 73, 78, 82, 91, 93
trade unions, 32, 39, 54, 81, 96, 110, 165, 172, 179, 182, 186, 204, 230, 257, 290, 306, 309–11, 365, 436n5
Transnistria, 411
Treaty on European Union. *See* Maastricht Treaty
Trente Glorieuses, 31, 41–*42*
Trichet, Jean Claude, 7
Turkey, 2, 4, 11, 13, 15–17, 20, 400, 416, 422, 425, 427; and the European Union, 9, 15, 124, 158, 294, 297–98
Tusk, Donald, *244, 247, 251*, 264–65, 270
Tymiński, Stanisław, 249–50

Ukraine, 14, 216, 235, 238, 405
unemployment, 27, 29–35, 37–39, 44, 46, 48, 61, 71–72, 74, 76, 118, 138, *170*, 186–88, *190*, 205, 257–58, 284, 292, 298, 305–6, 308, 311, 316–17, 390–92, 442n22
Union for Popular Movement (UMP, France), 26, 53, 64
Union of the Mediterranean, 60–61, 465, 437n20
unilateralism, 94, 204
United Arab Emirates, 59–60
United Kingdom, *67–68*, 119, 433n3; Atlanticism of, 88–89; economy of, 38, 70–74, 96, 149, 306–8; and England, 82, 86; and the European Union, 56, 88–92, 167, 278, 282–83, 286–88, 292, 294–95, 319; and immigration, 44, 373, 457n2; and Iran, 17; and the Iraq War, 158, 93–96; and NATO, 89, 413, 420, 427–28, 430; and Northern Ireland, 81–84, 366; political system of, 79–83, 97, 113, 150; and public spending, 74–76; and the radical right, 390; and Scotland, 81–83, 85–86; and Wales, 81–83, 85–86; and the war on terror, 18. *See also* Cold War and the United Kingdom, financial and economic crisis in the United Kingdom, North Atlantic Treaty Organization and the United Kingdom, United States and United Kingdom
UN. *See* United Nations
United Nations (UN), 404, 408; consent for military action, 126, 194, 235; and the Iraq War, 94, 204; and Scandinavia, 167, 192, 195, 197; and the United States, 428; and the West European Union, 413, *424*
United Nations High Commissioner for Refugees (UNHCR), 388
United States (USA): as a comparison with Europe, 2–3, 11, 17–19, 109, *170*–71, 177, 184, 186–87, 239, 300, 367, 382, 454n4, 458n11; domestic politics of, 211; economy of, *28*, 30, 38, 119, 284, 303–7, 309–12, 317; and European integration, 277; and France, 56–59, 60, 62, 93; and Germany, 93, 117, 120, 125–129, 130, 290; and immigration, 44, 229–30, 282, 381–82, 393; and Italy, 135, 141, 145–46; and NATO, 401, 403, 405, 410, 412, 416, 429–32, 458n7; and Russia,

235; and Scandinavia, 166, 194–96, 204; and Turkey, 16; and the United Kingdom, 88–89, 95, 282–83, 416; and the war on terror, 17–18, 88, 92–93, 96, 203, 417. *See also* financial and economic crisis in the United States, September 11, 2001

Universal Declaration of Human Rights, 352

USA. *See* United States

value added tax, 37

Van Rompuy task force, 6, 13, 324–25, 344, 346–47

Van Rompuy, Herman, 6, 12–13, 298, *330*, 336, 344

Veltroni, Walter, *134*, 155

Venice summit (1956), 280

Vietnam, 56, 198, 209

de Villepin, Dominique, 36–37, 43, 51, 64, 436n5

Vogel-Polsky, Elaine, 362

Wales. *See* United Kingdom and Wales

Wales Act, 85

Wałęsa, Lech, *247*–50, 253

weapons of mass destruction (WMD), 94, 399, 420, 426,

Warsaw Pact, 401–*402*, 404, 470–71

West European Union (WEU), 11, 194, 277, 282, 291, 401, 413–14, 431

Wilders, Geert, 389–90

Working Time Directive, 364

World Economic Forum, 41

World Trade Organization (WTO), 41, 469

World War I, 101–102, 167, 209, 234

World War II, 102, 104, *114*, 121–122, 124, *127*, 137–138, 165–67, 191–92, 210, 234, 277, 282, 308

xenophobia, 18, 48, 371, 393–94, 396

Yade, Rama, 48

Yeltsin, Boris, 210, 214, 215, 217–23, 225–28, 232–33, 235, 237, 239, 445n3

Yugoslavia, 126, 145, 292, 401

Ziobro, Zbigniew, 266

About the Contributors

Gianfranco Baldini is associate professor of political science at the University of Bologna. He is editor-in-chief of the annual publication *Italian Politics*, and coauthor, with Adriano Pappalardo, of *Elections, Electoral Systems and Volatile Voters* (2009).

Simon Duke is professor at the European Institute for Public Administration (EIPA) in Maastricht. He is author of *Beyond the Chapter: Enlargement Challenges for CFSP and ESDP* (2003).

Eric S. Einhorn is professor emeritus of political science at the University of Massachusetts, Amherst. He is author of *Modern Welfare States: Scandinavian Politics and Policy in the Global Age* (2003), together with John Logue.

Gabriel Goodliffe is assistant professor of international relations at the Instituto Tecnológico Autónomo de México. He is author of *The Resurgence of the Radical Right in France: From Boulangisme to the Front National* (2011).

Roberta Haar teaches international relations at Maastricht University. She researches in U.S. foreign policy and transatlantic relations and is coeditor of *Transatlantic Conflict and Consensus: Culture, History and Politics* (2009).

Jonathan Hopkin is senior lecturer in comparative politics at the London School of Economics. He is author of *Party Formation and Democratic Transition in Spain: The Creation and Collapse of the Union of Democratic Centre* (1999).

Erik Jones is professor of European studies at the SAIS Bologna Center of the Johns Hopkins University. He is author of *Economic Adjustment and Political Transformation in Small States* (2008).

R. Daniel Kelemen is associate professor of political science at Rutgers University. He is author of *Eurolegalism: The Transformation of Law and Regulation in the European Union* (2011).

John Logue was professor of political science at Kent State University. He is author of *Modern Welfare States: Scandinavian Politics and Policy in the Global*

Age (2003), together with Eric S. Einhorn. Professor Logue passed away in December 2009.

Benedicta Marzinotto is lecturer in political economy at the University of Udine and Research Fellow at Bruegel, Brussels.

Jonathon W. Moses is professor of political science at the Norwegian University of Science and Technology, Trondheim. He is the author of *International Migration: Globalization's Last Frontier* (2006).

Bruce Parrott is professor and director of Russian and Eurasian studies at SAIS Johns Hopkins University, Washington, D.C. He is author of "Empire and After: Russia and the Geopolitics of Eurasia in Historical Perspective," in Niklas Swanström (ed.), *Sino-Russian Relations in Central Asia and Beyond* (forthcoming).

Ben Stanley is Marie Curie Postdoctoral Fellow at the Institute for Public Affairs, Bratislava.

Ronald Tiersky is Joseph B. Eastman '04 Professor in Political Science at Amherst College. He is general editor of the "Europe Today" series and author of many books, including *François Mitterrand: A Very French President* (2003).

Saskia van Genugten is a Ph.D. candidate in European Studies at the School of Advanced International Studies (SAIS), The Johns Hopkins University. Her dissertation focuses on Italian and British relations with Libya.

John Van Oudenaren is director of the World Digital Library (www.wdl.org). He is coeditor, with Ronald Tiersky, of *European Foreign Policies: Does Europe Still Matter?* (2010).

Helga A. Welsh is professor of political science at Wake Forest University. She is coeditor and coauthor of volumes 9 (2006) and 10 (2010) of the e-publication *German History in Documents and Images*.